THE
NEW AMERICAN NATION
1775–1820

A Twelve-Volume Collection of Articles on the Development of the Early American Republic

Edited by

PETER S. ONUF
UNIVERSITY OF VIRGINIA

A GARLAND SERIES

THE NEW AMERICAN NATION
1775–1820

Volume
4

★

CONGRESS
AND THE
CONFEDERATION

Edited with an
Introduction by

PETER S. ONUF

GARLAND PUBLISHING, INC.
NEW YORK & LONDON
1991

Library of Congress Cataloging-in-Publication Data

Congress and the Confederation / edited with an introduction by Peter S. Onuf.
   p.   cm. — (New American nation, 1776–1815 ; vol. 4)
   Includes bibliographical references.
   ISBN 0-8153-0439-0 (alk. paper) : $49.99
   1. United States—Politics and government—1783–1789. 2. United States. Congress—History—18th century. I. Onuf, Peter S. II. Series.
   E164.N45   1991 vol. 4
   [E303]
   973s s—dc20   [973.3]   91-13165
                 CIP

Printed on acid-free, 250-year-life paper.
Manufactured in the United States of America

THE NEW AMERICAN NATION, 1775–1820

EDITOR'S INTRODUCTION

This series includes a representative selection of the most interesting and influential journal articles on revolutionary and early national America. My goal is to introduce readers to the wide range of topics that now engage scholarly attention. The essays in these volumes show that the revolutionary era was an extraordinarily complex "moment" when the broad outlines of national history first emerged. Yet if the "common cause" brought Americans together, it also drove them apart: the Revolution, historians agree, was as much a civil war as a war of national liberation. And, given the distinctive colonial histories of the original members of the American Union, it is not surprising that the war had profoundly different effects in different parts of the country. This series has been designed to reveal the multiplicity of these experiences in a period of radical political and social change.

Most of the essays collected here were first published within the last twenty years. This series therefore does *not* recapitulate the development of the historiography of the Revolution. Many of the questions asked by earlier generations of scholars now seem misconceived and simplistic. Constitutional historians wanted to know if the Patriots had legitimate grounds to revolt: was the Revolution "legal"? Economic historians sought to assess the costs of the navigation system for American farmers and merchants and to identify the interest groups that promoted resistance. Comparative historians wondered how "revolutionary" the Revolution really was. By and large, the best recent work has ignored these classic questions. Contemporary scholarship instead draws its inspiration from other sources, most notable of which is the far-ranging reconception and reconstruction of prerevolutionary America by a brilliant generation of colonial historians.

Bernard Bailyn's *Ideological Origins of the American Revolution* (1967) was a landmark in the new historical writing on colonial politics. As his title suggests, Bailyn was less interested in constitutional and legal arguments as such than in the "ideology" or political language that shaped colonists' perception of and responses to British imperial policy. Bailyn's great contribution was to focus attention on colonial political culture; disciples and critics alike followed his lead as they explored the impact—and limits—of "republicanism" in specific colonial settings. Meanwhile, the social historians who had played a leading role in the transformation of colonial historiography were extending their work into the late colonial period and were increasingly interested in the questions of value, meaning, and behavior that were raised by the new political history. The resulting convergence points to some of the unifying themes in recent work on the revolutionary period presented in this series.

A thorough grounding in the new scholarship on colonial British America is the best introduction to the history and historiography of the Revolution. These volumes therefore can be seen as a complement and extension of Peter Charles Hoffer's eighteen-volume set, *Early American History*, published by Garland in 1987. Hoffer's collection includes numerous important essays essential for understanding developments in independent America. Indeed, only a generation ago—when the Revolution generally was defined in terms of its colonial origins—it would have been hard to justify a separate series on the "new American nation." But exciting recent work—for instance, on wartime mobilization and social change, or on the Americanization of republican ideology during the great era of state making and constitution writing—has opened up new vistas. Historians now generally agree that the revolutionary period saw far-reaching and profound changes, that is, a "great transformation," toward a more recognizably modern America. If the connections between this transformation and the actual unfolding of events often remain elusive, the historiographical quest for the larger meaning of the war and its aftermath has yielded impressive results.

To an important extent, the revitalization of scholarship on revolutionary and early national America is a tribute to the efforts and expertise of scholars working in other professional disciplines. Students of early American literature have made key contributions to the history of rhetoric, ideology, and culture; political scientists and legal scholars have brought new clarity and sophistication to the study of political and constitutional thought and practice in the founding period. Kermit L. Hall's superb Garland series, *United States Constitutional and Legal History* (20 volumes, 1985), is another fine resource for students and scholars interested in the founding. The sampling of recent work in various disciplines offered in these volumes gives a sense of the interpretative possibilities of a crucial period in American history that is now getting the kind of attention it has long deserved.

Peter S. Onuf

INTRODUCTION

The history of the American union during the Revolution and under the Articles of Confederation (1781–1789) presents an apparent paradox. How could a central government that lacked the essential characteristics of a true sovereignty—the ability to levy taxes, or invoke coercive sanctions against states or citizens—have succeeded in guiding the Patriot cause toward ultimate victory? During most of the war, Congress operated without formal sanction: unwilling to recognize Virginia's extensive western land claims, Maryland refused to ratify the Articles until 1781. Even before ratification, nationalist reformers agreed, the loose confederation of states that the Articles created was fundamentally defective.

Historical judgments of the Confederation period inevitably have been shaped by the subsequent creation of a "more perfect union" under the federal Constitution. Federalist reformers highlighted the "imbecility" of the old regime, arguing that the union was on the verge of collapse before the "miracle" of the Constitutional Convention at Philadelphia. Reacting against the "critical period" argument and identifying the reform movement with a conservative reaction to the democratic impulses of the war years, Merrill Jensen undertook a full-scale rehabilitation of the Articles in his *The Articles of the Confederation* (1940) and *The New Nation* (1950). Though Jensen's interpretative framework survives only in attenuated form, his studies focused attention on the achievements of the first state and national governments and explicated some of the leading sources of political controversy— over land, commerce, and fiscal policy—that nationalist reformers eventually exploited.

The best modern account of the early Congresses, Jack N. Rakove's *The Beginnings of National Politics* (1979), eschews the progressive focus on class conflict, emphasizing instead the creative—and remarkably successful—efforts of Congressmen in organizing and administering the national war effort. Yet these efforts, culminating in Robert Morris's tenure as Superintendent of Finance (1781–1783), finally ran athwart the constraints of state particularism. And once victory was secured—and the state legislatures failed to ratify amendments to the Articles that would have secured Congress an independent revenue—nationalists began to recognize the futility of the reform movement.

The practical experience in national governance recounted by Rakove provided valuable precedents for the later federal regime.

But the sequence was by no means inevitable: indeed, Federalist depictions of the "critical period" reflected a massive crisis of confidence among frustrated nationalists. The challenge is to explain how political developments on the national level prepared the way for an ultimately successful constitutional reform campaign, notwithstanding the nationalists' mounting desperation.

Jensen pointed the way toward resolution of this historiographical conundrum in his early work on the creation of the national domain, the one clear success of the postwar Congresses. Federal lands in the new Northwest Territory constituted a substantial bond of union, a potential source of much-needed revenue, and opportunities for the development of interdependent interests. Furthermore, as I argue elsewhere, the massive renegotiation of state boundaries resulting from land cessions to Congress helped eliminate the chronic conflicts between large, "landed" states and the smaller, "landless" states that periodically threatened to immobilize Congress. Provisions in the territorial government ordinances for the creation of new states under Congress's supervision also pointed toward a more modest conception of states' rights that was compatible with a more powerful and effective central government.

The inadequacies of congressional government stood opposed to the broad range of powers—over war and peace and the conduct of foreign policy and other common concerns—that were set forth in the Articles. But the movement to augment Congress's powers never would have succeeded if state politicians could not have been persuaded that it was in the interest of their own governments to strengthen the union. The limitations and failures of the state governments thus provided the opportunity for reformers to make one last effort. In doing so, they sought to strike the "federal balance" implicit in their experience in the British Empire and compatible with Revolutionary commitments to individual rights, local self-government, and national independence.

Peter S. Onuf

ADDITIONAL READING

Thomas P. Abernethy. *Western Lands and the American Revolution*. New York: D. Appleton-Century, 1937.

Joseph L. Davis. *Sectionalism in American Politics, 1774–1787*. Madison: University of Wisconsin Press, 1977.

Jonathan R. Dull. *A Diplomatic History of the American Revolution*. New Haven: Yale University Press, 1985.

E. James Ferguson. *The Power of the Purse: A History of American Public Finance, 1776–1790*. Chapel Hill: University of North Carolina Press, 1961.

Jack P. Greene, ed. *The American Revolution: Its Character and Limits*. New York: New York University Press, 1987.

Merrill Jensen. *The Articles of Confederation: An Interpretation of the Social-Constitutional History of the American Revolution, 1774–1781*. Madison: University of Wisconsin Press, 1940.

———. *The New Nation: A History of the United States During the Confederation, 1781–1789*. New York: Alfred A. Knopf, 1950.

Jerrilyn Greene Marston. *King and Congress: The Transfer of Political Legitimacy, 1774–1776*. Princeton, NJ: Princeton University Press, 1987.

Peter S. Onuf. *The Origins of the Federal Republic: Jurisdictional Controversies in the United States, 1775–1787*. Philadelphia: University of Pennsylvania Press, 1983.

———. *Statehood and Union: A History of the Northwest Ordinance*. Bloomington: Indiana University Press, 1987.

Jack N. Rakove. *The Beginnings of National Politics: An Interpretive History of the Continental Congress*. New York: Alfred A. Knopf, 1979.

CONTENTS

Volume 4—Congress and the Confederation

Robert F. Berkhofer, Jr., "Jefferson, the Ordinance of 1784, and the Origins of the American Territorial System," *William and Mary Quarterly*, 1972, 29(2) (Third Series):231–262.

Peter S. Onuf, "Liberty, Development, and Union: Visions of the West in the 1780s," *William and Mary Quarterly*, 1986, 43(2)(Third Series):179–213.

Paul Finkelman, "Slavery and the Northwest Ordinance: A Study in Ambiguity," *Journal of the Early Republic*, 1986, 6: 343–370.

*Robert J. Taylor, "Trial at Trenton," *William and Mary Quarterly*, 1969, 26(4) (Third Series):521–547.

David M. Griffiths, "American Commercial Diplomacy in Russia, 1780 to 1783," *William and Mary Quarterly*, 1970, 27(3) (Third Series):379–410.

G. S. Rowe and Alexander W. Knott, "The Longchamps Affair (1784–86), the Law of Nations, and the Shaping of Early American Foreign Policy," *Diplomatic History*, 1986, 10(3): 199–220.

ACKNOWLEDGMENTS

Volume 4—Congress and the Confederation

Jack P. Greene, "The Background of The Articles of Confederation," *Publius*, 1982, 12(4):15–44. Reprinted with the permission of the North Texas State University. Courtesy of *Publius*.

Michael Lienesch, "Historical Theory and Political Reform: Two Perspectives on Confederation Politics," *Review of Politics*, 1983, 45(1):94–115. Reprinted with the permission of the University of Notre Dame. Courtesy of the *Review of Politics*.

Lawrence Delbert Cress, "Republican Liberty and National Security: American Military Policy as an Ideological Problem, 1783 to 1789," *William and Mary Quarterly*, 1981, 38(1) (Third Series):73–96. Originally appeared in the *William and Mary Quarterly*. Courtesy of Yale University Sterling Memorial Library.

Richard H. Kohn, "The Inside History of the Newburgh Conspiracy: America and the Coup d'Etat," *William and Mary Quarterly*, 1970, 27(2):187–220. Originally appeared in the *William and Mary Quarterly*. Courtesy of Yale University Sterling Memorial Library.

Kenneth R. Bowling, "New Light on the Philadelphia Mutiny of 1783: Federal-State Confrontation at the Close of the War for Independence," *Pennsylvania Magazine of History and Biography*, 1977, 101(4):419–450. Reprinted with the permission of the Historical Society of Pennsylvania. Courtesy of Yale University Sterling Memorial Library.

E. James Ferguson, "The Nationalists of 1781–1783 and the Economic Interpretation of the Constitution," *Journal of American History*, 1969, 56(2):241–261. Reprinted with the permission of the *Journal of American History*. Courtesy of Yale University Sterling Memorial Library.

E. Wayne Carp, "The Origins of the Nationalist Movement of 1780–1783: Congressional Administration and the Continental Army," *Pennsylvania Magazine of History and Biography*, 1983, 107(3):363–392. Reprinted with the permission of the Historical Society of Pennsylvania. Courtesy of Yale University Sterling Memorial Library.

Lance Banning, "James Madison and the Nationalists, 1780–1783," *William and Mary Quarterly*, 1983, 40(2) (Third Series):227–255. Originally appeared in the *William and Mary Quarterly*. Courtesy of Yale University Sterling Memorial Library.

Lawrence Delbert Cress, "Whither Columbia? Congressional Residence and the Politics of the New Nation, 1776 to 1787," *William and Mary Quarterly*, 1973, 32(4) (Third Series):581–600. Originally appeared in the *William and Mary Quarterly*. Courtesy of Yale University Sterling Memorial Library.

Merrill Jensen, "The Creation of the National Domain, 1781–1784," *Mississippi Valley Historical Review*, 1939, 26(3):323–342. Reprinted with the permission of Indiana University. Courtesy of Yale University Sterling Memorial Library.

Robert F. Berkhofer, Jr., "Jefferson, the Ordinance of 1784, and the Origins of the American Territorial System," *William and Mary Quarterly*, 1972, 29(2) (Third Series):231–262. Originally appeared in the *William and Mary Quarterly*. Courtesy of Yale University Sterling Memorial Library.

Peter S. Onuf, "Liberty, Development, and Union: Visions of the West in the 1780s," *William and Mary Quarterly*, 1986, 43(2) (Third Series):179–213. Originally appeared in the *William and Mary Quarterly*. Courtesy of Yale University Sterling Memorial Library.

Paul Finkelman, "Slavery and the Northwest Ordinance: A Study in Ambiguity," *Journal of the Early Republic*, 1986, 6:343–370. Reprinted with the permission of Indiana University, Department of History. Courtesy of Yale University Sterling Memorial Library.

Robert J. Taylor, "Trial at Trenton," *William and Mary Quarterly*, 1969, 26(4):521–547. Originally appeared in the *William and Mary Quarterly*. Courtesy of Yale University Sterling Memorial Library.

David M. Griffiths, "American Commercial Diplomacy in Russia, 1780 to 1783," *William and Mary Quarterly*, 1970, 27(3) (Third Series):379–410. Originally appeared in the *William and Mary Quarterly*. Courtesy of Yale University Sterling Memorial Library.

G. S. Rowe and Alexander W. Knott, "The Longchamps Affair (1784–86), the Law of Nations, and the Shaping of Early American Foreign Policy," *Diplomatic History*, 1986, 10(3):199–220. Reprinted with the permission of Scholarly Resources, Inc. Courtesy of Yale University Sterling Memorial Library.

The Background of The Articles of Confederation

Jack P. Greene
The Johns Hopkins University

I

In the summer of 1776, during initial debates over the Articles of Confederation, John Witherspoon, the learned president of Princeton University and a delegate to the second Continental Congress from New Jersey, reflected upon the astonishing events of the previous two years. "Honour, interest, safety and necessity," he observed, had conspired to produce "such a degree of union through these colonies, as nobody would have prophesied, and hardly any would have expected." As a result of this startling development, Witherspoon declared, it had suddenly become clear that "a well planned confederacy among the states of America" would contribute enormously to "their future security and improvement." "A lasting confederacy," he predicted, would not only "hand down the blessings of peace and public order to many generations" of Americans; it would also serve as a model and inspiration for the rest of the civilized world which, he hoped, might eventually "see it prosper by some plan of union, to perpetuate security and peace" over large portions of the globe.[1]

That Witherspoon was not alone in his surprise at the unity achieved by the colonies in their resistance to Britain between 1774 and 1776 or in his assessment of the promise of an American union has recently been emphasized by Jack N. Rakove. By far, the most important of these developments, Rakove has shown, were the exigencies arising out of the necessity of coordinating an effective resistance and waging a war against the strongest military power then existing in the western world. From the beginning, American leaders were aware that they had no chance of success unless they could maintain a high degree of "agreement on the principles and tactics of opposition" and avoid "the types of jealousy that had troubled American resistance in the early 1770s." Inexorably, this awareness pushed delegates to the Continental Congress in the direction of a

---

[1] John Witherspoon's Speech in Congress, [30 July 1776], in Paul H. Smith et al., eds., *Letter of Delegates to Congress* (Washington, D.C., 1976-), 4:584-587.

Publius: The Journal of Federalism 12 (Fall 1982) © Center for the Study of Federalism, Philadelphia

system in which Congress exerted extraordinarily extensive power, and thereby constituted a de facto national government.[2]

In this situation, Rakove has found, there was little interest during the first year of the war in creating "an enduring national state." But the surprising success of Congress in presiding over and organizing a coordinated defense effort quickly yielded a second short-term development that created additional pressures towards the formation of a continental union. This was the emergence among delegates of the hope that the colonies might achieve "a lasting Confederation" despite many perceived differences among them. As they came to grasp the potential for such a union, especially as it was spelled out for them by Thomas Paine and others during the first half of 1776, they began to feel that it would be a great tragedy if they did not seize as favorable an opportunity to accomplish such a noble end.[3]

Yet, as Rakove has also noted, two additional short-term developments combined both to delay codification and formal adoption of a continental confederation and to raise profound doubts about whether, as Joseph Hewes of North Carolina worried shortly after independence, delegates would ever be able to "modell it so as to be agreed to by all the Colonies."[4] First and most decisive during the first two years after independence was simply the press of other more urgent business. "The immensity of business created by the war," lamented the Virginia delegate, Richard Henry Lee, in August 1770, necessarily meant that "the Confederation goes on but slowly."[5]

Second, and of even greater long-term significance, was the rapid identification in 1775-76 of the enormously complex issues involved in trying to bring thirteen separate political entities into a broad continental union. "In such a Period as this, Sir, when Thirteen Colonies unacquainted in a great Measure, with each other are rushing together into one Mass," John Adams wrote presciently in November 1775, "it would be a Miracle, if Such heterogeneous Ingredients did not at first produce violent Fermentations."[6] The coming together of representatives from the several states inevitably produced not only a sense of common purpose in resisting Britain, but also a more intense awareness of the remaining differences in interest and orientation among the several colonies. Specifically, delegates discovered that they disagreed over certain fundamental issues involving representation, expenses, and western lands. By and

[2] Jack N. Rakove, *The Beginnings of National Politics: An Interpretive History of the Continental Congress* (New York, 1979), pp. 136-145.

[3] Ibid., p. 145; Silas Deane to Patrick Henry, 2 January 1775, in Smith, ed., *Letter to Delegates*, vol. 1, 291; Edmund Cody Burnett, *The Continental Congress* (New York, 1964), pp. 136-137.

[4] Joseph Hewes to Samuel Johnston, 28 July 1776, in Smith, ed., *Letters of Delegates*, 4:555.

[5] Richard Henry Lee to Thomas Jefferson, 25 August 1777, ibid., 7:551.

[6] John Adams to Samuel Osgood, 14 November 1775, ibid., 2:342.

large, the division over these issues was not sectional. Rather, as Merrill Jensen has pointed out, the "large colonies were pitted against the small ones; colonies with many slaves were in opposition to those with fewer; colonies that had no western lands contended with those that did."[7] But the delegates also quickly identified and articulated broad regional interests and contrasts between the southern and the eastern (New England) states, though no one initially seemed to be quite sure whether the middle states from Delaware to New York were closer to the southern or the eastern states.[8] Invariably, differences among the colonies in orientation, interest, and issues operated to make confederation, as John Adams predicted in May 1776, "the most intricate, the most important, the most dangerous, and delicate Business of all."[9]

If, as a result of Rakove's analysis, we now have a better understanding of the short-term developments beginning in late 1774 that both pushed the American colonies towards a continental union and made it difficult for them to contrive one, no one has yet considered systematically the several long-term preconditions that lay behind and shaped that process. This article is a preliminary effort in that direction. For purposes of analysis, it will divide those preconditions into two broad categories: those that inhibited and those that facilitated the formation of a permanent national union. It will conclude with some tentative observations on the ways those preconditions shaped that union in its initial form in the Articles of Confederation.

II

Certainly one of the most powerful preconditions operating to make achievement of a permanent union extremely difficult was the obvious dissimilarities among the colonies and the nearly ubiquitous judgment that they were far more impressive than any similarities. Such a perception had prevailed throughout the colonial period and had received widespread expression in the decades just prior to the Revolution. Thus, in 1760, less than fifteen years before the first beginnings of American national union, Benjamin Franklin had informed British readers that Britain's "fourteen separate governments on the maritime coast of the [North American] continent" were "not only under different governors, but have different forms of government, different laws, different interests, and some of them different religious persuasions and different manners." These differences, Franklin observed, gave rise to mutual suspicions and jealousies that were "so great that however necessary and desirable an union of the colonies has long been, for their common defence and security against their

---

[7] Merrill Jensen, *The Articles of Confederation: An Interpretation of the Social-Constitutional History of the American Revolution 1774-1781* (Madison, 1959), p. 56.
[8] See John R. Alden, *The First South* (Baton Rouge, 1961), pp. 33-73.
[9] John Adams to James Warren, 15 May 1776, in Smith, ed., *Letters of Delegates*, 3:678.

enemies, and how sensible soever each colony has been of that necessity, yet they have never been able to effect such a union among themselves, nor even to agree in requesting the mother country to establish it for them." Franklin was writing for the express purpose of allaying rising fears in Britain that the increasingly valuable colonies might rise up and throw off British control; but he expressed the conventional wisdom of his time.[10]

Indeed, prior to the Revolution, virtually every commentator on both sides of the Atlantic was entirely persuaded, with Franklin, that the extraordinary differences among the colonies made any form of union impossible. The validity of this conclusion seemed to be dramatically underscored by the fate of the Albany Plan of Union in 1754. This proposal for a limited defensive confederation against the French was not ratified by a single colony. Even worse, during the Seven Years' War, several colonies had shown very little concern for the welfare of their neighbors. When their assistance had "been demanded or implored by any of their distressed neighbours and fellow subjects," charged the metropolitan economist, Malachy Postlewayt, in 1757, some colonies had "scandalously affected delays" and "by an inactive stupidity or indolence, appeared insensible to their distressed situation, and regardless of the common danger, because they felt not the immediate effect of it."[11] "Being in a state of separation," each of the colonies, another metropolitan writer had complained during the war, acted "solely for its own interest, without regard to the welfare or safety of the rest," a situation that unfortunately "naturally begat jealousies, envyings, animosities, and even the disposition to do one another mischief rather than good."[12] It was an unfortunate fact, Henry Frankland admitted from Boston in September 1757, that the colonies were "all jealous of each other."[13]

How, contemporaries seem mostly to have thought, could it have been otherwise? In language very similar to that expressed by Franklin just four years earlier, Thomas Pownall, the former Massachusetts governor, in 1764 in his widely-read treatise on The Administration of the Colonies, explained the deep and manifold differences among the colonies. He predicted that "the different manner in which they are settled, the different

---

[10] Benjamin Franklin, Interest of Great Britain Considered (London, 1760) in Leonard W. Labaree et al., eds., The Papers of Benjamin Franklin (21 vols., to date, New Haven, 1959-), 9:90. On this point, see especially Jack P. Greene, "'A Posture of Hostility': A Reconsideration of some Aspects of the Origins of the American Revolution," in Greene and William G. McLoughlin, Preachers & Politicians: Two Essays on the Origins of the American Revolution (Worcester, 1977), pp. 5-46.

[11] Malachy Postlethwayt, Britain's Commercial Interest Explained and Improved (2 vols., London, 1757), in Jack P. Greene, ed., Great Britain and the American Colonies 1606-1763 (New York, 1970), p. 298.

[12] State of the British and French Colonies In North America (London, 1755), p. 54.

[13] Henry Frankland to Thomas Pelham, 1 September 1757, Additional Manuscripts 33087, 353f., British Library (London).

modes under which they live, the different forms of charters, grants, and frames of government they possess, the various principles of repulsion, . . . the different interests which they actuate, the religious interests by which they are actuated, the rivalship and jealousies which arise from hence, and the impracticability, if not the impossibility, of reconciling and accommodating these incompatible ideas and claims" would "obviously for ever" keep them "disconnected and independent of each other,"[14] a mere "rope of sand," in the words of another writer, the individual strands of which were all too "peculiarly attached to their respective constitutions of Government," forms of society, and interests ever "to relish a union with one another."[15]

Differences and animosities among the colonies appeared to be so deep that they became an important element in the calculations of both metropolitan officials and American resistance leaders during the controversies that preceded the Revolution. "The mutual jealousies amongst the several Colonies," Lord Morton assured Chancellor Hardwicke in the early 1760s, "would always keep them in a state of dependence."[16] Metropolitan strategy in the Coercive Acts, the measures that played such a crucial role in stimulating the final crisis that led to war and the American decision for independence, was based on the supposition that colonial opposition could easily be diffused by a policy of divide and rule, a policy pursued by the British government throughout the nine years of war.

Nor prior to 1774 were many American leaders very sanguine about their capacity even to offer a united resistance, much less to weld themselves together into a single political society. The inability of the colonists to maintain economic sanctions against Britain during the crisis over the Townsend Acts between 1768 and 1770 provided an object lesson in the difficulties of united action and exacerbated longstanding fears of internal division. These experiences and fears were certainly one of the more important deterrents to colonial revolt right through the mid-1770s.

Nor were such fears and the perceptions of diversity that underlay them quickly dissipated once united resistance began in the mid-1770s. Rather, close associations in the Continental Congresses seem both to have sharpened those perceptions and to have intensified the distrust that accompanied them. "The Characters of Gentlemen in the four New England Colonies," John Adams wrote to Joseph Hawley in November 1775, "differ as much from those in the others . . . as much as [in] several distinct Nations almost. Gentlemen, Men of Sense, or any Kind of Education in the other Colonies are much fewer in Proportion than in N. England,"

[14] Pownall, *The Administration of the Colonies* (London, 1764), in Greene, ed., *Great Britain and the American Colonies*, p. 306.
[15] "Some Thoughts on the Settlement and Government of Our Colonies in North America," 10 March 1763, Add. Mss. (Liverpool Papers) 38335, 74-77ff., British Library.
[16] As quoted by Sir Lewis Namier, *England in the Age of the American Revolution* (London, 1963), p. 276.

5

Adams thought, expressing his customary sectional pride: "Gentlemen in the other Colonies have large Plantations of slaves, and the common People among them are very ignorant and very poor. These Gentlemen are accustomed, habituated to higher Notions of themselves and the distinction between them and the common People, than We are." Ever the realist, Adams thought that nothing less than "a Miracle" could produce "an instantaneous alteration of the Character of a Colony, and that Temper and those Sentiments which its Inhabitants imbibed with their Mothers Milk, and which have grown with their Growth and strengthened with their Strength." [17]

More cautious delegates especially doubted that any effective or lasting union among such heterogeneous components could ever turn out well. "Their different Forms of Government—Productions of Soil—and Views of Commerce, their different Religions—Tempers and private Interests—their Prejudices against, and Jealousies of, each other—all have, and ever will, from the Nature and Reason of things, conspire to create such a Diversity of Interests, Inclinations, and Decisions, that they never can [long] unite together even for their own Protection," predicted Joseph Galloway: "In this Situation Controversies founded in Interests, Religion or Ambition, will soon embrue their Hands in the blood of each other." [18] Not just timid and future loyalists like Galloway, but also ardent proponents of continental union like John Adams, worried about the long-range prospects of a union. "I dread the Consequences of this Disimilitude of Character" among the colonies, wrote Adams, "and without the Utmost Caution . . . and the most considerate Forbearance with one another and prudent Condenscention . . . , they will certainly be fatal." [19]

These widespread perceptions of diversity among the separate states and regions and the many difficulties they created were not the only long-term source of anxiety that made people skeptical about the viability of a continental union. Bernard Bailyn has shown in detail the pervasiveness in early American politics of fears of the corrupting tendencies of power.[20] The particular difficulties of bringing a distant power to account had been indelibly impressed upon Americans during the long controversy with Britain after 1763. These painful lessons gave rise to a profound mistrust of central power that was readily transferable from the British government to an American national government. Such fears constituted a second precondition that delayed and affected the creation of a continental union. Having just separated from a strong central government, in some major part, because they had been unable to influence it in

---

[17] John Adams to Joseph Hawley, 25 November 1775, in Smith, ed., *Letters of Delegates,* 2:385.
[18] Joseph Galloway to [Samuel Verplanck], 30 December 1774, ibid., 1:288.
[19] Adams to Hawley, 25 November 1775, ibid., 2:385-386.
[20] Bernard Bailyn, *The Ideological Origins of the American Revolution* (Cambridge, 1967), pp. 55-93, and *The Origins of American Politics* (New York, 1968), pp. 41-58, 135-161.

their favor, much less to control it, many American leaders were understandably wary, as Merrill Jensen has repeatedly emphasized, of creating something similar in America.[21] More recently, Rakove has pointed out that this wariness rarely rose to the surface of public life during the early years of the War for Independence.[22] But it was so deeply embedded in public consciousness as to be easily reactivated by those who, like North Carolina delegate Thomas Burke, had an especially intense fear of power and were anxious lest, in the absence of adequate restraints, the members of a national government "would make their own power as unlimited as they please."[23] This suspicion and fear of central power meant that delegations of power to a nationwide government in the Articles of Confederation would necessarily be limited.[24]

The absence of positive examples in either theory or history constituted yet a third precondition that limited expectations and shaped attitudes about the form of a continental union. By 1787-88 assiduous scholars of the science of politics, such as James Madison and James Wilson, had analyzed existing literature on "Ancient & Modern Confederacies" exhaustively and systematically.[25] By contrast in the mid-1770s, no one was similarly prepared to put the problems of an extensive continental union in historical perspective. What American resistance leaders did know, however, discouraged all but a small minority from being very optimistic. As Gordon S. Wood has observed, "few Americans thought that . . . an extensive continental republic, as distinct from a league of states, was feasible."[26] This opinion derived in part from Montesquieu, the one reputable source of authority on the subject, who was of the opinion that liberty, as some later antifederalists phrased it, could not be preserved over an extensive territory "otherwise than by a confederation

---

[21] See Jensen, *Articles of Confederation,* and "The Articles of Confederation," in *Fundamental Testaments of the American Revolution* (Washington, 1973), pp. 49-80.

[22] Rakove, *Beginnings of National Politics,* pp. 1-239.

[23] Thomas Burke to Richard Caswell, 29 April 1777, in Smith, ed., *Letters to Delegates,* 6:672.

[24] A later corollary of this fear that a central government would run roughshod over the rights and powers of the constituent components of the union was that in America, as in Britain, not only power but wealth and talent, attracted by the great influence of a central government, would all flow from the peripheries to the center. Agrippa later articulated this fear succinctly during the debate over the constitution in 1787, predicting that the northern and southern states would "in a very short time sink into the same degradation and contempt with respect to the middle state[s] as Ireland, Scotland, & Wales are in with regard to England. All the men of genius and wealth will resort to the seat of government, that will be center of revenue, and of business, which the extremes will be drained to supply." Letters of Agrippa [James Winthrop], in Cecelia M. Kenyon, ed., *The Antifederalists* (Indianapolis, 1966), p. 157.

[25] See James Madison, "Ancient & Modern Confederacies," in William T. Hutchinson et al., eds., *The Papers of James Madison* (Chicago, 1962-), 9:4-24; Benjamin F. Wright, ed., *The Federalist* (Cambridge, 1961), pp. 171-185; and Robert Green McCloskey, ed., *The Works of James Wilson* (2 vols., Cambridge, 1967), 1:247-269.

[26] Gordon S. Wood, *The Creation of the American Republic 1776-1787* (Chapel Hill, 1969), p. 58.

of republics, possessing all the powers of internal government, but united in the management of their general and foreign concern," a theory that seemed to have been more than adequately borne out by the Americans' recent experience in the old British empire.[27]

Just as Montesquieu taught Americans that small republics linked together in a loose confederation had a better chance of surviving and preserving their citizens' liberty than large consolidated republics, so also did both historical and comtemporary examples. The people who contrived the first American national union were familiar with the confederated governments of the United Provinces of The Netherlands and the league of Swiss cantons, each of which was a limited confederacy that reserved considerable local autonomy to its constituent parts. From the works of Sir William Temple and Abbe Reynall, they understood that each of these confederations had serious deficiencies. Yet, their longevity constituted a strong recommendation for limiting grants of powers to a central government. Although some questioned the extent to which the Dutch had actually managed to preserve much liberty in their confederacy, the example still served as further confirmation of the correctness of Montesquieu's belief that the only viable kind of confederation among republics was one with sharply restricted powers.[28]

A fourth precondition inhibiting rapid formation of a permanent continental union .was the almost total absence of any sense of American national consciousness. Right down to the actual break with Britain, colonial national consciousness had been intensely British. All over the colonies, Americans took pride in their incorporation into the larger Anglophone world. Their ability to identify themselves as "free Englishmen, inheriting the liberties, rights, and culture of all British subjects was, for them, essential to the maintenance of a positive sense of identity. This "feeling of a community of values," traditions, language, religion, manners, interests, and identity between Britain and the colonies was powerfully enhanced by the colonies' close—and growing—commercial association with the metropolis.[29] Certainly, as one contemporary observer remarked, the colonies even as late as the early 1760s were more "directly connected with their Mother Country" than they were "with each other."[30]

---

[27] Address and Reasons of Dissent of the Minority of the Convention of the State of Pennsylvania, 1787, in Kenyon, ed., *Antifederalists*, p. 39. See also Wood, *Creation of American Republic*, pp. 356, 499, and Samuel H. Beer, "Federalism, Nationalism, and Democracy in America," *American Political Science Review* 72 (1978), 13.

[28] See Josiah Bartlett's Notes, [12 June-12 July 1776], John Adams' Notes of Debate, 30 July, 1 August 1776, John Witherspoon's Speech, [30 July 1776], and Benjamin Rush's Notes for a Speech, [1 August 1776], in Smith, ed., *Letters to Delegates*, 4:199-200, 568, 587, 592, 598-599; William Henry Drayton's Speech, 20 January 1778, in Hezekiah Niles, ed., *Principles and Acts of the Revolution in America* (New York, 1876), p. 563.

[29] Yehoshua Arieli, *Individualism and Nationalism in American Ideology* (Cambridge, 1964), pp. 45-49.

[30] "Some Thoughts on the Settlement and Government of Our Colonies," 74-77ff.

In view of these facts, it was scarcely surprising, as Franklin observed in 1760, that the colonies "all love[d] Britain much more than they love[d] one another."[31] By the middle decades of the eighteenth century, the colonists' pride in being British had, in Yehoshua Arieli's words, "all but obliterated" any "sense of separation and distinctiveness" that the colonists, especially New Englanders, might have felt earlier in the colonial period.[32] There was not "a single true *New England* Man, in the whole Province," exclaimed the Reverend John Barnard in 1734 from Massachusetts, the colony that had been most resistant to the benefits of metropolitan imperialism, cultural as well as economic and political, during the seventeenth century, who did not "readily" subscribe to the belief that "that form of Civil Government is best for us, which we are under, I mean the *British Constitution*."[33]

This widespread identification with Britain necessarily meant that, far from being exponents of American nationalism, the colonists exhibited "an intense personal affection, even reverence, for" British "leaders, institutions, and culture" and the most profound feelings of *British* nationalism.[34] Nor were these feelings at any time more intense than in the 1760s during the wake of the Seven Years' War. That so much of that war had been fought in the colonies, that the metropolitan government had made such a major effort to defend the colonies, and that the colonies had themselves—for the very first time—made, as they were persuaded, a substantial contribution of money and manpower to such a great national cause increased the immediacy and strength of colonial ties with Britain and produced a surge of British patriotism among the colonists, a surge that found expression in the confident expectation that they were now finally—or would soon be—"upon an equal footing" with Englishmen at home.[35]

Even the long and bitter controversy during the 1760s and 1770s could not wholly eradicate this deep-seated reverence for Britain. Throughout that controversy, as Samuel H. Beer has noted, the colonists "steadfastly claimed that they sought only freedom within the British empire, not freedom from it."[36] "So strong has been their Attachment to Britain" that "the Abilities of a Child might have governed this country," Connecticut delegate Oliver Wolcott said in May 1776 in expressing his dismay over the ineptness of the British government's handling of the colonies over the previous few years.[37]

[31] Franklin, *Interest of Great Britain Considered,* in *Franklin Papers,* vol. 9, 90.

[32] Arieli, *Individualism and Nationalism,* pp. 45-49.

[33] John Barnard, *The Throne Established By Righteousness* (Boston, 1734), as quoted by Paul A. Varg, "The Advent of Nationalism, 1758-1776," *American Quarterly* 16 (1964):172.

[34] Edwin Burrows and Michael Wallace, "The American Revolution: The Ideology and Psychology of National Liberation," *Perspectives in American History,* (1972), 6:275-276.

[35] *State of the British and French Colonies,* pp. 63-64.

[36] Beer, "Federalism, Nationalism, and Democracy," 11.

[37] Oliver Wolcott to Samuel Lyman, 16 May 1776, in Smith, ed., *Letters to Delegates.* 4:17.

In early 1776, Thomas Paine endeavored in *Common Sense* to make Americans aware of the many social and cultural unities among them and to articulate a vision of America's potential as a united republican political society that would serve as an example for the rest of the world. But not even Paine's persuasive rhetoric and exhilarating vision of Americans' common destiny in occupying a place of first importance in the unfolding course of history could immediately produce a powerful, subsuming national consciousness of the kind usually connoted by the word *nationalism*.[38] John Shy has shown that the War for Independence and, more especially, the behavior of the British Army and the widespread popular participation in the war, contributed to a kind of "hothouse nationalism,"[39] while the revolution itself provided Americans with an instant common past. But it would be at least two further generations before most Americans would give a high priority to American, as opposed to their own state or regional, loyalties. Becoming visibly manifest only in the mid-1760s, the process by which Americans began to think of themselves as "a people" was still in a primitive stage of development between 1775 and 1787.

The fifth, last, and in many respects the most important precondition that significantly inhibited and affected the development of a continental union was the long existence of the several states as separate corporate entities. By the time of independence, every one of the thirteen colonies except Georgia had been in existence as a distinct corporate body for at least nine decades, while the oldest colonies in the Chesapeake and in New England went back to the early decades of the seventeenth century. Consisting of a well-defined body of territory, each of these colonies had its own peculiar constitution, institutions, laws, history, and identity to which its inhabitants were, for the most part, both well-socialized and strongly attached. The thirteen colonies, Andrew C. McLaughlin has remarked, were, in fact, "thirteen distinct groups of people."[40]

Throughout the colonial period, the members of each of these distinct groups identified and defined themselves not only as members of the greater British world of which they were a part, but also in terms of their common residence and collective experiences and associations as members of the clearly delineated and separate corporate bodies that each of the colonies was and had long been. If, prior to the Declaration of Independence, none of these colonies was independent of Britain, they were, nonetheless, as many contemporary observers pointed out, wholly independent of each other.

[38] For an elaboration of this argument, see Jack P. Greene, "Paine, America, and the 'Modernization' of Political Consciousness," *Political Science Quarterly* 93 (1978):73-92.
[39] John Shy, "The American Revolution: The Military Conflict Considered as a Revolutionary War," in Stephen G. Kurtz and James H. Hutson, eds., *Essays on the American Revolution* (Chapel Hill, 1973), p. 155.
[40] Andrew C. McLaughlin, *The Confederation and the Constitution 1783-1789* (New York, 1962), p. 41.

That Americans thought of themselves as being organized into a series of independent corporate entities each of which had its own specific identity and characteristics that they had every intention of preserving to the fullest possible extent, was evident throughout the controversy with Britain between 1764 and 1776. From the Stamp Act crisis onward, as McLaughlin has pointed out, Americans claimed both individual liberty *and* "local liberty within the British empire." They demanded recognition on the part of the metropolitan government, not just of the individual rights of Americans as Englishmen and as men, but also "of the rights of the colonies, as bodies corporate, constituent members of the Empire."[41]

Similarly, the delegates to the First and Second Continental Congresses went off to defend not only individual rights but the corporate rights of the colonies—and they went as representatives not of the people at large, but of the colonies, those ancient corporate entities which retained their distinctive identities through the rapid series of changes in government—from colonial to provisional revolutionary to state—in the mid-1770s. Historians have frequently cited Patrick Henry's famous declaration at the First Continental Congress in the fall of 1774 that "the distinctions between Virginians, Pennsylvanians, New Yorkers, and New Englanders are no more. I am not a Virginian, but an American."[42] But few Americans managed to shed their provincial identities and acquire a new national one so.quickly. Rooted in their intimate associations with their native or adopted colonies, their deep local patriotism continued to be manifest during the Revolution in a strong determination to preserve the identity, authority, and distinctiveness of the several corporate entities to which they belonged. The difficulty of reconciling this determination with the desire to create a new national entity was perhaps the most perplexing problem facing American resistance leaders in their efforts to create a lasting continental union.

III

Although these five preconditions—1) the widespread tendency to emphasize differences among the colonies with a corresponding mutuality of suspicion among them, 2) fear of the aggrandizing tendencies of a remote central power, 3) existing theory about and contemporary examples of confederated republics, 4) the primitive state of American national consciousness, and 5) a strong sense in every colony of its identity as a distinctive corporate entity with an unquestioned commitment to preserve that identity—either retarded the adoption of, or set definite limits upon,

[41] Andrew C. McLaughlin, *Foundations of American Constitutionalism* (New York, 1961), pp. 132-133, 138; Jack P. Greene, *The Quest For Power: The Lower Houses of Assembly in the Southern Royal Colonies, 1689-1776* (Chapel Hill, 1963), pp. 438-453.

[42] John Adams' Notes of Debates, [6 September 1776], in Smith, ed., *Letters to Delegates*, 1:28.

the form and nature of a continental union during the late 1770s, still other and ultimately more powerful long-range developments helped to predispose American leaders towards some kind of permanent union.

Certainly, the most important of those was the remarkable social and cultural convergence experienced by those colonies beginning during the last decades of the seventeenth century. What makes that convergence so remarkable is the extraordinary diversity among the colonies at the time of their original settlement. Indeed, if one looks closely at the two major centers of English settlement on the North American continent during the first half of the seventeenth century, at the tobacco colonies of the Chesapeake and the Puritan colonies of New England, it would be difficult to imagine how any two areas composed almost entirely of Englishmen could have been any *more* different. About the only characteristics they had in common were their ethnic homogeneity, their ruralness, and, after the first few years, an abundant local food supply. In almost every other respect, they were opposites.

Within a decade after the settlement of Virginia in 1607, the Chesapeake societies were oriented toward the production of a single staple crop, tobacco, for the metropolitan market. The high profits for tobacco quickly made the reckless and single-minded pursuit of individual gain the central animating impulse and chief social determinant of the region. In quest of wealth that would take them back to the civilized comforts they had left behind in England, men greedily took risks, dispersed themselves over the land, and engaged in ruthless exploitation of labor. This highly market-oriented society was composed very heavily of landless single men, most of them English bond servants. With few families, the structure of its households more closely resembled those of nineteenth-century mining boomtowns. With a high death rate and a low birth rate, population increased very slowly and largely through immigration. The differential success rates characteristic of staple economies meant that wealth was concentrated in a relatively few hands and levels of social differentiation, based almost entirely upon wealth, were high. At the same time, the fragility of life and fortune and the lack of a clear connection between wealth and the traditional attributes of leadership as they were understood by Englishmen at home meant that political and social authority was weak, impermanent, and open to challenge and that the potential for social discord was great. The last thing that seemed to interest early Virginians, a later observer remarked, was the building of "a Country for posterity."[43]

---

[43] See Edmund S. Morgan, *American Slavery, American Freedom: The Ordeal of Colonial Virginia* (New York, 1975), and Thad W. Tate and David L. Ammerman, eds., *The Chesapeake in the Seventeenth Century: Essays on Anglo-American Society* (Chapel Hill, 1979). The quotation is from John Hammond, *Leah and Rachel* (London, 1656), in Clayton C. Hall, ed., *Narratives of Early Maryland 1633-1684* (New York, 1910), p. 286.

By sharp contrast, the Puritan colonies of New England had been settled by families in a single massive migration concentrated in the 1630s and motivated very largely by the desire to escape the religious impurity of Albion and to establish a city upon a hill, a true religious commonwealth that would serve as a model for the Christian world. Highly religious, with pronounced communal impulses, the inhabitants settled in nuclear households and in small villages organized around the church, villages that from the very beginning were conceived of as permanent. With no profitable staple, they engaged primarily in mixed subsistence agriculture and built societies that were far more egalitarian in terms of the distribution of wealth than those to the south. With a benign disease environment and a balanced sex ratio, mortality was low, fecundity high, and demographic growth rapid, primarily the result of natural increase. With a large number of visible leaders who obviously had all the attributes of sociopolitical authority among the initial immigrants and a high degree of cooperation between secular and clerical leaders, lines of authority were clear and the potential for contention and discord low.[44]

At least on the surface, these divergencies among the colonies seemed to increase over time as the Chesapeake colonies acquired a strong biracial character with the transition from European servant to African slave labor between 1680 and 1730 and with the establishment of two new—and also distinctive—nodes of settlement during the last decades of the seventeenth century. The so-called middle colonies, consisting of New York, conquered from the Dutch in 1664, New Jersey, Delaware, and Pennsylvania, settled by the English between 1664 and 1681, were characterized by profound ethnic, religious, and social diversity, rapid change, and, at least through their first decades of English control, high levels of public contention.[45] The other node, stretching out from Charleston on the South Carolina coast north into southern North Carolina and south into coastal Georgia, was similarly diverse. With rice, naval stores, and eventually indigo as enormously profitable staples, these colonies, at least at their center, were even more materialistic and more slave and African than the Chesapeake colonies. Many parishes in low-country South Carolina had a black-white ratio of from 7 to 9:1 and looked far more like the West Indian colonies of Barbados and Jamaica than any colonies to the north.[46]

---

[44] For summaries of the conclusions of recent literature on colonial New England, see John M. Murrin, "Review Essay," *History and Theory* 11 (1972):226-275, and Jack P. Greene, "Autonomy and Stability: New England and the British Colonial Experience in Early Modern America," *Journal of Social History* 7 (1974):171-194.

[45] See Patricia U. Bonomi, "The Middle Colonies: Embryo of the New Political Order," in Alden T. Vaughan and George A. Billias, eds., *Perspectives on Early American History: Essays in Honor of Richard B. Morris*, (New York, 1973), pp. 63-92, and Douglas Greenberg, "The Middle Colonies in Recent American Historiography," *William and Mary Quarterly*, 3d ser., 36 (1979):396-427.

[46] See Peter H. Wood, *Black Majority: Negroes in Colonial South Carolina from 1670 through the Stono Rebellion* (New York, 1974), and Converse D. Clowse, *Economic Beginnings in Colonial South Carolina 1670-1730* (Columbia, 1971).

13

As noted earlier, throughout the colonial period, most contemporaries continue to be far more impressed with dissimilarities among the colonies than with similarities. However, it is clear in retrospect that the colonies were becoming not less, but more alike during the century after 1680. This process can be seen in the gradual diminution of the sharp divergencies that had initially distinguished the Chesapeake from New England. The slow improvement of health conditions in the Chesapeake during the seventeenth century had led by the first decades of the eighteenth century to a balance of sex ratios and a more typically European family structure. Similarly, as tobacco profits settled to less spectacular and somewhat steadier levels, expectations among the successful of returning to England all but disappeared, the commitment to the Chesapeake became stronger, settlement became more compact and expansion more measured, and the devotion to staple production was less exclusive. Concomitantly, social, religious, and political institutions acquired more vigor; society became far more stable; and the communal impulse was much more evident, as Chesapeake society cohered around an emergent and authoritative socioeconomic elite, members of which exhibited all of the traditional attributes of social leadership as they strove successfully to assimilate themselves to the powerful cultural model of the English gentry. The new sense of coherence and community which was so strikingly manifest in Virginia after 1725 was, perhaps ironically, actually intensified among the free white population by the pressures toward racial solidarity created by the transition to African slave labor on the plantations.[47]

At the same time, in New England, the deterioration of health conditions by the mid-eighteenth century brought mortality to levels near those in the Chesapeake. Other developments also pushed the region closer to patterns of behavior and values toward which Virginians were moving. These developments included impressive population growth, a dispersion of people out from the original village centers to individual farms, an increasing differentiation of society and complexity of kinship networks, a growing diversity in many aspects of town life, acceleration of the economy as a result of rapid internal population growth and the increasing integration of the New England economy into the larger Atlantic economy, a slow attenuation of the social religious synthesis of the founders, a growing demand for and exhibition of autonomy among the sons of each successive generation, more individualism and more conflict within the public life of the towns, and a marked rise in geographical mobility. All of these developments weakened the bonds of community and pushed

[47] See Tate and Ammerman, eds., *Chesapeake in the Seventeenth Century*, pp. 206-296; Morgan, *American Slavery, American Freedom*, pp. 131-211, 295-362; and Jack P. Greene, "Society, Ideology, and Politics: An Analysis of the Political Culture of Mid-Eighteenth-Century Virginia," in Richard M. Jellison, ed., *Society, Freedom, and Conscience: The Coming of the Revolution in Virginia, Massachusetts, and New York* (New York, 1976), pp. 14-76, 191-200.

14

New England in the direction of greater individualism, personal autonomy, and social fluidity.[48]

Not just the Chesapeake and New England colonies, but the other continental colonies as well, were moving closer together in their configuration of socioeconomic and political life. The Carolinas and New York moved in the same direction as Virginia and Pennsylvania, which also began with a strong corporate and religious impulse, in the same direction as New England, only at a vastly more accelerated rate. Envision a hypothetical continuum running between the two poles of pure individualism and tight communalism at three different times—1660, 1713, and 1763—with each colonial area plotted along the line according to its dominant patterns. Such a continuum would show a steady convergence towards the center with, to take only the major continental colonies as examples, Virginia, South Carolina, and New York moving from individualism towards community and Massachusetts and Pennsylvania moving from community towards individualism until, by the last half of the eighteenth century, the differences among the colonies were less than they had been before.

New England was still more religious and had much lower levels of wealth concentration than the colonies to the south, while Virginia and South Carolina with their legions of slaves were certainly more strongly oriented toward acquisitiveness and more exploitative. But not even the presence of so many slaves in the southern colonies, certainly the most conspicuous difference between them and New England, was yet a crucial distinguishing feature. Though the ratio of black slaves of the free population decreased steadily from the most southern to the most northern colonies, slavery as late as 1770 was still an expanding institution in every one of the colonies that revolted except New Hampshire; and New York, Rhode Island, Pennsylvania, and New Jersey all had populations with a higher proportion of slaves than had the Chesapeake colonies as late as 1700 to 1710.[49]

The explanation for this growing convergence is to be found in two overlapping processes that were simultaneously at work in all the colonies. For purposes of analysis, they may be designated, rather crudely, as processes of Americanization and Anglicization. Distance from Britain, the looseness of British controls, the availability of land and other exploitable resources, and incorporation into the larger metropolitan economy and, increasingly, into the broad Atlantic trading system stretching from West Africa to the Caribbean in the south and North America to

---

[48] See especially, Murrin, "Review Essay," pp. 240-275; Greene, "Autonomy and Stability," pp. 187-193; Richard L. Bushman, *From Puritan to Yankee: Character and the Social Order in Connecticut, 1690-1765* (Cambridge, Mass., 1967).

[49] Population figures may be found in *Historical Statistics of the United States, Colonial Times to 1757* (Washington, 1960), p. 756.

western Europe in the north—all of these conditions combined to produce
levels of prosperity sufficient to support societies that were becoming
more developed, complex, differentiated, and pluralistic. They also stimulated the high levels of individual activity and expansiveness that underlay
the remarkable economic and demographic growth that characterized all
of the North American colonies through the middle decades of the
eighteenth century.

These developments also seem to have led throughout the colonies to
the development of "more autonomous personality types" that were impatient with authority and jealous of the personal independence which
was the chief defining quality of any fully competent man,[50] a fact appreciated by perceptive British officials for many decades prior to the
American Revolution. In his analysis of Britain's difficulties in America
during the 1760s and 1770s, William Knox, undersecretary for the colonies with experience as a royal officeholder in Georgia, declared that
conditions of both private and public life in America had strongly militated against the development of "all [of those] ideas of subordination and
dependence" that had traditionally been thought to be requisite for the
successful functioning of the British political system.[51] South Carolina
lawyer, Charles Pinckney, testified to the truth of Knox's observation
during the Philadelphia Convention of 1787, when he noted that all of
Britain's former colonies exhibited "fewer distinction of fortune and less
of rank, than among the inhabitants of any other nation."[52]

Along with the failure to establish a proper religious hierarchy and the
total absence of a middle or aristocratic estate, the wide distribution of
property referred to by Pinckney served to inhibit the emergence, as
Knox and many others pointed out, of whatever feelings "of subordination that property, ancestry or dignity of station . . . naturally excited"
among the British at home. The weakness of such feelings inevitably
meant that the political systems of the colonies were thoroughly
"tinctured with republicanism." In all the colonies, "the Democracy had
the leading influence and the general tendency," Knox thought, toward
"adoption of the commonwealth-mode," a general tendency that only
"increased with their wealth, & . . . their prosperity."[53] In the words of J.
R. Pole, "the American Colonies developed the characteristics of what
would later be known as a republican form of government many years
before they were to claim to be republican in principle."[54]

[50] See Burrows and Wallace, "American Revolution," pp. 287-288.
[51] Jack P. Greene, ed., "William Knox's Explanation for the American Revolution,"
William and Mary Quarterly, 3d ser., 30 (1973):299.
[52] Speech of Charles Pinckney, 25 June 1787, in Max Farrand, ed., *The Records of the
Federal Convention of 1787* (4 vols., 1911-1937), 1:398.
[53] Greene, ed., "Knox's Explanation," pp. 297-306.
[54] J. R. Pole, *The Seventeenth Century: The Sources of Legislative Power* (Charlottesville,
1969), p. 69.

Throughout the free segments of the Anglo-American population, from one region to the next, visitor after visitor reported that people in the colonies seemed to exhibit little respect for authority. "A fierce spirit of liberty," declared Edmund Burke, echoing a common opinion in March 1775, was "stronger in the English colonies, probably, than in any other people of the earth."[55] This pervasive and deeply engraved commitment to personal freedom and independence, said Samuel Williams, whose *History of Vermont,* published during the last decade of the eighteenth century, constitutes one of the first systematic analyses of the configuration of the emerging American society, "had been the constant product and effect, of the state of society in the British colonies" for "a century and a half," and, he should have added, of the social, economic, and physical forces that produced that society.[56]

If, as Williams observed, a "similarity of situation and conditions" had gradually pushed the colonies toward a similitude of society and values, more specifically, toward "that natural, easy, independent situation, and spirit, in which the body of the [free] people were found, when the American war came on," still a second major influence—growing Anglicization—was important in helping to erode differences among the colonies.[57] Partly, this development resulted from deliberate efforts by metropolitan authorities to bring the colonies under closer control, including gradual conversion of most of the colonies to royal provinces directly under crown supervision, the imposition of a common political system, at least at the provincial level, upon those colonies, strong pressures upon the five remaining private colonies to assimilate to that system, and the largely successful attempt, beginning in the 1650s, to subordinate the economies of the colonies to that of the metropolis. These efforts led both to the establishment of a common pattern of political institutions among the colonies and to an ever more intense political and economic involvement between metropolis and colonies. This growing involvement, together with an increasing volume of contacts among individuals and the improved communications that accompanied them, drew the colonists ever closer into the ambit of British life during the eighteenth century, provided them with easier and more direct access to English, Irish, and, increasingly, Scottish ideas and models of behavior, and tied them more closely to metropolitan culture.

As ties with the metropolis tightened, the pull of metropolitan culture increased, and the standards of the metropolis more and more came to be the primary model for colonial behavior, the one certain measure of cul-

[55] Edmund Burke, "Speech on Moving Resolutions for Conciliation with the Colonies," 22 March 1775, in Thomas H. D. Mahoney, ed., *Edmund Burke: Selected Writings and Speeches on America* (Indianapolis, 1964), pp. 131-132.
[56] Samuel Williams, *The Natural and Civil History of Vermont* (2 vols., Walpole, N. H., 1794), 2:431.
[57] Ibid., 429-430.

tural achievement for these provincial societies at the outermost peripheries of the British world. Throughout the colonies, and especially among the emergent elites, there was a self-conscious effort to anglicize colonial life through deliberate imitation of metropolitan institutions, values, and culture. Thus, prior to the mid-1770s, Anglo-Americans thought of themselves primarily as Britons, albeit Britons overseas. Contrary to the dominant opinion among earlier historians, colonial comparisons of the colonies with Britain did not usually come out in favor of the colonies. The colonists were not especially interested in identifying and celebrating what was distinctively American about themselves. Instead, so far as possible, they generally sought to eliminate those distinctions so that they might, with more credibility, think of themselves—and be thought of by people in Britain—as demonstrably British.[58]

As each of the colonies had during the century previous to the American Revolution become both more American and more British, as they increasingly assimilated to a common American social and behavioral pattern and to British cultural models, they became more alike. They shared similar institutions, a common identity as Britons overseas, a similar historical experience, a common political inheritance, the same political and social ideology, and similarly, though by no means equally, fragile structures of social and political authority. They were becoming, to one degree or another, more complex and pluralistic societies, and they all had an upward trajectory of demographic and economic growth. As William Grayson later remarked, they also displayed a conspicuous "similarity of laws, religion, language, and manners."[59]

There were still obvious differences, many of them rooted in the distinction between the slave-powered staple economies of the south and the mixed agricultural and commercial economies of the north; albeit, when John Dickinson worried in July 1776 about the eventual dissolution of the American union, he drew the line not between north and south, but between New England and the rest of the states.[60] Whatever the continuing variety among the new American states and to whatever extent that variety continued to impress contemporaries, their interests, "Trade, Language, Customs; and Manners," Benjamin Rush could credibly insist in congressional debate during the summer of 1776, were by no means "more divided than they are among . . . people in Briton."[61]

[58] A fuller discussion of this subject may be found in Jack P. Greene, "Search for Identity: An Interpretation of the Meaning of Selected Patterns of Social Response in Eighteenth-Century America," *Journal of Social History* 3 (1970):189-224. The contrary view is succinctly stated in Max Savelle, "Nationalism and Other Loyalties in the American Revolution," *American Historical Review* 68 (1962):904.

[59] Grayson's observation may be conveniently found in Kenyon, ed., *Antifederalists*, p. 282.

[60] "John Dickinson's Notes for a Speech in Congress," [1 July 1776], in Smith, ed., *Letters of Delegates*, 4:356.

[61] "John Adams' Notes of Debates," 1 August 1776, 592, and "Benjamin Rush's Notes for a Speech in Congress," [1 August 1776], in ibid., 592, 599.

This growing convergence was the single most important precondition for either the American Revolution or the emergence of an American national government and an American nationality. As the late David Potter reminded us, however, social and "cultural similarities alone will not provide a basis of affinity between groups." Nationalism and similar collective loyalties have to rest on "two psychological bases": the "feeling of a common culture *and* the feeling of common interest." "Of the two," he posited, "the concept of culture is, no doubt, of greater weight," but it cannot have its full effect without a mutual awareness of common interests.[62]

In the American case, a prior awareness of a common interest was a second necessary precondition even for a clear and full recognition of the existence of a common culture. As several scholars have argued, the emergence during the middle decades of the eighteenth century of intercolonial trading patterns and communications networks, an interlocking elite, closer interurban ties, and common participation between 1739 and 1763 in two wars against the neighboring colonies of foreign metropolitan powers resulted in the colonies becoming increasingly more interested in one another and perhaps even in the development of some nascent sense of American community. This development was in turn stimulated, to some degree, by the metropolitan penchant, especially evident during the mid-century intercolonial wars, for treating the continental colonies as a unit and describing them under the common rubric *American*.[63] Perhaps the most important point that can be made about the Albany Plan of Union in the early 1750s, in fact, a point that seems not to have been appreciated by anyone at the time, was not that it was universally rejected, but that it had been proposed and adopted by a conference of leaders in the first place. For its mere initiation manifested at least a rudimentary consciousness of the existence of some bases for an "American" union.

But Americans did not yet fully understand nor attach any special importance to the many and growing commonalities among them—as opposed to the similarities that linked them all to Britain—until the metropolis vividly impressed upon them that they had a common interest by challenging their pretensions to an equal status with Britons at home by new, restrictive measures between 1763 and 1776. In pointing out the seemingly vast differences among the colonies and stressing the extent to which those differences made united action improbable, Franklin had

[62] David M. Potter, "The Historians' Use of Nationalism and Vice Versa," *American Historical Review* 67 (1962):935, 949.

[63] See Albert Harkness, Jr., "Americanism and Jenkins' Ear," *Mississippi Valley Historical Review,* 37 (1950):61-90; Richard L. Merritt, *Symbols of American Community. 1735-1775* (New Haven, 1966); Michael Kraus, *Intercolonial Aspects of American Culture on the Eve of the Revolution, with Special Reference to the Northern Towns* (New York, 1928); and Carl Bridenbaugh, *Cities in Revolt: Urban Life in America. 1743-1776* (New York, 1955).

warned metropolitans in 1760, in words echoed both by himself and many later observers, that a "grievous tyranny and oppression" might very well drive the colonies to unite.[64] During the 1760s, many Americans had pointed out, in the words of Richard Henry Lee of Virginia, that the colonists' attachment to Britain could be preserved "on no other terms . . . than by a free intercourse and equal participation of good offices, liberty and free constitution of government."[65] But Lee's point was appreciated, virtually alone in Britain, by Burke when he pointed out that America's affection for Britain had always been conditional upon its continuing ability to carry "the mark of a free people in all" its "internal concerns" and to retain at least "the image of the British constitution."[66]

Britain's insistence upon treating the colonies as separate and unequal in the 1760s and 1770s was thus the contingent development that, in the words of Arieli, provided the "point of observation and comparison from which" the colonists could finally appreciate the many unities among them.[67] Increasingly during those years, they came to comprehend that, given existing attitudes among those in power in Britain, membership in the British Empire did not mean, for them, the equality as freeborn Englishmen to which they had so long aspired. Rather, it meant an inferior status equivalent, in the bitter words of Alexander Hamilton in 1774, only to those unworthy people in Britain who were *"in so mean a situation"* that they were "supposed to have no will of their own" and, according to the legal theorist Sir William Blackstone, therefore deserved no role in governing themselves.[68]

As the colonists slowly came to this comprehension, they began to lose their British nationalism and to develop, as grounds for asserting their own worthiness against their metropolitan antagonists, an awareness of their common interest in resisting metropolitan efforts to place them in a subordinate, unequal, and unBritish status. They developed as well an understanding of the common histories of the colonies as asylums for the oppressed and places where unfortunates could make new beginnings and of the many social and cultural similarities among them. Only then did they begin to acquire some sense of their possible "future power and imperial greatness" as a separate American people and to glimpse the potential for a comprehensive American political union.[69]

---

[64] Franklin, *Interest of Great Britain Considered*, in *Franklin Papers*, 9:90.

[65] Richard Henry Lee to Arthur Lee, 4 July 1765, in James C. Ballagh, ed., *Letters of Richard Henry Lee* (2 vols., New York, 1912-1914), 1:11. See also, among many expressions of similar beliefs, Robert M. Calhoon, "William Smith Jr.'s Alternative to the American Revolution," *William and Mary Quarterly*, 3d ser., 22 (1965):117.

[66] Burke, "Speech on American Taxation," 19 April 1774, in Mahoney, ed., *Edmund Burke*, p. 79.

[67] Arieli, *Individualism and Nationalism*, p. 45.

[68] Hamilton, *The Farmer Refuted*, [23 February] 1774, in Harold C. Syrett and Jacob E. Cooke, eds., *The Papers of Alexander Hamilton* (19 vols., New York, 1961-73), 1:106-107.

[69] Arieli, *Individualism and Nationalism*, pp. 67-68.

Still a third precondition that propelled leaders of American resistance toward a national union was their deep-seated and residual fears of disorder. Almost to a man, they took pride in the Anglo-Americans' devotion to liberty. But they knew from history and their own experience that the line between liberty and licentiousness was thin, and they worried that the notorious weakness of authority in America might lead to the breakdown of political institutions. Although the extent and depth of such fears varied from place to place, according to the strength of local political institutions and the cohesiveness of local elites,[70] they had partly justified the powerful anglicizing impulses among the colonies' emerging elites throughout the eighteenth century and had actually functioned as a powerful deterrent to revolution during the period from 1763 to 1776.

One of the most evident manifestations of these fears in the prerevolutionary period had been the belief that the British connection was essential to the continued political stability of the colonies. "We think ourselves happier . . . in being dependent on Great Britain, than in a state of independence," said an anonymous writer in the *New York Mercury* in 1764, "for then the disputes amongst ourselves would throw us into all the confusion, and bring on us all the calamities usually attendant on civil wars."[71] Given the weakness of authority in the colonies, many people feared with John Dickinson that without Britain's controlling power, Anglo-America would quickly degenerate into "a multitude of Commonwealths, Crimes and Calamities—centuries of mutual Jealousies, Hatreds, Wars and Devastations, until at last the exhausted Provinces shall sink into Slavery under the yoke of some fortunate conqueror."[72]

During the uncertain situation that obtained after 1774, such anxieties quickly translated into powerful fears of division and disunion and pushed congressional delegates more and more toward the view that a national union was essential, not simply to coordinate resistance and war against Britain, but to prevent internal chaos. At the time of the First Continental Congress, Joseph Galloway, the later loyalist, was one of the few to voice openly his anxieties about the ill effects that might arise from the absence of a central authority, without which, he observed in urging his fellow delegates to support his proposed plan of union, the colonies would be "destitute of any supreme direction or decision whatever, even to the settlement of differences among themselves."[73]

---

[70] See on this point Jack P. Greene, "Social Context and the Causal Pattern of the American Revolution: A Preliminary Consideration of New York, Virginia and Massachusetts," in *La Révolution Américaine et L'Europe* (Paris, 1979), pp. 25-63.

[71] *New York Mercury*, 27 August 1764, as quoted by Burrows and Wallace, "American Revolution," p. 191.

[72] John Dickinson to William Pitt, 21 December 1765, Chatham Papers, PRO 30/8/97, Public Record Office (London).

[73] Joseph Galloway, *Historical and Political Reflections on the Rise and Progress of the American Rebellion* (London, 1780), p. 77, as quoted by Jensen, *Articles of Confederation*, p. 69.

With war and independence, however, virtually all delegates from the most cautious to the boldest agreed that "Disunion among ourselves," as Witherspoon declared, was "the greatest Danger We have"[74] and that a formal union was absolutely essential not just to prosecute the war but, in the words of Richard Henry Lee, to secure "internal peace."[75] In the existing situation, complained Edward Rutledge, a delegate from South Carolina, "the Inhabitants of every Colony consider[ed] themselves at Liberty to do as they please upon almost every occasion."[76] Only a formal and lasting continental union, as Gouverneur Morris had earlier suggested, could "restrain the democratic spirit, which the constitutions and the local circumstances of the country had so long fostered in the minds of the people."[77] If the colonies remained "separate and disunited, after this war," predicted Witherspoon in urging a formal confederation upon Congress, "we may be sure of coming off the worse." Victory over Britain would surely be followed by "a more lasting war, a more unnatural, more bloody, and more hopeless war, among the colonies themselves."[78]

Still a fourth, and final, major precondition that strongly predisposed American resistance leaders toward a permanent continental union was their long-standing involvement with the de facto federal system of government in the old British Empire. According to metropolitan theory, Britain and its colonies constituted a single unitary state in which unqualified sovereignty lay in the metropolitan government, or more specifically—following the working out of "revolution principles" during the Revolutionary Settlement between 1688 and 1715—in the King, Lords, and Commons in Parliament assembled. Resting on strong medieval precedents involving the relationship between England and the crown's dominions outside the realm, including the Channel Islands, Anjou, Aquitaine, Gascony, Ireland, Wales, and the Isle of Man,[79] this theory was subscribed to by virtually all metropolitan commentators on the governance of the empire throughout the colonial period and had been "given its classic formulation" in 1765 during the first stages of the col-

[74] Adams' Notes of Debate, 30 July 1776, in Smith, ed., Letters of Delegates, 4:568.

[75] Richard Henry Lee to Landon Carter, 2 June 1776, in Letters of R. H. Lee, 1:198.

[76] Edward Rutledge to John Jay, [8 June 1776], in Smith, ed., Letters of Delegates, 4:175.

[77] Jared Sparks, The Life of Gouverneur Morris (3 vols., Boston, 1832), 1:26-27, as cited by Merrill Jensen, "Articles of Confederation," p. 57.

[78] Speech of Witherspoon, [30 July 1776], in Smith, ed., Letters of Delegates, 4:584-585. On the generalized extent of how the fear of disunion operated in favor of continental confederation in the mid-1770s, see the excellent analysis in Rakove, Beginnings of National Politics, pp. 135-215.

[79] A. F. M. Madden, "1066, 1776 and All That: The Relevance of English Medieval Experience of 'Empire' to Later Imperial Constitutional Issues," in J. E. Flint and G. Williams, eds., Perspectives of Empire (London, 1973), pp. 9-26. See also the earlier exchange on this subject by C. H. McIlwain, The American Revolution: A Constitutional Interpretation (New York, 1924), and Robert L. Schuyler, Parliament and the British Empire (New York, 1929).

onists' quarrels with Britain by Blackstone in his authoritative *Commentaries on the Laws of England.*[80]

Whatever the theory, the old empire, "as a practical working system," as Andrew C. McLaughlin pointed out almost fifty years ago, was "marked by the distribution rather than by the concentration of authority." "In the actual workings of the Empire, during several generations," McLaughlin argued, "there had been an Empire in which powers were parceled out among governments" with the metropolitan government exercising general powers "that could not well be exercised by the colonies—the post-office, naturalization, war and peace, foreign affairs, intercolonial and foreign commerce, establishment of new colonies, etc.—" and the colonial governments exerting de facto and virtually exclusive jurisdiction over almost all manners of purely local concern. In "actual *practice,* the empire of the mid-eighteenth century was a diversified empire; powers were actually distributed and exercised by various governments."[81] As William Smith, Jr., the noted New York lawyer, had pointed out in the mid-1760s, political arrangements within the British Empire had gradually drifted to a point where there was in fact a *"manifold . . . Partition,* of the *Legislative* Authority of the Empire."[82]

Failure to rationalize the existing imperial system in a way that satisfied both colonists and metropolitan officials was, however, the constitutional rock on which the old empire split. As it had gradually taken shape during the last decades of the seventeenth century, this "problem of imperial organization had been primarily discussed in terms, not of the locus of sovereignty, but of the question, as an anonymous Virginian put it in 1701, of "how far the Legislative Authority is in the Assemblies."[83] That is, to what extent—and in what cases—was the jurisdiction of colonial legislatures limited by the authority of the metropolitan government? Prior to the 1760s, the debate over this question focused not upon Parliament's authority over the colonies, which was, in any case, usually exerted only in very limited spheres relating to trade and other economic concerns of the empire as a whole, but upon whether the authority of the king and his ministers to bind the colonies by executive orders was limited by the requirement of colonial legislative consent. No theoretical resolution of this problem was ever achieved. In the meantime, however, the empire functioned with a rather clear demarcation of authority, with virtually all

[80] See H. T. Dickinson, "The Eighteenth-Century Debate on the Sovereignty of Parliament," *Transactions of the Royal Historical Society,* 5th ser., 26 (1976):189-210; Bailyn, *Ideological Origins,* p. 201.

[81] McLaughlin, *Foundations of American Constitutionalism,* pp. 133-138, and *A Constitutional History of the United States* (New York, 1935), p. 14.

[82] Calhoon, ed., "Smith's Alternative to Revolution," p. 114.

[83] Louis B. Wright, ed., *An Essay Upon the Government of the Plantations on the Continent of America* (San Marino, 1945), pp. 15-17, 23.

internal matters being handled by the governments of the respective colonies and most external affairs by the metropolitan government.[84]

That this was indeed the proper line and that it ought to have explicit constitutional recognition was the argument of Americans of almost all political persuasions in the pre-Revolutionary debate with Britain after 1764. Increasingly in this debate, they endeavored to demarcate the jurisdictional boundaries between Parliament and the colonial assemblies according to external and internal spheres of authority, with the former belonging to Parliament and the latter to the colonial assemblies. Regarding colonial demands as a direct challenge to metropolitan theory about the location of sovereignty within the empire, spokesmen for the metropolitan government insisted upon reducing the controversy to the single issue of sovereignty. They insisted that the logic of the indivisibility of sovereignty rendered any suggestion of qualifications upon Parliament's authority wholly absurd. The colonists resisted such reductionism and endeavored, unsuccessfully, to focus debate upon the seemingly more tractable and certainly less abstract problem of how power was or should be allocated in a political system composed of several related, but nonetheless distinct, corporate entities. For the colonists, resolution of their dispute with Britain seemed to require little more than the rationalization of existing arrangements within the empire.

But the continued insistence by metropolitan protagonists that the issue was nothing short of the location of ultimate authority eventually forced Americans in the late 1760s and early 1770s to consider their relationship with Britain in these terms. By 1774, they had agreed that, if the indivisibility of sovereignty required that Parliament had either total authority over the colonies or none, it had none. The colonies, they argued, were separate states, each with its own sovereign legislature. The British Empire was therefore "an imperial federation of sovereign states sharing and establishing unity in a single monarch."[85] In the later words of John Witherspoon, it was "a federal" and not "an incorporating Union," the colonies having always been independent "of the people or Parliament of England."[86]

In contrast to their metropolitan protagonists, American resistance leaders never seem to have attached central importance to the abstract question of the locus of sovereignty as opposed to the more immediate issue of the allocation of power. Thus, when they took their first concrete steps toward creation of a continental political system in 1774-76, they made it abundantly clear that they had no intention, in the words of the

---

[84] See the discussion in Greene, ed., *Great Britain and the American Colonies*, pp. xi-xlvii, and Greene, "'Posture of Hostility,'" pp. 41-46.

[85] Bailyn, *Ideological Origins*, pp. 223-225.

[86] Thomas Jefferson's Notes of Proceedings in Congress, [June 1776], and John Adams' Notes of Debates, 1 August 1776, in Smith, ed., *Letters of Delegates*, 4:161, 593.

North Carolina lawyer James Iredell, of permitting "the happiness of
millions" to be sacrificed to so "narrow and pedantic . . . a point of
speculation."[87] If, as Beer has noted, "theory . . . powerfully directed"
the work of the people who fashioned and pushed through the Federal
Constitution of 1787,[88] experience and exigency were much more evident
in shaping the earliest national political system under both the Continental
Congress and Articles of Confederation. The Americans' experience in
the old empire had accustomed them to living in a political system in
which there were functionally two interdependent levels of government,
each with its own sphere of authority. Reinforced, beginning in 1775, by
the palpable fact that resistance and war, general activities that "from the
necessity of the case, . . . could not well be exercised" by the individual
states, this experience also produced a strong disposition to recreate in
their new national situation a system in which political authority was
similarly allocated.[89]

In view of their long experience with a divided structure of authority, it
is not surprising, as Rakove has found, that, far from being "central to the
burgeoning Revolutionary . . . controversy between anti-Federalists and
continentalists," as Merrill Jensen and, more recently, Richard B. Morris
have affirmed,[90] the question of sovereignty "was never directly raised"
in 1775-76. In fact, "political exigencies imposed [such] powerful limits on
the sweep [and, one might add, depth] of formal constitutional thought"
that not even the problem of the proper allocation of authority "was at
first . . . carefully examined": "basic issues were neither clearly posed
nor well understood," and congressional discussions of confederation
"tended, like other issues, to be more deeply influenced by the demands
of resistance."[91]

In this situation, the federal structure of the new nation simply evolved
out of the colonists' experience in the old empire and the need to meet the
conditions of the war. Much as in the history of the old British Empire, a
working division of power between the Congress and the states, a division
along the very lines that had prevailed in the empire, quickly took shape.
In view of the intense suspicion of a remote central power exhibited by
American leaders both during the years prior to independence and in the
1780s, American leaders showed remarkably little aversion to endowing

---

[87] Don Higginbotham, "James Iredell and the Origins of American Federalism," in
George G. Suggs, Jr., *Perspectives on the American Revolution: A Bicentennial Contribution* (Carbondale, Ill., 1977), p. 107.
[88] Beer, "Federalism, Nationalism, and Democracy," p. 12.
[89] McLaughlin, *Foundations*, p. 138. See also John C. Ranney, "The Bases of American
Federalism, *William and Mary Quarterly*, 3d ser., 3 (1946):8-9.
[90] Richard B. Morris, "The Forging of the Union Reconsidered: A Historical Refutation of
the State Sovereignty over Seabeds," *Columbia Law Review* 74 (1974):1062; Jensen, *Articles of Confederation*.
[91] Rakove, *Beginnings of National Politics*, pp. xvi, 136, 162, 190.

the Congress with "legislative and administrative responsibilities unprecedented in the colonial past." Not even the intense theoretical discussion in 1776-77 of the form of the new republican state governments included much consideration of the relationship of those governments to Congress or to a permanent national union. At that point, Rakove has noted, Congress still commanded a degree of deference that "left it immune from close theoretical scrutiny." Perhaps more important, resistance leaders of all political persuasions seemed to have assumed that the pragmatic division of power that had taken shape during the early years of resistance would continue. That division, which had evolved, like that of the British Empire, without formal codification, saw the states handling all matters internal to them while the Congress was "endowed with substantial authority over matters of general concern."[92] The difference between a formal confederation and the existing union, John Adams blithely declared in April 1776, would be no greater than "that between an express and an implied Contract."[93]

IV

Thus, by the mid-1770s, three powerful long-range preconditions—growing social and cultural convergence among the colonies, an awareness of their common interest in opposing metropolitan efforts to curtail colonial rights and privileges, and fears of both disunion and the fragility of authority in American society—combined with short-term pressures created by war and the colonists' earliest experiences with united action to push American resistance leaders toward a permanent national continental union. A fourth precondition—their experience with a multi-tiered government under the old empire—predisposed them toward a federal union. Simultaneously, the five preconditions discussed in Section II—mutual suspicions and sharpened perceptions of differences, mistrust of distant power, available theories and models of federal organization, absence of national consciousness, and the long-standing existence of the states as distinctive corporate entities—made the actual codification of the ad hoc federal structure that had taken shape in 1774-76 extremely difficult.

Precisely how difficult was revealed with the very first effort to devise a suitable plan of confederation beginning in June 1776. On the surface, immediate issues involving representation, expenses, and western lands seemed to be most troublesome. Lurking behind these issues, however, was the old imperial problem of specifying a clear division of power among the two existing spheres of authority, a division that would give the central government sufficient power to meet its responsibilities—without compromising the political integrity of the individual states. Although it

[92] Rakove, *Beginnings of National Politics*, pp. 136, 148-149, 151, 172, 184-185.
[93] John Adams to James Warren, 16 April 1776, in Smith, ed., *Letters of Delegates*, 3:536.

clearly did not, as Edward Rutledge charged, destroy "all Provincial [state] Distinctions" or consolidate the states "into one unitary polity," the original plan of confederation drawn up by John Dickinson, a plan which, in Rakove's words "clearly intended to use confederation as a vehicle not only for defining the powers of Congress, but also for limiting the authority of the states," gave much too extensive powers to the Congress to satisfy the majority of delegates.[94]

During most of the present century, of course, historians assumed that the national government was actually the creation of thirteen sovereign states which retained all those powers not delegated to the Congress.[95] Since the publication of a seminal article by Curtis P. Nettels in 1960, however, this "contract theory" of the formation of the American union has been replaced by a new orthodoxy.[96] Following Nettels, Richard B. Morris, Samuel H. Beer, and Jack N. Rakove have each in turn attested to the validity of a national theory of the origins of American federalism according to which the national government "existed and functioned before the birth of any state" and "the source of authority for the various acts initiated by the Congress was 'the inhabitants of the several colonies, whom we represent.'" According to this interpretation, Congress as well as the states were the creation of "a single sovereign power, the people of the United States," while Congress "alone possessed those attributes of external sovereignty which entitled" the United States "to be called a state in the international sense while the separate States, possessing a limited or internal sovereignty, may rightly be considered a creation of the Continental Congress, which preceded them in time and brought them into being."[97]

But neither the old nor the new orthodoxy seems to be an adequate description of what happened. To be sure, the Congress existed before any of the new independent state governments. But these new state governments were merely the creations and the newest political instruments of old corporate entities, each of which preserved its well-defined territory and collective legal identity as it moved rapidly in 1775-76 from colony to provincial revolutionary society and to independent statehood. These distinctive corporate entities certainly preceded the existence of a new continental one.

Of course, Congress portrayed itself in various public documents from September 1774 onward as representing "the inhabitants of the several

[94] Edward Rutledge to John Jay, 29 June 1776, ibid., 4:388; Rakove, *Beginnings of National Politics*, pp. 155-157.

[95] See, especially, in addition to Jensen, *Articles of Confederation*, C. H. Van Tyne, "Sovereignty in the American Revolution: An Historical Study," *American Historical Review* 12 (1907):529-545.

[96] Curtis P. Nettels, "The Origin of the Union and of the States," *Proceedings of the Massachusetts Historical Society* 72 (1957-60):68-83.

[97] Morris, "Forging of the Union," pp. 1067, 1089; Beer, "Federalism, Nationalism, and Democracy," p. 12; Rakove, *Beginnings of National Politics*, pp. 173-174.

colonies."[98] During the debates over confederation a few delegates even argued that Congress should represent people rather than states.[99] But this view was strongly and successfully opposed at the time by those who, with Roger Sherman, insisted that "we are rep[resentative]s of States, not Individuals." Behind this view of the Congress as an assemblage of state representatives was the assumption, made explicit by John Witherspoon, that "Every Colony is a distinct Person."[100] Congress may have directed the colonies to form new state governments; but each of them retained, Witherspoon implied, its ancient legal identity as a distinctive corporate entity. In all probability, this view was strongly reinforced by the actual process of state constitution-making in 1776 and 1777, a process that had given explicit definition to and reaffirmation of the authority and legal identity of the states.[101]

The triumph of the view represented by Sherman and Witherspoon was evident in the fact that delegates to the Congress continued to be selected by the state governments both before and after the adoption of the Articles of Confederation which were ratified, not by the people at large, but by the states. The "Provincial Distinctions" cherished by so many of the delegates would not be obliterated by the Articles of Confederation.[102] The first American union would not be, as Beer has argued, representational, but territorial and corporate. Its source of authority lay not, as recent scholars have suggested, in the people of the United States, but in the states as corporate entities, which retained their separate identities and legal authority throughout the transition from colonies to states, from membership in the British Empire to membership in the new United States. As it had developed within the colonies prior to 1770, American government, as Beer has argued, was fundamentally government by consent as opposed to the "Old Whig constitution" in England, which was not representational but hierarchical and corporatist. To an important degree, however, America's first *national* government was a throwback to the old Whig constitution insofar as it represented the territorial and legal corporations of the states, not the people at large.[103]

But this is not to suggest that the older compact theory of the origins of American federalism, whereby a group of sovereign states created a national government, is correct. If few in Congress prior to the early 1780s intended to annihilate the identities of the individual states, yet, as

[98] Morris, "Forging of the Union," p. 1067.

[99] John Adams' Notes of Debates, 1 August 1776; Benjamin Rush's Notes for a Speech, [1 August 1776], in Smith, ed., *Letters of Delegates*, 4:592-593, 599-601. See also "Of the Present State of America," 10 October 1776, in Peter Force, comp., *American Archives*, 5th ser., 2:967-970.

[100] John Adams' Notes of Debates, 30 July, 1 August 1776, in Smith ed., *Letters to Delegates*, 4:568, 592.

[101] Rakove, *Beginnings of National Politics*, p. 167; "Of the Present State of America," p. 967.

[102] Edward Rutledge to John Jay, 29 June 1776, in Smith, ed., *Letters of Delegates*, 3:338.

[103] Beer, "Federalism, Nationalism, and Democracy," pp. 10, 12.

Rakove has argued with great cogency, the Congress had all along been "a national government" exerting an extraordinary degree of authority over the separate states. Moreover, the framers of the Articles of Confederation revealed their conscious intention to perpetuate this arrangement by vesting "certain sovereign powers in Congress" and subordinating "the states to its decisions." [104] During the war, most delegates probably agreed with William Henry Drayton that Congress should have no power that could "with propriety, be exercised by the several states." [105] But the declaration in Article 2 of the Articles of Confederation that "Each State retains its sovereignty, freedom and independence" was, ultimately, a fiction.[106] as Rufus King pointed out in the Philadelphia Convention in 1787, the states, under the Articles, lacked many of the fundamental attributes of sovereignty. "They could not," King said, "make war, nor peace, nor alliances, nor treaties." [107] The Articles of Confederation, as Gordon Wood has correctly remarked, on paper at least "made the league of states as cohesive and strong as any similar sort of republican confederation in history." [108] In doing so, the Articles simply gave formal sanction to an existing arrangement.

The process by which the American union was formed is thus too complicated to support either a national or a compact theory of its origins. The Continental Congress gathered to itself broad powers at the same time that the colonies, as old and continuing corporate entities, were changing themselves into states. What was clear throughout was that from the First Continental Congress on, the national union had involved a division of power in which, "in their separate spheres, both Congress and the states were to exercise certain functions of sovereign government." Inherited from the British Empire, such a division was thus "inherent in the nature of American union from the start" [109] and, as McLaughlin long ago pointed out, was perpetuated by the Articles of Confederation, which sought to specify the boundaries between the Congress and the state governments "with considerable precision." [110]

What was remarkable throughout this initial phase in the creation of an American union is that the issue—the location of sovereignty—which has received so much stress from modern historians, was so little emphasized by contemporaries. Much more interested in the practical problem of allocating power between the national and the state governments, members of Congress simply failed "to give serious attention" to the question of sovereignty. Even when Thomas Burke, the North Carolina delegate,

[104] Rakove, *Beginnings of National Politics*, pp. xvi, 184-185.
[105] William Henry Drayton's Speech, 20 January 1778, in Niles, ed., *Principles and Acts*, p. 363.
[106] Jensen, *Articles of Confederation*, p. 263.
[107] Morris, "Forging of the Union," p. 1064.
[108] Wood, *Creation of the American Republic*, p. 359.
[109] Rakove, *Beginnings of National Politics*, pp. 162, 172.
[110] McLaughlin, *Foundations*, p. 140.

raised it explicitly in Congress in early 1777, few of his colleagues exhibited much interest in pursuing it. Prior to the end of the War for Independence, Rakove concludes on the basis of these facts, that few Americans seemed to be "deeply interested in the nature of the union they were forming." Not only, as Gordon Wood has noted, did the war years yield no theoretical advance over the formulations of Blackstone, but the question of the locus of sovereignty remained "imperfectly understood" and a potential source of conflict and confusion.[111]

Although the problem of sovereignty "remained academic" in the late 1770s, it quickly became an important "practical issue" in the 1780s.[112] Wood has shown that the end of the war produced a reassertion of state authority and a corresponding diminution of central power, a development marked by a revival of that traditional distrust of remote power that had been so evident in the controversy with Britain in the 1760s and early 1770s and would be such a conspicuous feature of the debate over the Constitution of 1787. Ignoring the extraordinary power Congress had exercised during the war, observers in the mid-1780s could describe it, as did John Adams, as neither "a legislative assembly, nor a representative assembly, but only a diplomatic assembly." From this new and later perspective, the Congress by no means appeared to be, as Ezra Stiles observed, "a body in which resides authoritative sovereignty." There had obviously occurred, said Stiles, "no real cession of dominion, no surrender or transfer of sovereignty to the national council as each state in the confederacy," had remained "an independent sovereignty."[113]

The steady diminution in the actual power and status of the Confederation Congress during the 1780s provides yet further testimony to the continuing strength of the states and to the determination of their leaders to preserve their ancient identities. What was new and radical about the Federal Constitution of 1787, Wood has shown, was its embodiment of the new American Theory that sovereignty resided in the people at large and its incorporation of the idea of consent into the national government through the institution of direct election of members of the House of Representatives. These steps made American federalism, the "new" federalism of 1787, *representational*. What was old about the Federal Constitution was its endorsement of the continued sanctity of the identity of each of the states as separate territorial and corporate entities and their representation in the Senate. That provision insured that American federalism would continue to be, as it had been entirely under the Articles of Confederation, territorial as well as representational and not, as Beer recently argued, merely representational.[114]

---

[111] Rakove, *Beginnings of National Politics*, pp. 164, 174, 185; Wood, *Creation of the American Republic*, p. 353.
[112] Willi Paul Adams, *The First American Constitutions: Republican Ideology and the Making of the State Constitutions in the Revolutionary Era* (Chapel Hill, 1980), p. 50.
[113] Wood, *Creation of the American Republic*, pp. 355, 464, 580.
[114] Beer, "Federalism, Nationalism, and Democracy," pp. 12, 14-15.

Historical Theory and Political Reform: Two Perspectives on Confederation Politics*

Michael Lienesch

Among recent American historians, few topics have provoked more controversy than the character of the Confederation period. On one side, scholars like Forrest McDonald have contended that the era from the end of the revolutionary war to the creation of the federal constitution was a time of economic confusion and political chaos, a "critical period" in which popular protest became violent enough to threaten civil war. On the other side, critics of this view led by Merrill Jensen have argued that the period was in fact prosperous and relatively stable, that political protests were few and mostly well behaved, and that, in short, the "critical period" was really not very critical at all.[1] This article does not enter into this debate. Instead, it works from the premise that events are often less important than the perception of events. That is, actual conditions aside, it considers how Americans of the day perceived these conditions. In particular, it describes how they viewed their politics through the filter of their understanding of history.

While historians have written often about eighteenth-century ideas of history, and political theorists just as frequently about eighteenth-century ideas of politics, few have considered the relation between the two realms.[2] Recently, however, J.G.A. Pocock has produced a series of studies which has described in detail the importance of history in the shaping of early republicanism.[3] In

---

*I wish to thank the Earhart Foundation for supporting this study.

[1] Compare Forrest McDonald, *E Pluribus Unum: The Formation of the American Republic, 1776-1790*, 2nd ed. (Indianapolis, Ind., 1965), with Merrill Jensen, *The New Nation: A History of the United States During the Confederation, 1781-1789* (New York, 1950). For background, see Richard B. Morris, "The Confederation Period and the American Historian," *The William and Mary Quarterly*, Third Series, 13 (April 1956), 139-56.

[2] One notable exception is H. Trevor Colbourn, *The Lamp of Experience: Whig History and the Intellectual Origins of the American Revolution* (Chapel Hill, N.C., 1965).

[3] J.G.A. Pocock, *Politics, Language and Time: Essays on Political Thought and History* (New York, 1971), pp. 80-147; "Virtue and Commerce in the Eighteenth Century," *Journal of Interdisciplinary History*, 3 (Summer 1972), 119-34; and *The Machiavellian Moment: Florentine Political Thought and the Atlantic Republican Tradition* (Princeton, N.J., 1975), esp. pp. 3-9.

94

the most recent of these works, *The Machiavellian Moment,* Pocock showed how two diverse historical theories came to be combined in republican political thought: the cyclical concept of revolution, and the balanced model of constitutional stability. He described how these disparate themes were synthesized in the thought of James Harrington. But Pocock admitted that republican thought since Harrington has been a contradictory combination of these strains; *The Machiavellian Moment* traced some of the contradictions through the debates between the "court" and "country" politicians of eighteenth-century England. In a final chapter, Pocock made some suggestions on the application of these themes to early American politics.[4]

This study takes up where Pocock left off. First, it describes the divergence of cyclical and balanced theories of history in the early to mid-1780's. It then discusses how these conflicting historical logics helped form competing concepts of political reform, one revolutionary, the other constitutional. Finally, it shows how these theories influenced the perception of events, and how these perceptions in turn set the stage for constitutional conflict.

THE IDEA OF PERIODIC REVOLUTION

In republican theory, the earliest and most enduring theme has been the idea of revolution. Its origins lay in a cyclical concept of history. In the late eighteenth century, republicans drew on a vast set of sources to validate their view that historical events took place according to a pattern of decline and redemption. Their reading of classical history suggested that the ancient republics had followed a continuous cycle of founding, corruption, and reform. In Polybius, they found this historical process presented as a universal principle. Moreover, because they believed that in all ages similar causes produced similar effects, eighteenth-century republicans could apply cyclical theory to modern events. Thus they saw their own English history as a process in which Saxon liberties gave way to Norman oppression, only to be rescued by republican patriots reasserting their ancient prerogatives in the Magna Charta. In turn, as patriotism waned, the rights of Englishmen gave way again to the power of the Stuart kings, who themselves were overthrown by a new generation of republicans. With the Glorious Revolution, the cycle was

---

[4] See Pocock, *Machiavellian Moment,* pp. 462-552.

repeated. Bernard Bailyn has shown how this cyclical theory of history became pervasive in eighteenth-century republican thought.[5] By the end of the century, republicans everywhere were repeating the theme: "To revert to first principles is so essentially requisite to public happiness and safety," explained Dr. John Warren to an American Fourth of July audience in 1783, "that Polybius has laid it down as an incontrovertible axiom, that every State must decline more or less rapidly, in proportion as she recedes from the principles on which she was founded."[6]

Cyclical theory assumed both corruption and renewal. Applying the Polybian scheme to the history of modern republics, Machiavelli had suggested in the *Discourses* that the concerted action of virtuous citizens could return states from the final stages of decline to their original excellence. This theme contributed to creating the revolutionary strain in republicanism. It was repeated by the early Whig reformers like Harrington and Sidney, and, as Bailyn has shown, gained wide influence through the libertarian tracts of Trenchard and Gordon, who after 1688 called on their fellow republicans to rise up and recapture the liberties lost to scheming court politicians. Indeed, in the early eighteenth century even Tory conservatives like Bolingbroke would adopt the theory, arguing that a corrupted monarchy could be redeemed only by the introduction of a patriot prince. In effect, the popular idea of revolution implied restoration, the reversion to original principles. Before 1776 American revolutionaries had made this cyclical reform the basic tenet of their own republican protest, arguing not for a radical break from their colonial oppressors, but a conservative return to their original constitutional rights, what Sam Adams called that "true old English liberty." In fact, even following independence, some continued to make the case: the most effective means to the prevention of tyranny was to "frequently recur to *first principles*," the Reverend Joseph Buckminster observed in 1784, "as the only way of secur-

---

[5] See Bernard Bailyn, *The Ideological Origins of the American Revolution* (Cambridge, Mass., 1967), pp. 22-93. For background, see Caroline Robbins, *The Eighteenth-Century Commonwealthman* (Cambridge, Mass., 1959), pp. 3-21; Z. S. Fink, *The Classical Republicans*, 2nd ed. (Evanston, Ill., 1962), pp. 1-27; and Colbourn, *Lamp of Experience*, pp. 3-20.

[6] John Warren, *An Oration Delivered July 4th, 1783* . . . (Boston, Mass., [1783]), p. 6.

ing those rights, and of discovering the first encroachments of him who is *at heart* a tyrant."[7]

This cyclical theory implied a politics of resignation and rebellion. Revolutionary republicanism, assuming both declension and revision, combined long periods of watching and waiting with short bursts of protest. At best it was a psychologically demanding philosophy, for it required that citizens be constantly on guard against those ambitious leaders who would sacrifice public good for personal interest. The theory held that every ruler would sooner or later be corrupted by the prerogatives of power. Thus revolutionary republicans looked on their leaders as potential enemies. Buckminster explained: "Let us keep, not a *captious,* but, a *watchful* eye, over those in whose hands we place the reins of government. . . ." Americans had a duty to "support, encourage, and assist" rulers only so long as they "keep within the limits prescribed them by the Constitution." But as soon as leaders began to encroach on the rights of their subjects — and cyclical theory required that sooner or later they would "leap that impassible barrier" — citizens would need to act swiftly and surely to remove them, restoring their positions to more virtuous republican replacements. As to their fallen leaders, they had little sympathy: ". . . let them return to the walks of private life," Buckminster suggested, "and recover the feelings of the *subject,* which they may have almost lost in those of the *ruler.*"[8]

Revolutionary republicans did rely on some constitutional antidotes to corruption. The early Whig reformers like James Burgh had argued that the surest invitation to tyranny was to allow politicians to hold power for long periods. Accordingly they devised a series of constitutional checks to radically limit the length of public service. Gordon Wood has shown how American revolutionaries made use of these limits in their early attempts at constitution-making.[9] In all of the states, the tenure of office was

---

[7] Joseph Buckminster, Jun., A.M., *A Discourse Delivered in the First Church of Christ at Portsmouth* . . . (Portsmouth, N.H., 1784), p. 31. On Adams, see Colbourn, *Lamp of Experience,* p. 77. See also Bailyn, *Ideological Origins,* pp. 99-143. Perhaps the best account of this Copernican concept of revolution is Hannah Arendt, *On Revolution* (New York, 1963), pp. 34-40.

[8] Buckminster, *A Discourse,* p. 31. See Stow Persons, "The Cyclical Theory of History in Eighteenth Century America," *American Quarterly,* 6 (Summer 1954), 147-63.

[9] See Gordon S. Wood, *The Creation of the American Republic, 1776-1787* (Chapel Hill, N.C., 1969), pp. 127-244. Also helpful is Donald S. Lutz, *Popular Consent and Popular Control: Whig Political Theory in the Early State Constitutions* (Baton Rouge, La., 1980), pp. 53-84.

severely restricted. Revolutionary state constitutions varied widely, but in most of them elections were held annually, offices were
rotated (delegates limited often to three years service in six, or
four out of seven), and reelection was restricted. In the same manner, the powers of officials were strictly circumscribed, while the
liberties of the people were listed in detail. As a result, many of
the early documents ran to hundreds of pages, including the fares
of toll roads, the rates of local taxes, or the dates and times of
public meetings. The popular assumption was that when these
provisions were in need of revision, the document as a whole
would be due for replacement. In addition, in keeping with the
principle of periodic revision, most of the early constitutions included statutes of limitation for laws, and sometimes even for offices. The radically democratic Pennsylvania charter, for example, provided that the constitution itself be reviewed every seven
years. All told, the revolutionary constitutions seemed to institu-
tionalize the principle of cyclical reform. The Boston lawyer Benjamin Hichborn described the process: "But as the best of human
systems may involve in them the seeds of future danger to people's
rights, the constitution [the Articles of Confederation] has wisely
provided a periodical revision which must cure every possible
defect."[10]

Yet the theory of cyclical reform also required regular protest.
Constitutional checks went only so far. Periodically, power would
have to revert to its original source in the people. Revolutionary
republicans considered government to be a painful sacrifice made
to the sad realities of international conflict. They accepted the role
of the state in providing certain essential domestic services. But
beyond the basics, they thought of government as a usurper of
popular power. Stanley Elkins and Eric McKitrick have shown
how their backgrounds in colonial politics predisposed these
revolutionaries to be believers in direct democracy.[11] That is, they
assumed that citizens would play an active role in politics, not only at annual elections, but also in the petition drives, town
meetings, and mass assemblies that had been so common in the
prerevolutionary period.[12] As Hichborn said, the "right of

[10] Benjamin Hichborn, Esq., *An Oration, Delivered July 5th, 1784* . . . (Boston, Mass., [1784]), p. 13.

[11] See Stanley Elkins and Eric McKitrick, "The Founding Fathers: Young Men of the Revolution," *Political Science Quarterly,* 76 (June 1961), 200-206.

[12] On popular protest in the revolution, see Gordon S. Wood, "A Note on Mobs in the American Revolution," *The William and Mary Quarterly,* Third Series, 23 (October 1966), 635-42.

meeting together uncontrouled" was "among the first privileges, reserved to the individual. . . ." Without these popular protests, he suggested, the revolution would have been "conquered without a struggle." Hence the right of assembly had been repeatedly reaffirmed in the state constitutions, "expressly secured to the people."[13] As to any fears of disorder, revolutionary republicans maintained that popular participation would assure not only freedom, but stability. As "Agrippa" would put it, "No instance can be produced of any other kind of government so stable and energetick as the republican."[14]

It followed that in cyclical theory the ultimate remedy to corruption was revolution. Petitions and protests could serve as palliatives, but the only antidote to tyranny was periodic rebellion. After all, many of these revolutionary republicans were themselves experienced revolutionaries. For some, their entire public lives had been given to the cause of resistance. Having survived and thrived through almost a decade of revolutionary war, they saw rebellion as a natural, even normal state of political affairs. In the final analysis, Jefferson would write, the "irregular interpositions" of popular protests were the "only safeguard of the public liberty."[15] Republics did well to foster a spirit of rebellion: "The spirit of resistance to government is so valuable on certain occasions," he wrote to Abigail Adams, "that I wish it to be always kept alive."[16] Cyclical theory held that rebellion was a periodic purge to cure the diseases of the corrupt state, "a medicine," as Jefferson told Madison, "necessary for the sound health of government."[17] In short, to revolutionary republicans a little rebellion now and then was a good thing. As Jefferson concluded, in the most eloquent statement of the cyclical theory, "The tree of liberty must be refreshed from time to time with the blood of patriots and tyrants."[18]

The Idea of Constitutional Balance

The second strain in republican theory was the concept of constitution. Its origins lay in the twin themes of balance and excess,

---

[13] Hichborn, *Oration,* p. 5; 6.

[14] "Agrippa [James Winthrop]," letter to the *Massachusetts Gazette,* 14 January 1788, *The Complete Anti-Federalist,* ed. Herbert J. Storing (Chicago, Ill., 1981), 4:95.

[15] Jefferson to Edward Carrington, 16 January 1787, *The Papers of Thomas Jefferson,* ed. Julian P. Boyd (Princeton, N.J., 1950-), 11:49.

[16] Jefferson to Abigail Adams, 22 February 1787, *ibid.,* 11:174.

[17] Jefferson to James Madison, 30 January 1787, *ibid.* 93.

[18] Jefferson to William Stephens Smith, 13 November 1787, *ibid.,* 12:356.

ideas as important to constitutional republicans as cyclical renewal was to their revolutionary counterparts. Constitutional republicans held that well-ordered states required the well-ordered interplay of their parts. To these Aristotelians, the constitution of a state was not so much a document as a set of assumptions about the rights and responsibilities of each member of society. In the well-constituted regime, citizens would limit their own desires in order to secure the stability of the state. In the flawed system, on the other hand, they would throw off these limits, pursuing their own interests at the expense of social order. In the process, their excesses would create an imbalance between groups that would lead to conflict.[19] In a review of almost two hundred ancient revolutions, Aristotle had found repeated examples of the process. Furthermore, unlike Polybius, he saw no pattern of cyclical return. On the contrary, the revolutions of the ancient republics seemed to end all too often in civil war. Douglass Adair has shown that many eighteenth-century republicans embraced this constitutional theory; their reading of classical history pictured the ancient states beset by conflicts between kings and nobles, aristocrats and democrats, rich and poor.[20] In fact, they needed to look no further than the recent experience of states like Denmark and Holland to see examples of excess and imbalance.[21] Moreover, among certain Americans the threat of social breakdown came perilously close to home. For in the aftermath of revolution, anxious observers began to wonder whether social conflicts might not signal the continuation of revolution. It was entirely possible, observed Benjamin Thurston, writing as "Amicus Reipublicae," that American revolutionaries, having struggled so valiantly against a common political enemy, might soon find themselves at war with one another. He warned of the terrible consequences of such social conflict: "Every man's sword would be turned against his fellow, and mutual jealousy, resentment and malice, would operate in the acts of greatest cruelty. Our republics would become one general scene of plunder and slaughter."[22]

---

[19] On constitutional theory, see Bailyn, *Ideological Origins,* pp. 67-77.

[20] See Douglass Adair, "The Intellectual Origins of Jeffersonian Democracy: Republicanism, the Class Struggle, and the Virtuous Farmer" (Ph.D. diss., Yale University, 1943), pp. 96-121.

[21] See Gerald J. Gruman, " 'Balance' and 'Excess' as Gibbon's Explanation of the Decline and Fall," *History and Theory,* 1 (1961), 75-85.

[22] "Amicus Reipublicae [Benjamin Thurston]," *An Address to the Public, Con-*

In constitutional theory, the fear of excess was pervasive. Constitutional republicans, like all good republicans, assumed that an excess of power would create tyranny. But they also contended that an excess of liberty would lead to licentiousness. In the 1780's, certain American conservatives seemed determined to emphasize this trend towards lawlessness. Fundamentally, they believed that the abuse of power, while cause for concern, could never pose the threat to liberty that arose from an excess of license. According to the Reverend Moses Hemmenway, disorder was a form of debasement, as debilitating to free people as "the worst effects of slavery."[23] In addition, while republican citizens seemed all too aware of the abuses of excessive power, they tended to be lax in their fears of excessive freedom. Thus license posed a more subtle, almost insidious threat to the republic. Above all, these constitutional republicans could fear lawlessness because they saw it as a precondition to eventual tyranny. Their reading of classical history showed that once republics had declined into democratic disorder, demagogues and dictators would not be far behind. In particular, they read the history of the Roman republic as positive proof that popular discontent would lead to dictatorship. In 1783, constitutional republicans were predicting that the new nation would soon find itself travelling this same tragic path. "Amicus" made the case: ". . . all these civil commotions, . . . would probably introduce a government that was absolute; for if by experience it was evident, that our governments were overturned for want of energy, necessity would lead us to establish a government vested with more extensive power." In short, he contended, "Anarchy has a direct tendency to the introduction of tyranny. This is abundantly evident from the experience of ages."[24]

Without balance, republican government was impossible. From Aristotle on, constitutional thinkers had sought to control the excesses of one social order by counterpoising the assertions of another. In Polybius, Montesquieu, and the Commonwealth writers, the theme was elaborated into concepts of mixed govern-

---

taining Some Remarks on the Present State of the American Republicks, &c. (Exeter, N.H., [1786]), pp. 13-14.

[23] Moses Hemmenway, A.M., *A Sermon Preached Before His Excellency John Hancock, Esq.; Governor . . . of . . . Massachusetts, May 26, 1784 . . .* (Boston, Mass., 1784), p. 32.

[24] "Amicus," *Address,* p. 14.

ment, separation of powers, and checks and balances.[25] But in the early 1780's, these ideas seemed somehow out of place in America. The American states, after all, boasted neither feudal nobility nor hereditary monarch. Their own republican version of balanced government would be the creation of the federal convention, still several years in the future. Before that time, the ideal balanced government remained elusive.[26] At best, disparate thinkers could suggest such stopgaps as a stronger national government, more aristocratic influence, increased executive prerogatives. But by and large, constitutional theorists tended to see their own state as imbalanced and dangerously instable. In his *Defence of the Constitutions of Government of the United States,* John Adams made the classic indictment of this imbalance. Relying on Thucydides, he described in detail the conflicts between democratic and aristocratic parties that had been endemic to Greece during the Peloponnesian War: "The contagion spread through the whole extent of Greece; factions raged in every city; the licentious many contending for the Athenians, and the aspiring few for the Lacedemonians. The consequence was, seditions in cities, with all their numerous and tragical incidents." In the absence of balance, Adams contended, anarchy was succeeded by despotism. Nor did the despots put an end to conflict, for despotism evoked in turn further rebellions, resulting, he wrote, in "perpetual alterations of rebellion and tyranny, and the butchery of thousands upon every revolution from one to the other." The consequence was permanent warfare: without balanced constitutions, Adams concluded of the Greek states, "the pendulum was forever on the swing."[27]

To such constitutional conservatives, the purpose of written constitutions was to limit popular excess. They argued that revolutionary legislation had failed to check the trend from liberty to license. Indeed, the revolutionary constitutions had contributed to the instability of the new states. In his essay "The Vices of the Political System of the United States," James

---

[25] On the relation between mixed government, separation of powers, and balanced government, see W. B. Gwyn, *The Meaning of the Separation of Powers: An Analysis of the Doctrine from Its Origins to the Adoption of the United States Constitution* (New Orleans, La., 1965).

[26] On the problem of applying constitutional theory to American politics, see Wood, *Creation*, pp. 430-67.

[27] John Adams, "A Defence of the Constitutions of Government of the United States . . .," 1787, *The Works of John Adams,* ed. Charles Francis Adams (Boston, Mass, 1850-56), 4:285.

Madison described the hopelessly transitory quality of recent state government. "We daily see laws repealed or superseded, before any trial can have been made of their merits; and even before a knowledge of them can have reached the remoter districts within which they were to operate." Statutes had been revised repeatedly, sometimes duplicated, sometimes contradicted, sometimes both. The result, according to Madison, was a "luxuriancy of legislation."[28] In an explicit challenge to the principle of periodic revision, Madison denounced the "repealing, explaining, and amending laws" as "but so many monuments of deficient wisdom; so many impeachments exhibited by each succeeding against every preceding session. . . ."[29] Even more important to Madison was the fact that much of this legislation had been not only contradictory, but also unwise. Ambitious legislators had pursued private interest at the expense of public good. These self-interested politicians, he contended, had become so adept at presenting themselves as self-sacrificing public servants that the traditional check of frequent elections had been made meaningless: ". . . how easily," Madison observed, "are base and selfish measures, masked by pretexts of public good. . . ." In fact, he reported, the performance of the state legislatures had been disillusioning enough to lead many critics to ". . . question the fundamental principle of republican Government, that the majority who rule in such Governments, are the safest Guardians both of public Good and of private rights."[30]

Constitutional republicans saw democracy as an inherently instable system. As Elkins and McKitrick have shown, many constitutionalists had come of age in wartime, their political views being shaped by their national service in the army and congress, rather than the local experience of the militias or state legislatures.[31] Unlike their revolutionary counterparts, they were not predisposed to look kindly on direct democracy. Instead, they saw popular participation as an invitation, in Hamilton's words, to "violence and turbulence."[32] In keeping with Aristotelian

[28] James Madison, "Vices of the Political System of the United States," April 1787, *The Papers of James Madison,* ed. Robert A. Rutland (Chicago, Ill., 1962-), 9:353-54; 353.

[29] Madison, Federalist 62, *The Federalist Papers,* ed. Clinton Rossiter (New York, 1961), pp. 379-80.

[30] Madison, "Vices," *Papers,* 9:354.

[31] See Elkins and McKitrick, "Founding Fathers," p. 204.

[32] Hamilton, address to the federal convention, 18 June 1787, *Debates on the Adoption of the Federal Constitution . . . ,* 2nd ed., ed. Jonathan Elliot (Philadelphia, Pa., 1861-63), 5:203.

theory, they assumed that democracy would tend to degenerate into disorder, and ultimately, into anarchy. The purpose of a balanced polity, they contended, was to prevent this breakdown into mob rule. Thus they argued that republican rulers, because they governed in the interest of the people, deserved confidence and support, rather than the traditional criticism and skepticism. The affairs of government were complicated and difficult; sometimes officials made mistakes. Their errors, however, "ought not to disaffect us to our governments."[33] Indeed, because citizens had the right to remove officials at the next election, they had no reason whatsoever to engage in public protest. As "Amicus" argued, it "can never be justifiable to throw the states into a civil war which perhaps would continue years to obtain redress of grievances, when it might be effected within one year constitutionally, and without any dangerous or injurious consequences."[34] To constitutionalists, protest could only lead to what one called "the horrours of anarchy."[35] "Our civil constitutions and administrators must be supported," "Amicus" warned, "or we can reasonably expect nothing but national ruin."[36]

Above all, these constitutionalists feared revolution. The idea of imbalance suggested that democracy would decline first into anarchy, and then into despotism. Constitutional thinkers seemed unable to agree on whether future despots would come to power through foreign conquest or domestic insurrection. They debated the character of the despot, whether it would be military dictator or democratic demagogue. Above all, they speculated on the time it would take for popular protest to elicit some kind of authoritarian response. But few if any doubted the historical principle that disorder would lead back to a reinstitution of tyranny. Out of the chaos, some popular demagogue or military dictator would ride to power on the shoulders of the masses. "They will infallibly have a *Philip* or *Caesar*," John Dickinson would write of the American people, "to bleed them into soberness of mind."[37] Yet in time, the mob would tire of its protector, and revert again to revolution. On and on the conflict would continue, in what

---

[33] "Amicus," *Address,* p. 17.

[34] *Ibid.,* pp. 18-19.

[35] "Cassius [James Sullivan]," letter to the *Massachusetts Gazette,* 23 November 1787, *Essays on the Constitution of the United States . . .,* ed. Paul Leicester Ford (New York, 1892), p. 18.

[36] "Amicus," *Address,* p. 16.

[37] John Dickinson, "letters of Fabius, no. IV," 1788, *The Political Writings of John Dickinson, Esquire . . .* (Wilmington, Del., 1801), 2:107.

Hamilton would call the "perpetual vibration between the extremes of tyranny and anarchy."[38] To these constitutional conservatives, rebellion was the ultimate threat to the republic. As
"Amicus" said, it was "very impolitic to throw the public into convulsions, and attempt to overturn our government. . . ." Such
subversion, he argued, commonly constituted "high treason." In
fact, "Amicus" went on, it "is an offense that is capital, being an
attempt upon the life of every subject in the community."[39] In
constitutional theory, revolution, far from assuring the health of
the state, was a kind of political suicide. "Human nature," Adams
submitted, "is as incapable now of going through revolutions with
temper and sobriety, with patience and prudence, or without fury
and madness, as it was among the Greeks so long ago."[40]

CONFEDERATION POLITICS: THE REVOLUTIONARY PERSPECTIVE

In postwar America, historical theory influenced not only the
creation of political ideas, but also the perception of political
events. In particular, revolutionaries insisted on interpreting
many public issues in terms of the time-honored premise that
freedom would always be corrupted by power. Throughout the
revolutionary period, as Bailyn has shown, republicans had
warned of the first signs of corruption: ministerial influence,
unauthorized taxation, a standing army. Hence in 1783 they were
startled by the suggestion of leading constitutionalists that Congress create a strong executive branch made up of single departments run by single individuals. They were equally surprised by
the proposal that Congress be granted a taxing power, or impost.
But revolutionary republicans seemed nothing less than astonished at the plans of certain Continental army officers to resist
demobilization, combine forces with public creditors, and force
prompt payment of war debts. Among Whig republicans, the fear
of a standing army had always run deep. The professional army
of the eighteenth century, like the professional bureaucracy of the
twentieth, seemed to answer to no popular source of power. In the
hands of unscrupulous politicians, it could serve as a tool of tyranny. Thus, among revolutionary republicans, suspicion of military

---

[38] Hamilton, Federalist 9, *Federalist Papers*, p. 71.

[39] "Amicus," *Address*, p. 18; 28.

[40] Adams, "Defence," *Works*, 4:287. See also David Humphreys; Joel
Barlow; John Trumbull; and Lemuel Hopkins, *The Anarchiad: A New England
Poem*, ed. Luther G. Riggs (New Haven, Conn., 1861), p. 61: "They see no object, and perceive no cause;/ But feel, by turns, in one disastrous hour,/ Th' extremes of license, and th' extremes of power."

power led to outrage over the creation of the Society of the Cincinnati, the hereditary fraternal organization of former revolutionary
officers. Such secret societies, they reasoned, could only exist to
conspire against popular liberties. Before long, the new government would come under the ministerial control of these influential
military men. Furthermore, in the absence of an indigenous
aristocracy, such wealthy and well-bred leaders seemed like likely
candidates to establish themselves as a native nobility. In turn,
according to the revolutionary reading of history, a corrupt nobility would always seek to introduce a corrupt monarchy. Societies
such as the Cincinnati, warned Judge Aedanus Burke in a detailed denunciation, could only "perpetuate family grandeur in an
aristocratic Nobility, to terminate at last in monarchical
tyranny."[41]

For revolutionaries, many of the issues of the postwar period
pointed towards increasing aristocratic influence. In republican
theory, the fear of a corrupt feudal nobility had always been a
prominent theme, but in postrevolutionary America, the concern
with aristocratic corruption was, according to Wood, nothing
short of an obsession. Radical republicans were able to interpret
proposals to allow the return of Tory loyalists as part of a plan to
reintroduce an Anglophile aristocracy in America. More important, they feared the establishment of their own indigenous
aristocrats. In prerevolutionary America, popular discontent had
been held in check by a sense of deference to one's social
superiors. During the war, any resentment against persons of
privilege was easily redirected to the absentee English oppressors;
even the angriest petitioner could see that there could be no comparison between the heroic republican aristocrats whom they
followed into battle and the simpering, sycophantic lords from
whom they fought to be free. Following the war, however, resentment began to surface, as revolutionaries wondered whether certain republican gentlemen were not positioning themselves to take
up the prerogatives of aristocratic nobility. In particular, critics
pictured financiers like Silas Deane and Robert Morris as potential capitalist aristocrats. Behind many of the economic issues of
the time — proposals like the impost, the funding of state debts,
and the role of the national bank — they saw what Sam Adams

---

[41] "Cassius [Aedanus Burke]," *Considerations on the Society or Order of Cincinnati*
. . . (Charleston, S.C., 1783), p. 29. See also Jensen, *The New Nation*, pp. 54-84,
261-81.

called the "Seeds of Aristocracy."[42] Above all, revolutionaries feared an alliance between the landed and commercial classes. Throughout the period, they warned that conspiracies were afoot between the representatives of status and wealth to overturn the republic, and to "erect on the Ruins, a proper Aristocracy."[43] Besides, according to republican history, aristocracy was only one step along the road to more extreme forms of tyranny. Plans were already being made, warned the Reverend Jeremy Belknap in 1785, to create a "domineering aristocracy," "and what that will degenerate into," he continued, "let the histories of fallen republics tell. . . ."[44]

Ultimately, to revolutionary republicans the events of the period seemed to point towards a reintroduction of monarchy. Their recent experience with the unbridled power of a capricious king had led revolutionary lawmakers to limit wherever possible the prerogatives of their own republican executives. In most of the state constitutions, governors were all but powerless, lacking the ability to initiate legislation, levy taxes, veto bills, or, for that matter, to take almost any decisive action. Throughout the war, these feeble executives had proven unable to respond to wartime emergencies. By the mid-1780's, constitutional reformers in several states had begun to allot more powers to these pitiful officials. Yet many viewed such efforts with alarm, for to die-hard revolutionaries, any extension of executive power smacked of monarchy. In the late eighteenth century, monarchy was the most common political system in the Western world. Many European nations had managed to combine monarchical rule with a respect for constitutional liberties. At home, influential persons seemed to assume that Washington would soon be called on to play the role of republican king. Thus revolutionaries saw themselves as constantly on call to resist the reintroduction of monarchical rule. The memories of American patriots, they argued, were not so short; their own history showed that even well-intentioned

---

[42] Sam Adams, letter to Richard Henry Lee, 3 December 1787, *Anti-Federalists versus Federalists: Selected Documents,* ed. John D. Lewis (San Francisco, Calif., 1967), p. 160.

[43] Farmington [Connecticut] Revolutionary Records, 6 May 1783, cited in Jackson Turner Main, *The Antifederalists: Critics of the Constitution, 1781-1788* (Chapel Hill, N.C., 1961), p. 109.

[44] Jeremy Belknap, *An Election Sermon, Preached Before the General Court, of New-Hampshire . . .* (Portsmouth, N.H., 1785), pp. 19; 20. On the fear of aristocracy, see Wood, *Creation,* pp. 75-90, 475-99. See also E. James Ferguson, *The Power of the Purse: A History of American Public Finance, 1776-1790* (Chapel Hill, N.C., 1961), pp. 146-76.

monarchs like George III had ended as enemies of the people. As George Mason would tell the federal convention, the distance from benevolent executive to cruel tyrant was but "an easy step."[45]

Given their perception of postwar events, it is understandable that revolutionaries found themselves speaking often of the necessity for protest. Annual elections, frequent turnover, and periodic revisions were all essential. But when necessary, republicans had to be ready to resist. It was in this context that revolutionaries viewed the events surrounding Shays's Rebellion. Throughout the 1780's, local leaders in western Massachusetts had been calling conventions and circulating petitions aimed at preventing presumed abuses of power, meaning in particular the abuses of high taxes and frequent foreclosures. Nor were the protests without cause; the historian Robert East has shown that the Massachusetts legislature, controlled by creditor interests, had carried out fiscal and social policies that were harsh and unrealistic. East went so far as to suggest that the real reasons for popular rebellion could be found in these unjust measures.[46] Throughout the 1780's, protests had won wide popular support, including that of many persons of status and wealth. Shays and his men, far from ragged rabble, were for the most part respectable property owners.[47] In addition, the time-honored role of crowds in presenting petitions predisposed many to see even this somewhat disorganized display of resentment as a fairly conventional form of protest.[48] As for Shays, his band of farmers seemed surprisingly well behaved. Even conservative critics like George Richards Minot had to admit that the recourse to violence was in large part the responsibility of an anxious militia. Thus it is not surprising that many found themselves siding with these respectable rebels. (Minot himself estimated that one-third of the

[45] George Mason, address to the federal convention, 17 July 1787, *The Records of the Federal Convention of 1787,* ed. Max Farrand (New Haven, Conn., 1911-37), 2:35. See also Wood, *Creation,* pp. 132-43, 430-38, 543-47.

[46] See Robert A. East, "The Massachusetts Conservatives in the Critical Period," *The Era of the American Revolution,* ed. Richard B. Morris (New York, 1939), pp. 349-91.

[47] See Main, *The Antifederalists,* pp. 59-71.

[48] On the role of popular assemblies and political protest, see Lloyd I. Rudolph, "The Eighteenth Century Mob in America and Europe," *American Quarterly,* 11 (Winter 1959), 447-69; Pauline Maier, "Popular Uprisings and Civil Authority in Eighteenth-Century America," *The William and Mary Quarterly,* Third Series, 27 (January 1970), 3-35; and Wood, "A Note on Mobs in the American Revolution," pp. 635-42.

population was sympathetic.)[49] Many others seemed to find the protests cause for concern, though hardly for the ferocious response of the state and federal troops who routed the assembled farmers. In fact, observers like Jefferson could wonder from a distance how Shays and his men had managed to provoke such rage within the conservative ranks. After all, he wrote to William Carmichael, their protests were "not entirely without excuses."[50]

CONFEDERATION POLITICS: THE CONSTITUTIONAL VIEW

Constitutional republicans, relying on a different reading of history, viewed the same postwar events quite differently. Primarily, they saw popular excesses threatening the fragile balance that had maintained social order within the new republic. During the war, factional strife had been held in check by the common cause of rebellion. With peace, the disagreements of a decade had surfaced in continuing conflicts between creditors and debtors, merchants and farmers, easterners and westerners, "ins" and "outs." To constitutionalists, these contests suggested the breakdown of liberty into license, "unrestrained licentiousness," that threatened to "break through the laws of civil order, and destroy the peace of society. . . ."[51] Hence they began to call for a reassertion of the role of government in restoring the rough balance between power and liberty. The original object of government, "A Fellow Citizen" observed, was to ". . . restrain the turbulent passions of mankind, dispense justice, and support order and regulation in society. . . ." To these ends, the modern state required a strong national defense, an effective commercial system, and internal police forces. According to "Citizen," these powerful institutions posed no threat to republican freedom. On the contrary, he argued that republican citizens, realizing that these institutions promised to make their liberty and property secure, would render their government "cheerful obedience." As a result, such well-ordered republics would be strong enough to "withstand the rage of many tempests. . . ."[52] Constitutionalists recognized that these and other suggestions of increased state power would be greeted by howls of revolutionary protest. But many contended

---

[49] See George Richards Minot, *The History of the Insurrections, in Massachusetts* . . . (Worcester, Mass., 1788), pp. 5-29, 89-91, 103-05, 110-12. The estimate of "a third part of the Commonwealth" is in Minot, *History*, p. 105.

[50] Jefferson to William Carmichael, 26 December 1786, *Papers*, 10:633.

[51] "A Fellow Citizen," *The Political Establishments of the United States* . . . (Philadelphia, Pa., 1784), p. 3.

[52] *Ibid.*, pp. 5; 4; 5.

that without a stronger national state, factionalism could only lead to internal conflict. As "Citizen" reasoned, ". . . where the people are under no supreme authority, and are ultimately determined by individual and party opinions and resolutions, anarchy, and confusion must necessarily be the fatal consequence."[53]

In the same manner, postwar constitutionalists saw the breakdown of constitutional balance in the rise of class conflict. Many were quick to agree with their revolutionary colleagues on the threat posed to republican values by the rise of commercial wealth. Somewhat ironically, wealthy conservatives seemed to lead the way in the denunciation of commercialism. Constitutionalists saw no subtle alliance between status and wealth; on the contrary, they assumed that aristocracy and oligarchy were inimical. Even before the end of the war, representatives of the old agrarian elite had warned of the rising power of the new capitalist upstarts. After 1783, as landed patriots began to be defeated at the polls by merchant politicians, their warnings became lamentations. By 1786, established figures seemed ready to reassert themselves against those rising interlopers who, "by the brass in their face, or the gold in their purse," had pushed themselves into positions of power.[54] As John Adams explained, the role of selfless, self-sacrificing aristocrats was to hold government out of the grasp of the avaricious and ambitious rich.[55] The protestations of the landed class, many of whom were themselves enormously wealthy, often seem ironic. "The Rich will strive to establish their dominion & enslave the rest," Gouverneur Morris would tell the federal convention. "They always did. They always will."[56] But their protests were hardly hypocritical, for these self-professed aristocrats could fear oligarchy for the same reasons they feared democracy. Indeed, to them oligarchs were democratic figures. Above all others, Morris admitted, they feared those "opulent men whose business created numerous dependents to rule at all elections."[57] Constitutionalists like Morris realized that much popular opinion was decidedly opposed to any reintroduction of aristocratic influence. But these democratic protests, he concluded, would never drown out the simple truth

---

[53] *Ibid.*, p. 9. See Wood, *Creation*, pp. 543-47.

[54] Samuel Haven, D. D., *An Election Sermon, Preached Before the General Court, of New-Hampshire* . . . (Portsmouth, N.H., 1786), p. 12.

[55] On Adams, see Wood, *Creation*, pp. 574-87.

[56] Gouverneur Morris, address to the federal convention, 2 July 1787, *Records*, 1:512.

[57] *Ibid.*, 7 August 1787, *Records*, 2:209.

that "there never was, nor ever will be a civilized Society without an Aristocracy."[58]

To postwar constitutionalists, the trend of the times was to democratic despotism. Revolutionary republicans had always assumed that tyranny could exist only in the executive, that the popular branch could never be oppressive. After 1783, certain constitutionalists, in a sweeping rejection of Whig principles, began to argue that the people were every bit as capable of oppression as any monarch. Conservatives needed to look no further than the reckless actions of the state legislatures—the paper money schemes, tender laws, suspensions of debts, seizures of property. These ill-advised, intemperate measures were certain proof, as the scholarly James Wilson suggested, that *"legislature and tyranny . . .* were most properly associated."[59] Accordingly, many disillusioned conservatives found themselves questioning the very principle of popular sovereignty. The woeful weakness of the state governors suggested that the time had come, as one wrote, to "give life and vigour to the executive authority."[60] Some minced no words in their call for a strong executive. Of all forms of government, said "Fellow Citizen," that of "one man" was "best and most perfect."[61] Among constitutionalists, most apparently assumed that some form of monarchy was inevitable. There was, Benjamin Franklin observed, ". . . a natural Inclination in Mankind to kingly Government." Republican citizens, he wrote, would "rather have one Tyrant than 500. It gives them more of the Appearance of Equality among Citizens. . . ."[62] For the present, political opinion made a reintroduction of monarchical rule impossible. In 1787, John Dickinson admitted, a king was "out of the question."[63] Nevertheless, there was wide agreement that democratic disorder would eventually elicit some version of monarchical rule. To Hamilton, the trend was clear: ". . if we incline too much to democracy," he would tell the federal convention, "we shall soon shoot into a monarchy."[64]

[58] *Ibid.,* 6 July 1787, *Records,* 1:545.
[59] James Wilson, address to the federal convention, 15 August 1787, *Records,* 2:301.
[60] "Fellow Citizen," *Political Establishments,* p. 4.
[61] *Ibid.,* p. 9.
[62] Franklin, "Speech in the Convention, on the Subject of Salaries," 2 June 1787, *The Writings of Benjamin Franklin,* ed. Albert Henry Smyth (New York, 1905-07), 9:593.
[63] Dickinson, address to the federal convention, 2 June 1787, *Records,* 1:87.
[64] Hamilton, address to the federal convention, 26 June 1787, *Records,* 1:432.

In the minds of these conservative constitutionalists, postwar events pointed tragically towards anarchy. In constitutional theory, the return to first principles amounted to nothing more than the dissolution of government, the announcement that the constitution had come to an end. Popular protests would bring reversion to the state of war. As early as 1783, constitutional writers had been warning that the masses were "growing turbulent and ungovernable," that laws are "disregarded[,] civil officers insulted, and the constitution tottering to the foundation."[65] One year later they had found "internal broils" and "civil discord" that promised "horror and distress."[66] Well before any widespread protest, they had seen the "melancholy aspect" of "clamours and insurrections."[67] In short, constitutionalists had long been preparing to view Shays's Rebellion, or the next to come along, as the arrival of the predicted state of anarchy. As Douglass Adair suggested, their reading of history had prepared them to equate the respectable rebels of western Massachusetts ". . . with the blood-crazed citizens of ancient Corcyra, Syracuse, and Megira. . . ."[68] Thus it was no wonder that frantic conservatives could see this band of worried farmers as an army of mad anarchists, "Ignorant, wrestless desperadoes," a band of "mobish insurgents," leading a "deluded multitude."[69] James Sullivan would capture their fears: "Anarchy, with her haggard cheeks and extended jaws, stands ready," he wrote, "and all allow that unless some efficient form of government is adopted she will soon swallow us."[70]

To constitutionalists, the ultimate outcome of these events would be a return to tyranny. Their historical theory required that if anarchy went unchecked, it would end in dictatorship. All their attempts at balance — stronger central government, more aristocratic influence, increased executive prerogatives — had met with determined popular resistance. Accordingly they saw little hope for the present republican system. Through the waning days of the war, certain army officers led by Hamilton had spoken openly of establishing a military dictatorship. In 1783, as Merrill

---

[65] "Honorius," "An Address to the Officers of the Connecticut Line," *The Vermont Gazette,* 18 September 1783.
[66] "Fellow Citizen," *Political Establishments,* p. 3.
[67] "Amicus," *Address,* p. 20.
[68] Adair, "Intellectual Origins," p. 120.
[69] Abigail Adams to Thomas Jefferson, 29 January 1787, *The Adams-Jefferson Letters,* ed. Lester J. Cappon (Chapel Hill, N.C., 1959), 1:168.
[70] "Cassius [Sullivan]," letter to the *Massachusetts Gazette,* 23 November 1787, *Essays,* p. 15. See East, "Massachusetts Conservatives," p. 378.

Jensen has shown, it was only the determined opposition of General Washington that prevented a *coup d'etat*.[71] During the 1780's, Jensen reported, the talk of a dictator remained popular in conservative circles. By 1787, republican leaders had become worried that talk might soon become action: ". . . the best citizens," Jay wrote to Adams, "naturally grow uneasy and look to other systems."[72] Nor did their disillusionment with the republic seem likely to stop at limited reform. Those with property to protect, Jay observed, "prepare their minds for almost any change that may promise them quiet and security."[73] On the eve of the federal convention, observers could agree that the most serious danger to the new republic arose not from popular protest, but from authoritarian response. People in positions of power, Benjamin Rush confided to Richard Price, "not only all the wealthy but all the military men of our country . . . are in favor of a wise and efficient government." Most of them, he went on, were willing to allow "time, necessity, and the gradual operation of reason" to "carry it down." However, should incremental measures fail, Rush declared, *"force* will not be wanting to carry it into execution."[74]

CONCLUSION

In 1787, revolutionaries and constitutionalists met in the debates of the federal convention. At least in part, their positions were the product of their competing theories of history. On the whole, its opponents tended to interpret the federal constitution in light of the cyclical theory of history, viewing the new national government as the first stage of tyranny, the proposed Senate as an invitation to aristocracy, the more powerful executive as a potential republican king. In place of permanent government, they made the case for periodic renewal through a revitalization of the principles of the Confederation. At the extreme, there were some who held that the only antidote to corruption was another act of rebellion. But in the course of the Confederation period, many reflective revolutionaries had seemed to lose their faith in periodic rebellion. At the very least, they admitted to lacking the

---

[71] See Jensen, *The New Nation*, pp. 46-53.

[72] Jay to John Adams, 1 November 1786, *The Correspondence and Public Papers of John Jay*, ed. Henry P. Johnston (New York, 1890-93), 3:214.

[73] Jay to George Washington, 27 June 1786, *Correspondence*, 3:205.

[74] Benjamin Rush to Richard Price, 2 June 1787, *The Letters of Benjamin Rush*, ed. L. H. Butterfield (Princeton, N.J., 1951), 1:418.

stomach for another revolution. Instead, many began to consider the threat to order posed by periodic protest. With the creation of the Constitution, Antifederalists like George Clinton could admit that the Federalists had been right all along about the dangers of anarchy and tyranny: "I know the people are too apt to vibrate from one extreme to another," he confessed. "The effects of this disposition are what I wish to warn against."[75]

In the same manner, its supporters were inclined to view the new constitution as a response to historical imbalance. Shays's Rebellion was proof that the new nation was dissolving into civil war, and despotism could not be far behind. Thus they were predisposed to accept almost any alternative to anarchy and tyranny. But among these constitutionalists as well there was division between those moderate federalists who saw the salvation of the state in the new plan of government, and the more authoritarian nationalists who seemed ready to turn to force to create a unified nation. Even following the convention, the idea of counterrevolution would remain in the minds of these nationalists. For such persons, Jay had told Jefferson, nothing would suffice less than "systems in direct opposition to those which oppress and disquiet them."[76] The ardent Hamilton himself would warn of the dangers of this counterrevolutionary sentiment: "That the human passions should flow from one extreme to another, I allow is natural," he would tell the New York ratifying convention. "Hence the mad project of creating a *dictator*."[77]

Thus American republicans found themselves facing simultaneous threats of revolution and counterrevolution. Neither prospect was at all appealing. To review only the events of the postwar period, without also considering the perception of events, would be to overlook the consternation of these early republicans. For they viewed their times through the lens of history. In that regard, even the least significant issues seemed to magnify into cataclysmic contests. The historians have failed to recognize that it was not the times that brought on the constitutional crisis, but the popular perception of the times. For on one

---

[75] Clinton, address to the New York ratifying convention, 28 June 1788, *Debates*, 2:359.

[76] Jay to Jefferson, 27 October 1786, *Correspondence*, 3:213.

[77] Hamilton, address to the New York ratifying convention, 28 June 1788, *Debates*, 2:360.

point, revolutionaries and constitutionalists could agree: without some bold stroke, they seemed destined for conflict, "approaching a most interesting crisis," the Reverend Joseph Buckminster predicted, by which "will be decided the fate of this empire."[78]

---

[78] Joseph Buckminster, A. M., *A Sermon, Preached Before his Excellency the President . . . of the State of New-Hampshire, June 7, 1787* (Portsmouth, N.H., 1787), p. 27.

Republican Liberty and National Security:
American Military Policy as an
Ideological Problem, 1783 to 1789

Lawrence Delbert Cress

I N Congress and the army, concern about the American republic's peacetime security followed closely on the heels of the victory at Yorktown. The colonists had gone to war in 1775 committed to the classical republican axiom that only a militia, composed of "gentlemen, freeholders, and other freemen," could protect and preserve liberty.[1] The citizen-soldier was self-armed and locally organized, and thus was the only certain deterrent to what republican thinkers saw as the aggressive and tyrannical tendencies of centralized political authority. But the citizen in arms represented more than military prowess. Indeed, essayists and pamphleteers, comparing their fellow patriots with the enfranchised and economically independent citizens of ancient republics, considered the militiaman the embodiment of public virtue—an armed expression of the citizen's willingness to serve the common good. In short, publicists looked to the militia both as a deterrent to political oppression and as a symbol of republican values.[2]

Mr. Cress is a member of the Department of History at Texas A&M University. He would like to thank Charles Royster, Philander D. Chase, and Jack N. Rakove for their comments and suggestions.

[1] The phrase quoted here, and others of similar tone, was repeated often in resolutions passed at the local and provincial levels during the winter of 1774-1775. See, for example, Peter Force, ed., *American Archives . . .* , 4th Ser. (Washington, D.C., 1837-1846), I, 1022, 1032, 1145, II, 167-168.

[2] For the ideological framework of the Revolution see Gordon S. Wood, *The Creation of the American Republic, 1776-1787* (Chapel Hill, N.C., 1969), 46-118, passim; J.G.A. Pocock, *The Machiavellian Moment: Florentine Political Thought and the Atlantic Republican Tradition* (Princeton, N.J., 1975), 361-526, passim; Bernard Bailyn, *The Ideological Origins of the American Revolution* (Cambridge, Mass., 1967), 55-93; Edmund S. Morgan, "The Puritan Ethic and the American Revolution," *William and Mary Quarterly*, 3d Ser., XXIV (1967), 3-18; Charles Royster, " 'The Nature of Treason': Revolutionary Virtue and American Reactions to Benedict Arnold," *ibid.*, 3d Ser., XXXVI (1979), 164-167; Lance Banning, *The Jeffersonian Persuasion: Evolution of a Party Ideology* (Ithaca, N.Y., 1978), 22-69; and Lois G. Schwoerer, *"No Standing Armies!": The Antiarmy Ideology in Seventeenth-Century England* (Baltimore, 1974), 188-200. Writings that associated American

During the war years, however, that ideal had steadily eroded as the principal responsibility for national defense passed to an army modeled after the professional forces that served Great Britain. Self-interest replaced public virtue in the lexicon of military motivation, and centralization and professionalism were embraced by men vested with responsibility for national security.[3] John Adams, among other civilian leaders, resolved early in the fight for independence that Americans could not "reasonably hope to be a powerfull, a prosperous, or a free People . . . [without] a permanent Body of Troops." Within the army, George Washington was only the most senior officer who considered the militia ineffective and unreliable. He and many others agreed that duration enlistments—encouraged by pensions and bounties—seemed the only way to keep a skilled and disciplined army in the field. Noah Webster summarized the sentiment of a growing number when he concluded during the autumn of 1783 that "self-interest," not public virtue, "is the [operat?]ing principle of all mankind." "The truth is," he wrote, "no person will labour without reward—patriotism is but a poor substitute for food and clothing, but a much poorer substitute for Cash."[4] Certainly, by the war's end both the

society with the ancient republics include Simeon Howard, *A Sermon Preached to the Ancient and Honorable Artillery-Company* . . . (Boston, 1773); John Lathrop, *A Sermon Preached to the Ancient and Honorable Artillery-Company* . . . (Boston, 1774); Josiah Quincy, *Observations on the . . . Boston Port-Bill; With Thoughts on Civil Society and Standing Armies* (Boston, 1774); John Carmichael, *A Self-Defensive War Lawful* . . . (Philadelphia, 1775); David Jones, *Defensive War in a Just Cause Sinless* . . . (Philadelphia, 1775); Samuel Cooke, *The Violent Destroyed: And Oppressed Delivered* . . . (Boston, 1777); Charles Lee, *Strictures on a Pamphlet . . . on the Subject of Our Political Confusions* . . . (Philadelphia, 1774), also in *The Lee Papers* (New-York Historical Society, *Collections*, IV-VII [New York, 1872-1875]), IV, 162-166; "Plan of an Army, Etc.," *ibid.*, V, 383-389; and "A Sketch of a Plan for the Formation of a Military Colony," *ibid.*, VI, 323-330. See also essays reprinted in Force, ed., *American Archives*, 4th Ser., I, 1018n, 1063-1065, 1246-1247, II, 341-342, III, 219-221, and the annual orations commemorating the Boston Massacre delivered during the Revolutionary era, reprinted in Hezekiah Niles, ed., *Principles and Acts of the Revolution in America* . . . (Baltimore, 1822).

[3] Edward C. Papenfuse and Gregory A. Stiverson, "General Smallwood's Recruits: The Peacetime Career of the Revolutionary War Private," *WMQ*, 3d Ser., XXX (1973), 117-132; Arthur J. Alexander, "How Maryland Tried to Raise Her Continental Quotas," *Maryland Historical Magazine*, XLII (1947), 184-193; Charles W. Royster, "The Continental Army in the American Mind: 1775-1783" (Ph.D. diss., University of California, Berkeley, 1977), 191-192. See also the analysis of draft and enlistment laws passed in the states during the war years in Lawrence Delbert Cress, "The Standing Army, the Militia, and the New Republic: Changing Attitudes towards the Military in American Society, 1768 to 1820" (Ph.D. diss., University of Virginia, 1976), 162-163.

[4] Adams to Henry Knox, Aug. 25, 1776, in Edmund C. Burnett, ed., *Letters of the Members of the Continental Congress* (Washington, D.C., 1921-1936), II, 61, hereafter cited as *Letters of Cont. Cong.*; George Washington to the President of

virtue and the effectiveness of the citizen-soldier were in doubt. But if the citizenry could not be depended upon to serve the public good, what needed to be done to make the republic secure?

That question troubled the nation's military and political leaders in the aftermath of the war. The answer was by no means obvious. The war years had left Americans deeply divided over the implications of the militia's proven ineffectiveness. A good example of that division is found in the popular histories of the Revolution written during the 1780s by Mercy Otis Warren and David Ramsay. Both acknowledged the weakness of the militia, but for ideologically opposite reasons drew different conclusions from the nation's wartime experience. Warren considered inefficiency unavoidable. Ramsay believed military strength through an established army to be essential to the republic's security. Their divergent views help define the issues that informed the postwar debate over the nation's peacetime forces.[5]

Warren, whose three-volume *History of the Rise, Progress and Termination of the American Revolution* reflects a thorough grounding in the fear of standing armies that pervaded English radical whig tracts like John Trenchard's and Thomas Gordon's *Cato's Letters,* blamed Revolutionary military shortcomings on the erosion of republican values. She credited the mobilization of New England's citizen-soldiers after Lexington and Concord to a revival of public virtue (long dormant in America owing to the colonists' prolonged association with Britain's professional soldiers) sparked in large part by the Coercive Acts of 1774.[6] Unfortunately, she conceded, the martial spirit that had inspired American soldiers to heroic heights at Lexington and at Bunker Hill quickly evaporated, leaving the American army often undermanned and always poorly disciplined. Republicanism itself was partly to blame. "Unused to standing armies, and . . . impatient at the subordination necessary in a camp," Americans refused to enlist for more than a few months. But that was a minor factor compared with the "avaricious spirit" that crept into American society and destroyed the public virtue that had informed the initial call to arms. High enlistment bounties, the demand for half pay, and the founding of the

---

Congress[John Hancock], Sept. 24, 1776, in Walter Millis, ed., *American Military Thought* (Indianapolis, Ind., 1966), 9-11. Webster's ideas appear in letters published in the *Connecticut Courant* (Hartford), Sept. 9, 16, 30, and Oct. 14, 21, 1783.

[5] Ramsay published his *History of the American Revolution* in Philadelphia in 1789. Warren's *History of the Rise, Progress and Termination of the American Revolution* . . . was not published until 1805 when three volumes were released in Boston, but a substantial part of the writing was completed in the 1780s. William R. Smith, *History as Argument: Three Patriot Historians of the American Revolution* (The Hague, 1966), 34-39.

[6] Warren, *History,* I, 40-41, 43-45, 59-62, 66-67, 71-75, 91-97, 123, 157-160, 163, 311. See also Smith, *History as Argument,* 83-84, 88-91.

Society of Cincinnati—all reflections of the professional character of the American army—were only the most obvious manifestations of the spirit of self-aggrandizement that had jeopardized the struggle against tyranny during the war. Warren, well versed in the symptoms of corruption that had historically undermined republican liberties, argued that strict adherence to republican principles would have eased the problems that had plagued military and civil leaders. The military effort of a republic might be "hazarded by the unrestrained license of [its militia] soldiers," she wrote, but that was a small price to pay to avert the moral and political corruption inherent in an army enlisted for "an indefinite term."[7]

David Ramsay rejected the wisdom of *Cato's Letters*, arguing instead that the republic's wartime difficulties were the result of too much republicanism. He had little doubt that "the ideas of liberty and independence, which roused the Colonists to oppose the claims of Great Britain, operated against that implicit obedience which is necessary to a well-regulated army." "The principles of general liberty" used to justify mobilization had led the continental leadership to trust "too much in the virtue of their countrymen." At the same time, little attention had been paid to the need for "subordination and order in their army, which, though it intrenches on civil liberty, produces effects in the military line unequalled by the effusions of patriotism, or the exertions of undisciplined valour." Ramsay reasoned that the militia victories at Lexington, Concord, and Bunker Hill had caused many civilian leaders to believe that the yeoman farmer could meet the country's military needs. They had failed, however, to distinguish momentary gallantry from the perseverance necessary for continued success. The militia had not persevered, and the shortage of adequately trained soldiers had brought the republic " to the brink of destruction" more than once before independence was won.[8]

"The result of the [Revolutionary] experiment," Ramsay wrote, "was, that, however favourable republics may be to the liberty and happiness of the people, in the time of peace, they will be greatly deficient in that vigour and despatch, which military operations require, unless they imitate the policy of monarchies."[9] Assuming a sound defense to be prerequisite to civil liberty, he argued that no nation—republic or monarchy—could long endure without an army of well organized and disciplined regu-

[7] Warren, *History*, I, 177-178, 330-331, 362-363, 366-367, II, 187, 228, 236-239, III, 7, 268-280; Smith, *History as Argument*, 102-103. For an analysis of Warren's pervasive concern about public virtue and moral decay see Lester H. Cohen, "Explaining the Revolution: Ideology and Ethics in Mercy Otis Warren's Historical Theory," *WMQ*, 3d Ser., XXXVII (1980), 200-218.

[8] Ramsay, *History of Am. Rev.* I, 191, 200, 206, 233-234, 294, 304, 305, 330-331; Smith, *History aas Argument*, 59, 61-63.

[9] Quotation from Ramsay, *History of the United States, from their First Settlement as English Colonies, in 1607, to the Year 1808* ..., II (Philadelphia, 1816), 357. Similar ideas are in his *History of the Revolution*, I, 191-196, II, 98-99, 115-116, 124-125.

lars. Warren judged the militia adequate for military emergencies; just as important, she considered the citizen-soldier a measure of the republican virtue without which a republic could not long endure. This ideological conflict between the most popular historians of the Revolution went to the core of the debate over the military during the Confederation period. When the question of peacetime security fell to the army to ponder, its leadership considered both the military lessons and the ideological heritage of the Revolution. George Washington and his advisers showed on the one hand that fears of the regular army were exaggerated but on the other that an effective military establishment could be founded on the ideologically important militia. In Congress, however, ideological differences evoked strident debate. When Alexander Hamilton proposed to leave defense to the regular army and a continental reserve, he aroused a determined opposition united behind the classical republican axiom that standing armies in peacetime were incompatible with republican liberties.

In the spring of 1783, a congressional committee chaired by Hamilton asked the commander in chief to prepare a plan for the "interior defence" of the states commensurate "with the principles of our government."[10] Washington sought the opinions of such advisers as Inspector General Friedrich von Steuben, Chief of Artillery Henry Knox, Quartermaster General Timothy Pickering, and Adjutant General Edward Hand, as well as those of General Rufus Putnam, once the army's acting chief engineer, and George Clinton, governor of strategically important New York and formerly a brigadier general. Pickering, Knox, and Steuben were well versed in the military arts, and Putnam had extensive experience in the sophisticated art of fortification. These veteran soldiers knew that independence had not left the republic impregnable. Indian nations actively contested American territorial claims west of the Appalachian Mountains, and British and Spanish soldiers occupied positions on the republic's northern, western, and southern frontiers. Nevertheless, except for approximately seven hundred regulars left over from the wartime establishment, the nation's security depended on the same state-controlled and haphazardly organized militia system that had proven ineffective during the war.[11] Certainly, nothing Ramsay was to write later in the decade

[10] The congressional committee was formed on Apr. 4, 1783. Alexander Hamilton chaired the committee, which included James Madison, Samuel Osgood, Oliver Ellsworth, and James Wilson. See Madison, "Notes on Debates," Apr. 4, 1783, in William T. Hutchinson and William M. E. Rachal, eds., *The Papers of James Madison*, VI (Chicago, 1969), 432-443. See Hamilton to Washington, Apr. 9, 1783, in Harold C. Syrett *et al.*, eds., *The Papers of Alexander Hamilton* (New York, 1961-1979), III, 322, for the committee's request for a report from Washington. See also Richard H. Kohn, *Eagle and Sword: The Federalists and the Creation of the Military Establishment in America, 1783-1802* (New York, 1975), 41-42.

[11] Don Higginbotham, *The American War of Independence: Military Attitudes, Policies, and Practice, 1763-1789* (New York, 1971), 445-447; Kohn, *Eagle and Sword*, 41-42.

would have surprised the commander in chief's correspondents in 1783. They knew well the difficulties inherent in keeping an effective army in the field.

But though the need to create a reliable military force was foremost in their minds, Washington's advisers could not and did not ignore the ideological foundations of Revolutionary republicanism. Clinton, Hand, and Putnam, for example, understood the American suspicion of standing armies during peacetime. Pickering believed a "standing army would endanger our liberties." He, with Knox, considered the militia the "palladium of a free people."[12] Neither could these men have failed to note the renewed political influence—evident during the recent congressional debates over officer pensions—of persons who shared a profound ideological opposition to military professionalism.[13] Hence their analysis of the nation's military needs involved much more than a call for preparedness. Aware that any peacetime force would have to be acceptable to congressmen sympathetic to the assumptions of radical whiggery, these military leaders sought to reconcile the ideal of the citizen-soldier with the demonstrable effectiveness of a professional army. Personal ideological proclivities naturally led Pickering and Knox to devise plans compatible with the principles of radical whiggery. For others, most notably Steuben, a realistic assessment of the political atmosphere of the postwar years may have proven more influential. But no matter what their motives, they sought to create a military establishment that met both the ideological and the military needs of the republic.[14]

[12] The quotations and the following discussion are from a series of letters sent in Apr. 1783 to Washington from Jean Gouvion Apr. 16, from William Heath Apr. 17, from Henry Knox Apr. 17, from Timothy Pickering Apr. 22, from Rufus Putnam Apr. 25, with enclosures, "Thoughts on the Peace Establishment," and "For the Establishment of a Continental Militia," and from Edward Hand [Apr. 1783], "On the Peace Establishment," all in George Washington Papers, Library of Congress; from Jedediah Huntington Apr. 16, and from George Clinton Apr. 17, in Jared Sparks, ed., *Correspondence of the American Revolution . . .* (Boston, 1853), IV, 27-28, 28-29; and from Friedrich von Steuben, Apr. 15 and Apr. 21, in Washington Papers, Lib. Cong. Friedrich von Steuben, *A Letter on the Subject of an Established Militia . . .* (New York, 1784).

[13] Cress, "Standing Army, the Militia, and the New Republic," chap. 5.

[14] Historians have analyzed the military plans of 1783. John McAuley Palmer, *Washington, Lincoln, Wilson: Three War Statesmen* (Garden City, N.Y., 1930), 15-27, 55-69, 79-82, discusses the plans in the context of the post-World War I debate over the need for compulsory military training in 20th-century America. Walter Millis, *Arms and Men: A Study in American Military History* (New York, 1956), 42-46, comments on the plans in much the same context. Both Palmer and Millis note that Washington's militia plan went well beyond the decentralized militia system that existed in the states at war's end. Russell F. Weigley recognizes that Washington's plan did not envision a *levée en masse*, but he, too, associates Washington's thinking with the mass subscription "which historically has tied democratic political revolution to military revolution culminating in total war" (*Towards an*

Washington's advisers all believed that the militia must remain the principal instrument of national defense. Clinton pointed out that the "modern [European] system of military arrangements ... would be totally inadmissible with us." More enthusiastically, Knox described the militia as an institution that embodied "the ideas of freedom and generous love of ... country."[15] Nevertheless, the commander in chief's correspondents were uneasy with the classical republican notion that public virtue would ensure the citizen's willingness or ability to serve under arms. They also doubted that military service, unlike the franchise, should be regarded as one of the continual obligations of citizenship. Indeed, they contended that universal service was as militarily unreliable as it was socially disruptive. Steuben thought it "a flattering but ... mistaken idea—that every Citizen should be a Soldier," for "the use of arms is as really a trade as shoe or boot making," requiring an apprenticeship like any other craft. According to him, the failure to recognize the need for uniform training and discipline was the principal cause of "that want of confidence in themselves—that reluctancy to come out—that impatience to get home—and that waste of public and destruction of private property, which has ever marked an operation merely Militia." If the American states still sought to rely upon citizen-soldiers during peacetime, the assumptions behind militia service would have to be reassessed and the institution itself reorganized. With that end in mind, Washington's counselors uniformly recommended that a national militia system be established, one designed to keep a select group of citizens constantly prepared for military emergencies.[16]

Washington's correspondents agreed that militia units should be composed of citizens, substitutes discouraged, and blacks, mulattoes, and aliens excluded. Nevertheless, they perceived the militia in terms quite apart from the assumptions of classical republicanism. They insisted that only a selective approach to militia service could achieve the proficiency required for an effective force. Pickering, Putnam, Steuben, and Knox, for

American Army: Military Thought from Washington to Marshall [New York, 1962], 11-15). Don Higginbotham surveys the plans largely within the interpretive framework provided by Palmer and Weigley (*American War of Independence*, 441-445). Richard Kohn describes the plans submitted to Washington and traces the fate of his proposal in Congress, ultimately linking the ideas expressed in the plans with what he believes to be the Federalists' rejection of a militia defense in 1792 (*Eagle and Sword*, 40-53). Nevertheless, none of these historians have noted the differences among the plans presented to Washington, nor have they analyzed how these plans reflected efforts to blend Revolutionary republicanism with the military realities of the post-war period.

[15] Clinton to Washington, Apr. 17, 1783, in Sparks, ed., *Corr. of the Rev.*, IV, 28-29. Knox to Washington, Apr. 17, 1783, Washington Papers, Lib. Cong.

[16] Steuben, *Letter on Established Militia*, 7-8. Pickering to Washington, Apr. 22, 1783, Washington Papers, Lib. Cong.

example, proposed that the militia be classified by age, with the burden of service falling on the young. In a limited sense, militia duty would remain universal—all young men would bear arms—but the concept of universality was stripped of much of its former meaning. The general's advisers understood militia service to be an apprenticeship in arms designed to impart mastery of the martial arts rather than an expression of public virtue. "It would be otherwise," advised Steuben, "were courage the only qualification requisite in a Soldier." Indeed, he thought training would offer "no easy lesson[s] to a mind filled with ideas of equality and freedom." The advisers also separated the citizen's economic stake in society from the obligation to serve under arms. Men aged eighteen to twenty-four, the generals reasoned, not only did not have the family and economic obligations that would make such training unduly burdensome and impractical but could be called out in an emergency without disrupting the entire society. In time, Steuben noted, "a perfect knowledge of the duties of a soldier [would be] engraved on the mind of every citizen," creating "the best possible magazine for a Republic firmly established." Nevertheless, the war years had demonstrated, at least to these officers, that the American militia should no longer be regarded as the military manifestation of the civil constitution.[17]

While these militia plans suggest one mind on the need to reassess the assumptions behind militia service, they also reveal significant differences over the ideologically sensitive question of institutional control. Washington's advisers agreed that the militia must be systematically armed and organized but disagreed over the institutional apparatus required to accomplish that end. Historical circumstances supported decentralization; and, of course, a decentralized militia structure had long been considered an important deterrent to political tyranny. The lessons of the war, though, seemed to call for a degree of centralization theretofore unknown to the American militia.

Pickering, influenced by ideas common to the ideological position Warren represented, proposed a decentralized militia structure. He recommended that the states have charge of officering, training, and administering the militia. The Articles of Confederation vested the states with the responsibility to maintain a well-regulated militia; an inspector general paid and appointed by the continental government would be necessary only to insure that the states fulfilled their constitutional obligation. Pickering believed that an effectively organized state-militia system could meet the nation's military requirements while also continuing to provide a check against political tyranny. Indeed, the constitutional relationship between

[17] Pickering to Washington, Apr. 22, 1783; enclosure "For the Establishment of a Continental Militia," in Putnam to Washington, Apr. 25, 1783; Knox to Washington, Apr. 17, 1783, in Washington Papers, Lib. Cong. Steuben, *Letter on Established Militia*, 7-8, 11-15.

the continental government and the sovereign states prescribed in the Articles demanded a citizen militia devoid of all but the most basic forms of national control. Putnam, ideologically closer to the position espoused by Ramsay, proposed a highly centralized militia structure. Regimental officers would be appointed by state governors but commissioned by Congress, giving the Confederation government the final word in determining the character and composition of the officer corps. Militia regiments would be numbered without regard to states and organized in divisions commanded by congressionally appointed major generals. These generals and their staffs would be required to reside within the geographic areas they served—a concession to local supervision—but would be independent of state control. The entire system would be headed by the commander in chief of the Continental army. The smooth incorporation of militia manpower into the Continental army had been a chronic problem during the war, and it was to that problem that Putnam addressed his plan for militia reform. He ignored the militia's traditional obligation to oppose the centralizing drive of tyranny.[18]

Steuben was probably motivated more by a careful reading of the political climate than by ideological commitment; nevertheless, his plan best accommodated the need for military efficiency to the thorny issue of militia organization. He recommended that the militia be organized into self-sufficient legions, two each for New England and the South, and three for the mid-Atlantic states. The officer corps would be appointed and commissioned by the states, with appointment of general rank officers falling to the state providing the most men. State officials would supervise training, since drill would be conducted by state-appointed legion commanders. A provision allowing militiamen to take their arms and equipment home at the end of their three years of intensive training would further strengthen the militia's local ties without detracting from the institutional integrity of the national system. The seven militia legions would constitute a dependable twenty-one-thousand-man force able to respond to any emergency.[19]

Similar differences over the desirability of centralized military institutions surfaced when Washington's advisers considered the separate matter of the peacetime army. None of the general's counselors disputed the need for regular soldiers to man frontier garrisons: the constabulary duties of frontier forces had not since late in the seventeenth century been considered part of the responsibilities of the citizen-soldier.[20] Still, the plans for the organization and control of the regular army—like those for the militia—reflect the conflict between ideologically motivated demands for decentralization and the desire to create an effective and reliable military.

[18] Pickering to Washington, Apr. 22, 1783, and enclosure "For the Establishment of a Continental Militia," in Putnam to Washington, Apr. 25, 1783, in Washington Papers, Lib. Cong.
[19] Steuben, *Letter on Established Militia*, 11-15.
[20] Cress, "Standing Army, the Militia, and the New Republic," chap. 1.

Pickering, influenced by the assumptions of radical whiggery, never forgot that standing armies in peacetime had been used by ambitious men to oppress free people. He proposed an eight hundred-man frontier constabulary more regional than national in composition and organization. The frontier should be divided into regions, with the states in each region supplying continental troops and officers only for their own frontiers. States needing troops to protect their coastlines would use their own forces. Pickering recommended that no staff officers be commissioned. In the wartime Continental army, staff officers had been appointed by Congress, and Pickering wanted to prevent the peace establishment from falling under the influence of officers not dependent on the states for their commissions. He reasoned that forces serving under the scrutiny of the state assemblies would be least susceptible to corruption. Just as important, a decentralized command structure represented an obstacle to the oppressive propensities of centralized authority. Pickering did not intend to allow the frontier constabulary to become the germ of a standing army that might one day destroy the liberties secured through independence.[21]

Washington's other advisers recommended a larger and more centralized force. Steuben recognized that geographic isolation made a large standing army unnecessary. Nevertheless, he believed a legion of three thousand regulars and an engineer-artillery corps numbering one thousand strong—all under a continental command—to be necessary to guard the seaboard and frontier, and to meet the exigencies of war.[22] Putnam and Clinton were particularly concerned that Congress "preserve the great outlines of an army." Edward Hand endorsed the same approach. Specifically, he proposed that staff departments be continuously officered at wartime levels. Like the others, he wanted to ensure that the national government had a command structure able to organize and direct a large number of citizen-soldiers in the event of war. With Steuben, Clinton, and Putnam, Hand insisted that a force so conceived promised efficiency in arms without posing a threat to liberty.[23]

[21] Pickering to Washington, Apr. 22, 1783, Washington Papers, Lib. Cong.

[22] Steuben to Washington, Apr. 15, 1783, and "Peace Establishment" enclosure in Steuben to Washington, Apr. 21, 1783, ibid. The letter of Apr. 21 suggested a peacetime force of just under 5,000. Steuben refined that number to 4,000 and expanded upon the general plans in these letters in Letter on Established Militia, 2-7. For a similar view of the peacetime regular establishment see Gouvion to Washington, Apr. 16, 1783, Washington Papers, Lib. Cong.

[23] Putnam to Washington, Apr. 25, 1783, enclosure "Thoughts on the Peace Establishment," in Washington Papers, Lib. Cong. Clinton to Washington, Apr. 17, 1783, in Sparks, ed., Corr. of the Rev., IV, 29-31. Hand to Washington, "On the Peace Establishment" [Apr. 1783], Washington Papers, Lib. Cong. None of these men offered estimates of the size of the force needed to accomplish these ends. See also Huntington to Washington, Apr. 16, 1783, in Sparks, ed., Corr. of the Rev., IV, 27-28, and John Patterson to Washington, Apr. 16, 1783, Washington Papers, Lib. Cong.

No matter how the peacetime army was organized, all of the command-er in chief's correspondents believed that its enlisted ranks should be com-posed of men willing to make soldiering their occupation. Professionalism was needed in the officer corps as well. Steuben was the most outspoken on these points, arguing that the army's effectiveness depended upon the republic's willingness to view military service as a legitimate profession. Extended enlistments encouraged by attractive bounties would ensure a competent rank and file. Washington found less unanimity among his ad-visers on how to develop a skilled officer corps. Pickering opposed mili-tary academies, fearing that they would become the breeding ground for the same kind of decadent military elite that led Europe's corrupting ar-mies. He noted that the arts and sciences usually associated with military education were already being taught in American colleges, and he pro-posed that the republic rely on those institutions to prepare men for the officer corps. If military academies were established, he urged that they accept no more students than necessary to fill vacancies in the frontier constabulary.[24] Clinton shared Pickering's preference for a civilian educa-tion for the nation's regular officers, but he favored more formal instruc-tion under the tutelage of professors of military science located at a civilian college in each state. These civilian instructors would be super-vised by distinguished military leaders paid by the states. Under Clinton's plan, only those students receiving degrees in military science would be awarded commissions in the regular army.[25]

Steuben, Hand, and Knox held that military academies could best meet the republic's need for professionally trained officers. Indeed, they be-lieved that properly constituted academies could eliminate any need for a large standing army. Steuben's recommendations typified that point of view. He proposed founding military schools in New England, the mid-Atlantic states, and the South. Each would be organized within the Conti-nental army command and staffed by regular officers skilled in engineer-ing, artillery, and staff operations. The principal function of each academy would be to equip young officers to handle the problems of modern war-fare. But these academies were to be more than nurseries for regular army officers. Of the expected one hundred cadets graduating each year, no more than ten would be awarded commissions in the Continental army. Ninety percent of the graduates would return to civilian life, there to lead and train local militia units. In short, the academies would provide the cement for a unified system of defense consisting of the peacetime army and the select militia. They would serve as normal schools for instruction in military skills, and their graduates would prepare the citizenry to meet the military requirements of the nation. In time, the country would have

[24] Pickering to Washington, Apr. 22, 1783, Washington Papers, Lib. Cong.
[25] Clinton to Washington, Apr. 17, 1783, in Sparks, ed., *Corr. of the Rev.*, IV, 25-31.

not only a well-trained corps of regular army officers but also a well-regulated and disciplined select militia led by academy-trained officers.[26]

Washington distilled his advisers' ideas into a defense plan that reflected his own understanding of American republicanism as well as his concern for military effectiveness.[27] He held indisputable the need "to put the National Militia in such a condition as that they may appear truly respectable in the Eyes of our Friends and formidable to those who would otherwise become our enemies." The histories of Greece and Rome "in their most virtuous and Patriotic ages" and the contemporary security of Switzerland, the commander in chief noted, "demonstrate the Utility of such Establishments." Nevertheless, Washington clearly had doubts about what he considered to be the "primary position, and the basis of our system," the assumption "that every Citizen who enjoys the protection of a free Government, owes not only a proportion of his property, but even of his personal services to the defence of it." Like his correspondents, he believed that a dependable militia depended upon a reassessment of the assumptions traditionally associated with militia service and a reappraisal of the militia's historically decentralized organization.[28]

All citizens aged eighteen to fifty should be enrolled in the militia, but, the general noted, "amongst such a Multitude of People . . . there must be a great number, who from domestic Circumstances, bodily defects, natural awkwardness or disinclination, can never acquire the habits of Soldiers." Accordingly, while the practice of enrolling all adult males might be continued, Washington urged a classification system that placed the principal burden of training and service on volunteers willing to assume a three- to seven-year militia obligation. He considered entrusting that obligation only to "able bodied young Men, between the Age of 18 and 25" to be a viable but less desirable option. Service in the select militia would be encouraged by "such exemptions, privileges or distinctions, as might tend to keep alive a true Military pride, a nice sense of honour, and a patriotic regard for the public." This "Continental Militia" would be designed to resist "any sudden impression which might be attempted by a foreign Ene-

[26] Steuben to Washington, Apr. 21, 1783. Edward Hand explicitly endorsed the Steuben proposal in a letter to Washington [Apr. 1783]. Knox also suggested an academy plan similar to Steuben's, though it included provisions for separate naval and military academies. Knox to Washington, Apr. 17, 1783, in Sparks, ed., *Corr. of the Rev.*, IV, 27-28. Secretary of War Benjamin Lincoln also endorsed Steuben's plan. Lincoln to Hamilton, May 1783, Papers of the Continental Congress, Item 38, 317-330, National Archives. See also Palmer, *Washington, Lincoln, Wilson*, 62-65.

[27] Washington to Steuben, Mar. 15, 1784, in John C. Fitzpatrick, ed., *The Writings of George Washington* . . . (Washington, D.C., 1931-1944), XXVII, 360, hereafter cited as *Writings of Washington*. See also Weigley, *Towards an American Army*, 10-13, and Kohn, *Eagle and Sword*, 45.

[28] "Sentiments on a Peace Establishment," in Washington to Hamilton, May 2, 1783, *Writings of Washington*, XXVI, 388-389.

my," providing time for full-scale national mobilization. Washington also proposed that it be organized under the same rules and regulations as the regular army, and he hoped that veteran Continental army officers would be encouraged to assume command of militia units. These provisions would assure a national orientation for militia corps that would be geographically defined by state boundaries. Washington could still accurately claim that his select militia offered a system of defense free of the dangers inherent in "the Mercenary Armies, which have . . . subverted the liberties of allmost all the Countries they have been raised to defend," but clearly the idea of every citizen serving as part of the obligation of citizenship, as in the ancient republics, did not have a part in his understanding of how best to assure national security. Nevertheless, the militia, properly organized and thoroughly trained, retained in his scheme primary responsibility for the republic's defense.[29]

The need for military effectiveness dominated Washington's counsel that Congress keep a small regular army in the field. The commander in chief conceded that peacetime armies had proven dangerous in the past, and he recognized that American geography and ideology combined to make a force capable of defeating an invading European army both unnecessary and unacceptable. He advised, however, that current "circumstances" made a small number of regulars "not only safe, but indispensably necessary." He recommended a force of 2,631 officers and men, organized without regard to the states and entirely dependent upon Congress "for their Orders, their pay, and supplies." The commanding general would report directly to the secretary of war, and soldiers would be moved regularly from garrison to garrison in order to prevent the development of local associations "which often prove very detrimental to the [national] service." Washington proposed to staff the Continental army with longserving regular soldiers and professional officers. Initial recruits would serve three years, with later enlistments being based "upon Terms of similarity with those of the British": soldiers in Britain's peacetime army enlisted for life. Discipline would be strict, but the commander in chief expected few recruiting difficulties. "When the Soldiers for the War have frolicked a while among their friends, and find they must have recourse to hard labour for a livelyhood," he wrote, "I am persuaded numbers of them will reinlist upon almost any Terms." The isolation of frontier garrisons would require more officers, but Washington's suggestion of an expanded officer corps also reflected his determination to place the army's leadership in the hands of professionals. During an emergency the nation could look to these officers "well skilled in the Theory and Art of War" to fill the command positions in an expanded army, thus avoiding the confusion and delays involved in elevating untrained citizens to positions of command.[30]

[29] *Ibid.*, 389-394. Washington was willing to institute a draft to compel service in the select militia if that should become necessary.

[30] *Ibid.*, 374-385. On enlistments in the British peacetime army see J. W. Fortescue, *A History of the British Army*, II (London, 1910), 581-583.

Washington thought that the proposal prepared by Steuben offered the best means to train the army's officers. "That an Institution calculated to keep alive and diffuse the knowledge of the Military Art would be highly expedient," he wrote, "will not admit a doubt." Still, he recognized that academies might for the moment prove beyond the means of the young nation. "Until a more perfect system of Education can be adopted," he proposed that a number of "young Gentlemen" be trained in the art of war at posts manned by engineer and artillery corps officers. These cadets would fill vacancies in the regiments during peacetime. As "able Engineers and expert Artillerists," they would also represent an important addition to the republic's wartime capabilities.[31]

The commander in chief was not, nor for that matter were any of his advisers, recommending that the regular army replace the militia as the principal instrument for national security. Indeed, there is nothing in Washington's assessment of the republic's peacetime needs that suggests a desire to scrap the militia. His endorsement of Steuben's academy proposal suggests his interest in keeping a well-trained and ably officered militia. Even when Washington criticized himself for being guided by what "I thought *would*, rather than what I conceived *ought* to be a proper peace Establishment," his comment was aimed at his failure to recommend a more comprehensive militia system.[32] It was not an implicit endorsement of a large peacetime army. Indeed, if the country became wealthy enough to afford the luxury of "a standing Army adequate to our defence," the general thought the money would be better spent "building and equipping a Navy." Washington's intentions in 1783, as they would be later in his career, were to provide the Confederation with a systematically organized and carefully trained select militia that, together with a small regular army, could protect against surprise attack and provide the means for a quick and orderly popular mobilization in the event of actual war. Military efficiency was critical; but in the minds of General Washington and his advisers, the principal means to that end remained militia reform. As Washington put it, "our National Militia . . . is to be the future guardian of those rights and that Independence, which have been maintain'd so gloriously, by the fortitude and perseverance of our Countrymen."[33]

Hamilton received Washington's plan, along with Steuben's recommendation for a system of military academies, during the first week of May 1783.[34] He, however, proceeded to draft a military plan that ignored Washington's serious attempt at militia reform. Acknowledging that Congress had a "constitutional duty" to ensure that the states maintained a well-regulated militia, he urged the adoption of common organizational

[31] "Sentiments on a Peace Establishment," in Washington to Hamilton, May 2, 1783, *Writings of Washington*, XXVI, 396-397.
[32] Washington to Steuben, Mar. 15, 1783, *ibid.*, XXVII, 360.
[33] "Sentiments on a Peace Establishment," *ibid.*, XXVI, 375, 392.

and training systems. Nevertheless, Hamilton clearly did not intend the state militias to be an important part of the nation's defense system. He recommended that they assume only a limited obligation for service outside their territorial boundaries. Certainly, his suggestion that the militia be arranged by marital status was not designed to invigorate the institution. Single men would be required to attend six training sessions annually, and married men, four; in both categories the obligation for emergency service would extend to men fifty years of age. This proposal was but a pale reflection of the classification system recommended by Washington and his aides. Indeed, the proficiency and effectiveness that the commander in chief believed the select militia could bring to the national defense was to be provided, according to Hamilton's plan, by volunteers paid, supplied, and armed by the continental government. Conceived more as an auxiliary for the regular army than as an extension of the local militia, these units would train twice monthly as companies and once as regiments. In the event of war they would be obliged to serve three-year tours of duty wherever Congress ordered. To encourage the service of competent volunteer officers, Hamilton proposed that they hold rank on a par with regular continental officers.[34]

Hamilton urged that the regular army take primary responsibility for the republic's defense on the ground that it alone could provide the professionalism and the centralized organization necessary for an effective military. Indeed, his eagerness to relegate the state militia to obscurity was matched only by his determination to place the peacetime army on a national as well as professional footing. He proposed that Congress assume complete control over the recruitment of soldiers and the appointment of officers—functions left to the states by the Articles of Confederation—in addition to commanding, paying, and supplying the army. Since no state would fill an entire regiment, the appointment and apportionment of regimental officers would become needlessly complex if left to the states. Efficiency also justified congressional recruitment. Continental control would eliminate competitive enlistment bounties that would inevitably raise the

[34] Steuben's plan was delivered to Hamilton's committee by Richard Peters of Pennsylvania. Peters to Steuben, Apr. 23 and May 6, 1783, *Letters of Cont. Cong.*, VII, 150, 156. Secretary of War Benjamin Lincoln, working independently of Washington, also prepared recommendations for the peace establishment that were very similar to the commander in chief's. Lincoln to Hamilton, May 1783, and Lincoln's "Peace Establishment Plan" enclosed in Lincoln to the president of Congress, May 3, 1783, both in Papers of the Cont. Cong., Item 38, 317-330, 285-298.

[35] The complete text of Hamilton's report is in W. C. Ford *et al.*, eds. *Journals of the Continental Congress, 1774-1789* (Washington, D.C., 1904-1936), XXV, 722-743, hereafter cited as *Jours. Cont. Cong.* The comments concerning the militia are on pages 742-743. For summaries of Hamilton's report see Kohn, *Eagle and Sword*, 47-48, and Weigley, *Towards an American Army*, 14-15.

cost of national defense. To ensure proficiency and effectiveness, Hamilton recommended six-year enlistments for this three-thousand-man force as well as a highly paid and well-trained officer corps.[36]

Congress received Hamilton's proposals in mid-June 1783, at a time when the influence of Robert Morris and other proponents of expanded national power had begun to wane.[37] Four days later, without acting on the plan, Congress fled Philadelphia for Princeton to escape mutinous troops demanding back pay. The move revived a parochialist coalition led by Elbridge Gerry, David Howell, and Arthur Lee, and affiliated ideologically with the position articulated in Warren's *History*. The coalition, a loosely knit group bound by a common distrust of Robert Morris and his nationalist-minded followers, had recently failed to block the commutation of half pay to regular army officers. Determined to prevent the creation of a peacetime army, it now successfully used the tensions generated by Congress's hurried departure from Philadelphia to delay action on the report. In August, nationalists succeeded in inviting Washington to Princeton as part of an effort to revive debate; but Washington's visit produced only a flurry of committee meetings and a decision to postpone further discussion until October. By September, hope for passing Hamilton's plan had all but disappeared. Even the commander in chief found it wanting. Though Washington thought Hamilton's arrangement of the regular army generally adequate, he regarded the classification scheme and the proposal for a reserve force independent of the militia "not . . . well calculated to answer the object in view." He hoped Congress would organize a select militia after the fashion he had proposed. Meanwhile in Congress, parochialists pressed for the defeat of Hamilton's recommendations. They denied that Congress had constitutional authority to maintain troops in peacetime, linked the new impost proposal with the creation of a standing army, and charged that Hamilton's military plan was only another effort to expand congressional powers at the expense of state sovereignty. The October debates failed to produce a compromise, but Congress did formally agree that the vulnerability of the frontier required "some garrisons . . . to be maintained in time of peace at the expense of the United States."[38]

[36] *Jours. Cont. Cong.*, XXV, 722-738. Hamilton did not recommend a formal military academy, believing that "Military Knowledge is best acquired in service." Instead, he proposed that professors of mathematics, chemistry, natural philosophy, and civil architecture, and one drawing master be attached to the corps of engineers to provide advanced training in military arts. *Ibid.*, 732, 738.

[37] Burnett dates the report as submitted on June 17, as does Kohn. See *Letters of Cont. Cong.*, VII, xxvii, and Kohn, *Eagle and Sword*, 321, n. 26. Syrett dates the report as June 18, 1783, in *Hamilton Papers*, III, 378n. Kohn and Burnett are probably correct.

[38] The best discussion of the debate over the peace establishment during the summer of 1783 is Kohn, *Eagle and Sword*, 48-53. On the political significance of Congress's move to Princeton see Cress, "Whither Columbia? Congressional Resi-

Congress's move to Annapolis in November 1783 marked an end of efforts under the Articles of Confederation to build a Continental army capable of ensuring the nation's security. During the spring of 1784, the mood in Congress increasingly reflected the parochialists' claim that the Articles did not sanction a national army during peacetime. Repeatedly, parochialists criticized Hamilton's plan as an attempt to saddle the republic with an oppressive standing army. If Congress were allowed to raise a few men for a short time, nothing could prevent that body from extending the term of enlistment and enlarging the number of men under arms. Power, they argued, was inherently corruptive. Congressional control over a regular army and an elite reserve—the latter intended to supersede the state militias—would jeopardize the constitutional foundation of the Confederation. If no continental force were allowed, the militia would thrive, preserving that institution as the ultimate guarantor of civil liberties. "We have many brave and veteran officers to discipline the latter [militia]," wrote Elbridge Gerry, "but if a regular army is once admitted, will not the militia gradually dwindle into contempt? And where then are we to look for the defence of our rights and liberties?" After a stirring speech by Gerry charging that "standing armies in time of peace are inconsistent with the principles of republican governments, dangerous to the liberties of a free people, and generally converted into destructive engines for establishing despotism," Congress, on June 2, 1784, reduced the army to a handful of officers commanding eighty soldiers stationed at Fort Pitt and West Point. The next day, it "recommended" that Connecticut, New York, New Jersey, and Pennsylvania recruit from their militias a total of seven hundred men for a single year's service on the frontier. A year later, the term of service was extended to three years, and regulars replaced militiamen, but that measure was intended only to solve specific problems inherent in frontier duty; it in no way resolved the more basic question of the republic's peacetime security.[39]

---

dence and the Politics of the New Nation, 1776-1787," *WMQ*, 3d Ser., XXXII (1975), 582-588. See also Kenneth R. Bowling, "New Light on the Philadelphia Mutiny of 1783: Federal-State Confrontation at the Close of the War for Independence," *Pennsylvania Magazine of History and Biography*, CI (1977), 419-450. On Washington's reaction to Hamilton's plan see Washington, "Observations on an Intended Report of a Committee of Congress on a Peace Establishment," Sept. 8, 1783, in *Writings of Washington*, XXVII, 140-144. The congressional resolution on frontier defense is in *Jours. Cont. Cong.*, XXIV, 806-807. On the parochialist opposition to the peace establishment see the letters written by members of Congress during July and Aug. 1783, collected in *Letters of Cont. Cong.*, VII, 156, 167, 245, 263, 266, VIII, 842; and R. H. Lee to James Monroe, Jan. 5, 1784, in James Curtis Ballagh, ed., *The Letters of Richard Henry Lee*, II (New York, 1914), 287-289.

[39] On the mood in Congress against the peace establishment see accounts in *Letters of Cont. Cong.*, VII, 415, 434, 492-493, 546-547, 576, 603, VIII, 116, 197;

At the heart of the differences over the military needs of the Confederation stood the question of the compatibility of political liberty with military effectiveness. Antagonists were asking basic but different questions—questions determined by their understanding of how best to preserve a free society. Hamilton concluded that the preservation of republican liberties depended on the ability of the national government to field a body of trained soldiers able to repel attack. Moderate English whigs from Daniel Defoe to Adam Smith had reached the same conclusion, and it was in that tradition that Hamilton embraced a centralized and professional military establishment as necessary for and compatible with the survival of free institutions.[40] Parochialists believed that independence had eliminated the need for regulars. Equating professional soldiers with moral decay and political corruption, they, as had republican theorists in the line of James Harrington and Algernon Sidney, looked to the local militia as an expression of republican virtue and as a deterrent to tyranny. A decentralized militia composed of citizen-soldiers was admittedly inefficient; still, it alone could guarantee a free and stable republican constitution.[41]

Knox to Washington, May 28, 1784, in Sparks, ed., *Corr. of the Rev.*, IV, 68-69; and Massachusetts Delegation to the Massachusetts General Court, June 4, 1784, and Gerry to the Massachusetts General Court, Oct. 25, 1784, in James T. Austin, *The Life of Elbridge Gerry*, I (Boston, 1828), 432-433, 460-463. Gerry's speech is in *Jours. Cont. Cong.*, XXVII, 433-434. For the decision to reduce the army to 80 privates plus officers see *ibid.*, 524. On the 1785 resolution see *ibid.*, XXVIII, 28-29, 88-89, 223-224, 240-241, 247-248, 352-353, 390-391. The most complete discussion of Continental politics in 1784 and 1785 is in H. James Henderson, *Party Politics in the Continental Congress* (New York, 1974), 350-382. For an analysis centering on the political development of the army issue in the period see Kohn, *Eagle and Sword*, 54-62. See also Millis, *Arms and Men*, 38-46; C. Joseph Bernardo and Eugene H. Bacan, *American Military Policy: Its Development since 1775* (Harrisburg, Pa., 1955), 61-63; and Higginbotham, *War of American Independence*, 443-445.

[40] For example, see Daniel Defoe, *An Argument Shewing, That a Standing Army . . . Is not Inconsistent with a Free Government* (1698), in James T. Boulton, ed., *Selected Writings of Daniel Defoe* (London, 1965), 36-50; John Somers, *A Letter, Ballancing the Necessity of Keeping a Land-Force in Times of Peace . . .* (London, 1697); and [William Cobbett], *The Parliamentary History of England . . .*, X (London, 1812), *passim*. Adam Smith summarized the pro-army position that developed in England in *An Inquiry into the Nature and Causes of the Wealth of Nations* (1776), ed. Edwin Cannan (New York, 1937), 659-669, 738-739.

[41] For example, see Sten Bodvar Liljegren, *James Harrington's Oceana* (Heidelberg, 1924), 9-10, 16, 48-58; Algernon Sidney, *Discourses Concerning Government*, 3d ed. (London, 1751), 113-115; Robert Molesworth, *An Account of Denmark as It Was in the Year 1692* (London, 1694), 75-98, 123-137, 224-225, 258-268; John Trenchard, *A Short History of Standing Armies in England* (1698), in Trenchard and Thomas Gordon, *A Collection of Tracts*, I (London, 1751), 57-107; and James Burgh, *Political Disquisitions or, an Enquiry into Public Errors, Defects, and Abuses,*

Given the renewed influence of the parochialists in Congress, no peace establishment was acceptable that failed the test of classical republican theory. Had Congress considered the plans developed by Washington or Steuben instead of Hamilton's, its mood might at least have been conciliatory. The commander in chief and his head training officer understood the importance of the militia and looked to it as a primary guarantor of national security, though Congress most certainly would have questioned their insistence on a centralized command and a selective approach to service. No doubt Pickering's plan for a decentralized militia and a regionally organized frontier constabulary would have been more enthusiastically received than any other prepared in 1783. Yet even Pickering would have been criticized for not conceiving of militia duty as an expression of republican virtue. Needed was a peace establishment plan that not merely recognized the militia's role as a deterrent to political tyranny but also actually reinforced the republican virtue so important to republican theorists. The proposal prepared in 1786 by Secretary of War Henry Knox in response to a congressional request for a system of defense compatible with the military clause of the Articles met both requirements. Knox's *Plan for the General Arrangement of the Militia* is also noteworthy because during the early national period it became the touchstone for men—both Federalists and Republicans—committed to the republican tenets of the Revolution yet uneasy about the republic's capacity for defense.[42]

Republics, Knox argued, were inherently less responsive to military emergencies than monarchies. Deliberative government precluded executive tyranny but often at the expense of decisiveness. That made peacetime military preparedness particularly important. In America, however, peace had undermined national security, in part, Knox believed, because Americans were again exposed to the "effulgence of wealth" and the "seducing influence of luxury" that produced "a corruption of manners, destructive to a republic." A sound peacetime military structure, Knox reasoned, should sustain the martial spirit of the citizenry and "form the manners and habits of the youth, on principles of true republican magnanimity." A properly organized militia could do that. Specifically, he intended militia service to impart the basic republican concept "that the love of their country, and the knowledge of defending it, are political duties of the most indispensable nature."[43]

---

etc., II (London, 1775), 341-477, *passim.* See also Cress, "Radical Whiggery on the Role of the Military: Ideological Roots of the American Revolutionary Militia," *Journal of the History of Ideas,* XL (1979), 43-60.

[42] Historians who have taken note of the Knox plan have considered it only as a restatement of Washington's view of the postwar military establishment. See Palmer, *Washington, Lincoln, Wilson,* 86-94, and Millis, *Arms and Men,* 50-51. Neither Kohn, *Eagle and Sword,* nor Higginbotham, *War of American Independence,* discusses the Knox plan.

[43] Henry Knox, *A Plan for the General Arrangement of the Militia of the United States* ([Philadelphia], 1786), 1-6.

Knox's view of the militia as an instrument for instilling public virtue led him to envision a system aimed at classical republican ends while yet unencumbered by the ideal of universal service. He proposed that the burden of militia service would be borne by an "advanced corps" composed of young men aged eighteen through twenty—an age when youths were normally apprenticed to a trade or employed on a family farm. These young men could easily be committed to regular military training, he reasoned, since their labors usually provided their masters with excessive profits. Youths were more available than heads of households; they were also more receptive to "the splendor of military parade" because they were not distracted by family obligations. The "main" and "reserve" corps, composed respectively of men twenty-one through forty-five and forty-six through fifty-nine, would be required to serve in emergencies, but their main responsibility would be economic. These older men would be assessed for the cost of training, supplying, and equipping the advanced corps, as well as for supporting the families of men called to active service. "Although the substantial political maxim, which requires personal service of all the members of the community for the defence of the state, . . . is the main pillar of a free government, yet," argued Knox, the general welfare could best be served by a careful analysis of the obligations and responsibilities of the various age groups in society.[44]

Knox, however, had no intention of allowing the defense of the country to fall into the hands of politically and socially irresponsible youths. Borrowing from an early radical whig plan for militia reform, he pointed out that an important function of the annual "Camps of Discipline," to which members of the advanced corps would be sent for forty-two days each year, would be to "mould the minds of the young men, to a due obedience of the laws" as well as "instruct them in the art of war." Camps would be located near rivers and far from large cities: "The first is necessary for the practice of manoeuvers, the second to avoid the vices of populous places." Amusements would be limited to the military-related skills of running, swimming, and wrestling. Camp discipline would be designed to instill habits of industry and to discourage idleness and dissipation. Youths would be exposed to regular and concise discourses on the "eminent advantages of free governments to the happiness of society" and the importance of "the knowledge, spirit, and virtuous conduct of the youth" to such government. In short, every effort would be made to "form a race of hardy citizens, equal to the dignified task of defending their country," and to make military education "an indispensable qualification of a free citizen."[45]

[44] Ibid., 8, 11-14, 21-23, 25.
[45] Ibid., 18-19, 22-24. Knox borrowed extensively from Andrew Fletcher, A Discourse of Government with Relation to Militias, in The Political Works of Andrew Fletcher (London, 1737).

Under Knox's plan the continental war office would supply arms and accoutrements which each soldier would retain at the end of his tour with the advanced corps. Actual mobilization would be directed and supervised by state officials, though militiamen would be expected to serve during emergencies anywhere in the United States for a period not exceeding one year. This, Knox believed, gave the states the means by which to prevent misuse of the militia; yet it also ensured that the continental government would have access to a body of reliable soldiers. The plan required neither a large professional army nor mass mobilization, while still guaranteeing a well-armed citizenry capable of functioning as soldiers. The ranks of the army would be filled with men familiar with the moral, political, and military principles taught in the "Camps of Discipline." There would be no need to entrust "unprincipled banditti" with responsibility for "defending every thing that should be dear to freemen." In sum, Knox's militia plan would do what the adoption of republican constitutions had failed to do: it would "foster a glorious public spirit; infuse the principle of energy, and stability into the body politic; and give a high degree of political splendor, to the national character."[46]

Knox's proposal built upon the need—generally recognized by military planners—to reassess the classical republican idea that virtue would ensure military preparedness. The result was a bold attempt to satisfy the competing concerns for liberty and military efficiency that had informed the debate over national security since 1783. The secretary of war made the militia responsible for the nation's security, dismissing even the need for an expandable regular army. That represented an important recognition of the ideological tenor of Confederation politics. But the plan was more than simply a revival of the sensitivity to radical whig republicanism that had pervaded military planning before Hamilton sent his recommendations to Congress in 1783. If parochialists were most concerned about liberty and nationalists were most concerned about military efficiency, Knox proposed to meet these concerns by making the militia an agency of both military skills and republican values. The plan promised an effective military force as well as a virtuous citizenry. The republic's propensity to moral decadence, as well as the growing complexity of contemporary tactics, demanded a reassessment of the nation's military institutions. Yet Knox was convinced that a careful blending of ideological and practical considerations could ensure not only a strong national defense but also the perpetuation of traditional republican values and institutions.

The congressional committee that had commissioned the preparation of the plan gave it a favorable reading during September 1786. The plan also evoked a positive response from David Ramsay, who feared only "that our governments are too relaxed to bear any system which will be attended

[46] Knox, *Plan for the Militia*, 10-15, 20, 24-25, 30-34.

with so much time & expence."[47] Formal debate was forestalled by the meeting of the federal convention of 1787, but the basic elements of the plan continued to provide the starting point for militia reform through the early national period. In January 1790, Washington recommended the Knox plan—revised to reflect the national government's expanded constitutional powers—to Congress as the centerpiece of the new government's military establishment.[48] Federalists tried on several occasions during Washington's presidency to persuade Congress to found the republic's peacetime military strength on Knox's proposal for a republican militia.[49] Once in power, the Republican leadership also acknowledged the need to reassess the organization and composition of the republic's militia. Jefferson's determined effort to make the militia responsible for the republic's security "until the first moments of war"—best embodied in the select militia plan sent to Congress in 1805—depended on a conception of militia service akin to that recommended by Knox.[50] Though they often began with a far stronger commitment to the military implications of republican theory than had many Federalists, by the end of the Jefferson administration a host of Republican essayists embraced a similar view of the militia's place in the republic's system of defense.[51]

That both Federalists and Republicans failed to transform the decentralized, state-oriented militia into a dependable instrument of national secu-

[47] Congressional committee endorsement is in *Jours. Cont. Cong.*, XXXI, 642. Ramsay to Knox, Mar. 12, 1786, in Robert L. Brunhouse, ed., *David Ramsay, 1749-1815: Selections from His Writings* (American Philosophical Society, *Transactions*, LV, Pt. 4 [Philadelphia, 1965]), 98-99.

[48] Henry Knox to Speaker, House of Representatives, Jan. 18, 1790, in *[Annals of Congress] The Debates and Proceedings in the Congress of the United States . . .* (Washington, 1834-1853), II, 1st Cong., 2d sess., 2087-2107, hereafter cited as *Annals of Congress*.

[49] For example, see the call for militia reform led by Theodore Sedgwick and Jeremiah Wadsworth in *Annals of Congress*, IV, 3d Cong., 2d sess., 1067-1071, 1214-1220, 1233-1237; also *ibid.*, VI, 4th Cong., 2d sess., 1688-1691, 2099, 2223-2224, and 5th Cong., 2d sess., 1384-1386, 1772-1773. See also Washington's Eighth Address to Congress, Dec. 7, 1796, in *Writings of Washington*, XXXV, 319.

[50] Jefferson asked for militia reform during every year of his presidency except 1803. For his 1805 militia plan see James D. Richardson, comp., *The Messages and Papers of the Presidents, 1789-1902*, I (Washington, 1897), 385-386. The bill passed the Senate but never reached the House floor. *Annals of Congress*, XV, 9th Cong., 1st sess., 327-329, 1069-1075.

[51] See, for example, D[avid] Humphreys, *Considerations on the Means of Improving the Militia for the Public Defence* (Hartford, Conn., 1803). William Henry Harrison, "Militia Discipline," nos. 1 and 2, *National Intelligencer and Washington Advertiser*, Sept. 21 and Oct. 1, 1810. Unsigned essay, *ibid.*, Nov. 4, 1807; "On the Military Constitution of Nations," *ibid.*, Nov. 18, 1808; "Juriscola," *ibid.*, Oct. 17, 1810; "Aurora," *National Intelligencer* (Washington), Dec. 14, 1811.

rity indicates their common inability to overcome the deeply ingrained fear of any effort to place the militia at the disposal of a central political authority. Indeed, every attempt at serious militia reform during the early national period fell victim to the same ideologically inspired fears of political tyranny that had fired parochialist rhetoric during the 1780s. The institutional centralization implicit in the Knox plan proved unacceptable amidst the opposition to expanded executive power that characterized partisan dissent during much of the 1790s.[52] Jeffersonian plans for militia reform also succumbed to persistent congressional reluctance to accept the idea of a national militia.[53] Unable to incorporate the militia into the national military system, Federalists turned to the provisional army—a citizen reserve that, had it been organized, would have operated much like a national militia.[54] The Republicans, rejecting that approach, continued to the eve of the War of 1812 to urge reform of the existing militia structure as the best means to ensure national security.[55]

Republican ideology proved a significant consideration in the military planning that followed the Revolutionary war. The new republic's geographic isolation kept the issue of military preparedness from dominating national politics, but when the issue did come up, the classical republican commitment to the ideal of the citizen in arms could not be dismissed out of hand. The tone of postwar national politics ensured that the militia would not be ignored; but the intellectual foundations of the Revolution also shaped the peace establishment plans of the Confederation period. Washington and his advisers believed a combined militia/army system could be both militarily and ideologically sound. Though they differed among themselves over the need for institutional centralization, they all embraced the militia as the guarantor of the nation's defense. They also

[52] For example, see *Annals of Congress*, II, 1st Cong., 3d sess., 1851-1875, and III, 2d Cong., 1st sess., 418-423, 552-555, 574-579. See also *General Advertiser* (Philadelphia), Sept. 4, 25, 26, 27, Oct. 2, 20, 1794, and *Aurora. General Advertiser* (Philadelphia), Nov. 24, 1794. Also William Findley, *A Review of the Revenue System* (Philadelphia, 1794), 63-71.

[53] For typical congressional reaction to the Jeffersonian efforts to reform the militia see *Annals of Congress*, XII, 7th Cong., 2d sess., 521-522; *ibid.*, XV, 9th Cong., 1st sess., 327-329, 1069-1075; *ibid.*, XXI, 11th Cong., Appendix, 2409; Walter Lowrie and Matthew St. Clair Clarke, eds., *American State Papers*, I (Washington, D.C., 1832), 236, 256.

[54] *Annals of Congress*, VIII, 5th Cong., 2d sess., 1729-1731, 1734-1739, 1747, 1759. [Hamilton], "The Stand, No. VI"; Hamilton to Harrison Grey Otis, Dec. 27, 1798; Hamilton to Theodore Sedgwick, Feb. 2, 1799; Hamilton to Jonathan Drayton [*ca.* Oct.-Nov. 1790], in Syrett *et al.*, eds., *Hamilton Papers*, XXI, 438-449, XXII, 394, 453, XXIII, 599-602. James McHenry to John Adams, Dec. 24, 1798, printed in *Aurora. General Advertiser* (Philadelphia), Jan. 10, 1799.

[55] See Jefferson's and Madison's messages to Congress in Richardson, comp., *Messages of the Presidents*, I, 406-407, 410, 428-429, 476, 486-487.

agreed that the militia's continued importance depended upon a basic re-assessment of the nature of military institutions in a free society—a reassessment that ultimately led Knox to make the militia responsible for instilling republican values. The resounding defeat of Hamilton's plan, which ignored the militia's ideological significance, bespoke the importance of republican theory in military matters. The positive reception accorded Knox's 1786 plan pointed as well to the importance of ideology. His adaptation of classical republican perceptions of the militia to contemporaneous economic and military realities best accommodated the practical issues of military planning to the ideological foundations of American republicanism. That the Knox plan continued to provide the basis for attempts during the early national period to create a dependable peace establishment reflected the continuing importance of the nation's ideological origins in the ongoing effort to ensure an effective system of national defense.

The Inside History of the Newburgh Conspiracy: America and the Coup d'Etat

Richard H. Kohn*

L IKE so many of the old patriots who lived past their time, Timothy Pickering spent the twilight of his life refighting old political battles, attacking and defending reputations made decades before, or simply fleshing out the record for posterity. In 1820 Pickering received a letter from a stranger in New York asking for information about the anonymous addresses circulated at the Continental Army's Newburgh encampment in 1783. These addresses had very nearly brought the Army to mutiny and only a hastily called meeting by Washington had convinced the officers to reaffirm their loyalty to Congress. Pickering had been at camp those hectic days and his correspondent wanted the retired soldier's opinion of the origin of the addresses, their purpose, and the significance of the whole episode.

"On comparing the accounts," Pickering read, three interpretations were possible, all implying some kind of conspiracy. The first suggested a coup d'etat: the addresses were "part of a deliberate and studied plan, to break down the civil authority and to erect on its ruins, a military despotism." Only the "vast influence" of Washington averted this "dreadful catastrophe." The second explanation theorized that the conspiracy was merely artificial, a drama contrived to give "a sort of political and moral finishing to the character of Washington and the Army." The last, and most realistic, view was that the whole business had been part of a more complex plot to use the officers "as auxiliaries to the fiscal measures of that day." Specifically, the Army's discontent had been used to pressure first Congress, then the individual states, into accepting an amendment to the Articles of Confederation giving the national government power to tax imports. Both the first and second theories, Pickering's correspondent claimed, had little or no evidence in their support. But the third was in-

* Mr. Kohn is a member of the Department of History, The City College of the City University of New York.

triguing, supported by some "highly important and acknowledged facts" and by others "less known."[1]

Pickering's correspondent was none other than John Armstrong, Jr., who as a young major and aide-de-camp to General Horatio Gates, had written the addresses.[2] But because Armstrong had been only one of several actors in the larger drama and because the passage of time had blurred his memory, his conclusions were no more definitive than those of any contemporary. With only minor variations, however, historians have accepted his explanation. A group of the most prominent politicians in Congress, intent on strengthening the central government, fomented a mutiny in the Army to force Congress and the nation into adopting their program. No historian, however, has explained exactly how the conspiracy unfolded, or explained what its other purposes were. Some accounts have argued that it marked the first stage of a coup d'etat (though they never define the term), thus including Armstrong's "military despotism" interpretation.[3] Yet in many respects the incident remains a mystery. Were these politicians actually attempting to subvert the Articles of Confederation and substitute a

[1] "John Montgars" [John Armstrong, Jr.] to Pickering, Jan. 20, 1820, Timothy Pickering Papers, XXXI, 295, Massachusetts Historical Society, Boston.

[2] Armstrong used the pseudonym, he told Pickering, to avoid being "gazetted" as a writer of history, and to insure that Pickering's reply would not be prejudiced by knowing his correspondent. Armstrong to Pickering, Oct. 6, 1825, ibid., XXXII, 171. Although Edmund C. Burnett questions Armstrong's authorship of the addresses (Edmund C. Burnett, The Continental Congress [New York, 1941], 567), most historians disagree. Armstrong himself admitted writing them. See Armstrong to Horatio Gates, Apr. 29, 1783, Edmund C. Burnett, ed., Letters of Members of the Continental Congress (Washington, 1921-1938), VII, 155, n. 3; Gates to Armstrong, June 22, 1783, in George Bancroft, History of the Formation of the Constitution of the United States of America, 2d ed. (New York, 1882), I, 318. See also Armstrong's long review of William Johnson's Sketches of the Life and Correspondence of Nathanael Greene . . . (Charleston, 1822) in the United States Magazine, New Ser., I (1823), 1-44; John Armstrong, Jr., Letters Addressed to the Army . . . in 1783 (Kingston, N. Y., 1803).

[3] The major accounts are Bancroft, History of the Constitution, I, 76-101; Louis Clinton Hatch, The Administration of the American Revolutionary Army (New York, 1904), 142-178; John Corbin, Two Frontiers of Freedom (New York, 1940), 50-68; Carl Ferdinand Johnson, The Army and Politics, 1783-1784 (unpubl. M.A. thesis, University of Wisconsin, 1949); Merrill Jensen, The New Nation: A History of the United States during the Confederation, 1781-1789 (New York, 1950), 67-84; E. James Ferguson, The Power of the Purse: A History of Public Finance, 1776-1790 (Chapel Hill, 1961), 155-168; Forrest McDonald, E Pluribus Unum: The Formation of the American Republic, 1776-1790 (Boston, 1965), 22-29; James Thomas Flexner, George Washington in the American Revolution (1775-1783) (Boston, 1968), 467-508.

military government? The question is worth answering for several reasons. It would be the only known instance of an attempted coup in American history. The men involved—Pickering, Armstrong, Washington, Henry Knox, Alexander Hamilton, Robert and Gouverneur Morris, to name only a few—make the affair significant, since they and others who were in some way privy to the event were among the political elite of their generation. Finally, whether or not it was a plot to overthrow constituted authority, the Newburgh conspiracy raises imporant questions about the origin and development of American civil-military relations.[4]

Although the roots of the crisis went back years, the first stage began in late 1782. In the last week in December, Major General Alexander McDougall and Colonels John Brooks and Matthias Ogden rode into Philadelphia with a petition to Congress from the Army encamped at Newburgh. "We have borne all that men can bear—our property is expended— our private resources are at an end, and our friends are wearied out and disgusted with our incessant applications." The major grievance was pay. Officers and men had not received their salaries in months. More important, the officers were concerned about receiving the half-pay pensions promised by Congress in 1780. To the officers, half pay was "an honorable and just recompense for several years hard service" during which their "health and fortunes" had been "worn down and exhausted." But they feared, and with good reason, that its general unpopularity might induce Congress to repudiate the promise. Therefore, they were willing to accept a commutation of half pay to some equivalent lump sum payment. For all its moderation and plea for sympathy, however, the petition spoke in thinly veiled threats: "any further experiments on their [the Army's] patience may have fatal effects."[5]

The petition capped nearly six months of continual turmoil in the

[4] As anything approaching a coup d'etat, however, the Newburgh conspiracy never got off the ground. A few days after the addresses were circulated, Washington faced down the officer corps in a tense meeting. Three months later the Revolutionary Army dissolved. Analyzing the affair as a coup, then, becomes an analysis of an event that never even happened, using evidence that probably never existed, or was immediately destroyed because of its seditious implications. Yet if the events of the first months of 1783 did constitute an embryonic coup, a narrative—even one based on circumstantial evidence—can indicate the intentions of the leading participants.

[5] Henry Knox et al., "The address and petition of the officers of the Army of the United States," Dec. 1782, in Worthington C. Ford et al., eds., Journals of the Continental Congress, 1774-1789 (Washington, 1904-1937), XXIV, 291-293.

northern encampment. Earlier efforts to settle the pay problem with state governments had failed, and when Congress considered the question of half pay in the summer of 1782, the resurgence of all the old arguments in opposition only heightened the officers' desperation.[6] Pay and half pay, however, were only symptoms of a deeper malaise in Newburgh. Most officers were apprehensive about returning to civilian life. Many had been impoverished by the war while friends at home had grown fat on wartime prosperity. For all the long absence meant breaking back into a society that had adjusted to their absence, and in traditionally antimilitary New England, a society that would accord none of the advantages or plaudits that returning veterans normally expect. During those long, boring months of 1782, a growing feeling of martyrdom, an uncertainty, and a realization that long years of service might go unrewarded—perhaps even hamper their future careers—made the situation increasingly explosive.

In mid-November, their patience exhausted, the officers decided to petition Congress once more. Knox, the Massachusetts bookseller who had made his reputation as chief of artillery and one of Washington's protégés, drafted the address. In correspondence with Secretary of War Benjamin Lincoln, Knox carefully laid the groundwork for its reception in Philadelphia, and on his part, Lincoln took the utmost pains to press the seriousness of the situation on delegates in Congress.[7] From Philadelphia General Arthur St. Clair explained the political situation to McDougall's committee, and advised the officers to tell Congress "in the most express and positive terms" that unless action was immediate, it could expect "a convulsion of the most dreadful nature and fatal consequences."[8] Events were rapidly approaching a crisis. As one officer put it, "the Event of the Embassy *must* be agreeable" or the future could not be predicted.[9]

[6] Jensen, *New Nation*, 33-36; Burnett, ed., *Letters*, VI, 397-399, 405-408, 494, 514, 516, 518, 528. Rufus Putnam felt that if the committee was not given satisfaction by Massachusetts, the Army should not be trusted with arms. Putnam to Samuel Adams, Oct. 18, 1782, Samuel Adams Papers, New York Public Library, New York City. See also H. Ten Eyck to Henry Glen, Nov. 24, 1782, Henry Glen Papers, New York Public Library.

[7] Knox to Lincoln, Nov. 25, 1782, Lincoln to Knox, Dec. 3, 20, 1782, Henry Knox Papers, X, 123, 129, 155, Massachusetts Historical Society. See Knox's draft of the petition, *ibid.*, 171, 172.

[8] Dec. 1782, William Henry Smith, ed., *The St. Clair Papers* . . . (Cincinnati, 1882), I, 575. The formal instructions from the Army were much more moderate. See "Instructions from the Committee of the Army . . . ," Dec. 7, 1782, Alexander McDougall Papers, box 5, New-York Historical Society, New York City.

[9] Ebenezer Huntington to Andrew Huntington, Dec. 9, 1782, G. W. F. Blanch-

Although few in the Army knew it, the petition's timing was perfect. The same week that McDougall journeyed from Newburgh to Philadelphia, political conditions shifted abruptly in Congress. On December 24, Congress was shocked to learn that Virginia had repealed her ratification of the impost of 1781. Since Rhode Island had refused earlier to ratify, the measure was now dead.[10] Most shocked of all were Robert Morris and his clique of nationalist politicians who had been trying to increase the power of the national government since 1780. The impost had been the heart of their program, in the words of an opponent, "held out by them as the only means of restoring Public Credit, of preventing a Disunion of the States, and saving the Country from immediate ruin—in short . . . the infallible, grand Political Catholicon, by which every evil was to be avoided, and every advantage derived."[11] The significance of the impost followed naturally from the design of centralization. "Without certain revenues," Hamilton had predicted in 1780, "a government can have no power; that power, which holds the purse strings absolutely, must rule."[12]

The nationalists were overjoyed by McDougall's petition. James Madison saw immediately that it would "furnish new topics in favor of the Impost."[13] To pay any of the Army's claims, Congress would have to find new sources of money. Paper money would no longer circulate, and nationalists

---

field, ed., *Letters Written by Ebenezer Huntington during the American Revolution* (New York, 1914), 102. For the background in the Army, see Hatch, *Revolutionary Army*, 142-149; Johnson, Army in Politics, 6-13; Ferguson, *Power of the Purse*, 155-156; Samuel Shaw to John Eliot, Apr. 1783, Josiah Quincy, *The Journals of Major Samuel Shaw* . . . (Boston, 1847), 101-102. The Army at this time consisted of about 550 officers and over 9,000 enlisted men—at least officially. See William Barber, "Abstract of Musters for the Northern Army," Oct. 1782, McDougall Papers, oversize box. Robert R. Livingston's estimate (to John Jay, Aug. 9, 1782, Robert R. Livingston Papers, box 9, New-York Historical Society) was 12,000 men.

[10] James Madison, "Notes on Debates," Dec. 24, 1782, William T. Hutchinson and William M. E. Rachal, eds., *The Papers of James Madison* (Chicago, 1962–), V, 442. Interesting accounts of Rhode Island's action are Ferguson, *Power of the Purse*, 152-153, and McDonald, *E Pluribus Unum*, 20-22.

[11] Jonathan Arnold to the governor of Rhode Island, Jan. 8, 1783, Burnett, ed., *Letters*, VII, 7.

[12] Hamilton to James Duane, Sept. 3, 1780, Harold C. Syrett and Jacob E. Cooke, eds., *The Papers of Alexander Hamilton* (New York, 1961–), II, 404. This long letter is the blueprint of nationalism, and later, Federalism. Background on the nationalists and their financial program is in Jensen, *New Nation*, 54-67; Ferguson, *Power of the Purse*, 109-155; Clarence L. Ver Steeg, *Robert Morris: Revolutionary Financier* (Philadelphia, 1954).

[13] Madison to Edmund Randolph, Dec. 30, 1782, Hutchinson and Rachal, eds., *Papers of Madison*, V, 473. This letter dates McDougall's arrival at Dec. 29.

could argue that new foreign loans could not be floated without some visible means to meet interest payments. The only alternative was a new funding system; to the nationalists, this meant a new impost amendment. "In this situation what was to be done?" asked Hamilton later, recalling those critical days when the nationalists groped for some way to salvage their program. "It was essential to our cause that vigorous efforts should be made to restore public credit—it was necessary to combine all the motives to this end, that could operate upon different descriptions of persons in the different states. The necessity and discontents of the army presented themselves as a powerful engine."[14] The air of crisis and possible mutiny would bludgeon Congress into another impost. When Congress then presented it as a measure to repay its victorious army, the states and the public could not possibly refuse. "Depend on it," Gouverneur Morris wrote on January 1, "good will arise from the situation to which we are hastening."[15]

Against this background, the conspiracy began to unfold. Within twenty-four hours of arrival, McDougall and his officers conferred with Robert Morris.[16] Within another week, the nationalist leadership had convinced McDougall and his colleagues that the Army's only hope for payment lay in a new funding system. But unless McDougall and the Army cooperated fully, the nationalists threatened, "they would oppose" referring Army claims to the states "till all prospect of obtaining Continental funds was at an end."[17] McDougall's first task was to gain the support of the whole officer corps. On January 9, he wrote Knox on the possibility of uniting "the influence of Congress with that of the Army and the public Creditors to obtain permanent funds for the United states." It would, he added, "promise [the] most ultimate Security to the Army."[18] McDougall's second duty was to buttonhole individual congressmen, spreading rumors of the Army's uneasiness and the dire prospects if Congress refused satisfaction.

[14] Hamilton to Washington, Apr. 8, 1783, Syrett and Cooke, eds., *Papers of Hamilton*, III, 318-319.
[15] G. Morris to John Jay, Jan. 1, 1783, Jared Sparks, *The Life of Gouverneur Morris* . . . (Boston, 1832), I, 249. Hamilton said essentially the same thing, but with less optimism. Hamilton to George Clinton, Jan. 12, 1783, Syrett and Cooke, eds., *Papers of Hamilton*, III, 240.
[16] Diary entry, Dec. 30, 1783, Robert Morris Papers, II (Diary), 275, Library of Congress.
[17] McDougall to Knox, Jan. 9, 1783, McDougall and Ogden to Knox, Feb. 8, 1783, Burnett, ed., *Letters*, VII, 14, n. 2, 35n.
[18] McDougall to Knox, Jan. 9, 1783, *ibid.*, 14, n. 2.

The nationalists would take care of the rest. Not all of them were involved—only Hamilton and Robert and Gouverneur Morris, the assistant financier, for certain.[19] Other nationalists participated with varying degrees of enthusiasm. Some were uninformed of the machinations; others ignored them, willing to work for nationalist ends regardless of the means employed. Madison probably knew nothing directly of the manipulations behind the scenes. But he felt that without an increase in national authority, the union would collapse and the states would degenerate into small units warring with each other constantly.[20] In the weeks ahead, Madison's skill in debate and his incisive political understanding would perfectly complement the strategems of the nationalist floor leaders, Hamilton and James Wilson. After the Army had set the stage and spread the threats, the nationalists would forge an acceptable funding system and maneuver it through Congress.

On January 6, Congress received the Army memorial and referred it to a grand committee of one delegate from each state. The next day this com-

[19] The evidence against the three is circumstantial but damning. Robert Morris's official diary reveals frequent meetings with all the major participants, as well as machinations with Congress over funds for commutation. These activities—refusing funds at the grand committee meeting on Jan. 7 (below, p. 194), blocking attempts to raise money (below, p. 194), and the timing of his resignation, then the request to publicize it (below, pp. 194-195, 205), indicate a desire to heighten the crisis. Certainly he was one of the men who thought "continentally," as Hamilton put it (below, p. 214). Hamilton also directly described Morris's motives (Hamilton to Washington, Apr. 8, 1783, Syrett and Cooke, eds., Papers of Hamilton, III, 318-319). And when Washington confronted him with the charge, Morris's denial was weak and half-hearted (Morris to Washington, May 29, 1783, Francis Wharton, ed., The Revolutionary Diplomatic Correspondence of the United States [Washington, 1889], VI, 454). Hamilton's involvement is obvious from the text and citations that follow. He was on every important committee that acted on commutation; he tipped off Washington on Feb. 13, 1783 (below, n. 46); and he all but admitted his role to Washington (below, n. 28). Gouverneur Morris's role is more hidden. But letters to John Jay (above, n. 15), to Knox (below, n. 11), and to Nathanael Greene (Feb. 15, 1783, Sparks, Gouverneur Morris, I, 250-251) imply an active role. As Robert Morris's assistant, he was undoubtedly privy to most of the secret. He helped one of Hamilton's committees with commutation (G. Morris to Gov. Rutledge with enclosure, Feb. 3, 1783, Gouverneur Morris Papers, f. 720, Columbia University Library, New York City). And like his namesake, Gouverneur Morris thought "continentally."

[20] See the marginal note on his "Notes on Debates," Feb. 21, 1783, Gaillard Hunt, ed., The Writings of James Madison (New York, 1900-1910), I, 382n. Madison's correspondence and notes (ibid., and Hutchinson and Rachal, eds., Papers of Madison, and the James Madison Papers, Library of Congress and New York Public Library) indicate that he had no inside knowledge of nationalist intrigue. He did, however, deduce the broad outline of events.

mittee talked with Robert Morris. At a meeting marked by "loose conversation" on the "critical state of things," the financier stated "explicitly" that his office could not advance the Army any pay, and could not even promise any "until certain funds should be previously established."[21] On January 13, McDougall and the Army committee intensified the pressure. At a meeting with the grand committee, the officers depicted the resentment in camp in unmistakable terms. When a congressman asked them what, specifically, the Army might do if not satisfied, one colonel replied that Congress could expect "at least a mutiny." McDougall added that however prudent the officers and men might be, they were extremely angry. Brooks declared that "the temper of the army was such that they did not reason or deliberate cooly on consequences and therefore a disappointment might throw them blindly into extremities."[22] By the end of the conversation, the grand committee was convinced that a powder keg would explode in Newburgh unless Congress acted quickly. Therefore it appointed Hamilton, Madison, and John Rutledge of South Carolina to draft a report on the Army's claims, after consulting with Robert Morris to determine the monetary resources at the Confederation's disposal. Pressure tactics were working. Soon the tense and solemn mood of the meeting with McDougall pervaded the halls of Congress.[23]

For the next ten days, while Hamilton and the committee prepared a report on the Army's claims, Morris and his associates maneuvered to bring consideration of a new revenue system before Congress. Using the full weight of his personal prestige and the authority of his office as arbiter of national finance, Morris delayed congressional efforts to refurbish the old Confederation taxing system and turned aside initiatives to seek new foreign loans.[24] On January 22, the grand committee submitted its report. In the midst of debate the financier suddenly tendered his resignation. In a bitter letter he declared that his own integrity and position as financier

[21] Madison, "Notes on Debates," Jan. 6, 7, 1783, Hunt, ed., *Writings of Madison*, I, 303-305.
[22] Madison, "Notes on Debates," Jan. 10, 13, 1783, *ibid.*, 308, 310-313.
[23] *Ibid.*, 313; Madison and Joseph Jones to the governor of Virginia, Jan. 14, 1783, Abner Nash to James Iredell, Jan. 18, 1783, Burnett, ed., *Letters*, VII, 16, 19.
[24] Diary entries, Jan. 15, 30, 31, 1783, Robert Morris Papers, II (Diary), 283, 293, show Morris trying to torpedo Congress's attempts to put a valuation of lands taxing system into effect. For his action on foreign loans, see Madison, "Notes on Debates," Jan. 17, 1783, Hunt, ed., *Writings of Madison*, I, 317. For an indication of his motives, see Hamilton to Washington, Apr. 8, 1783, Syrett and Cooke, eds., *Papers of Hamilton*, III, 319.

were "utterly unsupportable" because of the Confederation's financial distress. If "permanent provision for the public debts of every kind" was not established by the end of May, he threatened, Congress would have to find a new superintendent.[25]

In the wake of Morris's resignation, the strain of McDougall's scare campaign, and the urgency of the Army's unquestioned discontent, the nationalists gained their first victory. On January 25, after three days of debate on Hamilton's report, Congress agreed to leave the first two claims of the Army—present pay and the settlement of unpaid salaries—to Morris's discretion. To support his efforts, it promised to "make every effort in [its] power to obtain from the respective states substantial funds, adequate to the object of funding the whole debt of the United States."[26] Nationalist tactics had worked beautifully; a new revenue system was now before Congress under circumstances that made its adoption imperative.

But the nationalist victory was incomplete. The heart of the report was a provision for commuting half pay into an outright grant, the one point which would solidly wed the Army's interests to those of other public creditors. Twice on January 25 the nationalists tried to shove the measure through, but both times a coalition of New England and New Jersey delegates voted nay. Rhode Island and Connecticut were bound by instructions from their legislatures to oppose half pay in any form, and other eastern congressmen well knew the popular aversion to anything resembling pensions. The nationalists dropped the matter for the moment. Congress referred it to a committee of five, including Hamilton and Wilson, and then turned its attention to a new impost proposal.[27]

Despite this setback, the nationalist program seemed on the surface to be faring well. But in reality, the Morrises and Hamilton were stymied at several points. Knox's silence—it had been three weeks since McDougall had written to him—was ominous. Unless the officer corps cooperated, by keeping up or increasing the pressure from Newburgh and agreeing not to

---

[25] Morris to the president of Congress, Jan. 24, 1783, Wharton, ed., *Revolutionary Diplomatic Correspondence*, VI, 228-229. For the reaction in Congress, see Madison, "Notes on Debates," Jan. 24, 1783, Hunt, ed., *Writings of Madison*, I, 322-323. An indication of Morris's strategy is in Hamilton to Washington, Apr. 8, 1783, Syrett and Cooke, eds., *Papers of Hamilton*, III, 319.

[26] Ford *et al.*, eds., *Journals of Continental Congress*, XXIV, 94-95.

[27] *Ibid.*, 93-95, 97-98; Madison, "Notes on Debates," Jan. 25, 27, 28, Feb. 4, 25, 1783, Hunt, ed., *Writings of Madison*, I, 327-343, 356, 386; Rhode Island delegates to the governor of Rhode Island, Feb. 11, 1783, Burnett, ed., *Letters*, VII, 29.

seek half pay from the states, the whole nationalist design could collapse. A second problem was tactical. Even after a month of crisis politics, nationalist maneuvers were still masked. But to a man like Arthur Lee, an old hand at political infighting and anti-Morris for years, their stratagems were becoming obvious. He would not be bluffed. "A majority of the Army at least," he told Samuel Adams, "will remember that they are Citizens, and not lend themselves to the tory designs, as I verily believe this is, of subverting the Revolution. . . ."[28] Lee and other antinationalists benefited mightily when Hamilton, overly excited in debate over the impost, openly suggested using the Army claims to force national funds on the states. The opposition "smiled at the disclosure," noted Madison, saying "in private conversation, that Mr. Hamilton had let out the secret."[29]

The greatest obstacle of all, however, was Congress's reluctance to adopt commutation. Hamilton's committee of five, appointed in January to reshape the measure, recommended it again on February 4, but New England opposition remained adamant and subsequent debate led nowhere. Commutation was critically important. The fear of a mutinous Army might prod Congress into resolving national revenues, but the state legislatures, scattered over the continent far from the Army's potential grasp, would not necessarily ratify such an amendment. The Confederation must be committed to paying the huge sums commutation entailed; then like it or not, the states would have to agree to the revenue system or abandon a long-standing promise to the nation's Army. For this reason, the Morrises and Hamilton were willing to use any tactic that could ram commutation down congressional throats.[30]

Overshadowing all these obstacles was the likelihood that news of a peace treaty would arrive at any moment. Peace was the one contingency that could not be manipulated by the nationalist leadership. Should definite word arrive, the crisis would be over, the need to buttress national authority lost, and the nightmares of mutiny dispelled in the euphoria of victory. Peace would also destroy the Army's political leverage. No longer

[28] Lee to Adams, Jan. 29, 1783, Burnett, ed., *Letters*, VII, 28.
[29] Madison, "Notes on Debates," Jan. 28, 1783, Hunt, ed., *Writings of Madison*, I, 335-336, and 336n.
[30] Nationalist thinking can be gleaned from Madison, "Notes on Debates," Feb. 4, 1783, *ibid.*, 356-357; G. Morris to Knox, Feb. 7, 1783, McDougall and Ogden to Knox, Feb. 8, 1783, Burnett, ed., *Letters*, VII, 34n-36n; Hamilton to Washington, Feb. 13, Apr. 8, 1783, Syrett and Cooke, eds., *Papers of Hamilton*, III, 253-255, 317-321; G. Morris to Greene, Feb. 15, 1783, Sparks, *Gouverneur Morris*, I, 250-251.

needed, it would be quickly demobilized to allow the rank and file to return home for spring planting. Nationalist leaders understood these possibilities all too well.[31] When commutation lost for the second time, on February 4, they began the preparations to use force.

The second stage in the plot began on February 8, when Brooks left Philadelphia to corner Knox and commit the Army to the nationalist program. In his dispatch pouch, Brooks carried two letters for Knox. One, from McDougall and Ogden, reported to the entire Army in detail on the political situation and emphasized the dim prospects for commutation.[32] The other was a personal message from Knox's "dear friend" Gouverneur Morris, lamenting the state of the nation and pleading for a union of the officers with other public creditors to enact permanent taxes. "The army may now influence the Legislatures," intimated Morris, "and if you will permit me a Metaphor from your own Profession after you have carried the Post the public Creditors will garrison it for you."[33] Four days later a secret letter, more explicit, more conspiratorial, and more pressing, left Philadelphia for Knox. Under a prearranged pseudonym, McDougall told him that the Army might well have to mutiny in order to gain its just due —declare publicly that it would not disband until it could be paid and assured of commutation. Such a move would be very dangerous, he admitted; Knox should wait for definite instructions. Meanwhile their friends would decide whether to introduce a motion to this effect on the floor of Congress. "But the Army," he added, "ought not to lose a moment in preparing for events."[34]

[31] See, for example, R. Morris to Washington, Oct. 16, 1782, Robert Morris Collection, Henry E. Huntington Library, San Marino, Calif.; McDougall to Knox, Feb. 19, 1783, Burnett, ed., *Letters*, VII, 50, n. 3.

[32] McDougall and Ogden to Knox, Feb. 8, 1783, Burnett, ed., *Letters*, VII, 35n-36n. This was sent to different lines. See the entry for Feb. 15, 1783, in a long series of documents which appears to be an official record of the Army proceedings for redress, in the Knox Papers, LIII, 161.

[33] G. Morris to Knox, Feb. 7, 1783, Burnett, ed., *Letters*, VII, 34n. Since the two letters are dated so closely, and because Morris's was so incriminating, it is likely that Brooks carried both.

[34] "Brutus" to Knox, Feb. 12, 1783, Knox Papers, XI, 120. I am indebted to Miss Mary-Jo Kline, formerly of the John Jay Papers, Columbia University, for identifying "Brutus." She pointed out that while McDougall partially masked his handwriting in the letter, he did not do so for the address. Compare the handwriting of the addresses in the two "Brutus" letters (*ibid.*, 120, 165) with that of the McDougall letter of Feb. 19, 1783 (*ibid.*, 139). Also, Knox never mentioned "our friend B—" except in two letters to McDougall (Mar. 3, 12, 1783, McDougall Papers, box 6).

Although these overtures to Knox vaguely implied the use of force, nationalist leaders were not scheming counterrevolution. Any plans that even suggested a coup were unrealistic. Later Hamilton admitted that while some leaders entertained "views of coercion," most agreed with his assessment that the "ar[my] would moulder by its own weight and for want of the means of keeping together. The soldiery would abandon their officers. There would be no chance of success without having recourse to means that would reverse our revolution."[35] The British had tried for years to capture Congress, and failed. A country so dispersed geographically, with so many conflicting interests and groups, so many local sources of power and authority, could never be united by the bayonet, especially in the face of deeply rooted traditions of antimilitarism. The attempt would only bring on chaos and civil war, exactly the conditions the nationalists wished to avoid. The whole thrust of the nationalist effort was toward strengthening national authority. A coup would simply destroy it.

What the nationalists wished when they sent Brooks back to Newburgh was the active cooperation of Knox and the other leaders of the Army's effort for redress.[36] Should all the rumors and parliamentary maneuvers in Philadelphia fail, a declaration by the Army that it would not disband might frighten Congress into passing commutation, then another funding system to raise the money. Such a declaration, while constituting only a passive mutiny, would definitely convey overtones of more positive action

[35] Hamilton to Washington, Mar. 25, 1783, Syrett and Cooke, eds., *Papers of Hamilton*, III, 306.

[36] John Brooks's role and activities are the least understood of any individual's in the whole incident—and they are crucial. I have reconstructed it from obscure circumstantial evidence. His role in the meeting with the grand committee (above, p. 194) implies that he was working solidly with the nationalists. That he was entrusted with the first direct meeting between the people in Philadelphia and those at Newburgh implies this also. He arrived on Feb. 13 (entry for Feb. 13, 1783, Newburgh records, Knox Papers, LIII, 161), but he drops out of all surviving evidence until the Mar. 15 meeting, when he was solidly behind Washington as Knox's helper in drawing up the resolutions reaffirming the Army's loyalty to Congress. It is possible that Knox convinced him not to play the nationalists' game. Pickering suspected this (to Gates, May 28, 1783, Pickering Papers, V, 313). It is also possible that Brooks tipped off Washington as Armstrong later told Gates (Apr. 29, 1783, Burnett, ed., *Letters*, VII, 155, n. 3) and as Pickering agreed (to Gates, May 28, 1783, Pickering Papers, V, 313). But it is likely that if he did, he was *instructed* to do so, since Hamilton himself tipped off Washington less than a week after Brooks left Philadelphia (below, p. 202). Certainly Brooks remained in the good graces of Washington and the nationalists judging by the offices he was offered in the 1790s (see Samuel Eliot Morison in *DAB* s.v. "Brooks, John").

in the future, perhaps even a military takeover. Congress would have no choice: accept commutation or risk the consequences. The dangers in this scheme were considerable. In the first place, a statement by the Army that it would not lay down its arms would disgrace the national government. It would proclaim to the world that in its first breath of independence, the United States was unwilling to do its victorious soldiery justice. Secondly, it might mark the first step in a wholly unpredictable chain of events. No one could possibly foresee the consequences of the military's declaring its independence from the civil power. Yet in the first week of February, anticipating the worst, the Morrises and Hamilton were willing to take the chance. Knox and the other leaders in Newburgh were responsible men, and could be depended upon to keep the situation in hand.[37]

The nationalists did have another alternative, one they were eventually forced to use and one that historians of the conspiracy have never fully understood. If an incident had to be staged in Newburgh, they could foment a real mutiny among the officers. But it was even more risky since it would have to involve not only a confrontation with Congress, but also with the military's legitimate leadership. For several days they had known of a dissident element in camp which could be persuaded to force an explosion, though the manipulations required would be far more delicate than the rather direct approaches they were making to Knox. There was a group of young officers, a small extremist wing of the corps, which was angrier, more dogmatic and hotheaded, and which fumed at Washington's moderate leadership.[38] Unlike many older officers, these men had grown up in the Army and had less to look forward to on returning to civilian life. They sensed more deeply the impending loss of their military status and privilege.[39] These Young Turks naturally gravitated to Gates, the "hero of

[37] A good indication of nationalist thinking at this time is "Brutus" [McDougall] to Knox, Feb. 12, 1783, Knox Papers, XI, 120. Hamilton spelled out the general nationalist design in two letters to Washington, Mar. 25, 1783, Apr. 8, 1783, Syrett and Cooke, eds., *Papers of Hamilton*, III, 305-306, 317-321.

[38] An indication of this hotheadedness is Armstrong to Gates, Apr. 22, 29, May 9, 30, June 26, 1783, Burnett, ed., *Letters*, VII, 150, n. 4, 155, n. 3, 160, n. 3, 175, n. 3, 199, n. 2.

[39] Only three members of this group can be identified for certain: Armstrong, Christopher Richmond, and William Barber—all involved in the writing and circulation of the addresses (Gates to Armstrong, June 22, 1783, Bancroft, *History of the Constitution*, I, 318). Two other *very likely* suspects are William Eustis (see *ibid.*) and Pickering (see Pickering to Gates, May 28, 1783, Pickering Papers, V, 313). Armstrong was 24, Eustis 29 years old. Richmond's and Barber's ages are unknown. Most officers who served as aides, secretaries, and staff assistants were under 30.

Saratoga," an overbearing and sensitive general whose bad blood with Washington was longstanding. Gates's pretensions had suffered for years. For him the discontent in Newburgh could be used to recoup his reputation, and, incidentally, to snatch the Army away from his rival. Fed by disillusionment, frustration, and personal dreams of glory, Gates and his young zealots evidently lost all sense of reality and began planning a full-fledged coup d'etat. The exact nature of the group and its plans will probably never be known. But there are strong hints that they talked of replacing Congress and ruling themselves, either as individuals under a new form of government or through a military dictatorship.[40]

Apparently they approached Robert Morris in January.[41] The financier, recognizing in them another tool should an uprising in Newburgh prove necessary, cynically encouraged their hope for a coup.[42] It was far safer, of course, to rely on Knox. Under regular leadership, a declaration by the officers that they would not disband would represent the united voice of

[40] The most direct evidence for the existence of a Gates cabal is Rufus King, "Notes on a conversation with William Duer," Oct. 12, 1788, in Charles R. King, *The Life and Correspondence of Rufus King* (New York, 1894-1900), I, 621-622. But Armstrong's correspondence in Burnett, and other correspondence (usually to or from Gates) in the Gates Papers (New-York Historical Society) and the papers of Walter Stewart (Library of Congress and New-York Historical Society) show a close connection and friendship between Gates, Armstrong, Barber, Stewart, and Richmond. And after Mar. 1783, it is overladen with references to conversations between members of the group. The addresses, Gates's own dislike of Washington, and Armstrong's later correspondence show their mood. This and other evidence indicates an anti-Washington group, and by Gates's own admission (to Armstrong, June 22, 1783, Bancroft, *History of the Constitution,* I, 318) these men were responsible for the addresses on signal from "friends in congress and in the administration." Gates of course disclaimed thought of a coup, but William Duer's information from Armstrong indicates otherwise. That Hamilton tipped off Washington and spread rumors of this group (below, pp. 202, 204, and Jones's letter, p. 207) is further evidence.

[41] Duer told King that the conspirators approached Morris ("Notes on conversation," Oct. 12, 1788, King, *Rufus King,* I, 621-622). January is a guess. It is unlikely that the date would be in 1782, before Gates and the young officers knew whether the Army would petition Congress for redress, or what course the agitation in Newburgh would take. It was certainly before Feb. 4, since Armstrong implied that Brooks could have been the agent to inform them of Morris's help (Armstrong to Gates, Apr. 29, 1783, Burnett, ed., *Letters,* VII, 155, n. 3). I have found no evidence other than some routine letters that the nationalists and Gates people were in direct contact. The oblique reference to the financier and the Army crisis in Gates's letter to Richard Peters (Feb. 20, 1783, Sol Feinstone Collection, American Philosophical Society, Philadelphia, Pa.) suggests strongly that no direct correspondence took place.

[42] This is speculation. It figures, however, since Morris needed contacts in the Army in January. And afterwards, Armstrong's story to Duer implied that the Gates group was encouraged by Morris.

the whole Army. The Gates cabal could never speak for all the officers, most of whom revered Washington. Yet Gates and his men, if handled with cunning, could be used to kindle an insurrection in camp that might very well scare Congress more, especially if the mutiny were partially directed against Washington's authority. The scheme, however, involved a desperate gamble. If Gates successfully snatched the Army from Washington, the military takeover and civil war the nationalists were determined to avoid might become reality. Furthermore, the nationalists mistrusted Gates. Hamilton, for one, considered him a personal enemy since Gates and the young congressman's father-in-law, General Philip Schuyler, had been sworn enemies for years; Hamilton's other patron, Washington, looked on Gates with equal disdain.[43] But if they could not push their program through Congress, and if Knox would not cooperate, then Hamilton and the Morrises would have no choice but to use Gates.

In the first week of February, using Gates was only a last resort. Then on February 13, news arrived in Philadelphia that George III, in a speech to Parliament, had mentioned preliminary articles of peace signed between Great Britain and the United States. While the report was only hearsay, the nationalists thought peace was certain, even "hourly expected."[44] Haste was now imperative. Though Knox had yet to be heard from, the nationalists now felt that they must prepare to use Gates just as a safeguard. The plan was simple. Through him, they would incite a mutiny in the Army— spark the explosion—then make certain it was immediately snuffed out.[45]

[43] Two years earlier, Hamilton had considered Gates his "enemy personally" (to James Duane, Sept. 6, 1780, Syrett and Cooke, eds., *Papers of Hamilton*, II, 420). See also Broadus Mitchell, *Alexander Hamilton* (New York, 1957-1962), I, 146-152; Jonathan Gregory Rossie, The Politics of Command: The Continental Congress and Its Generals (unpubl. Ph.D. diss., University of Wisconsin, 1966), Chaps. VIII-XI, XIII-XIV; John C. Miller, *Triumph of Freedom, 1775-1783* (Boston, 1948), 253-261.

[44] Elias Boudinot to Greene, Feb. 13, 1783, Burnett, ed., *Letters*, VII, 42-43. See also diary entry, Feb. 13, 1783, Robert Morris Papers, II (Diary), 302. There had been rumors of a preliminary treaty for several days. See James Craig to Isaac Craig, *Monthly Bulletin of the Carnegie Library of Pittsburgh*, XVI (1911), 196-197. Not everyone, however, thought peace was certain. An indication of the ambiguity is in Charles Pettit to Greene, Feb. 26, 1783, Nathanael Greene Papers, William L. Clements Library, Ann Arbor, Mich.

[45] There is no direct evidence of a plan. My reconstruction is based on the timing of Hamilton's letter (see next paragraph), the fact that Washington was tipped off, and later events. Ogden told Armstrong later that the plan had gone awry because Brooks tipped off Washington (Armstrong to Gates, Apr. 29, 1783, Burnett, ed., *Letters*, VII, 155, n. 3). Duer had the same information ("Notes on conversation," Oct. 12, 1788, King, *Rufus King*, I, 622) in slightly garbled form. Given Hamilton's

It was a treacherous double game, fraught with uncertainty. But to the nationalists, the whole future of the country was at stake. The only alternative to the disintegration of the confederacy was the impost, or some other measure which could effectively shore up the central government. On the other hand, fomenting a mutiny might produce the same result: anarchy, civil war, and an end to the Confederation. The whole venture cut a fine line between parallel disasters.

The other side in the double game, the means by which the convulsion would be harnessed, was Washington, the patient, persevering commander whom the nationalists knew would never brook direct military interference in politics. The same day that the king's speech arrived, the nationalists readied Washington for the coming storm. Hamilton began his letter by pointing out the injustice the Army felt and the possibility that the oncoming peace would justify its fears. In a political sense, however, the Army might assure itself justice while at the same time easing the country's financial dilemma. "Urged with moderation," Hamilton argued, its claims could "operate on those weak minds which are influenced by their apprehensions more than their judgments; so as to produce a concurrence in the measures which the exigencies of affairs demand." This pressure might "add weight to the applications of Congress to the several states." The problem, however, would "be to keep a *complaining* and *suffering army* within the bounds of moderation." This would be Washington's duty, "*to take the direction*" of the Army's anger, preserving its confidence in him without losing that of the nation. "This will enable you," added the commander's former aide-de-camp, "in case of extremity to guide the torrent, and bring order perhaps even good, out of confusion." But Washington should prepare for the worst. He should know that there was a real danger of the Army rejecting his leadership. Many officers, Hamilton noted, felt that "delicacy carried to an extreme prevents your espousing its interests with sufficient warmth." Although obviously false, this feeling tended "to impair that influence, which you may exert with advantage, should any commotions unhappily ensue."[46]

---

direct tip-off, I think Ogden's story about Brooks was a nationalist fake, planted in order to cover themselves and explain to the Gates group why the scheme had not worked and why Washington was so obviously prepared.

[46] Hamilton to Washington, Feb. 13, 1783, Syrett and Cooke, eds., *Papers of Hamilton*, III, 253-255. In a postscript, Hamilton said: "General Knox has the confidence of the Army and is a man of sense. I think he may be safely made use of." Jensen (*New Nation*, 71) interprets this letter as sounding out Washington either

Brooks was already in Newburgh when Hamilton's letter arrived, trying to establish direct channels between the nationalists and Knox. His activities, however—with whom he spoke and what information was passed—remain clouded.[47] Undoubtedly he talked to Washington and to Knox, to whom he delivered McDougall's report and Gouverneur Morris's letter.[48] Knox was the pivot in the nationalist scheme. As the leader in all the agitation at Newburgh since mid-1782, as a friend of the most important officers, and as a respected member of Washington's military family, Knox could best influence the corps to cooperate. But Knox was also extremely cautious. While he sympathized deeply with nationalist goals, he was first and foremost a soldier with his career tied to Washington's and to the reputation of the Army. Not only were these plans risky, potentially damaging to the Army's image, but they would throw him into direct conflict with his patron. The Massachusetts general would not risk a show of force. He undoubtedly said as much to Brooks, and on February 21, he wrote McDougall and Gouverneur Morris to the same effect. "I consider the reputation of the American Army as one of the most immaculate things on earth," he told McDougall; "we should even suffer wrongs and injuries to the utmost verge of toleration rather than sully it in the least degree."[49] The Army could exert no pressure except when directed by the "proper authority."[50] Otherwise, its influence "can only exist in one point, and that to be sure is a sharp point which I hope in God will never be directed than against the Enemies of the liberties of America."[51]

---

to lead or join the mutiny and coup. I disagree, and interpret the letter as a simple tip-off of a possible explosion—Hamilton "coaching" Washington, as Ferguson (*Power of the Purse*, 159-160) puts it. Certainly it was a tip-off: Knox knew what was happening, and the postscript was obviously insurance should Washington not get the point. Second, it is inconceivable to me that Hamilton or any nationalist could possibly think Washington, after his record since 1775, would countenance, much less join, direct military interference in politics. Hamilton knew him too well.

[47] For Brooks's mission, see the reasoning in n. 36 and 45.

[48] Entry for Feb. 13, 1783, Newburgh records, Knox Papers, LIII, 161; Knox to McDougall, Mar. 3, 1783, McDougall Papers, box 6.

[49] Knox to McDougall, Feb. 21, 1783, Knox Papers, XI, 148.

[50] Knox to G. Morris, Feb. 21, 1783, *ibid.*, 150.

[51] Knox to McDougall, Feb. 21, 1783, *ibid.*, 148. There is circumstantial evidence that Knox wavered. Brooks arrived on Feb. 13, but Knox did not write these letters until Feb. 21. And on Mar. 11, after the first address appeared, Washington wrote Knox immediately to come from West Point and help. But Knox claimed ice in the river prevented a quick trip (Knox to Washington, Mar. 11, 1783, Knox Papers, XII, 15). Knox may have been waiting to see which side to join.

The final stage of the conspiracy began when Knox's rebuffs reached
Philadelphia, near the end of February. The nationalists acted without
hesitation.[52] For the last three weeks their efforts in Congress had been
losing momentum. The impost proposal was mired in violent arguments
over detail. The nationalists could not muster enough votes without con-
ceding both the appointment of collectors by the states and a limitation on
the number of years the measure would be in effect. Even worse than the
debates and interminable delays was the appearance of antinationalist
counterattacks on the very foundations of the impost. On February 18,
Rutledge and John Francis Mercer proposed that all the revenue from any
impost be appropriated for the exclusive use of the Army—for salaries and
half pay—rather than to provide generally for the restoration of public
credit. The restriction cleverly reversed the chief nationalist argument—
that permanent funds were needed to satisfy the Army's claims—and thus
attacked the whole concept on an impost as adding to the strength of the
central government.[53]

Although nationalist leaders easily blocked these attacks, it was obvious
that the impost would not pass strictly on its own merits. Immediately they
shifted attention to commutation. Again, however, the house deadlocked.
New Englanders, still mindful of the unpopularity of pensions in their region, continued to vote in opposition. At one point the nationalists had to
choke off an attempt to recommend half pay back to the states.[54] Faced
with such obstacles, the nationalists amplified their campaign of rumor.
Washington, they hinted, was losing control of the officers; the Army
would not lay down its arms, would declare so soon, and had even made
plans to support itself in the field.[55] By the end of the month, the Massachusetts delegation and Oliver Wolcott, Sr., of Connecticut had swung over

[52] My guess is that the letters arrived Feb. 25. The trip from Newburgh to Philadelphia took three to six days, depending on the weather. Since the nationalists acted
on Feb. 26, the letters probably arrived on the twenty-fifth or twenty-sixth. The
nationalists' lack of hesitation is indicated by the speed of McDougall's letter to
Knox (Feb. 26) and Robert Morris's quick request to make his resignation public
(see below, p. 205).
[53] Madison, "Notes on Debates," Feb. 18-20, 1783, Hunt, ed., *Writings of Madison*, I, 370-371, 374-378.
[54] Madison, "Notes on Debates," Feb. 25-28, 1783, *ibid.*, 386, 390-393, 394; Ford,
et al., eds., *Journals of Continental Congress*, XXIV, 145-151, 154-156.
[55] For the rumors, see Madison to Randolph, Feb. 15, 25, 1783, "Notes on Debates," Feb. 20, 1783, Hunt, ed., *Writings of Madison*, I, 368n, 378-379, 384n-385n;
Jones to Washington, Feb. 27, 1783, Burnett, ed., *Letters*, VII, 61.

to commutation. But threats were not enough. The air of crisis and the shaky coalition supporting commutation could evaporate at a moment's notice. It had been over two weeks since word of the king's speech. Now, with Knox's refusal to help, it was the last possible moment for action.

On February 26, the nationalists opened their final offensive. To incite the Army, McDougall penned one last frenzied letter to Knox, suggesting that there was no hope left for the officers' claims and that the Army might soon be split into separate detachments to prevent rebellion.[56] In a similar move, Robert Morris requested permission to make his resignation public, in order not to mislead those who had "contracted engagements" with him. The explanation sufficed, and "without dissent or observation" Congress agreed. News of his resignation, as he well realized, would rock the Army and call into question the whole fabric of Confederation finance. After a short wait to let these maneuvers take effect, the nationalists alerted Gates.[57]

The emissary was Walter Stewart, a Pennsylvania colonel, former aide of Gates, and now inspector of the Northern Army.[58] His trip would arouse no suspicion, since illness had kept him home in Philadelphia and he would be rejoining the Army by direct order of the commander-in-chief.[59] Stewart reached the cantonment on Saturday, March 8. If he followed custom, he called first on Washington, then rode the three miles southeast from Newburgh to Gates's headquarters at the Edmondson house.[60] Although there is no record of the meeting, Stewart undoubtedly pledged Morris's support

[56] "Brutus" [McDougall] to Knox, Feb. 27, 1783, Knox Papers, XI, 165. This does not imply that the nationalists were still using Knox. McDougall may not have known of the decision to use Gates. Second, Knox was still a firm contact, and such an obviously fabricated rumor would have to be spread very secretly, under a pseudonym.

[57] Madison, "Notes on Debates," Feb. 27, 1783, Hunt, ed., *Writings of Madison,* I, 390; Ford *et al.,* eds., *Journals of Continental Congress,* XXIV, 151. Morris's request (to the president of Congress, Feb. 26, 1783) is in Wharton, ed., *Revolutionary Diplomatic Correspondence,* VI, 266. The original letter of resignation was published in the *Freeman's Journal* (Philadelphia), Mar. 5, 1783.

[58] Gates called Stewart "a kind of agent from our friends in congress and in the administration" (Gates to Armstrong, June 22, 1783, Bancroft, *History of the Constitution,* I, 318). Armstrong remembered later that Stewart was very nationalist in his financial views (Armstrong to Jared Sparks, May 19, 1833, John Armstrong, Jr., Photostats, New-York Historical Society) and McDonald tabs Stewart (McDonald, *E Pluribus Unum,* 27) as a holder of a large amount of public securities.

[59] See Washington to Baron Steuben, Feb. 18, 1783, John C. Fitzpatrick, ed., *The Writings of George Washington . . .* (Washington, 1931-1944), XXVI, 143.

[60] See the map of the cantonment by [Simeon] DeWitt, 1783, in the New-York Historical Society.

for any action the officers might take and assured Gates and his followers that the public creditors were fully behind them. Apparently nothing passed that hinted of the nationalists' preplanned treachery, and Stewart probably knew as little of their true intentions as Armstrong and Gates. The officers and their ambitious leader still thought that the first initiatives had been theirs, and that Morris was the unwitting tool, influenced by "hopes of future greatness, which he might promise himself in case of success, by having the sole direction and control of the Finances."[61] In any case, Gates had been waiting for the signal.[62] The die was cast.

Within hours rumor flew around camp that "it was universally expected the Army would not disband untill they had obtained justice," that the public creditors would join the officers in the field, if necessary, to redress their grievances, and that many in Congress looked favorably on the venture.[63] Then on Monday morning, the conspirators published anonymously a call for a meeting of all field officers and company representatives for Tuesday morning at eleven o'clock, to consider McDougall's report of February 8 and to plan a new course of redress. Simultaneously, William Barber, Stewart's assistant in the inspector's department, took several copies of an unsigned address to the adjutant's office where officers from various lines assembled each morning to receive general orders.[64] When the officers saw it, and later, as copies circulated around the encampment, bedlam ensued.

Written by Armstrong and copied by Christopher Richmond, another of Gates's aides, the first of the famous Newburgh Addresses urged the officers to forget "the meek language of entreating memorials" and "change the milk-and-water style" of their last petition to Congress. In the most

[61] King, "Notes on conversation," Oct. 12, 1788, King, *Rufus King*, I, 622. See also Armstrong to Sparks, May 19, 1833, Armstrong Photostats.

[62] There is no record of Stewart's meeting with Gates. But judging by the rumors that began circulating (see next paragraph) and by what Armstrong told Duer (King, "Notes on conversation," Oct. 12, 1788, King, *Rufus King*, I, 622), Stewart undoubtedly pledged Morris's help. The story of Brooks's treachery (see n. 45 above), accepted by Gates and Pickering (Pickering to Gates, May 28, 1783, Pickering Papers, V, 313), suggests that the Gates group was unaware of the tip-off sent to Washington. Stewart definitely told the Gates group to act. See Gates to Armstrong, June 22, 1783, Bancroft, *History of the Constitution*, I, 318; Washington to Hamilton, Mar. 12, 1783, Syrett and Cooke, eds., *Papers of Hamilton*, III, 286.

[63] Washington to Hamilton, Mar. 12, 1783, Syrett and Cooke, eds., *Papers of Hamilton*, III, 286.

[64] Armstrong to Sparks, May 5, 1835, Armstrong Photostats; Gates to Armstrong, June 22, 1783, Bancroft, *History of the Constitution*, I, 318; Armstrong, *Letters . . . to the Army*, 3, and 3n.

inflammatory rhetoric, Armstrong recalled the Army's suffering and glory, comparing them with "the coldness and severity of government," and the country's ingratitude to the men who had placed it "in the chair of independency." Whom would peace benefit? Not the officers, who could only look forward to growing "old in poverty, wretchedness and contempt." Could they, he asked, "consent to wade through the vile mire of dependency, and owe the miserable remnant of that life to charity, which has hitherto been spent in honor?" If so, they would be pitied, ridiculed, for suffering this last indignity. They had bled too much. They still had their swords. "If the present moment be lost, every future effort is in vain; and your threats then, will be as empty as your entreaties now." In a menacing reference to Washington, Armstrong demanded that they "suspect the man who would advise to more moderation and longer forebearance." Draw up one last remonstrance, Armstrong argued, without "the sueing, soft, unsuccessful epithet of memorial," and send it to Congress as an ultimatum. If the terms of the December petition were met, the Army would keep its faith. If not, the Army would have its alternatives—"If peace, that nothing shall separate them [Congress] from your arms but death: if war, that courting the auspices, and inviting the direction of your illustrious leader, you will retire to some unsettled country, smile in your turn, and 'mock when their [Congress's] fear cometh on.' "[65]

Washington, shocked and dismayed, realized that the officers were about to plunge "themselves into a gulph of Civil horror."[66] But he had expected the explosion for some time. He had understood the hints Hamilton had dropped the previous month, even to the point of suspecting Gates —"the old leven"—of again working to undermine him "under the mask of the most perfect dissimulation and apparent cordiallity."[67] Joseph Jones, Washington's friend from Virginia then sitting in Congress, had that very week reported rumors in Philadelphia that the Army would not disband and that there were "dangerous combinations" working against the commander.[68]

Though not surprised, Washington still faced a "predicament" as "critical and delicate as can well be conceived," one he had fought through-

[65] Ford et al., eds., Journals of Continental Congress, XXIV, 295-297.
[66] Washington to Hamilton, Mar. 12, 1783, Syrett and Cooke, eds., Papers of Hamilton, III, 287.
[67] Washington to Hamilton, Mar. 4, 1783, ibid., 278.
[68] Jones to Washington, Feb. 27, 1783, Burnett, ed., Letters, VII, 61.

out the war and which, at this point, never seemed closer to crushing him in the middle.[69] On the one hand, he could in no sense compromise Congress's jurisdiction over the military. On the other, the officers' temper had turned so ugly, and so directly in conflict with civil authority, that a refusal to stand on their side—perhaps any counsel of moderation—might cost him his position and authority. Yet Washington never wavered. He was certain that "the sensible, and discerning part of the army" could hardly "be unacquainted" with his faithful service, that by the sheer power of his personality and the officers' almost filial devotion to their commander, he could continue, as he wrote Hamilton, to hold them "within the bounds of reason and moderation."[70]

In his first move, Washington threw the conspirators on the defensive. On Tuesday morning he issued general orders which objected to the address and invitation to a meeting as "disorderly" and "irregular." An assembly with his personal approval would take place at noon on Saturday to discuss McDougall's letter from Philadelphia. The senior officer present—undoubtedly Gates—would preside, and, implying his own absence, Washington requested a full report of its deliberation afterwards.[71] The ploy had possibilities. Five days hiatus might cool down passions. In any event, Washington fully planned to attend the meeting and confront the officers in person, with Gates in the chair, strictly circumscribed by procedure and unable to speak out or manipulate the proceedings.[72]

Gates and his men immediately countered with a second address designed to soften Washington's reproach. In fact, they claimed the general obviously approved of their actions. A meeting on Saturday hardly differed from one on Tuesday, since it would consider the same agenda. The "solemnity" of his order "sanctified" their appeals, added unanimity, and

[69] Washington to Hamilton, Mar. 4, 1783, Syrett and Cooke, eds., *Papers of Hamilton*, III, 278.

[70] *Ibid.*

[71] General orders, Mar. 11, 1783, Fitzpatrick, ed., *Writings of Washington*, XXVI, 208.

[72] This, evidently, was Washington's strategy. See Washington to Hamilton, Mar. 12, 1783, Syrett and Cooke, eds., *Papers of Hamilton*, III, 287. Washington's other preparations are less clear. He called for Knox immediately, but the latter was delayed (Knox to Washington, Mar. 11, 1783, Knox Papers, XII, 15). Washington also published Congress's resolve of Jan. 25 promising action on pay (general orders, Mar. 13, 1783, Fitzpatrick, ed., *Writings of Washington*, XXVI, 221-222). He also did a little personal persuading to win over important officers. See William Gordon, *The History of the . . . Establishment of the . . . United States . . .* (London, 1788), IV, 356; Charles Brooks, *History of the Town of Medford . . .* (Boston, 1855), 138.

would "give system" to the proceedings. And, the officers were reminded, "it cannot possibly lessen the *independence* of your sentiments."[73]

On Saturday morning tension was high. Officers from every unit stationed near Newburgh trudged up the low hill to the newly constructed log and board public meeting building which Washington had ordered built in December to encourage more intercourse and "sociability" among officers of different states. The "New Building" consisted chiefly of a large low-ceilinged room, about seventy by forty feet, with a small stage and lectern at one end.[74] As Gates opened the proceedings, the commander in chief entered and asked permission to address the gathering. Gates could hardly refuse, and Washington mounted the stage. Instead of pleading for delay, he took the offensive, denouncing the anonymity of the first summons to a meeting as "unmilitary" and "subversive of all order and discipline." Then he attacked Armstrong's first address directly, maligning its motives, its appeal to "feelings and passions" rather than "reason and good sense," and its "insidious purposes." "I have been a faithful friend to the army . . . ," Washington declared, "the constant companion and witness of your distresses." No one present could possibly suppose he was "indifferent to its interests." Yet either of the alternatives proposed in the address was simply a "physical impossibility." Would the officers leave wives and children and all their property to desert the country "in the extremest hour of her distress," to "perish in a wilderness with hunger, cold and nakedness?" Or worse, could the Army actually contemplate "something so shocking" as turning its swords against Congress, "plotting the ruin of both, by sowing the seeds of discord and separation" between military and civil? "My God!" Washington exclaimed, "What can this writer have in view, by recommending such measures? Can he be a friend to the army? Can he be a friend to this country? Rather is he not an insidious foe?"

Again Washington raked the motives of the secret writer, especially the insinuation that strong, independent men should suspect the man of

[73] The second address is also in Ford *et al.*, eds., *Journals of Continental Congress*, XXIV, 298-299.

[74] Benjamin Walker to Steuben, Jan. 23, 1783, F. W. A. Steuben Papers, New-York Historical Society. For descriptions of the building, see E. M. Ruttenber and L. H. Clark *et al.*, comps., *History of Orange County, New York* . . . (Philadelphia, 1881), 226; John J. Nutt, comp., *Newburgh: Her Institutions, Industries and Leading Citizens* . . . (Newburgh, 1891), 36-37. The building has been reconstructed outside New Windsor, N. Y.

moderation. It was merely a trick, he said, to suppress open discussion, to take away freedom of speech so that "dumb and silent, we may be led, like sheep, to the slaughter." Then Washington reminded the officers of their duty and the disgrace that would follow any step that might sully the Army's glory or tarnish its deserved reputation for courage and patriotism. Congress, like any large body "where there is a variety of different interests to reconcile," moved slowly. But ultimately it would justify the Army's faith, and Washington pledged himself "in the most unequivocal manner" to press its case. With a final appeal to reason and virture and a plea to reject any wicked "attempts to open the flood-gates of civil discord" and "deluge our rising empire in blood," Washington ended his formal speech.[75]

He then produced Joseph Jones's letter as proof of Congress's good intentions. After reading the first paragraph, Washington paused, fumbled in his vest, found the spectacles Dr. David Rittenhouse had sent him in February, and put them on. Unaffectedly, the tall general murmured that he had grown gray in the service of his country, and now found himself going blind. The assemblage was stunned. A year's frustration, a week's excitement and expectation, then the unbearable strain of confronting their beloved commander, seemed to hang suspended in that one moment. In his speech, Washington had stood them at the abyss, forced them to face the implications of rash action—civil war, treason, and the undoing of eight years' effort. The contrast with this simple dramatic gesture, an act that blended Washington's charismatic influence with the deepest symbolic patriotism, was overpowering. The tension, the imposing physical presence of the commander in chief, the speech, and finally an act that emotionally embodied the Army's whole experience, combined all at once and shattered the officers' equanimity. Spontaneously they recoiled. Some openly wept.[76]

[75] The speech is in Ford et al., eds., Journals of Continental Congress, XXIV, 306-310.
[76] Although some officers later denied a letter had been read, others remembered it. For the meeting and its impact, see James V. Armstrong to George Bancroft, Mar. 22, 1865, Edward Hand to William Irvine, Apr. 19, 1783, Bancroft Transcripts, America, 1783, I, 131, 202, New York Public Library; Pickering to Gates, May 28, 1783, David Cobb to Pickering, Nov. 9, 1825, Nicholas Fish to Pickering, Nov. 30, 1825, Pickering's notebooks [1827], Pickering Papers, V, 313, XXXII, 183, 185, XLVI, 115-119, 176-179, 328-333; Philip Schuyler to Stephen Van Rensselaer, Mar. 17, 1783, in Benson J. Lossing, The Life and Times of Philip Schuyler (New York, 1873), II, 427n; Bernardus Swartwout's journal, Mar. 15, 1783, Miscellaneous Papers, New-York Historical Society; Bancroft, History of the Constitution, I, 97-98.

Gates's plans disintegrated. Sitting helpless on the podium, he watched the officers' resolve evaporate in a wave of emotion. In a moment Washington was gone, the meeting now firmly in the grasp of his lieutenants. First Knox moved to thank the commander for his speech. Then, after the McDougall report and other documents were read, Rufus Putnam moved to appoint Knox, Brooks, and another officer to bring in resolutions. After a brief interval, Knox returned with motions that repeated the Army's "attachment to the rights and liberties of human nature" and its "unshaken confidence" in Congress, and asked the commander in chief to write Congress again on the Army's behalf. The officers accepted these unanimously, declaring their "abhorrence" and "disdain" of the "infamous propositions" advanced in the addresses, and their "indignation [at] the secret attempts of some unknown persons to collect officers together, in a manner totally subversive of all discipline and good order."[77] Only Pickering, of all the men present, stood up and objected, angry at the officers' hypocrisy in damning "with infamy two publications which during the four preceding days most of them had read with admiration [and] talked of with rapture."[78] But the assemblage was too exhausted to respond, and the meeting adjourned.

Even as the officers left the hall, news of the incident was on the way to Philadelphia. Tuesday afternoon Washington had posted copies of the addresses and his general orders. Coming on the heels of other serious

---

The best description of the scene is Samuel Shaw to John Eliot, Apr. 1783, Quincy, *Journals of Shaw*, 104.

[77] Ford *et al.*, eds., *Journals of Continental Congress*, XXIV, 310-311. I am convinced that the whole meeting was managed by Washington and his confidants. Knox's later career testifies to his fidelity to Washington. Putnam had drafted a speech deprecating the addresses (Knox Papers, XII, 22), perhaps as a draft for Washington, or to deliver himself at the meeting should it be necessary. Also, there is evidence that one of Washington's aides, David Humphreys, moved through the crowd during the general's speech (Pickering to Armstrong, July 15, 1825, Pickering Papers, XVI, 46), perhaps gauging the speech's impact on the officers so that others —Knox, Putnam, Brooks—could take appropriate action.

[78] Pickering to Samuel Hodgdon, Mar. 16, 1783, Pickering Papers, XXIV, 145. Pickering left doubts as to whether he objected openly. See Pickering to Gates, May 28, 1783, Pickering's notebooks [1827], *ibid.*, V, 313, XLVI, 115-119, 176-179, 328-333; Pickering to his wife, Mar. 16, 18, 1783, Timothy Pickering Papers (microfilm), Essex Institute, Salem, Mass. Gordon states that no one objected (Gordon, *History of United States*, IV, 357-358), while Duer claimed Pickering spoke (King, "Notes on conversation," Oct. 12, 1788, King, *Rufus King*, I, 622). Gen. Hand stated: "Some grumbling from Old Pa., but the vote nem. con." (Hand to Irvine, Apr. 19, 1783, Bancroft Transcripts, America, 1783, I, 202). In any case, Pickering evidently did not side openly with the Gates group.

problems, the "alarming intelligence" induced "peculiar awe and solemnity . . . and oppressed the minds of Congs. with an anxiety and distress which had been scarcely felt in any period of the revolution."[79] Immediately the nationalists seized the initiative. As an embarrassment to the men involved, the committee appointed to consider Washington's dispatches consisted exclusively of opponents of commutation and the impost.[80] Both measures had languished for days. The explosion in Newburgh, properly represented, would add new urgency.

The one obstacle left to commutation was Eliphalet Dyer, a Connecticut delegate who reflected his constituents' dislike of pensions and felt bound by his instructions to oppose half pay in any form. Earlier in March he had agreed that if his vote alone blocked the measure he would consent. But at the crucial moment, he had surprised everyone by voting nay, quibbling over one insignificant provision.[81] When Congress heard from Washington on March 17, Dyer, though shaken, stubbornly refused to allow fear, instead of "great principles of right and justice" to stampede the proceedings.[82] Two more days of uncertainty, however, weakened him. Badgered by the nationalists and McDougall, told that only he prevented the measure, that he had become the focus of resentment from everyone in the army, that commutation was more publicly acceptable than half pay, that it alone "would quiet and pacify the Army," Dyer caved in.[83] On March 20, he introduced a motion for passage, "extorted from him," said Madison,

[79] Madison, "Notes on Debates," Mar. 17, 1783, Hunt, ed., Writings of Madison, I, 407.

[80] Ibid.

[81] Ford et al., eds., Journals of Continental Congress, XXIV, 176, 178-179; William Floyd to George Clinton, Mar. 12, 1783, McDougall to Knox, Mar. 15, 1783, Burnett, ed., Letters, VII, 72, 72, n. 2. For Dyer's consistency on the question, see Larry R. Gerlach, "Connecticut and Commutation, 1778-1784," Connecticut Historical Society Bulletin, XXXIII (1968), 53-55.

[82] Dyer to Gov. Trumbull, Mar. 18, 1783, Jonathan Trumbull, Jr., Papers, Correspondence with Congressmen, I, 17, Connecticut Historical Society, Hartford. Dyer's bravado belies the mood of the letter. John Adams characterized Dyer in 1775 as "long winded and roundabout—obscure and cloudy. Very talkative and very tedious, yet an honest, worthy Man, means and judges well." Diary, Sept. 15, 1775, L. H. Butterfield et al., eds., Diary and Autobiography of John Adams (Cambridge, Mass., 1961), II, 173.

[83] Dyer to Trumbull, Apr. 12, 1783, J. Trumbull, Jr., Papers, Correspondence with Congressmen, I, 22. Dyer said later that his vote ruined his political career of 25 years in Connecticut. See Dyer to Washington, Aug. 18, 1789, George Washington Papers, 7th Ser., IX, 89, Library of Congress.

"by the critical state of our affairs."[84] Two days later, a committee of Hamilton, Dyer, and one other delegate submitted a report recommending five years full pay to all officers entitled to half pay. With Connecticut now in agreement, commutation passed. The impact of Newburgh and the apprehension of something worse converted even such confirmed nationalist opponents as Arthur Lee and John Francis Mercer.[85]

Superficially, the nationalist intrigue had worked well, and within another month a new impost amendment had also passed Congress. But the result was not a nationalist victory. The impost contained such a jumble of compromises, so many concessions to sectional jealousy and state sovereignty, that even Hamilton could not bring himself to vote for it. It was limited to twenty-five years, the revenues restricted to paying debts, and its enforcement uncertain since the states would appoint collectors. Yet it was all the nationalists could muster since news of peace had arrived on March 12, the Army was disintegrating, and Robert Morris's resignation was public.[86] Even as they girded for the effort to sell the new funding measure to the states, the nationalists' political star was waning.

The same day that Congress voted its approval of commutation, it received Washington's speech and the proceedings of the March 15 meeting. Even though some apprehension lingered over the Army's mood, the news dissipated "the cloud" of fear and "afforded great pleasure" to the delegates.[87] Instead of receiving the suspicion and distrust its flirtation with mutiny deserved, the Army emerged from the Newburgh affair with enhanced prestige and honor. Few knew how close to calamity the officers had really come. The public record belied any conspiracy. It showed a loyal officer corps rejecting the seductions of despair despite deep and abiding grievances. "Though intended for opposite purposes," remarked Knox, the affair "has been one of the happiest circumstances of the war, and will

[84] Madison, "Notes on Debates," Mar. 20, 1783, Hunt, ed., *Writings of Madison,* I, 420.
[85] Madison, "Notes on Debates," Mar. 22, 1783, *ibid.,* 421-422; Ford *et al.,* eds., *Journals of Continental Congress,* XXIV, 202-203, 207-210.
[86] Ford *et al.,* eds., *Journals of Continental Congress,* XXIV, 188-192, 256-261; Stephen Higginson to Theophilus Parsons, Sr., Apr. [7], 1783, Burnett, ed., *Letters,* VII, 123; Madison to Thomas Jefferson, Apr. 22, 1783, Julian P. Boyd, ed., *The Papers of Thomas Jefferson* (Princeton, 1950-), VI, 262-263; Ferguson, *Power of the Purse,* 164-167.
[87] Madison, "Notes on Debates," Mar. 22, 1783, Hunt, ed., *Writings of Madison,* I, 421; Ford *et al.,* eds., *Journals of Continental Congress,* XXIV, 210n.

set the military character of America in a high point of view."[88] Most officers were equally ecstatic and wanted the proceedings published. "The whole transaction ought to be *known*," crowed David Humphreys, Washington's young aide. "It will do honour to the Army . . . honour to the Country . . . honour to human Nature."[89]

Within two months, the addresses, Washington's speech, the resolutions of the March 15 meeting, and a few other documents were printed from one end of the country to the other.[90] But only a few people perceived the darker overtones of those hectic three months. Jedidiah Huntington, one of the leaders in the Army's agitation, had predicted that "the Matter [would] wear as great a Variety of Guises as there may be Persons to tell the Story," but no one was talking.[91] It was Washington, standing in the eye of the storm, who deduced more than anyone. It occurred to him and to others at Newburgh, he told Hamilton, that the scheme had been hatched and matured in Philadelphia, that Robert Morris had very likely been the culprit, and that for selfish reasons the politicians had been toying with the Army. With some evasion, Hamilton admitted almost every one of these accusations. He told Washington that the group under suspicion, the "most sensible the most liberal," the men "who think continentally," had been working to include the Army with other public creditors "in order that

[88] Knox to Lincoln, Mar. 16, 1783, Knox Papers, XII, 26.
[89] Humphreys to Lincoln, Mar. 19, 1783, in Frank Landon Humphreys, *Life and Times of David Humphreys* (New York, 1917), I, 270.
[90] *Boston Gazette*, Apr. 21, 28, 1783; *Connecticut Courant* (Hartford), Apr. 15, 1783; *Connecticut Gazette* (New London), Apr. 25, 1783; *Freeman's Journal* (Phila.), Apr. 2, 1783; *Virginia Gazette* (Richmond), July 12, 19, 26, 1783; *Gazette of the State of Georgia* (Savannah), June 5, 12, 19, July 10, 1783.
[91] Huntington to A. Huntington, Mar. 18, 1783, Connecticut Historical Society, *Collections* (Hartford, 1923), XX, 460. For a sampling of reactions to the event, see North Carolina delegates to the governor of North Carolina, Mar. 24, 1783, Boudinot to the Marquis de Lafayette, Apr. 12, 1783, Burnett, ed., *Letters*, VII, 100, 136; Jefferson to Washington, Apr. 16, 1784, Boyd, ed., *Papers of Jefferson*, VII, 106-107; John Murray, *Jerubbaal, or Tyranny's Grave Destroyed* . . . (Newburyport, Mass., 1784), 44; "Brutus" [Robert Yates], *New York Journal and Weekly Register*, Jan. 24, 1788. Benjamin Gale was a particularly perceptive private citizen, but his sources of information are unknown. See the *Conn. Courant* (Hartford), Sept. 2, Oct. 7, 1783; Phillip D. Jordan, Jr., "Connecticut Anti-Federalism on the Eve of the Constitutional Convention, A letter from Benjamin Gale to Erastus Wolcott, February 10, 1787," *Conn. Hist. Soc. Bull.*, XXVIII (1963), 14-21; Gale's address to the Killingworth Town Meeting, Nov. 12, 1787, Benjamin Gale Papers, Beinecke Library, Yale University, New Haven, Conn. Most of these suspicions came from antinationalists. And they came closest to the truth. See, for example, Mercy Warren, *History of the . . . American Revolution* (Boston, 1805), III, 271-272.

the personal influence of some, the connections of others, and a sense of justice to the army as well as the apprehension of ill consequences might form a mass of influence in each state in favour of the measures of Congress." Physical coercion, he emphasized, was impossible, though at times the country's prospects seemed so hopeless that "could force avail" he would be sorely tempted. With all these confessions, however, Hamilton knew the secret would be safe with Washington. Besides the general's own sympathy for the nationalist effort to strengthen the central government, he had benefited too much from the incident ever to hurl public charges. Like the Army itself, Washington's reputation for honesty and unshakable devotion to the government and to the Revolution had been enhanced enormously. And in the final analysis, Hamilton noted wryly, those who could piece together the real story "would be puzzled to support their insinuations by a single fact."[92]

With the intrigue submerged beneath favorable public reaction, the Army again became a nationalist tool, this time to gain ratification of the impost.[93] But in New England commutation sparked such a popular outcry that some states refused to ratify a revenue system that would finance military bonuses. The hubbub over commutation, and then over the Society of Cincinnatus, which New Englanders discovered in early winter, 1783, delayed ratification for months. Nationalist leaders had pulled off a daring stroke in early 1783. Perhaps the impost would never have been revived without pressure from the Army, pressure which they had applied with

[92] Hamilton to Washington, Mar. 17, 25, Apr. 8, 1783, Washington to Hamilton, Mar. 12, 31, Apr. 4, 16, 1783, Syrett and Cooke, eds., Papers of Hamilton, III, 290-293, 305-306, 317-321, 286-288, 309-311, 315-316, 329-330. Hamilton understood Washington's reputation and political future, and he wanted to stay in Washington's good graces. To deny the accusation of plotting would have been dangerous in the extreme since Hamilton had no idea how much information Washington had, or from what source. But Hamilton of course claimed that he and his friends had been working through Washington and had not been neglecting the Army's interest. To admit otherwise, and especially to admit working with Gates, would have killed Hamilton forever in Washington's eyes.

[93] See the Address and Recommendations to the States by . . . Congress . . . (Philadelphia, 1783), 83. This pamphlet was drawn up by a committee of Hamilton, Madison, and Oliver Ellsworth to sell the impost, but Hamilton claimed Madison was the sole author. See Ford et al., eds., Journals of Continental Congress, XXIV, 277; Madison, "Notes on Debates," Apr. 26, 1783, Hunt, ed., Writings of Madison, I, 454; Hamilton to Edward Carrington, May 26, 1792, Syrett and Cooke, eds., Papers of Hamilton, XII, 427. In a circular letter to the state governors, Washington also used the Army claims to buttress the impost request (June 8, 1783, Fitzpatrick, ed., Writings of Washington, XXVI, 488-489, 491-492).

sinister precision. But in the end their strategy almost backfired. By joining the Army to the impost through commutation, they furnished anti-impost forces with a popular issue that delayed the measure's ratification and took the momentum out of the campaign's first, and most crucial, phase.[94] Ironically the Army, responsible for the passage of the impost, was in part responsible for its demise.

Many details of the Newburgh affair will never be known. The questions are endless: how much of the plot Brooks or Stewart, the two messengers to the Army, knew; whether or not others were involved with the Morrises, Hamilton, and McDougall; or even how much McDougall himself understood of the complex manuevering in Congress and at Newburgh. There is no way of telling how united the nationalist leadership was, either in terms of objectives or on strategy at various points. It is even unclear whether one individual or the nationalist leaders together first perceived the opportunities and coordinated the different moves. But while the Morrises and Hamilton clearly realized the seditious nature of their undertaking, and did at one point consider using force to gain their ends, it is highly unlikely that a coup was consciously intended. If they had planned the military overthrow of the Confederation, they would have made the preparations in secret without spreading rumors and threats that could only warn Congress. Given Hamilton's feelings about Gates, they would have chosen a more reliable, popular, and personally acceptable military leader. And in no case would they have warned Washington of a coming upheaval in camp, as Hamilton did in the second week of February. As skillful politicians, nationalist leaders were aware of the American prejudice against professional armies and military interference in politics. They hoped to strengthen national authority in the United States, not discredit and destroy it. That they were willing to risk destroying the government in order to enlarge its power speaks only for their methods and their desperation, not their ultimate goals.

[94] For reactions to commutation, see John Chester to Lt. Col. Ebenezer Huntington, Sept. 21, 1783, Worthington C. Ford, ed., *Correspondence and Journals of Samuel Blachley Webb* (New York, 1893-1894), III, 247; William Williams to the president of Congress, Nov. 1, 1783, Papers of the Continental Congress, Item 66, I, 248-253, Record Group 360, National Archives, Washington. Madison told Randolph (Sept. 8, 1783, Hunt, ed., *Writings of Madison*, II, 16) that the agitation "had increased to such a degree as to produce almost a general anarchy." See also Jackson Turner Main, *The Antifederalists: Critics of the Constitution, 1781-1788* (Chapel Hill, 1961), 84-102, 106-109; William H. Glasson, *Federal Military Pensions in the United States* (New York, 1918), 43-49.

Above all, a coup was a practical impossibility in the America of 1783, and the nationalist leaders knew it. The Army was not composed of the rootless, determined band of janissaries loyal only to a commander that such an adventure demanded. "Even among the officers, whose situations were similar," Brooks recalled forty years later, "there could have been no union in the pursuit of an object of ever doubtful legitimacy: Washington himself could not have effected it." Officers and soldiers alike had other loyalties, not only political but to "parents and other relations, perhaps wives and children, who were dear to them, and to whose society they were anxiously wishing to be restored." For the rank and file, a call to revolt "would have been but the watch word for them to abandon their veteran companions, and return to their friends and firesides."[95]

Nor were the conditions those that have typically spawned coups d'etat in modern times. Even though the Continental Congress was weak, there was no political vacuum in the country. State and local authorities were strong; the extremist groups or grinding class conflicts that precipitate chaos, revolution, and military interference were comparatively insignificant. The officer corps was not, as in other countries that have experienced military takeovers, drawn from one particular social stratum, nor by and large did it identify itself as a separate caste with its own traditions and loyalties, despite feelings of common danger and paranoia over half pay. Unlike the armies of most new nations, America's military did not view itself as the arbiter between contending forces of traditionalism and modernization. Quite often, new nations face tribal, religious, and geographical differences that create two conflicting groups, one in favor of maintaining traditional social forms and institutions, the other favoring modernization of institutions and full utilization of modern technology. The armies in these countries find themselves interfering in politics to save national authority and encourage modernization.[96] The United States, however,

---

[95] Brooks to Pickering, Sept. 6, 1823, Pickering Papers, XXXII, 17.
[96] Edward Shils, "The Military in the Political Development of the New States," in John J. Johnson, ed., *The Role of the Military in Underdeveloped Countries* (Princeton, 1962), 7-67. For the conditions of military intervention, see S. E. Finer, *The Man on Horseback: The Role of the Military in Politics* (London, 1962), Chaps. 4-6; Morris Janowitz, *The Military in the Political Development of New Nations: An Essay in Comparative Analysis* (Chicago, 1964). It could be argued that the conflicts between nationalists and antinationalists, Federalists and Antifederalists, and Federalists and Republicans represented a similar struggle between traditionalism and modernization. The one fought for an urban, commercial, and early industrial orientation—modern in terms of what developed later—while the other wanted the country to take a rural, agrarian direction. And it is true that America

had legitimate political leaders and institutions, working within well-developed traditions that drew strength from a set of widely held beliefs. Most important of all, it had a tradition of legitimacy in governmental forms despite a recent revolution, and rigid, well-defined traditions of civilian dominance of the military. It was this tradition of civilian supremacy and the prejudice against standing armies that assured that any coup, or even the attempt, would plunge the country into bitter civil war. And it is the presence of this tradition, unstained by any contrary experience, that has saved the United States from the coup d'etat ever since.

Although the composition of the Army and the government and various political, geographic, and social conditions made a coup impossible, the country did face a crisis in early 1783, a crisis whose significance cannot be overstated. The traditions of civilian supremacy and antimilitarism were powerful and immediate, but they were still young. England's struggle with Cromwell and military interference was barely a century old. There the civil-military relationship had since developed without friction because the military drew its leadership from the same aristocracy that ran the government. The identity of interests between the leaders of the two organizations and the constant interchange of men from positions in one to those in the other made military interference almost irrelevant.[97] The United States, however, was a republic without a closed, sharply defined elite; given its political predispositions, it could never construct so vague a civil-military relationship, or allow its military institutions to become an extension of one particular group or class.

Secondly, the traditions of civilian dominance and antimilitarism, while strongly entrenched attitudes, had been tested in a *national* political arena

---

had strong religious and sectional differences at the time. But I believe that behind these conflicts lay a widely accepted set of values, attitudes, and traditions, and that America's internal differences pale in comparison with those of other new nations. For a differing view, see Seymour Martin Lipset, *The First New Nation: The United States in Historical and Comparative Perspective* (New York, 1963), Pt. I.

[97] England at this time probably conformed most closely to Janowitz's "aristocratic" model of civil-military relations. See his "Military Elites and the Study of War," *Journal of Conflict Resolution*, I (1957), 9-18. For examples of the interchange between the British Army and the government, see Stephen Saunders Webb, Soldiers and Governors: The Role of the British Army in Imperial Government and the Administration of the American Colonies, 1689-1722 (unpubl. Ph.D. diss., University of Wisconsin, 1965). Good discussions of civil-military relations are Samuel P. Huntington, *The Soldier and the State: The Theory and Politics of Civil-Military Relations* (Cambridge, Mass., 1957), esp. Chap. IV; Louis Smith, *American Democracy and Military Power: A Study of Civil Control of the Military Power in the United States* (Chicago, 1951), esp. Chap. I.

for only eight years. Throughout the war, the potential conflict between Congress and the Army and the implications of such conflict worried leaders in both institutions. Both sides had striven mightily to preserve the form and the substance of military subordination. Each understood that while state political and civil-military traditions were strong, nationally there were few precedents, and those that did exist were weak. One false step could be disastrous. The tradition of military subordination to the civil, in terms of its origins and its implementation on the national level, was still raw in early 1783, in a sense untested, and, at a time when great precedents were being set, extremely vulnerable.

A full-fledged coup d'etat—in the modern sense of the military displacing the regular government and substituting itself or a set of men or a specific political system of its own choosing—was not the problem in 1783. But there are different degrees of intervention that can take a variety of different forms.[98] The Newburgh incident was a case of outside pressure on the normal political process similar in its operation to modern lobbying. What distinguished it, however, was the threat of more direct intervention. Furthermore, it could have led to more serious events. Had Washington not interceded, the officer corps might very well have taken Armstrong's advice. What followed would not have been the kind of venture that required the determination and the united action of which Brooks, and others, knew the corps incapable. It would have been a passive mutiny, a declaration of independence from the nation by the military, and it would in all probability have precipitated a major political and constitutional crisis. Instead of a small, forgotten event at the close of the war, submerged beneath the joy of independence and the return of peace, it would have become a major happening, widely known and remembered, affecting the politics of the whole period. Long into the future it would have cast a pall of suspicion on any military institution the new republic created. In an oblique way, at a crucial point in the nation's development, it would have eroded the tradition of civilian control.

Once civilian control is violated, even by the most halting attempt, a certain purity is irretrievably lost. The bond of trust between the military and society at large evaporates. A new, corrupting element, something previously unthinkable partly because it has never been at-

[98] The categories are described excellently in Finer, *Man on Horseback,* Chaps. VII-XI. Also see Samuel P. Huntington, ed., *The Changing Patterns of Military Politics* [*International Yearbook of Political Behavior Research,* III] (Glencoe, Ill., 1962), esp. the introduction and the essays by Harold Lasswell, David Rapoport, and Martha Derthick.

tempted, is injected into the political process. Once this happens, an aura of automatic rejection is shattered. The possibility of military overthrow then forever lurks in the background, corroding legitimate political activity until the very conditions that provoke its use become more real. No matter how sacred the tradition, how deep rooted the consensus, or how powerful and legitimate the governmental forms, direct military interference in politics makes the coup a new political-constitutional alternative for generations to come.[99]

The Newburgh affair was significant for what did not happen. No tradition was broken and no experience with direct military intervention occurred to haunt the future direction of American political life. The only precedent set, in fact, positively reaffirmed Anglo-American tradition: the first national army in American history explicitly rejected military interference and military independence from civilian control. The disbanding of the Revolutionary Army without a damaging incident assured that civil-military relations for the foreseeable future would be an administrative rather than a political problem. America did stand at the crossroads in March 1783. Today, as one weighs an impossible number of variables and attempts to judge the alternatives without the certainty that hindsight normally offers, the significance of the event is vague and indistinct. Perhaps contemporaries understood the question more clearly. To them the shape of the country's political institutions, even whether or not the disparate sections could live together in union, was uncertain. Thomas Jefferson was describing a general feeling when he claimed "that the moderation and virtue of a single character has probably prevented this revolution from being closed as most others have been by a subversion of that liberty it was intended to establish."[100]

[99] In their excellent and thoughtful, but fundamentally improbable, novel, *Seven Days in May* (New York, 1963 [orig. publ., New York, 1962]), Fletcher Knebel and Charles W. Bailey II make this point explicitly. After blocking the attempted coup by Gen. James M. Scott, Pres. Jordan Lyman goes to elaborate lengths to cover up the affair. He explains away the resignations of the conspirators—even at the risk of further unpopularity—and rewards several characters to insure silence. Lyman knew instinctively, the authors imply, that any knowledge that a coup had been attempted would make a future attempt possible simply because it had been tried previously—a kind of reverse precedent predicated on a "we can do it better" psychology. See *ibid.*, 85, 140-141, 301, 371-372.

[100] Jefferson to Washington, Apr. 16, 1784, Boyd, ed., *Papers of Jefferson*, VII, 106-107. The letter generally concerns the problem of the Cincinnati.

THE
Pennsylvania
Magazine
OF HISTORY AND BIOGRAPHY

New Light on the Philadelphia Mutiny of 1783: Federal-State Confrontation at the Close of the War for Independence

LATE in life, Federalist Timothy Pickering made a habit of putting on paper any historical or political tidbit which confirmed his bias about the evils of things Jeffersonian. A conversation with Richard Peters, an old friend and fellow revolutionary, inspired him to record some remarks about an event thirty-five years into the past: the two-week mutiny at Philadelphia in June 1783. Had Pennsylvania Supreme Executive Council President John Dickinson called up the militia on that occasion, Pickering argued in his notebook, Philadelphia would have remained the capital of the United States; America would have saved not only the millions it had wasted by building Washington, D. C., but would also have avoided the disastrous measures adopted during the presidencies of Thomas Jefferson and James Madison.[1]

[1] Vol. 51, p. 236, Timothy Pickering Papers, Massachusetts Historical Society. Pickering was stationed at Newburgh in the spring of 1783 and went to Philadelphia with the soldiers sent to restore order. Part of the research for this article was conducted under a grant from the National Endowment for the Humanities. The author wishes to thank Paul Smith, Richard Kohn, and Joseph Davis for their help.

419

The climax of the mutiny had occurred on June 21, 1783. On that day a few hundred soldiers, primarily of the Continental Army's Pennsylvania Line, acting on their own initiative, had demonstrated at the State House. The demonstration was only the last and most public scene in several months of dramatic disturbance within the Continental Army. But its importance to the latter phases of the Revolution was considerable. It brought about the first major confrontation between a state and the United States government. It raised the question of how much police power republican governments should exert. It resulted in the departure of Congress from Philadelphia after years of futile attempts to do so. It convinced some Americans of the necessity of Congress having exclusive jurisdiction over any place which eventually became the permanent capital of the new country. And most importantly, it killed the ailing movement within Congress for a stronger federal government.

Peters, an important figure in the events surrounding the mutiny, had not been convinced in 1783 that Dickinson and Pennsylvania rather than Congress was to blame for Congress leaving Philadelphia. Peters believed then that the question of responsibility would "always remain a Matter of Opinion upon which each may decide from possibly opposite Motives."[2] However, most other supporters of a stronger Congress at the time, who did not suffer Peters' conflict of interest as a Pennsylvanian in Congress, blamed Dickinson. Historians, too, have generally shared Pickering's view and the June 21 demonstration has come to symbolize the weakness of Congress under the Articles of Confederation. They have repeated the story of disgruntled Continental soldiers surrounding an insolvent and impotent Congress which could not even convince the State of Pennsylvania to protect it.[3] The symbolism is justified; but

---

[2] Undelivered Motion, [July 26–30], 1783, Edmund C. Burnett, ed., *Letters of Members of the Continental Congress* (Washington, 1921–1938), VII, 329–330, hereinafter cited as *LMCC*. See note 64 below for my dating of this document.

[3] The most detailed account of the mutiny is Varnum L. Collins, *The Continental Congress at Princeton* (Princeton, 1908). Collins portrays a Congress unsupported by Pennsylvania. Louis C. Hatch, *The Administration of the American Revolutionary Army* (New York, 1904) is shorter but more balanced in its interpretation. Most recently, H. James Henderson, *Party Politics in the Continental Congress* (New York, 1974), recognizes the complexities surrounding the mutiny, but writes as if Congress were in session during the demonstration and as if there were no connection at all between the centralists and the soldiers.

the evidence[4] shows that Congress was not the object of the demonstration and that Congress and its supporters attempted to use the incident to assert the authority and even the supremacy of the federal government at a time when public support for Congress was dissipating rapidly. As for John Dickinson, he had refused to be intimidated by either Congress or the mutinous soldiers.

The Philadelphia Mutiny grew out of the troubles which confronted the United States during the spring of 1783. Its immediate origins lay in the dangerous question of how to disband the Army and settle the complex financial accounts of the soldiers. After the dark days of 1780, when the war for independence almost collapsed, such centralists in Congress and the states as James Madison, Alexander Hamilton, Elias Boudinot, Charles Thomson, Richard Peters, Oliver Ellsworth, Gouverneur Morris and John Dickinson had a renewed opportunity to strengthen the central government. ("Centralist" is used here in preference to "nationalist" because only a vocal minority of them sought a national government, supreme over the states. The idea of a national government was not popular with Americans in 1783 and the term was generally avoided.) By 1783, with peace at hand and the value of a strong central government more subject to public doubt, their program was ailing and their leader, Robert Morris, was threatening to resign as

4 Several of the major actors in the mutiny left accounts. The undated four-page account of Elias Boudinot, President of Congress, is among his papers at the Library of Congress, hereinafter, Boudinot Account. Alexander Hamilton, chairman of the congressional committee to treat with Pennsylvania, placed two reports on the *Journals of Congress* on July 1, 1783. In addition he recorded his view of the mutiny (based for the most part on the minutes which he kept and which are no longer extant) in a lengthy September 1783 letter to John Dickinson, the extant part of which is in Harold C. Syrett and Jacob E. Cooke, eds., *The Papers of Alexander Hamilton* (New York, 1961—), III, 438–458, hereinafter, Hamilton Account. John Dickinson gave his version of the mutiny in a message to the Pennsylvania Assembly dated Aug. 18, 1783, which is in *Colonial Records* [of Pennsylvania] (Philadelphia, 1852–1853), XIII, 654–666, hereinafter, Dickinson Account. A draft of the message in the R. R. Logan Dickinson Papers, Historical Society of Pennsylvania (HSP), varies only slightly from the published version. Col. Richard Humpton, commander of the Philadelphia Barracks, sent his account to the President of Congress in late June 1783; it is in RG 360, Item 38, folios 3–[10], National Archives and Records Service, hereinafter, Humpton Account.

Superintendent of Finance. A clear sense of constitutional crisis gripped Congress at Philadelphia and spread throughout the Union. The crisis involved Robert Morris and legislative versus executive supremacy within the federal government; the power of the federal government in relationship to the states; the belief that Philadelphia was a modern Capua, ridden with luxury and political corruption; the newspaper publication of secret documents released by a congressman; the threat of military intervention in civilian affairs; and a host of immediate problems to be solved by the new country. Congressman James Madison had predicted in February that the next six months would determine whether the Revolution would end in "prosperity and tranquility, or *confusion and disunion*."[5] The overriding question was whether or not, in the wake of peace, the states could be held together in anything more than a symbolic union.

In desperation, some centralists used certain disgruntled army officers and other public creditors in what became known as the Newburgh Conspiracy. Commander-in-Chief George Washington was deeply disturbed by the uprising at Newburgh, particularly because he believed civilians at Philadelphia were responsible. One of the resolutions adopted by the officers, after Washington's masterful coup-de-grace to the conspiracy, declared an unshaken confidence in Congress and a conviction that it would not disband or *disperse* the Army until the accounts of both officers and soldiers were settled. "I fix it as an *indispensable* Measure," Washington informed a congressman, "that previous to the Disbanding of the Army, all their accounts should be completely liquidated and settled." Washington also warned his former aide-de-camp Alexander Hamilton, the congressman with whom he had the most confidential correspondence, that "unhappy consequences would follow" any attempt by Congress to disband the troops or separate the Lines prior to a settlement.[6]

In a series of decisions, however, the centralists acted in Congress

---

[5] Madison to Edmund Randolph, Feb. 25, 1783, William T. Hutchinson, *et. al.*, eds., *The Papers of James Madison* (Chicago, 1962–), VI, 286, hereinafter, *Madison Papers*.

[6] Washington to Theodorick Bland, Apr. 4, 1783, Washington to Hamilton, Apr. 4, 16, 1783, John C. Fitzpatrick, ed., *The Writings of George Washington* (Washington, 1931–1944), XXVI, 285–296, 342.

to disperse the Army prior to a settlement. Robert Morris considered a settlement of accounts for thousands of soldiers before the expensive Army was disbanded to be totally out of the question. The settlement involved the different laws and procedures of the states, Congress, and various departments within the Army. In addition to back pay and cash bounties, the government of the United States and the several states had to consider tax free land titles, clothing allowances, and other rations in the computations. Each soldier needed to be treated individually because the accounts varied enormously. Morris knew they would take years to settle, and he held to his position adamantly, pointing out that the longer the Army was retained, the less likely it would be to go home peacefully. Hamilton recommended Morris' position to Congress on May 23, but Congress balked. Three days later Hamilton, without the support of Morris, proposed and Congress adopted a compromise. Instead of an immediate disbandment, the troops which had enlisted for the duration of the war (but not those which had enlisted for a three-year term) would be furloughed to their homes, pending a discharge once the definitive treaty of peace had been ratified. There was neither provision for a settlement of accounts nor even a word of appreciation for the soldiers.[7]

Washington shared the disgust of the officers at Newburgh when he ordered the furlough without settlement on June 2. Three days later Major General William Heath, commander of the Army's Eastern Department, presented Washington with a moderate, reasoned "Address of the Generals and Officers Commanding the Regiments and Corps" which implored him as their friend and general to intervene with Congress. The address asserted that the furlough was a ploy by Congress to avoid a settlement. The officers urged him to amend his June 2 order to make acceptance of furloughs voluntary. Washington replied immediately, assuring the officers that Congress had done everything in its power to obtain justice for them but that the states had not complied with its requests. Nevertheless, in a rare showing of independence from

[7] Worthington C. Ford, *et. al.*, eds., *Journals of the Continental Congress, 1774–1789* (Washington, 1904–1937), XXIV, 358, 364; E. James Ferguson, *The Power of the Purse* (Chapel Hill, 1961), 179–181; Morris to Hamilton, Peters, and Nathaniel Gorham, May 15, 1783, *Hamilton Papers*, III, 356–361; Morris Diary, May 27, 1783, Robert Morris Papers, Library of Congress (DLC).

Congress, made possible only because of the provisional articles of peace, Washington adopted the suggestion of his officers and issued orders declaring that each soldier could decide for himself whether or not to accept furloughs. Washington transmitted the memorial and his response to Congress with a covering letter indicating his support for the officers. Washington's letter with its enclosures reached Congress on June 11 and was referred to a committee which recommended on June 19 that Congress agree to Washington's variation respecting furloughs. Congress so resolved; but it is clear from the events which transpired that some highly placed civilians and military officials disapproved and sought to conceal Washington's concession from soldiers in Pennsylvania.[8]

While Washington had for the second time in less than three months prevented an explosion at Army Headquarters, there were junior officers of the Pennsylvania Line in Philadelphia who were not to be calmed. Sergeant James Bennett was walking on Second Street early in June when he was stopped by two officers of his Line, Lieutenant John Sullivan, an Irishman, and Captain Henry Carbery, a Marylander. The latter had been on inactive service following a settlement with Pennsylvania after the Line's serious 1781 Mutiny. The two men took Bennett into the Doctor Franklin Tavern and told him they understood that Congress had recently adopted a yet-to-be published resolution dismissing the Army without a settlement of its accounts. They said that the only way to obtain a settlement was for the Line to take up arms in its own behalf, and, if the soldiers would do this, Carbery and Sullivan promised to lead the men to a place where they would receive the justice due them. Partly as a result of this meeting, rumor of a dispersal without settlement spread among the soldiers stationed at Philadelphia.[9]

Confirmation of the rumor came with the arrival of the furloughed Maryland Line from Newburgh on the night of June 12,

---

[8] Pickering to Samuel Hodgdon, June 7, 1783, Pickering Papers, XXXIV, 207; Washington to Morris, June 3, 1783, Washington, General Orders, June 2, 6, 1783, Fitzpatrick, *Washington*, XXVI, 463–467, 471–472; John Pierce to Morris, June 6, 1783, Washington to Boudinot, June 7, 1783, with enclosures, RG 360, Item 165, folio 653, Item 152, Vol. XI, folio 295; Ford, *Journals*, XXIV, 403.

[9] Francis B. Heitman, *Historical Register of Officers of the Continental Army* (Washington, 1914), 143, 527; Deposition of Sgt. James Bennett, July 1, 1783, RG 360, Item 38, folios 65–[66].

and the belated announcement of the furlough (but not Washing-- ton's modification of it) the next morning. This was too much for the war-hardened soldiers, most of whom had not received any cash pay since 1782 and some of whom were veterans of the 1781 mutiny. A board of sergeants immediately submitted a mutinous memorial to Congress declaring "We will not accept your furloughs and de- mand a settlement." Congress was indignant and referred the matter to Secretary at War Benjamin Lincoln, who along with General Arthur St. Clair, commander of the Continental troops in Pennsylvania, immediately took "prudent and soothing measures." St. Clair issued Washington's order on June 6 suspending furloughs for any men who chose not to accept them. Most of the dissatisfied soldiers at Philadelphia (unlike the soldiers at Newburgh) refused furloughs, just as the men who had suppressed the order expected, and remained mutinous. They disobeyed orders to march to barracks in small towns well outside the state and federal capital. Even as the Maryland Line, which had supported the June 13 memorial to Congress, went home, veterans of the Pennsylvania Line who had been serving in the Southern Army arrived by ship from Charleston, South Carolina.[10]

Meanwhile Sergeant Christian Nagle, a seven-year veteran of the Line stationed at Lancaster, received anonymous letters from Phila- delphia, apparently written by Lieutenant Sullivan. The letters communicated the designs of the troops at the capital. Nagle shared the news with other soldiers, insisting that justice would never be done unless they took matters into their own hands. Thus, when the officers announced the furlough without a settlement (but not Washington's moderation of it) at Lancaster on the evening of June 16, the angry men were prepared. Armed soldiers, primarily inexperienced recruits, set out the next morning for Philadelphia to join the mutiny already in progress.[11]

[10] Humpton Account, folio 3–[6]; John Armstrong to Horatio Gates, June 16, 1783, LMCC, VII, 189–190n; "Notes on Debates," June 13, 1783, Madison to Edmund Randolph, June 17, 1783, *Madison Papers*, VII, 141, 158–159; Collins, *Princeton*, 10.

[11] Collins, *Princeton*, 14; Richard Butler to Dickinson, William Henry to Dickinson, June 17, 1783, RG 360, Item 38, folios 37, 123; Affidavit of Benjamin Spyker, Jr., June 28, 1783, Samuel Hazard, ed., *Pennsylvania Archives*, Series I (Philadelphia, 1852–1856), X, 577. Spyker's affidavit is an account of what he heard Sgt. Christian Nagle declare about the mutiny after Nagle fled to Berks County. It is not clear about the timing of events, it is second hand, and little of its bravado is supported by other documentation.

On Thursday, June 19, Pennsylvania President John Dickinson left the State House and hurried to the office of his friend Robert Morris for advice. ·It was common practice for centralists such as Dickinson to consult with their leader. Congress had recently given Morris a vote of confidence and he had not resigned. Although his influence had declined, he remained the man one went to see if one sought results.[12] Even though Dickinson was the governor of a state, he had always been deeply committed to a strong central government. In response to the centralists' calls for strengthening the Union during the spring of 1783, Dickinson was preparing at the time of the mutiny a series of proposals to make to the powerful Pennsylvania Assembly at its next session in August. He would support federal taxation and commercial regulations.[13]

On this visit to Morris' office, Dickinson was worried about two letters he had just received by express from Lancaster reporting that armed soldiers were on the road to Philadelphia. The letters asserted that the mutiny had originated at the capital, that the soldiers planned to rob the Bank of North America for their pay, and that they would likely be joined by men stationed at York. Dickinson asked Morris what should be done. Call up the local militia immediately, Morris advised. Dickinson returned to the State House where the Council had sent the letters downstairs to a Congress which, given peace, was rapidly declining in both attendance and public opinion.[14]

Congress appointed a committee of three prominent allies of Morris to confer with Pennsylvania and to take appropriate measures. Pennsylvania's Richard Peters, Connecticut's sole delegate Oliver Ellsworth, and New York's sole delegate Alexander Hamilton, a freshman member, who, like Peters, was considered a military expert, composed the committee. President of Congress Elias Boudinot needed a chairman on whom he could rely and he appointed Hamilton. The two men were not only centralists but also personal friends; Hamilton had spent his first year in America a decade earlier in Boudinot's Elizabethtown, New Jersey, home.[15]

12 Morris Diary, May 3, June 19, 1783; Ford, *Journals*, XXIV, 284–285.

13 Dickinson to Charles Thomson, June 12, 1783, Thomson Papers, DLC.

14 Butler to Dickinson, Henry to Dickinson, June 17, 1783, RG 360, Item 38, folios 37, 123; Council Minutes, June 19, 1783, *Colonial Records*, XIII, 603.

15 Ford, *Journals*, XXIV, 402–405n; Broadus Mitchell, *Alexander Hamilton, Youth to Maturity, 1755–1788* (New York, 1957), Chapter 4.

Frustrated by the feebleness of Congress, the twenty-seven-year-old Hamilton assumed the lead in the unfolding drama. From at least Saturday night until Tuesday, he, rather than Congress or its President, would determine the response of the federal government in its dealings with Pennsylvania.

For the temperate Dickinson the crisis of a state presidency was at hand. His reputation as the first intercolonial Revolutionary hero had suffered after he refused to sign the Declaration of Independence, and the attacks against his character when he stood for the Council in 1782 (while serving as President of Delaware) had been so vicious as to stain his character even to the present. With his reputation at stake, he paid close attention to public opinion throughout the mutiny and its aftermath. Neither he nor the finally victorious Republican Party of Pennsylvania, which he represented, could afford to mishandle the affair. It did not wish to give ammunition to its opponents just prior to the all-important October 1783 election of the first Council of Censors, a body which had the authority to propose changes in the state Constitution opposed by the Republicans. Thus the local political situation acted to fortify Dickinson's caution. His strategy throughout the mutiny was moderation rather than force, aimed at cooling passions and preventing bloodshed. As an advocate of restraint Dickinson clashed with Hamilton during the mutiny itself and in their official versions of what had occurred. As a result, he was seen as a champion of states' rights and his reputation suffered even more.[16]

When the Hamilton Committee met with Dickinson and the Council on Thursday afternoon, Hamilton recommended that Pennsylvania use its militia to disperse the soldiers, or at least keep them on the west bank of the Schuylkill River. But Council opposed the use of force until an outrage had been committed. It was uncertain that the city militia, men who several years earlier had joined a mob attack on the home of James Wilson, could be relied upon to take up arms against soldiers whom they credited with having secured independence. A call of the militia which was disobeyed

[16] Robert L. Brunhouse, *The Counter-Revolution in Pennsylvania, 1776–1790* (Harrisburg, 1942), Chapters 2–4; Madison to Randolph, June 30, 1783, *Madison Papers*, VII, 205–207; Elias to Elisha Boudinot, June 23, 1783, *LMCC*, VII, 195. I am indebted to Milton E. Flower, Dickinson's biographer, for sharing insights into his subject's personality.

would hazard the authority of the state (and the reputation of Dickinson). Besides, it took time to put the militia in readiness. Finally, Council reasoned, the soldiers claimed they had come to Philadelphia only for a settlement of accounts due them, and there was no proof that they intended violence. Therefore, after mature deliberation, Council resolved that "the language of invitation, and good humour became more advisable than any immediate exertion of authority."[17] Pennsylvania, which had exclusive jurisdiction over affairs within its boundaries, had made its decision; Congress, which had no jurisdiction over the capital of the United States at Philadelphia, had to obey Pennsylvania's decision.

Hamilton was astonished by Pennsylvania's response. Consequently, he ordered Assistant Secretary at War William Jackson to use every effort short of force to keep the soldiers from entering the city. Jackson first consulted Robert Morris and then rode out to the troops. The soldiers from Lancaster, numbering about seventy to eighty men after desertion along the route, were not convinced.[18]

On Friday morning, June 20, the soldiers, under the command of Sergeant Nagle, marched into the Philadelphia Barracks where Congress' War Office had made special provision for them. As the day wore on, several events fanned dissatisfaction among the Philadelphia and Lancaster troops. Assistant Paymaster Philip Audibert informed the barracks commander, Colonel Richard Humpton, that he had received orders that no soldiers were to be given any more payroll certificates—which Morris offered as part of the furlough in lieu of cash for three months pay—unless they also accepted the terms of Congress' furlough as it stood prior to Washington's modification. The order was illegal since Congress had approved Washington's modification the day before.

Who issued the inflammatory order to Audibert is uncertain. Secretary at War Lincoln and Paymaster General John Pierce were not in Philadelphia at the time, and it would have been uncharacteristic for Assistant Secretary at War Jackson to take the initiative. The order must have come from the Office of the Superintendent of

17 Ford, *Journals*, XXIV, 413–414; Council Minutes, June 20, 1783, XIII, 603; Dickinson Account, 654.
18 Hamilton to Jackson, June 19, 1783, *Hamilton Papers*, III, 397; Morris Diary, June 19, 1783.

Finance. Audibert and Jackson had consulted Robert Morris about the soldiers apparently before the order was issued, but Morris, who supported pay certificates even for those refusing furlough, denied responsibility the next morning.[19]

Most likely the order was issued by the man who shared Morris' office, birthday, and political philosophy, Assistant Superintendent of Finance Gouverneur Morris. Gouverneur enjoyed intrigue, and was a "person of no principle, a downright Machiavelian Politician," according to a contemporary. Indeed, Washington pointed to him as the man who had built the "groundwork of the superstructure" that became the Newburgh Conspiracy. Gouverneur Morris had reflected two months after Newburgh that he was "content . . . *again to labor and to hazard* but neither time nor circumstance *will permit anything now.*"[20] The Philadelphia Mutiny provided another circumstance for intrigue and his role in it points to him as the man who probably instructed Audibert.

By evening the troops at the barracks were more restive than at any time since their memorial to Congress a week earlier. All were openly upset by the order to stop their back pay. In addition, the Lancaster men considered ridiculous and insulting a decision by the Hamilton Committee and Robert Morris earlier in the day that they be paid only upon their return to Lancaster. In the midst of this tension, Hamilton, Jackson, and Gouverneur Morris visited the soldiers at the barracks. Some soldiers believed the three came in their official capacities, perhaps even on higher authority. Apparently

---

[19] Humpton Account, folios [6]-7; Morris Diary, June 17, 20, 21, 1783 (Morris' statement about pay for the soldiers in the diary on June 7 meant that those who accepted furlough should be paid first); Dickinson Account, 654; "Vox Populi," (Philadelphia) *Freeman's Journal*, July 23, 1783. The author of this important piece was someone who apparently had access to the soldiers, Congress, and the Council. Col. Humpton, who was sympathetic to the soldiers, is the most likely person because the article is similar in its coverage to the account which he submitted to Congress and both place great emphasis on the events which drove the soldiers to their action. Congress was critical of Humpton's furlough of the soldiers after the mutiny and he had good reason to be annoyed with that body. Another possible author is John Armstrong, Jr., the author of the Newburgh Addresses and the Secretary to Council at the time of the mutiny.

[20] William Gordon to Gates, Feb. 26, 1783, *Massachusetts Historical Society Proceedings*, LXIII, 488; Washington to Hamilton, Apr. 16, 1783, *Hamilton Papers*, III, 330; Morris to Gen. Nathaniel Greene, May 18, 1783, Greene Papers, DLC.

Gouverneur Morris took the lead in the meeting, allegedly urging
the troops to accept the unamended original furlough even though
it did not provide for a settlement of accounts, and promising the
men one month's pay in *cash* so that they could go home in a
"genteel manner." Imagine, the soldiers later complained to the
Pennsylvania Council, the feelings of those "sons of liberty who
have freed their country from Tyranny, and secured America's
Independence and a honorable peace" upon hearing the "generous
expressions of that honorable gentleman."[21] The visit quieted the
troops only in the sense that it convinced the doubters that drastic
action was necessary.[22] Before the soldiers went to sleep Friday
night, Carberry and Sullivan spent fifteen minutes talking to Nagle
and a few other sergeants outside the barracks.[23]

On Saturday June 21 Dickinson again visited Robert Morris.
Morris repeated his recommendation for a militia call on the grounds
that the authority and dignity of the United States were threatened.
At 12:30 the long drum roll to assemble sounded at the barracks.
Edgy officers hastily abandoned their mess. The soldiers refused
orders to disband, and soon marched out of the barracks under the
command of sergeants. Supposedly known only to a few, their
destination was the State House six blocks away. Their plan, one
of the sergeants swore later, was to obtain authority from President
Dickinson and General St. Clair to appoint a committee to represent them in settling their accounts with Pennsylvania. The soldiers
knew that Congress would not be meeting since it was Saturday,
and that only their state's Supreme Executive Council would be in
session at the State House. The decision to turn to the state for
redress was more than a reaction to their treatment by Congress a
week earlier and by the federal officials the night before. It was a
realistic assessment of the constitutional and financial realities of

---

21 Address of the Mutineers, RG 360, Item 38, folios 33–[34]; Ford, *Journals*, XXIV,
414–415; Spyker Affidavit, 577–578.

22 Humpton later informed Congress that the soldiers appeared "a little easier" the next
morning (Humpton Account, folio 7), and assured Gouverneur Morris in the presence of
Robert Morris that, contrary to anonymous newspaper reports, the visit had quieted the
troops. Morris Diary, Sept. 2, 1783.

23 Deposition of Sgt. Solomon Townsend, July 2, 1783, RG 360, Item 38, folio 49–[50].

the United States in 1783: Pennsylvania was simply wealthier and more important than the federal government.[24]

The Council, with Dickinson presiding, had just convened when it heard the approaching drum rolls and piping fifes. Soon about thirty well-ordered troops with fixed bayonets under the command of Sergeant John Robinson came into view below the Council Chamber windows. The soldiers formed in front of the State House and delivered to the Council, by way of its secretary, a crude note demanding authority to appoint new officers for the purpose of assuming command and redressing grievances. Dickinson and the Council were allowed twenty minutes to comply "or otherwise we shall instantly let in those injured soldiers upon you and abide by the consequences." The note was penned by either Sullivan or Carbery. While the Council was in the process of unanimously rejecting the demands, about 250 more armed soldiers under the command of Sergeant Nagle arrived. They posted sentries at the State House doors and at the avenues surrounding the building; they had previously left others at the munitions store houses throughout the city. However, the soldiers allowed free entry and exit from the State House.[25]

Meanwhile, congressmen were gathering in their chamber on the first floor of the State House, most probably arriving between the two groups of soldiers. They had been summoned into emergency session on thirty minutes notice. President Boudinot issued the summons at the suggestion of Hamilton who reported that the soldiers were in an ugly mood and might rob the Bank that evening.[26]

24 Morris Diary, June 21, 1783; Humpton Account, folio 7; Deposition of Sgt. Richard Murthwaite, June 30, 1783, RG 360, Item 38, folio [74]. Hamilton was unwilling to give the soldiers credit for understanding the constitutional and financial realities of 1783 America, stating that they turned to Pennsylvania because of either "artifice or confusion of ideas" (Hamilton Account, 456). The soldiers, however, knew that their State would play a vital role in the settlement of accounts. It had promised them various bounties throughout the war in land, money, and rations as inducements to enlist or remain in service; particularly after 1780, Pennsylvania had assumed the pay of its Line, sometimes following specific requests from Congress. By 1783 Pennsylvania had issued $1,673,000 to its Line. *Pennsylvania Magazine of History and Biography*, XXVII (1903), 504; Ferguson, *Purse*, 180–181.

25 Dickinson Account, 655; Council Minutes, June 21, 1783, XIII, 605; Murthwaite Deposition, June 30, 1783, folio [50]; Townsend Deposition, July 2, 1783, folio [74]; Chevalier de La Luzerne to Comte de Vergennes, June 21, 1783, Correspondence Politique, Etats-Unis, XXIV, microfilm, DLC.

26 Boudinot Account, [1]; "Vox Populi," *Freeman's Journal*, July 23, 1783.

Did Hamilton knowingly send Congress into the midst of an armed confrontation or did he merely want Congress in session to discuss the mood of the soldiers?

The weight of the evidence, particularly the timing of Boudinot's summons, indicates that Hamilton either knew or surmised what was about to happen when he convinced Boudinot to call the session.[27] No delegates indicated that they arrived at the State House after the soldiers, but a business firm stated that they "assembled in their Chamber after the Soldiery had beset the State House." Dickinson's account carries more weight because it was a report to the Pennsylvania Assembly and because no spokesman for the United States, Hamilton in particular, ever denied it: "Upon the alarm the members were specially ["hastily" in the draft version] summoned by their President, and at the place to which the soldiers were moving. For what purpose they were so summoned, we have not been informed."[28]

Hamilton's motives, at least in part, can be surmised. The prospect of Continental troops petitioning their state rather than Congress for redress was not a flattering one for the centralists, and the demonstration provided them with an opportunity to once again assert the claims of Congress. Hamilton knew as well as anyone the antimilitary bias of Americans and hoped perhaps that a military demonstration against Congress would be the source of badly needed public support for the federal government. Although there is no evidence to show that Hamilton intended to stimulate

[27] The problem is to be precise about the timing of Boudinot's summons and the troop assembly. Boudinot officially informed Washington three hours after the summons that he had called Congress to meet at one P.M.; Humpton officially informed Congress later that the troops assembled at twelve-thirty. Thus Hamilton, who insisted to Dickinson that he had prompt intelligence of the soldiers' activities during the mutiny, could have known of the demonstration, in addition to the general restlessness, prior to the summons. In his postmortem notes on the mutiny, Boudinot—and the question of a cover-up must be raised—stated that he summoned Congress at twelve to meet at twelve-thirty, making it impossible for either Hamilton or himself to have known that the troops had assembled. His still later claim in a private letter that the soldiers decided to march on the State House after learning of his summons is not only unconfirmed but also ignores the fact that the soldiers paid no attention to the congressmen during the demonstration. Boudinot to Washington, 4 P.M., June 21, 1783, Boudinot to the Ministers Plenipotentiary at Paris, July 15, 1783, *LMCC*, VII, 193, 222; Humpton Account, folio 7; Hamilton Account, 444–445; Boudinot Account, [1].

[28] Chaloner and White to ————, June 22, 1783, Chaloner and White Letter Book, HSP; Dickinson Account, 665.

such an outburst when he, along with Gouverneur Morris and Jackson, had visited the men at the barracks the evening before, he apparently saw the opportunity on Saturday and quickly manufactured a confrontation.

At least two congressmen from each of six states and one from a seventh state came to the special session. The second delegate from the seventh state never arrived, and Congress never achieved a quorum. The constitutional body known as "Congress" was consequently never surrounded or even threatened on June 21. No entry was placed on the Journals, and the congressmen within the building quickly realized that they were not the object of the demonstrators. Dickinson, however, carried the soldiers' demand and Council's unanimous rejection of it downstairs to the congressmen. He explained the difficulties involved in calling the militia and offered his opinion that unless some outrage on persons or property was committed it should not be called out. Dickinson returned to the Council Chamber. Congressman Ralph Izard proposed that the congressmen leave the building, but it was agreed instead that they would remain until three o'clock, the usual time of Congress' weekday adjournment. The ignored congressmen further decided, should a quorum form, not to transact any business whatsoever, and in particular not to accept any propositions directed to them by the soldiers, should any be sent.

Meanwhile, General St. Clair worked out an agreement with the soldiers to end the demonstration. He asked the Council if it would attend a conference with a committee of commissioned and decommissioned (this would include Carbery) officers, to be appointed by the soldiers? St. Clair believed the soldiers might be prevailed upon to return to the barracks if the Council so agreed. Dickinson returned to the congressmen and inquired of Boudinot if it was agreeable with them for the Council to hold the conference proposed by St. Clair. The President of Congress declared it was. Whereupon the Council consented to receive a state of claims from the soldiers "if decently expressed and constitutionally presented."[29]

29 Council Minutes, June 21, 1783, XIII, 605; Hamilton to Clinton, June 29, 1783, *Hamilton Papers*, III, 407; Boudinot Account, [1]; Madison, Notes on Debates, June 21, 1783, Virginia Delegates to Gov. Benjamin Harrison, June 24, 1783, *Madison Papers*, VII, 176–177, 189–191. The implication of Madison's notes is that Congress was in session and it is the prime source of that misinformation.

Since the arrival of the first soldiers, citizens had been massing at the State House. Liquor from taverns in the area was widely served and excitement mounted. Congressman James Madison observed that while "no danger from premeditated violence was apprehended," the drinking might lead "to hasty excess." As the soldiers got drunk they cursed loudly and occasionally pointed bayonetted muskets at the first floor windows a few inches above their heads. Just because congressmen were on the first floor looking straight into the demonstration, while the Supreme Executive Council looked down upon it from upstairs, did not make Congress the object of the confrontation. Three o'clock arrived and the congressmen passed through the sentries and into the mass of drinking demonstrators and citizens. Other than shouts and curses, only one incident occurred. A citizen pointed out Boudinot as the President of Congress and yelled that he should not be allowed to escape. Private Andrew Wright and a small group of soldiers accosted Boudinot and ordered him back to the State House. Sergeant Solomon Townsend, however, came up, apologized to Boudinot, and lectured the men on the respect due their superiors. St. Clair soon thereafter informed the soldiers of the Council's willingness to meet with a negotiating committee. While there were some cheers at the announcement, on the whole the soldiers milled about unable to agree who should present their case. Finally, the sergeants directed the men back to the barracks in order to decide there. The demonstration was over, and the Council adjourned just after four P.M. Robert Morris, who had fled to the country home of a business associate, returned to Philadelphia, allegedly regretting his flight as an overreaction.[30]

Immediately upon reaching his home, Boudinot sent an express to General Washington at Newburgh requesting him to advance a body of dependable troops on Philadelphia. Boudinot informed Washington that he was not writing with the authority of Congress

30 "Notes on Debates," June 21, 1783, *Madison Papers*, VII, 177; Townsend Deposition, folio [50]; Boudinot Account, [2]; Dickinson Account, 656; La Luzerne to Vergennes, June 21, 1783, Correspondence Politique; Jonathan Buyers to William Irvine, July 1, 1783, Irvine Papers, HSP; William Clayton to Horatio Gates, June 23, 1783, Miscellaneous Manuscripts, New York Public Library; Morris Diary, June 21, 1783; "The Reminiscences of David Hayfield Conyngham, 1750-1834 . . .," *Proceedings and Collections of the Wyoming Historical and Genealogical Society*, VIII (1904), 221.

but at the request of the members present. Boudinot also summoned congressmen back to the State House for another special session at six P.M. This time a quorum formed and secret resolutions were placed on the Journals: Washington was ordered to march troops on Philadelphia; the Hamilton Committee was instructed to seek effectual measures in support of public authority from the Pennsylvania Council; and, if the Council did not respond promptly or adequately, Congress agreed to remove either to Princeton or Trenton by the end of the week.[31] With the mouth of the Hudson still in British hands and with Delaware so intimately linked to Pennsylvania, Congress had to choose between Maryland and Boudinot's home state of New Jersey. Maryland lost out, apparently because of a lack of votes to pull Congress southward, because only one Maryland delegate was attending, and because soldiers of the Maryland Line had participated in the mutinous June 13 memorial to Congress. Congress delegated to the Hamilton Committee full authority to recommend a removal if it saw fit.

All seven states attending concurred in the resolves. Pennsylvania, which could have prevented the adoption of the removal resolution, agreed because its centralist delegation favored supporting the claims of the federal government and because it was clearly understood that the removal was to be *temporary*, only until order was restored. Boudinot sent the resolves off to Washington Sunday morning, concluding that "this wound to the dignity of the Federal Government should not go unpunished."[32] The authority and dignity of the government, in the form of a confrontation with the State of Pennsylvania, had replaced the settlement of accounts as the central issue of the mutiny in all but the soldiers' minds.

While Congress adopted its secret resolutions on the evening of June 21, between twenty and thirty of the mutinous soldiers met at the Sign of the Three Tuns Tavern on Race Street. Carbery and Sullivan assured the men that they would have their pay in a day or two if they remained sober and created no further disturbances.

[31] Boudinot to Washington, 4 P.M., 11 P.M., June 21, 1783, *LMCC*, VII, 194; Boudinot Account, [3]; "Notes on Debates," June 21, 1783, *Madison Papers*, VII, 177; Ford, *Journals*, XXIV, 410; James McHenry to Thomas S. Lee, June 28 [26?], 1783, McHenry Papers, DLC.
[32] Peters to Thomas FitzSimons, July 26, 1783, Boudinot to Washington, 11 P.M., June 21, 1783, Peters, Undelivered Motion, [26–30 July], 1783, *LMCC*, VII, 194, 234, 329–330.

The meeting selected Captains Henry Carbery, Jonas Symonds, John Steele, James Christie, and Lieutenants John Sullivan and William Houston to represent them in the negotiations with Pennsylvania. Elsewhere in Philadelphia that Saturday night, Robert Morris called on Dickinson at his home and advised him once again to call up the militia.[33]

Rumors of violence were widespread on Sunday and Monday as the Hamilton Committee and the Pennsylvania Executive Council met to discuss the situation. The Committee informed Pennsylvania that Congress expected the state to call up the militia, but Pennsylvania refused on grounds that the citizens of Philadelphia remained convinced of the peaceful intent of the soldiers, of the justice of their demands, and of a happy outcome to the negotiation arranged by St. Clair and consented to by Pennsylvania and the congressmen at the State House during the Saturday demonstration. The Hamilton Committee requested the response in writing but Pennsylvania refused; it would correspond only with Congress, not with one of its committees. Although Congress had put the heaviest pressure it could on Pennsylvania—a threat to remove the federal capital and all it represented in prestige and money for the local economy—the State not only refused to buckle under to the federal government's demand for a militia call but also used the opportunity to confirm its supremacy over a congressional committee. It was an ironical role for Dickinson and Pennsylvania whose commitments to strong central government were well known.[34]

Hamilton barely controlled his rage—a rage fed by congressional impotence—at the state's "weak and disgusting position." He considered its refusal to transact business with his committee in writing further evidence of Pennsylvania's disrespect for the federal government, and made that incident a central issue in the federal-state confrontation.[35]

---

[33] Deposition of Sgt. Joseph Morgan, July 1, 1783, Bennett Deposition, July 1, 1783, Townsend Deposition, July 2, 1783, RG 360, Item 38, folios 51, 54–[55], 67–69; Morris Diary, June 21, 1783.

[34] Benjamin Rush to John Montgomery, July 2, 1783, *LMCC*, VII, 201n; Chaloner and White to ————, June 22, 1783, Chaloner and White Letter Book; Council Minutes, June 22, 1783, XIII, 606, 608–609; Dickinson Account, 656–661; Hamilton Account, 440–445; Ford, *Journals*, XXIV, 416–418.

[35] Hamilton to Gov. George Clinton, June 29, 1783, *Hamilton Papers*, III, 408.

On Tuesday Robert Morris' office was abuzz. Hamilton and the Pennsylvania delegation advised the Superintendent that Congress would likely leave that afternoon. Secretary of Congress Charles Thomson called on Morris to make arrangements for the removal. In the meantime, the Council met with the militia's field officers to seek their advice about a mobilization, explaining that Congress would likely leave Philadelphia if there were no call. The field officers recommended against a call unless the proposed negotiation failed, the demands of the soldiers became unreasonable, or if an outrage were committed. The Council accepted the advice, but nevertheless urged them to have their companies in readiness.[36]

Prior to adjourning for the day, Council received a letter from Captain Christie, president of the soldiers' negotiating committee, informing it that his committee had reached an honorable arrangement with the sergeants for representing their interests. The sergeants would present their proposals via the negotiating committee the next day. After Council adjourned, Dickinson read a note from Boudinot informing him that Congress had left for New Jersey.[37]

Why had the reluctant Hamilton, who later claimed to have been willing to delay removal until the last minute if necessary to secure a militia call, changed his mind? He was of course under great pressure from members of Congress, chief among whom was his friend Boudinot. When General St. Clair informed Hamilton that he thought the soldiers' proposals were actually new demands, and when Dickinson had yet to inform him of the results of the Council's meeting with the militia field officers, Hamilton gave in. He and Ellsworth signed a letter recommending removal to New Jersey, but Ellsworth's name was scratched out apparently after Peters refused to sign. Hamilton, however, asserted later that he, Ellsworth, and St. Clair understood Peters to believe that the committee had no alternative. Hamilton, who always implied that Congress was in session on the afternoon of June 21, drafted a proclamation which Boudinot signed after rewriting some phrases, including words that implied Congress had adopted its Saturday resolutions during the

[36] Morris Diary, June 24, 1783; Council Minutes, June 24, 1783, XIII, 609–610; Dickinson Account, 661–663.

[37] Council Minutes, June 24, 1783, XIII, 610; Dickinson Account, 663; Dickinson Notations, *Pennsylvania Archives*, Series 1, X, 60.

demonstration. The proclamation gave the impression that Congress was meeting during the demonstration. Boudinot informed federal officials (Hamilton got to Robert Morris with the news first) and the congressmen about the proclamation, requesting that it be kept secret until Congress was safely out of town.[38]

West of Fort Pitt, out in that vast wilderness to which the United States in Congress Assembled had all but secured title from Britain if not from the states, the summer sun was still shining on a rising empire. Yet, that Congress, its faithful Secretary, and its Secretary of Finance, as a result of a unanimous vote of the states present, were on the road for Princeton. What had motivated a politically divided Congress to adjourn to New Jersey in the wake of a nonviolent demonstration which was not even aimed at it? Three reasons stand out. First, was the fear of a few delegates that the mutiny of the Lancaster and Philadelphia soldiers was not an isolated event. Congress was beginning to hear about mutinies throughout the states. Was there a grand design behind it all? Had the flame suppressed at Newburgh been rekindled, two delegates pointedly wondered? Was the Revolution to be subverted, as had been so often the case in history, "by the swords of a mutinous or victorious Army?"[39] Second, the federal government desperately needed more political power and public support. The mutiny provided a final, unexpected opportunity to assert the claims of that government and to rally public opinion to its support. Centralists knew they took a great risk in removing from Philadelphia because some people, particularly in Europe where public credit was at stake, might interpret the removal as an act of weakness instead of strength.[40] But its temporary nature and the triumphal return of Congress to its capital when order was restored made the risk worth taking. Some centralists such as Madison, and moderates such as the two North Carolina delegates, questioned the need for the removal, but they saw the necessity of asserting Congress' right to

---

[38] Hamilton Account, 447–448; Dickinson Account, 662; Hamilton to Boudinot, June 24, 1783, Hamilton's draft of the proclamation, June 24, 1783, Boudinot Papers, DLC; Madison to Hamilton, Oct. 16, 1783, *Madison Papers*, VII, 383.

[39] North Carolina Delegates to Gov. Alexander Martin, Aug. 1, 1783, *LMCC*, VII, 246–247.

[40] On the prestige and power of Congress in 1783, see Hamilton, "Defense of Congress," [July 1783], *Hamilton Papers*, III, 426–430. On Hamilton's awareness of the dangers of a removal see his letter to Madison, June 29, 1783, *ibid.*, III, 409, and Hamilton Account, 447.

protection where it resided. As the North Carolina delegates expressed it to their governor, "the respect which we owe to the Sovereign State we have the honor to represent, required that we should leave a city in which protection was expressly refused us, even though there had not been other motives more closely connected with the public safety."[41] The third reason deserves special attention. "The prevailing idea" in Philadelphia, Hamilton noted on a visit back to the city, "is that the actors in the removal of Congress were influenced by the desire of getting them out of the city. . . ."[42]

Except for two periods when the British Army drove Congress out of Philadelphia, that city had been the American capital since 1774, but for a variety of reasons congressmen had long been unhappy about it. Philadelphia was an expensive place to live. The pressures of a large commercial city, including mob action, repeatedly interfered with Congress' independence, and, some feared, even threatened the existence of a Republic. Further, because of its proximity to Congress, the government of Pennsylvania had exercised more influence over the affairs of the Union than had other states. Congress similarly had an unnatural effect on Pennsylvania politics. Several conflicts between the two governments (Gouverneur Morris had been the central figure in the most heated) had occurred. In response to offers of capital sites from New York and Maryland, Congress had agreed early in June 1783 to select a post-war capital in October.[43]

Although some centralists had indicated their desire to leave Philadelphia prior to the June mutiny, decentralists such as Stephen Higginson and Samuel Holten of Massachusetts, Jonathan Arnold of Rhode Island, Arthur Lee and Theodorick Bland of Virginia, and Ralph Izard of South Carolina were particularly anxious to leave.[44]

41 North Carolina Delegates to Gov. Alexander Martin, Aug. 1, 1783, *LMCC*, VII, 248. See also Eleazer McComb to President Nicholas Van Dyke of Delaware, June 30, 1783, *ibid.*, 206–207.

42 To Madison, July 6, 1783, *Hamilton Papers*, III, 412.

43 On Congress' troubled residence at Philadelphia from 1774 to 1783, see Brunhouse, *Counter-Revolution*, Chapters 2–4; and my forthcoming book on the location of the United States Capital.

44 Nathaniel Gorham to Caleb Davis, June 4, 1783, Caleb Davis Papers, Massachusetts Historical Society; Ellsworth to Gov. Jonathan Trumbull, June 4, 1783, *LMCC*, VII, 180. Although the decentralists did not oppose all efforts to strengthen the central government, they were vigilant in their belief that the federal government should be the creature of supreme states.

They had come to see Congress' residence at Philadelphia as the symbol of all that was evil in the post-1780 centralist vision of a strong federal government. Lee complained in 1782 that "the residence of Congress in the bosom of *Toryism* . . . is as impolitic as it is unjust," and he had repeated in 1783 that "Congress have set too long in a City where every man affects the Politician. . . . They must move to some Spot where they will have a better chance to act independently."[45] These men welcomed the opportunity to escape from Philadelphia and "Morrisonian slavery." They had attempted without success to remove Congress from Philadelphia when Dickinson first informed Congress that soldiers from Lancaster were on the road for the city.[46]

In addition to the reasons for leaving which pushed from Philadelphia, there was also a pull. Certain Middle States delegates, well aware of the financial and other benefits of the residence of Congress, saw in the mutiny an opportunity to get Congress into their own state and this influenced their conduct, though probably not to the extent that the Pennsylvanians believed. Maryland's sole delegate, James McHenry, was convinced that if his state's troops had not joined in the mutinous June 13 memorial to Congress, he could have effected his "favorite scheme"—making Annapolis the American Hague.[47]

President Boudinot more than any other seized the opportunity. "I wish Jersey to show her readiness on this occasion as it may fix Congress as to their permanent residence," he prompted his brother at home. From the Governor of New Jersey he sought assurance that the citizens and the state would show Congress more respect than Pennsylvania and its citizens had: "the Honor and dignity of the United States are at stake." Boudinot also reminded the Governor, who already had "good reason" to think that Congress would prefer New Jersey to either Maryland or New York for its permanent capital, that even a temporary removal would benefit their state. Boudinot told the Governor that if Congress came to New Jersey it would go to Princeton, not Trenton. Boudinot chose

---

45 To Francis Dana [?], July 6, 1782, to ————, May 1783, *LMCC*, VI, 379, VII, 156.
46 John Scott to Arthur Lee, Aug. 20, 1783, Lee Papers, quoted by permission of the Houghton Library, Harvard University; "Notes on Debates," June 19, 1783, *Madison Papers*, VII, 165.
47 To Thomas S. Lee, June 28 [26?], 1783, McHenry Papers.

Princeton—a decision made before the Hamilton Committee recommended removal—because he knew the town well. He had lived there from boyhood through college and had married into its most prominent family. The fact that Trenton, like Philadelphia, was the residence of a state government may have influenced him also. Madison, who like Ellsworth and other delegates knew the village from college days, noted later that Princeton was chosen over Trenton because it was the least unfit of the two towns.[48]

Nevertheless, it was Hamilton more than Boudinot who was accused by the Pennsylvanians and others of using the mutiny to take Congress ultimately to his own state. "I am told," he informed Madison less than a week after Congress left Philadelphia, "that this insinuation has been pointed at me in particular." He sought testimony from Madison so that his friends could vindicate him. In particular he asked Madison to confirm that he had in fact urged delay in leaving Philadelphia.[49] Madison confirmed, as did Boudinot and Dickinson, that Hamilton had opposed removal except as a last resort,[50] but Madison also gave a centralist ally in Virginia reason to comment "that two of the members of the Committee were disposed to advise the President to the Measure which his inclination encouraged them to adopt I have no doubt. . . . Mr. H———'s excuse for concurring in the measure is by no means satisfactory."[51]

It is impossible to determine how much Hamilton, who was the central figure in the removal, acted from such a motive. He clearly supported the effort of New York to obtain the capital and lamented to its Governor after the removal that New York's offers of space at Kingston had not been more liberal. "It is probable if they had been, the scales would incline in our favour. . . . I need not urge the advantages that will accrue to a state from being the residence of

---

[48] Elias to Elisha Boudinot, June 23, 1783, *LMCC*, VII, 195; Boudinot to Gov. William Livingston, June 23, 1783, Boudinot Papers; Livingston to the Assembly, June 12, 1783, *Henkels Catalog No. 860* (1901), item 548; George Boyd, *Elias Boudinot* (Princeton, 1952), Ch. 1; "Notes on Congress' Place of Residence," [c. Oct. 14, 1783], *Madison Papers*, VII, 379.

[49] June 29, July 6, 1783, *Hamilton Papers*, III, 408–409, 412.

[50] Madison to Hamilton, Oct. 16, 1783, *Madison Papers*, VII, 382–383; Boudinot to Rush, July 25, 1783, Boudinot Papers; Dickinson Account, 662.

[51] Joseph Jones to Madison, July 14, 1783, *Madison Papers*, VII, 222–224n1.

Congress."[52] On the other hand, Hamilton never implicated himself. Whatever effect the desire of New Yorkers to obtain the capital had on Hamilton's conduct during the mutiny, he never escaped the insinuation. An allegory published in Philadelphia asserted that the ship *Congress* after escaping all sorts of dangers during the Revolution, including "Lee shores," had sunk, and that some members "were privy to the sinking" desiring that she should be "moored hereafter, at a new warf lately built on the North [Hudson] River." Even the grave did not spare Hamilton and his friend Boudinot from the allegations.[53]

After Congress left Philadelphia, the mutiny quickly subsided. Boudinot's proclamation was posted throughout the city Tuesday night only to be torn down by soldiers and disgusted citizens. Expectations of violence were still adrift Wednesday morning when Council and an exhausted Dickinson (he had stayed awake all night because of a rumored attack on the Bank which never materialized) called out 100 militia to secure the government from insult and the State and City from injury.[54]

As word spread among the citizens that Congress had "decampt in the night," Captains Christie and Symonds of the soldiers' negotiating committee arrived at the State House. They brought a written apology from the sergeants for their behavior in front of the State House as well as a denial and condemnation of any such desperate acts as an attack on the Bank. The two officers also had the soldiers' proposals with them. All but the last, which requested a pardon, concerned settlement of the Line's accounts. The soldiers apologized separately for their behavior on Saturday but claimed in their own defense that they had been inflamed by the three federal officials who had visited them at the barracks the night before. In particular they pointed to one whom they did not name: "Had not that particular Gentleman . . . spoke as he did, the troops

---

52 Hamilton to Clinton, June 29, 1783, *Hamilton Papers*, III, 408.

53 (Philadelphia) *Independent Gazetteer*, Aug. 9, 1783. A writer in the *American Register* asserted in 1809 (V, 379) that the removal had been contrived by Boudinot and Hamilton to get Congress first to New Jersey and, later, to New York City.

54 (Philadelphia) *Pennsylvania Gazette*, June 28, 1783; Rush to Montgomery, June 27, 1783, Lyman H. Butterfield, ed., *The Letters of Benjamin Rush* (Princeton, 1951), I, 302; Dickinson Notations, *Pennsylvania Archives*, Series 1, X, 60; Council Minutes, June 25, 1783, XIII, 611.

would not [have] assembled." The soldiers requested that they receive one half of all the pay due to them before accepting furlough; that the rest be paid in interest bearing certificates—but not the worthless kind they had received previously; and that arrangements be made to settle their accounts—the clothing, rations, land patents, and other special gratuities promised when they had enlisted.[55]

Council refused to consider the proposals until the soldiers made a full and satisfactory submission to Congress. Christie and Symonds agreed to so inform the soldiers but warned the Council that the soldiers might respond violently because they "did not think they had offended Congress, as their intention on Saturday was only to apply to Council." When the two Captains left, Council raised its militia call to 500 men. On his return to the barracks, Christie opened a cryptic note from Carbery and Sullivan to one of the sergeants. Christie and Symonds took it to Colonel Humpton, who along with the sergeants, went to Dickinson. Convinced that the note meant that the two ringleaders had fled, the sergeants considered themselves betrayed. Humpton proposed, and Dickinson agreed, that the officers and sergeants should return to the barracks to convince the soldiers to submit, and in this they were successful.[56]

Benjamin Rush was one of several citizens involved in these negotiations. He believed that he was the key figure in convincing the soldiers to submit. Since the soldiers were worried that should they do so unconditionally they would be punished, Rush went to Dickinson who promised to plead their case to Congress if they laid down their arms. The soldiers were at first dubious, but agreed to go as a group to Dickinson's home near the State House if Rush would come along as security. Very sympathetic to the sufferings of the soldiers and a lover of the limelight, Rush agreed immediately. With the exception of the Lancaster troops, the soldiers—with Rush placed among the leaders at the front—marched to Dickinson's in the evening. Dickinson came out, stood on a table, and addressed

[55] Christopher Marshall Diary, June 25, 1783, HSP; Council Minutes, June 25, 1783, XIII, 612; Dickinson Account, 664; Bennett to Council, June 25, 1783, Address of the Mutineers, June 25, 1783, RG 360, Item 38, folios 29-[30], 33-[38].

[56] Asserting that they had been the sole instigators of the mutiny, the two men went to London. Both later returned to the United States.

them by candlelight. He lectured on their "unprecedented and heinous fault," promised to recommend their pardon to Congress, and demanded as proof of their reformed disposition that they join the militia to reduce the Lancaster troops should they not leave Philadelphia within twenty-four hours.[57] Dickinson then informed Boudinot that the mutiny was over.

On Thursday, just as Boudinot received Dickinson's letter, most of the Lancaster troops submitted at morning roll call. By nightfall all were on the road home. Dickinson informed Boudinot on Thursday night and again on Friday morning that the situation in Philadelphia had returned to normal. There had been no property damage or injury to life during the entire two-week mutiny. Because of the temporary nature of the removal, Dickinson and other Philadelphians expected Congress to return immediately.[58] Few dreamt Congress would wait more than seven years.

Washington did not adopt Boudinot's suggestion that he personally lead the troops from Army Headquarters to Philadelphia. Instead, Washington dispatched General Robert Howe and 1,500 men of the Massachusetts Line. Even though it knew the mutiny was over, Congress, on July 1, ordered Howe to march to Philadelphia. It also adopted Hamilton's motion for Howe to bring to trial all army personnel involved in the mutiny and to examine fully all circumstances related to it. Howe was cautioned to consult with the Pennsylvania Council on all matters touching civil authority.[59] The General remained in Philadelphia for several weeks and probably did more than anyone to ease tensions. He took depositions from participants and witnesses, and by the end of July several men were court-martialed. The court-martial acquitted Captain Christie, Captain Symonds, and Lieutenant Houston. John Steele, the fourth member of the soldiers negotiating committee was not court-martialed. The other two members of the committee, Sullivan and

---

[57] Council Minutes, June 25, 1783, XIII, 611–612; Dickinson Account, 664–665; draft of Dickinson Account, Dickinson Papers, HSP; Humpton Account, folios [8]–9; Dickinson Notations, Pennsylvania Archives, Series 1, X, 60; Rush to [John Adams], April 1812, Rush Papers, Library Company of Philadelphia, HSP.

[58] Dickinson to Boudinot, June 25, 26, 27, 1783, RG 360, Item 38, folios 127, 135, 143, National Archives.

[59] Boudinot to Washington, June 26, July 1, 1783, LMCC, VII, 200, 208; Ford, Journals, XXIV, 411-413.

Carbery, had fled. Sentenced to whippings were gunner Lilly, drummer Horn, and privates Thomas Flowers and William Carman. Sentenced to death by hanging were the two sergeants who had led the demonstration, John Morrison and Christian Nagle. Pennsylvania requested pardons for all the men, and Nagle and Morrison petitioned Congress for pardon. Mary Morris and Mary Dickinson signed both petitions thus indicating their husbands' positions. While Congress pardoned all parties sentenced, it struck from the resolution praise to the army for submitting so long to innumerable wants and hardships and the statement that the troops involved in the mutiny had submitted quickly. Congress also voted special thanks to Howe for his conduct during "the delicate investigation of so atrocious an offense." By then Paymaster General John Pierce had begun the settlement of accounts authorized by Congress early in July, a task he had not completed when he died five years later. And in October, Congress discharged the army it had furloughed in May.[60]

Many observers of the mutiny were convinced that civilians with deep designs were behind the affair, and that Carbery and Sullivan were mere pawns in a grand design. James Mercer punned to his brother at Congress to "sift every thing to the bottom as it [Congress] will discover some Capital movers in this nefarious business." Madison was convinced that the "real plan and object" lay in "profound darkness," and Hamilton and Boudinot believed that much more than the settlement of accounts had been at stake. General Howe informed Boudinot at the end of his investigation that "the ultimate ends . . . of this horrid transaction were of greater magnitude and of deeper design than as yet can be made to appear." Nevertheless, there is no evidence to support such contentions and they appear as unfounded as all of the other rumors which circulated in Philadelphia during the mutiny.[61]

[60] Ford, *Journals*, XXIV, 426–427, 509–510, 514, XXV, 564–567, 703; RG 360, Item 38, folios 151, 185–187, 189; Boudinot to Howe, Sept. 13, 1783, *LMCC*, VII, 297; *Pierce's Register*, introduction.

[61] James to John Mercer, July 15, 1783, Mercer Papers, Virginia Historical Society; Madison to Thomas Jefferson, Sept. 20, 1783, *Madison Papers*, VII, 354; Hamilton Account, 457; Boudinot to Rush, July 25, 1783, Boudinot Papers; Howe to Boudinot, Sept. 2, 1783, RG 360, Item 38, folio 119.

The summer of 1783 was filled with charges and countercharges between the partisans of Pennsylvania and those of Congress over the necessity of the move to Princeton and the degree of blame due Congress or Pennsylvania. At the official level, Hamilton and Ellsworth prepared a report describing their committee's dealings with Pennsylvania in the wake of the demonstration. Ellsworth believed it would "exhibit the President, and Council of Pennsylvania to the World, in such colours as will not be very pleasing to the brave, and virtuous part of the community."[62]

Peters, who refused to join Hamilton and Ellsworth in the report because he objected to its contents, was disgusted by Congress' refusal to return to Philadelphia: "It seems to be the Plan of some to while away the Time here 'till it is too late to remove anywhere before the Period fixed for a final Resolution for our permanent Residence. . . . Our City is scarcely mentioned [among possible sites] lest if we should get there we should never get out." He thought of putting something on the Journal of Congress to counteract the Hamilton-Ellsworth report, and as July wore into August he drafted a resolution to effect a return to Philadelphia.[63] Its seven lengthy whereas clauses were in effect the minority report of the Hamilton Committee. Peters argued that Congress should go back to Philadelphia because Pennsylvania had consented to the removal on June 21 on the sole ground that it was to be temporary; because the decision by Dickinson and the Council to negotiate with the soldiers appeared to the public to have resolved the mutiny without bloodshed; and because a continued refusal to return might necessitate an investigation into the mutiny by Pennsylvania. Such an investigation, if its conclusions differed from the investigation already initiated by Congress, Peters threatened, might obstruct federal plans and occasion a dangerous breach between Congress and a state which had constantly shown its disposition to support the federal government. Most importantly, Peters observed that a return to Philadelphia (since it would necessitate the votes of members whose known object was to locate the permanent capital somewhere other than Philadelphia) would avoid the appearance

---

[62] Ford, *Journals*, XXIV, 416–421 (Hamilton's report on the events preceding the demonstration is on pages 413–416); Ellsworth to Reed, July 1, 1783, *LMCC*, VII, 209–210.
[63] To Thomas FitzSimons, July 26, 1783, *LMCC*, VII, 233–234.

that "the Supreme Government of the United States," had left Philadelphia "for private or partial Motives." Peters never submitted his motion, and on August 14, despite assurances from Dickinson and the Council that its return was sincerely desired, Congress easily defeated a motion to return to Philadelphia.[64] Thus, the temporary removal became permanent.

Pennsylvania never conducted an investigation of the mutiny. However, Dickinson believed the report which Hamilton and Ellsworth had placed on the Journals of Congress was a gross distortion, and he delivered his interpretation of the mutiny to the Pennsylvania Assembly in August. The Assembly, still hoping to woo Congress back, did not, as was customary, order the message printed. Dickinson consequently had it published anonymously in the press. The message was self-justifying of course, but it raised fundamental questions about Congress' motives in removing. It argued that Congress reacted improperly to a matter which was between Pennsylvania and its Line; and that the Council and General St. Clair, with the approval of the congressmen at the State House during the demonstration, acted to calm a potentially inflammatory situation by agreeing to a negotiated settlement. Dickinson seldom mentioned Hamilton by name in his message but it was clear whom he blamed for Congress' behavior.[65] The French Minister believed the message left the impression with the public that the removal of Congress was not due to Dickinson but instead to Hamilton who had "soured the climate by spreading rumors" during the mutiny in hopes that Congress "would reside in his State."[66]

Hamilton was pained when he read the message in the newspaper. In response he penned, but apparently never sent, a more than 5,000 word letter to Dickinson defending himself and asserting the

---

[64] Undelivered motion to Return to Philadelphia, [July 26–30], 1783, *LMCC*, VII, 329–330. Burnett published the document under the date of [Oct. 10?, 1783], on the assumption that it was related to the debate on the permanent and temporary residence of Congress. Internal evidence indicates that it was written soon after an address from the citizens of Philadelphia reached Congress on July 24, perhaps even prior to Congress' response to it on July 28. Peters left Congress on August 14 after it voted not to return to its former capital.

[65] Dickinson Account, 654–666; James to James Madison, Sr., Aug. 30, 1783, *Madison Papers*, VII, 294; Frederick Muhlenberg to Peters, Aug. 30, 1783, Peters Papers, HSP.

[66] To Vergennes, Nov. 1, 1783, Correspondence Politique, XXVI.

supremacy of the United States government in the matter. Hamilton completely rejected Dickinson's contention that the dignity of Congress was "only *accidently* and *undesignedly* offended." It was immaterial whether the soldiers had memorialized Pennsylvania or Congress, the insult to the latter was the same. Indeed, the insult was not so much to Congress as it was to government and public authority in general. Nor was there any weight to Dickinson's contention that there was no danger. It was a "deliberate mutiny of an incensed soldiery carried to the utmost point of outrage short of assassination . . . an armed banditti of four or five hundred men" who might in "a fit of intoxication . . . make the city a scene of plunder and massacre." These soldiers "were reduced by coertion [on the part of Congress] not overcome by mildness [on the part of Pennsylvania]" as Dickinson had insisted.

"The Multitude," Hamilton knew, would likely "conclude that the affair was of triffling consequence," that Congress "discovered a prudish nicety and irritability about their own dignity" while Council "were more temperate, more humane and possessed of greater foresight." The bias in favor of an injured army, "the propensity of the human mind to lean to the speciousness of professed humanity rather than to the harshness of authority," the imperfect notions of what is due to public authority in an infant popular government, and "the insinuating plausibility of a well constructed *message*," will all act, he complained to Dickinson, to support the multitude in its conclusion.[67]

For Hamilton a "chain of ideas" naturally connected the removal of Congress from Philadelphia with its weakness and want of public support. "New governments emerging out of a revolution, are naturally deficient in authority," wrote Hamilton in a piece intended for the Philadelphia press in July. "This observation applies with peculiar force to the government of the union; the constitutional imbecility of which must be apparent to every man of reflection." The fault lay in the Constitution, not in its administration, and when Congress made attempts to strengthen itself it was "branded with the imputations of a spirit of encroachment and a lust of power." "To be happy," the states "must have a stronger

67 Hamilton Account, 438–460.

bond of Union and a Confederation capable of drawing forth the resources of the Country."[68]

Dickinson and Hamilton sought to establish their own veracity in their analyses of Congress' response to the mutiny. Each man wrote not only for immediate vindication but also for history. Both versions are necessary to understand what happened and why. Hamilton believed that the necessity of asserting the dignity and supremacy of the federal government justified the means Congress employed. Dickinson believed otherwise, but his defense of Pennsylvania in the confrontation with the federal government did not diminish his commitment to the same end as Hamilton. Along with his message on the mutiny, he also submitted one which urged Pennsylvania to institute new efforts to strengthen the federal government. Despite agreement on the necessity of supporting the dignity and powers of Congress, the two adversaries disagreed about the means Congress employed during and after the mutiny to assert it. Historians have always settled the dispute in favor of Hamilton and the federal government.

The constitutional crisis which faced the United States in the spring of 1783 ended when Congress left Philadelphia. It was resolved in favor of continued state supremacy within the federal government and of executive dependence on Congress. For centralist allies Hamilton and Dickinson, among many others, this meant five more years of struggle. No upsurge of public support for Congress grew out of the mutiny, and in the process centralists lost the stability and concentration of political and financial power which had supported them at Philadelphia. Instead, Congress wandered about the Middle States for eighteen months until it settled, as the Philadelphians had predicted in the wake of the mutiny, at New York City. The only benefit to the centralists from the mutiny was the great push it gave the novel American concept that a central government should have exclusive jurisdiction over the place at which it resided. But even that would take years to accomplish. When it was proposed on the floor of Congress in September 1783, the decentralists, whose rapidly ascending influence in Congress was evident in the refusal to return to Philadelphia, easily turned the

[68] Defense of Congress, [July 1783], *Hamilton Papers*, III, 426–430.

idea aside.[69] "You will readily conceive that a recollection of the events which have taken place these six months past give me the most pungent pain," the Philadelphia centralist, Secretary of Congress Charles Thomson, complained to the momentarily retired Richard Peters in January 1784. "Oh that it could be obliterated from the annals of America and utterly effaced from my memory!"[70]

When John Dickinson died in February 1808, Congress had just turned back the efforts of a New Jersey congressman to abandon the District of Columbia in order to return to Philadelphia. Members of both houses unanimously agreed to wear black crepe on their left arms as a testimony of *national* gratitude.[71] The United States government at the time of Dickinson's death bore little resemblance to the government which had asserted in 1783 that it had been surrounded by armed soldiers and unprotected by Dickinson and Pennsylvania. In 1783 a federal government, still in its infancy and seeking a larger share of the political power in America for itself, had considered itself doubly insulted. It chose to interpret the insults in such a way as to appeal for the public support it desperately needed, basing that appeal on the popular concept of civilian control of the military and on the dignity owed Congress by the government of the state in which it resided. The real insult to the United States in June 1783 was devastating in its implications: Continental soldiers under the command and control of Congress ignored the federal government and sought instead to settle their accounts with the State of Pennsylvania. This fact, and not the assertion that Congress left because it had been surrounded by soldiers and unprotected by Pennsylvania, is the reason why the mutiny and subsequent removal of Congress is an appropriate symbol of the lack of power and prestige of the federal government in 1783.

Madison, Wis.   KENNETH R. BOWLING

[69] See *LMCC*, VII, 302n, and my forthcoming book on the location of the United States Capital for information on the debate over the jurisdiction of Congress.

[70] Jan. 19, 1784, *LMCC*, VII, 421.

[71] Joseph Gales and W. W. Seaton, comps., *Annals of Congress* (Washington, 1834–56), XVII, 234, XVIII, 1532–1579, 1648.

The Nationalists of 1781-1783 and the Economic Interpretation of the Constitution

E. JAMES FERGUSON

Iɴ spite of such leaders as George Washington, Alexander Hamilton, James Madison, Robert Morris, and others who were later enrolled among the Founding Fathers, the Nationalist movement of 1781-1783 has not made a distinct impression on historical interpretations of the early national period. Surprisingly, it is seldom brought into disputes over the economic background of the Constitution—a matter to which it is precisely relevant.[1]

It should make a difference to historians that constitutional revision and Hamiltonian funding were first linked together not in 1787, not in 1790, but in the closing years of the Revolution. The movement to reorganize the central government was started by the Nationalists of 1781-1783. They coupled economic with political objectives, formulated a program, and lined up a body of actual and potential supporters for whom such a program had a special appeal. The merger of political and economic goals was organic, and the essential elements of Hamiltonian funding were adopted with the Constitution.

The effort to strengthen Congress began in 1780, in many ways the most discouraging year of the war, when military defeats and the depreciation of paper money seriously undermined patriot morale. Congress, convinced that any further output of Continental currency would destroy what little value it still had, ended emissions late in 1779—a courageous act, but one that left it without funds. As long as Continental currency had value, Congress

Mr. Ferguson is professor of history in Queens College.

[1] Modern studies that bring out the implications of the Nationalist movement most explicitly are Clarence L. Ver Steeg, *Robert Morris: Revolutionary Financier: With an Analysis of his Earlier Career* (Philadelphia, 1954); Merrill Jensen, *The New Nation: A History of the United States During the Confederation, 1781-1789* (New York, 1950), and E. James Ferguson, *The Power of the Purse: A History of American Public Finance, 1776-1790* (Chapel Hill, 1961). The economic phases of the movement are implicit throughout Robert A. East, *Business Enterprise in the American Revolutionary Era* (New York, 1938); and the political aspects are treated in George Bancroft, *History of the Formation of the Constitution of the United States* (2 vols., New York, 1882).

·241·

enjoyed a freedom of action incommensurate with its constitutional powers under the still unratified Articles of Confederation. The stoppage of emissions disclosed its weakness.[2]

Any political change appealed to some persons more than to others and could be expected to have differential effects upon various groups of the population. In principle, central government was antithetical to liberty, which most Americans associated with local self-rule. Since the war had begun, however, there had been second thoughts on this matter. To the extent that state governments had fallen under "popular" influence, people who had opposed democratic tendencies favored a stronger central authority as the only available check upon abuses of local majorities. This sentiment was most articulated at the time by elite groups in the middle states, but it was a predisposing influence everywhere and certainly an element in the support for political reform.[3]

The drive for political reform was associated with changes in economic policies. By 1780, the war was supported by massive confiscations; state and federal officers seized what they needed. The people at large were surprisingly patient under these impositions, yet there was widespread resentment against arbitrary acts of government.[4] Other irritants were legal tender laws and economic controls. Such regulations were a general nuisance.[5] Merchants, especially, felt victimized by economic legislation. It could be and was argued that regulations were hopeless, that the answer to high prices and the scarcity of goods was to abolish restraints on trade, and that the solution to governmental fiscal problems was deep taxation and the abandonment of paper money. Such proposals were impractical under the circum-

[2] Worthington C. Ford, ed., *Journals of the Continental Congress, 1774-1789* (34 vols., Washington, 1904-1937), XV, 1019-20. On the constitutional point, see James Madison to Thomas Jefferson, May 6, 1780, Edmund C. Burnett, ed., *Letters of Members of the Continental Congress* (8 vols., Washington, 1921-1936), V, 128-29.

[3] The affinity between central government and political elitism is the central theme of Merrill Jensen, *The Articles of Confederation: An Interpretation of the Social-Constitutional History of the United States* (Madison, 1940). This is made explicit in his concluding statement, pp. 239-45. The same phenomenon in late colonial times is discussed in Edmund S. and Helen M. Morgan, *The Stamp Act Crisis: Prologue to Revolution* (Chapel Hill, 1953), 11-20. With his talent for the pungent and invidious phrase, Gouverneur Morris supposed in 1774 (as paraphrased by his biographer) that an American central government would "restrain the democratic spirit, which the constitutions and local circumstances of the country had so long fostered in the minds of the people." Jared Sparks, *Life of Gouverneur Morris . . . in the Political History of the United States* (3 vols., Boston, 1832), I, 27.

[4] On the magnitude of confiscations, see Ferguson, *Power of the Purse*, 57-64.

[5] Oscar and Mary F. Handlin, "Revolutionary Economic Policy in Massachusetts," *William and Mary Quarterly*, IV (Jan. 1947), 3-26; East, *Business Enterprise*, 195-212. See also Curtis P. Nettels, *The Emergence of a National Economy: 1775-1815* (New York, 1962), 27-29.

stances, but existing policy was so clearly bankrupt that a case could be made for moving in another direction. Although merchants and other businessmen made profits amidst inflation and in the teeth of economic controls, sound money and free trade were better suited to their ethics and presumably to their interests.[6]

A different group of recruits to the cause of stronger government was the officer corps of the Continental army from Washington down. After the capture of General John Burgoyne and the formation of the French alliance, military victory seemed within sight; yet, at this very point, the American war effort faltered. In the winter of 1779-1780, the Continental army suffered as much as at Valley Forge. "We begin to hate the country for its neglect of us," warned Hamilton in 1780.[7] The officers wanted a government that could raise, pay, clothe, feed, and arm enough troops to win the war.

A more direct interest in stronger central government was that of the public creditors. As Congress fell into insolvency, it ceased paying interest on the public debt. The creditors, who emerged as a political force in 1780, had reason to urge the establishment of a government capable of paying its debts.[8]

The converging influence of these groups began to affect state and federal policy and to create a disposition toward stronger central government, more "authority," less "liberty" in the conduct of public affairs, and, in the economic sphere, sound money and the abandonment of restraints on trade.[9] The formula appealed primarily to the elite, especially in the middle states, to merchants in general, and to special interest groups such as the army officers and the public creditors. It would be a distortion, however, to attribute the Nationalist impulse wholly to the interest or influence of par-

[6] East, *Business Enterprise*, 207, describes the repudiation of paper currency in 1781 as a victory for the "rising conservative movement" in which the viewpoint of merchants and lawyers figured prominently. Robert Morris, who frequently expressed himself on this point, looked forward in 1781 to the time when, by the removal of the "detestable tribe" of economic restrictions, people would possess "that freedom for which they are contending." Robert Morris to the Governors of North Carolina, South Carolina, and Georgia, Dec. 19, 1781, Francis Wharton, ed., *The Revolutionary Diplomatic Correspondence of the United States* (6 vols., Washington, 1889), V, 58-59.

[7] Alexander Hamilton to James Duane, Sept. 3, 1780, Harold C. Syrett, ed., Jacob E. Cooke, assoc. ed., *The Papers of Alexander Hamilton* (13 vols., New York, 1961-   ), II, 406.

[8] "Original Documents: A Hartford Convention in 1780," *Magazine of American History*, VIII (Oct. 1882), 688-89; Bancroft, *History of the . . . Constitution*, I, 14-16; Ferguson, *Power of the Purse*, 149-52.

[9] Jensen, *New Nation*, 45-53; East, *Business Enterprise*, 207-12; Jennings B. Sanders, *Evolution of Executive Departments of the Continental Congress, 1774-1789* (Chapel Hill, 1935), 3-5.

ticular groups. The controlling factor was a national emergency which called for new measures. The degree of support, which the proposal to confer additional powers on Congress eventually received in all the states, shows that leaders at every level were alarmed by the critical state of the war and persuaded that something drastic had to be done about it.

The man who more than anyone else worked out the Nationalist program and gave the movement some degree of organization was Morris. Congress, impressed by the urgent need for reform, appointed him superintendent of finance in 1781. A wealthy Philadelphia merchant, a leader of the conservative anti-constitutionalist party in Pennsylvania, and a security holder, he combined in his own person most of the elements of the Nationalist movement. From long and outstanding service in Congress he had gained an unequalled mastery of congressional administrative and business affairs. He was widely respected, also widely hated, but such duties and powers were soon conferred upon him that he became a virtual prime minister—the real director of congressional policy from the time he took office in the spring of 1781 until the close of the war. Morris proved to be a superb administrator. He was also a statesman, the first in the line of the nation's early financial ministers who tried to steer its institutional development from the treasury.[10]

Associated with Morris were some of the outstanding leaders of the later movement for the Constitution. Madison, who attended Congress from 1780 to 1783, was a strong Nationalist; and he backed Morris' program. In 1782, Hamilton served as Morris' tax receiver, a kind of personal representative, in New York, before moving on to Congress to become one of the most uncompromising advocates of a national system. In the army the foremost influence for Nationalist reform was Washington. Although his military position kept him out of civil administration, he continually urged Congress and the country to give more power to the central government.

The Union was a league of states rather than a national system because Congress lacked the power of taxation. This was not an oversight. In drafting the Articles of Confederation, Americans registered their hatred of centralized European systems and their high regard for liberty—which they associated with the supremacy of local government—by denying Congress the power to tax. As Congress needed money to execute its functions, it was in principle dependent on the states at every turn. In practice, it had some leeway, for it could issue paper money and contract loans at home and abroad.

[10] Robert Morris is entitled to a place in the line of succession that includes Hamilton and Albert Gallatin. Although Ver Steeg in his excellent study compares Robert Morris with Hamilton, he does not give Morris enough credit. Ver Steeg, *Robert Morris*, 193-99.

By 1780, however, its leeway was pretty well used up. Paper money was failing fast, and neither foreign nor domestic loans were ever large enough to sustain more than a fraction of the expense of fighting the war.[11]

Early in 1781, after a last futile effort to revive Continental currency, Congress struck at the heart of its problem by requesting the states to grant a permanent 5 percent duty on imports to be collected by federal officers and placed at Congress' disposal. As an amendment to the Articles of Confederation, the impost resolution had to be ratified by every state legislature. Congress at first brought it forward as a war measure, a way of securing an income wholly under federal control and, therefore, acceptable to European nations as security for additional loans then being sought. Within a few months, however, the capture of Cornwallis and signs that Britain was ready to make peace altered its significance. The impost, and whatever federal taxes might later be added to it, were to be a fund for discharging the entire Revolutionary debt.[12]

The impost breached the primary restriction upon congressional authority and was the essential first step in building an effective central government. Of equal importance was federal control of the Revolutionary debt itself. That a federal debt existed at all was inconsistent with the structure of the Union. Congress, it is true, had authority to contract loans, but, since it lacked the taxing power, it could not guarantee repayment. Under the Articles of Confederation, Congress was supposed to get money from requisitions on the states. This system never worked, not entirely because the states were negligent, but because their fiscal systems were geared to local priorities and the use of state currency. With the best of motives, the states could often meet Continental requisitions only with great difficulty, if at all. In a country in which the operative fiscal systems were those of thirteen local and diverse entities, a federal debt was an anomaly.[13]

More compatible with the structure of the Union was the procedure outlined by the Articles of Confederation for dealing with the expenses of the Revolution. Each state was to be assessed according to the value of its landed property. When requisitions proved to be ineffectual, the logical solution—one in harmony with the political system—was to give each state its share of the debt and let each state pay in its own way. In fact, something like this began to happen during the last years of the war. Various states

[11] Foreign loans became an important resource for Congress only in 1781 as the fighting drew to a close. Ferguson, *Power of the Purse*, 125-31, 333n.

[12] *Journals*, XVIII, 1033-36, XIX, 110-13; Madison to Edmund Pendleton, May 29, 1781, Burnett, ed., *Letters*, VI, 103-04. The grant of the impost was to be coextensive with the existence of the Revolutionary debt.

[13] Ferguson, *Power of the Purse*, 29-31, 140-41, 221-28.

began to settle accounts for debts owed to citizens and soldiers. They absorbed all kinds of claims—not only claims against the state governments but also claims against Congress. There was a good chance that the entire mass of unsettled debts would slip into state possession.[14]

Loss of the debt portended disaster to the Nationalist movement. Without a debt there would be little reason to ask for the taxing power, since, when the war was over, paying the debt was about the only thing that Congress would need much money for. Led by Morris, the Nationalists rejected the idea that the states should take over any part of the federal debt. "There is in it," wrote Morris, "a principle of disunion implied which must be ruinous." The debt belonged wholly to Congress. "The creditors trust the Union, and there can be no right to alter the pledge which they have accepted for any other, even for a better one, without their free consent."[15] The obligation to the creditors could be honored only if Congress itself possessed the means of payment. Even if requisitions worked, which they obviously did not, they would not do. Nothing would avail but the impost and other federal taxes. In short, Morris and the Nationalists made payment of the debt contingent upon a revision of the Articles of Confederation to give Congress the taxing power. "The political existence of America," Morris declared, "depends on the accomplishment of this plan."[16]

Morris tried to make sure that unsettled claims against Congress would remain a federal obligation, and at his suggestion Congress resolved in 1782 to send commissioners to all parts of the country to register federal debts due to civilians.[17] The next year Congress declared the large sums owed to the Continental army to be a federal responsibility and refused to allow the states to assume payment of them.[18] Under Morris' guidance the Nationalist Congress clung to the federal debt and enlarged it. At the close of the war, the debt consisted of about $11,000,000 in loan office certifi-

[14] Ibid., 141-44, 180-83, 203-04.

[15] Robert Morris to Governors of Massachusetts, Rhode Island, New York, Delaware, Maryland, and North Carolina, July 27, 1781, Wharton, ed., Diplomatic Correspondence, IV, 608.

[16] Robert Morris to Nathaniel Appleton, April 16, 1782, ibid., V, 311. Robert Morris exempted the federal debt from the general expenses of the Revolution which were to be apportioned on the states. Robert Morris to President of Congress, Aug. 28, 1781, ibid., IV, 674-75. At his insistence, Congress refused to allow the states credit for payments they had made to their own lines in the Continental army. Robert Morris to Governor of Rhode Island, June 26, 1782, ibid., V, 524; Robert Morris to Daniel of St. Thomas Jenifer, March 12, 1782; Report on the New Jersey Memorial, Sept. 27, 1782; to Receivers of the several States, Oct. 5, 1782, Official Letterbook C, 97-99, Official Letterbook D, 231-34, 277-78, Robert Morris Papers (Manuscript Division, Library of Congress); Journals, XXIII, 629-31. Congress backed down from this position, April 13, 1785. Ibid., XXVIII, 261.

[17] Journals, XXII, 82-86.

[18] Ibid., XXIV, 206-10. See Ferguson, Power of the Purse, 156-57.

cates—the government bonds of the Revolution. By 1786, when the bulk of the unsettled accounts had been examined and new securities issued in recognition of claims against Congress, the debt had risen to more than $28,000,000.[19]

A debt this large was justification enough for the impost, indeed for a whole battery of federal taxes. It was a "bond of union" in the sense of creating a need to confer additional powers upon Congress. It was a bond of union in still another way. The fact was well understood that funding the English national debt had consolidated the Revolution of 1689 by creating a vested interest in the new regime. Irrespective of historical examples, however, the primacy of economic self-interest was a maxim seldom challenged in the eighteenth century. If the federal debt could be funded—that is, the interest regularly paid by means of the import and other federal taxes —security holders throughout the nation could be expected to give their loyalty to the central government. Economic self-interest was that "active principle of the human mind" the Nationalists sought in order to weaken the identification of Americans with their states and generate allegiance to the Union.[20] As Morris phrased it in a report to Congress: a peculiar advantage of domestic loans was that "they give stability to Government by combining together the interests of moneyed men for its support, and consequently in this Country a domestic debt, would greatly contribute to that Union, which seems not to have been sufficiently attended to, or provided for, in forming the national compact."[21]

Up to this point Nationalist objectives were political—to secure federal taxes and to bond the Union with the cement of self-interest. It was the economic program associated with constitutional revision, however, that gave the movement its particular character. The pursuit of political ends by economic means was certain to have economic consequences, some of them integral to and inseperable from the political changes being sought, and others not necessary, perhaps, but closely related to them.

One necessary result was an increase in business capital. That Congress,

[19] The foreign debt of about $11,000,000 was generally conceded to be a federal obligation and did not affect constitutional issues. On the foreign debt in the postwar era, see Ferguson, *Power of the Purse*, 234-38.

[20] The quotation is out of context. It is taken from a comment on Hamilton's funding program by Oliver Wolcott, Jr. Hamilton to Oliver Wolcott, Sr., March 27, 1790, George Gibbs, ed., *Memoirs of the Administration of Washington and Adams From the Papers of Oliver Wolcott* (2 vols., New York, 1846), I, 43.

[21] Robert Morris to President of Congress, Aug. 5, 1782, *Journals*, XXII, 432. His report was dated July 29, 1782. Robert Morris expected the Bank of North America to create the same kind of unifying appeal. Robert Morris to John Jay, July 13, 1781, Wharton, ed., *Diplomatic Correspondence*, IV, 563, 568-69; Robert Morris to Benjamin Franklin, July 13, 1781, *ibid.*, IV, 568-69.

if fortified by taxation, would fund the debt was certain; otherwise, its improved status could not be actualized, and it must remain a shadow, its powers unexerted. And funding was certain to create domestic capital. After interest payments on the debt ceased in the closing years of the war, the $11,000,000 in loan office certificates, which then comprised the federal debt, had depreciated in market value. If the securities were funded, if regular taxes like the impost were devoted to paying the interest, their market value could be expected to rise, increasing the wealth of the holders.

Morris in 1782 submitted a funding program to Congress remarkably similar to Hamilton's plan in 1790. He recommended a new loan in which old securities would be received at face value in exchange for new securities. After considering a discrimination between original and present holders, he rejected it as detrimental to the public interest. In outlining his plan, he proposed that only the interest be provided for, that payment of the principal be deferred to the indefinite future, and that, in the meantime, a sinking fund be employed to purchase and retire outstanding securities. Funding on this basis, he argued, would immediately benefit the nation. Since interest on invested capital in the United States was higher than the interest payments required to support the debt, the new capital created by funding, if properly invested, would bring a net increase in national income. Moreover, since the securities were held by propertied men, the gains from an increase in security values would go to persons in a position to use them not for consumption but for investment. As Morris phrased it, funding would distribute property "into those hands which would render it most productive." He also expected that it would encourage foreign investment in federal securities. He considered the inflow of money a clear gain to the country, since Americans could employ money at rates of return higher than the interest paid to foreign investors. In short, a national debt was an economic as well as a political blessing.[22]

An increase in domestic capital implied, if it did not entail, the founding of commercial banks. Despite a growing need for banks, none had existed in colonial times, and American businessmen had been forced to rely very largely on credit extended by British merchants. But as was demonstrated

[22] Robert Morris' report, dated July 29, 1782, is the fullest theoretical exposition of his views. *Journals*, XXII, 429-46; Wharton, ed., *Diplomatic Correspondence*, V, 619-34. He was thinking not only of the existing loan office debt but also of the enlarged federal debt that would result from the settlement of claims already under way. In his last official communication before he retired from office, he expressed his confidence that the debt would one day be funded and added that it was "a commercial problem which admits of absolute demonstration that the punctual payment of interest on our debts will produce a clear annual gain of more than such interest can possibly amount to." Robert Morris to President of Congress, Sept. 30, 1784, *ibid.*, VI, 822.

by the establishment of banks in Philadelphia, New York, and Boston during and after the Revolution, American businessmen were ready to start banking enterprises with money they had made in the war. Funding the debt would provide more capital for such projects. Banking operations, in turn, would multiply the effect of the capital generated by funding, for, as was well understood, banks could expand loans to several times the reserves actually on hand.[23]

Note issues by banks were a prospective substitute for state paper money. In trying to cope with the shortage of coin and dearth of credit facilities— perennial problems of America's economy—colonial governments had employed paper currency, issuing it in public expenditures and in making loans to farmers. It was fiat money, not redeemable in gold or silver, based instead on anticipation of tax receipts and the repayment of loans. In colonial times the paper money system had worked pretty well. Businessmen in most colonies, if not always enthusiastic, were reconciled to it as the only thing possible under the circumstances. What confidence they had in it was destroyed, however, by the depreciation that occurred during the Revolution.[24] In a more democratic age, propertied men had lost faith in the integrity of legislative bodies; they were afraid that popularly controlled legislatures would deliberately undermine the currency in order to wipe out private and public debts. They wanted to end the paper money system. Because it was unlikely that the country could acquire enough coin or bullion to afford a metallic circulating medium, the only alternative was banks of issue whose notes would serve as a medium of exchange. Funding the Revolutionary debt was a way of solving this problem. The capital created by

[23] Robert Morris to Robert Smith, July 17, 1781, Wharton, ed., *Diplomatic Correspondence*, IV, 582; Alexander Hamilton to James Duane, Sept. 3, 1780, Syrett, ed., *Papers of Alexander Hamilton*, II, 415.

[24] For an appraisal of colonial experience with paper money and a bibliography of the subject up to the date of publication, see E. James Ferguson, "Currency Finance: An Interpretation of Colonial Monetary Practices," *William and Mary Quarterly*, X (April 1953), 153-80. The reorientation of scholarly opinion as to colonial monetary practices has become pretty general. It has been embraced with particular enthusiasm by the new economic historians, who are highly interested in the function of colonial currency and land banks in promoting economic development. See Ralph L. Andreano, ed., *New Views on Economic Development: A Selective Anthology of Recent Work* (Cambridge, Mass., 1965), 41-56. The current reappraisal is judiciously stated by Curtis P. Nettels, who writes that in the middle colonies land banks were prudently managed and "realized the benefits claimed for them," but that serious depreciation took place in Massachusetts, Rhode Island, and South Carolina. (He might have added that the depreciation was at an early date in South Carolina and that for forty-five years before the Revolution the colony's currency was stable.) Nettels concludes by saying that it was the depreciation that occurred during the Revolution that evoked "impassioned opposition" to paper money during the 1780s—the main reason being that creditors no longer trusted the legislatures. Nettels, *Emergence of a National Economy*, 80-81.

funding, placed in banks, would provide backing for bank note emissions, which, if on a sufficient scale, would afford a stable currency beyond reach of popular legislatures. The paper money era might well be brought to an end if state governments could be induced to give up paper emissions altogether and conduct their finances by borrowing from banks.[25]

During his term of office, Morris organized the nation's first bank, the Bank of North America, which began operations in 1782.[26] Its capital was only $400,000, not considered a large sum (Morris was able to raise this amount only by buying $254,000 in shares for the government), and it was entirely specie. Morris was aware that he might have employed public securities as part of the bank's capital if the value of securities had been supported by regular interest payments. But, since no interest was being paid, he dared not include them in his venture.[27] In other respects, however, his plans demonstrated how well he had defined his goals and the means to reach them. He hoped to expand the bank's capital to the point where it would be "a principal pillar of American credit." He intended, as soon as possible, to bring about a retirement of federal and state paper money and to replace it with bank notes. In fact, he made a start in this direction by floating a mercantile currency consisting of Bank of North America notes and his personal notes. In 1782 and 1783, he had about $1,000,000 of this paper outstanding. It passed at par, or nearly so, in all parts of the country. It was readily accepted by merchants and received as legal tender by most of

[25] For an expression of these ideas, see *Journals*, XVIII, 1157-64, in which a committee report of December 18, 1780, envisages a bank note currency; also, Robert Morris to Franklin, July 13, 1781; Robert Morris to Governors of the States, Sept. 4, 1781, Wharton, ed., *Diplomatic Correspondence*, IV, 562-63, 693; Madison to Pendleton, Feb. 25, 1782, Burnett, ed., *Letters*, VI, 305-06; Hamilton to Robert Morris, April 30, 1781, Syrett, ed., *Papers of Alexander Hamilton*, II, 620, 623-24, 627-30.

[26] *Journals*, XX, 545-48. Wharton, ed., *Diplomatic Correspondence*, IV, 565-68; *Journals*, XXI, 1187-90.

[27] Employing federal securities as bank stock was proposed in Congress, April 12, 1781, *Journals*, XIX, 381. In the plan for a bank which he submitted to Robert Morris, Hamilton suggested that land be accepted as partial payment for shares. Robert Morris replied that he had thought of "interweaving a security" in the bank's capital, but had given up the idea as too risky. Hamilton to Robert Morris, April 30, 1781; Robert Morris to Hamilton, May 26, 1781, Syrett, ed., *Papers of Alexander Hamilton*, II, 621-22, 645-46. See also the plan of a bank Hamilton sent to Duane, Sept. 3, 1780, *ibid.*, II, 400-18. Businessmen already employed securities like money in making payments to one another. In his statement of accounts published in 1785, Robert Morris expressed his continuing faith in the potential economic uses of the public debt, saying: "A due provision for the public debts would at once convert those debts into a real medium of commerce. The possessors of certificates, would then become the possessors of money. And of course, there would be no want of it among those who having property wish to borrow provided that the laws and administration are such, as to compel the punctual payment of debts." Robert Morris, *A Statement of the Accounts of the United States of America During the Administration of the Superintendant of Finance* (Philadelphia, 1785), ix.

the states.[28] Morris' larger plans for the bank were too optimistic; certainly they were unrealized. Yet they failed of at least partial accomplishment mainly because they were predicated upon political reforms which did not come to pass.

Owing in no small degree to Morris' leadership, what one might call a mercantile capitalist reorganization of the country's economic institution had become integrated with constitutional revision. Between 1781 and 1783, Morris, as virtual director of congressional policy, set forth a system that fully anticipated the later Federalist program: a government invigorated by taxation; a funded debt whose increase in market value would augment business capital; a national bank that would enhance the effect of capital accumulation, afford commercial credit, and provide a nongovernmental circulating medium beyond reach of state legislatures. Morris in 1783 even proposed the federal assumption of state debts.[29] The measures that constituted this system, and to a large extent the rationale behind them, were communicated to Congress. To what extent they were known to the country at large, or their implications grasped by persons unversed in economic reasoning, can only be conjectured; but the system and the logical relationship of its parts were plainly visible to anyone who was informed about congressional affairs.

The Nationalist movement declined rapidly at the end of the war. Although ratified by all but one state, the impost amendment of 1781 failed; hence, the debt was not funded and the economic reforms contingent upon funding did not materialize. The Bank of North America severed its connection with the government and never became a national institution. Morris lost influence over congressional policy and retired from office with his major goals unaccomplished. Yet the elements which the Nationalists had put together survived and perpetuated a need to execute their program. They had, in effect, created a national debt, vested title to it in Congress, and aroused a general expectation that the debt would be paid by means of federal taxes. In 1783, Congress submitted another request for the impost grant to the states, and for several years there was a reasonable chance of its adoption.[30]

[28] On the plans, see Robert Morris to Jay, July 13, 1781; Robert Morris to Franklin, July 13, 1781, Wharton, ed., *Diplomatic Correspondence*, IV, 562-65, 568-71. Nettels is perceptive, but no more perceptive than Robert Morris himself, in seeing the implications of the flotation of currency. Nettels, *Emergence of a National Economy*, 32-33. See Robert Morris to Hamilton, Oct. 5, 1782, Syrett, ed., *Papers of Alexander Hamilton*, III, 177-79.
[29] Robert Morris to President of Congress, Aug. 26, 1783, Papers of the Continental Congress, No. 137, III, 33-40 (National Archives); Ferguson, *Power of the Purse*, 209-10.
[30] Jefferson, among others, was hopeful of the impost's adoption. Jefferson to Madison, May 7, 1783, Julian P. Boyd, ed., *The Papers of Thomas Jefferson* (17 vols., Princeton, 1952-   ), VI, 265-67.

In 1786 a new crisis reinvigorated the movement for constitutional reform. Shays' Rebellion, the paper money scandal in Rhode Island, and lesser disturbances in other parts of the country rekindled conservative fear of "unchecked democracy." Perhaps the lowest common denominator of the motives of the Founding Fathers was the desire to impose restraints upon majority rule in order to preserve a republican form of government. But sentiments like this were hardly new in 1786. What gave them peculiar urgency at this time was not entirely the disorders caused by the postwar economic depression; it was the fact that the movement to strengthen the central government had come to a dead end.

After the war, Congress and the states contested for possession of the Revolutionary debt and the consequent exercise of taxing power.[31] As the all-but-unanimous agreement upon the impost amendment showed, there was a general consensus that the Union needed to be "patched together," that Congress should be allowed to fund the debt, and that, for this reason, it should be given a limited power of taxation. Yet, the impost was not unanimously ratified; and, as requisitions on the states did not raise much money, Congress lacked funds to discharge interest on the debt. Congress was in the anomalous position of asserting ownership of the debt, but not being able to pay it.

The states claimed the debt. Responding to appeals from their own citizens who were federal creditors, the states paid interest on the debt with certificates and paper money. States redeemed federal securities by accepting them for taxes and in the sale of land. Some states went further. By 1786, Maryland, Pennsylvania, and New York had carried out a transaction by which they gave their citizens state securities in exchange for federal securities. In this and other ways, various states absorbed more than $8,000,000 in securities—a sum approaching one third of the principal of the federal debt. As other states planned similar action, there was a distinct possibility that most of the debt would soon be absorbed by the states or converted into state debts.

As this unhappy prospect materialized, the impost ran into fatal difficulties. The only state that had not ratified it in one form or another by 1786 was New York. The legislature then approved it, but with stipulations that Congress would not accept. To make matters worse, Congress discovered that the earlier ratifications of Pennsylvania and Delaware were, for quite different reasons, also unacceptable. The Pennsylvania legislature refused to reconsider its position.[32]

[31] The analysis that follows is based on Ferguson, *Power of the Purse*, 220-42.
[32] *Journals*, XXX, 439-44; James Monroe to Madison, Sept. 12, 1786, James Madison Papers (Manuscript Division, Library of Congress).

That seemed to be just about the end of the impost amendment. In despair, Congress entertained the idea of distributing the debt among the states. The procedure proposed was simple: give each state its share of the total debt and allow it to pay its share in any way it pleased. Such a step was practical and in accord with the political realities of the Confederation.[33] It signified, however, the complete abandonment of the plan for strengthening the central government. Furthermore, a distribution of the debt was certain to promote disintegrative tendencies in the Union. When the states permanently committed their taxes to the justifiable purpose of paying Congress' creditors, it was not hard to foresee that Congress would be left with attenuated functions, little revenue, and no excuse to ask for more. Self-interest would no longer cement the Union; it would bind the creditors to their states.

The failure of the impost amendment in 1786 had a note of finality, for the absorption of the federal debt by the states destroyed any real hope of securing unanimous ratification in the future. Constitutional revision as heretofore projected had failed; some other way had to be found to achieve it. The Philadelphia Convention took place in this context. The Founders met not only to protect government from the mob but also to save the nation from disunion. It should be added that the crisis was a prospective, not an existent, one. By 1787 the country was recovering from economic depression, and it had no overwhelming problems. The real crisis involved the future of the Union.

The Philadelphia Convention of May 1787 exploited a general consensus favorable to reform and the force of economic interests in stronger central government which had arisen since the war, particularly in the matter of federal regulation of trade.[34] Throwing out the Articles of Confederation altogether, the Convention drafted a plan for a national government with powers exceeding anything the Nationalists of 1781-1783 had dared to imagine. All the delicate questions of state interest upon which the impost foundered were swept aside by the grant of unlimited power of taxation to Congress,[35] a power which George Mason observed "clearly discovers that

[33] Committee report of Aug. 17, 1786, *Journals,* XXXI, 521-23. See John Henry to Governor of Maryland, Aug. 30, 1786, Burnett, ed., *Letters,* VIII, 455-56.
[34] For a discussion of federal regulation of trade, see Nettels, *Emergence of a National Economy,* 66-75.
[35] Duties on exports were excepted. In the struggle over ratification, the Antifederalists tried to limit congressional taxing power. Every state convention that attached amendments to its ratification requested that federal revenues be restricted to indirect taxes in the first instance, that additional sums be raised by requisitions, and that federal collection of taxes within the states be permitted only if the states themselves did not deliver the money. This proposal was considered by the first Congress, along with other amendments, but voted down thirty-nine to nine in the House of Representatives and not included among the

it is a national government and no longer a Confederation. . . ."²⁶ Another Nationalist objective was nailed down by prohibiting the states from issuing paper money. So deep was the aversion of the Convention to fiat money that it considered denying the power to issue it even to Congress, but decided in the end to preserve this last resource for emergencies.

As the new government was being formed, the Nationalist economic program advanced in mere anticipation of its fulfillment. Federal securities sold in the market before 1787 at ten-to-fifteen cents on the dollar. But because the states paid interest on them or accepted them for land sales, they were a good investment at that price; and speculators bought them up. The evidence indicates that the bulk of the securities changed hands during the mid-1780s. By 1790, at least 80 percent, and almost certainly an even higher percentage, had been sold by the original holders to people of means who bought them for speculative purposes.³⁷ After the Constitutional Convention met, the market value of securities rose and continued to go up with every step taken in instituting the new government. At the beginning of 1787, the market value of the entire debt, principal and interest, can be estimated at $7,332,000. Three years later, in December 1789, as Hamilton was about to deliver his report on funding, the market value had shot up to about $16,628,000—a gain since the beginning of 1787 of about $9,296,000.³⁸

amendments sent out to the states for ratification. Jonathan Elliot, ed., *The Debates in the Several State Conventions on the Adoption of the Federal Constitution* (2nd ed., 5 vols., Philadelphia, 1861), I, 175-77, 322-23, 325, 326, 336, II, 545; U. S. Congress, *Annals of Congress: The Debates and Proceedings in the Congress of the United States* (42 vols., Washington, 1834-1856), I, 773-77. See "Luther Martin's Letter on the Federal Convention of 1787," in Elliot, ed., *Debates*, I, 368-69.

²⁶ Elliot, ed., *Debates*, III, 29.

³⁷ This is the market value of "final settlement certificates" issued in satisfaction of military and civilian claims. Loan office certificates, which represented money loaned to the government during the war, were generally higher, about twenty cents on the dollar. On speculation in the public debt, see Ferguson, *Power of the Purse*, 251-86.

³⁸ These estimates could be refined by exhaustive research without altering them very substantially. The principal and interest have been estimated by collating figures in the following documents: Statement of the Liquidated and Loan Office Debt to Dec. 31, 1786, Papers of the Continental Congress, No. 141, Vol. II (National Archives); Statements of the Financial Affairs of the late Confederated Government, United States, Finance (Manuscript Division, Library of Congress); *American State Papers, Finance: Documents, Legislative and Executive of the United States* (5 vols., Washington, D.C., 1832-1834), I, 12-13, 27, 239; Albert Gallatin, "A Sketch of the Finances of the United States," Henry Adams, ed., *The Writings of Albert Gallatin* (3 vols., Philadelphia, 1879), III, 124-27. Although only $27,569,000 of the debt was settled by December 31, 1786, the amount due in 1789 ($28,344,833) seems a more reliable figure because unsettled claims had value. By December 31, 1789, the principal of the debt was reduced by $960,915 received in payment for public lands; the amount was then $27,383,000. The accumulated interest due on December 31, 1789, has been computed by deducting a year's interest ($1,643,035) from the amount stated in Schedule D of Hamilton's funding report as due on December 31, 1790. *American State Papers: Finance*, I, 27-28.

In January 1790, Congress received Hamilton's report on public credit and began to draft a funding act. Many people outside Congress thought that to give one hundred cents on the dollar for securities that had for years sold at no more than one sixth or one eighth of that amount was not only unjust but unnecessary. The alternative was somehow to deal with the debt at its depreciated market value rather than its nominal value, a procedure which Congress and the states had often adopted. One way to accomplish this was to distinguish between original and secondary holders and to pay the full value of securities to original holders but only the market value to secondary purchasers. Since at least 80 percent of the debt had been transferred and the highest market value at which securities had ever sold had been about fifty cents on the dollar, this plan would have cut the federal debt nearly in half. Hamilton alluded to this idea in his report, but dismissed it as adverse to public credit.[39]

There were only a few repudiationists in Congress. Three or four members of the House of Representatives wanted to revalue the debt. Their proposition never reached the stage of definition, but it had to do with reducing securities to market value.[40] In the Senate, William Maclay pushed a scheme to accomplish the same result by other means. He proposed to fund securities at the low rate of 3 percent interest and redeem them not in cash

In the establishment of market values at the beginning of 1787, higher values of up to thirty-seven cents on the dollar in Pennsylvania and forty cents in Maryland were given to principal securities issued in these and other middle states that were funded or otherwise supported by state governments. Higher values were also assigned to loan office as opposed to final settlement certificates issued in adjustment of army and civilian claims. On the market value of securities, see Ferguson, *Power of the Purse*, 253. The market value of indents and unpaid interest has been rated at thirteen cents on the dollar. In the estimates of market values in December 1789, the principal securities have been rated at forty-seven cents on the dollar, indents and accumulated interest at thirty-three cents. These estimates are on the high side, but they reflect what New York speculators were quoting. The market fluctuated violently on the eve of Hamilton's report, prices ranging from forty cents to as high as fifty-two cents. See William Constable to Robert Morris, Dec. 17, 1789; Constable to Garret and Cottringer, Dec. 29, 1789; Constable to Thomas Fitzsimons, Jan. 1, 1790; Constable to John Inglis, Jan. 4, 1790; Constable to Robert Morris, Jan. 4, 1790; Constable to Gouverneur Morris, Jan. 7, 1790, William Constable Letterbook, 1782-1790, Bayard-Campbell-Pearsall Collection (New York Public Library). Lower prices are quoted for Boston but a flurry of speculation raised them to New York levels late in 1789. Joseph Standcliffe Davis, *Essays in the Earlier History of American Corporations* (2 vols., Cambridge, Mass., 1917), I, 339. See Andrew Craigie to Leonard Bleecker, Dec. 19, 1789; Craigie to Samuel Rogers, Jan. 11, 1790, Box 3, Andrew Craigie Papers (American Antiquarian Society); Henry Jackson to Henry Knox, Dec. 27, 1789, Henry Knox Papers (Massachusetts Historical Society).

[39] Hamilton, "Report Relative to a Provision for the support of Public Credit [Jan. 9, 1790]," Syrett, ed., *Papers of Alexander Hamilton*, VI, 73-75. Hamilton added that the idea was "sometimes" suggested of making good the difference to the original possessor, but he did not feel it necessary to discuss this. On repudiationists, see Albert Gallatin's "Sketch of the Finances," Adams, ed., *Writings of Gallatin*, III, 124, 127, 129, 148.

[40] *Annals of Congress*, I, 1148-49, 1160-62, II, 1182, 1300.

but only by receiving them in the sale of western lands.[41] The effect would have been to keep securities nearly at current market levels and enable the government to retire them at their depreciated value as the holders offered them in bidding for western lands.

Repudiation was rejected in both houses. To advocate it was regarded as disgraceful as well as antifederal. To those concerned with implementing the political revolution that had just occurred, it was unthinkable. The proceedings of the first Federalist Congress were dominated by the logic that related sovereignty to taxation and taxation to the payment of the Revolutionary debt. Everywhere in the country congressional action on the debt was awaited as a decisive test of the difference between the new regime and the Confederation. Repudiation would have been a self-denying act, a rejection of the birthright of functions and powers conferred by the Constitution. Moreover, as Hamilton and his supporters argued, it would have undermined public credit. Any substantial scaling down of security values or discrimination between holders would have set a precedent inimical to the right of all future holders of securities to payment in full. Confidence in the government's promises, and in its securities, would have been shaken right at the beginning.[42] Finally, a repudiation would probably have ruined the valuable credit the United States possessed in Holland. Dutch bankers had invested heavily in American domestic securities at relatively high prices.

The only issue that caused any stir in the House debate over funding was Madison's motion to discriminate between original and secondary holders. His plan called for giving full value to original holders; holders of alienated securities were to get only the highest market value, presumably 50 percent. However, the remaining 50 percent was to be restored to the original holders who had sold out at a discount. Madison's proposal had a strong element of justice on its side, but it is important to note that it was not a repudiation. As a Nationalist of long standing and a Virginia gentleman, Madison carefully dissociated himself from the repudiationists and refused to join them. Since his scheme called for funding the debt at its face value and paying 6 percent interest, it represented fuller payment than Hamilton's plan, which called for an immediate interest rate of about 4.5 percent. Madison's proposal neither appeased the popular desire for repudiation nor furthered the political and economic objectives of the supporters of the new regime; hence, it had few adherents in Congress.[43] It was voted

---

[41] William Maclay, *The Journal of William Maclay, United States Senator from Pennsylvania, 1789-1791* (New York, 1927), 195-96.

[42] Conceivably, if the debt had been funded on the basis of a repudiation or a discrimination between holders, the credit of the government might have been reestablished afterward by regular payments. But this would have been a work of time.

[43] Maclay fumed against Madison for his refusal to line up with the repudiationists.

down in the House thirteen to thirty-six—nine of the minority votes being those of Virginia delegates—and it was never advocated in the Senate.[44] It seems, on the whole, to have been little more than a political maneuver designed, among other things, to make a show of opposition without offering a real alternative and to court favor among Virginians who had sold out to northern speculators.[45]

Congress in the end funded at face value the Revolutionary debt, both principal and interest, in the amount of some $42,000,000. There was no promise ever to pay the principal of the debt, only the interest; however, a sinking fund was created to purchase securities in the market and retire them. This scheme was in outline what Morris had proposed in 1782, but there was one important modification of the earlier Nationalist formula. To insure that Congress would have enough revenue to pay interest on the federal debt and also on the state debts, whose assumption was contemplated, Hamilton proposed that, for a period of ten years, the interest be reduced to about 4.5 percent. So much he threw to the repudiationists on the ground of higher necessity, and, notwithstanding the outcries of federal creditors, Congress adopted this provision.[46] Congress saved Hamilton from further ventures into financial unorthodoxy by rejecting, as Morris had once rejected, the idea of offering payment in western lands. Congress struck out all the alternatives except specie payment or the equivalent.[47]

The assumption of state debts was in a different category from the funding of the federal debt. It was not essential to the new political establishment and was, therefore, an arguable proposition. It did, however, bear a visible relationship to national unity, and this consideration was probably foremost in Hamilton's mind. Its purpose was to sidestep divisive issues and reconcile particular states—Massachusetts and South Carolina—to the

"Madison's [system] yields no relief as to the burden, but affords some alleviation as to the design the tax will be laid for; and is, perhaps on that account more dangerous, as it will be readier submitted to. . . . He will see Congress in no light than as one party. He seems to prescribe to them to follow laws already made, as if they were an executive body"; whereas, in Maclay's opinion, Congress' duty was to mediate on principles of justice between a few thousand security holders and the mass of the taxpayers. When Madison's motion was defeated, Maclay wrote: "The obstinacy of this man has ruined the opposition." But as Maclay's own remarks show, there was little opposition to Hamilton's proposal respecting the federal debt either in the House or the Senate. Maclay, *Journal*, 194-95, 197.

[44] *Annals of Congress*, II, 1298; Irving Brant, *James Madison, Father of the Constitution, 1787-1800* (New York, 1950), 298-99.

[45] Ferguson, *Power of the Purse*, 297-302.

[46] Robert Morris held out in the Senate for 6 percent. Maclay, *Journal*, 313-15.

[47] The final act departed from Hamilton's original proposals in other details, notably in funding accumulated interest at 3 percent rather than on equal terms with the principal, by rating old Continental currency at 100 rather than at forty-to-one of specie, and by funding state securities at a slightly lower rate of interest than federal securities. *The Public Statutes at Large* (Boston, 1848), I, 138-44.

Union by equalizing the financial burdens left over from the war. For exactly the same reasons, Morris had suggested it in 1783.[48] The matter was more urgent in 1790 because Congress had taken over import duties and deprived indebted states of income. But assumption, which was contrary to the economic interest of several states, ran into heavy opposition, failed once in the House, and passed only as a result of the well-known trade that placed the national capital on the Potomac. Politically, its service to national unity was debatable. It appeased Massachusetts and South Carolina, and this may have been necessary at the time, but it raised lasting resentment in Virginia, North Carolina, and a few other states.[49] Economically, its contribution to Nationalist objectives was more demonstrable. It added $18,300,000 in funded securities to the federal debt, piled up another thick layer of business capital, and converted another body of creditors to national loyalty.

The next year Congress put the finishing touches on the Nationalist economic structure by incorporating the first Bank of the United States. State paper money was prohibited by the Constitution, and banks were now the only source except, possibly, for the federal government, of the paper medium that the country's economy required. The Bank of the United States was to be a truly national institution, with a capital of $10,000,000 and the authority to establish branches about the country. Federal securities, now the "real medium of commerce" that Morris had once envisaged, were directly transformed into bank capital as purchasers of shares were allowed to pay three fourths of their subscription in securities and one fourth in specie.

The demand for securities created by this transaction drove prices up to par. Early in 1792, when securities reached this level, the market value of the federal debt, including principal and accumulated interest, can be estimated at $32,378,000. The market value of federal and state debts combined, according to Hamilton, was $43,800,000.[50] Even if the rise in the value of state securities brought about by assumption is disregarded, the appreciation of the federal debt alone since the beginning of 1787 had been

[48] See note 29.
[49] Gallatin observed in 1796: "The additional debt laid upon the Union by the assumption, so far from strengthening government, has created more discontent and more uneasiness than any other measure." Adams, ed., *Writings of Gallatin*, III, 131.
[50] *American State Papers, Finance*, I, 149-50. In the computation of the value of the debt, the ratio between the different kinds of securities that were funded was projected over the unfunded debt. The prices Hamilton gave in April, 1792 in purchasing for the sinking fund were used to compute the market value. Hamilton to William Seton, April 4, 1792, Syrett, ed., *Papers of Alexander Hamilton*, XI, 225-26. On the value of the combined debt, see Hamilton to Washington, Aug. 18, 1792, *ibid.*, XII, 232-33. At the time that Hamilton wrote, stocks had risen above par to a value of over $50,000,000.

a little over $25,000,000. A share of the profits after 1788 went to foreign capitalists, who invested heavily in the domestic debt; and their security purchases brought a voluminous flow of capital into the United States.[51] Within the means available, the economic revolution envisaged by the Nationalists had been accomplished.

What bearing does the Nationalist movement of 1781-1783 have upon the interpretation of the Constitution? First, the economic content of the earlier movement does not necessarily imply that economic motives were primary in the actual process by which the Constitution was drafted and adopted. It does not discount the range of the Constitution's appeal to many elements of the population: to gentlemen fearful of disorder, to frontiersmen desirous of military protection, to merchants and mechanics interested in federal trade regulation, and to all kinds of people who were disgusted by the erratic government of the Confederation or alarmed by the threat of disunion. Such considerations cut across economic, class, and sectional lines; and, in 1787, they fairly well united the country's elite behind the Constitution. For this reason, it is impossible to sustain Charles A. Beard's distinction between realty and personalty interests among the gentlemen at the Convention, who, if they were so divided, were doubly united in the determination to erect barriers against popular misrule.

Second, a review of Nationalist antecedents does not tend to maximize the role of crass economic interest in the adoption of the Constitution. Certainly, there were a good many individuals who held stakes in the new government too great to be gainsaid. In 1790, the 280 largest security holders had $7,880,000, nearly two thirds of the federal securities for which ownership can be exactly established from the records. The top 100 holders had $5,000,000.[52] Beneath them was a segment of the propertied class whose holdings were large enough to imply crass economic motive. Yet, if security holders were an influential group, they were only a small fraction of the

[51] That funding "created" new capital is of course debatable. Gallatin was perceptive enough to advance in 1796 the argument that it merely redistributed national income. Whatever the process, however, funding generated *effective* capital for investment—a fact which Robert Morris and Hamilton never questioned. It should also be noted that Gallatin differed with Hamilton as to the benefits from foreign investment. See Hamilton's "Report on the Subject of Manufactures," Syrett, ed., *Papers of Alexander Hamilton*, X, 278-79, 295-96, and Gallatin's "Sketch of the Finances," Adams, ed., *Writings of Gallatin*, III, 146-48.

[52] Ferguson, *Power of the Purse*, 284-85. Most of the largest holders were brokers who did not own all the securities registered in their names; hence, the figures might seem to overstate the degree of concentration. However, nearly all the records relative to $18,000,000 (out of a total of about $40,000,000) have been almost completely destroyed. These were of securities registered at the treasury, in which the really great interstate speculators, foreign as well as domestic, tended to invest. If these records were available, the degree of concentration would undoubtedly appear much higher than is suggested by the figures given here.

population; and their motives have to be regarded as mixed. Superimposed upon what might be interpreted as a crass interest was the general allegiance of merchants and businessmen to institutional reforms long sponsored by the Nationalists, a group value system that elevated their endorsement of the Constitution and the Hamiltonian financial program to the level of moral principle.

What can be said with certainty is that the Constitution does have an economic interpretation,[53] one that does not have to be elucidated by doubtful attempts to construct the inner motives of the Founders or depend upon a Beardian or anti-Beardian assessment of the role of security holders. The relationship of economic goals to constitutional revision was neither fabricated nor foisted on the country by interested men; it was organic. If the government was to be strengthened, it had to exercise the taxing power and pay the debt. The profits of speculators were incidental—the price that had to be paid for any degree of centralized authority, even for what most of the Antifederalist leaders were ready to accept in 1787. It is hard to find a prominent man who did not admit the necessity of paying the debt and who, thereby, acquiesced in speculative gains and the advantages to be conferred on the North as opposed to the South.[54] Other Nationalist objectives, such as currency reform and the promotion of banks, were not essential to constitutional reform, yet they were inherent in the funding of the debt and made almost mandatory by the constitutional prohibition of paper money. If the nation wanted a stronger government, it had to accept part or all of the mercantile capitalist formula of economic change.

Thus, an historical necessity existed, which would continue as long as payment of the federal debt impinged upon political reform. If the establishment of a new frame of government had been delayed until circumstances changed—until the debt had disappeared and the nation faced the international crises of the French Revolution—it might well have come in a different guise. In the period immediately after the War of Independence, however, constitutional revision entailed the realization of a mercantile capitalist economic program. The Nationalists of 1781-1783 composed the formula, kept it current after the war by preserving the federal debt, and in some measure committed the nation to an acceptance of at least their basic

[53] For a powerful summary of the economic effects of the establishment of the national government, see Nettels, *Emergence of a National Economy*, 89-108.

[54] Writing in 1796, Gallatin, leading spokesman of the Republicans on financial matters, said that Republicans had never disputed the necessity of funding the debt, although he suggested mildly that they would have preferred a discrimination between creditors. He himself had no objection to the way the debt was funded. Gallatin, "Sketch of the Finances," Adams, ed., *Writings of Gallatin*, III, 128, 148.

goals.[55] In 1787 the desire to form a more adequate government had many sources, but in certain fundamental ways the Nationalists had determined under whose auspices and to what ends the reorganization of the Union would take place.

[55] "The situation of our public debts and the very great embarrassments which attended all our concerns on that account, were the *principal* causes, of that revolution which has given us the Constitution." Letter on Hamilton's funding proposals dated New York, Feb. 3, 1790, *Maryland Journal and Baltimore Advertiser*, Feb. 12, 1790.

The Origins of the Nationalist Movement of 1780-1783: Congressional Administration and the Continental Army

HISTORIANS HAVE GENERALLY AGREED that the Nationalist movement of 1780-1783 emerged during the nadir of the Revolutionary War and sought to increase the powers of the Continental Congress. While noting the serious military reverses the Continental army suffered in 1780 and the near collapse of the nation's financial structure during this period, some scholars have located the beginnings of the movement in 1781 and have identified the motivations of the Nationalists as economic self-interest and political conservatism rather than wartime experiences or revolutionary patriotism. Such an interpretation portrays the Nationalists as a coalition of reactionary interest groups attempting to roll back the democratic gains of the Revolution; or it pictures them as trying to protect their investments; or it sees them as grasping for government back-pay and pensions. In all these interpretations the Nationalists appear as little more than conservatives in revolutionary clothing who exploited the army's defeats and the nation's economic distress in an attempt to restore aristocratic rule and gain financial advantage.[1]

*The author would like to thank Ken Beeth, John Catanzariti, Douglas Greenberg, James H. Kettner, Lucy Kerman, John M. Murrin, James Oakes, Charles Royster, Eugene R. Sheridan, and Paula B. Shields for their criticism and encouragement.

[1] Of the numerous studies of the Nationalists, the most important include Merrill Jensen, "The Idea of a National Government during the American Revolution," *Political Science Quarterly*, LVIII (Sept. 1943), 356-79; Jensen, *The New Nation: A History of the United States during the Confederation, 1781-1789* (New York, 1950), pt. I; E. James Ferguson, *The Power of the Purse: A History of American Public Finance, 1776-1790* (Chapel Hill, N.C., 1961), pt. 2; Ferguson, "The Nationalists of 1781-1783 and the Economic Interpretation of the Constitution," *Journal of American History*, LVI (Sept. 1969), 241-61. See also H. James Henderson, *Party Politics in the Continental Congress* (New York, 1974), chaps. 10-12. For a denial of the existence of a Nationalist party, see Jack N. Rakove, *The Beginnings of National Politics: An Interpretive History of the Continental Congress* (New York, 1979), 323-24.

A reexamination of the origins, composition, program, and purpose of the Nationalist movement reveals first that the initial impulse to strengthen the national government began in 1780, not 1781. Second, this impulse emerged primarily from the failure of congressional administrative policies and the terrifying consequences of military defeat. The realization that the war might actually be lost prompted popularly-elected state legislatures to call for increasing the powers of the central government and to send Nationalists to Congress to effect the change. Nationalists agreed on the broad goal of augmenting the powers of the Continental Congress, disagreed on the best means of achieving that goal, and, in the end, proved to be as inept as the localists who opposed them. At bottom, Nationalists' adherence to republican ideology undermined their administrative effectiveness. Yet none of these aspects of the Nationalist movement can be understood unless it is first placed in the context of Congressional administration of the Continental army and of the states' obstruction of logistical operations.

By almost any standard, congressional administration of the Continental army was inadequate through the war, as evidenced by the failure to furnish the army with sufficient food, clothing, camp equipment, and medical supplies.[2] In 1775-1776, Congress tried to meet its responsibility to supply the army by haphazardly employing congressional committees, creating rudimentary staff departments, and calling upon military commanders, state officials, and private citizens to assist in the war effort. The results were disappointing and the army was ill-served. In 1777, Congress rationalized supply operations, relied more heavily on the staff departments, decentralized responsibility, and introduced a system of public accountability. That too failed. In 1778, Congress reversed itself by centralizing the quartermaster and commissary departments, abandoning restraints on department chiefs, and handsomely remunerating staff officers. And under the leadership of Quartermaster General Nathanael Greene and Commissary General Jeremiah Wadsworth, these reforms proved effective. But relief was short-lived: by late 1779 the army once again lacked every necessity and was on the verge of disbanding.

---

[2] This and the next two paragraphs are based on E. Wayne Carp, *"To Starve the Army at Pleasure": Continental Army Administration and American Political Culture, 1775-1783* (Chapel Hill, forthcoming), Introduction, chaps. 1-3.

Congress's efforts at reform were bound to fail because of the strength of America's localistic perspective, a frame of mind common to colonists from all walks of life. Localism was both a product of the colonists' English cultural heritage—in New England, especially, opposition to Stuart centralism manifested itself in a deep suspicion of central authority and a desire to preserve an established way of life—and a tradition of self-government at the town and county level. Regional, religious, and ethnic differences, the isolation of rural life, the distance between seaboard and hinterland, and poor transportation and communication systems reinforced a narrow world view. Americans' predilection for provincial tendencies made them insular, parochial, and selfish, with all the strengths and weaknesses a restricted vision of the world provides. Localism contributed to colonial intolerance of strangers, exemplified in New England's system of warning out and in the mistreatment of religious minorities, such as Anglican persecution of Baptists in Virginia. But it also created the framework within which the colonists launched and nurtured their successful experiment in self-government and defended their liberties against encroachments.

Thus, state and local authorities had their own set of priorities, shaped by political practices in the colonial era, that defeated congressional attempts to centralize logistical operations. State officials and magistrates believed that their primary responsibility was to protect the citizens of their state, county, or town. They feared the army intensely and went to great lengths to uphold the primacy of the civil power over the military. As a result, they were fundamentally committed to defending their own territory from British attack and to equalizing the burdens of the war among their inhabitants, in defiance of national priorities. The consequence of state and local provincialism was constant disruption of logistical operations as staff officers struggled against state interference with the drafting of military supply officers into militias and state refusal to cooperate in drawing up impressment statutes. Repeatedly, state and local officials subordinated the needs of the army to the sanctity of private property and the liberties of their constituents.

Pennsylvania authorities' interference with continental supply operations exemplifies the problem of localism with which staff officers had to contend throughout the war. Staff personnel complained that key workers employed as assistant deputy quartermasters, wagonmasters, and teamsters were called upon by state officials to perform militia duty and threatened with fines if they failed to comply. The fines levied by Pennsylvania authorities in August 1780 on Commissary General Ephraim Blaine's assistants for non-performance of militia duty were so prohibitive that the men quit the army and returned home. The consequences of departure from Philadelphia were severe: without the assistants, according to Blaine, "I must be under the necessity of shutting up my office and all Business cease."[3] Similarly, Colonel Benjamin Flower, Commissary General of Military Stores, protested to Pennsylvania's President Thomas Wharton that a contract entered into for "a large quantity of Shott and Shells" would go unfilled because all of the furnace's workmen had been drafted into the militia. Though Pennsylvania was the worst offender, the identical problem existed in most of the other states.[4] To avoid state interference with supply personnel, staff officers wanted their men exempted from militia service. Exemption would protect current workers but, staff officers believed, would also encourage others to volunteer for employment in the staff departments.[5]

State authorities viewed the matter differently. They claimed they did not object to exemption from militia duty per se, but only to abuses of the exemption policy. A few states could even point to statutes already on the books exempting artisans, wagon drivers, post masters, and post

[3] Ephraim Blaine to the President of Congress, Aug. 15, 1780, Papers of the Continental Congress, microfilm, M-247, Reel 182, Item 165, I, 328 (National Archives, Washington, D.C.) (Hereafter cited as PCC.)
[4] Benjamin Flower to President Wharton, M / 2, 1778, *Pennsylvania Archives*, eds., Samuel Hazard *et al.* (Philadelphia and Harrisburg, 1852-1935), First Series, VI, 463 (hereafter cited as *Pa. Arch.*). For additional complaints of state militia policy, see George Washington to President Wharton, Apr. 10, 1778, *ibid.*, 405-6; Andrew Taylor to Pierre Van Cortlandt, Aug. 19, 1777, *Journals of the Provincial Congress, Provincial Convention, Committee of Safety and Council of Safety of the State of New York 1775-1776-1777* (Albany, N.Y., 1842), II, 498; George Rice to Thomas Jefferson, Mar. 24, 1781, *Papers of Thomas Jefferson*, eds., Julian P. Boyd *et al.* (Princeton, N.J., 1950-); William Rippey to John Davis, June 12, 1778, Peter Force Collection (John Davis Papers), microfilm, Reel 79, Library of Congress, Washington, D.C. (hereafter cited as Davis Papers); Jacob Cuyler to George Clinton, May 19, 1780, *Public Papers of George Clinton, First Governor of New York*, ed., Hugh Hastings (New York, 1899-1914), V, 726-27 (hereafter cited as *Clinton Papers*); Gustavus Risberg to Charles Stewart, Oct. 23, 1779, Charles Stewart Papers, New York State Historical Association, Cooperstown, New York.
[5] Rippey to Davis, June 12, 1778, Davis Papers, Reel 79.

riders as evidence of their support for the army.[6] State officials said
they disapproved of attempts to evade militia service and avoid payment
of a substitute by serving as staff personnel for as little as a month or
two. One solution, proposed by the Pennsylvania Council, was to
prescribe a fixed term of enlistment—anywhere from nine months to a
year—for men who served in the staff departments.[7] Though a reasonable idea, it was never enacted. Instead, in their zeal to meet their
militia quotas and apprehend shirkers, state officials continued to dis-
rupt continental supply operations by depriving staff officers of needed
personnel. Although motivated by the best of intentions, state policies
undermined the war effort in the name of the war effort.[8]

When staff officers were unable to supply the army adequately, they
turned to impressment—the taking of civilian property with or without
the owner's permission and leaving with the citizen a promise to pay in
the form of Quartermaster or Commissary certificates. By 1778, state
legislatures had enacted into law elaborate impressment statutes that
gave town and county magistrates a major role in impressment. In
theory, state authorities expected magistrates to both mediate between
the army and inhabitants and provide the troops with supplies. In
practice, magistrates often protected citizens and harassed and delayed
military supply officials.[9]

Pennsylvania, however, which bore the brunt of impressment
operations during the army's encampment at Valley Forge, did more
than pass laws to control staff officers. To protect citizens from military
impressment, Pennsylvania's General Assembly created in January
1778 a separate administrative system to procure wagons for the army.
In this scheme, the Quartermaster General applied to the state's Wag-
onmaster General, who would in turn issue the necessary orders to his

[6] *The Statutes at Large: Being a Collection of All the Laws of Virginia*, ed., William Waller
Hening (Richmond, Virginia, 1809-1823), X, 177, 425; *Acts and Resolves, Public and Private,
of the Province of Massachusetts Bay* (Boston, 1869-1922), V, 729.
   [7] Clinton to the Mayor and Corporation of Albany, June 2, 1778, *Clinton Papers*, III, 388;
Pennsylvania Council to Washington, Apr. 13, 1778, *Pa. Arch.*, First Series, VI, 416.
   [8] This is a direct paraphrase of an idea expressed about Congress by Marcus Cunliffe in
"Congressional Leadership in the American Revolution," *Leadership in the American Revolution*,
Library of Congress Symposium on the American Revolution (Washington, D.C., 1974), 48.
   [9] Carp, *"To Starve the Army,"* chap. 4.

county deputies, thus removing the military from contact with the populace.[10] Later steps taken by Pennsylvania authorities reveal how serious they were about protecting their citizens. When complaints continued, the power to impress in Pennsylvania was lodged solely in the hands of the Council of Safety from whom all military officers, even General Washington, had first to secure permission to impress.[11]

The need to consolidate citizen support for the new revolutionary regimes contributed to state authorities' hostility toward impressment. When fighting commenced in 1775, the political legitimacy of the new state governments was not in every case automatically conferred. In such states as New York, where loyalists and secessionists in the northeastern counties of the state challenged the central revolutionary government, and Pennsylvania, where disagreement over the newly instituted Constitution of 1776 encouraged opposition to the state's revolutionary leadership, impressment added to the instability of the new regimes by increasing the number of disaffected citizens.[12]

Pennsylvania's Council of Safety expressed these fears when refusing to implement a congressional resolution in 1777 urging it to seize blankets for the army. Though the Council recognized the seriousness of the army's need for supplies, it feared that the "intrusion upon the private property of individuals [would] be unavoidably resented, as a grievance arising from the Constitution." And by identifying the fundamental law of Pennsylvania with the policy of impressment, state officials were apprehensive "that it will greatly weaken and disable the Council from performing essential services."[13] In this case, Pennsyl-

[10] *The Statutes at Large of Pennsylvania from 1682 to 1801*, eds., James T. Mitchell and Henry Flanders (Harrisburg, Pa., 1896-1915), IX, 181-82:

[11] *Ibid.*, 384-87; Elizabeth Cometti, "Impressment During the American Revolution," in *The Walter Clinton Jackson Essays in the Social Sciences*, ed., Vera Largent (Chapel Hill, N.C., 1942), 102.

[12] For the relationship between impressment and the increase in disaffection, see Jonathan Bayard Smith to Joseph Reed, Feb. 21, 1778, *Letters of Members of the Continental Congress*, ed., Edmund C. Burnett (Washington, D.C. 1921-1936), III, 94 (hereafter cited as *LMCC*). For the problem of political legitimacy in New York, see Edward Countryman, "Consolidating Power in Revolutionary America: The Case of New York, 1775-1783," *Journal of Interdisciplinary History*, VI (Winter 1976), 645-77. For the constitutional problems in Pennsylvania, see Richard Alan Ryerson, *The Revolution Is Now Begun: The Radical Committees of Philadelphia, 1765-1776* (Philadelphia, 1978); Robert L. Brunhouse, *The Counter-Revolution in Pennsylvania, 1776-1790* (Philadelphia, 1942).

[13] Supreme Executive Council to the President of Congress, Sept. 17, 1777, *Pa. Arch.*, First Series, V. 630.

vania authorities preferred to strengthen long-term support for the regime rather than to give short-time aid to the army. Also implicit in Pennsylvania's decision was a recognition of the need to tread lightly on constituents who annually voted on the government's policies.

State impressment laws effectively protected citizens but they made it extremely difficult for staff officers to supply the army in emergencies. Pennsylvania's refusal to include in its wagon law of 1778 a clause allowing the army to impress carriages in a crisis is an excellent example of state authorities' interference with continental supply operations. The convoluted logic guiding the Pennsylvania Council's decision is worth quoting in its entirety to convey the state's distrust of military supply officers:

> Notwithstanding there is no provision in the Law for cases of real emergency, it is nevertheless the opinion of Council that there may be instances which will fully justify the Quartermaster General, his deputies and the officers commanding detachments in impressing Waggons. If the Law had given authority to the military to impress, there would have been some reason to fear that very little attention would have been paid to the regular mode of calling upon the Farmers, whereby the burthen might possibly be very unequal.[14]

In essence, Pennsylvania authorities declared they would not permit the army to take wagons because the military would abuse the privilege; nevertheless, in emergencies impressment was permissible, though expressly prohibited by statute. Staff officers were thus invited to act without sanction of law but risked prosecution should their judgment prove wrong. State laws such as Pennsylvania's contributed to the distress of the Continental army.

Congress paid little heed to these problems with the states. Indeed by 1780, Congress was so deeply troubled by the increasing evidence of national bankruptcy that it adopted on February 25, 1780, the system of specific supplies by which the states assumed responsibility for provisioning the army. In the act's final form, each state was assigned specific quotas and was required to collect and deliver provisions to various magazine sites designated by the commander in chief.

---

[14] Pennsylvania Council to vvashington, Apr. 13, 1778, *ibid.*, VI, 416. See also Pennsylvania Council to Nathanael Greene, Apr. 18, 1778, *Pennsylvania Colonial Records. Minutes of the Supreme Executive Council of Pennsylvania* (Harrisburg, Pa., 1852-1853), XI, 467.

From its inception the system of specific supplies worked poorly. Congressional administrative oversights and failure to keep informed of the states' internal affairs contributed to the system's lack of success. But state legislatures' sluggish response to congressional resolves, in some cases willful disregard of them, and states' reliance on uncooperative local officials compounded the problem. In addition, state and local authorities now discovered at first hand what staff officers had been charging for the past year: supplies could not be purchased without money; engrossers and speculators were everywhere; and the French, with specie in hand, preempted state purchasers, especially in Maryland and Connecticut. At bottom, the problem was financial. State treasuries were empty, towns bankrupt, continental currency worthless, and the marketplace glutted with Quartermaster and Commissary certificates. At every level of government—national, state, and local—the system of specific supplies had failed.[15]

Aside from sending a committee to army headquarters, Congress's only reaction to the breakdown of the system of specific supplies was to rely even more heavily on the states. As Rhode Island's Congressman Ezekiel Cornell despairingly noted, Congress wished

> to see their States without control (as the term is) free, sovereign, and independent. If anything appears difficult in regard to supply, etc., what can we do? Why, we can do nothing; the States must exert themselves; if they will not, they must suffer to consequences.[16]

Cornell's disgust at Congress's passivity presaged a widespread sentiment which began in August, 1780, to gain adherents for increasing the powers of Congress. Forming the backdrop to the movement was the worsening state of Continental finances, the mutiny of the Connecticut line, and the inability of the states to comply with congressional tax requisitions or supply quotas. Between May and September, 1780, three additional events immediately galvanized revolutionaries to advocate strengthening the authority of Congress. Disastrous military defeats in South Carolina at Charleston on May 12 and at Camden on August 16 dealt an almost mortal blow to the revolutionary war effort. At Charleston, General Benjamin Lincoln surrendered a force of more

---

[15] Carp, *"To Starve the Army,"* chap. 7.
[16] Ezekiel Cornell to Greene, July 21, 1780, *LMCC*, V, 281.

than 3,300 men, the largest single loss of American soldiers during the Revolutionary War. Three months later, at Camden, in the bloodiest battle of the war, the Americans suffered their worst defeat: the British killed or wounded more than 1,000 Continental soldiers and decisively routed General Horatio Gates' army. Upon reassembling, only 700 soldiers of the original 4,000-man army showed up. Finally, the treason of General Benedict Arnold dramatized the weakness of the Continental army and sent shock waves through the country.[17]

Rather than demoralizing Americans, these events awakened revolutionaries from the apathy they had slipped into during the past two years.[18] The loss of Charleston, according to one observer, had the effect of reviving "a spirit unknown since the year 1776, a spirit which is fast pervading the mass of the community."[19] The hoped for revival of the *rage militaire* of 1775 never occurred, but among a significant number of revolutionaries the very real possibility of losing the war provided the main impetus to advocate new ways to win.

The Nationalist movement of 1780-1783 was a product of these supply failures and military reverses. Its dominant aim was to win the war, and its supporters believed the only way to do that was to strengthen the powers of Congress. Army officers and popularly elected state legislatures were its major proponents. What these groups had in common and what compelled them to act was either their first-hand acquaintance with the army's plight or their knowledge of Congress's impotence in commanding the resources and cooperation of the states.

As early as October, 1779, Nathanael Greene, who as Quartermaster General was painfully aware of the disruption of military operations resulting from Congress's inability to furnish his deputies with money,

[17] For the battles of Charleston and Camden, see Christopher Ward, *The War of the Revolution*, ed., John Richard Alden (New York, 1952), II, chaps, 61, 65. Statistics on soldiers captured, wounded, and killed are from *The Toll of Independence: Engagements and Battle Casualties of the American Revolution*, ed., Howard H. Peckham (Chicago, 1974), 70, 74. On the reaction to Arnold, see Charles Royster, "'The Nature of Treason': Revolutionary Virtue and American Reactions to Benedict Arnold," *William and Mary Quarterly*, 3d Ser., 36 (Apr. 1979), 163-93.

[18] Charles Royster, *A Revolutionary People at War: The Continental Army and American Character, 1775-1783* (Chapel Hill, N.C., 1979), 284-86.

[19] William Houston to John Jay, July 10, 1780 in *The Correspondence and Public Papers of John Jay*, ed., Henry P. Johnson (New York, 1890-1893), I, 380n. See also Michael Scott Patterson, "From Revolution to Constitution: The Forging of the National Republic, 1776-1787," Ph.D. diss. (University of North Carolina, 1971), 70-71.

advocated "a new plan of civil constitution," one which permitted Congress at once to be more independent of the states and to exercise more control over them.[20] General Washington fully shared Greene's view, basing his opinion on the unreliability of the states in providing for the army. "One state will comply with a requisition of Congress," he wrote Virginia Congressman Joseph Jones on May 31, 1780, "another neglects to do it. A third executes it by halves, and all differ either in the manner, the matter, or so much in point of time, that we are always working up hill, and ever shall be."[21] In the following months, Washington reiterated his dissatisfaction with state jealousies, stubbornness, and delays, and he repeatedly called for "an entire new plan" that would lodge ample powers in Congress "adequate to all the purposes of the War."[22] Without this crucial reform, Washington was convinced that "our Independence fails and each Assembly under its present Constitution will be annihilated, and we must once more return to the Government of Great Britain, and be made to kiss the rod preparing for our correction."[23]

The first step in achieving this goal was upgrading the quality of congressmen. Washington believed that the states must send the ablest and best men to Congress, men who understood the country's interests and the need to increase congressional powers.[24] Other revolutionaries agreed with him. As early as the Valley Forge winter of 1777-1778, Benjamin Rush and Alexander Hamilton criticized the absence of outstanding patriots in Congress and decried the lack of effective congressional leadership.[25] A year later in March, 1779, similar thoughts

[20] Greene to [?], Oct. 29, 1779, quoted in William Johnson, *Sketches of the Life and Correspondence of Nathanael Greene. . .*(Charleston, S.C., 1822), I, 144. See also PCC, Reel 46, Item 39, I, 209; Reel 193, Item 173, V, 161.

[21] Washington to Joseph Jones, May 31, 1780 in *The Writings of George Washington from the Original Manuscript Sources, 1745-1799*, ed., John C. Fitzpatrick (Washington, D.C., 1931-1944), XVIII, 453.

[22] *Ibid.*, XX, 242. For additional expressions of Washington's need to strengthen Congress's powers, see 117, XXI, 164, 183, 320. See also Harold W. Bradley, "The Political Thinking of George Washington," *Journal of Southern History*, 11 (Nov. 1945), 473-74.

[23] Washington to Custis, Feb. 28, 1781 in *Writings of Washington*, ed., Fitzpatrick, XXI, 320.

[24] *Ibid.*

[25] Benjamin Rush to Patrick Henry, Jan. 12, 1778 in *Letters of Benjamin Rush*, ed. L.H. Butterfield (Princeton, N.J., 1951), I, 182; Alexander Hamilton to Clinton, Feb. 13, 1778 in *The Papers of Alexander Hamilton*, eds., Harold C. Syrett and Jacob E. Cooke *et al.* (New York, 1961-1979), I, 427 (hereafter cited as *Hamilton Papers*).

about congressmen crossed Washington's mind, prompting him to ask, "where are our men of abilities?"[26] The answer was that many revolutionaries preferred to serve at the state level as governors and legislators. It was extremely difficult to overcome the attraction to high state office, the traditional locus of power and distinction in colonial society. In addition, state service had the added appeal of being near the comforts of family and home. The high turnover rates in Congress suggest that this was no small enticement. Service in Congress proved to be arduous, tedious, inconvenient, and expensive. Coupled with its lack of power, loss of deference and prestige, and manifest ineffectiveness, Congress had become by 1779 a distinctly unattractive place in which to serve one's country.[27]

The Nationalists hoped to attract superior individuals to Congress by replacing congressional executive boards with a single administrator at the head of each department. Boards needed to be abolished because they extinguished the passion which "topped all others in the eighteenth-century hierarchy of passions": the love of glory and fame.[28] It followed from this belief that "men of the first pretensions" were reluctant to serve on boards because they would "be less conspicuous, of less importance, have less opportunity of distinguishing themselves." But by allowing individuals to take charge of a department and by conferring "real trust and importance" on the office, gifted and enterprising men would be attracted to Congress and the management of the war greatly improved.[29] Seen from this perspective, the form the Nationalist program assumed was prompted not only by the desperate circumstances of the war, but also by the desire to make Congress more appealing to men of ability and ambition.

The idea of restructuring congressional administrative boards was

[26] Washington to Mason, Mar. 27, 1779 in *Writings of Washington*, ed., Fitzpatrick, XIV, 301.

[27] Rakove, *Beginnings of National Politics*, chap. X; Arnold M. Pavlovsky, "'Between Hawk and Buzzard': Congress as Perceived by Its Members, 1775-1783," *Pennsylvania Magazine of History and Biography*, 101 (July 1977), 349-64. In New Hampshire, even state government service was viewed as a hardship. See Jere R. Daniell, *Experiment in Republicanism: New Hampshire Politics and the American Revolution, 1741-1794* (Cambridge, Mass., 1970), 126.

[28] Gerald Stourzh, *Alexander Hamilton and the Idea of Republican Government* (Stanford, Calif., 1970), 106.

[29] Hamilton to Duane [Sept. 3, 1780], *Hamilton Papers*, II, 405. For an excellent discussion of the role of fame in Hamilton's conception of human nature, see Stourzh, *Hamilton*, 99-106.

only one part of the most comprehensive plan put forth by any Nationalist in 1780. The plan was advanced, not surprisingly, by an army officer, Lieutenant Colonel Alexander Hamilton, who—having fought at the Battle of Long Island, wintered at Valley Forge and witnessed the fruitless attempts to fight a war without sufficient men, money, or matériel—developed strong convictions about what changes were needed at the national level. Though comprehensive, Hamilton's program was neither extreme nor atypical. In one form or another, most of the ideas Hamilton proposed were widely shared and would eventually be implemented by Congress. In a lengthy letter written in September, 1780, to Congressman James Duane, Hamilton went quickly to the heart of the problem: "The fundamental defect is a want of power in Congress." Congressional powerlessness was a product of uncontrollable state sovereignty—the states, jealous of their independence, reserved to themselves the right to reject congressional resolves—and a timid and indecisive Congress which lacked the means or energy to provide for the exigencies of the war. As a result, Congress was overly dependent on the states.[30]

To counteract the influence of the states, Hamilton called for a reversal of the balance of power within the Confederation by vesting Congress with "complete sovereignty," making it both more independent of the states and more efficient.[31] Specifically, he proposed that Congress be granted a permanent revenue—for that government "which holds the purse strings absolutely, must rule"—by giving it the power to tax the states.[32] In addition, Congress should appoint "great officers of state—A secretary for foreign affairs—A President of War—A President of Marine—A Financier"—to succeed congressional executive boards.[33] With congressional revenue assured and its administrative apparatus centralized, Hamilton believed that the army could finally be built into a respectable fighting force. He recommended that Congress put the army on a more permanent footing and insure its loyalty by making good on the depreciation of the soldier's pay

[30] Hamilton to Duane [Sept. 3, 1780], *Hamilton Papers*, II, 401.

[31] *Ibid.*, 407-408. Hamilton quickly qualified the meaning of "complete sovereignty" by adding "except as to that part of internal police, which relates to the rights of property and life among individuals and to raising money by internal taxes." In enumerating those areas over which Congress should have complete sovereignty, Hamilton gave first place to military affairs and second place to commercial matters.

[32] *Ibid.*, 404.

[33] *Ibid.*, 408.

and by conferring half-pay for life on officers. To provide the army with supplies, that being "the pivot of every thing else," Hamilton proposed abolishing the state supply system. In its place, he called for "a foreign loan, heavy pecuniary taxes, a tax in kind, [and] a bank founded on public and private credit."[34] He suggested two methods to carry this program into effect. The first was for Congress simply to assume the discretionary powers needed and which, according to Hamilton, it already possessed. But Hamilton was not optimistic about this strategy because he believed Congress would shrink from such a bold expedient. The second method, in which he had more confidence, was to call a convention of states, whose delegates would possess sufficient wisdom and power to implement the necessary changes in the balance of power between Congress and the states.[35]

That the movement to strengthen Congress should originate among army officers is readily understandable. They witnessed the states' inability to provide for the army, observed the damage caused by the refusal of the states to cooperate with Continental measures, and, most important, feared that the failure of the states to support the army would result in the Revolution's collapse. Yet it should be pointed out, if only because it is easy to overlook what is so often taken for granted, that Continental officers' first impulse during those discouraging months in late 1780 was to seek civilian solutions to military problems. In the flurry of rancorous letters Continental officers wrote to each other during 1780, in which they acidulously condemned the people's lack of virtue and the "supi[ne]ness & stupidity" of civil authorities, the most radical method they advanced to redress their grievances was simply to petition Congress. Significantly, they never contemplated a coup d'etat against the national government: the tradition of civilian primacy over the military continued inviolate.[36]

[34] *Ibid.*, 411, 406.
[35] *Ibid.*, 407. See also Hamilton to Isaac Sears [Oct. 12, 1780], 472-73.
[36] For a perceptive and more detailed treatment of this theme, see Richard H. Kohn, "American Generals of the Revolution: Subordination and Restraint," in Don Higginbotham, ed., *Reconsiderations on the Revolutionary War: Selected Essays,* Contributions in Military History, No. 14 (Westport, Conn., 1978), 104-23 (quotation from 114). For Continental officers' growing disenchantment with American society, see Royster, *Revolutionary People at War,* 311-20. For several insightful accounts of how inadequate support of the army created Nationalist sentiment, see Charles Royster, *Light-Horse Harry Lee and the Legacy of the American Revolution* (New York, 1981), chap. 3; Roger J. Champagne, *Alexander McDougall and the American Revolution in New York* (Schenectady, N.Y., 1975), 169-170; David McLean, "Timothy Pickering: Citizen-Soldier of the Revolution," in Neville Meany, ed., *Studies of the American Revolution* (South Melbourne, Australia, 1976), 133, 138-41.

State governments were the second major group to advocate increasing the powers of Congress. This point needs to be underscored because it reveals that support of the Nationalist movement was widespread and popular. During the war, legislative bodies became even more representative of colonial society as artisans and ordinary farmers filled assembly halls and as backcountry areas gained seats in the legislature. Between 1774-1779, in New York, for example, the men who once dominated the streets and extralegal committees now ruled the state's assembly and senate. Similarly, in Pennsylvania by 1776, the old Assembly leaders had been overthrown, their places taken by men of the mechanic, or middle classes. Likewise in Connecticut, a political revolution occurred between 1779-1782 as citizens' anger with the way the state waged war resulted in an unprecedented turnout of incumbent office-holders.[37] That the Nationalist movement received popular support is surprising only if one views the Nationalists as a conservative, economically motivated group of aristocrats attempting to overturn the political rule of equalitarian radicals. Because the movement to strengthen the power of Congress was primarily a response to the desperate military situation of 1780, these Progressive categories make little sense. New York's Governor George Clinton, for instance, was at once the principal architect of Antifederalism in the Empire State and one of the staunchest advocates of Congress exercising implied powers. According to Clinton, if Congress did not have the requisite powers "it ought to have them." Indeed, "these were powers that necessarily existed in Congress and we cannot suppose that they should want the Power of compelling the several States to their Duty and thereby enabling the Confederacy to expel the common Enemy." Inspiring Clinton's analysis was his awareness of the British army camped in New York City, British-provoked Indian attacks on New York's western frontier, and widespread disaffection throughout the state.[38]

[37] Jackson Turner Main, "Government by the People: The American Revolution and the Democratization of the Legislatures," *William and Mary Quarterly*, 3rd Ser., 23 (July 1966), 391-407; Edward Countryman, *A People in Revolution: The American Revolution and Political Society in New York, 1760-1790* (Baltimore, 1981), chap. 8; Ryerson, *Revolution Is Now Begun*, chap. 8; Richard Buel, Jr., *Dear Liberty: Connecticut's Mobilization for the Revolutionary War* (Middletown, Conn., 1980), 207-8.

[38] Clinton to the President of Congress, Feb. 5, 1781 in PCC, Reel 81, Item 67, II, 358; E. Wilder Spaulding, *His Excellency George Clinton: Critic of the Constitution* (New York, 1938), 119-20. For Clinton's Antifederalism, see Jackson Turner Main, *The Antifederalists: Critics of the Constitution 1781-1788* (Chapel Hill, N.C., 1961), 138, 148; Spaulding, *Clinton*, chap. XIII. For conditions in New York, see Countryman, "Consolidating Power in Revolutionary America," 645-78.

Other state governments threatened by British military power or unable to comply with congressional resolves shared Clinton's desire to strengthen Congress. They acted on this concern in two ways: by electing nationalist-minded men to Congress and by taking the lead in initiating conventions of states. As early as October, 1779, New York and Virginia, two states most seriously menaced by British military operations, sent four Nationalists to Congress. The New York Assembly elected Philip Schuyler and Robert R. Livingston. Schuyler, an aristocratic, wealthy landlord was a veteran of the Great War for the Empire and had been elected to Congress in 1775. At the commencement of the war, he had the distinction of being appointed one of the four Major-Generals under Washington and had commanded the troops of the Northern Department until 1777. Livingston, graduate of King's College, member of the bar, and former delegate to Congress in 1775-1776, was politically conservative and had only reluctantly accepted America's decision for Independence. Nevertheless, he remained a revolutionary and was active in state politics. From Virginia came Joseph Jones and James Madison, both strong Whigs, who in the Convention of 1776 were members of the committee that drafted the state's constitution and Declaration of Rights. These men joined two long-standing members of Congress who shared their Nationalist views, New York's James Duane and South Carolina's John Mathews.[39] Although these men were of different economic status, social background, and political persuasion, they could all agree on the need to increase the powers of Congress.

During most of 1780 the Nationalists were a distinct minority in Congress. As a result, they had little success in implementing their program or relieving the distress of the army. Their one major resolution, calling on the states to levy a one percent impost on exports and imports, was easily defeated. And those resolutions that were referred to committee, a motion to reorganize the department of foreign affairs and another one to revise the civil executive departments, became bogged down in Congress's institutional inertia. In their one administrative achievement, the reorganization of the Hospital Department, the cure

---

[39] *Dictionary of American Biography*, s.v. "Jones, Joseph," "Livingston, Robert R.," "Madison, James," "Schuyler, Philip." Livingston's activities in Congress can be followed in George Dangerfield, *Chancellor Robert R. Livingston of New York 1746-1813* (New York, 1969). For Madison, see Irving Brant, *James Madison* (New York, 1941-1961), II. For Schuyler, see Martin H. Bush, *Revolutionary Enigma: A Re-appraisal of General Philip Schuyler of New York* (Port Washington, N.Y., 1969), 148-49.

proved worse than the disease. Cutting back on medical personnel and expenses was no way to improve the soldiers' health. The ineffectiveness of the national government became increasingly evident.[40]

With the army unable to keep men in the field for lack of food and clothing and with Congress standing by helplessly, several New England states in the summer of 1780 decided that more drastic measures were required if the war were to be won. To express their views, they met in a series of conventions. The first, composed of delegates from New Hampshire, Connecticut, and Massachusetts, met in Boston from August 3 to 9, 1780, to promote measures for strengthening the war effort. The Boston Convention passed thirteen resolutions, most of which exhorted the others states to redouble their efforts to comply with congressional resolves regarding the collection of taxes and the provision of supplies and recruits to the army. The twelfth resolution, however, sounding an entirely new note, called on the states to "invest their Delegates in Congress with powers competent for the government and direction of. . .national affairs" and also urged that all matters concerning the nation as a whole "be under the superintendency and direction of one supreme head." In effect, these New England states were asking Congress to assume sufficient power to coerce all the states into doing their duty with respect to the army. Upon adjourning on August 9, the delegates called for another convention to be held at Hartford in early November and invited New York and Rhode Island to attend.[41]

Upon receiving the report of the Boston convention and noting its contents "with Pleasure," Governor Clinton laid it before the New York Assembly.[42] The Assembly fully shared Clinton's assessment of the "defects in the present System, and the Necessity of a supreme and coercive Power in the Government of the States" and on September 26 voted to send commissioners to Hartford. "Unless Congress [is] au-

[40] Carp, "To Starve the Army," chap. 8.
[41] The Public Records of the State of Connecticut, ed., Charles J. Hoadly and Leonard W. Labaree (Hartford, Conn., 1894-), III, 559-64. The most comprehensive account of the Boston Convention is in William Winslow Crosskey and William Jeffrey, Jr., Politics and the Constitution in the History of the United States (Chicago, Ill., 1953-1980), III, 136.
[42] Clinton to the New York Assembly, Journal of the Assembly of the State of New York, microfilm ed., Records of the States of the United States, ed., William Sumner Jenkins (Washington, D.C., 1949), N.Y., A. 1b., Reel 4, unit 1, entry for Sept. 7, 1780.

thorized to direct uncontrollably the Operations of War, and enabled to enforce a Compliance with their Requisitions," the Assembly asserted, "the Common Force can never be properly united."[43] Two weeks later, on October 10, New York spelled out exactly what it meant by enforcing a compliance. Should any state fail to provide its quota of men, money, provisions, or other supplies, the Assembly wrote its congressional delegates, Congress must "direct the Commander-in-Chief, without delay, to march the Army. . .into such state; and by a Military Force, compel it to furnish its deficiency."[44] Like the other states, the New York's Assembly's justification for this unprecedented and radical action was the fear of the revolution's imminent collapse and the urgent need for concerted action to prevent it. Rhode Island likewise agreed to send delegates.

The Hartford Convention, which met from November 11 to 22, was in many respects similar to its predecessor: its delegates again urged the states to execute promptly every congressional resolve relating to the army's support. They went beyond the Boston Convention's resolves, however, by calling for Congress to lay taxes upon "specific Articles, or duties or imposts."[45] Even more far-reaching, a measure of the states' desperation over the future of the revolution, was their recommendation that Congress confer upon General Washington the power "to induce the several States to a punctual compliance with the requisitions which have been or may be made by Congress for supplies for the year 1780 and 1781."[46] In effect, the Hartford commissioners asked Congress to make George Washington a military dictator. Finally, in a cover letter to the President of Congress, the commissioners endorsed the idea of centralizing congressional executive boards and recommended the appointment of a man of "Talents, abilities, and integrity" to manage the nation's finances.[47]

In other ways, the states demonstrated the depth of their commitment to winning the war. While state commissioners sat in conventions, state

[43] Address of the New York Assembly to Clinton, *ibid.*, entry for Sept. 9, 1780.
[44] Resolutions of the New York Assembly, Oct. 10, 1780, *LMCC*, V, 445 n. 6.
[45] *Records of the State of Conn.*, III, 564-74 (quotation from 571).
[46] *Ibid.*, 571.
[47] *Ibid.*, 573. For other accounts of the Hartford Convention, see Crosskey and Jeffrey, Jr., *Politics and the Constitution*, III, 535 n. 21; Patterson, "From Revolution to Constitution," 82-84.

legislatures gave bite to their proposals by sending an additional contingent of Nationalists to Congress to put them into effect. Significantly, most of the new Congressmen had served in the Continental army. From New Hampshire came General John Sullivan, a lawyer who had fought in every major engagement of the war, had commanded the Newport Expedition of 1778, and had laid waste to the Seneca lands in Western Pennsylvania and New York in 1779. The Rhode Island legislature elected Generals Ezekiel Cornell and James Mitchell Varnum, who had participated in the siege of Boston and the Battle of Long Island. Cornell, a self-educated mechanic, had served as Deputy Adjutant General and distinguished himself at the Battle of Rhode Island in August, 1778. Varnum, a lawyer admitted to the Rhode Island bar in 1771, had been with Washington at Valley Forge and was later made Commander of the Department of Rhode Island. Also returned to Congress was John Witherspoon, the Presbyterian clergyman, who immigrated to America in 1768 to become President of the College of New Jersey (Princeton). Witherspoon, first elected to Congress in 1776, was an enthusiastic signer of the Declaration of Independence. During his three-year tenure, he served on more than one hundred committees and became a staunch advocate of centralizing the civil executive departments.[48]

The Nationalists had been given a mandate. How they would implement it remained to be seen. Before Robert Morris took *de facto* command of the movement in May, 1781, the Nationalists acknowledged no leader. They were an abrasive, individualistic group united less by their economic status or social position than by their contempt for Congress's impotent and lethargic management of the war and by their conviction that the powers of Congress had to be strengthened if the war were to be won.

But although they agreed that Congress's powers needed to be increased, the Nationalists were not of one mind over the best means to

---

[48] *Dictionary of American Biography*, s.v. "Cornell, Ezekiel," "Sullivan, John," "Varnum, James Mitchell," Witherspoon, John." Sullivan's activities in Congress are related in Charles P. Whittemore, *A General of the Revolution: John Sullivan of New Hampshire* (New York, 1961), chaps. X-XI. For Witherspoon, see Varnum Lansing Collins, *President Witherspoon: A Biography* (2 vols., Princeton, N.J., 1925), II, chap. I. A fourth general, Alexander Champagne, was elected to Congress from New York but served only thirty-seven days, from Jan. 17 to Mar. 2, 1781. His brief career in Congress is discussed in Champagne, *McDougall*, 170-71.

achieve their goals. Rather, as is characteristic of a heterogeneous group thrown together to solve a problem during a crisis of unprecedented magnitude, the Nationalists advocated different measures at different times and even disagreed among themselves. In the fall of 1780, the most common solution proposed was to call a convention of states which would vest Congress with authority to coerce "those States which Refuse to comply with reasonable requisitions." This plan was especially popular with army officers in and out of Congress who viewed it as a quick, forceful, and legal method to secure their ultimate end, the success of the Revolution.[49] The Hartford Convention's resolves, presented to Congress on December 12, in great measure fulfilled these Nationalists goals, but a good many in Congress, including other Nationalists, shrank from the use of military force, even when sanctioned by civil authority. "Few persons have a high opinion of or confidence in Gen. Washington than myself or a greater desire of having vigorous executive powers put into the hands of persons at the head of our affairs either in the military or civil department," John Witherspoon declared to the Governor of New Jersey on December 16, "yet that resolution is of such a nature that I should never give my voice for it unless you or my constituents should specifically direct it, perhaps *even not then*." Revolutionaries' fear of concentrating power in the hands of the military was too strong to be easily overcome even in an emergency.[50]

With the rejection of the resolves that would have authorized Congress to use force against the states, Nationalists' efforts to strengthen Congress focused on centralizing the civil executive departments and securing a permanent revenue for Congress. In the aftermath of the mutiny of the Pennsylvania Line on January 1, 1781, and with reports circulating that the mutineers were heading for Philadelphia, a renewed

[49] John Sullivan to the President of New Hampshire, Oct. 2, 1780, *LMCC*, V, 397. Other officers included Philip Schuyler, Alexander Hamilton, and Nathanael Greene. See Edmund Cody Burnett, *The Continental Congress* (New York, 1941), 487-88.

[50] John Witherspoon to the Governor of New Jersey, Dec. 16, 1780, *LMCC*, V, 487 (emphasis in the original). See also Duane to the Governor of New York, Nov. 14, 1780, 445; Burnett, *Continental Congress*, 485. The issue of using military force against the states was raised in March 1781 by a congressional committee composed of James Madison, James Duane, and James Mitchell Varnum. The committee's report, which favored the use of force, was deferred until May and overwhelmingly rejected in August 1781. See *Journals of the Continental Congress, 1774-1789*, eds., Worthington C. Ford *et al.* (Washington, D.C., 1904-1937), XIX, 236, XX, 469-71, 773 (hereafter cited as *JCC*); Rakove, *Beginnings of National Politics*, 289-91.

sense of urgency pervaded Congress. In the following weeks, measures
that had languished in committee for months or which earlier had been
easily voted down were now brought before Congress and approved. To
handle foreign policy matters, Congress established on January 10,
1781, the position of Secretary for Foreign Affairs.[51] On February 3,
an amendment to the yet unratified Articles of Confederation proposed
by John Witherspoon and seconded by North Carolina's militant
spokesman for state rights, Thomas Burke, was approved, vesting
Congress with the power to levy a duty of five percent *ad valorem* on
imports and prize goods.[52] Four days later, Congress approved a plan
prepared primarily by James Duane, creating the posts of Secretary at
War, Secretary of Marine, and the Superintendent of Finance.[53] With
these reforms, the Nationalists hoped to achieve two of their foremost
goals: the efficient administration of the army and the establishment of
an effective power for Congress to tax the states.

The Nationalists were unanimously in favor of abandoning congressional boards, but they were less united on the question of the impost. Reflecting the Nationalists' tactical differences, their individualism, and the absence of a strong party leader, prominent Nationlists
such as James Madison, John Sullivan, Joseph Jones, and John Witherspoon voted against the impost.[54] Defections from the Nationalists'
ranks were compensated for by unexpected support from localists such

[51] *JCC*, XIX, 143; Burnett, *Continental Congress*, 490-91. For the mutiny of the Pennsylvania Line, see Carl Van Doren, *Mutiny in January* (New York, 1943).

[52] *JCC*, XIX, 102-03, 105-06, 110-13. The clearest summary of the complicated history of
the impost is the editor's note in *The Papers of Robert Morris 1781-1784*, eds., E. James
Ferguson *et al.* (Pittsburgh, Pa., 1973-), I, 395-97 (hereafter cited as *Morris Papers*). For
Burke's *volte-face*, see John S. Watterson, "Thomas Burke, Paradoxical Patriot," *The Historian*,
41 (Aug. 1979), 676; Elisha Douglas "Thomas Burke, Disillusioned Democrat," *North
Carolina Historical Review*, 26 (Apr. 1949), 173.

[53] *JCC*, XIX, 126-28; Edward P. Alexander, *A Revolutionary Conservative: James Duane of
New York* (New York, 1938), 144-45.

[54] Madison's about-face was pragmatic. He thought the measure too strong and would be
voted down by the states. See Brant, *Madison*, II, 211-12. For an insightful analysis of
Madison's inconsistent Nationalism, see Lance Banning, "James Madison and the Nationalists
1780-1783," *William and Mary Quarterly*, 3d Ser., 40 (Apr. 1983), 227-55. Sullivan's biographer suggests that his inconsistency might be explained either by not wanting to alienate his
state's commercial interests or by his dislike of Thomas Burke with whom he almost fought a
duel in 1777. See Whitemore, *General of the Revolution*, 164. I have been unable to discover
why Witherspoon or Jones voted against the impost. Witherspoon may have believed the
amended version of his motion too weak.

as Virginia's Theodorick Bland and Massachusetts's James Lovell, who usually opposed any resolve that even hinted at diminishing state power.[55] Localists' support of Nationalist measures is testimony to the widespread fear that the Revolution might indeed fail.

Although broad-based, the congressional consensus was a fragile one as localists remained apprehensive about concentrating power in the hands of individuals. Hence, the question of who would head up the new civil executive posts led inevitably to temporizing as the two factions wrangled over nominations. An extreme example of this tendency was Congress's lengthy delay in filling the position of Secretary at War. General John Sullivan was a strong candidate for the post, but the opposition of Samuel Adams was sufficient to defer a final decision on the matter until October 31, 1781. On that date Congress settled upon Major-General Benjamin Lincoln to perform the duties of Secretary at War, but he did not arrive in Philadelphia until November 20 and did not have the Department of War fully functioning until sometime in January, 1782, nearly three months after the victory at Yorktown.[56] Similar delays, though not as extensive, characterized the appointment of officials to the posts of Secretary of Foreign Affairs, Secretary of Marine, and Superintendent of Finance.[57]

Even if the localists were entirely to blame for preventing nominees from taking office promptly, it is evident from the Nationalists' reorganization of Congress's top managerial posts that they were every bit as deficient in administrative expertise as their predecessors. A surprising lack of boldness and a reliance on previous administrative practices characterized the Nationalists' reform of the civil executive departments. Most striking was the similarity that the powers and responsi-

[55] *JCC*, XIX, 111-12; Henderson, *Party Politics*, 273-75.

[56] The genesis of the office of the Secretary at War is fully covered in Harry M. Ward, *The Department of War, 1781-1795* (Pittsburgh, Pa., 1962), 7-11. For Adams's objections to Sullivan, see Sullivan to Washington, Mar. 6, 1781, *LMCC*, VI, 11-12; William V. Wells, *The Life and Public Services of Samuel Adams*. . .(Boston, 1865), III, 128-30; Jennings B. Sanders, *Evolution of the Executive Departments of the Continental Congress 1774-1789* (Chapel Hill, N.C., 1931), 98-99.

[57] For the delay in appointing the Secretary for Foreign Affairs, see Sanders, *Executive Depts.*, 110. For the Secretary of Marine, see Champagne, *McDougall*, 171-72. For the Superintendent of Finance, see RM to the President of Congress, Mar. 13, 1781, *Morris Papers*, I, 18; Clarence L. Ver Steeg, *Robert Morris: Revolutionary Financier: With an Analysis of his Earlier Career* (Philadelphia, 1954), 59-61; Ferguson, *Power of the Purse*, 118.

bilities of the new department chiefs bore to those of the congressional boards they were replacing: their functions were still mostly clerical. Thus, the Secretary at War was not authorized to direct military strategy, but, like the Board of War before him, empowered only to keep military records, communicate congressional orders and resolves to the army, and report to the Finance Department estimates of the army's manpower, supply, and pay needs. The power of directing the war remained divided between the Secretary at War, the Finance Department, the Congress, the commander in chief, and the states.[58] Similarly, the Nationalists envisioned the new Secretary for Foreign Affairs not as the architect of America's foreign policy, but rather as Congress's amanuensis, a mere recorder and transmitter of congressional foreign policy initiatives.[59]

The Nationalists likewise never spelled out exactly how any of these reforms would alleviate the army's logistical problems. The impost is a good example of the Nationalists' administrative myopia. Because the impost passed Congress in the form of an amendment to the unratified Articles of Confederation, it needed the unanimous consent of the states. No one in Congress, least of all the Nationalists, should have placed much faith in prompt action by the states. Moreover, even if the tax were quickly approved by the states, it would yield only about $500,000 to $700,000: "A trifle when compared with our wants," observed John Mathews.[60] Thus there was a curious split between the ideological importance of vesting Congress with the power to tax the states, which was great, and the actual effect such a measure would have on reducing the army's distress, which was small.

The disjunction between broad objectives and specific means was especially noticeable in the new position of Superintendent of Finance, a post which would figure prominently in facilitating the army's march to Yorktown. In the congressional instructions outlining the office's responsibilities, the only mention made of logistical matters was the general statement that the Superintendent of Finance would "direct and control all persons employed in procuring supplies for the public service." But the bulk of the Financier's duties, like those of the Board

[58] Ward, *Department of War*, 13.
[59] Dangerfield, *Livingston*, 144.
[60] Quoted in Burnett, *Continental Congress*, 481.

of Treasury, consisted of monetary matters involving revenues, expenditures, the public debt, and the settlement of accounts.[61] These were important issues, but restoring the nation's fiscal integrity was a long-term project, and it is difficult to see how the Nationalists thought the Superintendent would immediately help the army. Thus, in practice, the Nationalists' prescription for winning the war was just as ineffective and visionary as their adversaries' program of relying on the states. The only difference between them was the Nationalists' powerful faith in the capacity of individual genius to surmount administrative difficulties and provide the leadership necessary to win the war. Necessity, Robert Morris, and the passage of time would prove their faith well founded.

When Robert Morris, the most prominent and influential merchant in America, accepted the position of Superintendent of Finance on May 14, 1781, he had no intention of assisting the army with its logistical problems.[62] Nor did his plans for reviving the nation's financial health promise any immediate relief for Washington's troops. Aside from proposing the establishment of a national bank three days after accepting office, Morris had no specific blueprint for rescuing the country from bankruptcy.[63] Rather, at the outset, he saw his task as Superintendent of Finance in terms of two basic objectives: first, to raise revenues—which he acknowledged was Congress's responsibility—and second, to expend the funds in the most frugal and honest manner. This last goal he believed to be "the most Essential part of the duty of the Superintendent of Finance. He must ever have it in View to reduce the Expenditures as nearly as possible to what in Reason and Justice they ought to be."[64]

---

[61] *JCC*, XIX, 126.

[62] The best biography is Ver Steeg, *Robert Morris*. See also Ferguson, *Power of the Purse*, chaps. 6-8; Elizabeth Miles Nuxoll, "Congress and the Munitions Merchants: The Secret Committee of Trade During the American Revolution, 1775-1777" Ph.D. diss. (City University of New York, 1979). For RM's reluctance to become involved in the army's logistical problems, see RM to the President of Congress, May 14, 1781, *Morris Papers*, I, 62-63, 97, 205-06; Victor L. Johnson, "Robert Morris and the Provisioning of the American Army During the Campaign of 1781," *Pennsylvania History*, 5 (Jan. 1938), 8; Ver Steeg, *Robert Morris*, 72-73.

[63] Ver Steeg, *Robert Morris*, 72-73; Henderson, *Party Politics*, 291.

[64] RM to a Committee of Congress, Mar. 26, 1781, *Morris Papers*, I, 22. For additional examples of Morris's insistence on the need of frugality and retrenchment, see 92, 95, 222-23, II, 79, IV, 119; Ver Steeg, *Robert Morris*, 74.

This point cannot be overemphasized. For at the heart of every financial measure Morris would eventually propose was the belief that the country had been brought to financial ruin by waste, extravagance, and the lack of systematic administration. These practices, he believed, had prolonged the war in two ways. They had destroyed public credit and undermined widespread support for the revolution. Thus, all of Morris's subsequent actions were designated to restore public credit and revive popular support for the war. "If I can regain for the United States the Confidence of Individuals so as they will trust their property and exertions in the hands of Government," Morris wrote the Governor of Virginia, "our Independence and Success are certain but without that Confidence we are nothing."[65] Morris understood that within the weak framework of the Articles of Confederation, "the people must be wooed and won to do their duty." By slashing expenditures, eliminating wasteful practices, and introducing order and regularity into the army's administrative procedures, Morris hoped to convince the people that America's government merited their support.[66]

The same ends—the attraction of new sources of revenue, the restoration of the public credit, and the revival of the people's confidence in the revolution—were behind Morris's plans to establish a national bank and a mint, to reorganize the Treasury, to issue "Morris notes," and most importantly, to fund the Confederation's debts.[67] But above all

[65] *Morris Papers*, IV, 46-47, I, 97.

[66] RM to Benjamin Franklin, Sept. 27, 1782, in *The Revolutionary Diplomatic Correspondence of the American Revolution* ed., Francis Wharton (Washington, D.C., 1889), V, 774. See also RM to the President of Congress, Sept. 21, 1781, *Morris Papers*, II, 323; RM to Greene, Apr. 24, 1782, *ibid.*, V, 50.

[67] Ver Steeg, *Robert Morris*, chaps. IV-V; Ferguson, *Power of the Purse*, chap. VII. The role of merchants and public creditors in the origins of the Nationalist movement has been vastly overemphasized. What is most striking about this earlier period is the *lack* of support the Nationalist financial program received from the very economic interests it was purportedly designed to serve. Thus, for example, the mercantile community demonstrated a remarkable lack of interest in subscribing to the Bank of North America. On this point, see *Morris Papers*, I, 315 n. 3, II, 69, III, 121 n. 1; Ver Steeg, *Robert Morris*, 84. In addition, rather than pleasing public creditors, Morris's financial program was initially denounced by them. Public creditors' hostility was directed at Morris's recommendation to halt the practice of giving loan office certificates in lieu of the interest due them and at his proposal in June 1782 to stop further payment of interest on loan office certificates in bills of exchange on France. For the adverse reaction of public creditors to Morris's program, see *Morris Papers*, III, 460; 482; V, 398n. For the order stopping interest payments in loan office certificates, see III, 50-51, V, 397n-99n.

else, Morris's financial program was designed to win the war. A financially revitalized America would have the effect on England of a psychological Yorktown. In Morris's vision of winning the war, there was no need for planning military strategy, for fighting battles, or for paying soldiers. Once Great Britain perceived America's fiscal resolve, the tangible sign of a people determined to fight for their liberty, it would quickly sue for peace.

In a circular written in October, 1781, Morris laid out the logic connecting the nation's financial integrity to winning the war. Working backward from the effect to the cause, Morris told the state governors he was "thoroughly convinced that the Enemy must ask Peace, whenever we are in a Condition vigorously to prosecute the War; and that we shall be in that Condition, whenever our Affairs are reduced to order and our Credit restored; and that for these Purposes, nothing more is necessary than a proper System of Taxation."[68] Conversely, the only thing that kept England in the war, its one hope, was for "the Derangement of our Finances" to continue. Should the states ratify the impost and put the national government in possession of an adequate revenue "that Hope must cease."[69] Morris was convinced that England would capitulate rather than continue fighting against a united and solvent America. Although Morris's financial policies resulted in making America safe for public creditors and also laid the groundwork for America's economic expansion in the 1780s, they were not designed with those ends in mind. Their origins stemmed from the developments of the war and Morris's genuine desire to see America "independent, Really and Truly independent, Independent of our Enemies, of our Friends, of all but the Omnipotent."[70]

Ironically, Morris spent the better part of his first four months in office intervening in and directing the Continental army's logistical operations. On August 7, 1781, in the company of Richard Peters, a member of the Board of War, Morris journeyed to army headquarters

---

[68] *Morris Papers*, III, 88.

[69] *Ibid.*, 482, 88; RM to James Lovell, July 29, 1782, *Rev. Dipl. Corr.*, ed., Wharton, V, 624, 828.

[70] *Morris Papers*, IV, 196. For variations on this theme, see 375-76, 402, 383, 495, 515, 551. Cf. Jensen, "Idea of a National Government," 366-67; Ferguson, *Power of the Purse*, 121; Rakove, *Beginnings of National Politics*, 303-05.

at Dobbs Ferry, New York, where for a week (August 11-18), he held high level discussions with the commander in chief. With a dedication to frugality that would have brought smiles to the faces of Samuel Adams and Richard Henry Lee, Morris proposed eliminating posts, cutting back soldiers' pay, economizing on hospital expenses, reducing the number of regiments, abolishing franking privileges for officers, and curtailing the expenditures for military stores, provisions, and forage.[71] These proposals were temporarily shelved, however, when on the afternoon of August 14, Washington learned that a French fleet of 29 warships carrying 3,000 men was sailing for Chesapeake Bay and would be arriving in mid-October. Washington immediately recognized the possibility of trapping the British with the aid of French sea power and countered Morris's program of retrenchments by asking for increased logistical support.[72]

Morris complied with Washington's request, and for the next month, while keeping creditors at bay and fending off insistent requests for money from staff officers, he plunged into the complexities of transporting and supplying the army on its four hundred mile march from the Hudson to the York. Morris ultimately succeeded in this last major logistical operation of the war and deserved a large portion of credit for the victory at Yorktown. Success was due largely to the fact that planning, direction, and responsibility were centralized in the person of Robert Morris.[73]

After Yorktown, Morris never lost sight of the means which he believed would bring an end to the war—the collection of tax revenues, the prudent expenditure of government funds, and the restoration of public credit. All else was subordinated to these goals. His commitment not to allow "any Consideration to divert me from that Line which Reason points out as my Duty to walk in," boded ill for the troops.[74] If push came to shove, the soldiers would be sacrificed for the greater

---

[71] *Morris Papers*, II, 75-76. For the background of RM's meeting with Washington, see the headnote, 73-74; Ver Steeg, *Robert Morris*, 74.

[72] Ver Steeg, *Robert Morris*, 74; Douglas Southall Freeman, *George Washington: A Biography* (New York, 1948-1957), V, 309; Henry P. Johnston, *The Yorktown Campaign and the Surrender of Cornwallis 1781* (New York, 1881), 83.

[73] Carp, "To Starve the Army," chap. 8. For the preparations of the Yorktown campaign, see Johnston, *Yorktown Campaign*, chaps, IV-V.

[74] *Morris Papers*, IV, 119.

good: the revival of public credit. Nowhere is this better revealed than in Morris's implementation of the contract system to feed the army.

In December, 1781, Morris began to extend to the entire army the system of contracts he had earlier used as Agent for Pennsylvania to supply that state's military posts. Morris was attracted to the contract system because he was convinced it was "the cheapest, most certain, and consequently the best, mode of obtaining those articles, which are necessary for the subsistence, covering, cloathing, and moving of an Army."[75] Sealed, competitive bidding would keep the price per ration down to a minimum, while also allowing Morris to eliminate transportation and personnel costs, shut down expensive military posts, and save on paying for wastage and spoilage. The contractors were sure to provide a sufficient number of good rations because if they failed to supply an adequate amount, they would deprive themselves of a portion of the profits. Likewise, if they supplied bad rations "the Contractors will suffer the loss of it when condemned, so that they are bound in Interest to take care that the Beef put up be of a good quality."[76] As with the Bank of North America, Morris sought to harness economic self-interest to serve the public good.

Morris was overly optimistic in trusting to economic self-interest to solve the army's supply problems. In the hands of grasping merchants, a contract, even with arbitration clauses written into it, was a frail reed to lean upon: the agreement's stipulations could be shoddily complied with or simply ignored. This was the experience of Washington's troops fed by "Mr. Comfort Sands, wrongly named so," whose firm was awarded the contracts for West Point and the Moving Army.[77] Sands, a New York merchant, whose putative maxim in trade was "that no poor person can be honest," did everything in his power to grow prosperous at the expense of the public. He was arrogant to army officers, punc-

[75] *Ibid.*, 482-83. For examples of contracts, see I, 207, 299.

[76] *Ibid.*, III, 428, 179, V, 175; Ver Steeg, *Robert Morris*, 106-07.

[77] The Moving Army consisted of fighting troops not assigned to a specific post. For the contracts, see *Morris Papers*, III, 342-47, IV, 525-30, 497 n. 8, 530n-31n; Ver Steeg, *Robert Morris*, 142-51. The quotation is from John Campbell to Hugh Hughes, Apr. 20, 1782, Hugh Hughes Letterbooks, 5, New-York Historical Society, NYC.

tilious to a fault, and mendacious in negotiations.[78] Not surprisingly, disputes between Sands and the army arose as early as March, 1782, and by May the complaints were legion, if not exactly novel. For it was the same litany heard throughout the war: spoiled flour, rotten meat, bad rum, and adulterated whiskey. Adding insult to injury, the soldiers were made to walk upwards of three miles from camp to where the food was issued, a spot chosen to suit the contractor's convenience.[79]

The army in the South fared no better, albeit for different reasons. Because Morris was adamantly opposed to deficit spending, he required the states to continue to meet congressional tax and supply requisitions. He would not bail them out, believing that their reasons—"that each had done [the] most, and that the people are not able to pay Taxes"— were pretexts for "Langour and Inexertion."[80] As a result of Morris's fiscal triage, the contract system was not extended to the Southern army until the middle of 1782. Consequently, throughout much of 1782, Nathanael Greene's army suffered and almost disbanded because it was forced to rely on state supplies and impressment. When Greene complained, Morris turned aside his requests for aid and blithely consoled his friend: "You therefore my Dear Sir must continue your Exertions with, or without Men, Provisions, Cloathing or pay, in hopes that all Things will come right at last."[81]

[78] For Sands's character, see Herman Swift to Heath, Mar. 26, 1782, Papers of George Washington, microfilm ed. (Library of Congress, Washington, D.C.), Ser. 4, Reel 83 (hereafter cited as Washington Papers). "Minutes of Conversation of Colonel Humphreys and Jonathan Trumbull, Jr.," May 6, 1782, Reel 84; Washington to the Superintendent of Finance, May 17 [-25], 1782, Writings of Washington, ed., Fitzpatrick, XXIV, 287-88, 283-85. For Sands's maxim in trade, see D. Carthy to William Duer, July 2, 1787, William Duer Papers, II, 27 (New-York Historical Society, New York City).

[79] Heath to Benjamin Lincoln, Mar. 27, 1782, Washington Papers, Ser. 4, Reel 83. For the complaints, see Heath to Sands, Mar. 1, 1782, ibid.; Writings of Washington, ed. Fitzpatrick, XXIV, 259; 467-68. See also the fine discussion and sources in the Morris Papers, V, 212-14 n. 6; Ver Steeg, Robert Morris, 142-43, 146. Sands denied all charges of misconduct. For his defense, see Sands and Company to Humphreys and Trumbull, Jr., May 11, 1782, Washington Papers, Ser. 4, Reel 84; Sands and Company to the Committee of Field Officers of the Army, May 14, 1782, ibid., Reel 85. For the army's logistical problems during the war, see Carp, "To Starve the Army," chap. 3.

[80] RM to Greene, Apr. 24, 1782, Morris Papers, V, 50. Referring to the states, RM remarked, "If complaints of Difficulties were equivalent to Cash I should not complain that the [tax] quotas are unpaid." RM to Daniel of St. Thomas Jenifer, June 11, 1782, 380.

[81] Ibid., 50. For RM's refusal to supply the southern troops, IV, 406-09, 410 n. 4; V, 237-38 n. 1, 492-93, 35-37. See also Theodore Thayer, Nathanael Greene: Strategist of the American Revolution (New York, 1969), 396-97; Johnson, Sketches of the Life of Nathanel Greene, II, 315-17.

In the following months, although the army grew to nearly 14,000 men by late 1782, its logistical problems disappeared, mainly as a result of the ensuing peace that brought stability and regularity to administrative affairs.[82] Few soldiers now complained of a lack of supplies. On February 5, 1783, Washington wrote, "I have. . .the satisfaction of seeing the troops better covered, better clothed, and better fed than they have ever been in any former Winter Quarters."[83] After seven and a half years, Washington finally had an army ready to fight. Five weeks later, Congress received the provisional peace treaty from Paris.

* * * *

The Nationalist movement of 1780-1781, initiated by army officers and popularly elected state legislatures, was a reaction to economic chaos and military defeat. Both these groups had experienced firsthand the consequences of Congress's inefficient administration of the war and the defects of relying on weak and obstructive state governments to provide men and supplies for the army. But what is surprising is not that Nationalists emerged in 1780 but that they were supported by their philosophical opponents, the localists, who had been adamantly opposed to increasing the powers of Congress. Localist participation in the Nationalist coalition is a true measure of the magnitude of the economic and military crisis. At stake was the fate of the Revolution.

Once in power, however, Nationalist administrative theory and practice had much in common with earlier congressional management of the war. In particular, the Nationalists, like the localists, distrusted the military, abhorred fraud and extravagance, and passionately believed in the need to reduce drastically public expenditures. Their commitment to these republican values insured that their direction of the war would be as ineffective as former attempts had been. Only Robert Morris's decision to forsake republican austerity, combined with French military aid, prevented the Nationalists' administrative principles from endangering American victory at Yorktown. Nor did

---

[82] *The Sinews of Independence: Monthly Strength Reports of the Continental Army*, Charles H. Lesser, ed. (Chicago, 1976), 240.
[83] Washington to Heath, Feb. 5, 1783, *Writings of Washington*, ed. Fitzpatrick, XXVI, 97.

the Nationalists succeed in their effort to increase the powers of Congress. Their strongest measure, the impost, went down to defeat by the refusal of a single state, Rhode Island, to ratify it.[84] But although they were administratively inept, the Nationalists achieved their ultimate goal: not the restoration of aristocratic rule or the enrichment of public creditors, but Independence.

Princeton University   E. WAYNE CARP

---

[84] Irwin H. Polishook, *Rhode Island and the Union 1774-1795* (Evanston, Ill., 1969), chap. 3; Ver Steeg, *Robert Morris*, 129-31; Ferguson, *Power of the Purse*, 152-54.

James Madison and the Nationalists, 1780-1783

Lance Banning

IN the Continental and Confederation Congresses, wrote Irving Brant, James Madison "endeavored to establish . . . national supremacy—first by a return to the original authority Congress lost when it stopped printing money and became financially dependent upon the states, next by recognition of implied powers in the Articles of Confederation, then by the vigorous exercise of powers whose validity could not be challenged, finally by amendment of the articles to confer new powers upon Congress."[1] While subsequent biographers of Madison have challenged Brant on lesser points, both they and other students of Confederation politics have generally affirmed his central theme. Current scholarship portrays the young Virginian as an eager, dedicated nationalist throughout his years of congressional service, one of a group of reformers often referred to as "the nationalists of 1781-1783."[2]

Several elements of this familiar portrait are misleading. They impede a better understanding of Madison's personal development and erect unnecessary obstacles to attempts to comprehend his later career. They also obscure some vital differences among the nationalistic reformers of the

Mr. Banning, who is preparing a biography of Madison, is a member of the Department of History at the University of Kentucky. He wishes to thank the John Simon Guggenheim Foundation for a grant to aid research and Ralph Ketcham, Harold Schultz, Willi Paul Adams, Charles F. Hobson, and Drew R. McCoy for comments on an earlier version of the article, as well as to acknowledge benefits received between drafts from Jay Kinney, "James Madison's Nationalist Persuasion" (senior honors thesis, University of Texas at Austin, 1980).

[1] Brant, *James Madison*, 6 vols. (Indianapolis, Ind., 1941-1961), II: *The Nationalist*, 418.

[2] Ralph Ketcham, *James Madison: A Biography* (New York, 1971), 126-134; Merrill D. Peterson, ed., *James Madison: A Biography in His Own Words* (New York, 1974), 51, 69-71; E. James Ferguson, "The Nationalists of 1781-1783 and the Economic Interpretation of the Constitution," *Journal of American History*, LVI (1969), 241-261. Important monographs identifying Madison with a group of nationalistic reformers include Merrill Jensen, *The New Nation: A History of the United States during the Confederation, 1781-1789* (New York, 1950); E. James Ferguson, *The Power of the Purse: A History of American Public Finance, 1776-1790* (Chapel Hill, N.C., 1961); H. James Henderson, *Party Politics in the Continental Congress* (New York, 1974); and Joseph L. Davis, *Sectionalism in American Politics, 1774-1787* (Madison, Wis., 1977).

early 1780s—differences with critical implications for the more successful effort for reform that came at the decade's end.

Prevailing views do not explain that Madison first rose to prominence in Congress as a determined advocate of Virginia's special interests. For months, those interests reinforced his inclination to *resist* unauthorized extensions of congressional authority—an inclination deeply rooted in his Revolutionary creed. But a commitment to Virginia and the Revolution also called with growing urgency for change. Day by day, while British forces devastated the deep South and then turned toward Virginia, Congress groped for one expedient and then another to keep an army in the field. Victory at Yorktown put an end to the danger that the South might be torn from the Confederation, but the agonizing crawl toward peace brought difficulties nearly as severe. While Madison continued to defend his state's distinctive interests, he came increasingly to favor significant additions to the powers of Congress.

Still, Madison's acceptance of the need for fundamental change was limited and halting. Until the fall of 1782 he supported several reforms with obvious reluctance, often as a product of his alarm for Virginia or for the Revolutionary cause. Even in his final months of congressional service, when he allied himself with Robert Morris and others to push Congress toward the reforms of 1783, he proved unable to accept the ultimate objectives of his allies. James Madison was not a "nationalist" during the early 1780s—not, at least, in several of the senses commonly suggested by that term. His cooperation with the Morrisites did not reflect a concord of opinion. On the contrary, the course of the cooperation suggestively prefigured the confrontation with Alexander Hamilton that would eventually divide the Federalists of 1789 into the warring parties of the 1790s.

When Madison retired from Congress, he intended to reenter the Virginia legislature to advocate compliance with Confederation treaties and acceptance of the congressional recommendations of 1783. But he did not yet favor a complete departure from the Articles of Confederation. He had been pushed, not pulled, toward national supremacy. He had developed doubts about the program and intentions of his former allies. Developments would push him farther in a nationalistic direction in the years ahead. By the time of the Virginia Plan of 1787, he would see some very positive advantages in a program of centralizing reform. And yet the doubts he carried with him from the early 1780s would also help to shape his subsequent career. The content of Madison's nationalism was not just different from, but incompatible with, the centralizing vision of other nationalists who gathered, first, around the old Confederation's superintendent of finance and, after 1789, around the new republic's secretary of the Treasury. This incompatibility had quite important consequences, often overlooked, during the crisis of 1783. It would become explicit after a new federal government had been approved.[3]

[3] It is not sufficient to concede, as several influential authors do, that there were differences between Madison and the nationalists from the Middle States. The

JAMES MADISON

229

Madison presented his credentials to the Continental Congress at a gloomy juncture in the history of the Confederation. North America was near the end of the most severe winter in a generation. At Morristown, where the continentals were enduring hardships more extreme than at Valley Forge, George Washington wondered how he could keep his hungry, unpaid troops together when their three-year enlistments began to expire. In December 1779 Congress had turned to requisitions of specific supplies to feed the army. On March 18, 1780, the day Madison arrived in Philadelphia, Congress devalued the continental dollar at a rate of forty for one and threw responsibility for generating new bills of credit on the states. Desperate as these decisions were, the long delay in reaching them had brought congressional prestige to a point as low as its power. During 1779, while precipitate inflation threatened to choke the army's supplies, Congress had erupted in bitter public controversy over peace terms, the diplomatic establishment, and the mutual accusations of Silas Deane and Arthur Lee.[4]

While Madison was aware of all these problems and had labored in particular to collect his thoughts on the financial crisis, the desperate condition of affairs hit him with redoubled force as soon as he began to view it from the central government's perspective. Soon after his arrival, he warned Gov. Thomas Jefferson that "the course of the revolution" had seen no moment "more truly critical than the present." The army was "threatened with an immediate alternative of disbanding or living on free quarter." The treasury was empty. Public credit was exhausted. Congress complained "of the extortion of the people, the people of the improvidence of Congress, and the army of both." Congress recommended measures to the states, and the states separately decided whether it was expedient to comply. "Believe me, Sir, as things now stand, if the states do not vigorously proceed in collecting the old money and establishing funds for the credit of the new, . . . we are undone."[5]

---

caveat is commonly lost in the generalization when it is entered at all. For example, in *Power of the Purse*, 158-160, Ferguson writes that Madison "was not in the inner councils of the Morris group," at least during the Newburgh Affair. Yet Ferguson, with Brant, describes the Virginian as "an unwavering Nationalist," a phrase he usually defines in terms of Morris's objectives. The reader may fairly infer that what distinguished Madison from the inner group was that he was "less intransigent" in his insistence on a common program (*ibid.*, 166). Other authors make no distinction between Madison and the Morrisites, sometimes with disturbing consequences. For a recent example see James H. Hutson, "Country, Court, and Constitution: Antifederalism and the Historians," *William and Mary Quarterly*, 3d Ser., XXXVIII (1981), 337-368.

[4] Charles Royster, *A Revolutionary People at War: The Continental Army and American Character, 1775-1783* (Chapel Hill, N.C., 1979), 299-300; Edmund Cody Burnett, *The Continental Congress* (New York, 1941), 401-403; Jack N. Rakove, *The Beginnings of National Politics: An Interpretive History of the Continental Congress* (New York, 1979), 255-274.

[5] Madison to Jefferson, Mar. 27, 1780, *The Papers of James Madison*, 14 vols. (Chicago and Charlottesville, Va., 1962-   ), II, 6. Hereafter cited as *Madison*

The shock that seems apparent in Madison's early letters to Virginia is a most important clue to understanding his career.[6] Forced to grapple daily with the nation's problems through the Confederation's most difficult years, he would never forget the desperation he often felt. Having occupied the station that he did, he found it impossible to see American affairs in the manner that he might have seen them had he never left Virginia. His later letters repeatedly comment on the different perspectives of those who comprehended problems from a national vantage and those who were immersed in local concerns.[7] And yet these early letters may also easily mislead. They do not justify the view that Madison attempted to extend congressional authority from the beginning of his service.

At twenty-nine, the youngest man in Congress, Madison was shy, weak-voiced, and diffident. Through his first six months of service, he made no motions and probably never entered a debate. Authorities agree that Congress was preoccupied with war and relatively free of factional division during the spring and summer of 1780, months marked by military disaster in the Carolinas, continuing depreciation of the currency, and the failure of specific supplies to meet the needs of the northern army, in which mutinies erupted in May and June. The optimism sparked by the financial reforms of March quickly gave way to virtually unanimous alarm over the army's condition and to a general opinion that so much reliance on the states might have to be replaced by broader congressional authority.[8]

Madison plainly shared the general sense of crisis and national humiliation.[9] He seems to have agreed with Joseph Jones, his senior colleague in Virginia's delegation, that Congress had surrendered too much of its power to the states.[10] He certainly agreed that the situation demanded prompt ratification of the Articles of Confederation.[11] How much farther

---

Papers, vols. 1-7 were edited by William T. Hutchinson and William M. E. Rachal and vols. 8-14 by Robert A. Rutland *et al.* I have modernized spelling and punctuation and given abbreviations in full throughout this article.

[6] As Ketcham notes in *James Madison*, 101.

[7] See, especially, Madison to Edmund Randolph, May 20, 1783, *Madison Papers*, VII, 59.

[8] See the secondary sources cited in nn. 2 and 4, together with Worthington Chauncy Ford *et al.*, eds., *Journals of the Continental Congress, 1774-1789*, 34 vols. (Washington, D.C., 1904-1937), XVI-XVII, and Edmund C. Burnett, ed., *Letters of Members of the Continental Congress*, 8 vols. (Washington, D.C., 1921-1936), V. The latter works are hereafter cited as *Jours. Cont. Cong.* and *Letters Cont. Cong.*

[9] See, especially, Madison to Jefferson, May 6, 1780, *Madison Papers*, II, 19-20.

[10] Madison to John Page, May 8, 1780, to Jefferson, June 2, 1780, and to Jones, Oct. 24, 1780, *ibid.*, 21-22, 37-38, 145-146. On June 19, 1780, Jones wrote to Washington, "Congress have been gradually surrendering or throwing upon the several states the exercise of powers they should have retained. . . . Congress is at present little more than the medium through which the wants of the army are conveyed to the states. This body never had or at least . . . exercised powers adequate to the purposes of war" (*Letters Cont. Cong.*, V, 226-227).

[11] Madison to Edmund Pendleton, Sept. 12, 1780, *Madison Papers*, II, 81-82.

he might have been willing to go to strengthen the federal hand is impossible to say. But there is nothing in his surviving papers through the end of 1780 that confirms the common suggestion that he was ahead of other delegates in accepting the need for centralizing reforms. Rather, there are several hints that he persisted somewhat longer than did most in the hope that such extensive change might be unnecessary. The want of money, he protested, "is the source of all our public difficulties." One or two million guineas "would expel the enemy from every part of the United States" and "reconcile the army and everybody else to our republican forms of governments, the principal inconveniences which are imputed to these being really the fruit of defective revenues." The troops, he thought, could be as well equipped "by our governments as by any other if they possessed money enough."[12]

By the time he wrote these words, Madison had been thrust into a role of greater visibility in Congress, though hardly as an advocate of centralizing change. On September 6 he seconded a motion in which Jones presented Virginia's terms for the western cession that Congress had recommended as necessary to assure ratification of the Articles. Almost immediately, Jones, to whom the delegation had deferred on this vital issue, departed for Virginia to attend his ailing wife and to persuade the legislature to complete the cession. Appointed to the committee to consider Jones's motion, Madison shared prominently from this point on in all congressional deliberations concerning the west—not least because he feared that his remaining colleagues in Virginia's delegation, John Walker and Theodorick Bland, were not sufficiently alert to the commonwealth's long-term interests. On September 16, with Kentucky much in mind, he suddenly entered the ongoing controversy over Vermont, whose independence Bland favored, with a set of resolutions looking toward a congressional settlement that would have placed the rebellious territory firmly under the jurisdiction of either New Hampshire or New York.[13] Moreover, when Congress received the committee's report on the Virginia cession and agreed to strike a clause voiding private purchases from the Indians, Madison voted against the altered resolutions, although Bland

---

[12] Madison to Pendleton, Nov. 7, 1780, *ibid.*, 166. For additional hints of his persistent hope that problems could be solved within the present structures, see Madison to Jefferson, May 6, 1780, and to John Page (?), May 8, 1780, *ibid.*, 19-20, 21.

[13] Madison, "Resolutions Respecting Vermont Lands," Sept. 16, 1780, *ibid.*, 87-88. On Sept. 19, 1780, Madison wrote Jones that he believed a decision should be made "on principles that will effectually discountenance the erection of new governments without the sanction of proper authority" (*ibid.*, 90). Jones's reply of Oct. 2, 1780, strengthens the impression that the Virginians, who were faced with a weak secession movement in Kentucky, had their own interest very much in view. Of the agitation for Vermont's independence, Jones said, "Such excrescences should be taken off on their first appearance. . . . We know not what may be the consequences if Congress shall countenance by precedent the dismembering of states" (*ibid.*, 106).

and Walker cast the delegation's vote in favor of the committee's recommendations.[14]

For all his wish to help prepare the way for the completion of the Confederation, Madison would always stubbornly resist any cession that would not confirm his state's exclusion of the claims of the great land companies. Recognition of these claims, in his opinion, could transfer a great treasure "from the public to a few land mongers."[15] It would also imply an improper congressional jurisdiction over the northwest. Through all the months ahead, while the terms of a cession remained a periodic subject of controversy, Madison insisted that Virginia's sovereignty was absolute within the whole of its chartered bounds. He denied that Congress had a valid, independent claim to the lands northwest of the Ohio River and maintained that Congress could acquire legitimate authority only by accepting a cession on Virginia's terms.[16]

Meanwhile, Madison's preoccupation with the west and his determination to defend state interests prompted him to take a major role in deliberations over a potential treaty with Spain. With most of the delegates from the frightened South, Madison favored close cooperation with France. He quickly established close relationships with the Chevalier de La Luzerne and the secretary of the French legation, François de Barbé-Marbois.[17] He has often been identified as a member of a "French party," and French agents described him as "devoted to us." Yet La Luzerne also characterized him as "not free from prejudices in favor of the various claims of Virginia, however exaggerated they may be."[18] Certainly, these claims made Madison a difficult friend of France on the issue of America's relationship with Spain.

Aware that Spain would not complete a treaty that might threaten its position in Louisiana, French emissaries sought American flexibility on the question of a western boundary and on American pretensions to a right to navigate the Mississippi River. No one in Congress was *less* flexible on these issues than the young Virginian. The original instructions for a

---

[14] *Jours. Cont. Cong.*, XVIII, 916. For the issue of the western lands to this point see Thomas Perkins Abernethy, *Western Lands and the American Revolution* (New York, 1937), chap. 19, and Peter Onuf, "Toward Federalism: Virginia, Congress, and the Western Lands," *WMQ*, 3d Ser., XXXIV (1977), 353-374. Onuf's insistence that a resolution of this issue was, for many Virginians, a prerequisite for support of stronger federal power has been particularly helpful.

[15] Madison to Jones, Oct. 17, 1780, *Madison Papers*, II, 136-137.

[16] For now, Madison swallowed his "chagrin" over the decision of Oct. 10 and urged Virginians to proceed with the cession. He insisted that Virginia could still accomplish the exclusion of the companies simply by attaching to its act of cession a condition voiding private claims, perhaps even a provision that "no private claims be complied with" in the cessions of any state (*ibid.*). See also Madison to Jones, Sept. 19, 1780, *ibid.*, 89-90.

[17] Jones to Madison, Oct. 9, 1780, *ibid.*, 120-121; Madison to Jones, Oct. 24, 1780, *ibid.*, 145; Brant, *Madison*, II, 77-79.

[18] Quoted in Brant, *Madison*, II, 14.

Spanish treaty were entirely to his liking. When the hard-pressed Geor-
gians and South Carolinians moved to abandon Congress's original
insistence on free navigation of the Mississippi, Madison forced postponement of a reconsideration despite the anxiety he suffered when his stand
embroiled him in another conflict with Bland. He trusted, he told Jones,
"that Congress will see the impropriety of sacrificing the acknowledged
limits and claims of any state" without that state's consent.[19] And when he
wrote Governor Jefferson to seek a resolution of the difference between
himself and Bland, he indicated that the desperate military situation in the
South had not sufficed to make him think that Virginia should agree to
purchase a Spanish pact at the price of the navigation of the Mississippi or
its western claims. He also asked for specific instructions as to what the
delegates should do if Congress made concessions on either matter
without Virginia's consent.[20]

By the end of his first year of service, Madison had become a
congressman with whom his fellows reckoned. Early in 1781 he was
mentioned as a candidate for the position of secretary for foreign affairs.[21]
Created in January, this post was the first of four executive offices
established by Congress while Virginia and Maryland were acting to
complete the ratification of the Articles. Congress made these important
administrative changes, culminating in the appointment of Robert Morris
as superintendent of finance, without a serious division. Madison supported them, although his surviving papers are entirely silent on the subject.
In the years ahead, he would become something of an administration man
in Congress. He was willing to see a good deal of executive initiative,
normally supported the secretaries' recommendations, and seems often to
have been called upon by Morris and Robert R. Livingston, the secretary
for foreign affairs, to guide their proposals through Congress.[22]

Madison's support for executive efficiency should not be confused with
a determined nationalism. In close conjunction with the creation of
executive departments, Congress asked the states for power to levy a 5
percent duty on foreign imports and began a broad consideration of the
adequacy of the newly ratified Articles. Analyzing these deliberations of
the spring and summer of 1781, most students of Confederation politics
have identified Madison as one of the leaders of a nationalistic push.
Failing to secure endorsement of a federal power to coerce delinquent
states, it is said, Madison conducted a campaign to expand federal

[19] Madison to Jones, Nov. 25, 1780, *Madison Papers*, II, 203. See also Madison
to Jones, Dec. 5, 1780, *ibid.*, 224.

[20] Virginia Delegates in Congress to Jefferson, Dec. 13, 1780, *ibid.*, 241-242.

[21] Thomas Burke to William Bingham, Feb. 6 (?), 1781, *Letters Cont. Cong.*, V,
562-563.

[22] "I have always conceived the several ministerial departments of Congress to
be provisions for aiding their counsels as well as executing their resolutions"
(Madison to James Monroe, Mar. 21, 1785, *Madison Papers*, VIII, 255-256).

authority by means of a doctrine of implied congressional powers.[23] This interpretation rests on a partial reading of the evidence and smothers a deep and obvious ambivalence in Madison's position during this time of important reforms. It also raises an imposing barrier to understanding how he would arrive at the position he would occupy by 1793.

What we know of the critical decisions of 1781 can be reduced to a few essentials. On February 3 John Witherspoon moved that the states be asked to grant Congress the power to superintend the nation's commerce and an exclusive right to levy duties on imports. This motion was defeated, four states to three. Then, by the same margin, Congress approved a recommendation of power to levy a 5 percent impost. Madison and Jones overrode Bland to cast Virginia's vote *against* both proposals.[24] At some point Madison prepared a substitute resolution, which seems the best clue to his current preference: "That it be earnestly recommended to the states, as indispensably necessary to the support of public credit and the prosecution of the war, immediately to pass laws" levying a 5 percent duty on foreign imports and vesting Congress with power to collect and appropriate the funds to discharge the principal and interest of its debts. The language plainly suggests that while Madison wanted this revenue and favored congressional collection, he did not currently favor an independent congressional power to levy the tax or to use it for any purpose except to provide for the debt.[25] On this issue and on the question of congressional superintendence of commerce, he was not willing to extend congressional authority as far as many of his fellows would have liked.

Similar conclusions can be reached about the episode that may appear to offer the strongest evidence for Madison's early participation in a nationalistic thrust. During the spring and summer of 1781, a progression of three congressional committees considered ways to strengthen the Articles. Madison served on the first of these committees and wrote its report,

[23] Madison "used every strategem to expand" congressional power "indirectly," moving to give Congress power to prohibit trade with Britain, to permit impressment of supplies, etc. (Ketcham, *James Madison*, 114). This accords closely with the longer discussion in Brant, *Madison*, II, chap. 8: Madison believed in "easy discovery of implied powers where none were expressly stated" (p. 110). Defeated on the matter of the coercive power, he drove "to the same end by specific legislation based on implied powers" (p. 111). "Forced by necessity, Congress adopted one specific measure after another which Madison put before it, based on implications of power" (p. 118).

[24] *Jours. Cont. Cong.*, XIX, 110-113.

[25] Madison, "Motion on Impost," Feb. 3, 1781, *Madison Papers*, II, 303-304. At the end of May, Madison was still not as unequivocal an advocate of this independent federal revenue as he would come to be. He defended congressional collection as necessary to prevent diversion of the funds to state uses and as less disruptive of the states' internal governance than Pendleton feared. But he confessed that a congressional right to collect an impost might require a confidence in Congress "greater perhaps than many may think consistent with republican jealousy" (Madison to Pendleton, May 29, 1781, *ibid.*, III, 140-141).

which recommended an amendment authorizing Congress "to employ the force of the United States" to compel delinquent states to fulfill their "federal obligations."[26] Madison's biographers have correctly pointed out that he regarded the coercive power as implicit in the Articles and was quite serious about employing this formidable tool at a time when Virginians were complaining bitterly about inadequate northern support. He even wondered whether Congress, by seeking an amendment, should risk a denial by the states of a power it already possessed by implication.[27] But it is equally important to recall the nature of Madison's defense of the proposed amendment. While a coercive power was implicit in the Articles, his report maintained, the absence of a more "determinate and particular provision" could lead to challenges by recalcitrant states. Moreover, it was "most consonant to the spirit of a free constitution that . . . all exercise of power should be explicitly and precisely warranted." A preference for explicit grants of power was a theme to which the Virginian would return repeatedly in the months—and, of course, the years—ahead.[28]

In 1781 Madison insisted on the existence of implied congressional powers in the case of coercion of delinquent states. He assumed the presence of implied powers—logically at least—when he moved to tighten the embargo on trade with Britain and to authorize Gen. Anthony Wayne to impress supplies on his march to Virginia. So, however, did virtually the whole of Congress, for neither of these motions generated constitutional debate. Each advocated an extension or renewal of measures that Congress had long employed. They are not sufficient grounds for concluding that Madison was engaged in a campaign to extend congressional authority. Apart from the coercion of the states, the incidents that have been cited to support the view that he was deliberately attempting to enlarge congressional authority uniformly involved measures that were obvious derivatives of the power to make war, and no one had to torture the Articles to support them.[29] Ordinarily, Madison was demonstrably wary of

[26] Madison, "Proposed Amendment of Articles of Confederation," Mar. 12, 1781, *ibid.,* III, 17-19.

[27] Madison to Jefferson, Apr. 16, 1781, *ibid.,* 71-72, in which he argued that the grant of a coercive power was necessary because of the "shameful deficiency" of some of the "most capable" states and the "military exactions" to which others, "already exhausted," were consequently exposed. Note also the remark that a federal navy, which Madison conceived to be the proper tool of coercion, merited support for a "collateral reason." "Without it, what is to protect the southern states for many years to come against the insults and aggressions of their northern brethren?"

[28] Madison's most eloquent denunciation of legislative trangressions of constitutional limitations would come in his "Memorial and Remonstrance against Religious Assessments [in Virginia]," 1785, *ibid.,* VIII, 295-306.

[29] The single issue on which Madison, who was frantically working to rush assistance to Virginia, might be fairly accused of torturing the Articles saw him argue that five states should be sufficient to form a quorum for ordinary business. Thomas Rodney Diary, Mar. 5, 1781, *Letters Cont. Cong.,* VI, 8.

the doctrine of implied powers. His regard for written limitations of authority and charter boundaries between the powers of the nation and the states is clear.

Madison's position on a national bank is one of many illustrations of the point. With nearly all his colleagues, he favored the appointment of Robert Morris, conceded the financier's extraordinary conditions for acceptance, and supported the superintendent's attempts to finance the Yorktown campaign and to preserve the public credit from absolute collapse. The bank was a partial exception. Morris submitted his proposal for a bank on May 17, 1781, three days after accepting his office, two weeks after the Virginia delegates had reported the final collapse of the currency, and one week after the Virginia legislature had been forced to flee from Richmond. On May 26 Madison nevertheless distinguished himself as one of only four congressmen to oppose a resolution endorsing the superintendent's plan, believing that the Articles conferred no federal power to create a corporation. On December 31 Madison apparently acquiesced in the ordinance of incorporation itself, but not without some agony. "You will conceive the dilemma in which . . . circumstances placed the members who felt on the one side the *importance* of the institution, and on the other a want of power and an aversion to assume it," he wrote. Unwilling to frustrate the financier, disappoint the army, or break an implicit promise to subscribers, worried congressmen had felt able to do no more than insert a resolution by Edmund Randolph recommending actions by the states to give the bank's charter validity within their bounds. "As this is a tacit admission of a defect of [federal] power, I hope," Madison explained, "it will be an antidote against the poisonous tendency of precedents of usurpation."[30]

The bank was not the only issue on which Madison revealed the limits of his continentalism and his inclination to insist on strict construction of the Articles. On May 28 Congress received La Luzerne's request for a definition of its terms for peace. Through the summer and into the fall of 1781, countered at every turn by Witherspoon and opposed by the French and the frightened delegates from the deep South, Madison fought a losing battle to make the western claims of the United States—or, at minimum, the western claims of Virginia—part of the peace ultimata. Failing that, he sought to make these claims a necessary part of any commercial treaty with Great Britain.[31] During the same months he continued to worry about growing congressional sentiment in favor of independence for Vermont, not least because he suspected that "some of the little states . . . hope that such a precedent may engender a division of some of the large ones."[32] The question of western cessions was slowly

---

[30] Madison to Pendleton, Jan. 8, 1782, *Madison Papers*, IV, 22-23. See also Virginia Delegates to Benjamin Harrison, *ibid.*, 19.

[31] *Ibid.*, III, 133; *Jours. Cont. Cong.*, XX-XXI, *passim;* Brant, *Madison*, II, 137-140, 143-146.

[32] Madison to Pendleton, Aug. 14, 1781, *Madison Papers*, III, 224.

working its way through a Congress hostile to Virginia's conditions.[33] Madison ended the year thoroughly angered over the congressional temperament. He counseled Virginians against despair. Congress, he explained to Jefferson, had not adopted "the obnoxious doctrine of an inherent right in the United States to the territory in question." He hoped that Jefferson would try to counteract "any intemperate measures that may be urged in the legislature." Yet he freely declared his opinion that the congressional proceedings were "ample justification" for a legislative revocation of the cession and a remonstrance against interference in Virginia's jurisdiction, as well as ample indication that the legislature should "in all their provisions for their future security, importance, and interest . . . presume that the present union will but little survive the present war."[34]

Through the spring of 1782, as he completed his second year in Congress, Madison remained preoccupied with Vermont and the western cession. He continued to work to block Vermont's admission as an independent state. He questioned congressional authority, feared the consequences of the precedent for Virginia, and resisted the addition of another state to the forces of the easterners and the landless block in Congress.[35] He also sought to force a decision on the Virginia cession, which he perceived as intimately connected to the struggle over Vermont.[36] When Congress stalled, postponing a decision indefinitely, Madison suggested to Arthur Lee that it would not be "consistent with the respect we owe to our own public characters nor with the dignity of those we serve to persist longer in fruitless applications" for a congressional decision. Instead, the delegation would request instructions from the legislature, "who will certainly be fully justified in taking any course . . . which the interest of the state shall prescribe."[37] Madison hoped the

[33] See Virginia Delegates to Thomas Nelson, Oct. 9, 16, 23, 1781, *ibid.*, 281-282, 286-288, 293, and Randolph to Nelson, Nov. 7, 1781, which reported the delegation "almost worn down with motions respecting your cession. . . . Virginia is . . . not merely destitute of friends but surrounded by those who labor to retrench her territory" (*Letters Cont. Cong.*, VI, 259-260).

[34] Madison to Jefferson, Nov. 18, 1781, *Madison Papers*, III, 307-308.

[35] With every indication of approaching hostilities between the Green Mountain men and the authorities of New Hampshire and New York, Madison groaned, it might be necessary to accept congressional interposition despite the constitutional and practical arguments against it. "It is very unhappy that such plausible pretexts, if not necessary occasions, of assuming power should occur. Nothing is more distressing to those who have a due respect for the constitutional modifications of power than to be obliged to decide on them" (Madison to Pendleton, Jan. 22, 1782, *ibid.*, IV, 38-39).

[36] Madison to Pendleton, Apr. 23, 1782, *ibid.*, 178; Madison to Randolph, May 1, 1782, *ibid.*, 196-197. See also Madison's memorandum, "Observations Relating to the Influence of Vermont and the Territorial Claims on the Politics of Congress," May 1, 1782, *ibid.*, 200-203.

[37] Madison to Lee, May 7, 1782, *ibid.*, 217-218.

legislature would continue firm. The delegation even determined at one point to make its support for measures pressuring recalcitrant states to approve the impost "subservient to an honorable" decision on the cession.[38]

Madison's positions on the impost, on a national bank, and on the west should warn against identifying him with a group of nationalistic reformers during his first two years and more in Congress. The more closely one examines this interpretation, the larger grow the problems. H. James Henderson, for example, explicitly follows Brant in portraying the Virginian as a consistent, energetic nationalist,[39] yet Henderson's quantitative studies afford poor support for this view. The cluster-bloc analysis for 1780 places Madison in a New England-Virginia bloc on the fringes of an "Eastern Party," which was the home of most of the old radicals who remained in Congress and which voted quite differently from the Southern and New York blocs, whose members Henderson identifies with a nationalistic thrust.[40] The table for 1781 places Madison in a separate Virginia bloc, which was the most loosely attached of the four groupings within a dominant "Middle-Southern Coalition."[41] The analysis for 1782, when divisions were dominated by the issues of Vermont and the west, associates Madison with a separate Virginia group within a "Southern Party," which opposed a "Northern Party" with New England and Middle States blocs.[42] Only during 1783 does the analysis of roll calls place Madison firmly within a nationalistic coalition.

For the months between the spring of 1780 and the fall of 1782, the evidence permits few generalizations about Madison's congressional position, and these must differ markedly from the conclusions most scholars have drawn. Madison *did* consistently advocate a harmonious relationship between the United States and France, although no one in Congress was a more persistent or effective *opponent* of American concessions to French or Spanish desires on the matters of the western boundaries or the Mississippi River. By the summer of 1782, Madison's desire for close relations with the French and his appreciation of Benjamin Franklin's contribution to such relations prompted him to take a leading role in

[38] Madison to Randolph, *ibid.*, 220.

[39] Henderson, *Party Politics*, 249.

[40] *Ibid.*, 250-251, and chap. 10 *passim.*

[41] *Ibid.*, 288-289. Indeed, if I read Henderson correctly, his reason for placing the Virginia bloc in this coalition is the link between Randolph, Jones, and some of its marginal members and the Pennsylvania-Maryland bloc, which was the core of the "Middle-Southern Coalition." This, of course, has little to do with Madison's own position, which might fairly be characterized as eccentric. Henderson sees the "Middle-Southern Coalition" of 1781 as opposed to a "New England Group" more on matters of foreign policy than on domestic issues, yet Madison often found his closest allies in the arguments over peace terms among the Massachusetts men.

[42] *Ibid.*, 295.

opposition to the maneuvers of his Virginia colleague Arthur Lee, whose enmity toward Franklin and suspicion of the French Madison denounced as portending a revival of the party controversies of 1779.[43] The younger man's dislike of Lee was compounded by the latter's vendetta against Robert Morris, whom Madison normally supported.[44]

Through the fall of 1782, however, Madison did not conceive of Congress as divided into pro- and anti-Morris parties, nor is it possible to identify him with a group intent on national aggrandizement. He did not vote that way across a range of issues. On the impost and the national bank he sided with the handful of congressmen most resistant to centralizing reform. Moreover, one may search in vain through his surviving papers through most of 1782 for any indication that he was even aware of a reformist push toward greater national authority, much less identified with one. Far from seeking subtle means to extend the constitutional boundaries of congressional power, he seems to have been a strict constructionist of sorts. He was not invariably consistent on the point; he consciously departed from the principle when exigencies required. But he departed from the principle with obvious reluctance and concern. Madison's fundamental inclination was to insist on charter definitions of authority, on *both* the full assertion of powers confided to the central government and genuine regard for the authority left to the states. If this could lead him to support coercion of delinquents, it could also—and more often— lead him to defend states' rights.[45]

Nowhere was this more evident than on the matter of Virginia's western claims, the issue that distinguished Madison most clearly from the majority in Congress. Historians have emphasized the young man's role in the creation of a national domain, and it is also necessary to remember that he frequently wrote home to urge adoption of the impost and compliance with other congressional recommendations. Madison was certainly no localist. Neither was he *principally* a defender of the states' constitutional preserves. Contemporaries nonetheless saw him correctly as a dedicated servant of Virginia. He was willing to subordinate his desire for the impost and the cession to his determination to exclude the speculators from the west and to defend Virginia's jurisdictional claims. He opposed congressional control of commerce. He shared with most Virginians an intense suspicion of New England and an acute resentment of the obvious congressional jealousy of the Old Dominion. When he discussed congressional divisions, he identified his foes as easterners, Pennsylvania speculators, and members from the landless states. He could not commit himself consistently to centralizing change while these remained his dominant

[43] Madison to Randolph, July 23, 1782, *Madison Papers*, IV, 435; Madison, "Comments on Instructions to Peace Commissioners," *ibid.*, 436-438.

[44] Madison to Randolph, June 4, 1782, *ibid.*, 313.

[45] For additional defenses of state preserves and attempts to determine "constitutional" boundaries see *ibid.*, 195-196, 298, 391-394, 410-412, 444-445.

concerns. He would not be unaffected by these feelings when his perspective changed.

In the fall of 1782, as Congress anxiously awaited news from its peace commissioners in Paris, circumstances slowly altered Madison's preoccupations. Deliberations on Vermont and the cession took turns to his liking.[46] At the same time, the Confederation government drew ever nearer to financial collapse. The superintendent of finance had completed his administrative reforms of the Department of the Treasury, put the Bank of North America into operation, enlarged the supply of usable paper by issuing the "Morris Notes," and urged a settlement of accounts between the nation and the states as the first step toward funding the general debt. But the states were increasingly in arrears on their requisitions—Virginia notoriously so. Rhode Island had not approved the impost. Pressure from unpaid public creditors was mounting, and Morris had seized the occasion of one of their memorials to deliver his most important paper on public finance. Dated July 29, 1782, this report insisted that additional general revenues must be added to receipts from the impost and the anticipated sales of western lands in order to meet current expenses and pay the interest on the debt. By fall, however, Congress had done no more than requisition additional funds for the interest due the creditors.[47]

Through the fall, Madison still served as something of an administration man in Congress. His views accorded closely with the financier's when the clamors of soldiers and civilian creditors led two states to contemplate assuming a portion of the Confederation's financial responsibilities. Reporting for a committee assigned to consider New Jersey's warning that the state might be compelled to pay its line out of funds intended for its annual quota, Madison insisted that "the federal constitution" provided that costs for the common defense be paid from the common treasury.[48] He also served with John Rutledge and Alexander Hamilton on a committee that managed to dissuade the Pennsylvania assembly from adopting a plan to pay its civilian federal creditors from state funds.[49] As before, he defended the authority confided to the general government, just as he insisted on respect for the written limitations on its power. He continued to guard Virginia's interests, not only in deliberations on the cession and Vermont, but also in early considerations of adjustments of

[46] Madison, "Notes on Debates," Nov. 14, 1782, *ibid.*, V, 273-274 (hereafter cited as "Notes"); Madison to Randolph, Sept. 10, Nov. 5, 1782, *ibid.*, 115-116, 242-243.

[47] For the evolution of and action on Morris's proposals, besides sources cited in nn. 2 and 4, see Clarence L. Ver Steeg, *Robert Morris: Revolutionary Financier* (New York, 1954), chap. 5, and 123-129. Morris's report is in *Jours. Cont. Cong.*, XXII, 429-446.

[48] Madison, "Report on Payment of New Jersey Troops," *Madison Papers*, V, 173-177.

[49] "Notes," Dec. 4, 1782, *ibid.*, 363-364.

state accounts. On the latter issue he could not agree entirely with the superintendent.[50]

Rather suddenly, the budding crisis burst. Events propelled the Virginian toward a leading role in the war years' most important effort to extend the powers of Congress. In December 1782 a deputation from the angry army arrived in Philadelphia to demand immediate pay for the private soldiers and firm assurances to the officers that they would receive the half-pay pensions promised them in 1780. Then, on Christmas Eve, a humiliated Madison was compelled to tell the fundless Congress that Virginia had rescinded its approval of the impost, destroying all remaining hope that the proposal of 1781 might provide the required relief. Soon thereafter, Robert Morris committed himself to an all-out push to win approval of his plans. The superintendent feared that the end of the war would ruin an unrepeatable opportunity for strengthening congressional authority and securing the general revenues necessary to restore public credit and promote peacetime prosperity. As rumors of a preliminary treaty of peace grew louder and unrest in the army assumed an ominous tone, a "movement for uniting the support of the public creditors—civil and military—emanated . . . from the Office of Finance."[51]

On January 6 Congress received the army's memorial. The following day a grand committee met with Morris, who informed them that the finances would not permit any payments at present or any assurances of future pay until general funds were established for the purpose. On January 9 the financier informed another committee that accounts abroad were overdrawn and secured permission for one more draft on foreign funds despite that fact. On January 17 he told the army deputation that one month's pay could be provided from this draft, but that no other provisions could be made without congressional action. At the same time, he advised Congress against further applications for foreign loans. Finally, on January 24, without warning, he submitted a letter announcing that he would resign at the end of May if permanent provision had not been made for the public debt. The superintendent declined to be "the minister of injustice."[52]

The letter from the financier jarred Congress, which began a full-scale consideration of funding the following day. Moreover, some of Morris's supporters took it as a signal for a concentrated effort to enlist extra-congressional pressure for independent federal revenues, especially from the army. For two months Congress battled over funding and commutation of the half-pay pensions amidst growing rumors that the army might

---

[50] Morris's advice, "in rigid adherence to his maxims of public faith," as Madison put it, was that state surpluses of old continentals be credited at the official rate of 40-1. The eastern states particularly had retired great quantities at far lower rates. Madison opposed ratios of 40-1, 75-1, 100-1, and even 150-1. "Notes," Nov. 26, 1782, ibid., 321-322; Madison to Randolph, Dec. 3, 1782, ibid., 356-357.

[51] Ver Steeg, Morris, 166-177, 185-187, quotation on p. 169.

[52] Ibid., 171.

refuse to disband. At camp, agitation culminated in the Newburgh Addresses of March 10 and 12, 1783.[53]

The major elements of Madison's response seem clear.[54] Through most of February, the Virginian, who served on all the key committees to confer with the army deputation and with Morris, was in close agreement with the superintendent on the measures necessary to resolve the crisis. As a guardian of Virginia's interests, he would not accept the financier's proposal that state surpluses of the old continentals be credited at the official rate of forty to one, nor would he support a tax on acreages of land. And yet, despite Virginia's instructions to oppose any departure from the present mode of apportioning taxes (which required an assessment of land values), he joined with Hamilton and James Wilson, the superintendent's closest supporters in Congress, to insist that the present rule of apportionment was unworkable and must be changed. And while he shared the general congressional resentment of Morris's threat to resign, he agreed with the financier that Congress must have both an impost and additional general revenues to meet its constitutional responsibilities.[55]

With Madison restrained by Virginia's preference for requisitions based on the Articles' rule of apportionment, Wilson and Hamilton took the early lead in advocating independent revenues collected by Congress, while Bland and Arthur Lee led the opposition. Then, on January 28, Madison entered the debate with one of the most impressive speeches of his congressional years. It was unnecessary, he remarked, to argue the necessity of paying the public debt, since "the idea of erecting our national independence on the ruins of public faith and national honor must be horrid to every mind which retained either honesty or pride." No one,

---

[53] The precise nature of the relationship between army radicals and the nationalists and public creditors supporting Morris is undiscoverable. Interpretations range from Henderson's suggestion that Hamilton and Gouverneur Morris, who was Robert's assistant at the Treasury, made "hesitant and uncoordinated" efforts to encourage continuing verbal protests from the army (*Party Politics*, 332-335), through an argument that Hamilton and both Morrises conspired to provoke a coup d'etat by the group around Gates and then to alert Washington in time to squelch it. For the latter see Richard H. Kohn, *Eagle and Sword: The Federalists and the Creation of the Military Establishment in America, 1783-1802* (New York, 1975), chap. 2, and C. Edward Skeen, "The Newburgh Conspiracy Reconsidered," With a Rebuttal by Richard H. Kohn, *WMQ*, 3d Ser., XXXI (1974), 273-298. I suspect a declaration of an intent to disband was more than Hamilton or R. Morris wanted from the army, but it is clear that the Morrisites urged the army to look to Congress, not to the states, for satisfaction of its demands and used the agitation at camp to generate an atmosphere of crisis in Philadelphia. All authorities agree that Madison was not involved in contacts with the army.

[54] Madison's "Notes on Debates," the single most important source for the crisis of 1783, make it possible to follow developments daily. My discussion is based primarily on these (*Madison Papers*, VI, *passim*), and on *Jours. Cont. Cong.*, XXIV.

[55] Madison to Randolph, Jan. 22, 1783, *Madison Papers*, VI, 55. For the response to Morris's letter see "Notes," Jan. 24, 1783, *ibid.*, 120.

though, continued to suppose that Congress could rely on "a punctual and unfailing compliance by thirteen separate and independent governments with periodical demands of money." Nor could Congress reasonably depend on the states to make separate, permanent provisions for the debt. Innumerable occasions would arise for diversion of such funds to state uses, while the conviction of every state that others would fail to meet their obligations would ultimately stop such separate provisions completely. The situation called imperatively for "the plan of a general revenue operating throughout the United States under the superintendence of Congress." The alternative, as Pennsylvania's recent conduct showed, would be state assumptions of federal responsibilities. "What then," he asked, "would become of the Confederation?" What would be the reaction of the army? "The patience of the army has been equal to their bravery, but that patience must have its limits."

Madison denied that general revenues would contravene the principles of the Confederation. Congress was already vested with the power of the purse. "A requisition of Congress on the states for money is as much a law to them as their revenue acts, when passed, are laws to their respective citizens." The Articles authorized Congress to borrow money. If provision for the resulting debt could be made in no other way, then "a general revenue is within the spirit of the Confederation."[56]

With this speech of January 28, Madison seized a leading role in the attempt to win congressional approval of general revenues. He became, indeed, floor general of the effort, although his specific proposals could still be distinguished from those of Hamilton or Wilson by their southern flavor. Viewing the congressional support for an assessment of lands as an insuperable barrier to prior approval of general funds, Madison supported a motion to move the discussion of a mode of assessment ahead of the debate on independent revenues. Hamilton, who saw that the Virginian was trying desperately to bridge the gap between the congressional majority and Morris, quickly fell in line with Madison's attempts to untie procedural knots.

The strategy eventually misfired. By the end of January, even Lee and Bland were moving toward support of a modified impost. Madison argued quietly and effectively for a commutation of the half-pay pensions. Yet the New England and New Jersey delegates continued to resist, provoking him, at one point, to cry out that he was "astonished to hear objections against a commutation come from states in compliance with whose objections against the half-pay itself this expedient had been substituted."[57] Even worse, Congress managed, to Madison's surprise, to agree on a method for assessing lands, although he voted consistently against the plan that was finally approved.[58] Madison had anticipated that a full

[56] "Notes," Jan. 28, 1783, *ibid.*, 143-147.
[57] "Notes," Feb 4, 1783, *ibid.*, 187.
[58] *Jours. Cont. Cong.*, XXIV, 137. Madison condemned the plan as contrary to the Articles because it required a return of population as part of the formula for making an assessment (*Madison Papers*, VI, 256, 195-198, 209, 213, 215-216, 247).

discussion of the possibility of an assessment would convince others, as he was convinced, that the Articles' rule for apportioning requisitions was unworkable. Instead, Congress agreed on a procedure, and the commitment of many members to a first recourse to taxes based on such apportionments remained a major obstacle to approval of general revenues.

The problem was immediately apparent when John Rutledge and Virginia's John Francis Mercer moved to apply the proceeds from a new impost exclusively to the debt due to the army. Madison helped to defeat this proposal on February 18, only to hear Hamilton and Wilson follow with a motion that Congress open its doors to the public when matters of finance were under debate. The Virginian shared the general dislike of this surprising motion, which was greeted with adjournment, and he queried the Pennsylvania delegation privately about it. The Pennsylvanians told him that they had put themselves in a delicate position with their legislature by persuading it to drop its plans for state payments to civilian creditors and simply wished their constituents to know where they stood. "Perhaps the true reason," Madison suspected, "was that it was expected the presence of public creditors, numerous and weighty in Philadelphia, would have an influence" on congressional proceedings.[59]

Congress had already heard Hamilton urge a general revenue on grounds that worried several members. "As the energy of the federal government was evidently short of the degree necessary for pervading and uniting the states," the New Yorker had argued, "it was expedient to introduce the influence of officers deriving their emoluments from and consequently interested in supporting the power of Congress."[60] The subsequent attempt by Hamilton and Wilson to open Congress itself to a powerful lobby reinforced a gathering impression that several advocates of general funds hoped the public creditors would press both the state and federal legislatures into a grant of independent revenues to Congress.[61] Madison was obviously uncomfortable with the expression of such desires.[62]

At just this point the pressure from the army neared its peak, encouraged, if not deliberately provoked, by some of the Philadelphia

---

[59] "Notes," Feb. 18, 1783, *Madison Papers*, VI, 251.

[60] "Notes," Jan. 28, 1783, *ibid.*, 243.

[61] See also Nathaniel Gorham's comment, "Notes," Feb. 18, 1783, *ibid.*, 249-250, and the famous letter of Feb. 7, 1783, in which Gouverneur Morris wrote to Gen. Henry Knox: "If you will permit me a metaphor from your own profession, after you have carried the post, the public creditors will garrison it for you" (*Letters Cont. Cong.*, VII, 34n-35n).

[62] Among other indications, he entered an interesting footnote to the portion of Hamilton's speech quoted above: "This remark was imprudent and injurious to the cause which it was meant to serve," since this sort of influence was precisely what made the states resist a collection by Congress. All the members who shared this fear "smiled at the disclosure." Bland and Lee said privately that Hamilton "had let out the secret" ("Notes," Jan. 28, 1783, *Madison Papers*, VI, 143n).

advocates of general revenues. On February 19, with members openly referring to the threat from the army,[63] Rutledge renewed the motion to appropriate the impost exclusively to the soldiers' needs. Again, Hamilton "strenuously" opposed "such a partial dispensation of justice," suggesting that "it was impolitic to divide the interests of the civil and military creditors, whose joint efforts in the states would be necessary to prevail on them to adopt a general revenue." Mercer countered that he opposed "a permanent debt supported by a permanent and general revenue," believing "it would be good policy to separate instead of cementing the interest of the army and the other public creditors."[64]

On the following evening, February 20—after another day of angry debates—Madison joined Hamilton, Nathaniel Gorham, Richard Peters, and Daniel Carroll at the home of Congressman Thomas FitzSimons. Hamilton and Peters, whose military backgrounds and contacts seemed to make them best informed, told the gathering that the army had definitely decided not to lay down arms until its demands were satisfied; a public declaration would soon announce this intent, and "plans had been agitated if not formed for subsisting themselves after such a declaration." Washington, the two ex-officers announced, "was already become extremely unpopular among almost all ranks from his known dislike to any unlawful proceeding," and "many leading characters" were working industriously to replace him with Horatio Gates. Hamilton said that he had written the commander to alert him to these schemes, urging him to lead the army in any plans for redress, "that they might be moderated." If these revelations were intended to intensify the pressure for the taxes Morris wanted, the strategy could not have been more misconceived. With only Hamilton dissenting, the group of delegates agreed that the temperament of Congress made it impossible to secure any general revenues beyond the impost.[65] Several must have silently concluded that the temper of the army would permit no more delay.

The meeting at FitzSimons's was a critical event for Madison. On the morrow, he rose in Congress for a speech in which he once again defended general revenues as consistent with "the principles of liberty and the spirit of the constitution." But he "particularly disclaimed the idea of perpetuating a public debt," and he admitted that he was now convinced that Congress would have to limit its recommendations to the impost and a "call for the deficiency in the most permanent way that could be reconciled with a revenue established within each state separately."[66] Before this speech of February 21, Madison had worked in close

[63] FitzSimons and Williamson both said openly that they hoped the army would not disband. Williamson added, "If force should be necessary to excite justice, the sooner force were applied the better" ("Notes," ibid., 260-261).

[64] Ibid., 259-261. Wilson agreed with Hamilton that "by dividing the interest of the civil from that of the military creditors provision for the latter would be frustrated."

[65] "Notes," Feb. 20, 1783, ibid., 265-266.

[66] "Notes," Feb. 21, 1783, ibid., 270-272.

conjunction with Morris and his congressional spokesmen. From this point forward, he was determined to construct a compromise of which they disapproved. On March 6, his alternative proposals for restoring public credit were reported from committee. Although Morris, Hamilton, and Wilson continued to resist, the proposals were accepted in amended form on April 18, and Madison was assigned to draft an address to the states. Already, on March 17, Congress had received Washington's report on the resolution of the Newburgh Affair.[67]

Madison's separation from the other advocates of general revenues has commonly been seen, when it is mentioned, as a straightforward product of his conviction that only a compromise could resolve the urgent crisis.[68] More was certainly involved. Beginning with his speech of February 21, Madison took pains to distance himself from suggestions that a "permanent" federal debt could be a useful tool for strengthening Congress and the union. He insisted that he would concur "in every arrangement that should appear necessary for an honorable and just fulfillment of the public engagements and in no measure tending to augment the power of Congress which should appear unnecessary."[69] Madison was out of sympathy, by now, with both the immediate tactics and the ultimate objectives of Hamilton, Wilson, and Morris. He was, indeed, no longer certain of the patriotism and republicanism of some of his fellow advocates of general funds.

Morris's report of July 29, 1782, had advocated general revenues

[67] Madison initially envisioned a comprehensive scheme to resolve several recurrent controversies among the states as well as to secure the revenues required by Congress. Recommendations of an impost and of additional, though separate, state appropriations for servicing the debt would be linked with completion of the western cessions, a federal assumption of state debts, and an abatement of proportions owed by various states upon a settlement of accounts in favor of those states whose abilities had been most impaired by the war. Congress struck the assumption of state debts from the proposal and disjoined the various elements that Madison had meant as a package whose parts would all depend on approval of the others. After excision of assumption from the plan, Madison decided against further attempts to rejoin its parts. He feared that the final plan had "no bait for Virginia," yet hoped that "a respect for justice, good faith, and national honor" would secure the state's approval (see esp. "Notes," Feb. 26, 1783, *ibid.*, 290-292, "Report on Restoring Public Credit," Mar. 6, 1783, *ibid.*, 311-314, and Madison to Jefferson, May 20, 1783, *ibid.*, 481). Morris's report on Madison's proposals approved an assumption of state debts, but preferred to turn the impost into a tariff, still insisted on the need for other congressional revenues (a land tax, a house tax, and an excise), objected to the limitation of the impost to 25 years, and urged congressional appointment of collectors. For Wilson's and Hamilton's continuing attempts to secure Morris's objectives see "Notes," Mar. 11, 20, 1783, *ibid.*, VI, 322-325, 370-372.

[68] Brant, *Madison*, II, chap. 15; Ferguson, *Power of the Purse*, chap. 8, where Madison's authorship of the proposals of April 18 is not mentioned.

[69] "Notes," Feb. 21, 1783, *Madison Papers*, VI, 272.

adequate to meet the government's ordinary operating expenses as well as to manage the debt. These revenues would be collected by officers appointed by Congress, and they would continue as long as the debt existed. For all of Madison's insistence that such measures were within the spirit of the present constitution, no one had expressed a clearer understanding that independent federal revenues would mean a fundamental alteration in the balance of power between Congress and the states.[70] It was this fundamental change that Arthur Lee opposed and Morris, Hamilton, and Wilson found so difficult to relinquish. It was this that Madison first favored and then abandoned in his speech of February 21. He gave it up, not simply because he was more flexible than some of his allies, but because it was not for him, as it was for some of them, an object worth the risks it came to entail. He gave it up, moreover, because it had become increasingly clear that several advocates of general revenues had ulterior objectives he did not share.

All of the original supporters of general funds regarded a dependable federal revenue as essential to the restoration of public credit and probably to the very survival of the Confederation. All of them regarded a provision for regular payment of the interest on the debt as a critical test of national character and an indispensable security against the day when it might be necessary to borrow again. Not all of them, however, actually wished to see the debt retired, nor did the superintendent's plan provide for payment of the principal. Contemporary critics realized this when they condemned a "permanent" or "perpetual" debt, and historians increasingly agree that several of the advocates of general funds looked beyond the reestablishment of public credit toward management of the debt in such a fashion as to promote economic development and to advance a particular variety of political centralization. Properly funded, as Morris put it, the mass of "dead" certificates of debt could rise in value, become "a sufficient circulating medium" for the country, and provide the capital for more intensive economic development.[71] Simultaneously—to use the vivid current metaphor—the obligations of the federal government would become a new "cement" of union. Looking to Congress for their salaries, pensions, or other claims, civilian creditors, the discharged soldiers, and the officers appointed to collect federal taxes, together with merchants doing business with the national bank, would "unite the several states more closely together in one general money connection" and "give stability to government" by combining in its support.[72]

[70] While Congress "exercised the indefinite power of emitting money . . . they had the whole wealth and resources of the continent within their command." Since shutting the presses, they are "as dependent on the states as the king of England is on the Parliament. They can neither enlist, pay, nor feed a single soldier, nor execute any other purpose but as the means are first put into their hands" (Madison to Jefferson, May 6, 1780, *ibid.*, II, 19-20).

[71] Report of July 29, 1782, *Jours. Cont. Cong.*, XXII, 435-437.

[72] Morris to John Jay, July 13, 1781, quoted in Ferguson, *Power of the Purse*, 123-124; *Jours. Cont. Cong.*, XXII, 432.

Hamilton had been thinking in similar fashion since the beginning of the decade. His private correspondence and his anonymous newspaper series, "The Continentalist," repeatedly insisted on the necessity of creating among the nation's leadership a class of influentials tied to the federal government and capable of counterbalancing the influentials currently tied to the states. Genuine federal power, he argued, required a union of the government's resources with those of a monied and office-holding class directly dependent on that government for promotion of its economic interests.[73]

Consciously seeking to replicate developments in England after the Revolution of 1689, several of the nationalists of 1783 sought to bind fragmented segments of the American elite into a single interest intimately connected with the federal government, much as it was thought that the ministers of William III had once attempted to create a "monied interest" that might counterbalance the Tory gentry.[74] It is not a gross exaggeration to suggest that these reformers proposed to use the national debt to create a single nation—or at least an integrated national elite—where none existed in 1783. They envisioned the emergence in America of a facsimile of those linked forces of government, the military, commerce, and finance that ordinarily fell in line behind a ministry in power and lent stability to the British system—interests that the English had in mind when they referred broadly to the forces supporting the "court." Imagining a national greatness predicated on an imitation of the political and economic strengths of England, nationalists such as Hamilton and Morris were prepared to risk some further clamors from the army, if not to feed the agitation, for the sake of general funds. But Madison, who was preoccupied with the defense of a republican revolution and who would never see

[73] See, especially, the letters to an unknown recipient (n.d.), to James Duane (Sept. 3, 1780), and to Robert Morris (Apr. 30, 1781) in Harold C. Syrett et al., eds., *The Papers of Alexander Hamilton*, 26 vols. (New York, 1960-1979), II, 234-251, 400-418, 604-635, together with the conclusion of "The Continentalist," ibid., III, 99-106.

[74] Ferguson was first to see that the Morris nationalists understood and wished to replicate "the role of funded debt and national bank in stabilizing the regime founded in Britain after the revolution of 1689." As historians have more fully explored the character of the 18th-century British regime and the thinking of the English "court"—a term Ferguson did not employ—the implications of this desire have increasingly emerged (*Power of the Purse*, 289-290, and passim). A preliminary exploration of the course of "court" thinking in America is Lance Banning, *The Jeffersonian Persuasion: Evolution of a Party Ideology* (Ithaca, N.Y., 1978), 126-140, and passim. Since then a host of useful contributions have appeared; see particularly Drew R. McCoy, *The Elusive Republic: Political Economy in Jeffersonian America* (Chapel Hill, N.C., 1980); John M. Murrin, "The Great Inversion, or Court versus Country: A Comparison of the Revolution Settlements in England (1688-1721) and America (1776-1816)," in J.G.A. Pocock, ed., *Three British Revolutions: 1641, 1688, 1776* (Princeton, N.J., 1980), 368-453; and Pocock, "1776: The Revolution against Parliament," ibid., 265-288.

Great Britain as a proper model for America, was not. He did not quarrel with the Morrisites or join with Lee and Mercer. Neither was he ignorant of the implications when he disclaimed a desire for a perpetual debt.

Always sensitive about his reputation for consistency, Madison added to his record of his speech of February 21 a lengthy footnote explaining why he had earlier favored the general revenues he now saw as unattainable. This should be read with care, for it suggests the gulf between his motives and those of some of the other reformers, as well as the extent of his discomfort with their views. "Many of the most respectable people of America," he reflected—and it is hard to see whom he had in mind if these "respectable people" did not include the circle of public creditors, army officers, and congressmen that radiated from the Office of Finance— "supposed the preservation of the Confederacy essential to secure the blessings of the revolution and permanent funds for discharging debts essential to the preservation of union." If they were disappointed, he imagined, their ardor in the cause might cool, and in a "critical emergence" they might "prefer some political connection with Great Britain as a necessary cure for our internal instability." Madison himself had not been able to see how "the danger of convulsions from the army" could be obviated without general funds, which also seemed the surest method for preventing "the calamities" sure to follow from continuing disputes among the states. Without general funds "it was not likely the balances would ever be discharged. . . . The consequence would be a rupture of the Confederacy. The eastern states would at sea be powerful and rapacious, the southern opulent and weak. This would be a temptation. The demands on the southern states would be an occasion. Reprisals would be instituted. Foreign aid would be called in by first the weaker, then the stronger side, and finally both be made subservient to the wars and politics of Europe."[75] Collapse of the union would inevitably bring the collapse of the republican revolution in its wake.[76]

Concern for the republican experiment, distrust of the New Englanders, and doubts about the motives of his fellow advocates of general funds may all have contributed to Madison's original decision to support this strengthening of Congress. What is certain from the February memorandum is that all these fears contributed importantly to his decision to *abandon* general revenues in favor of a complex compromise designed to satisfy the army, put an end to the recurrent disagreements that had

[75] "Notes," Feb. 21, 1783, *Madison Papers*, VI, 272.

[76] Madison's fullest (and most fervent) explanation of the inseparable connection he perceived between union and the republican revolution would come in his speech of June 29, 1787, to the Constitutional Convention. Max Farrand, ed., *The Records of the Federal Convention of 1787*, rev. ed. (New Haven, Conn., 1966 [orig. publ. 1937]), I, 464-465. Without the union, the people of every state would see their liberties crushed by powerful executives, standing armies, and high taxes—instruments, by the way, that several nationalists of the early 1780s hoped to create. See also Madison's *Federalist* #41.

periodically disrupted Congress, and do these things *without* so large an alteration of the federal system. Madison did not simply conclude that it was inexpedient to delay a resolution of an urgent crisis. Rather, as he saw more clearly the directions that some of the nationalists wished to take, as he heard from credible sources the growing rumors of intrigues between the capital and the camp at Newburgh, he deliberately drew back.[77] He believed, as Washington believed, that it was profoundly dangerous to delay the satisfaction of the soldiers' demands by continuing to insist on a solution that a majority in Congress would not approve. He had also come to be uneasy at the prospect of the corollaries that Morris's solution seemed to imply. In his "Address to the States" of April 26, 1783, Madison urged the legislatures to approve the new financial plan because it was the *smallest* departure from the Articles of Confederation that could be reconciled with the necessity of providing for the debt.[78]

This was not just special pleading. Through all his years in Congress, Madison had shown a genuine regard for what he often called the "constitutional" boundaries of congressional power. Respect for written limitations of authority was near the center of his republican convictions, as was his regard for national honor. The balance of power between the federal government and the states was always, by comparison, a secondary concern. He thus stood in between the Morrisites and their opponents, genuinely swayed by what he heard from both. By 1783, some nationalists already wished for a convention that would thoroughly transform the federal system.[79] Madison was not prepared for reforms so extreme.[80] He

[77] It is likely that Madison saw the letter to Jones in which Washington suggested that the first Newburgh Address was written in Philadelphia and that the agitation at camp was ultimately attributable to Robert or, more likely, Gouverneur Morris. Madison later remarked that from "private letters from the army and other circumstances there appeared good ground for suspecting that the civil creditors were intriguing in order to inflame the army" and secure general funds ("Notes," Mar. 17, 1783, *Madison Papers*, VI, 348).

[78] "Address to the States by the United States in Congress Assembled," *ibid.*, 489. Madison admitted that the plan departed from the principles of the Confederation—a point about which he was not entirely happy—yet challenged opponents to "substitute some other equally consistent with public justice and honor and more conformable to the doctrines of the Confederation" (Madison to Randolph, May 20, 1783, *ibid.*, VII, 59).

[79] Hamilton drafted a congressional resolution calling for a convention shortly before he retired from Congress, then decided there was too little support to introduce it (Syrett *et al.*, eds., *Hamilton Papers*, III, 420-426). There is disagreement among Ver Steeg, Rakove, and Ferguson as to whether Morris also hoped for a structural transformation of the system.

[80] Hamilton mentioned his desire for a convention in a debate of Apr. 1, 1783 ("Notes," *Madison Papers*, VI, 425). Stephen Higginson, who favored the idea, told Henry Knox in 1787 that he had "pressed upon Mr. Madison and others the idea of a special convention. . . . But they were as much opposed to this idea as I was to the measures they were then pursuing to effect, as they said, the same thing" (*Letters Cont. Cong.*, VII, 123n).

was willing, unlike Lee or Mercer, to accept a centralizing solution to the difficulties the Confederation faced. But this was not his principal objective. He approved a tilting of the federal balance only in the sense and only to the point that he conceived it necessary for the preservation of a union without which the republican experiment could not survive. And he was not immune to fears that certain federal measures might prove incompatible with what he called the "spirit" or the "principles" of liberty.[81] He thus specifically disclaimed a wish for the sort of political centralization that other advocates of funding seemed to have in mind. In January he agreed with Morris that greater powers for Congress were necessary to resolve a crisis of the Revolution. By April he had changed his mind about how far the swing should go. He did not articulate a systematic explanation of his discontent with the emerging program of other continental-minded men to achieve political centralization by fiscal means—perhaps not even to himself. This would await developments after 1789, when their desires assumed more substantial shape. It would also require a further evolution of Madison's own views. By 1783, experience had taught him that congressional reliance on the states for revenue endangered both the character and harmony of the union. But he was not yet ready to conclude, with Hamilton, that the Articles of Confederation were irredeemably defective in their fundamental principles, and he had yet to formulate a truly nationalistic program of his own.

Madison stayed on in Congress until his term expired on October 31, 1783. Through his final months of service, with peace at hand and the financial plan on its way to the states for their decision, he was cast once more in his familiar role as servant of Virginia. Although he struggled unsuccessfully to locate the seat of the federal government on the Potomac River, he had the satisfaction to be present when his old opponents finally decided to give ground on Virginia's terms for a western cession. On September 13 deliberations opened on a compromise that was finally accepted with only Maryland and New Jersey in dissent. Madison

---

[81] A day-by-day reading of his "Notes on Debates" is necessary for a full understanding of the antinationalists' influence on Madison and his growing anxiety for resolution of the crisis; but see particularly the "Notes" for Feb. 27, 1783. Mercer charged that commutation tended "in common with the funding of other debts to establish and perpetuate a monied interest" that "would gain the ascendance of the landed interest . . . and by their example and influence become dangerous to our republican constitutions." Madison protested that commutation was a compromise intended to conciliate those to whom pensions were obnoxious. Now opponents stigmatized commutation as well. Paying the principal of the debt at once was clearly impossible, but funding was said to be "establishing a dangerous monied interest." Madison "was as much opposed to perpetuating the public burdens as anyone," but felt that funding could not be more contrary to "our republican character and constitutions than a violation of good faith and common honesty" (*Madison Papers*, VI, 297–298).

and Jones were content, and their efforts helped secure Virginia's agreement on December 22, 1783.[82]

Madison's pleasure at the outcome of this old dispute was mixed with disappointment over his state's initial rejection of the other congressional recommendations of 1783.[83] When he retired from Congress, he intended to reenter the Virginia House of Delegates to work for the enactment of the state reforms initiated by Jefferson, who had replaced him at the seat of the federal government, and to urge the state's compliance with the Treaty of Paris and the financial proposals of 1783. Pursuing these objectives, he visited George Mason on the journey home and found the great man more favorably inclined than he had anticipated toward the measures he desired. "His heterodoxy," Madison reported, "lay chiefly in being too little impressed with either the necessity or the proper means of preserving the Confederacy."[84]

For Madison, the "proper means" had very recently come to include one significant addition to the powers sought by Congress. In fact, it was his wish for this reform that set him on the path he was to take to the Constitutional Convention. As late as the spring of 1783 he had been reluctant to deliver to the federal government extensive powers over commerce. He had resisted even a commercial treaty with Great Britain, because he feared that an agreement, eagerly desired by northern shippers, could be purchased only with concessions that would sacrifice the planting states' ability to satisfy their most essential needs. "It cannot be for the interest of" Virginia, he had written Randolph, "to preclude it from any regulations which experience may recommend for its thorough emancipation" from the British monopoly over its trade.[85] As he neared retirement, though, Madison had read with alarm the earl of Sheffield's *Observations on the Commerce of the American States,* which argued that Great Britain could maintain its dominant position in trade with the United States without dismantling its restrictive navigation laws.[86] By autumn he had seen the British proclamation of July 2, 1783, which confined most American trade with the West Indies to British bottoms.[87] "Congress," he

---

[82] "Notes," June 10, 20, 1783, *ibid.*, VII, 125-126, 167-168; letters of these months to Jefferson and Randolph, *ibid., passim;* Abernethy, *Western Lands and the Revolution,* 270-273. On Sept. 17, and Oct. 8, 1783, two essays appeared in the *Pennsylvania Journal, and the Weekly Advertiser* (Philadelphia) over the signature "The North American." Examining the critical situation of federal affairs, these urged an alteration of state and federal constitutions that would transfer sovereignty to the central government and render the states subordinate units. Brant drew important support for his portrait of Madison as a nationalist by arguing that the Virginian was the author and that only in these anonymous essays did he reveal the real direction of his thinking. I agree with the editors of the *Madison Papers* that this attribution was mistaken (VII, 319-346).

[83] Madison to Randolph, June 24, 1783, *Madison Papers,* VII, 191-192.

[84] Madison to Jefferson, Dec. 10, 1783, *ibid.,* 401-403, quotation on p. 401.

[85] Madison to Randolph, May 20, 1783, *ibid.,* 59-62, quotation on p. 61.

[86] Madison to Randolph, Aug. 30, 1783, *ibid.,* 295-296.

[87] Madison to Randolph, Sept. 13, 1783, *ibid.,* 314-315.

now reported, "will probably recommend some defensive plan to the states. . . . If it fails . . . it will prove such an inefficacy in the union as will extinguish all respect for it."[88]

Madison reentered the Virginia assembly with his thoughts much occupied with the state's economic situation. In the same letter to Jefferson in which he reported on his visit with Mason, he described the Old Dominion's commercial condition as "even more deplorable than I had conceived." The note of shock is reminiscent of the note of alarm about the state of the union in his letters from Philadelphia as a beginning congressman. Detection of this note is similarly important to an understanding of his career. As Drew R. McCoy has explained, Madison conceived a proper course of economic development to be critical to the success of the republican experiment. This course required the breaching of mercantilist restrictions on American trade.[89] But the congressional request for power to retaliate against the British was denied. Madison's attempts to break the British stranglehold with new state regulations were gutted by the demands of local interests in Virginia's legislature.[90] The congressional recommendations of 1783 also failed to win approval from the states, among which tensions mounted.

By the end of 1784 Madison was willing, if not yet eager, to see a constitutional convention to amend the Articles of Confederation.[91] By August 7, 1785, if not much before, he was fully persuaded that America's commercial ills could not be corrected by state actions, such as those he had attempted in Virginia. Congressional superintendence of commerce, he now argued, was "within the reason of the federal constitution. . . . If Congress as they are now constituted cannot be trusted with the power, . . . let them be chosen oftener . . . or, if any better medium than Congress can be proposed, by which the wills of the states may be concentered, let it be substituted. . . . But let us not . . . rush on certain ruin in order to avoid a possible danger."[92]

It was, in short, the obvious inability of the states to grapple separately with the economic difficulties of the postwar years that first led Madison to think in terms of a thoroughgoing alteration of the federal system. It was his profound discontent with the measures many states adopted in response to the postwar depression—measures he considered contrary to the liberal principles of the Revolution—that would complete his change of stance and lead him to assume the major role in preparing the Virginia Resolutions.[93] Before his retirement from the Confederation Congress,

---

[88] *Ibid.*, 315.

[89] Madison to Jefferson, Dec. 10, 1783, *ibid.*, 401; McCoy, *Elusive Republic*, esp. chap. 3.

[90] McCoy, "The Virginia Port Bill of 1784," *Virginia Magazine of History and Biography*, LXXXIII (1975), 288-303.

[91] Madison to Richard Henry Lee, Dec. 25, 1784, *Madison Papers*, VIII, 201.

[92] Madison to Monroe, *ibid.*, 333-336.

[93] Two of many passages are particularly revealing of Madison's route to the Virginia Plan. "Most of our political evils"—paper money, indulgences for

there had been little evidence that he would favor, much less author, such a plan.

During his years in Congress, James Madison made several major contributions to the movement to strengthen the central government. His role in the Virginia cession and his authorship of the congressional recommendations of 1783 identified him as a prominent reformer. When he retired from Congress, everyone expected him to lead the continental-minded forces in his state assembly. Yet Madison had never been a nationalist by instinct, as some of the reformers of the early 1780s were. He had never shared the fascination with an English model of administration and political economy. His contributions to reform were always shaped and limited by a concern that certain centralizing changes might endanger both the interests of Virginia and the Revolution's most essential goals.

Through the years in Congress, Madison had ordinarily attributed the difficulties of the central government to the clashing interests of the different states, in which he was continuously involved, and to the disabilities that all the states experienced as a result of war. He had hoped that peace would meliorate these problems.[94] He did not deeply challenge the purposes or structure of the federal government as defined by the Articles of Confederation. He did not deeply question the republican regimes established in the states by the early Revolutionary constitutions. Only after he left Congress and went home to struggle year by year in the assembly with advocates of paper money, tax abatements, and assessments for religion, only as he grew increasingly distressed with poorly drafted and inconstant legislation, only when he could no longer hope that the parochial objectives of the states could be reconciled with the continuation of the union, was Madison compelled to reexamine the most fundamental assumptions of his republicanism. Only then did he conclude that accusations he had once dismissed as calumnies on republican government—charges of inconstancy, weakness, and oppression of minorities—were true of small republics and could be overcome only by "extending the sphere."[95]

At the Constitutional Convention, nonetheless, Madison still sought, as he insisted, a genuinely republican remedy for the ills of republican government. In 1787, as before, his fundamental purpose was to nurture and defend a Revolutionary order of society and politics. He remained, as

---

debtors, etc.—"may be traced up to our commercial ones, as most of our moral may to our political" (Madison to Jefferson, Mar. 18, 1786, *ibid.*, 502). In the Convention, June 6, 1787, Madison stated that foreign relations, national defense, and protection against interstate disputes were not the only concern; additional security for private rights was also a necessary object. "Interferences with these were evils which had more perhaps than anything else produced this convention" (Farrand, ed., *Records*, I, 134).

[94] See the sketch printed in Farrand, ed., *Records*, III, 542-543.
[95] *Federalist* #10.

he had always been, a nationalist at certain times, on certain issues, and within the limits of his Revolutionary hopes. Grasping this, it may seem less surprising that he quickly moved into the opposition to Alexander Hamilton's proposals for the new regime.

Hamilton may well have been "affectionately attached" to the cause of republican government.[96] As secretary of the Treasury he nevertheless attempted to "administer" the new American republic toward a future incompatible with Madison's desires.[97] Of all the nationalists of 1783, Hamilton had had the clearest vision of a nation integrated on a British model. After 1789 his foreign policy and constitutional constructions were intimately related to this vision. Both served an economic program intended to create a counterbalance to the influence of state attachments by tying the interests of a critical segment of the American elite to the fortunes of the central government. If Hamilton had seen a little deeper into the assumptions of his occasional ally, he might have been less startled when Madison rebelled.

Hamilton and Madison both understood that the United States had no equivalent of England's national elite. For Madison, this fact was an essential precondition of the promise that the new Constitution might effect a genuinely republican solution to the nation's ills. Liberty, as he conceived it, demanded both a government dependent on the body of the people and security for the fundamental rights that had been threatened in the states by majority control. The pluralistic structure of American society, which would be mirrored in the pluralistic character and conduct of its leaders, was the most important guarantee that a responsive federal government would not prove equally at odds with the protection of the civil liberties of all. For Hamilton, by contrast, pluralism was America's great weakness. A government consistent with promotion of the common good and security for private rights was not to be attained except by policies designed to overcome the centrifugal inclinations of the American order. Hamilton's economic program, calculated to encourage the appearance of a unified elite whose interests would divorce them from the localistic inclinations of the American majority, was deliberately intended to subvert the social and economic structure on which Madison believed a federal republic had to rest. In the Virginian's stands in the old Congress—his hostility to speculative gain at public expense, his profound distrust of Britain, his inclination to respect constitutional definitions of authority, and his eventual disagreement with the more determined advocates of general funds—lay several warnings that his thinking did not really share "the same point of departure" as Hamilton's own.[98] After 1789, Madison refined and made explicit principles that had already influenced him in 1783.

[96] As he insisted in a letter to Edward Carrington, May 26, 1792 (Syrett et al., eds., *Hamilton Papers*, XI, 426-445).

[97] Madison's word in an interview with Nicholas P. Trist, Sept. 27, 1834 (Farrand, ed., *Records*, III, 533-534).

[98] Hamilton to Carrington, May 26, 1792, Syrett et al., eds., *Hamilton Papers*, XI, 426-445.

Whither Columbia?
Congressional Residence and the Politics of the New Nation, 1776 to 1787

Lawrence Delbert Cress*

IN 1790 Congress adopted legislation that moved the nation's capital from New York to Philadelphia, with the stipulation that a new capital city be built on the banks of the Potomac River by 1800. This was not the first time that Congress had acted on the question of the location of the national government. Repeatedly, over a period of more than two years—from 1782 to 1784, when New York was designated the temporary residence of Congress and the decision was taken to fix its permanent site in open country near the falls of the Delaware—the representatives of the confederated states had grappled with the issue. Their deliberations involved important sectional interests, both political and economic, and these considerations were associated with basic attitudes toward the power and function of central government, federally conceived, in a republican society. The wanderings of Congress during the Confederation period were also related to the declining political fortunes of the proponents of a stronger national government and the subsequent reaffirmation of the limited government prescribed in the Articles of Confederation. The debates over the location of the capital thus provide insights both into the nature of factional divisions in Congress at the close of the period of nationalist ascendancy and into the complex relationship between ideology and sectional self-interest that influenced the decision-making process in Congress during the 1780s.

The Continental Congress had been meeting in Philadelphia for nearly two years when independence was declared in July 1776. During the next two years Congress was forced to flee Philadelphia twice to avoid capture by British regulars. General William Howe's advance into New Jersey in December 1776 sent Congress south to Baltimore until late February 1777. In September 1777 Howe threatened once more; again Congress fled

* Mr. Cress is a graduate student at the University of Virginia.

Philadelphia, first to Lancaster, then on to York, where the delegates remained until the British evacuated the Quaker City in June 1778.[1]

Congressional wanderings during the war years were the result of military necessity. Yet throughout the period an uneasiness about residence in Philadelphia existed that sprang both from the anti-urban bias of republican ideology and from resentment of the political influence Philadelphia exerted over the deliberations of Congress.[2] This uneasiness was never strong enough to cause Congress to leave Philadelphia, but it did manifest itself in several plans concerned with the postwar location of Congress. Some New England delegates considered establishing a migratory legislature that would move regularly about the Confederation. An "ambulatory Congress," they reasoned, would give each state an opportunity to host that body, thus precluding excessive influence over its decisions by the interests of a particular locale. An alternative proposal that Congress purchase land on which to build a new federal city reflected

---

[1] Robert L. Brunhouse, *The Counter-Revolution in Pennsylvania, 1776-1790* (Harrisburg, Pa., 1942), 23-25; Edmund Cody Burnett, *The Continental Congress* (New York, 1941), 210, 309-310, 339-340; Thomas Burke, "Abstract of Debate," Feb. 8, 1777, Burke Papers, Southern Historical Collection, University of North Carolina, Chapel Hill. This document and many others have been examined at the Library of Congress, where the American Revolution Bicentennial Committee is preparing a new edition of *Letters of Delegates to Congress, 1774-1789*. Thomas Burke, "Abstract of Debates in Congress," Feb. 26, 1777, in Walter Clark, ed., *State Records of North Carolina, 1777-1790* (Winston and Goldsboro, N. C., 1895-1905), XI, 385; Edith Rossiter Bevan, "The Continental Congress in Baltimore, Dec. 20, 1776, to Feb. 27, 1777," *Maryland Historical Magazine*, XLII (1947), 21-28; Gaillard Hunt, ed., *Journals of the Continental Congress, 1774-1789* (Washington, D. C., 1904-1937), VIII, 742; William Duane, ed., *Extracts from the Diary of Christopher Marshall, Kept in Philadelphia and Lancaster, during the American Revolution, 1774-1781* (Albany, N. Y., 1877), entry for Sept. 29, 1777.

[2] George Washington to Thomas Johnson, Jr., Aug. 5, 1774, in John C. Fitzpatrick, ed., *The Writings of George Washington* (Washington, D. C., 1931-1944), III, 235; Silas Deane to Thomas Munford, Oct. 16, 1774, letter privately owned by Robert J. Sudderth, Jr., Lookout Mountain, Tenn.; Deane to Elizabeth Deane, Sept. 23, 1774, Deane Papers, Connecticut Historical Society, Hartford; William Whipple to John Langdon, Dec. 24, 1776, Elywin Papers, Library of Congress; Richard Henry Lee to Patrick Henry, Dec. 18, 1776, Samuel Adams to Mrs. Adams, Dec. 19, 1776, in Edmund C. Burnett, ed., *Letters of Members of the Continental Congress* (Washington, D. C., 1921-1936), II, 178, 179; Francis Lightfoot Lee to Landon Carter, Jan. 14, 1777, Lee-Ludwell Papers, Virginia Historical Society, Richmond; Whipple to Josiah Bartlett, Jan. 13, 1777, Bartlett Papers, Dartmouth College Library, Hanover, N. H.; William Williams to Jonathan Trumbull, July 5, 1777, Oliver Wolcott to Mrs. Wolcott, June 5, 1778, in Burnett, ed., *Letters*, II, 401, III, 278; Bartlett to Langdon, July 13, 1778, Bancroft Collection, New York Public Library, New York City; Francis Lewis to George Clinton, Aug. 18, 1779, William Floyd to Clinton, Dec. 21, 1779, Nathaniel Peabody to Bartlett, Dec. 24, 1779, in Burnett, ed., *Letters*, IV, 382, 544, 549.

much the same intent. Both plans offered ways to free congressional deliberations from state and local influences while providing a means of escaping the moral depravity of Philadelphia's urban environment.[3]

Periodic attempts were made to move Congress out of Philadelphia during 1778 and 1779. But after a brief revival of the issue in 1780, the residency question lay dormant for nearly three years, while the southern campaign, fiscal problems, peace negotiations, the demobilization of the army, the ratification of the Articles, and the problem of western lands dominated the congressional calendar.[4] During this period, a shift in the locus of power in Congress from New England to the middle states contributed to the physical stability of Congress. The "eastern bloc"—the source of earlier agitations to remove Congress from Philadelphia—had dominated deliberations from 1774 to 1779 under the able leadership of Samuel Adams and Richard Henry Lee. The demand for more efficient management of the war effort and the retirement of key members of the eastern bloc during the winter of 1779-1780 shifted power to the nationalist faction, led by Robert Morris, the Philadelphia merchant and financier.

By 1781 the nationalists, backed by a strong coalition of middle and southern state delegates, had overhauled the executive machinery of Congress and were advocating a 5 percent impost, continental funding of the public debt, and half-pay for life for army officers. Wide southern support for the nationalists' program was related to the critical military situation in the South during 1781 and reflected the South's fear of being severed from the rest of the Confederation if peace should be declared on the heels of a major British victory south of the Potomac. The end of hostilities and the renewal of debate over such regionally sensitive issues as the western lands during 1782 tended to fragment the southern wing of the coalition, leaving the nationalist faction composed primarily of delegates from the middle states, together with several prominent southerners, among whom were James Madison and Joseph Jones of Virginia and Daniel Carroll of Maryland. During 1783 this nucleus of nationalists continued to seek the enlargement of congressional power and the creation of a solid fiscal foundation for the federal government.[5]

[3] John Adams to Mrs. Adams, Mar. 7, 1777, in Burnett, ed., Letters, II, 291; Benjamin Rush to George Morgan, Nov. 8, 1779, in L. H. Butterfield, ed., Letters of Benjamin Rush, I (Princeton, N. J., 1951), 245. The editor notes correctly that this letter was probably written on Dec. 8, 1779.
[4] Hunt, ed., Journals, XV, 1134, 1139, XVI, 293. See also Burnett, ed., Letters, V, 15, n. 4.
[5] Herbert James Henderson, "Political Factions in the Continental Congress, 1774-

Nationalists saw the seeds of American greatness not only among the sturdy yeoman farmers who symbolized the Revolution's mythical Saxon heritage, but also in the embryonic commercial and metropolitan centers of the North American continent. Their support of congressional residence in Philadelphia reflected the business-oriented and urban-centered vision of leading spokesmen like Morris. Practically, the presence of Congress was estimated to be worth an additional $100,000 in annual trade for the city's merchants. This economic windfall, together with the nationalist outlook of Philadelphia's merchant community, gave the nationalists important "out-of-doors" support for their policies as long as Congress remained in Philadelphia. Nevertheless, the economics of residency tended to weaken nationalist solidarity, inasmuch as southern nationalists, ever eager to secure a major commercial center for their region, parted company with their northern allies whenever the capital seemed within reach. This temptation was particularly prevalent within the Maryland and Virginia delegations.[6]

The centralist energies of the nationalist faction aroused a republican opposition that was united more in opposition to nationalist programs than in support of any policies of its own. This "parochialist coalition" included Elbridge Gerry, Stephen Higginson, and Samuel Osgood of Massachusetts, David Howell and William Ellery of Rhode Island, Arthur Lee and Theodorick Bland of Virginia, and Ralph Izard and John Gervais of South Carolina.[7] Although the coalition was a negative if not artificial

---

1783" (Ph.D. diss., Columbia University, 1962), 314-322; H. James Henderson, "The Structure of Politics in the Continental Congress," in Stephen G. Kurtz and James H. Hutson, eds., *Essays on the American Revolution* (Chapel Hill, N. C., 1973), 165-166, 174-176, 186-187; H. James Henderson, "Constitutionalists and Republicans in the Continental Congress, 1778-1786," *Pennsylvania History*, XXXVI (1969), 131-137; H. James Henderson, *Party Politics in the Continental Congress* (New York, 1974), 319-320; Jackson Turner Main, *The Antifederalists: Critics of the Constitution, 1781-1788* (Chapel Hill, N. C., 1961), 72-102. The term "eastern bloc" is appropriated from Henderson.

[6] Arthur Lee to Francis Dana, June 6, 1782, A Member of Congress to [?] [1783], Ezra L'Hommedieu to Clinton, Aug. 15, 1783, in Burnett, ed., *Letters*, VI, 379, VII, 156, 266. Burnett credits the anonymous letter to Arthur Lee, dating it sometime in May 1783. Henderson, "Constitutionalists and Republicans," *PH*, XXXVI (1969), 138; Henderson, "Political Factions," 317-318; Henderson, *Party Politics*, 338-339.

[7] The nomenclature of the political configurations in the Continental Congress has always been a problem for historians of the Confederation Period. For the present essay the term "anti-nationalist" was rejected because it seemed to imply a positive program and the possibility of continued political coherence once the nationalist faction had collapsed. The designation "parochialist" is used because of the special character and function of the coalition. The coalition sprang from a negative reaction to nationalist programs and had little potential for political unity once the

alliance, motivated primarily by the political challenge of the nationalist ascendancy, it reflected the multiple ideological and sectional strains that affected congressional politics during the 1780s. The coalition drew from regionally oriented blocs that were products of pragmatic as well as ideological commitments, and it achieved its greatest coherence on issues that transcended regional boundaries. Eastern and southern members of the coalition regularly found themselves divided over such issues as western lands, officers' pensions, and national finance, but the coalition was in solid agreement that Morris and men of his type represented one of the gravest dangers to the young nation. To these delegates, the elimination of the influence exercised over the councils of government by Morris and the "wealthier citizens" of Philadelphia was essential to the survival of republican government. The removal of Congress from Philadelphia was one way to reduce that influence.[8]

If Morris represented a threat to limited government, his base of operation, Philadelphia, connoted a threat to the public virtues necessary to the success of republicanism. To parochialists, the moral decay and social disorder in America's growing commercial centers seemed to encourage decadence and corruption in the government at the very time that republican virtues were needed most. The parochialist coalition viewed the removal of the capital from Philadelphia not only as a cure for the centralizing tendencies of Morris's nationalists but also as a means of returning the nation to the wholesome values of a simpler, agrarian society.[9] This commitment to republicanism was important in generating anti-Philadelphia sentiment in Congress, but the parochialists could not agree among themselves on where the capital should be located. Attempts to settle this question brought forth old regional prejudices and sectional antagonisms that bespoke the basic sectional character of politics in the Continental Congress.

---

nationalist faction declined. The unity of the coalition often depended directly upon the relationship of a particular issue to the ambitions of Robert Morris and his nationalist followers. Although Elbridge Gerry did not arrive in Congress until later in 1783, he is included here because of the leadership role he assumed in the coalition by the summer of 1783.

[8] Henderson, "Constitutionalists and Republicans," *PH*, XXXVI (1969), 131, 138; Henderson, "Political Factions," 311-312, 315-319; Henderson, *Party Politics*, 341; Anonymous to Theodorick Bland, Nov. 17, 1782, Stephen Higginson to Bland, Jan. 1784, in Charles Campbell, ed., *The Bland Papers* . . . , II (Petersburg, Va., 1840), 95-97, 113-114.

[9] Member of Congress to [?] [1783], Samuel Osgood to J. Adams, Dec. 7, 1783, in Burnett, ed., *Letters*, VII, 156, 378; James T. Austin, *The Life of Elbridge Gerry*, I (Boston, 1828), 450-451; Henderson, *Party Politics*, 338-341.

The first serious discussion of moving the government from Philadelphia since 1780 occurred in Congress during the winter of 1782-1783.[10] Dissatisfaction over conditions in the Quaker City dated back to 1774, but always before the realities of war or the strength of the nationalist faction had militated against leaving the city. By the end of 1782, however, the promise of peace, the breakup of the southern wing of the nationalist faction, and the coalescing of the parochialists had combined to make the relocation of the capital a political possibility. Throughout the next two years the problem of finding a permanent home was never far from the mind of any congressman.

During the spring of 1783, even before Congress officially solicited recommendations for its permanent residence, offers to host the government began arriving. These offers were significant principally for their expression of the civic pride of communities that were seeking national fame and fortune. In mid-March, Kingston, New York, that state's capital until British troops burned it in 1777, offered Congress one square mile of land overlooking the Hudson River. The town's motive was clearly economic. As the residence of Congress, Kingston would attract a supply of people and money with which to rebuild itself. Kingston residents expressed their willingness to accept the full civil authority of Congress, but the official offer of jurisdiction sent by the New York legislature proposed only limited congressional control. Disputes over property, civil suits involving inhabitants of Kingston and citizens outside of its boundaries, and all criminal matters were to be tried in the state courts. Local residents were to remain subject to taxes and other assessments levied on citizens of New York.[11]

In May the Maryland legislature offered Congress a three-hundred-acre site in Annapolis. The statehouse, the governor's mansion, and a public circle were included, and the state promised to build thirteen official residences for the delegates of each of the states. The mayor and councilmen of Annapolis informed Congress of the many amenities of life on the Chesapeake and voiced the willingness of local residents to accept broad congressional jurisdiction over their affairs. Maryland state officials, however, were willing to grant Congress only the jurisdiction "necessary [to

---

[10] Anon. to Bland, Nov. 17, 1782, in Campbell, ed., *Bland Papers*, II, 95-97. This letter is also of interest because it indicates that persons outside Congress were aware of the regional and possibly ideological configuration of politics in the Continental Congress.

[11] Papers of the Continental Congress, Item 46: 1-10, Library of Congress; Alphonso Trumpbour Clearwater, *The History of Ulster County, New York* (Kingston, N. Y., 1907), 205-215.

insure] the Honor, Dignity, convenience, and safety of that body." This important limitation reflected the reluctance of most states to grant extensive extraterritorial powers to the federal government.[12]

Meanwhile the Virginians in the Congress were attempting to interest skeptical members of the Maryland delegation in a plan to have Virginia and Maryland jointly offer Congress a site near the falls of the Potomac River in the vicinity of Georgetown.[13] This proposal was appealing for several reasons. The conditions of communication and transportation in 1783 made it advisable for the government to be both centrally located and readily accessible. This meant that the capital had to be situated somewhere between the Hudson and Potomac rivers, preferably in reach of oceangoing vessels. Virginia and Maryland were the only southern states geographically eligible to host the capital, and a site acceptable to both states was important if the South hoped to present a unified position on the residency issue. The Georgetown site, besides meeting the geographic requirements, offered a means of guaranteeing sectional solidarity.

Georgetown also had the potential of winning the support of the parochialist coalition. Southern members of the coalition, including Lee and Bland of Virginia and Benjamin Hawkins of North Carolina, had no trouble endorsing the site. Georgetown was as far removed from the nationalist establishment in Philadelphia as any parochialist might wish. Furthermore, southern parochialists saw the location on the Potomac as a means of gaining a much-needed commercial outlet for the upper South. With the aid of these key southern parochialists, the proponents of Georgetown hoped to unite the economic interests of the South with the anti-Philadelphia bias of the parochialist coalition, thus gaining enough votes to move the capital to the Potomac.[14]

In early June 1783, Congress decided to put off formal consideration of a permanent residence until October in order to give other states an opportunity to propose additional sites.[15] For the moment, Congress

[12] Continental Congress Papers, Item 46: 15-19, 32-33.

[13] Maryland never formally joined Virginia in nominating the Georgetown site. For obvious reasons, Marylanders favored locating Congress in Annapolis and normally backed the Potomac site only when hopes for Annapolis were dim.

[14] Benjamin Harrison to Virginia Delegates, May 17, 1783, James Madison to Edmund Randolph, July 28, 1783, in William T. Hutchinson and William M. E. Rachal, eds., *The Papers of James Madison*, VII (Chicago, 1971), 49-50, 256-257; Virginia Delegates to Harrison, Apr. 10, 1783, Madison to Randolph, Oct. 13, 1783, North Carolina Delegates to Gov. Alexander Martin, Oct. 24, 1783, in Burnett, ed., *Letters*, VII, 133-134, 332-333, 353-354.

[15] President of Congress [Elias Boudinot] to the Several States, June 10, 1783, in Burnett, ed., *Letters*, VII, 192.

seemed certain to stay in Philadelphia at least another six months. Then on June 24 the threat of armed troops again forced Congress to leave Philadelphia. Unable to persuade the Executive Council of Pennsylvania to call out the militia to control an angry regiment of the Continental Army demanding back pay, an outraged Congress adjourned across the Delaware River to Princeton, New Jersey,[16] where it convened on June 30, intending to stay only until order was restored in Philadelphia. Soon, however, most delegates agreed that the circumstances of their departure necessitated that Congress insist on an official request for their return from the Pennsylvania Executive Council.[17] The parochialist coalition, finding Congress at last freed from Philadelphia, was determined not to go back. The coalition believed that Morris's influence was declining daily while Congress remained in Princeton and hoped that continued residence there would eventually force his resignation as superintendent of finance.[18]

The nationalist faction, for its part, pressed for an immediate return to Philadelphia. Failure to do so, the nationalists contended, would not only have an adverse effect on government credit at home and abroad but would hinder peace negotiations. Speaking for the interests of the city, a Pennsylvania nationalist, John Montgomery, raised the threat of his state's separation from the Confederation if Congress did not comply. Such leading Virginia nationalists as Madison and Jones were also influenced by sectional considerations. They believed that only a return to Philadelphia would prevent a site selection based solely on the availability of accommodations for Congress, a criterion that would give Annapolis a clear advantage over undeveloped Georgetown, their preferred site.[19]

16 "Preface," *ibid.*, xix, xxii; Elias Boudinot to Elisha Boudinot, June 23, 1783, *ibid.*, 195; Alexander Hamilton to Elias Boudinot, June 24, 1783, Boudinot Papers, Lib. Cong. For a detailed account of politics and business in Princeton see Varnum Lansing Collins, *The Continental Congress at Princeton* (Princeton, N. J., 1908).

17 Hunt, ed., *Journals*, XXIV, 423; Continental Congress Papers, Item 46: 59, 63-64, 67, 71; John Montgomery to Rush, July 8, 1783, in Burnett, ed., *Letters*, VII, 216; Charles Thomson to William White, July 8, 1783, Society Collection, Historical Society of Pennsylvania, Philadelphia; Joseph Jones to Madison, July 14, 1783, in Worthington Chauncey Ford, ed., *Letters of Joseph Jones, of Virginia, 1777-1787* (Washington, D. C., 1889), 126-128.

18 A. Lee to St. George Tucker, July 21, 1783, Earl Gregg Swem Library, College of William and Mary, Williamsburg, Va.; David Howell to Nicholas Brown, July 30, 1783, Nicholas Brown Papers, John Carter Brown Library, Providence, R. I.; Higginson to Nathaniel Gorham, Aug. 5, 1783, in Burnett, ed., *Letters*, VII, 252.

19 Edmund Pendleton to Madison and Jones, July 21, 1783, in David John Mays, ed., *The Letters and Papers of Edmund Pendleton, 1734-1803*, II (Charlottesville, Va., 1967), 455-456; Montgomery to Rush, June 30, 1783, Rush to Montgomery, July 2, 1783, Madison to Randolph, July 8, 1783, in Burnett, ed., *Letters*, VII, 205, 201n-

Meanwhile Congress continued to receive proposals concerning its permanent residence. The New Jersey legislature tendered Congress £30,000 in specie to defray the cost of procuring land and erecting buildings in any New Jersey community that petitioned for congressional residence. Trenton, Nottingham, Newark, New Brunswick, and Elizabethtown all filed petitions under these terms before the summer was over.[20] In July the Virginia Assembly offered one hundred acres of land near the falls of the Potomac. A sum of £100,000 was promised to finance the construction of necessary accommodations. If the capital were built across the river at Georgetown, £40,000 would be allocated to meet construction expenses. Virginia also offered a three-hundred-acre tract in Williamsburg, should Congress desire immediate accommodations. This proposal included the use of the old statehouse and the governor's mansion, besides £100,000 for the construction of "hotels" in which to house the delegations.[21]

In Congress, pressure was mounting for a firm decision concerning its winter residence. Many New England delegates advocated remaining in Princeton pending a final decision on permanent residence. Other delegates recommended adjourning temporarily to Annapolis or New York City, where more ample accommodations were available.[22] Madison, Jones, and Hugh Williamson, a North Carolina nationalist, supported a return to Philadelphia. Their thinking was based in the sectional and ideological realities of congressional politics. If Congress returned to Philadelphia, these delegates reasoned, the anti-Philadelphia votes of the parochialists could be combined with solid southern support, including that of the southern nationalists, for the proposal to move Congress permanently to the Potomac. The only serious threat to this eastern-southern entente would arise from the possibility that the New Englanders might opt for a more centrally located residence. Finding little support for

202n, 219; Rush to Montgomery, July 4, 1783, Rush to Elias Boudinot, Aug. 2, 1783, in Butterfield, ed., *Letters of Rush*, I, 304-305, 307-308; Madison to Thomas Jefferson, July 17, 1783, in Julian P. Boyd *et al.*, eds., *The Papers of Thomas Jefferson* (Princeton, N. J., 1950-   ), VII, 318-319.

[20] New Jersey House of Assembly Resolution, June 18, 1783, Continental Congress Papers, Item 46: 39-41; Hunt, ed., *Journals*, XXIV, 422. Copies of the Nottingham, Trenton, New Brunswick, and Elizabethtown offers are in the Continental Congress Papers, Item 46, 43-46, 83-84, 95-96, 105-110. The Newark offer is in Hunt, ed., *Journals*, XXIV, 439.

[21] Continental Congress Papers, Item 46: 155-157; Hunt, ed., *Journals*, XXIV, 494.

[22] Richard Peters to Thomas Fitzsimons, July 26, 1783, Gratz Collection, Hist. Soc. Pa.; Hugh Williamson to William Blount, Aug. 4, 1783, Blount Papers, North Carolina Archives, Raleigh; Williamson to Martin, Aug. 4, 1783, in Burnett, ed., *Letters*, VII, 251; James McHenry to T. S. Lee, June 28, 1783, Miscellaneous MSS, United States Naval Academy, Annapolis, Md.

moving Congress directly to Annapolis, Carroll and James McHenry of Maryland also endorsed the plan to go back to Philadelphia. Their motives were similar to those of Madison, Jones, and Williamson, except that the Marylanders hoped to persuade Congress to move on to Annapolis. These delegates from the upper South also recognized that a return to Philadelphia had the added advantage of reducing the likelihood that middle state delegates would be willing to ally with the eastern delegates to relocate Congress somewhere outside the Quaker City.[23]

Congress took several preliminary votes on the residency question during August 1783. Determined to block a return to Philadelphia, Howell of Rhode Island and Bland of Virginia, both important members of the parochialist coalition, moved to adjourn Congress to the Quaker City. Their strategy was to force a vote on the issue before the nationalists were able to persuade Pennsylvania's Executive Council officially to invite Congress to return. After the pro-Philadelphia delegates, led by James Wilson and Richard Peters of Pennsylvania, failed to delay consideration, the Howell-Bland resolution was soundly defeated. With Madison and Jones absent, Virginia voted solidly against the measure, while Williamson's vote for Philadelphia left the North Carolina vote evenly divided. Only Pennsylvania and Maryland supported the measure.[24]

With Philadelphia at least temporarily disposed of, members of the parochialist coalition began to consider alternative sites. Southern parochialists, attuned to sectional priorities, advocated residence near Georgetown, but New England delegates had other ideas. Their region being geographically ineligible, the New Englanders were particularly sensitive to the power and influence the capital would bring to its host. Eastern delegates feared that residence on the Potomac would only increase the "aristocratic" influence of the South in Congress. They preferred a site in New Jersey. That state's central location made it easily accessible, and its small size precluded undue influence on the councils of government. Just as important, it had no potential for commercial development and

[23] McHenry to Gov. Paca, July 26, 1783, Hall of Records, Annapolis; Madison to Randolph, July 28, 1783, in Hutchinson and Rachal, eds., *Madison Papers,* VII, 256-257; McHenry to Paca, Aug. 9, 1783, Madison to Randolph, Aug. 18, 1783, in Burnett, ed., *Letters,* VII, 254, 268.

[24] Hunt, ed., *Journals,* XXIV, 484, 506-509; Clifford L. Lord, ed., *The Atlas of Congressional Roll Calls,* I: *The Continental Congresses and the Congresses of the Confederation, 1777-1789* Cooperstown, N. Y., 1943), C 0973, C 0977, C 0978, C 0979. This volume contains mapped vote distributions for every recorded roll call in Congress beginning in 1777. Abiel Foster to Bartlett, Aug. 23, 1783, Bartlett Papers.

so would long preserve the purity of its "republican principles and manners." Some New Englanders recommended permanently locating Congress in Princeton, called the "Montpelier of America" by one enthusiastic delegate. The town was small; it lacked the commercial development that made Philadelphia unacceptable, and it was free of yellow fever and other epidemics that regularly plagued cities like Philadelphia and New York. New Englanders also believed that Princeton's location between New York and Philadelphia would assist in preventing either city from dominating Congress.[25]

During September 1783 Congress received more residency offers. The Pennsylvania Assembly, guaranteeing that the "Honor and dignity" of Congress would be maintained, offered the Pennsylvania statehouse and its adjoining buildings for the temporary use of Congress while a permanent site was being selected and reminded Congress that Philadelphia was still available as a permanent seat.[26] The assembly also forwarded an invitation from the citizens of Germantown, a small farm community located six miles from Philadelphia. The strategy behind this proposal was to offer Congress an alternate residence that would not represent a serious threat to the nationalist interests of Philadelphia.[27]

From New York came an offer of the Manor of Morrisania, the large estate of Lewis Morris, brother of Gouverneur Morris and a signer of the Declaration of Independence. Overlooking the East River where it joins the Harlem, Morrisania boasted a saltwater harbor that would never be closed by ice—an advantage, Morris noted, not enjoyed by sites located on inland rivers. Its location also made a surprise attack by a foreign fleet highly unlikely since the enemy would have to sail the entire length of the Long Island Sound undetected. The number of small towns in the area, together with the militia strength of New York City, gave Morrisania the greatest concentration of potential fighting men anywhere in the country. Morris noted by comparison that some populated areas in

[25] Howell to Thomas Carder Hazard, Aug. 6, 1783, Howell to Moses Brown, Aug. 24, 1783, Moses Brown Papers, Rhode Island Historical Society, Providence; Howell to N. Brown, July 30, 1783, Brown Papers; Higginson to S. Adams, Aug. 21, 1783, Rhode Island Delegates to Gov. William Greene, Sept. 8, 1783, in Burnett, ed., *Letters*, VII, 271-272, 286-287; Johann David Schoepf, *Travels in the Confederation [1783-1784]*, trans. and ed. Alfred J. Morrison, II (Philadelphia, 1911), 41-42.

[26] Hunt, ed., *Journals*, XXV, 530-531.

[27] The same basic proposal arrived from Germantown on three different occasions, July 26, Sept. 11, and Dec. 24, 1783. Continental Congress Papers, Item 45: 117-121, 137-139; Hunt, ed., *Journals*, XXIV, 451, 553; Pendleton to Madison and Jones, Oct. 6, 1783, in Mays, ed., *Letters and Papers of Pendleton*, II, 458.

the country were inhabited by persons "Principled by religion against bearing arms" and thus incapable of defending a capital city. Still other areas, he said, were populated by slaves who could not be trusted with arms and whose presence limited the fighting potential of their masters.

Also recommending Morrisania was its proximity to New York City, a major terminal for packet boats traveling to and from Europe. At Morrisania Congress could enjoy the advantages of residence near a commercial center without being exposed to the "dangers of those mobs and tumults, so naturally incident to great cities." Morris offered to have his manor and the adjoining borough of West Chester, an area of over twenty-five square miles, separated from New York state and placed under the complete authority of Congress.[28]

The degree of jurisdiction Congress was to have over the seat of government was an issue not taken lightly in the states or in Congress. Even before Congress had been humiliated by the failure of Pennsylvania to rescue it from the rebellious troops that harassed the delegates in Philadelphia, it had become clear that the national government needed a large measure of authority over its immediate surroundings. After rejecting the limited jurisdiction in the Kingston offer, Congress appointed an ad hoc committee in early July 1783 to consider the problem. The committee recommended on September 22 that a district should be ceded to Congress and made totally exempt from the authority of the ceding state. Congress would control the appointment of judges and the executive administration of the district, while local residents would be governed by municipal representatives of their own choosing.[29] That the recommendations of the committee were never adopted reflected the delicacy of the problem. Congress was far from certain where its authority should end and the rights of local citizens should begin. Local leaders feared that federal jurisdiction would lead to the violation of the fundamental rights of representation, placing local inhabitants under the control of a legislature they had no part in electing. There also was the fear that Congress would be an ineffective administrator of criminal justice, causing its domain to become the "hiding place of all the scoundrels upon the Continent and like the Churches of Italy, a refuge from justice."[30]

[28] Lewis Morris to Congress, Sept. 20, 1783, Continental Congress Papers, Item 46: 125-129; Martha J. Lamb and Mrs. Burton Harrison, *History of the City of New York: Its Origin, Rise, and Progress*, II (New York, 1880), 280-281.

[29] Hunt, ed., *Journals*, XXIV, 376, XXV, 428; Continental Congress Papers, Item 46: 93, Item 23: 161. Members of the ad hoc committee were James Duane, Jacob Read, Samuel Huntington, James Wilson, McHenry, and Peters.

[30] Madison to Randolph, July 28, 1783, Pendleton to Madison, Sept. 1, 1783,

In early October 1783 Congress opened what it hoped would be the final debate on the residency issue. The increased power of the parochialist coalition—due in part to resignations and poor attendance by the nationalist faction—made two sites clear favorites, one near Lamberton, New Jersey, at the falls of the Delaware, and the other at the falls of the Potomac, near Georgetown. The leading candidacy of these sites reflected the fundamental commitment on the part of the parochialist coalition to locate the capital away from the pressures of local populations and from the influence of merchant and commercial groups already established in the larger cities. The new republic had created its own form of government; now it would create its own capital on a scale and style consonant with its civil ideals. As Versailles expressed the central power and grandeur of Louis XIV, so the American capital would express the limited sovereignty and republican simplicity inherent in the Declaration of Independence and the Articles of Confederation.[31] The parochialist coalition's unity on the residency issue did not extend, however, beyond its basic commitment against an urban location. Thus on October 7, when the vote was taken, the division was basically sectional. The Delaware and Potomac sites received the solid support of their respective regions, leaving to New England the deciding votes. As expected, the New Englanders unanimously endorsed the Lamberton site.[32]

Southerners were far from satisfied with this decision, and after a move for reconsideration failed by one vote, they let it be known that they might ally with nationalists in the middle states to return the capital at least temporarily to Philadelphia. To this veiled threat was coupled a suggestion that they might oppose legislation to fund construction of the capital at Lamberton. Since nine votes were necessary to pass money bills, the southerners were warning that they might vote to return for a time to Philadelphia and then refuse to provide the funds necessary to build

---

"Memo on Jurisdiction," undated and unsigned but in Madison's hand, in Hutchinson and Rachal, eds., *Madison Papers*, VII, 256-257, 300, 357; John Armstrong to General Gates, June 9, 1783, in Burnett, ed., *Letters*, VII, 182n-183n.
[31] Henderson, *Party Politics*, 338; notes prepared by Madison for Jefferson concerning the residency question, ca. Oct. 14, 1783, in Hutchinson and Rachal, eds., *Madison Papers*, VII, 378-380; Higginson to S. Adams, Aug. 21, 1783, Rhode Island Delegates to Greene, Sept. 8, 1783, Huntington to Trumbull, Oct. 22, 1783, Osgood to J. Adams, Dec. 7, 1783, in Burnett, ed., *Letters*, VII, 271-272, 286-287, 346, 378-379; Alexander Gillam to A. Lee, Nov. 29, 1783, Lee Family Papers, University of Virginia, Charlottesville.
[32] Hunt, ed., *Journals*, XXV, 654-658; Lord, ed., *Atlas*, C 1026, C 1029, C 1031; Madison to Randolph, Oct. 13, 1783, in Burnett, ed., *Letters*, VII, 332.

the new capital unless it were located on the Potomac, thus leaving Congress in the nationalist stronghold.[33]

Eastern parochialists quickly realized that the South would have to be accommodated. Gerry of Massachusetts, seeking to reunite the parochialist coalition that had split on Lamberton, proposed that two capital cities be built, one on the Delaware and the other on the Potomac. A revitalized parochialist alliance led by Gerry and Arthur Lee and reinforced by a handful of southern nationalists repealed the Lamberton decision on October 20, and on the next day pushed through Congress a dual residency plan. It created an ambulatory government that would move regularly between twin capitals on the Delaware and the Potomac. Annapolis and Trenton were then designated as alternate temporary residences until accommodations could be built at the permanent sites.[34]

Middle-state representatives were exasperated by the sudden and successful maneuvering of the eastern and southern delegations. Elias Boudinot of New Jersey, the president of Congress, accused the South of having deceived the eastern delegates and charged that a "solid foundation for future divisions" had been laid by the decision. Charles Thomson of Pennsylvania, the secretary of Congress, declared the plan would bring

---

[33] Just who masterminded this southern strategy is not clear. The best accounts of southern maneuvering to gain support from New England for a reconsideration of the Lamberton decision are in the letters of New England delegates; unfortunately, their comments are couched in sectional terminology. Since Virginia and Maryland had the most to gain from a vote to reconsider, it is probable that the main organizers of the southern strategy came from those states. Madison and Daniel Carroll had connections with the nationalist faction in the middle states and both had supported a return to Philadelphia earlier. Arthur Lee and Bland were probably also involved since they had close political ties with the eastern branch of the parochialist coalition. The leadership of Madison and Carroll probably lent credence to the notion that the South was ready to ally with the middle states, while Lee and Bland kept communications open with the reluctant New Englanders. Since the southern states from Maryland to South Carolina (Georgia being absent) voted as a bloc both on the Lamberton question and on subsequent balloting on dual residency, it is probably also reasonable to suggest that the southern states were solidly together in attempting to persuade New England to reconsider its preference for Lamberton. Madison to Randolph, Oct. 13, 1783, Massachusetts Delegates to the Massachusetts Assembly, Oct. 23, 1783, Osgood to J. Adams, Dec. 7, 1783, in Burnett, ed., *Letters,* VII, 332-333, 349-350, 378-379; Williamson and Hawkins to Martin, Oct. 24, 1783, in Clark, ed., *N. C. State Recs.,* XVI, 908-910.

[34] Connecticut Delegates to Trumbull, Oct. 9, 1783, Foster to Meshech Weare, Oct. 28, 1783, Massachusetts Delegates to the Massachusetts Assembly, Oct. 23, 1783, Osgood to J. Adams, Dec. 7, 1783, in Burnett, ed., *Letters,* VI, 328, 348, 349-350, 378-379; Higginson to Bland, Jan. 1784, in Campbell, ed., *Bland Papers,* II, 113-114; Hawkins to John Gray Blount, Oct. 22, 1783, in Alice Barnwell Keith, ed., *The John Gray Blount Papers,* I (Raleigh, N. C., 1952), 123-124; Stephen Higginbotham to A. Lee, Nov. 1783, Lee Family Papers; Lord, ed., *Atlas,* C 1043, C 1044, C 1045, C 1049, C 1050, C 1051, C 1052; Hunt, ed., *Journals,* XXV, 675-714.

the nation to the "brink of ruin and calamity." "If the public treasury were full of money," he wrote, such plans might be considered with patience, but "talk of building cities, when they [Congress] can scarcely furnish money to buy paper on which to draw . . . them," could only be considered foolish.[35]

Francis Hopkinson, a nationalist from Philadelphia, charged sardonically that the plan must be a scheme to avoid the "irregular workings" of the European "machines" of state. American politicians, he wrote, hoped to draw the "thirteen wheels" of the American machine into regular and unified motion by affixing a giant pendulum in the sky which would swing between the Potomac and the Delaware. Hopkinson suggested building a wooden equestrian statue of George Washington large enough to contain all the members of Congress. This statue would be floated from one capital to the other by way of the Chesapeake Bay. Alternatively, government buildings might be constructed of light wood and fitted with sails and bellows, like those in Cyrano de Bergerac's *Voyages to the Moon and the Sun*. Hopkinson calculated that these mobile buildings would allow Congress to travel between the Potomac and the Delaware in approximately four days.[36]

Dual residency was far from a frivolous proposition to New Englanders, for they regarded it as yet another way of preserving the independence and republican purity of the national government. The plan had the additional advantage of avoiding the jealousies that might arise if Congress chose to reside at a single site. The purpose of the plan was not to make the federal government more accessible to the people of the republic; rather, it was to free the government from the pressures of particular local interests. These New Englanders, who traced their political ancestry to the Radical Whigs of Augustine England, had no faith in the system of influence and corruption that kept the British Parliament in working order. Governmental mobility would make extensive systems of patronage economically unfeasible. Continuous travel would necessitate the smallest of bureaucracies, staffed by men devoted to the commonweal, not to their private purses. Just what the system would mean to the political effectiveness of Congress was not clear. Presumably, the hardship of public service would leave only the most dedicated, if not the most wealthy, in positions

[35] Elias Boudinot to Robert R. Livingston, Oct. 23, 1783, Boudinot to R. Morris, Oct. 23, 1783, in Burnett, ed., *Letters*, VII, 347, 348; Thomson to Hannah Thomson, Oct. 17, 1783, Miscellaneous MSS, American Philosophical Society, Philadelphia.

[36] Francis Hopkinson, *Miscellaneous Essays and Occasional Writings . . .*, I (Philadelphia, 1792), 179-183; Schoepf, *Travels*, trans. and ed. Morrison, II, 384-386.

of responsibility. The congressional work load would also have to be small enough to be handled by the small traveling bureaucracy, thus eliminating the danger of an ever-expanding government. As a Rhode Island delegate phrased it, "A perambulatory Congress favors republicanism—a permanent one tends to concentrate power, Aristocracy and Monarchy."[37]

Southern nationalists and parochialists alike viewed dual residency principally as a temporary measure, allowing them more time to persuade Congress to settle permanently on the Potomac. Georgetown was within easy reach of all the states, and the recent expansion of settlement into the southwest placed it nearer the country's population center than any other site under consideration. The addition of new states would eventually create enough votes to bring the capital to the Potomac. The South seemed only to need more time.[38]

On November 4, 1783, Congress left Princeton, intending to convene in Annapolis on November 26. The representatives who gathered in Maryland's capital differed substantially from preceding delegations, both in mood and in political configuration. The nationalist faction that had dominated Congress for nearly three years had all but disappeared. The relocation of Congress outside Philadelphia, disagreements over federal fiscal policy, and differences over the organization of the West had cut deeply into the faction's power during the summer of 1783. Its strength was further eroded when nationalist-oriented governments in Pennsylvania and New York were replaced by more parochial administrations, resulting in corresponding changes in those states' congressional delegations. These developments were symptomatic of growing parochial sentiment both in Congress and in the states as the end of the war approached. The decline of the nationalists reduced the ideological urgency that had marked congressional deliberations during the period of nationalist ascendancy. Important issues, which formerly had divided nationalist from republican, came increasingly to be viewed primarily in terms of state and sectional self-interest. This significant alteration in the mood of Congress

[37] Huntington to Trumbull, Oct. 22, 1783, Massachusetts Delegates to the Massachusetts Assembly, Oct. 23, 1783, Osgood to J. Adams, Dec. 7, 1783, Howell to Greene, Dec. 24, 1783, in Burnett, ed., *Letters*, VII, 346-347, 349-350, 378-379, 397; Hawkins to John C. Blount, Oct. 22, 1783, Blount Papres; Gillam to A. Lee, Nov. 20, 1783, Lee Family Papers; Higginson to Gerry, Nov. 5, 1783, Higginson Miscellaneous MSS, New-York Historical Society, New York City.

[38] Jefferson to Francis Eppes, Nov. 10, 1783, Jefferson to Harrison, Nov. 11, 1783, Jefferson to George Rogers Clark, Dec. 4, 1783, in Boyd *et al.*, eds., *Jefferson Papers*, VI, 349-350, 351-353, 371; Virginia Delegates to Harrison, May 13, 1784, in Burnett, ed., *Letters*, VII, 524.

was manifested in a dramatic drop in attendance and in the gradual collapse of the parochialist coalition, which had depended on the presence of a strong nationalist faction for much of its internal cohesion.[39]

The decline in ideological fervor cut deeply into support for dual residency. Congress had been meeting in Annapolis for only a short time when New England delegates began to reconsider the wisdom of building two capital cities. They were bothered by persistent reports from diplomatic missions that congressional mobility was having adverse effects on European confidence in the stability of the American government.[40] Just as important, some New Englanders were beginning to fear that the "aristocratic, even monarchic tendencies" of southern politics were as dangerous to the preservation of republicanism as the nationalists had been. By mid-February Congress was filled with talk of building a single federal residence near Trenton.[41]

Even southerners admitted that without the support of New England, Congress could not hope to remain long near the Potomac. Nevertheless, in early April, delegates from Maryland and Virginia made a final attempt to keep Congress in the upper South. James Monroe suggested that Maryland and Virginia be allowed to credit any funds advanced for construction at Georgetown against future requisitions by the federal government, but this proposal was rejected. A few days later Thomas Jefferson moved that Congress hold its fall session at Alexandria. That resolution gained only the vote of Virginia in balloting that reflected a growing sentiment in Congress to return to a more central location. An attempt to keep Congress in Annapolis was also decisively rejected. Hopes of keeping Congress near the Potomac were finally dashed on

[39] Henderson, *Party Politics*, 318-343, 353-356; Henderson, "Political Factions," 322-323; Henderson, "Constitutionalists and Republicans," *PH*, XXXVI (1969), 140; Washington to Clinton, Sept. 11, 1783, in Fitzpatrick, ed., *Writings of Washington*, II, 148; Kenneth R. Rossman, *Thomas Mifflin and the Politics of the American Revolution* (Chapel Hill, N. C., 1952), 177-180; Mifflin to R. R. Livingston, Feb. 20, 1784, Robert R. Livingston Papers, Massachusetts Historical Society, Boston.

[40] Peace Commissioners in Paris [J. Adams, Benjamin Franklin, and John Jay] to Elias Boudinot, Sept. 10, 1783, in J. J. Boudinot, ed., *The Life, Public Services, Addresses and Letters of Elias Boudinot, LL.D., President of the Continental Congress*, I (Boston, 1896), 380; Jefferson to Madison, Dec. 11, 1783, Jefferson to marquis de Chastellux, Jan. 16, 1784, in Boyd *et al.*, eds., *Jefferson Papers*, VI, 381, 466-467.

[41] Osgood to Higginson, Feb. 2, 1784, Howell to Jonathan Arnold, Feb. 21, 1784, Gerry to Higginson, Mar. 4, 1784, Samuel Dick to Thomas Sinnickson, Mar. 18, 1784, Gerry to Samuel Holten, Apr. 21, 1784, Ephraim Paine to R. R. Livingston, May 24, 1784, in Burnett, ed., *Letters*, VII, 430-432, 451, 461, 472, 498, 534; Gerry to S. Adams, Mar. 4, 1784, Samuel Adams Papers, New York Public Lib.; Jefferson to Madison, Feb. 20, 1784, in Hutchinson and Rachal, eds., *Madison Papers*, VII, 424.

April 26, 1784, when Congress confirmed its earlier decision to hold its winter session in Trenton. No one in Congress took this decision to represent a continuing commitment to dual residency; rather, it was a clear signal to most delegates that Congress would not soon be returning south of Pennsylvania.[42]

Congress adjourned on June 3, 1784, leaving the responsibility of moving the government from Annapolis to Trenton to the newly organized Committee of States. When the delegates gathered in Trenton in late October, they again faced the problem of residency. Frustrated by inadequate accommodations in the New Jersey town, they quickly revoked the dual residency plan in favor of a single seat of government. Only the South held out for dual residency, still hoping to use it as a means to bring the capital to the Potomac. There being no serious prospect that Congress would return to Philadelphia, voting on a new permanent residence reverted to the sectional alignment by which the Lamberton site had been endorsed in October 1783. After rejecting Georgetown by a lopsided margin, Congress designated an undeveloped two- or three-square-mile site near the falls of the Delaware as the future capital of the United States. The land was to be purchased from either Pennsylvania or New Jersey, depending on the better offer. New York City was then selected as the temporary capital. Accommodations there were sufficient both for the government and for foreign diplomats, and even those delegates who might have been politically distressed by New York's urban and commercial liabilities approved it as a temporary resort for they were certain that the city was located too far north to become the permanent residence of Congress.[43]

The move to New York marked the end of the debate on residency in the Continental Congress. Hoping for only a short tenure in New York, many delegates felt they had at last developed a workable plan for a national capital commensurate with their conception of republican government. Through the creation of a federal district under congressional

[42] Hunt, ed., Journals, XXVI, 221-225, 293-294; Jefferson to Madison, Apr. 25, 1784, Edward Hand to Jasper Yeates, May 3, 1784, in Burnett, ed., Letters, VII, 500, 511.
[43] Samuel Hardy to Harrison, Nov. 7, 1784, R. H. Lee to Thomas Lee Shippen, Nov. 10, 1784, John Francis Mercer to Madison, Nov. 12, 1784, James Monroe to Madison, Nov. 15, 1784, Monroe to Henry, Jan. 1, 1784, in Burnett, ed., Letters, VII, 607-608, 608, 609, 612, VIII, 1; Gerry to J. Adams, Feb. 15, 1785, Elbridge Gerry Papers, Lib. Cong.; Lord, ed., Atlas, C 1110, C 1232, C 1230; Hunt, ed., Journals, XXVI, 224-225.

control they expected to avoid state interference and to insure order in the immediate area. By building a new federal city they believed Congress would be able to govern effectively without pressure from commercial interests or the threat of urban agitation and mob manipulation. By settling at one site they proposed to end the constant inconvenience and loss of time involved in frequent moves and to establish a center that would insure attendance and encourage national unity. Indeed, it was becoming increasingly clear to many congressional leaders that a truly national focal point was necessary even for a union of confederated states.[44]

The contest over the location of the capital was illustrative of the complex mixture of sectional and ideological considerations that operated within the factional construct of politics in the Continental Congress. No region was insensitive to the economic and political advantages to be derived from the presence of the capital. New England, geographically ineligible to host the government, was concerned that the new site not increase the influence in Congress of powerful states like Virginia and Pennsylvania. The middle states saw economic gain and political power in the continued residence of Congress within the region. To the South, securing the capital meant not only the acquisition of an important economic center but opportunities for increased political influence. In addition, ideological considerations were never far below the surface. To nationalists and parochialists alike the residence of Congress in Philadelphia was connected with a vision of a strong, centralized federal government. Nationalists, especially in the middle states, continually maneuvered for a return to the politically congenial environs of Philadelphia's merchant community. Parochialists, sensing the failing strength of the nationalist faction once Congress left Philadelphia, pushed to relocate the capital in a setting more consonant with their vision of a virtuous agrarian nation. In the upper South, the agrarian bias of the parochialists merged with the expansive republicanism of Madison and others to make the relocation of the capital part of a larger plan for the establishment of a republic founded on expanding domestic agriculture and a growing export trade. Although Congress opted for the more comfortable accommodations of New York late in the winter of 1784, its parochialist members were still determined to build a capital commensurate with the civil

---

[44] Joseph Gardner to John Bayard, Feb. 11, 1785, Massachusetts Delegates to the Massachusetts Assembly, Feb. 12, 1785, Virginia Delegates to Henry, Feb. 13, 1785, in Burnett, ed., *Letters*, VIII, 28, 30-31, 33-36; R. H. Lee to Washington, Feb. 27, 1785, in James Curtis Ballagh, ed., *The Letters of Richard Henry Lee*, II (New York, 1914), 339; Monroe to Henry, Jan. 1, 1785, in Burnett, ed., *Letters*, VIII, 1.

ideals embodied in the Articles of Confederation. The plan to locate the capital at an isolated site on the banks of the Delaware was a manifestation both of the realities of sectional politics and of the ideological commitment to the preservation of simple republican virtues that pervaded congressional politics between the decline of the nationalists in 1783 and the ratification of the Constitution in 1787.

THE CREATION OF THE NATIONAL DOMAIN, 1781-1784

By MERRILL JENSEN

The creation of the national domain at the end of the American Revolution entailed the performance of two outwardly simple acts: (1) the cession of western lands by the states laying claim to them; and (2) the acceptance of those cessions by the government of the United States. The apparent simplicity of these actions at once disappears as one turns to the history of the years between the surrender of various state claims to the Old Northwest, and the creation of the national domain by the Confederation Congress through its acceptance of the claims surrendered. By March, 1781, Congress was in possession of the New York, Connecticut, and Virginia cessions, but Congress did not accept the Virginia cession of the Old Northwest and thereby lay the foundations of the national domain until March, 1784. An account of the causes of this three year delay illuminates a phase of the history of the West and of national politics at the close of the American Revolution.[1]

The cessions of state claims to the Old Northwest came only after a long and confused struggle during the course of which the landless state of Maryland refused to ratify the Articles of Confederation and thus prevented the union of the thirteen states. Maryland refused to ratify the Articles until Congress should be given some control over western lands. In her various demands Maryland consistently exempted from the proposed congressional control and disposition, those areas of land in the West which had been purchased from the Indians before the outbreak of the Revolution. This exemption was designed to protect the Illinois, Wabash, and Indiana companies, which had made such purchases and whose membership was made up largely of important business men and politicians of Maryland, Pennsylvania, and New Jersey.

[1] The controversy over the West during the early part of the Revolution, which resulted in land cessions from the various states, is treated in Merrill Jensen, "The Cession of the Old Northwest," THE MISSISSIPPI VALLEY HISTORICAL REVIEW (Cedar Rapids, 1914—), XXIII, 1936, pp. 27-47.

All the land company purchases and claims lay within the charter bounds of Virginia, and after 1776 that state promptly investigated and declared them null and void. The land speculators therefore turned to the Continental Congress as the only political organization which might be manipulated in their interest. They soon conceived of Congress as a sovereign body which had inherited the powers and prerogatives of the British government, including of course, the power to control lands west of the Appalachians. Such ideas were of little moment at the time. The most effective measure was Maryland's desperate refusal to ratify the Articles of Confederation until the states with western lands could be forced or persuaded to surrender their claims to Congress.

In the course of time and for various reasons, Virginia ceded her claims to the territory northwest of the Ohio River. Prior to her act of cession, however, her delegates in Congress sought from Congress certain guarantees as to the future disposal of the region to be ceded. Congress agreed to these demands with one all-important exception: Congress flatly refused to declare null and void all purchases from Indians in the region to be ceded.

Nevertheless Virginia ceded her claims to the Old Northwest and carefully attached to her act of cession all the conditions previously demanded, including the requirement that Congress nullify the land company purchases. Virginia politicians had no intention of allowing Maryland and Pennsylvania speculators to preempt anything that Virginians might surrender. The Virginia cession was followed by Maryland's ratification of the Articles of Confederation, although Maryland's ratification did not mean that her citizens had surrendered their hopes. The Maryland legislature made it perfectly plain that it still objected to the claims of the landed states and that it still hoped to share in the profits to be derived from the West.[2] Thus the Virginia

[2] See the message of the Maryland House of Delegates to the Maryland Senate, the Senate's reply, and the instructions to the Maryland delegates in Congress in St. George L. Sioussat, "The Chevalier De La Luzerne and the Ratification of the Articles of Confederation by Maryland, 1780-1781," *The Pennsylvania Magazine of History and Biography* (Philadelphia), LX, 1936, pp. 415-417. Professor Sioussat feels that if men like Thomas Johnson, Samuel Chase, and Charles Carroll had been governed solely by their interests in the Illinois-Wabash Company, they ought to have stuck by their guns and refused to ratify the Articles. *Ibid.*, LX, 406, n. 32.

cession of the Old Northwest did not mark the end of the controversy. The history of the next three years is the history of re-doubled efforts on the part of the land companies and their adherents: efforts directed toward the sole end of evading the obnoxious conditions attached to the Virginia cession and which Congress must accept before the cession could become final, and the national domain a reality.

The requirement that Congress should void all purchases in the territory ceded was aimed directly at the Illinois-Wabash group, which included such leading men of Pennsylvania and Maryland as Robert Morris, James Wilson, Samuel Chase, Thomas Johnson, and Charles Carroll of Carrollton. The required guarantee of Virginia's remaining territory to her was designed to thwart the Indiana Company, which included such important men as Benjamin Franklin, Samuel and Thomas Wharton, and George Morgan. Naturally these companies and their representatives in Congress fought to evade the unwelcome conditions attached to the Virginia cession. They attempted to do this in two ways. On the one hand they sought to establish the sovereignty of Congress over the regions at stake. On the other they sought to secure an unrestricted cession from Virginia, thereby leaving the land companies to the none-too-virtuous discretion of Congress. Neither idea was followed consistently and sometimes both were urged at once as expediency seemed to dictate.[3]

But it must be remembered that that policy had proven fruitless, as the Maryland House of Delegates explained to the Maryland Senate on January 29, 1781. Furthermore, the activity of the Illinois-Wabash Company and other companies after 1781, and the support of them by the Maryland delegates is inferential proof that Maryland had not surrendered her interests even though she had given up one part of her program: that is, refusing to ratify the Articles of Confederation.

[3] It is not to be supposed that the land companies were the only force in opposition to Virginia's claims. There was the less tangible, though no less real jealousy of the small states for the larger. Yet when one considers that George Morgan of the Indiana Company was one of the most powerful influences in New Jersey politics, it is difficult to make an accurate evaluation of the relative parts played by interests and emotions, even in the small states.

Another factor was the New York-Vermont controversy, which had been going on since the outbreak of the Revolution, and which was utilized by both sides as circumstances seemed to warrant. There is evidence to indicate that New York's cession itself was motivated more by a desire to get support in the Vermont affair rather than by any conviction that the New York claim was worth very much either to New York or Congress.

When the Virginia delegates delivered the act of cession to Congress in March, 1781, they naively assumed that Congress would soon accept it. One of them wrote Richard Henry Lee, "The Covert manoeuvers of the land Jobbing Companies are so well known, and so fully discovered, that few of their abettors will be hardy enough to oppose it in its fullest latitude."[4] But Richard Henry Lee, who had had more experience with Congress and with land companies, made a far more accurate prediction of what the future was to disclose. Shortly after the Virginia assembly passed the act of cession, Lee explained to Samuel Adams that it would complete the confederation, but that he feared its acceptance would be delayed or defeated in Congress. He wrote:

It will bar the hopes, of some powerful confederated Land jobbers, who have long had in contemplation immense possessions in this ceded country, under pretence of Indian purchases, and other plausible, but not solid titles. . . . The modes and methods, which these artists pursue, are well understood. . . . They pretend great friendship and concern for the Indepen[den]cy, the Union, and Confederation of America, but by circuitous means, attack and destroy those things, that are indispensible to those ends. Hitherto the avarice and ambition of Virginia, has prevented Confederation — Now when Virginia, has yielded half, and more than half her Charter Claim, the argument will be applied to the terms as improper, and for certain purposes perhaps it may be said, that the quantity ceded is not enough — in short anything that can operate the delay and defeat of a measure, calculated to sever us completely from Great Britain, and to preclude the avaritious views of certain Land mongers, will be industriously pressed.[5]

Since the opposition to the Virginia cession of 1781 was directed chiefly at the conditions attached to it which thwarted the hopes of the land companies, there is at least strong probability that the land companies were the chief forces behind that opposition.

Of course, as has been said, it is difficult if not impossible "to establish a direct connection between selfish motives and public acts. In the present state of research, the historian, like contemporary Virginians, is compelled to trust to inference." Clarence W. Alvord, *The Illinois Country 1673-1818, The Centennial History of Illinois* (Springfield), I, 1920, p. 381, n. 6.

[4] Theodorick Bland to Lee, March 5, 1781, Edmund C. Burnett, ed., *Letters of Members of the Continental Congress* (Washington, 1921-1936), VI, 7.

[5] To Samuel Adams, February 5, 1781, in James C. Ballagh, ed., *The Letters of Richard Henry Lee* (New York, 1911-1914), II, 214-215.

Richard Henry Lee's predictions were fulfilled promptly and accurately. Within two weeks of the presentation of the Virginia cession to Congress, Congress received memorials from George Morgan on behalf of the Indiana Company; from James Wilson on behalf of the Illinois-Wabash Company, of which he was now president; from Benjamin Franklin and Samuel Wharton on behalf of the Vandalia Company; and from William Trent, Samuel Wharton, and Bernard Gratz on behalf of George Croghan; these were later followed by yet another memorial from Trent on behalf of the Indiana Company.

The Indiana Company stated that it had presented its case to Congress in the past, and emphasized the present willingness and even anxiety of the company to have the matter decided by Congress, "by whom alone, it is presumed, a proper and competent Decision can be made." The memorial requested the appointment of a day for hearing all the parties concerned. Franklin's and Wharton's petition on behalf of the Vandalia Company was a long recital of the events in the history of that scheme since the treaty at Fort Stanwix in 1768. They maintained that the company had acquired title to the land in question, although they admitted that the instrument of conveyance had never been delivered. But they appealed to Congress for justice as a body having jurisdiction: "Your Honors have now succeeded to the Sovereignty of the Territory in question."[6]

These land company memorials were referred to the same committee to which had been referred the cessions from the various states. The report of this committee made it evident that the land companies had persuasive ways. The original resolutions of Congress asking for land cessions were completely ignored by the committee. Those original resolutions had refused to consider the question of "right" to the West, holding it subordinate

[6] Papers of the Continental Congress (Library of Congress), no. 77, f. 206, 167-201, 226-229; ibid., no. 41, X, f. 87-98. The memorial on behalf of George Croghan took particular pains to point out the inconsistent policy of the Virginia Assembly with regard to western claims. In the same session in which it had denied Croghan's claims, it had validated sales from Croghan to Virginians from the very claims it had earlier nullified. Such actions on the part of the Virginia Assembly really had an inner consistency in that the Virginia legislature usually promoted the welfare of its own citizens as opposed to those of other states. Journals of the Continental Congress, 1774-1789 (Washington, 1904 —), XIX, 99-100, 253, 264; XX, 534; XXI, 784.

to expediency and to the necessity of securing the cessions of all
the states, no matter how vague their "rights" might be.[7] Now,
the committee on cessions upheld the contentions of the land
speculators of the landless states and of the representatives of
those states in Congress. Its report declared it inexpedient to
accept the cessions with conditions attached. Instead, the committee defied the landed states by proposing a resolution to the
effect that there were already lands belonging to the United
States and that a committee should be appointed to dispose of
such lands for the payment of the debts of the United States.[8]

By dint of much maneuvering, the Virginians brought this
report before Congress in October, 1781, and forced it into the
hands of a new committee.[9] The issue was clear-cut: should the
decision be made upon the basis of the resolutions asking for
the cessions, or should the whole question of the territorial rights
of the ceding states be reopened for discussion?[10]

The personnel of the new committee made it obvious that the
latter was to be the case. It was composed of one delegate each
from the landless states of Maryland, Pennsylvania, New Jersey, Rhode Island, and New Hampshire.[11] After some experience
with this committee, James Madison declared that apprehensions
for Virginia's western interests were not unfounded for "an
agrarian law is as much coveted by the little members of the
Union, as ever it was by the indigent citizens of Rome."[12] This
committee called before it the various claimants including New
York, Connecticut, and the land companies. The Virginia delegates flatly refused to present any evidence of their claims and
asserted that such jurisdiction on the part of Congress was contrary to the Articles of Confederation.[13] This was perfectly true

[7] *Journals*, XVII, 559-560, 580, 586, 806-807.
[8] *Ibid.*, XX, 704.
[9] *Ibid.*, XXI, 784, 1032.
[10] Virginia Delegates to Governor of Virginia, October 9; 1781, Burnett, *Letters*, VI, 235.
[11] *Journals*, XXI, 1032. The men were Elias Boudinot of New Jersey, James M. Varnum of Rhode Island, Daniel of St. Thomas Jenifer of Maryland, Thomas Smith of Pennsylvania, and Samuel Livermore of New Hampshire.
[12] James Madison to Edmund Pendleton, October 30, in Gaillard Hunt, ed., *The Writings of James Madison* (New York, 1900-1910), I, 160. Edmund Randolph char-
acterized the situation as "the disgust and jealousy conceived against Virginia." To Governor of Virginia, November 7, 1781, Burnett, *Letters*, VI, 259.
[13] Virginia Delegates to Governor of Virginia, October 9, 1781, Burnett, *Letters*,

but it had no effect. The committee continued its work unhindered by constitutional restraints or by Congress, although the Virginia delegates insisted that Congress should interfere.[14]

When the committee delivered its report to Congress on November 3, 1781, it was at once evident that minds capable of evolving such concepts as the devolution of sovereignty, had found with ease a new and far more plausible expedient for evading the unwelcome fact of Virginia's practical control over the West. The old arguments of "common right" to the West arising out of the expenditure of "common blood and treasure" had proven singularly ineffective. The theory of the devolution of sovereign powers from the British government to the Continental Congress was even less convincing. Now, the cession of New York's "shadowy title held from the Six Nations of Indians"[15] was seized upon as covering not only the region ceded by Virginia, but also the region south of the Ohio which Virginia asked to be guaranteed to her. The report recommended acceptance of the New York cession because it was based upon the claims of the Six Nations, and these, the committee declared, were paramount to all other claims. For the same reason the Virginia cession was to be rejected as was the guarantee of her remaining lands to her. Her lands south of the Ohio, said the committee, had been separated from her by the King in Council before the Revolution and then sold to individuals. Thus in theory Virginia was to be confined to the region east of the Alleghenies. The committee, however, recommended that Virginia should reconsider her act of cession and by a "proper act," cede "all claims and pretensions of claims to the lands and country

VI, 235; Edmund Randolph to Governor of Virginia, November 7, 1781, *ibid.*, 259-260.

[14] *Journals*, XXI, 1057-1058; Virginia Delegates to Governor of Virginia, October 16 and 23, 1781, Burnett, *Letters*, VI, 242-243, 246.

[15] Clarence E. Carter, ed., *The Territorial Papers of the United States* (Washington, 1934 —), II, 5, n. 6. Burke A. Hinsdale, *The Old Northwest* (New York, 1899), chap. xi, contains a discussion of the basis of the various claims to the Northwest. Whatever the comparative legal validity of the various claims, the most important element at the time was Virginia's practical control of the West, so far as any control at all was exercised. The importance of Virginia's claim was clearly demonstrated by the fact that even when Congress accepted the New York cession in the fall of 1782, Congress made no effort to take any steps on the basis of the title derived from the New York cession. See also, Alvord, *The Illinois Country*, 383.

beyond a reasonable western boundary," such cession to be free from all conditions and restrictions.

The report then turned to a consideration of the land company claims. The Indiana claim to land south of the Ohio River was declared valid and Congress was urged to confirm it. Likewise the claims of George Croghan were declared legal. The American members of the Vandalia group were to be reimbursed by new land grants to the extent of their expenses in the Vandalia project. But the Illinois-Wabash petition was rejected on the grounds that the purchases had been made without public authority and because the region in question really belonged to the Six Nations.[16] The denial of the Illinois-Wabash claims in this report is a peculiar maneuver. Its adherents were powerful in Congress at the time, Robert Morris being in the ascendancy as superintendent of finance. Possibly the land company group was ready to surrender the region northwest of the Ohio in the peace negotiations in the hope of getting the lands they desired from Great Britain once the war was over. Such was the belief of James Madison and Luzerne, the French envoy. Furthermore, the votes on the new instructions of June, 1781, which placed the matter of boundaries at the discretion of the peace commissioners, point very strongly in the same direction. Three members of the committee on cessions, Livermore, Varnum, and Jenifer, had consistently voted to give discretion to the commissioners, even to the extent of allowing them to give up lands southeast of the Ohio River.[17] While the evidence is circumstantial it is at least worthy of note. Certainly the Illinois-Wabash Company was not crushed by its apparent failure to receive congressional recognition in the report.

The report thus presented to Congress in November, 1781, was not acted upon for over a year. It was impossible to secure a vote of seven states either for or against it.[18] The Virginia delegates were at last seriously alarmed and asked George Mason and Thomas Jefferson to prepare a statement of Vir-

[16] *Journals*, XXI, 1098; XXII, 225-232.

[17] Thomas P. Abernethy, *Western Lands and the American Revolution* (New York, 1937), 285; Edward S. Corwin, *French Policy and the American Alliance of 1778* (Princeton, 1916), 300-306; *Journals*, XX, 605-607, 608-610, 611-619, 625-628.

[18] Madison to Edmund Pendleton, November 13, 1781, Hunt, *Madison Writings*, I, 161-162; *Journals*, XXI, 1113-1114.

ginia's legal rights in the case. Madison pointed out that the opinion of the committee was not necessarily the opinion of Congress, since the committee was composed of members who he declared were "systematically and notoriously" in opposition to all western claims. He admitted, however, that Virginia had ample cause for the revocation or suspension of her cession, and warned that in making plans for the future, the state should assume that the existing union would not long survive the end of the war.[19]

By the spring of 1782 the question of cessions was badly entangled with the controversy over Vermont and the possibility of its admission to the Confederation. The New England States were said to desire Vermont within the union in order to strengthen the relative position of their section. Hence, they supported the landless states in order to secure support for the admission of Vermont. The landless states on the other hand, supported the admission of Vermont in order to secure New England votes for their western policy. Each group knew full well that the alliance would terminate abruptly once the end of either was achieved, so each was interested in delaying a decision while maneuvering for an advantage.[20] The situation was further complicated because New York had apparently been bidding for support in the Vermont affair by making a cession of her dubious claims. The agents of Vermont and those of "the land-mongers" wrote Madison, "are playing with great adroitness into each others' hands."[21]

The land companies were by this time exceptionally well represented in Congress. James Wilson, president of the Illinois-Wabash Company and one of the great speculators of the day,

[19] James Madison to Thomas Jefferson, November 18, 1781, Burnett, *Letters*, VI, 264-265. The Virginia assembly in its spring session in 1782, appointed Thomas Jefferson, George Mason, Edmund Randolph, Arthur Lee, and Dr. Thomas Walker a committee to draw up a statement of Virginia's right to the West. Nothing seems to have been done officially, although George Mason wrote a long letter to Edmund Randolph in which Virginia's claims were set forth in detail. See Kate M. Rowland, *The Life of George Mason, 1725-1792* (New York, 1892), II, 23-33, 64-66; Thomas Jefferson to James Madison, March 24, 1782, Paul L. Ford, ed., *The Writings of Thomas Jefferson* (New York, 1892-1899), III, 52-54.

[20] James Madison, "Observations in Vermont and Territorial Claims" [May 1, 1782], Burnett, *Letters*, VI, 340-341.

[21] To Edmund Randolph, May 1, 1781 [1782], *ibid.*, 340.

was a member of Congress from Pennsylvania. Samuel Wharton, a leader in the Vandalia and Indiana companies, was in Congress as a member from Delaware, and, although memorials in his behalf before Congress pleaded the sadness of his bankrupt estate, he yet found funds to treat the members "with magnificent Dinners." Arthur Lee declared, "These Agents are using every art to seduce us and to sow dissention among the States, I think they are more dangerous than the Enemy's Arms. Every Motion relative to Vermont and the Cessions of the other States is directed by the interests of these Companies." [22]

In April the Virginia delegates sought from Congress some decision on the Virginia cession so that they could report to the Virginia assembly during its spring session. Madison insisted that the land companies were "the radical impediment," and that whenever Virginia proposed a decision, "every artifice that could perplex the case was immediately exerted." [23] Madison failed to tell the whole story, however, for at this time the Virginia delegates were engaging in tactics most offensive to the land companies and their representatives in Congress. When the report on cessions came up for discussion, Arthur Lee moved that its consideration should be postponed until each member of Congress had declared, upon roll-call, whether or not he was interested in any of the land companies affected by the proposed cessions. Lee declared that his "purifying declaration," as he called it, "was evaded by three days chicane." It was met by flurries of counter motions aiming to avoid any such official declaration of holdings in the companies concerned. [24]

From this time on, whenever the report on cessions came up for consideration, the Virginia delegates asked the members of Congress to explain their connections with land companies. Each time the demand was met by a series of counter motions which usually ended with a motion to adjourn when nothing else proved adequate to escape the unpleasant persistence of the Virginians. Finally, on May 6, 1782, consideration of the report was postponed *sine die* as the only way out of the dilemma of the

[22] To Samuel Adams, April 21, 1782, *ibid.*, 331.
[23] To Edmund Pendleton, April 23, 1782, *ibid.*, 336-337.
[24] *Journals*, XXII, 184, 191-194; Arthur Lee to Samuel Adams, April 21, 1782, Burnett, *Letters*, VI, 331.

land company members and supporters.[25] The Virginia delegates therefore decided to place the issue before the Virginia assembly and stated that, with regard to the West, the assembly would be fully justified in taking whatever steps Virginia's interests should dictate.[26]

Congress, however, found it impossible to ignore the potential federal revenue to be derived from the creation of a national domain. It needed money and the sale of western lands was its most obvious resource of securing money. In July, 1782, therefore, the committee on finance urged some decision concerning the cessions of the back lands.[27] The only result of this suggestion, however, was to throw Congress once more into a futile debate on the subject of "right" to the West, a basis for discussion which had not in the past and could not in the future be made to square with the facts of practical politics.[28]

In the fall of 1782 the Virginia delegates once more took the offensive when Theodorick Bland moved that Congress accept all the state cessions, regardless of the conditions attached to them. But once more the only result was a series of futile motions and evasions which but thinly disguised the real issue.[29] Some members of Congress realized that such tactics would never result in any profit. It was obvious to the more disinterested that even if Congress did have some legal right to western lands, enough of the states thought the contrary to prevent a vote favorable to its claims. There was even less chance, said Madison, that they would support "coercive measures to render the title of any fiscal importance." It was equally obvious that the states with western land claims might open land offices, as Virginia had done once, issue patents to land, and protect the execution of their claims without any hindrance except "the clamors of individuals within and without the doors of Congress."[30]

25 *Journals*, XXII, 223-225, 234-235, 240-241; James Madison to Edmund Randolph, May 14, 1782, Hunt, *Madison Writings*, I, 193.

26 Madison to Arthur Lee, May [7], 1782, Burnett, *Letters*, VI, 345-346.

27 *Journals*, XXII, 423; David Howell to Governor of Rhode Island, July 30, 1782, Burnett, *Letters*, VI, 402-403.

28 Charles Thomson, "Notes on Debates," July 31, 1782, Burnett, *Letters*, VI, 409.

29 *Journals*, XXIII, 550-551.

30 Madison to Edmund Randolph, September 10, 1782, Hunt, *Madison Writings*, I, 232.

It was apparently the realization of this fact that induced John Witherspoon of New Jersey to bring in a series of compromise resolutions. These were to the effect that the states which had not yet made cessions should do so; that the states which had not made cessions in accordance with the wishes of Congress should reconsider their actions; and finally, that the decisions of the ceding states with regard to private property within the ceded areas should not be altered without the consent of the states concerned.[31] This last resolution was the core of the controversy. The members from the landless states attacked and defeated this guarantee that Congress would not interfere with the Virginia decisions nullifying the land company claims.[32]

This was the first open and positive victory that the landless states had won on the floor of Congress and they were confident they could now carry out the rest of their program.[33] As soon as seven states favorable to their plans appeared, they voted acceptance of the New York cession in accordance with the report which had been made almost exactly a year before. By thus accepting the New York cession, Congress in theory escaped the necessity of a cession from Virginia.[34] Practically, however, nothing was done except to add pages to the *Journals* and irritation to the hearts of the Virginians. Virginia was in control of the West. She had no intention of handing it over to the speculators of the landless states, whatever her intentions might be with regard to her own speculators. Virginia did want to surrender the region northwest of the Ohio to Congress and her politicians on the whole continued to urge that this end be accomplished in spite of the apparent determination of a majority in Congress to favor the desires of the land speculators.

The land companies engaged in a renewed campaign for congressional help during the spring of 1783. James Wilson, as delegate from Pennsylvania, once more argued the case of his Illinois-Wabash Company. He insisted that there were lands lying beyond the bounds of the particular states. He even argued that the land south of the Ohio had never belonged to Virginia

[31] *Journals*, XXIII, 551-553.

[32] September 25, 1782, *ibid.*, 604-606.

[33] Daniel Carroll to Daniel of St. Thomas Jenifer, October 8, 1782, Burnett, *Letters*, VI, 498.

[34] October 29, 1782, *Journals*, XXIII, 693-694.

and he urged openly that the Allegheny Mountains should be made the western boundary of that state.[35] His activity was countered by the Virginia delegates, who now offered to compromise. by urging Congress to accept the Virginia cession with all its conditions, except the provision which required a guarantee to her of the region south of the Ohio River. The Virginia delegates declared that they took this step in order to sound out the disposition of Congress and because, they said, "We considered it as our duty to produce if possible some decisive determination on a matter so important to the welfare of our state, and of such consequence to the U States in General."[36]

The very next day a memorial of the Indiana Company was read to Congress. The memorial spoke of the "illustrious example of Justice" on the part of the Six Nations and the British King and implied an invidious contrast with the "indecision of Congress." The document sought to pluck hardened congressional heart-strings by pleading that among the memorialists were "numbers of aged and distressed Widows and helpless orphans." Justice so long delayed, it declared, was as injurious as justice denied. The "true Policy, which is always found in National Justice" should move Congress to dictate an order for the immediate settlement of the case in accordance with the committee report in favor of the Indiana Company claim.[37]

This request was ignored and the Virginia proposal was given to a committee which soon decided that Congress should first make a decision on the report of November 3, 1781, so far as that report related to the Virginia cession. Congress immediately turned over the Virginia section of the report to a new committee upon which the extremists of the Middle States were but poorly represented.[38] This committee delivered its report

[35] James Madison, "Notes on Debates," April 9, 1783, Hunt, *Madison Writings*, I, 444-445; *Journals*, XXIV, 271.

[36] Virginia Delegates to Governor of Virginia, April 29, 1783, Burnett, *Letters*, VII, 153; Rhode Island Delegates to Governor of Rhode Island, April 23, 1783, *ibid.*, 148; *Journals*, XXIV, 271-272.

[37] Papers of the Continental Congress, no. 41, X, 99-104. William Trent presented a memorial on behalf of the Vandalia group which was read May 1, 1783. Michael Gratz and William Powell, executors of the estate of George Croghan, presented a memorial which was read May 7. See Papers of the Continental Congress, no. 77, f. 222-225, and no. 41, III, 493-496.

[38] *Journals*, XXIV, 271, 381, n. 2. This second committee was composed of John Rutledge, Oliver Ellsworth, Gunning Bedford, Nathaniel Gorham, and James Madison.

to Congress on June 6, 1783. The report represented the views of those really interested in the creation of a national domain and it wisely referred back to the resolutions of October, 1780, requesting land cessions from the states. One by one it took up the various conditions attached to the Virginia cession of January, 1781, and disposed of them in a manner satisfactory to the Virginians. The committee held that the original resolutions asking for cessions provided for the first condition demanding that the territory ceded should be divided into states not more than one hundred and fifty and not less than one hundred miles square, and that these states should be admitted to the union with the same "rights of sovereignty, freedom and independence as the other states." The committee recommended that commissioners should be appointed to determine the "reasonable" military expenses incurred by Virginia in the Old Northwest and to liquidate the account. The French inhabitants of the region, who had become citizens of Virginia, should be guaranteed their rights and possessions and United States troops should be stationed there as Virginia demanded. The report declared reasonable the fourth and fifth conditions which related to land bounties for George Rogers Clark and his troops, as well as for regular Virginia troops in the region ceded.

The sixth condition required that the lands ceded should be considered a common fund for all the United States, present and future, to be shared according to the "general charge and expenditure." The seventh condition was the famous one demanding the nullification of all land company purchases in the region ceded. The eighth condition asked Congress to guarantee Virginia's remaining territory to her. In discussing these demands the committee arrived at a general formula which gave to Virginia what she demanded without at the same time making any specific guarantees. The sixth condition was declared reasonable and acceptable. This condition was held to be sufficient on the point of land company purchases and therefore a statement on the seventh condition was unnecessary. Finally the committee declared that Congress could not guarantee Virginia's territory to her without entering into a discussion of Virginia's right to the land in question. The committee declared such a guarantee both unnecessary and unreasonable. If the land really belonged to Virginia the Articles of Confederation were a sufficient guarantee. If the land did not belong to Virginia there was no reason for such a guarantee. The important thing, declared the committee, was for Virginia to make a cession in conformity with the report and for Congress to accept such a cession once it was made.[39]

Madison predicted correctly that this report would meet with much opposition as it "tacitly" excluded "the pretensions of the companies."[40] Promptly the delegates from the Middle States demanded postponement. The Delaware delegates declared that they were expecting instructions. A New Jersey delegate said he must first transmit the plan to his constituents. The Maryland delegates were not present and their presence was felt necessary before a decision could be made. Other members of Congress wanted an immediate decision. Alexander Hamilton joined these, but he asserted the "right" of the United States to western lands and moved an amendment to the report in favor of the land company claims. The upshot of the argument was that Congress gave its President permission to send informal notification of the time set for consideration to the land companies, to the Maryland delegates, and to others concerned.[41]

When the report was taken up for further debate on June 20, the New Jersey delegates presented a "representation and remonstrance" from their legislature. This document damned the Virginia cession as "partial, unjust and illiberal," and recapitulated the various proceedings of the New Jersey legislature in which it had stated the "just and incontrovertible claims of this State to its full proportion of all vacant territory." The New Jersey legislature expressed itself as incapable of sitting silent while one state sought to aggrandize itself by keeping property which had been procured "by the common blood and treasure of the whole." "On every principle of reason and justice," it continued, "[the land] is vested in Congress for the use and general benefit of the Union they represent." Therefore, the

[39] *Journals*, XXV, 559-563. This report was delivered to Congress June 6, but it does not appear in the *Journals* until September 13, 1783, at which time it was agreed to by Congress.

[40] Madison to Edmund Randolph, June 10, 1783, Hunt, *Madison Writings*, I, 475-476, n. 1.

[41] *Ibid.*

New Jersey legislature demanded that Congress reject the Virginia cession and call upon Virginia "to make a more liberal surrender of that territory of which they claim so boundless a proportion." [42] Further discussion was shut off, Madison said, "there being seven States only present and the spirit of compromise decreasing." [43]

Consideration was thus finally delayed until September, when the Maryland delegates once more sought to establish the principle that there were lands lying without the bounds of any particular state and that Congress had succeeded to the sovereignty over them. Maryland had not relinquished her rights and interests in the West when she acceded to the Confederation, declared her delegates. Congress should appoint committees to determine the lands that lay beyond the boundaries of the several states. [44] Maryland had learned nothing in the school of practical politics of the past seven years. Only New Jersey supported her demands. Congress was at last passing from the control of the landless states whose motives were a compound of jealousy and private interest. Other problems and other interests were coming to the fore as the Revolution drew to a close. For more than a year the financial difficulties of Congress had caused more and more men to look toward the sale of western lands as a likely source of revenue with which to handle the public debt. In fact it was a discussion of the financial difficulties of Congress which put in motion the train of events leading to the ultimate creation of the national domain. [45]

Another reality which Congress faced was the necessity of fulfilling or denying the promises made to the soldiers of the

[42] *Journals*, XXIV, 407-409. The document, dated June 14, had been in the hands of the New Jersey delegates for some time and unfairness was complained of because they had not presented it to Congress earlier. The somewhat lame reply of one of the New Jersey delegates was that they feared that the news of it might hasten the opening of a land office in Virginia. The delegate, Clark, declared that he was hopeful that Congress would yet limit the western extension of Virginia. See Madison, "Notes on Debates," Hunt, *Madison Writings*, I, 481-482.

[43] Madison, "Notes on Debates," June 20, Hunt, *Madison Writings*, I, 482.

[44] September 13, 1783, *Journals*, XXV, 554-558.

[45] See Joseph Jones to Washington, February 27, 1783, Worthington C. Ford, ed., *Letters of Joseph Jones of Virginia* (Washington, 1889), 97-98; Stephen Higginson to Samuel Adams, May 20, 1783, Burnett, *Letters*, VII, 168; David Howell to Governor of Rhode Island, December 24, 1783, *ibid.*, 397; Madison, "Notes on Debates," April 17, 1783, Hunt, *Madison Writings*, I, 451-452.

army back in 1776. At that time Congress had promised land bounties to those who would enlist for the duration of the war. It was a promise born of desperation for Congress had then had no land to give. But now the war was over, and in the Newburgh Petition the officers of the army demanded fulfillment of the old promise.[46] Washington backed their demands with the weight of his vast influence,[47] and when released from the command of the army, he spent time with Congress furthering the cause of the army officers who hoped for land grants north of the Ohio River. He pointed out that which was becoming increasingly plain: that while Congress and Virginia were debating, the West was being settled by those whom Washington called "Banditti," who were not only depriving the officers of their just rewards, but who were also sowing the seeds of Indian war.[48] The danger of Indian war was growing ever greater as uncontrolled emigration pushed farther and farther into Indian country and came into violent contact with its inhabitants.[49]

As a result of these various influences and difficulties, Congress accepted the report of June, 1783, which, as Madison said, "tacitly" excluded the land companies from congressional consideration, and upon the basis of which Virginia was to be asked for a new cession of the Old Northwest. Massachusetts, Rhode Island, Connecticut, New York, Pennsylvania, Virginia, and North and South Carolina voted for the report. Only Maryland and New Jersey persisted in wanting to continue the fruitless struggle.[50] The New York delegates explained their own agreement on the grounds that the matter could be settled only by compromise and that it would leave to Congress an immense

[46] Archer B. Hulbert, ed., *The Records of the Original Proceedings of the Ohio Company* (Marietta, 1917-1918), I, xxvi-xxviii. The petition was dated June 16, 1783.

[47] Washington to President of Congress, June 17, 1783, Worthington C. Ford, ed., *The Writings of George Washington* (New York, 1889-1893), X, 267-270; *Journals*, XXIV, 421, n. 2.

[48] Washington to Henry Knox, September 23, 1783, Ford, *Washington Writings*, X, 319-320; Washington to Chevalier De Chastellux, October 12, 1783, *ibid.*, X, 324; Jefferson to Governor Benjamin Harrison, November 11, 1783, Ford, *Jefferson Writings*, III, 343-344.

[49] Washington to James Duane, September 7, 1783, Ford, *Washington Writings*, X, 303-312; *Journals*, XXV, 534, n. 2, citing a letter from Brigadier-General William Irvine "respecting settlements beyond the Ohio and the consequent danger of an Indian War."

[50] *Journals*, XXV, 564. New Hampshire's one nay vote did not count.

tract of country which was "daily overrun by lawless men (who endanger by their Rashness a new Indian War): and which might be improved to great public Advantage." Finally, as they pointed out, the compromise would tend to settle a question which had proven a great obstacle to the conduct of public business, and which might have been a source of internal contention and convulsion.[51]

The issue was at last placed squarely before the Virginia assembly where it had been in dispute for some time. Many Virginians, and particularly George Mason, were bitter against the intrigues of the land companies and were dubious of the intentions of a Congress which was openly charged to be under their influence.[52] A second obstacle proved to be the land-hunger of Virginia officers who looked upon the lands set aside for them south of the Ohio River as barren and inadequate, and who demanded that the assembly grant them lands across the Ohio.[53] A committee of the assembly proposed to grant the officers their desires, and even more, to give them an additional quantity and to pay for the expenses of location as well. This idea met with the hearty support of Patrick Henry, once more on the road back to political favor. Furthermore, he expressed himself in favor of bounding the state reasonably, but instead of ceding the parts beyond the limits established, he was for laying them off into small republics. Joseph Jones, who earnestly desired a cession to Congress, opposed such schemes and was able to stop them temporarily.[54]

Nevertheless, the demand of the Virginia officers for lands northwest of the Ohio caused many members of the assembly to urge the withdrawal of the act of cession. Point was lent to their arguments by the fact that Congress had neither accepted the cession nor assigned any reasons for delay. The best that the friends of the cession could do was to set a date in the future,

[51] New York Delegates to Governor of New York, September 19, 1783, Burnett, *Letters*, VII, 300-301.

[52] Address from the Citizens of Fairfax County to the County Representatives in the Virginia House of Delegates, May 30, 1783, Rowland, *George Mason*, II, 51. This address was written by George Mason.

[53] Joseph Jones to James Madison, May 31, 1783, Ford, *Letters of Joseph Jones*, 110.

[54] Ford, *Letters of Joseph Jones*, May 31, June 6, 1783, pp. 110, 113-114; Jefferson to Madison, June 17, 1783, Ford, *Jefferson Writings*, III, 333-334.

after which the cession would be withdrawn unless accepted by Congress.[55]

It was at this juncture that the news of the compromise report of June, 1783, reached Virginia. The assembly showed no inclination to take up the matter since it was not an act of Congress. Furthermore, the report did not "fully remove the fears of our people respecting the Indian purchases and grants to companies. Their jealousy of Congress on that head is very strong."[56] Matters stood thus until late in the fall of 1783, when Virginia was faced with the official action of Congress accepting the report which agreed to, in one form or another, the conditions attached to the Virginia cession of 1781. Joseph Jones presented a bill accepting the compromise offered by Congress, and on December 20, 1783, Virginia made a second cession of her claims to the Old Northwest.[57] No specific conditions were attached. The generalities of the act of cession like those of the compromise report of Congress, however, were clearly designed to preserve the West for the United States as a whole.

On March 1, 1784, Congress accepted the second Virginia cession of the Old Northwest and thereby became the owner of a national domain. New Jersey was the only state to vote against acceptance. Maryland was unrepresented in Congress.[58]

The national domain was at last a reality. Congress speedily

[55] Joseph Jones to James Madison, June 8, June 14, 1783, Ford, *Letters of Joseph Jones*, 114, 117-118.

[56] *Ibid.*, June 21, 121-122. In a letter of June 28, Jones reported, "It will be vain to attempt relaxing the clause respecting the companies." *Ibid.*, 125.

[57] *Journal of the House of Delegates of the Commonwealth of Virginia* [October-December, 1783] (Richmond, 1827), 53, 69, 70, 79; Ford, Joseph Jones to Madison, October 30, 1783, *Letters of Joseph Jones*, 132; Jones to Jefferson, December 21, December 29, 1783, *ibid.*, 133-135, 135-136.

[58] *Journals*, XXVI, 112-117. Jefferson's account of the discussion in Congress before final acceptance is in his letter to Governor Benjamin Harrison, March 3, 1784, Ford, *Jefferson Writings*, III, 411-412.

The Indiana Company sought once more to secure the intervention of Congress before the acceptance of the Virginia cession. The company had become so influential in New Jersey politics that the New Jersey legislature had appointed George Morgan, agent of the company, as agent of the state of New Jersey. As agent for the state, he brought the claim of the Indiana Company before Congress as the claim of the state of New Jersey, and thus attempted to force Congress to arbitrate the matter as a dispute between state and state in the manner provided by the Articles of Confederation. The attempt was frustrated, but the Indiana Company was to live many more years and to have its effect on the political life of the nation.

put in motion measures that led to the adoption of ordinances for the survey and disposal and for the government of the national domain. Military control of the more lawless inhabitants was provided for. A policy of making treaties with the Indian inhabitants was adopted. In all these matters the Confederation Congress showed both vigor and originality and laid a substantial portion of the foundation upon which was based a great deal of the subsequent policy of the government of the United States toward the national domain.

Jefferson, the Ordinance of 1784, and the Origins of the American Territorial System

Robert F. Berkhofer, Jr.*

CURRENT interpretations of the origins of the United States territorial system generally rest upon two fundamental readings of events of the time accepted as fact. Because Jefferson as committee chairman wrote the report that became, as amended by the Continental Congress, the Ordinance of 1784, historians presume he was primarily responsible for the basic governmental policies proclaimed in the document. Therefore they interpret its provisions for new states mainly in light of how they understand his political philosophy. Because the Northwest Ordinance repealed the one of 1784, historians generally portray the latter as a repudiation of the former document specifically and of Jefferson's liberal philosophy in general. Close attention, however, to the chronology of precedents, the evolution of the Ordinance of 1784, and Jefferson's voting record on it challenges the larger role usually attributed to him in the composition of the document. Reexamination of Jefferson's correspondence, the evolution of the Northwest Ordinance, and the opinions of the time raises questions about the relationship between the two ordinances as traditionally ascribed by their leading interpreter.[1] These doubts suggest the need for a newer and more sophisticated history of the origins of the American territorial system.

* Mr. Berkhofer is a member of the Department of History, University of Wisconsin.

[1] Francis S. Philbrick in his long introduction to *The Laws of Illinois Territory, 1809-1818* (Illinois State Historical Library, *Collections*, XXV [Springfield, Ill., 1950]), ccl-ccclxiii, praises Jefferson's plan because it embodied revolutionary idealism and faith in frontier democracy, while he condemns the Northwest Ordinance as a reactionary scheme designed to exploit western settlers for the benefit of eastern conservatives. See also Philbrick, *The Rise of the West, 1754-1830* (New York, 1965), 120-133. Cf. the classic work of Merrill Jensen, *The New Nation: A History of the United States During the Confederation, 1781-1789* (New York, 1950), 352-359. How easy it is for even a careful scholar to slip from mentioning Jefferson's drafting of the committee report to claiming for the sage from Monticello all its chief ideas and those of the Ordinance of 1784 may be seen in Merrill D. Peterson, *Thomas Jefferson and the New Nation: A Biography* (New York, 1970), 279-286.

On March 1, 1784, "the Committee appointed to prepare a plan for the temporary government of the Western territory" presented its report, in the handwriting of Jefferson, to the Continental Congress sitting in Annapolis. It coincided with and was the result of Virginia's cession by deed to Congress of her claim to the territory north and west of the Ohio River. The deed created for the first time a national domain for the "United States in Congress Assembled" to govern and, equally important from the viewpoint of the Confederation treasury, to sell. The deed and the creation of the domain represented the culmination of a long dispute over the Old Dominion's claims to the trans-Appalachian West. Throughout the controversy, but incidental to the main issues, references to the formation of new states in the West served as precedents for Jefferson's report and shaped its main provisions.

Although states other than Virginia also claimed lands in the trans-Appalachian West upon the basis of the vague boundaries stated in their founding charters, no other state's claims embraced so vast a territory as those of the Old Dominion, which included not only the area between the Appalachian Mountains and the Ohio River but also the huge acreage beyond that became known as the Old Northwest. Its very extensiveness made the claim the focus of opposition. Moreover, with seven states "landed" according to charter claims and six "landless," the even balance produced a long drawn out fight that even Virginia's cession in 1784 only partially resolved.

The rhetoric of the controversy focused upon whether Virginia (and by implication other landed states) should retain all rights to the entirety of its claims for its exclusive private advantage or whether, regardless of original charter limits, these lands should benefit all the states fighting the war. Behind the rhetoric lay a diverse set of men and motives on both sides,[2] although both agreed from the beginning upon one principle: whoever controlled the trans-Appalachian West, the area should enjoy new independent governments. As the cession controversy moved through its phases so too did the ideas about the nature of these new governments.

[2] For an analysis of motives as well as the story, cf. Merrill Jensen, "The Cession of the Old Northwest," *Mississippi Valley Historical Review*, XXIII (1936-1937), 27-48; Jensen, "The Creation of the National Domain, 1781-1784," *ibid.*, XXVI (1939-1940), 323-342; Thomas P. Abernethy, *Western Lands and the American Revolution* (New York, 1937), 162-287; Rudolf Freund, "Military Bounty Lands and the Origins of the Public Domain," *Agricultural History*, XX (1946), 8-18; and Jack M. Sosin, *The Revolutionary Frontier, 1763-1783* (New York, 1967), 151-160.

Since the conflict originated in the vagueness of boundaries specified in the colonial charters, the cession dispute was hardly new in 1776. Rather it was in many ways a continuation of the earlier fights among the colonies and their land speculators over rival land claims and political jurisdiction in the trans-Appalachian West. Independence changed the final authority from Parliament to Congress and the official actors from colonies to states. The change shifted concern from how to go about erecting new royal colonies, if any, in the West to whether there would and ought to be new governments in the West as well as what ought to be their nature. The transition in thinking was rapid and may be traced in the documents of 1776.

Although the idea of giving Congress power to limit state boundaries had been discussed earlier in the halls of Congress,[3] the initial draft of the Articles of Confederation first presented the issue officially on July 12, 1776. Composed by John Dickinson from "landless" Pennsylvania, Article XVIII gave Congress the right to limit the boundaries of those states with extended western charter claims. Significantly, he stipulated that Congress would create "new colonies" in these areas "to be established on the Principles of Liberty."[4] Virginians not only opposed in Congress this proposed interpretation of the Confederation's powers but also reasserted their claims in the new state constitution. Jefferson, angered by the attempts to deny his state's sovereignty over the West, was largely responsible for the strong wording of the clause on this subject in the Virginia constitution. In a draft of a proposed constitution for his state, he avowed among other things:

The Western and Northern extent of this country shall in all respects stand as fixed by the charter of [   ] until by act of the Legislature one or more territories shall be laid off Westward of the Alleghaney mountains for new colonies, which colonies shall be established on the same fundamental laws contained in this instrument [i.e., as in Virginia's Constitution], and shall be free and independent of this colony and of all the world.[5]

[3] Article V of Benjamin Franklin's proposed Articles of Confederation, July 21, 1775, in Worthington C. Ford *et al.*, eds., *Journals of the Continental Congress, 1774-1789* (Washington, D. C., 1904-1937), II, 196.
[4] Article XVIII, *ibid.*, V, 550-551, July 12, 1776. In a subsequent version, this section was omitted in Article XIV. See *ibid.*, 682.
[5] Third draft, in Julian P. Boyd, ed., *The Papers of Thomas Jefferson* (Princeton, N. J., 1950-   ), I, 362-363. That Jefferson was responsible for the inclusion of this provision can be seen in a comparison of his various drafts for the Virginia

For Jefferson's strong statement on "new colonies," the Virginia Convention substituted a vaguer wording: the possibility that "one or more Territories shall hereafter be laid off, and Governments established Westward of the *Allegheny* Mountains."[6] Upon learning of this specific provision in their neighboring state's constitution, the Maryland Convention passed unanimously a resolution opposing Virginia's claim to the West and declared that "such lands ought to be considered as a common stock, to be parcelled out at proper times into convenient, free and independent governments."[7] As much as the Maryland and Virginia Conventions differed upon the proper bounds of the Old Dominion, both, however, saw new "governments" arising in the trans-Appalachian West.

After this initial debate, all subsequent references to western governments were in terms of new states rather than colonies—the transition from colonial to independent thinking on the question was completed. Delegates talked about new states when the Articles came up for debate during the next year, and Maryland and other landless states' representatives tried to restore the power of Congress to limit western boundaries.[8] All their efforts failed, and so the final version of the Articles submitted to the states for discussion and ratification in November 1777 followed the wishes of the landed states in regard to boundaries.[9] Without some such provision, however, the Articles remained unacceptable to Maryland, and by early 1779 she alone remained outside the Confederation.

Resolution of this crisis was to come by means of Virginia's cession of her boundary claims to Congress, because she could cede upon her conditions while Congress gained control of the lands, which was what many of the opposition wanted. In fact, as early as September 1778 a congressional Finance Committee dominated by delegates from landless

---

Constitution and the final version *ibid.*, 344, 352-353, 362-363, 383, and the notes thereto. See also Boyd's introduction.

[6] *Ibid.*, 383. This probably does not refer to the extension of county governments, because it implies separating the territory from Virginia.

[7] *Proceedings of the Convention of the Province of Maryland, Held at The City of Annapolis, on Wednesday, the fourteenth of August, 1776* (Annapolis, Md., 1776[?]), 49, Oct. 30, 1776.

[8] Ford *et al.*, eds., *Jour. Cont. Cong.*, IX, 806-808, esp. 806, Oct. 15, 1777.

[9] *Ibid.*, 915-923, Art. IX. Both Edmund C. Burnett, *The Continental Congress* (New York, 1941), 213-230, 237-241, 248-258, 341-345; and Merrill Jensen, *The Articles of Confederation: An Interpretation of the Social-Constitutional History of the American Revolution, 1774-1781* (Madison, Wis., 1940), trace the evolution of the Articles of Confederation.

states suggested such a solution. In its report the committee recommended that Congress call on the several states having "large uncultivated territory" to cede upon certain terms. Among these terms were: "That it be covenanted with the States that the Lands set off shall be erected into separate independent States, to be admitted into the Union, to have a Representation in Congress, and to have free Governments in which no Officers shall be appointed by Congress, other than such as are appointed through the other States."[10] Not until the fall of 1780 did congressmen find a formula acceptable to both sides. On September 6 Congress agreed to a report recommending cession but forbearing to decide on the relative merits of Maryland's and Virginia's claims and counterclaims over the boundary issue.[11] On October 10 Congress further resolved at the behest of the Virginia delegates that all such ceded lands "shall be disposed of for the common benefit of the United States, and be settled and formed into distinct republican states, which shall become members of the federal union, and have the same rights of sovereignty, freedom and independence, as the other states. . . ." The resolution also specified, at Virginia's insistence, "that each state which shall be so formed shall contain a suitable extent of territory, not less than one hundred nor more than one hundred and fifty miles square, or as near thereto as circumstances will admit."[12] This resolution became the basic foundation for subsequent cession and the creation of new states.

Factors other than reports and resolutions, however, caused the Virginia General Assembly to vote on January 2, 1781, to cede all claims northwest of the Ohio River with many conditions attached detrimental to the private land speculators of the landless states. Included in the conditions was the recommendation of October 1780 about the nature and size of the new states. For reasons other than the cession Maryland at long last signed the Articles of Confederation on March 1, 1781.[13] Neither act settled the controversy, for those who opposed Virginia's conditions or hoped to gain territory south of the Ohio River now sought

[10] Ford *et al.*, eds., *Jour. Cont. Cong.*, XII, 931, Sept. 19, 1778. The Virginia delegate on the committee favored some form of compromise. See Richard Henry Lee to Patrick Henry, Nov. 15, 1778, in James C. Ballagh, ed., *The Letters of Richard Henry Lee*, I (New York, 1911), 452-453.

[11] Ford *et al.*, eds., *Jour. Cont. Cong.*, XVII, 806-807.

[12] *Ibid.*, XVIII, 915, with crossed-out words omitted. For the original motion by the Virginia delegates, see *ibid.*, XVII, 808, Sept. 6, 1780.

[13] Cf. Sosin, *Revolutionary Frontier*, and Burnett, *Continental Congress*, with Jensen, *The New Nation*, on the reasons for Virginia's and Maryland's actions.

to block congressional acceptance. So successful were they in their tactics that three years were to pass before Congress accepted the cession and thereby created a national domain to sell and to rule. Each side had enough votes to thwart the other's wishes but too few to gain its own ends, and only forces generated by the ending of the war finally brought both cession by Virginia and acceptance by Congress. Both army officers and congressional delegates, with prospects of peace and cession near, discussed the nature of new state governments in more detail, thereby ushering in the final phase of discussion on the topic before the official report of Jefferson's committee.[14]

A combination of the army officers' specific request for a new state or "colony" in the West and the Virginia condition on the size of new states reached the floor of Congress in mid-1783 by way of Theodorick Bland. As a member of the congressional Finance Committee, which dealt with the so-called Newburgh Conspiracy in the spring, Bland had been concerned about the bounties and back pay owed the army. As a Virginia delegate, he had long fought for congressional acceptance of his state's cession upon her conditions. On June 5, 1783, he combined both ends by moving that Congress accept Virginia's cession in order to finance its promises to the army. As part of his proposal, he requested fellow lawmakers create from the cession a territory of unspecified boundaries and ordain:

That the said territory shall be laid off in districts not exceeding two degrees of Latitude and three degrees of Longitude each, and each district in townships not exceeding [   ] miles square. . . . That each of the said districts shall, when it contains 20,000 male inhabitants, become and ever after be and constitute a separate, Independent free and Sovereign state, and be admitted into the union as such with the privileges and immunities of those states which now compose the union.[15]

Thus he translated the size of the new states from the Virginia amendment of October 1780 into geographical terms, and he added the number of inhabitants necessary for admission to statehood. All this suggests that

14 The so-called Pickering Plan may be found in Octavius Pickering, *The Life of Timothy Pickering*, I (Boston, 1867), 546-549. The petition of the army officers, June 16, 1783, is in William P. and Julia P. Cutler, *Life, Journals and Correspondence of Rev. Manasseh Cutler, LL.D.*, I (Cincinnati, 1888), 159-167.

15 Ford *et al.*, eds., *Jour. Cont. Cong.*, XXIV, 385.

Congress may have been considering western government in more specific terms by mid-1783.

Certainly congressmen were discussing new statemaking by the fall of that year. Unfortunately this discussion must be reconstructed solely from the amendments offered during the formulation of postwar Indian policy. George Washington called the interconnection of illegal white settlement, peace with the Indians, and the formation of a new state to the attention of the chairman of the Indian Affairs Committee in a lengthy letter dated September 7, 1783. To maintain peace with the Indians as well as to preserve an orderly, well-regulated white society in the West, Washington recommended the confinement of the unruly frontiersmen to only a portion of the trans-Ohio West. For this purpose, a new state should be established for the white settlers and a strict line of separation between red and white men enforced. He also suggested two possible limits for the new state, either a large state embracing Detroit within its bounds or a smaller state. If Congress chose the latter, he thought the remainder of the land that his larger state would have embraced should eventually form a second state.[16]

In accord with Washington's views, the report of the Indian Affairs Committee asked whether Congress should appoint a committee to lay off a new state in the West and devise a plan for its "temporary government." This recommendation led eventually to the appointment of the committee and to Jefferson's report, but congressional debate over this aspect of the Indian report and its implications for the Ordinance of 1784 has been obscured and confused by the particularly bad editing of the report and its amendments in the modern edition of the *Journals of the Continental Congress*. The resultant confusion and scarcity of evidence demand extensive quotation of the relevant portions of the report and the subsequent amendments for clarification.[17]

The Committee on Indian Affairs delivered its report in two parts on two different dates. The original report of September 19 mentioned

[16] George Washington to James Duane, Sept. 7, 1783, in John C. Fitzpatrick, ed., *The Writings of George Washington* . . . , XXVII (Washington, D. C., 1938), 133-140.

[17] Ford *et al.*, eds., *Jour. Cont. Cong.*, XXV, 680-695, confuses the sequence of events by running both parts of the report under the date of the final adoption and a day after the debate on the amendments to it. The confusion is compounded by combining both parts of the report and the amendments into one text so it all appears in a form it never had in actuality.

only the need for a strict separation of Indians and whites,[18] but the idea was not developed to include the possibility of a new state until the further report of September 22. In a long paragraph deserving full quotation, the report followed Washington's reasoning on the unattractive character of frontiersmen and the consequent need for good government and then went on to suggest the appointment of another committee to achieve that purpose:

And lastly your committee beg leave to observe that they do not offer the measures which they suggested as a sufficient security against the increase of feeble, disorderly and dispersed settlements in those remote and wide extended Territories; against the depravity of manners which they have a tendency to produce, the endless perplexities in which they must involve the administration of the affairs of the United States, or against the calamities of frequent and destructive wars with the Indians which reciprocal animosities, unrestrained by the interposition of legal authority must naturally excite.—Nothing in the opinion of the committee can avert those complicated and impending mischiefs, or secure to the United States the just and important advantages which they ought to derive from those Territories, but the speedy establishment of government and the regular administration of justice in such District thereof as shall be judged most convenient for immediate settlement and cultivation.— Your committee therefore submit it to the consideration, whether it is not wise and necessary that a Committee be appointed to report to Congress on the expediency of laying out a suitable district within the said territory, and of erecting it into a distinct government for the accommodation of such as may incline to become purchasers and inhabitants, as well as for doing justice to the army of the United States who are entitled to lands as bounty or in reward for their services, with instructions to such committee to devise a plan for the temporary government of the inhabitants and the due administration of justice, until their number and circumstances shall entitle them to a place among the States in the Union; when they shall be at liberty, to form a free constitution for themselves not incompatible with the republican principles which are the basis of the constitutions of the respective States in the union. But if Congress conceive it doubtful whether the powers vested by the Instrument of Confederation and perpetual union are competent to the establishment of such government, that then the committee be instructed to

[18] The original draft of this report is found in Papers of the Continental Congress, Item 30, foll. 35-43, Record Group 360, National Archives. A printed version is *ibid.*, fol. 193.

prepare and report to Congress a proper address to the respective States for remedying the defects of the said instrument in this respect.[19]

The report ended with Washington's two suggestions for state boundaries. In the minds of committee members, such new states would have to pass through some period of temporary government before achieving permanent government, an idea that received further development during the debate on the second half of the long paragraph.

In the debates on the report what was not amended is as revelatory of congressional thinking on western statemaking as what was amended. The first part of the long paragraph pointing out the desirability of establishing government in the West in light of the nature of the settlement pattern and the character of frontiersmen was never controverted, if lack of amendment reflects lack of discussion. On the other hand, the second part of the paragraph after the second dash was debated extensively on October 14. From the evidence of the journal and the amendment slips in the Papers of the Continental Congress, Elbridge Gerry of Massachusetts offered an amendment apparently to specify more precisely that Congress was solely responsible for the creation of any temporary government in the new state:

Your committee therefore submit it to consideration, whether it will not be wise and necessary, when the State of Virginia shall close with conditions of Congress in the session of the Western Territory as soon as circumstances shall permit, to erect a part thereof District of the Western Territory into a distinct Government, as well for doing Justice to the Army of the United States, who are entitled to Lands as a Bounty or in reward of their Services, as for the accommodation of such as may incline to become purchasers and Inhabitants, and in the interim to appoint a committee to report a plan, which to be poll [?] consistent with the principles of the Confederation, for connecting with the Union by a temporary Government the said purchasers and Inhabitants of the said District, untill their Number and circumstances shall entitle them to form for themselves a permanent government, [illeg.] permanent constitution for themselves and as citizens of a free sovereign and independent state shall be admitted to a representation in the Union.[20]

Samuel Huntington of Connecticut added a clause to bring Gerry's amendment in line with the stipulations of Congress and the previous

---

[19] This is the printed version considered by Congress, *ibid.*, fol. 199. Cf. the handwritten draft, *ibid.*, foll. 181-185.

[20] *Ibid.*, Item 36, fol. 343. Cf. Ford *et al.*, eds., *Jour. Cont. Cong.*, XXV, 678.

conditions of cession: "Provided such Constitution shall not be incompatible with the republican principles which are the basis of the Constitutions of the respective states in the Union."[21] According to the official journal, David Howell of Rhode Island then moved to postpone consideration of the Gerry amendment in favor of his own paragraph allowing the inhabitants of the new state a greater say in their own government:

Y[ou]r Com[mitt]ee recommend it as necessary and expedient as soon as circumstances will admit to lay off a suitable district within the said territory and to erect it into a distinct government as well as for doing justice to the army of the United States, who are entitled to lands as a bounty or in reward of their services as for the accommodation of such as may incline to become purchasers and inhabitants, and for this purpose a com[mitt]ee be appointed with instructions to said committee to devise and report a plan for the government of the inhabitants and the due administration of justice, which if agreeable to the settlers shall be their form of temporary government until their number and circumstances shall entitle them to a place among the States in the union; when they shall be at liberty to form a free constitution for themselves not inconsistent with the republican principles which are the basis of the constitutions of the republican States in the Union.[22]

Howell's amendment was voted down in favor of Gerry's amendment by six states to three with three more states insufficiently represented to vote. So the final report as adopted by Congress and entered upon the journal contains the first half of the original paragraph before the second dash unchanged and Gerry's amendment becomes a full second paragraph.[23] The task of drawing up a plan of temporary government was immediately given to a committee of three. To this committee was also referred the now omitted last part of the original report containing Washington's suggested boundaries.[24]

[21] Written on the side of Gerry's motion, Papers of the Continental Congress, Item 36, fol. 343, R. G. 360.

[22] Ibid., Item 36, fol. 421. According to Gaillard Hunt, editor of Jour. Cont. Cong., XXV, 679n, the motion is in the handwriting of James McHenry and Abraham Clark, but these names are crossed out on the side of the original and the names of Howell and William Ellery substituted. In the manuscript "form of" was struck out and "temporary" was inserted later.

[23] Cf. the versions in Ford et al., eds., Jour. Cont. Cong., XXV, 693-694, with the original published Journals of Congress: Containing Their Proceedings from November 2, 1782, to November 1, 1783, VIII (Philadelphia, 1800), 309.

[24] According to notation on the side of that portion of the printed report in

The process indicates how far congressional thinking had proceeded in planning the nature and extent of government for the western territory. All congressmen seemed agreed upon the necessity, given the nature of frontiersmen, for some form of good government there. Furthermore, most believed that Congress should provide such government without consulting the wishes of the inhabitants. Only five congressmen plus his fellow Rhode Islander supported Howell's position, while sixteen favored Gerry's position on temporary government.[25] Less clear from Howell's wording is whether he and his supporters wished to make any distinction between temporary and permanent government in the new state, but it is certain that those who followed Gerry did want to provide just such a distinction. In fact, that reason seems as much behind the Gerry amendment as his desire to remove the say of the new state's inhabitants in the planning of their government. Lastly, whether Congress discussed the number of states is unclear, since Washington's plan for a single state of whatever size in the beginning was not specifically amended but merely passed along to the new committee.

Only after all this discussion of new statemaking had occurred did Jefferson take his seat in Congress during November 1783. He immediately became chairman of a succession of committees that finally eventuated in the committee to prepare "a plan for the temporary government of the western territory." Also appointed on February 3, 1784, to serve with him were Howell and Jeremiah T. Chase of Maryland.[26] On February 21 committee member Howell, in a long letter to his friend and former congressional colleague, Jonathan Arnold, revealed that the committee had agreed on a report but had not yet presented it to Congress.[27] He then proceeded to give in detail the outline of the report as finally delivered on March 1, the same day on which Congress also formally received the second deed of cession from Virginia. That the report took no more than two and a half weeks for completion during a busy time for all committee members tends to confirm that Congress

---

Papers of the Continental Congress, Item 30, fol. 199, R. G. 360; and Ford *et al.*, eds., *Jour. Cont. Cong.*, XXV, 695.

[25] The vote is recorded in Ford *et al.*, eds., *Jour. Cont. Cong.*, XXV, 679.

[26] Julian Boyd straightens out the succession of the committees and the dates of their appointment in *Jefferson Papers*, VI, 584-585.

[27] David Howell to Jonathan Arnold, Feb. 21, 1784, in William R. Staples, *Rhode Island in the Continental Congress . . .* (Providence, R. I., 1870), 478-482.

had discussed western statemaking at length in connection with Indian affairs before Jefferson arrived in Congress. Such certainly was Howell's impression, for he wrote that "the mode of government, during the infancy of these states, has taken up much time, and was largely debated at Princeton last summer."[28] Jefferson reached Princeton just as Congress was preparing to move to Annapolis, so his effective term began at the new location.

Certainly the protracted debate first over cession and then over Indian affairs had dictated the main outlines of the report long before Jefferson arrived on the scene. As a result of the cession controversy, the committee had to operate within a framework that specified the size (and possibly the shape) of the new states, provided for eventual statehood only after some form of temporary government, and required both the temporary and permanent governments to be republican in form. Likewise, the debate over Gerry's and Howell's amendments to the Indian affairs report indicates that congressmen had discussed at some length the possible role of the new settlers' voice in the creation of temporary government. Boundaries had been proposed in the plans of the army officers and in Washington's letter to the Indians Affairs Committee. The subject of prohibiting slavery had come up outside Congress, and the idea of a covenant between Congress and the new states within its chambers. Even the length of time before statehood had been mentioned in a pamphlet by Tom Paine.[29] Thus Jefferson's contribution to the report appears to be less than scholars previously assumed. At the same time, Howell's role may have been greater than merely remembering the congressional debates prior to Jefferson's arrival. Detailed consideration of the report's content and the votes on amendments points further in this direction and enables us to speak more clearly about Jefferson's and Howell's roles.

Regardless of their roles or the previous discussion, the report of March 1, 1784, was the first detailed plan for western government the Congress considered and recorded.[30] The very first resolution fulfilled both the promise made by Congress in event of cession and one of

[28] *Ibid.*, 479.
[29] Thomas Paine, *Public Good, Being An Examination Into the Claim of Virginia to the Vacant Western Territory, and of the Right of the United States to the Same* . . . (Philadelphia, 1780), 38.
[30] A thoroughly annotated version of the report is in Boyd, ed., *Jefferson Papers,* VI, 603-607.

Virginia's conditions for cession: "Resolved, that the territory ceded or to be ceded by Individual states to the United states shall be formed into distinct states. . . ." The remainder of the paragraph specified the boundaries of the proposed states. Each state would extend two degrees of latitude from north to south counting from thirty-one degrees northward. Parallels drawn through the Falls of the Ohio and the mouth of the Great Kanawha River would determine east to west dimensions.

Probably this paragraph contained Jefferson's main contribution to the report. His ideas had evolved from previous proposals for creating only one or two states to forming six to fourteen or more, including, as a result, lands still unceded.[31] As Julian Boyd has pointed out, his originality lay in delineating boundaries on both ceded and yet to be ceded lands. He also showed boldness in recommending immediate division into the full number of states required by the Virginia amendment of October 10, 1780. Thus he rejected the possibility of preliminary government in one or more territories before drawing state boundaries, as Washington and others had suggested.

Jefferson's boundaries included lands south of the Ohio River still claimed by Georgia and North and South Carolina as well as by Virginia. He now advocated that his state should cede more than it already had and incorporated that belief in the report.[32] Even before the report was presented to Congress or the deed executed, he urged James Madison: "For god's sake push this at the next session of assembly." In explanation he argued, "It is for the interest of Virginia to cede so far immediately; because the people beyond that will separate themselves, because they will be joined by all our settlements beyond the Alleghaney if they are the first movers."[33] In a letter to George Washington during debate on the report, he expressed his thoughts even more succinctly: "I hope our country [Virginia] will of herself determine to cede still

[31] Boyd traced the development of Jefferson's ideas on this aspect of the report, *ibid.*, 588-594, 600-602.

[32] How long Jefferson had favored this position is unclear. Although he provided in his draft of the Virginia Constitution for the separation of some of the western portion of Virginia to form independent states, he also favored setting up the Kentucky region as a new county in 1776. See Boyd's editorial note, *ibid.*, I, 564-568. Again in 1778 and 1779 Jefferson favored the establishment of a Virginia land office to sell the lands and so obviously was not acting on the idea of splitting off this territory from the Old Dominion at that time. *Ibid.*, II, 133-167.

[33] Jefferson to James Madison, Feb. 20, 1784, *ibid.*, VI, 547.

further to the meridian of the mouth of the Great Kanhaway. Further she cannot govern; so far is necessary for her own well being."[34]

These sentences hint at the reasoning behind Jefferson's proposed geography for the West. The fear of western separation derived from larger considerations of political ideology common to the leaders of the period. For governments to remain republican, he and others believed the size of the state must be small enough to preserve the homogeneity of the interests, opinions, and habits of the citizens; otherwise a stronger, more centralized government than desirable for republicanism would be needed to extend its influence to the far corners of the state. The larger the territory of a government, the more likely that it would embrace diverse interests as a result of different climates and economic concerns. Accordingly, trans-Appalachian settlers would probably break away from eastern control in general and Virginia governance in particular, because they would have different interests from those of the inhabitants on the eastern seaboard. Furthermore, the limited force that a republican government would presumably exert could not possibly reach settlers so far removed from the center of that government. For its own good government as well as that of the trans-Appalachian West, therefore, Virginia ought to cede all territory beyond that which she could govern according to republican ideals of maintaining a homogeneity of interests among the state's population. Such reasoning prompted the original Virginia restriction that states should be no larger than one hundred fifty miles square.[35] Later, in protesting James Monroe's alteration of his proposed state sizes, Jefferson advanced the same reasons for retaining small states.[36] Small states, in sum, guaranteed the economic and political bases essential to republicanism, for the old states no less than the new ones.

When Jefferson set forth specific boundaries for the new states, however, he violated the sizes stipulated in Virginia's conditions of cession and in the instructions to his committee. According to the maps of the time, particularly one by Thomas Hutchins that Jefferson probably

[34] Jefferson to Washington, Mar. 15, 1784, *ibid.*, VII, 25.
[35] For earlier views on the connection between sizes of states and the force of republican government, see R. H. Lee to Henry, Nov. 15, 1778, in Ballagh, ed., *Letters of Richard Henry Lee*, I, 452-453; and Joseph Jones to Jefferson, June 30, 1780, in Boyd, ed., *Jefferson Papers*, III, 472. The whole conception is the focus of Cecelia M. Kenyon, "Men of Little Faith: The Anti-Federalists on the Nature of Representative Government," *William and Mary Quarterly*, 3d Ser., XII (1955), 3-43. See also Gordon S. Wood, *The Creation of the American Republic, 1776-1787* (Chapel Hill, N. C., 1969), 499-506.
[36] See below, 257-258.

thought most trustworthy, only the states between the meridians of the Great Kanawha and the Falls of the Ohio reasonably approximated the stipulated size. Even they approached the maximum, for they were approximately two degrees latitude by three degrees longitude or roughly 140 by 150 miles. The states between the Falls of the Ohio and the Mississippi generally exceeded the maximum, measuring approximately two by five or six degrees or roughly 140 by 250 or more miles.[37] One may guess that Jefferson deliberately violated the stipulated areas for geopolitical considerations. As Howell explicated the geography of the report, "There are to be three tiers of states:—One on the Atlantic [original thirteen], one on the Mississippi, and a middle tier. The middle tier is to be the smallest, and to form a balance betwixt the two more powerful ones."[38] Jefferson selected his meridian lines for the abstract idea of balance and from fear of conflict between large and small states. He further selected the Great Kanawha as one of the lines, because it provided for the separation of Kentucky that its residents had already threatened and yet gave Virginia access to the western trade by potential canal route from the Ohio River along the Great Kanawha and James Rivers.[39] All in all, the proposed boundaries constituted nothing less than a grand plan for the entire trans-Appalachian West according to Jefferson's ideological geography and his perception of Virginia's interests.

For governing the new settlers, the report established a series of stages, as Howell termed them, from temporary to permanent govern-

[37] These measurements are derived from the geographical knowledge available to Jefferson. The difficulties of measuring and counting in early American geography are demonstrated with special attention to Jefferson in John K. Wright, *Human Nature in Geography: Fourteen Papers, 1925-1965* (Cambridge, Mass., 1966), 205-247. Jefferson's own estimates of Virginia's extent are given in Queries I and II of his *Notes on the State of Virginia* (1787), ed. William Peden (Chapel Hill, N. C., 1955), 3-16. That Jefferson probably considered Thomas Hutchins's "A New Map of the Western Parts of Virginia . . . " of 1778 the most accurate available to him is indicated by his use of it in combination with his father's map for the map to accompany the *Notes on Virginia*. For that reason, I have relied for my measurements primarily on Hutchins's map and his accompanying *Topographical Description of Virginia, Pennsylvania, Maryland, and North Carolina, Comprehending the Rivers Ohio . . . Illinois, Mississippi . . . and . . . Containing Mr. Patrick Kennedy's Journal up the Illinois River . . .* (London, 1778). Cf. the observations of William D. Pattison, *Beginnings of the American Rectangular Land Survey System, 1784-1800* (Chicago, 1957), Chap. 1, for similar points.

[38] Howell to Arnold, Feb. 21, 1784, in Staples, *Rhode Island,* 479.

[39] Jefferson provides a lengthy rationale for that meridian in his letter to Madison, Feb. 20, 1784, in Boyd, ed., *Jefferson Papers,* VI, 547-548.

ment to statehood and admission to Congress. The "first stage"[40] allowed the settlers of any new state upon their own petition or by the authority of Congress to meet together to form a "temporary government" by adopting the constitution and laws of one of the original states. When the population of a new state reached twenty thousand free inhabitants, the settlers entered the second stage by receiving authority from Congress to call a convention "to establish a permanent constitution and government for themselves." Admission of delegates from a new state to Congress was possible when the number of its free inhabitants equaled that of the least populated original state, provided two-thirds of the states in Congress consented. Until that time any new state could, after establishment of temporary government, send a delegate to Congress with the right to debate but not to vote.

Though the report distinguished between temporary and permanent government according to the Gerry amendment to the committee's instructions, participation of the settlers in their own governance was definitely more in the spirit of Howell's attempted amendment, as the wording of the provision for the initial stage of government indicated:

That the settlers within any of the said states shall, either on their own petition, or on the order of Congress, receive authority from them, with appointments of time and place for their free males of full age to meet together for the purpose of establishing a temporary government, to adopt the constitution and laws of any one of these [original] states, so that such laws nevertheless shall be subject to alteration by their ordinary legislature, and to erect, subject to a like alteration, counties or townships for the election of members for their legislature.[41]

Certainly Howell in his long letter to Arnold interpreted these provisions as giving the settlers the initiative in establishing and participating fully in each stage of government.[42]

Scholars have long wondered why the report denied to the settlers the privilege of naming their states if they were granted self-government from the beginning.[43] Again Howell seems to supply the clue, for in his

[40] In calling this the "first stage" I follow committee member Howell's designation in his letter to Arnold, Feb. 21, 1784, in Staples, *Rhode Island*, 480. Cf. Jack E. Eblen, *The First and Second United States Empires: Governors and Territorial Government, 1784-1912* (Pittsburgh, 1968), 22, who uses first stage in another way.
[41] The bracketed "original" appeared in the printed version of the report according to Boyd, ed., *Jefferson Papers*, VI, 666, n. 13.
[42] Howell to Arnold, Feb. 21, 1784, in Staples, *Rhode Island*, 480.
[43] E.g., Boyd's discussion in *Jefferson Papers*, VI, 598.

explication of the first stage of government he observed that "settlers will always readily know in which of the states they are, for the states are to be named as well as numbered. . . ."[44] The report named the states, but Jefferson had a map in Paris with the new states numbered.[45] Whether specified as Michigania, Cherronesus, Assinisipia, Pelisipia, and six other classical and patriotic names as in the report or merely located by number, the inference is obvious: such a device seemed necessary precisely to facilitate self-government. Settlers would know exactly, by name or by number, in which little republic they lived, so they could go more quickly about the business of erecting governments.

The report stipulated five provisos for both temporary and permanent governments. They, like other parts of the report, appeared consistent with much of previous congressional thinking. That the new states "shall for ever remain a part of the United states of America" appears the very reason for the existence of the report, as does the vague wording of the second condition: "That in their persons, property and territory they [the governments] shall be subject to the government of the United states in Congress assembled, and to the Articles of confederation in all those cases in which the original states shall be so subject." The plight of the Confederation treasury and the pressures that generated compromise over cession seem adequate to explain the stipulation that new states pay their share of federal debts, but the long argument over the original states' obligations in financing the Confederation probably reinforced the point. The first part of proviso four, "that their respective governments shall be in republican forms," copied the wording of a number of congressional resolutions and the Virginia cession deed, but the prohibition upon the new states admitting to citizenship a person holding a hereditary title was probably original with Jefferson. He certainly felt strongly upon the subject, especially about the dangers to republicanism of the secret Society of Cincinnati as he indicated when he explained to Washington why Congress later dropped the provision.[46] The prohibition of slavery in any of the new states after 1800, which

---

[44] Howell to Arnold, Feb. 21, 1784, in Staples, *Rhode Island*, 480.

[45] The so-called Jefferson-Hartley map, in Boyd, ed., *Jefferson Papers*, VI, 592-593. Thomas Paine in his *Public Good*, 38, suggested that the first step in setting up a new state in the West would be to mark off its boundaries.

[46] Jefferson to Washington, Apr. 16, 1784, in Boyd, ed., *Jefferson Papers*, VII, 105-107, and notes thereto.

Timothy Pickering had proposed earlier, was a reform as dear to Howell as to Jefferson.[47]

The last paragraph of the report formed the covenant suggested by the finance committee in 1778:

That the preceding articles shall be formed into a Charter of Compact[,] shall be duly executed by the President of the U. S. in Congress assembled under his hand and seal of the United States, shall be promulgated, and shall stand as fundamental constitutions between the thirteen original states, and those now newly described, unalterable but by the joint consent of the U. S. in Congress assembled and of the particular state within which such alteration is proposed to be made.

No stronger form of language existed at the time to convince the settlers of new states that Congress intended to carry out its part of the bargain promised in the plan for government in return for their remaining in the Confederation. If the settlers followed the rules outlined, then Congress promised eventual statehood in the union on a par with the original states.

Essentially, then, the report embraced five aspects: a delineation (or bounding) and naming of the proposed states, provisions for the creation of temporary and permanent governments, a set of provisos upon which these governments were to be formed, and a charter of compact. In many ways, the document appears a recapitulation of the original states' political evolution with a colonial agent, taxation without and then with representation, and finally admission to statehood upon attaining a free population equal to that of the least populous original state. The report intended to guarantee the success of republicanism, even to the extent of requiring, during the period of temporary government, the selection of a constitution from one of the original states. It assured the union of the Confederation through the document itself, especially by the promise embodied in the compact. Just how consciously this process imitated the political growth of the colonies into states and confederation must be left to another place.

Debate upon the document proceeded in two phases. The report, ac-

[47] The best guide to Jefferson's ambivalent views on the black man and the institution of slavery is Winthrop D. Jordan, *White Over Black: American Attitudes Toward the Negro, 1550-1812* (Chapel Hill, N. C., 1968), 429-481. Brief mention of Howell's antislavery activities may be found in James F. Reilly, "The Providence Abolition Society," *Rhode Island History*, XXI (1962), 33-48.

cording to Secretary Charles Thomson's endorsement, was delivered March 1, read March 3, assigned for consideration March 8, and recommitted March 17. A revised report, again in the handwriting of Jefferson, was delivered and read March 22.[48] From a comparison of the two reports we can tell what was in dispute during the period. The main change was omission of the state names.[49] Subsequent debate suggests that the deletion reflected opposition to the settlers' participation in temporary government, for without self-government at the beginning, the new states need not be designated by name. Another change was the first of many that sought to fix exactly the number of states which had to consent to the admission of a new state as the Confederation enlarged.[50]

It was, however, during consideration of the second report from April 19-23 that Congress revealed in its journal basic disagreements and made major alterations. Soon after debate began Jefferson lost two of his cherished reforms which had been written into the provisos. On the first day the clause prohibiting slavery came under immediate attack. Jefferson and Howell voted for retention of the clause as did all the delegates north of the Mason-Dixon Line, but those from Maryland and South Carolina plus Jefferson's colleagues from Virginia voted for striking the clause. Since North Carolina's representatives divided and New Jersey was insufficiently represented, the antislavery forces lacked but one state of attaining their goal.[51] The next day the delegates struck by a large vote the clause withholding citizenship to persons claiming hereditary titles. As Jefferson explained the defeat to Madison, congressmen did not approve of such honors but they thought the ordinance "an improper place to encounter them."[52]

Obvious concern about the relationship between Congress and the new state governments prompted considerable change in the number and order of the provisos. The ambiguous second proviso gave much trouble

[48] Boyd, ed., *Jefferson Papers*, VI, 607-613, again provides a well-annotated version.

[49] According to Boyd, the elimination of the state names occurred in stages, first the dropping of one and then the omission of all. *Ibid.*, 607, n. 25.

[50] See also Ford *et al.*, eds., *Jour. Cont. Cong.*, XXVI, 251, 252. The problem in phrasing this provision is explained by Jefferson in his elucidation of the deficiencies of the Articles of Confederation in Boyd, ed., *Jefferson Papers*, X, 27-28, Query 8.

[51] Jefferson explained the closeness of the vote to Madison, Apr. 25, 1784, *ibid.*, VII, 118.

[52] *Ibid.*

in phrasing. In original form, it read: "That in their persons, property and territory they shall be subject to the government of the United states in Congress assembled, and to the Articles of confederation in all those cases in which the original states shall be so subject." Apparently in debate unrecorded in the Journal of Congress, the words "in their persons, property and territory" were deleted.[53] On April 20, the Connecticut representatives moved to simplify the proviso further, leaving it to read simply: "That they shall be subject . . . to the articles of Confederation in all those cases in which the original States shall be so subject." Both Jefferson and Howell voted with Gerry and the majority to adopt this wording; Chase voted against the motion.[54] Subsequently, and again in unrecorded debate, Congress added some words to the end: "and to all the Acts and Ordinances of the United States in Congress assembled conformable thereto."[55] And so what Congress had once voted down, it restored later in another guise.

This teeter-totter of wording probably reflected the course of debate on the degree of congressional authority over the new states as well as on the changing nature of the first stage of government. That it related to the latter question is indicated by the motion to alter even the wording of the heading for all the provisos by striking "temporary and" from the introductory sentence of the section, which read: "Provided that both the temporary and permanent governments be established on these principles as their basis."[56] But only the two sponsors favored such an alteration, and so the words remained. That the argument over the second proviso involved the relationship of congressional authority to the new state governments may be seen in the nature of other provisos added during debate.

Interestingly enough, Jefferson seconded Elbridge Gerry's motion to add another proviso, "That the lands and improvements thereon of non-resident proprietors, shall in no case be taxed higher than those of residents within any new State" before admission into Congress. Howell opposed this attempt to benefit absentee owners and speculators by moving to delete "and improvements thereon." Jefferson with Gerry and Chase and the majority of delegates opposed Howell's motion, but he

[53] *Ibid.*, VI, 611, n. 13.
[54] Ford *et al.*, eds., *Jour. Cont. Cong.*, XXVI, 248-249, Apr. 20, 1784.
[55] Boyd, ed., *Jefferson Papers*, VI, 611, n. 15, and in final ordinance, *ibid.*, 614.
[56] Ford *et al.*, eds., *Jour. Cont. Cong.*, XXVI, 249-250, Apr. 20, 1784.

won because South Carolina's delegates divided. Howell then attempted to amend the wording further by striking that portion of the proviso limiting its effect to the period before statehood but lost overwhelmingly, with Jefferson, Chase, and Gerry all opposing him once again. Finally, on a vote to agree to Gerry's original motion with Howell's first deletion, seven states voted yes, two no, and two divided. In this final tally, Jefferson along with Chase and Gerry voted in favor of prohibiting discriminatory taxation while Howell disapproved the whole proviso.[57]

Thus, by the end of this aspect of the debate, the number, the order, and the content of the provisos upon which the new states' temporary and permanent governments were to be formed had undergone considerable change in the direction of specifying the rights of the Confederation over new state governments. The same tendency also appeared in two additional provisos adopted without record of debate. In the final draft the third proviso prohibited state governments from interfering with prior disposal of the land by Congress or with its conveyance of title to purchasers. The fifth proviso forbade a tax on the lands owned by the federal government.

The climax of the debate came in discussion of the extent of congressional control over settlers before and during the period of temporary government. On April 22 Elbridge Gerry offered and Jefferson seconded a motion to revise the wording of the report's paragraph on the subject to read:

That on the petition of the settlers on any territory so purchased of the Indians, or otherwise obtained and sold to individuals, or on the order of Congress, authority may be given by Congress with appointment of time and place, for all free males of full age, being citizens of the United States, and owning lands or residing within the limits of their state, to meet together for the purpose of establishing a temporary government. . . .[58]

Although Gerry apparently meant to bring the wording in line with a concurrent Indian affairs report,[59] his motion opened old wounds from the conflict between landed and landless states over cession and revived the argument over the original instructions to Jefferson's committee. Five states divided in voting with only four solidly aye and two nay. The

[57] *Ibid.*, 257-259, Apr. 21, 1784.
[58] *Ibid.*, 256. Cf. with the original wording above, 238.
[59] According to Boyd, ed., *Jefferson Papers*, VI, 605, n. 2.

negative votes cast by Howell and Chase as opposed to Jefferson's aye indicates the solidarity of the landless states more than who opposed Gerry's instructions in committee.

With congressmen so divided, Jacob Read of South Carolina moved to place the settlers under magistrates and laws selected solely by Congress until the stage of permanent government was reached. All three members of the committee plus Gerry voted for this imposition of congressional authority before and during temporary government.[60] Although three state delegations divided and New Jersey was still insufficiently represented to vote, the motion failed to pass by only one state, since six states voted in favor.[61] Thus compromise was indicated, and so two days later Gerry offered a new paragraph to be inserted before the final charter of compact: "That such measures as may from time to time be necessary not inconsistent with the principles of the confederation are reserved for and shall be taken by Congress to preserve peace and good order among the settlers in any of the new States, previous to their assuming a temporary government as aforesaid."[62] Read again wished to substitute for this amendment his earlier one to impose congressional officials and laws upon the settlers before and during the first stage. Only the two landless states of Maryland and Pennsylvania voted solidly for it this time, but other delegates favored Read's motion. Howell and Jefferson sided with the majority against the substitution.[63] According to Boyd, Jefferson brought forth at this moment the needed substitute compromise amendment, although Gerry received credit for it in the official journal.[64] As finally adopted, it read: "That measures not inconsistent with the principles of the Confederation, and necessary for the preservation of peace and good order among the settlers in any of the said new states, until they shall assume a temporary government as aforesaid, may from time to time, be taken by the United States in Congress assembled."[65] Thus did the argument come around half circle to the original report.

[60] Ford *et al.*, eds., *Jour. Cont. Cong.*, XXVI, 259-260, Apr. 21, 1784, Boyd, ed., *Jefferson Papers*, VI, 612, n. 26, argues that Jefferson voted for the measure because he knew it would be defeated. There is no evidence on the point, but this interpretation of the vote seems too ingenious and unnecessary in light of Jefferson's overall voting record.
[61] Ford *et al.*, eds., *Jour. Cont. Cong.*, XXVI, 259-260.
[62] *Ibid.*, 274.
[63] *Ibid.*, 274-275, Apr. 23, 1784.
[64] The various versions are given in Boyd, ed., *Jefferson Papers*, VI, 613, n. 26.
[65] Cf. the various phrasings as given *ibid.*

These reversals in position during the debate indicate that congressmen were unsure just how much autonomy they should allow frontiersmen in setting up their own initial governments and how much authority Congress should retain in selecting magistrates and adopting laws, especially before but also during the stage of temporary government. Jefferson's and Howell's vacillation in voting on these two positions proves that they too shared their colleagues' uncertainty. The record shows clearly that both agreed to the strict imposition of congressional authority over the settlers before the organization of permanent government as well as the vaguer, final compromise on authority before temporary government.

More significant than the two men's vacillation, or that of all congressmen, was the remarkable continuity in the controversy from Gerry's and Howell's amendments to the Indian affairs report to the final compromise. Throughout the entire debate the basic alternatives remained the same. Only individuals' specific positions varied at different times. At best, one can only conclude that the final vote and wording was but one point in a continuing debate not yet resolved and that neither Jefferson nor Howell had decided at this particular moment upon the final disposition of the matter any more than had their colleagues in Congress. That this was the case gains added confirmation from the subsequent evolution of the Northwest Ordinance.

Having decided upon the final wording of the paragraph on the extent of congressional authority before the formation of the first stage of government, Congress adopted on April 23, 1784, the amended report as a formal ordinance with all but one state favoring passage.[66] As the New Hampshire delegates explained, because of the conditions of the Virginia cession and the extent of territory involved, establishment of government for the West created "much difficulty" for Congress.[67] In particular, the changed order of the provisos and their contents and the new paragraph on congressional authority inserted before the charter of compact manifested this difficulty. These and other changes tended to establish greater congressional control over the new states before admission to Congress and particularly before the period of temporary

[66] Ford *et al.*, eds., *Jour. Cont. Cong.*, XXVI, 275-279. Cf. the version given in Boyd, ed., *Jefferson Papers*, VI, 613-615.
[67] New Hampshire delegates to Meshech Weare, May 5, 1784, in Edmund C. Burnett, ed., *Letters of Members of the Continental Congress* (Washington, D. C., 1921-1936), VII, 514.

government. On the other hand, delegates left major portions of the original report unrevised and presumably did not debate or question them. Although the provisions for the first stage of government received extensive debate, those for the second stage went undiscussed. Neither was there dispute over the population requirement for statehood or the principle of admitting new states into Congress, but congressmen spent much time in wording the exact procedure for admission. The charter of compact and the provisos stipulating that the new states must remain part of the Confederation and maintain republican governments continued into the final ordinance untouched by revision. Similarly, the proviso on sharing the federal debt appeared unchanged in the final ordinance.

Both the altered and unaltered wording and the votes on the various versions provide inferential evidence about the authorship of the original report. Items not discussed imply fundamental agreement upon those aspects of statemaking and perhaps suggest that Congress had considered them before Jefferson's arrival. Absence of debate upon the number of stages in the formation of government and the transition points of each stage likewise hints at previous discussion and perfection of these aspects of the plan before Jefferson took his seat. The continuity in the positions initially represented by Gerry's and Howell's amendments to the Indian affairs report upon the relationship of Congress to the new states and its authority over their inhabitants before statehood shows that Jefferson joined sides already formed upon the issue. Since he voted with Gerry rather than Howell when there was a division of opinion among the two men, one may conclude that he viewed the West and frontiersmen more as did the delegate from Massachusetts than the one from Rhode Island. Moreover, a comparison of his votes with those of Chase and Howell implies he acted as the balance wheel between the two men in preparing the original committee report. Although he shared Howell's outlook more consistently than Chase's, Jefferson did not agree entirely with Howell on congressional authority over the new settlers.[68] Thus

[68] The actual number of times the various men voted alike as pairs is compared in the following table, which shows the per cent of agreement of the 4 men on the 13 votes.

	Jefferson	Gerry	Howell	Chase
Jefferson	—	100	67	50
Gerry	100	—	67	50
Howell	67	67	—	36
Chase	50	50	36	—

we must conclude that the report of March 1, 1784, resulted as much from previous congressional discussion as translated by Jefferson and especially Howell as from the original ideas of the statesman from Virginia.

Not even Jefferson's originality in bounding and naming the new states survived untouched by congressional revision. When Congress moved to assert greater authority over the frontiersmen during initial settlement, the interesting names proposed by Jefferson were no longer necessary to facilitate early participation in self-government and were accordingly struck. Congress retained Jefferson's idea of planning for states to be formed from lands yet to be ceded as well as those already ceded, but it reversed his order of determining latitudinal boundaries in order to avoid appearing to count chicks before they hatched. Instead of fixing boundaries at two degree intervals northward from thirty degrees latitude, the final ordinance specifies that the counting proceed southward from forty-five degrees. Perhaps the change accommodated the feelings of landed states which had yet to cede their claims.[69] Thus the final version of the Ordinance of 1784 retains the basic pattern of Jefferson's geography at the expense of eliminating its two boldest elements. This congressional rebuff to his grand scheme of ideological geography for the West did not prevent Jefferson from drafting an elaborate plan for the disposition of the public domain before he left for France as ambassador.[70] After his departure, Congress adjourned in June 1784, and so the fate of his political ideology as embodied in the

That Jefferson voted more frequently with Gerry than the other members of the committee may be seen in a table comparing the records of the four men on all the votes they had in common as pairs during the 1783-1784 session.

	Jefferson	Gerry	Howell	Chase
Jefferson	—	76	60	60
Gerry	76	—	63	60
-Howell	60	63	—	43
Chase	60	60	43	—

In both tables the percentages represent the agreement on votes in which the men in each pair were both present and voting. All the men did not vote on all the possible votes together for at times one or the other of a pair would be absent. My colleague, Allan Bogue, generously made available the computer program he developed for tabulating these percentages. I would like to thank him for the program and the Graduate Research Committee of the University of Wisconsin for the funds to run the program.

[69] No record of debate exists on the change, but see Boyd, ed., *Jefferson Papers*, VI, 610, n. 5.

[70] Report, *ibid.*, VII, 140-147.

restricted size of new states and the land system as well as in the whole ordinance for western government remained in the hands of future congressmen.

The man chiefly responsible for the two major differences between the Ordinances of 1784 and 1787 was Jefferson's young friend James Monroe. He was the first to propose altering the size and number of the states in the West in order that there would be two to five large ones,[71] just as he served as chairman of the committee that produced the first report in a long series that provided a new scheme of temporary and permanent government for those states. Under this plan the inhabitants were to be governed from the beginning of settlement by a governor and secretary, a council of five members, and a court of five judges—all appointed by Congress—under laws of one of the original states. In the new second stage, the people would be governed by their own elected assembly with a governor and council appointed by Congress. During this period the governor could convene, prorogue, or dissolve the assembly at will. Only during this second stage could the territory have a nonvoting delegate to Congress. Permanent government based on principles of the inhabitants' choice came only with statehood and admission into Congress.[72] With some changes these proposals regarding the number of states and the nature of the stages survived long debate to become the basis of the Ordinance of 1787.[73]

As was his wont, Monroe reported his activities to his friend in France. After summarizing the new scheme of government proposed by his committee, Monroe concluded that "the most important principles of the act at Annapolis [Ordinance of 1784] are you observe preserv'd in this report."[74] Apparently Jefferson agreed with Monroe's point, for he did not complain in his reply or subsequently about the arbitrary nature of the government provided during the first stage under his fellow Virginian's plan or under the Ordinance of 1787. All the letters

---

[71] According to the preamble to the report, Ford *et al.*, eds., *Jour. Cont. Cong.*, XXX, 132, Mar. 2, 1786. For the figures originally recommended by the committee, see James Monroe to Jefferson, May 11, 1786, in Boyd, ed., *Jefferson Papers*, IX, 510.

[72] Ford *et al.*, eds., *Jour. Cont. Cong.*, XXX, 251-255, May 10, 1786, give the report.

[73] A heavily annotated copy of the document is presented in Clarence E. Carter, ed., *The Territorial Papers of the United States*, II (Washington, D. C., 1934), 39-50.

[74] Monroe to Jefferson, May 11, 1786, in Boyd, ed., *Jefferson Papers*, IX, 511.

usually cited by historians to prove Jefferson's opposition to the extension of congressional authority during the early stages of government, when read in the context of his ideological geography, refer more to the proposed alteration in the size of the new states than to the nature of their government. His reply to Monroe seems ambiguous on this point until read in its entirety:

With respect to the new states were the question to stand simply in this form, How may the ultramontane territory be disposed of so as to produce the greatest and most immediate benefit to the inhabitants of the maritime states of the union? the plan would be more plausible of laying it off into two or three states only. Even on this view however there would still be something to be said against it which might render it at least doubtful. But it is a question which good faith forbids us to receive into discussion. This requires us to state the question in it's just form, How may the territories of the Union be disposed of so as to produce the greatest degree of happiness to their inhabitants? With respect to the Maritime states nothing, or little remains to be done. With respect then to the Ultramontane states, will their inhabitants be happiest divided into states of 30,000 square miles, not quite as large as Pennsylvania, or into states of 160,000 square miles each, that is to say three times as large as Virginia within the Alleghaney? They will not only be happier in states of a moderate size, but it is the only way in which they can exist as a regular society. Considering the American character in general, that of those people particularly, and the inergetic nature of our governments, a state of such extent as 160,000 square miles would soon crumble into little ones. These are the circumstances which reduce the Indians to such small societies. They would produce an effect on our people similar to this. They would not be broken into such small pieces because they are more habituated to subordination, and value more a government of regular law. But you would surely reverse the nature of things in making small states on the ocean and large ones beyond the mountains. If we could in our consciences say that great states beyond the mountains will make the people happiest, we must still ask whether they will be contented to be laid off into large states? They certainly will not; and if they decide to divide themselves we are not able to restrain them. They will end by separating from our confederacy and becoming it's enemies. We had better then look forward and see what will be the probable course of things. This will surely be a division of that country into states of a small, or at most of a moderate size. If we lay them off into such, they will acquiesce, and we shall have the advantage of arranging them so as to produce the best combinations of interest. What Congress has already done in this matter is an argument the more in favour of the revolt of those states against a different arrangement, and of their acquiescience under a continuance of that. Upon this plan we treat them as fellow citizens. They will have a just share in their own government, they will love us, and pride themselves in an union with us. Upon the other we treat them as subjects, we govern them, and not they themselves; they will abhor us as masters, and break off from us in defiance. I confess to you that I can see no other turn that these two plans would take, but I respect your opinion, and your knowlege of the country too much, to be over confident in my own.[75]

In the context of the full paragraph, the conclusion refers to the difference between his plan and Monroe's in terms of the size of states with its long-run implication for republican governments more than the imposition of arbitrary colonial government at the beginning of settlement. Separation would come from the different interests of the settlers beyond the mountains and from their character as frontiersmen, not from the type of government provided by Congress during the initial period of settlement. From Jefferson's point of view, large states increased the probability of diverse interests in a state while the tendency of frontiersmen to disobey any government derived from the wildness of their physical environment. Geography and his view of man's self-interest, not governmental arrangements, lay at the base of his criticism of Monroe's plan.

Jefferson's ideological geography and not the mode of initial government explained his opposition to subsequent developments, too, as when he raised the same issue of state size in discussing the threatened closing of the Mississippi to western commerce:

I find Congress have reversed their division of the Western states, and proposed to make them fewer and larger. This is reversing the natural order of things. A tractable people may be governed in large bodies; but in proportion as they depart from this character, the extent of their government must be less. We see into what small divisions the Indians are obliged to reduce their societies. This measure, with the disposition to shut up the Missisipi give me serious apprehensions of the severance of the Eastern and Western parts of our confederacy. It might have been made the interests of the Western states to remain united with

[75] Jefferson to Monroe, July 9, 1786, *ibid.*, X, 112-113.

us, by managing their interests honestly and for their own good. But the moment we sacrifice their interests to our own, they will see it better to govern themselves. The moment they resolve to do this, the point is settled. A forced connection is neither our interest nor within our power.[76]

His fear of separation makes sense only in terms of his assumptions about the geographical determination of men's interests and the necessity for founding republican government upon a population of homogeneous interests and therefore living in a small area.

That Jefferson should disregard the question of arbitrary government was as natural as his spirited defense of his primary contribution to the Ordinance of 1784. The first stage under Monroe's plan provided for a system of government during the period before the formation of temporary government under the Ordinance of 1784 that was consistent with the congressional resolution that Jefferson, Howell, and others supported during the debates upon the original report. Such was Congress's thinking as represented by the new paragraph inserted in the final version of the 1784 ordinance. Thus Monroe's plan apparently seemed to him and to other congressmen an extension and clarification of the basic policy adopted by Congress in the earlier ordinance. The first statement of such a view occurred in May 1785, in the report of an Indian Affairs Committee of which Monroe was chairman. Discussing the reasons for administering an oath of allegiance to the people in the Illinois country, the committee argued:

The State of Virginia having also relinquished her right of jurisdiction, and no government being as yet established over the said Inhabitants and settlers upon the principles of the resolutions of the 23ᵈ. of April 1784, they are of Course free from any express engagements or allegiance to the Union whatever. The Committee considering it as highly improper, that any body of Men should inhabit any part of the territory within the United States without acknowledging its authority; suggest that the [Indian] Commissioners be instructed to administer to the said Inhabitants an Oath of allegiance or fidelity. . . .[77]

The same notion lay behind Monroe's interpretation of his committee's task of considering the extension of government over the whole of the Old Northwest because of illegal American settlement there. "It

[76] Jefferson to Madison, Dec. 16, 1786, *ibid.*, 603. Cf. Jefferson to Madison, June 20, 1787, *ibid.*, 481.

[77] Ford *et al.*, eds., *Jour. Cont. Cong.*, XXVIII, 331, May 3, 1785.

will be determin'd," Monroe stated, "what authority Congress will exercise over the people who may settle within the bounds of either of the new Sta[tes] previous to the establishment of a temporary government, whether they will leave them to themselves or appoint majistrates over them."[78] In the mind of Monroe the vexatious problem of congressional authority over the initial settlements in the new states—one that went back to the Gerry and Howell amendments in 1783—had not been resolved in mid-1786. Thus it is apparent why Monroe considered the plan of temporary government proposed by his committee not a violation of "the most important principles" of the Ordinance of 1784, but an extension plugging a loophole in his friend's report that had long posed a perplexing problem to Congress.

Monroe's terminology suggests, moreover, that the Ordinance of 1784 was merely a framework of general rules for the establishment of government in the West and that a specific system had yet to be worked out by further congressional action. Jefferson presented a somewhat similar view of the ordinance in discussing the defects of the Articles of Confederation in the *Encyclopédie Methodique* (1786). He pointed out the need for a general rule for the admission of new states into the Union in the following words: "It becomes necessary to agree what districts may be established into separate states, and at what period of their population they may come into Congress. The act of Congress of April 23, 1784, has pointed out what ought to be agreed on."[79] In this view of the matter, the Ordinance of 1784 represented an incomplete set of resolutions about fundamental principles, or a policy statement, while the Northwest Ordinance was a specific system designed to effectuate those principles. That the latter in accomplishing this implementation moved in the direction of more arbitrary government during the early settlement of the new states meant it followed a trend already well established during the evolution of the Ordinance of 1784 and reflected the political currents of the day toward centralization of government.

Such an interpretation clarifies the legal status of the 1784 Ordinance

[78] Monroe to Jefferson, June 16, 1785, in Boyd, ed., *Jefferson Papers*, VIII, 217-218. This was in accord with the charge to the committee, Ford *et al.*, eds., *Jour. Cont. Cong.*, XXX, 139n. Cf. the wording in the frequently cited letter of Monroe to John Jay, Apr. 20, 1786, in Burnett, ed., *Letters of Members of Congress*, VIII, 342.
[79] Boyd, ed., *Jefferson Papers*, X, 14.

before the Northwest Ordinance repealed it. The debate has revolved about its application: whether the 1784 Ordinance was or could have been applied to the Old Northwest before the subsequent ordinance superseded it. Thus historians have concerned themselves mainly with how Indian occupation and English influence prevented settlement by many Americans and, more importantly, establishment of congressional jurisdiction over the region. Essentially, then, the issue of legal status is phrased in terms of whether the United States in Congress Assembled exercised de facto control in addition to de jure title in the Old Northwest. According to this view, to the degree that Congress possessed and asserted actual authority, then the 1784 Ordinance was in effect. Although such reasoning may be relevant to the larger history of the ordinance, it is beside the point insofar as its legal status is concerned. It fails to consider the nature of the ordinance as conceived by congressmen of the time. That status was, I argue, a statement of principles that required passage of a more specific system to implement its resolutions on the early phases of settlement in the new states. To the extent that the 1787 Ordinance provided such a system for the principles of 1784, it was an extension of congressional thinking embodied in the original report of Jefferson's committee and the earlier ordinance. Insofar as it duplicated provisions of the 1784 document, it made the previous one unnecessary. To the degree that the Northwest Ordinance created new provisions for the governance of western settlers, it superseded the other ordinance.

For all these reasons, the Northwest Ordinance repealed the set of resolutions passed on April 23, 1784. Thus the 1787 document should be considered more an extension and replacement than a repudiation of the Ordinance of 1784, and the process of transition is best studied in light of the slow evolution of the two documents.[80] No one man was primarily responsible for either document, and consensus upon basic republican goals and principles explains the contents of the two ordinances as much as conflict over the application of those ideals to western inhabitants. That substantial differences exist between the provisions of

[80] The beginnings of such a reinterpretation may be found in Eblen, *First and Second Empires,* Chap. 1; and Robert F. Berkhofer, Jr., "The Republican Origins of the American Territorial System," in Allan G. Bogue, *et al.,* eds., *The West of the American People* (Itasca, Ill., 1970), 152-160.

the two ordinances is undeniable, but these dissimilarities should not obscure the fundamental ideas and attitudes pervading both documents or the consistency of the trend to greater Confederation control over the territories in the period 1783-1784 as well as in the years between then and the adoption of the Northwest Ordinance.[81]

[81] The overall similarities of the two ordinances as a result of the general intellectual climate of the times is the theme of my article, "The Northwest Ordinance and the Principle of Territorial Evolution," forthcoming in a book of essays on the history of the territories to be published by the National Archives, John P. Bloom, editor.

Liberty, Development, and Union: Visions of the West in the 1780s

Peter S. Onuf

AFTER the Revolution, American policymakers looked west with mingled expectation and anxiety. They entertained high hopes for the growth of national wealth and power through expansion of settlement and addition of states. At the same time, in darker moments, they feared that the opening of the West would release energies that might subvert social order and destroy the union. Images of anarchy and disorder in postwar America were drawn from, and projected onto, the frontier. Semisavage "banditti," squatters, and land speculators were seen spreading over the western lands. European imperial powers—British to the north, Spanish to the south and west—supposedly stood ready to exploit frontier disorder and Indian discontent.[1] The success of the American experiment in republican government thus seemed to depend on establishing law and order on the frontier.

As republican ideologues, Americans found the idea of territorial expansion profoundly unsettling. History demonstrated that republics were vulnerable to decline and decay as citizens turned toward private pursuits. Would vast new opportunities for individual improvement—or for escape from the restraints of the "civilized" East—subvert republican virtue?[2] Would Americans be able to preserve the wide distribution of property, the "happy mediocrity" that students of James Harrington

Mr. Onuf is a member of the Humanities Department, Worcester Polytechnic Institute. This article was written during his tenure as a National Endowment for the Humanities Fellow at the American Antiquarian Society, Worcester, and was delivered at a Conference on the Land Ordinance of 1785, held at Temple University in April 1985 and sponsored by the Center for the Study of Federalism and the Liberty Fund. Acknowledgments: I wish to thank Robert Dykstra, James Henretta, Cathy Matson, Andrew Cayton, Robert Berkhofer, and Drew R. McCoy for helpful criticism.

[1] On the "critical period" see Peter S. Onuf, *The Origins of the Federal Republic: Jurisdictional Controversies in the United States, 1775-1787* (Philadelphia, 1983), 173-185. See also Frederick W. Marks III, *Independence on Trial: Foreign Affairs and the Making of the Constitution* (Baton Rouge, La., 1973).

[2] The literature on republicanism is voluminous. See particularly Gordon S. Wood, *The Creation of the American Republic, 1776-1787* (Chapel Hill, N.C., 1969), and J.G.A. Pocock, *The Machiavellian Moment: Florentine Political Thought and the Atlantic Republican Tradition* (Princeton, N.J., 1975).

considered essential to the broad distribution of power?[3] Expansion also raised the familiar issue of size. Montesquieu and other writers warned Americans that republicanism was best suited to small states and that a republic's effective authority progressively diminished as it expanded.

During the mid-1780s the West presented a challenge to both policy-makers and ideologists. Once the states began to relinquish their western claims, Congress had to organize, distribute, and defend the new national domain. In view of the nation's straitened circumstances, congressmen were determined that land sales would cover the costs of western government; they also expected that these sales eventually would help discharge the burdensome national debt. The realization of these goals hinged on the market for western lands. Were they valuable enough, now or in the foreseeable future, to attract sober and industrious settlers? The answer depended on Congress's ability to protect new settlements and on the region's prospects for economic development. Would farmers be able to get their crops to market? Would merchants and manufacturers be attracted west, thus creating local markets as well as links to the outside world?

This article will explore the ideological implications of these policy imperatives. Regardless of their prior political preferences, policymakers were compelled to embrace a vision of an economically developing, commercial frontier. But the endorsement of private enterprise implicit in this program for western development was at odds with long-cherished republican premises. American republicans needed to invent a new vision of their future prospects that would transcend and invalidate the grim predictions of republican theory. Advocates of territorial expansion had to portray the private pursuit of profit—the impulse that would draw purchasers into the western land market—as the source of national wealth and welfare.

Prescriptions for commercial development of the frontier challenged the conventional opposition of self-interest and public interest. Opponents of expansion argued that the centrifugal force of private enterprise pushing outward the frontiers of settlement threatened to weaken the states and subvert republican liberty. In response, promoters of western development boldly asserted that private interest, properly channeled,

---

[3] Benjamin Franklin, "Consolation for America, or remarks on her real situation, interests, and policy," *American Museum*, I (Jan. 1787), 7. My discussion of attitudes toward economic development relies heavily on Michael Lienesch, "Development: The Economics of Expansion," a chapter in his forthcoming book, *New Order of the Ages: The American Constitution and the Making of Modern Republican Thought*. For a fine treatment of the relation between expansion and republican ideology see Drew R. McCoy, *The Elusive Republic: Political Economy in Jeffersonian America* (Chapel Hill, N.C., 1980), and for an analysis of development themes in antebellum political ideologies see Major L. Wilson, *Space, Time, and Freedom: The Quest for Nationality and the Irrepressible Conflict, 1815-1861* (Westport, Conn., 1974).

was the true foundation for liberty and prosperity in an expanding "republican empire." This assertion suggested a broad reconception of the relation between public and private realms. In effect, promoters of expanding economic opportunity in agriculture, commerce, and manufacturing in the West—and by extension throughout the union—redefined liberty. For them, "a Love of liberty" and "a spirit of enterprize" were complementary, perhaps even identical, impulses in the forming of American character.[4]

In May 1784 a student orator at the College of Philadelphia captured the sense of opportunity and adventure that helped transform republican premises: "A new country, partly uninhabited, and unexplored, presents the fairest opportunity to the industrious and enterprising, of making most useful and curious discoveries—of serving mankind, and enriching themselves." How, exactly, the "noble, patriotic desire of serving mankind and ourselves" would advance the cause of republicanism was not yet altogether clear.[5] But the formulation of a coherent western policy in the years after the Peace of Paris suggested the shape of things to come.

The far-receding hinterland evoked grandiose visions of future greatness. It also presented problems that demanded immediate attention. Congressmen had to formulate effective policies for novel conditions, knowing that a few false steps could transform the dream of western development into a nightmare of lawlessness, frontier warfare, and disunion. The challenge was to regulate the westward thrust of settlement in ways that would strengthen the union, preserve peace with the Indians and neighboring imperial powers, and pay the public debt while permitting enterprising settlers to pursue their own goals. Congress's response, embodied in the western land and government ordinances of 1784-1787, was to attempt to create a legal and political framework conducive to both regional and national economic development. Promoters of western expansion believed that the commercial development of the frontier would increase the population and wealth of the entire union; most important, it would produce a harmony of interlocking interests without which union itself was inconceivable.

Enthusiastic reports about the fertility of America's inland empire made

[4] Introductory Remarks to [David Humphreys], "The Happiness of America," *Columbian Magazine*, I (Oct. 1786), 67. Joyce Appleby provides a useful analysis of contemporary notions of liberty in *Capitalism and a New Social Order: The Republican Vision of the 1790s* (New York, 1984), 16-23. My interpretation of American liberal thought relies heavily on Appleby's writings. Marshall Berman, *All That Is Solid Melts into Air: The Experience of Modernity* (New York, 1982), has helped me see "development" as an act of imagination or "dream." For a discussion of early attempts to define the new American character, focused on *Columbian Magazine*, see Lawrence J. Friedman, *Inventors of the Promised Land* (New York, 1975), 3-43.

[5] Oration Delivered at Commencement, University of Philadelphia, May 7, 1784, *Columbian Magazine*, I (Oct. 1786), 84, 85.

economic development on an unprecedented scale seem possible, even natural; the dangers of disorderly expansion made planning seem imperative. The western lands problem thus forced Americans to think in new ways about their future. They began to make crucial new connections between private enterprise, economic growth, and the national destiny. Such thinking undoubtedly came easily to "commercial republicans" dedicated to the pursuit of profit and imbued with a spirit of free trade.[6] But the necessity of wartime sacrifice and public-spiritedness inhibited the open advocacy of enterprise. After the war, conflicts among farmers, merchants, and manufacturers over the direction of economic policy reinforced traditional misgivings about the place of private interests in public life. Ironically, it was in opening the way west—precisely where European philosophers saw *homo Americanus* escaping the baneful reach of commerce and preserving his republican virtue in rustic simplicity—that American expansionists saw an unprecedented opportunity for a higher synthesis of agriculture, commerce, and manufactures.[7] For them, the development of the frontier would be a movement forward in the history of civilization, not a refuge from it. In the West, interests so often in conflict in long-settled parts of the country would be harmonious and interdependent: farmers needed merchants to find markets; by processing local products and supplying farmers' basic needs, manufacturers would help the new settlements avoid unequal terms of trade with the outside world. Even Jefferson, the patron saint of agrarian localism, promoted the development of commercial agriculture on the frontier.[8] Only by rapidly developing the frontier economy and integrating it into the national economy could the West be preserved for the union, and the union itself be perpetuated.

In many ways, the debate over how to begin disposing of the national domain, culminating in the land ordinance of May 20, 1785, anticipated the reconception of the American union later embodied in the Federal

[6] On "commercial republicans" see Ralph Lerner, "Commerce and Character: The Anglo-American as New-Model Man," *William and Mary Quarterly*, 3d Ser., XXXVI (1979), 3-26.

[7] For European perceptions of Revolutionary America see Durand Echeverria, *Mirage in the West: A History of the French Image of American Society to 1815* (Princeton, N.J., 1957), and Horst Dippel, *Germany and the American Revolution, 1770-1800*, trans. Bernhard A. Uhlendorf (Chapel Hill, N.C., 1977).

[8] For Jefferson's interest in developing commercial links between Virginia and the West see his letters to Madison and Washington, Feb. 20, Mar. 15, 1784, in Julian P. Boyd et al., eds., *The Papers of Thomas Jefferson* (Princeton, N.J., 1950-), VI, 547-548, and VII, 25-27, hereafter cited as *Jefferson Papers*. Appleby emphasizes Jefferson's role as "an early advocate of the commercial exploitation of American agriculture" in "What Is Still American in the Political Philosophy of Thomas Jefferson," *WMQ*, 3d Ser., XXXIX (1982), 287-309, quotation on p. 295. Virginian expansionists are discussed in Marc Egnal, "The Origins of the Revolution in Virginia: A Reinterpretation," *ibid.*, XXXVII (1980), 401-428.

Constitution.[9] Policymakers faced a "critical period" in the West: frontier lawlessness threatened Congress's tenuous hold over the domain recently created by state land cessions. The federal lands were potentially an "amazing resource" for paying off Revolutionary war debts: on the day the land ordinance passed, Richard Henry Lee exulted that "these republics may soon be discharged from that state of oppression and distress" caused by indebtedness.[10] But if settlers refused to pay Congress for their lands and looked beyond the United States for markets for their produce, disunion would inevitably follow. Westerners would then "become a distinct people from us," George Washington predicted. "Instead of adding strength to the Union," they would become "a formidable and dangerous neighbour," especially if they turned to Britain or Spain for protection.[11] In effect, by fracturing the continent, the loss of the West would recreate European conditions in America. The weakness of the new nation in conventional military terms would then be telling. This disintegration was precisely what Americans—"the hope of the world"—had to avoid, according to Anne Robert Jacques Turgot, the French economist and statesman. America must never become "an image of our Europe, a mass of divided powers contending for territory and commerce."[12]

Not only did the United States stand to forfeit tremendous economic resources and a vast area for growth by failing to maintain federal

[9] The ordinance is printed in Worthington Chauncey Ford *et al.*, eds., *Journals of the Continental Congress, 1774-1789*, 34 vols. (Washington, D.C., 1904-1937), XXVIII, 375-381, hereafter cited as *Jours. Cont. Cong.* For its legislative history see Payson Jackson Treat, *The National Land System, 1785-1820* (New York, 1910), 15-40, and Paul W. Gates, *History of Public Land Law Development* (Washington, D.C., 1968), 59-74. William D. Pattison, *Beginnings of the American Rectangular Land Survey System, 1784-1800* (Chicago, 1957) is useful in clarifying the differences between the 1785 ordinance and previous proposals. Malcolm J. Rohrbough, *The Land Office Business: The Settlement and Administration of American Public Lands, 1789-1837* (New York, 1968), 3-25, offers a good introduction to the history of the ordinance in practice.

[10] "An honest chearful citizen," "A word of consolation for America," *American Museum*, I (Mar. 1787), 188; Lee to Samuel Adams, May 20, 1785, in Edmund C. Burnett, ed., *Letters of Members of the Continental Congress*, 8 vols. (Washington, D.C., 1921-1936), VIII, 122, hereafter cited as *Letters Cont. Cong.* Though Virginians were unusually sensitive to the debt issue, a broad consensus supported this use of the national domain. A writer in the *Independent Chronicle: and the Universal Advertiser* (Boston), Apr. 14, 1785, thought land sales revenue would help provide tax relief for manufacturers.

[11] Washington to Henry Knox, Dec. 5, 1784, in John C. Fitzpatrick, ed., *The Writings of George Washington from the Original Manuscript Sources, 1745-1799*, 39 vols. (Washington, D.C., 1931-1944), XXVIII, 4.

[12] M. Turgot to Dr. Price, Mar. 22, 1778, appendix to Richard Price, *Observations on the Importance of the American Revolution . . .*, 2d ed. (London, 1785), in Bernard Peach, ed., *Richard Price and the Ethical Foundations of the American Revolution* (Durham, N.C., 1979), 215-224, quotation on p. 222. This letter and the Price pamphlet were widely excerpted in contemporary American newspapers.

authority in the West, but it would also become increasingly vulnerable to disunion and counterrevolution. Most commentators agreed that the alternative to expansion was disintegration; even the most superficial knowledge of western conditions confirmed that such fears were well grounded. This mix of hope and fear was characteristic: the West was thus a mirror for Americans in the critical years after the Revolution.

I. LIBERTY

Congress had to decide quickly how to organize and sell the western lands. The rapid movement of settlers and speculators across the Ohio jeopardized congressional authority in the region and threatened to embroil the frontiers in Indian warfare. As congressional land policy was debated and defined in 1784-1785, attention focused on what kinds of settlers should be encouraged to move into federal territory as well as on the proper organization of new settlements. Congressmen had to establish a context and limits for private enterprise that would secure and advance the public interest. In doing so, they groped toward a working, practical definition of republican liberty.

Deliberations began in earnest when a committee headed by Thomas Jefferson reported a land ordinance on April 30, 1784, only a few weeks after Congress had finally come to terms with Virginia on conditions attached to that state's cession of its trans-Ohio claims. The 1784 proposal, authored by Jefferson and Hugh Williamson of North Carolina, introduced the idea of dividing the western lands by a perfect grid keyed to the new state meridian lines in the companion government ordinance of April 23.[13] But the related questions of how purchasers were to locate their lands (that is, the process by which they would acquire good title) and of how much they would pay became locked in an intersectional stalemate. At first, southern and middle state congressmen favored indiscriminate locations: settlers would identify desirable lands, pay the land office, take out warrants, and run surveys. The Jefferson-Williamson proposal rationalized this system: holdings could be located anywhere on the public lands but would have to conform to the grid pattern. New Englanders objected to the scattering of settlement and the speculation in prime locations that this plan would predictably encourage. They sought instead to sell surveyed townships to associations of purchasers actually intending to settle in the Ohio country.

The debate over the best way to sell lands and organize settlement might never have been resolved—a transcript of congressional delibera-

---

[13] The report, drafted by a committee also including David Howell of Rhode Island, Elbridge Gerry of Massachusetts, and Jacob Read of South Carolina, is in *Jours. Cont. Cong.*, XXVI, 324-330. On the authorship question see Pattison, *American Rectangular Survey*, 38-39, and Williamson to Gov. Alexander Martin, July 5, 1784, in Walter Clark, ed., *State Records of North Carolina*, XVII (Goldsboro, N.C., 1899), 80-83.

tions "would fill forty Volumes," William Grayson reported—if Congress's hand had not been forced.[14] Settlers would not wait. The fertility of the Ohio Valley was already common knowledge; there emigrants would find "the finest land in the world," according to geographer Jedidiah Morse.[15] John Filson's popular firsthand account of "the Present State of Kentucke," published in 1784, reported and encouraged mass migration down the Ohio.[16] The "amazing" growth of the Kentucky District, just across the river from the national lands, made westward migration seem a powerful natural force, a veritable human "torrent."[17] The Ohio lands would be next. Even before the Virginia cession was completed, the region was settling with "amazing rapidity."[18] Washington, an astute observer with an extensive personal interest in the fate of the West, was convinced that the "spirit for emigration" could not be restrained. But if "you cannot stop the road," he told his fellow Virginian Richard Henry Lee, then president of Congress, "it is yet in your power to mark the way; a little while and you will not be able to do either."[19]

The landrush westward, both actual and predicted, forced congressional action. A western Pennsylvanian described the "impatience" of would-be settlers in the Ohio region who were waiting for Congress to define its land policy. If terms were not attractive, he warned, "Congress will lose the only opportunity they ever will have of extending their power and influence over this new region." People "will go and settle themselves down, and not only locate for themselves, but enter into some sort of

[14] Grayson to Timothy Pickering, Apr. 27, 1785, in *Letters Cont. Cong.*, VIII, 106. Grayson's correspondence gives the fullest account of these discussions. Also see his letters to Washington, Apr. 15, May 8, 1785, *ibid.*, 95-97, 117-119, and to Madison, May 1, 28, 1785, in William T. Hutchinson *et al.*, eds., *The Papers of James Madison* (Chicago, 1962-   ), VIII, 274-277, 284-285, hereafter cited as *Madison Papers*.

[15] Morse, *Geography Made Easy . . .* (New Haven, Conn. [1784]), 112. Pelatiah Webster called them "the richest wild lands in the world" in "An Essay on the Extent and Value of Our Western Unlocated Lands . . . ," Apr. 25, 1782, in his *Political Essays on the Nature and Operation of Money, Public Finances, and Other Subjects* (Philadelphia, 1791), 485-500, quotation on p. 490.

[16] Filson, *The Discovery, Settlement and Present State of Kentucke . . .* (Wilmington, Del., 1784).

[17] "Extract of a letter from a gentleman in the western country," Dec. 22, 1785, *Maryland Journal* (Baltimore), Apr. 4, 1786. For similar imagery see Edmund Randolph, *History of Virginia*, ed. Arthur H. Shaffer (Charlottesville, Va., 1970), 272-273.

[18] William Ellery and Howell to Gov. William Greene, Sept. 8, 1783, in William R. Staples, *Rhode Island in the Continental Congress . . .*, ed. Reuben Aldridge Guild (Providence, R.I., 1870), 447.

[19] Washington to Lee, Dec. 14, 1784, in Fitzpatrick, ed., *Washington Writings*, XXVIII, 12. For Washington's famous comment that "you might as well attempt . . . to prevent the reflux of the tide, when you had got it into your rivers," as attempt to stem the westward flow of population see Washington to Grayson, Apr. 25, 1785, *ibid.*, 138.

covenant to protect each other, and make their new title good."[20] This was not an idle threat. The writer may have seen one of the many handbills that proclaimed mankind's "undoubted right to pass into every vacant country" and challenged Congress's power to sell the Ohio lands.[21] Exploiting the long history of jurisdictional confusion in the region and questioning the legitimacy of congressional pretensions not positively authorized by the Articles of Confederation, the sponsors of this message proposed to organize a new state. Separatist movements elsewhere, notably in Vermont, the Wyoming Valley, and western North Carolina, represented efforts to wrest control of public lands from particular states. Given its notorious weakness, Congress was at least equally vulnerable to separatist agitation. Rhode Island's delegates had made the connection explicit. "Now is the critical juncture," they reported in late 1783. "In the course of a few years the [Ohio] country will be peopled like Vermont. It will be independent, and the whole property of the soil will be lost forever to the United States."[22]

The character and scope of challenges to national property and jurisdiction became clearer in the months between the Jefferson-Williamson proposals and the adoption of a revised ordinance in May 1785. As congressmen learned more about the frontier, southern and northern views on western policy began to converge. In effect, southerners, particularly influential Virginians, came to accept the necessity of ensuring compact settlement and of maximizing revenue by a more systematic sale of lands than was practiced in their own states. The prevailing confusion about titles in the southern backcountry resulting from indiscriminate locations directed their attention to the need for a rational system of surveys. (One writer noted that in some places in Kentucky there were "8 or 10" overlapping claims: "whoever purchases there, is sure to purchase a lawsuit.")[23] Financial needs and strategic considerations made a coherent, township settlement pattern increasingly attractive. Virginians were particularly concerned about national indebtedness and, no less, about the vulnerability of the state's Kentucky District to Indian attack.

The shift toward the township form did not mean that southerners were suddenly convinced of the superiority of Yankee civilization. James Madison thought the New Englanders' predilection for reserving town lots for the support of religion smelled "strongly of an antiquated Bigotry."[24] But Virginians and Marylanders intrigued by the lucrative

[20] News of Congress's land ordinance evidently had not reached the writer. "P. W.," "Extract of a letter from Bedford, Pa.," n.d., *Independent Chronicle*, Aug. 25, 1785.

[21] Advertisement signed by John Emerson, Mar. 12, 1785, in William Henry Smith, *The St. Clair Papers: The Life and Public Services of Arthur St. Clair . . .*, 2 vols. (Cincinnati, Ohio, 1882), II, 5n.

[22] Ellery and Howell to Gov. Greene, Sept. 8, 1783, in Staples, *Rhode Island in Congress*, ed. Guild, 447.

[23] "Extract of a letter," Dec. 22, 1785, *Md. Jour.*, Apr. 4, 1786.

[24] Madison to James Monroe, May 29, 1785, in *Madison Papers*, VIII, 286.

commercial potential of trade links with the Ohio country saw reason to favor a more systematic land policy that would lead, predictably, to larger, denser, and therefore more productive settlements. At the same time, political idealists like Jefferson who hoped to see republican institutions take root as soon as possible also supported compact settlements.

Squatters had already begun leapfrogging across the Ohio and forming widely scattered, unauthorized settlements. Intruders on the public lands were encouraged by the return of peace and by the apparent inability first of Virginia and then of Congress to control their movements. Even if squatters could be made to pay for their lands—a doubtful proposition— the scattering of settlement would retard the development of commercial agriculture and discourage further purchasers. Congress would thus lose revenue from land sales while becoming liable for the costs of defending dispersed, strategically vulnerable settlements that were bound to pro- voke the Indians. Mismanagement of the frontier would jeopardize one of Congress's few likely sources of revenue.

Squatters became a problem as the potential uses and "public" character of the public lands were clarified. Before the Virginia cession, squatting had not been a conspicuous or pressing problem for state authorities who were characteristically intent on promoting westward expansion for commercial or speculative reasons. However much they might lament unauthorized settlement, they often found it difficult in practice to distinguish between legal and illegal settlers. They perceived, or preferred to perceive, no essential difference between squatting and legitimately locating a prospective property holding; squatters simply had not yet perfected their titles by warrant and survey.

According to southern practice, good title was the culmination of a series of steps—from location to survey—and of its successful defense against counterclaimants. This was the system, modified to preclude controversy over property lines, that Jefferson and Williamson first proposed to extend across the Ohio. Not surprisingly, at this time Jefferson did not see squatters as a problem; in a sense he did not "see" them at all. He "rather doubt[ed]" that anyone had settled across the Ohio. Even granted that there were such settlers, he continued, "these very people will be glad to pay the price which Congress will ask to secure themselves in their titles to these lands."[25] In other words, squatters could be left in place, to be transformed retroactively into legitimate settlers— the first purchasers of the public domain.

But Jefferson's position could not be sustained: the conception of the squatter as imperfect but more or less perfectible citizen-farmer on which it was premised was progressively undermined. Jefferson himself en- dorsed the new policy orientation embodied in the 1785 land ordinance. The act provided for prior survey of federal lands, thus avoiding the entire process of title perfection that characterized southern policy. Acknowl-

[25] Jefferson's comment [May 4, 1784] on G. K. van Hogendorp's essay "On Western Territory," in *Jefferson Papers*, VII, 220n.

edging that Congress would have to take a more active role than he had first expected in preparing land for sale, Jefferson wrote James Monroe from Paris that the adopted system represented an improvement over his own proposals "in the most material circumstances": "I am much pleased with your land ordinance."[26] Under the Jefferson-Williamson plan, Congress simply would have imposed regularity on unauthorized and undirected settlement. But Congress would take the initiative under the 1785 ordinance: as soon as seven ranges of townships, each six miles square, had been surveyed, commissioners of the continental loan office would offer federal lands for competitive bidding at public sales in each of the old states. No land would be sold for less than a dollar per acre in specie or its equivalent.

The desire to transform the western lands into valuable property as swiftly as possible prompted a broad indictment of scattered, illegal settlements. Congressmen recognized, of course, that the market price depended on various factors, including clear title, the supply of land for sale, access to markets, fertility, and other intrinsic values. While locating *ad libitum* made sense for individual settlers who, as purchasers, were looking for good lands at nominal prices, it would retard regional economic growth and thus work against the settlers in the long run. The public interest in revenue from land sales and in maintaining a peaceful (inexpensive) frontier thus seemed to converge with the private interest of westerners in the future prosperity of their new communities.

There was no room for squatters in this picture. The squatters' chief sin was their inability—or unwillingness—to pay for their lands. Drafters of the land ordinance were also determined to neutralize the traditional preemptive advantage enjoyed by squatters and speculators: location, survey, and sale were to be rationalized and centralized. Success of the new land policy hinged on the government's being able to offer unencumbered titles. This meant clearing squatters off the land, by force if necessary.

Congress's subsequent military operations against illegal settlements beyond the Ohio were justified by conventional ideas about the character of frontier people. Settlers supposedly reverted to barbarism as they pushed beyond the frontiers of civilization: the stages of historical development defined by social science were reversed when projected across progressively emptier spaces. Thus, according to Benjamin Rush, the "first settler" in a new country "is nearly related to an Indian in his m[a]nners."[27] Such logic could lead Congressman David Howell of Rhode Island to imagine "combinations [of] . . . Indians and disaffected, or

[26] Jefferson to Monroe, Aug. 28, 1785, *ibid.*, VIII, 445.

[27] "A citizen of Pennsylvania" [Benjamin Rush], "Account of the Progress of the Population, Agriculture, Manners, and Government in Pennsylvania," *Columbian Magazine*, I (Nov. 1786), 120. See the helpful discussion in Lienesch, "Development," in his *New Order*. See also Ronald L. Meek, *Social Science and the Ignoble Savage* (Cambridge, 1976).

corrupted white people" if "depressed and disorderly settlements pre-vail[ed] over these lands."[28] Of course, "disorderly" whites were more likely to fight with the "savages" and to drag everyone else into their disputes.[29] Such lawless violence threatened the orderly progress of settlement. Alternatively, white intruders in the Northwest were likened to wild animals, "roaming" or "rambling" across the trackless wilderness. (Speculators seeking out prime sites were like "Wolves," Washington wrote.)[30] This characterization was most memorably expressed in Crève-coeur's *Letters from an American Farmer:* on the frontier men "are often in a perfect state of war" with each other and with "every wild inhabitant of these venerable woods. . . . There men appear to be no better than carnivorous animals of a superior rank."

Warnings about reversion to savagery reflected concern that frontier settlers were, in Crèvecoeur's words, "placed still farther beyond the reach of government, which in some measure leaves them to themselves."[31] This lack of restraint clarified the limits of republican liberty. Unflattering images of semisavage settlers and speculators showed the dangers of rampant privatism—the impulse to pursue private interest at public expense, the very antithesis of the new American idea of liberty as a higher synthesis of private and public realms. Private interest and enter-prise had to be contained within a context that guaranteed productive activity and mutually beneficial exchange. But the discipline of the marketplace, like the rule of law, barely reached the new settlements. Accordingly, the West provided refuge and new opportunities for "the scum and refuse of the Continent."[32] The predatory impulses of these "Rascals," who survived "by hunting and stealing," were recognizable to civilized easterners, themselves restrained by the accumulated force of law

[28] Howell to Gov. Greene, Feb. 1, 1784, in Staples, *Rhode Island in Congress,* ed. Guild, 472.

[29] Webster, "Essay on Western Lands," in his *Political Essays,* 495; Washington to Duane, Sept. 7, 1783, in Fitzpatrick, ed., *Washington Writings,* XXVII, 133-140; report of congressional committee on the West, Oct. 15, 1783, *Jours. Cont. Cong.,* XXV, 693-694.

[30] For typical comments on the effects of unrestrained movements of squatters and speculators see Washington to Read, Nov. 3, 1784, in Fitzpatrick, ed., *Washington Writings,* XXVII, 486, and Pickering to Gerry, Mar. 1, 1785, in Octavius Pickering, ed., *The Life of Timothy Pickering,* 4 vols. (Boston, 1867-1873), I, 505. The Washington quotation is from Washington to Williamson, Mar. 15, 1785, in Fitzpatrick, ed., *Washington Writings,* XXVIII, 108.

[31] J. Hector St. John de Crèvecoeur, *Letters from an American Farmer* (New York, 1957 [orig. publ. London, 1782]), 42-43.

[32] Washington refuted characterizations such as this, often found in contempo-rary British writings (Washington to Rev. William Gordon, Apr. 10, 1787, in Fitzpatrick, ed., *Washington Writings,* XXIX, 200). Contemporary American attitudes toward westerners are briefly assessed in Robert F. Berkhofer, Jr., "The Northwest Ordinance and the Principle of Territorial Evolution," in John Porter Bloom, ed., *The American Territorial System* (Athens, Ohio, 1973), 45-55, at 50-51.

and custom.[33] The lawless West released the selfish impulses held in check in the "civilized" East, thus representing the negation of republican liberty.

Unbounded privatism was seen to jeopardize the security and prosperity of the new nation. In pursuing their immediate private interests, frontier settlers casually ignored laws enacted by representatives of the sovereign people. To secure dubious land claims or commercial concessions they appeared willing to betray the Revolution itself by erecting their own independent governments or by submitting to British or Spanish imperial authority. The history of frontier politics during and after the war (Vermont was again the most obvious example) convinced congressmen that a vacuum of effective authority in the trans-Ohio region was a standing invitation to enemies of the Revolution, domestic and foreign.[34] War against the squatters was thus imperative. Otherwise, the Virginia delegates predicted in late 1783, the Ohio lands "wou'd not only remain profitless to the United States, but wou'd become a prey to lawless banditii [sic] and adventurers, who must necessarily have involv'd us in continued Indian wars and perhaps have form'd Establishments not only on dissimilar principles to those which form the basis of our Republican Constitutions, but such as might eventually prove destructive to them."[35] If such "establishments" represented the antithesis of the new American republics, the motivations of their would-be founders were all too familiar. Significantly, the "banditii" who infested the public domain preyed on *lands:* they would make their fortunes by exploiting the demands of bona fide settlers. In polite language, these predators were land speculators, a highly evolved species who ventured into the wilds only because of their prospective market value. Given the expected torrent of emigration, they understood that "very great advantages may be made by those who are early in their adventures and speculations."[36]

---

[33] "Extract of a letter from Louisville," Oct. 19 [1784], *Md. Jour.*, Mar. 1, 1785.

[34] "The authority of the Congress, can never be maintained over those distant and boundless regions," Lord Sheffield predicted in 1783: "her nominal subjects will speedily imitate and multiply the examples of independence" ([John Baker Holroyd], *Observations on the Commerce of the American States with Europe and the West Indies* . . . , 2d ed. [London, 1783], 104-105). The British press gleefully reported pervasive "anarchy" throughout America after the peace: "Letter from Suffolk, Va.," June 1, 1785, *London Chronicle*, Aug. 6, 1785, in Samuel Cole Williams, *History of the Lost State of Franklin*, rev. ed. (New York, 1933), 87-88, and "Sketches of the Present Times," *The Times* (London), Feb. 2, 1786. For a discussion of American anarchy by a Jamaican writer see *Falmouth Gazette and Weekly Advertiser*, Sept. 10, 1785.

[35] Delegates to Gov. Benjamin Harrison, Nov. 1, 1783, in *Letters Cont. Cong.*, VII, 365.

[36] "Extract of a letter," Dec. 22, 1785, *Md. Jour.*, Apr. 4, 1786. On the role of "land jobbers" in creating the new state of Franklin see "Extract of a letter from Washington county," Dec. 15, 1784, *Freeman's Journal: or, the North-American Intelligencer* (Philadelphia), Feb. 2, 1785. On land speculation and separatism

Why were policymakers so hostile to speculators? The obvious answer is that speculators threatened to usurp the government's role in the western land market. By preempting prime sites at nominal prices and waiting for rising demand to make them valuable, speculators would be enriched while the public would gain little from Congress's investment in organizing and protecting the West. There were political implications to this substitution. If Congress could not create, alienate, and guarantee land titles, it could not, for practical purposes, govern at all. But one's impression of congressional hostility to speculators must be carefully qualified. Framers of congressional western policy were not opposed to private participation in the land market: buying and selling by individuals and companies would necessarily be profit-oriented and to some degree speculative. Policymakers did not expect that purchasers would always be settlers. But they were determined that Congress would control the land market. The dollar-an-acre minimum price precluded extensive speculation; meanwhile, Congress would withhold a vast reserve of lands to be surveyed and brought to market over a long period of time.

The attack on speculators is prominent in the correspondence of George Washington, one of many Virginians heavily involved in western land speculation. It was not enterprise or speculation as such that disturbed Washington. Rather, he was opposed to the headlong pursuit of private advantage at the public expense, and at the expense of the future prosperity of the region and of the nation as a whole. In other words, efforts to control western settlement—and thus to restrain land speculation—represented an attempt to balance and reconcile private and public interests, to fashion a working definition of liberty appropriate to a dynamic and expanding political economy. The challenge was not to suppress speculation but rather to direct it toward the public good.

Washington's ambivalent position as a speculator warning against speculation reflected not only his assessment of the strategic situation but his state's controversial campaign to cede the Ohio country unencumbered by private claims. Out-of-state land companies, not claims by other states or by Congress, presented the chief challenge to Virginia's western jurisdiction; the state's invalidation of private purchases from the Indians was the stumbling block in resolving the protracted impasse over congressional acceptance of the cession.[37] As a consequence, Virginians were sensitive to the conflict between private speculation and public interest in the ceded area, even though the state's land system made such a distinction impossible where the state retained jurisdiction. The result was that the same sort of activity—squatting, locating prime sites, speculating—seemed perfectly acceptable (or at least unavoidable) south of the Ohio while it was seen as a threat to vital national interests across the river.

---

generally see Thomas Perkins Abernethy, *Western Lands and the American Revolution* (New York, 1937).

[37] Onuf, *Origins of the Federal Republic*, 75-102.

Washington warned that Congress should not "suffer" that "wide extended Country to be over run with Land Jobbers, Speculators, and Monopolisers or even with scatter'd settlers."[38] Indeed, the lack of restraint encouraged by the apparently unlimited stock of free land seduced squatters, who otherwise might have been content with eking out a marginal subsistence, into dreaming speculators' dreams. This unrestrained speculative impulse, not the more modest ambition of making a living off the land, best explained the strategically dangerous overextension of settlement. The "rage for speculating in, and forestalling" Ohio lands was contagious, Washington wrote Jacob Read in November 1784. The upshot was that "scarce a valuable spot within any tolerable distance of [the Ohio River], is left without a claimant. Men in these times, talk with as much facility of fifty, a hundred, and even 500,000 Acres as a Gentleman formerly would do of 1000 acres. In defiance of the proclamation of Congress, they roam over the Country on the Indian side of the Ohio, mark out Lands, Survey, and even settle them."[39]

Washington's letter betrays the anxieties of a "Gentleman" confronting a mad scramble for wealth in which a man's social standing and even his capital resources were of no account. In such a world, there was no difference between settlers and speculators, or between good and bad speculators: everyone was an "adventurer." But Washington and other policymakers also showed that they understood that the unconstrained pursuit of wealth destroyed wealth. If all the potentially valuable locations were brought to market at once, they would have no value—even for speculators. If, Timothy Pickering wrote, Congress opened up the entire Northwest, permitting "adventurers . . . to ramble over that extensive country"—as they did under the southern system of indiscriminate locations—"the best lands would be in a manner *given away*."[40] Furthermore, in Washington's view, the larger the area opened to settlement, the more "extensive" the "field for Land jobbers and Speculators." The result would be to "Weaken our Frontiers [and to] exclude Law, good government, and taxation to a late period."[41] But "compact and progressive Seating" would discourage speculators and multiply the number of "useful citizens," thus advancing the "public interest."[42]

The authors of congressional land policy were determined to prevent widespread speculation in the Northwest. Here, at least, the distinction between private and public interest was apparent: the land had to be kept clear of squatters and speculators so that Congress could bring something of value to market. Further, in order to keep up land values and land sales

[38] Washington to Duane, Sept. 7, 1783, in Fitzpatrick, ed., *Washington Writings*, XXVII, 133.

[39] Washington to Read, Nov. 3, 1784, *ibid.*, 486.

[40] Pickering to Gerry, Mar. 1, 1785, in Pickering, ed., *Life of Pickering*, I, 505.

[41] Washington to Knox, June 18, 1785, in Fitzpatrick, ed., *Washington Writings*, XXVIII, 168.

[42] Washington to Williamson, Mar. 15, 1785, *ibid.*, 108.

revenue Congress had to regulate the available supply and encourage competition for an artificially scarce resource. This meant compact settlement by townships. Conversely, the government had to prevent widely scattered settlements that increased the risk of Indian wars. War would destroy the market for federal lands while putting further strain on an overextended treasury.

In its deliberations on land policy, Congress was forced to define the role of individual interest and enterprise in developing the West. The stock figures in contemporary accounts of frontier life—semisavage squatters, outlaws, speculators, and other unsavory "adventurers"—represented the dangerous excesses of unrestrained privatism. At the same time, policymakers relied on the properly regulated pursuit of private interest to promote the wealth and power of the American union. The distinction between private enterprise and privatism made it possible to identify a positive relationship between individual liberty and the public good.

II. DEVELOPMENT

Makers of policy for the West promoted the commercialization of the frontier in order to gain much-needed revenue from the sale of federal lands. A policy that maximized land values by controlling the available supply and clustering new locations near existing settlements and transportation routes would also make the frontier easier and less costly to defend. From both financial and strategic perspectives western development was an immediate, practical imperative. But for more enthusiastic commentators, economic development served loftier goals. For them the new nation's prosperity and power depended on the commercial conquest of western nature.

The key issue for political economists who contemplated the productive potential of the West was whether Congress would implement policies that would guarantee development. As Enos Hitchcock posed the question to a convocation of the Society of the Cincinnati at Providence, Rhode Island, on July 4, 1786, would the United States

rise superior to all her enemies, and extend her hospitable arms for the reception of the oppressed every where? How would the inexhaustible sources of agriculture be continually pouring into her lap, wealth and opulence; opening every avenue to commerce, and extending it from pole to pole? How would the rapidity of her population cover the vast tracts of uncultivated lands, now the rendezvous of wild beasts, with virtuous and useful inhabitants?[43]

For Hitchcock and other proponents of constitutional reform, one

[43] Hitchcock, *A Discourse on the Causes of National Prosperity* . . . (Providence, R.I. [1786]), 24.

obvious answer to these questions was the institution of a stronger federal union. Certainly, the generally perceived weakness of Congress inhibited effective enforcement of its land policy. But wealth would not pour forth from the western cornucopia by simple fiat, even of a powerful central government. Instead, the vast project of development could succeed only by mobilizing private initiatives. The ultimate strength—even the survival—of the union depended on the resulting growth of national population and wealth.

Congressional land policy, it appeared, would determine not only the pace of settlement but also the ultimate size of western population. Proponents of western development suggested that too rapid and unorganized settlement in advance of, and at the expense of, the development of markets and transportation facilities would retard long-term population growth. Just as disorganized settlement jeopardized revenues from land sales, it also endangered the region's—and the nation's—long-term prospects for economic growth: the promise of the West could easily be forfeited.

The vision of western abundance, as well as more practical policy considerations, led to a significant divergence between the views of Americans and of Europeans sympathetic to republicanism about the character of continental expansion. Looking at the new world from afar, European writers hoped that Americans would sustain a pastoral balance between nature and civilization as they pushed out across the West, thus avoiding the excesses of commercial civilization. They had a "whole world to people," wrote Mirabeau: "From the sea, quite beyond the mountains, stretches out an immense territory, which must be covered with cottages, with peasants, and with implements of husbandry."[44] This would be a world without commerce, a physiocratic utopia. English radical Richard Price also predicted that Americans would "spread over a great continent and make a world within themselves." Both writers were captivated by the image of America as an agrarian paradise peopled by an "independent and hardy yeomanry, all nearly on a level."[45] Neither made the connections

----

[44] [Honoré Gabriel de Riquetti], Count de Mirabeau, *Reflections on the Observations on the Importance of the American Revolution* ... [by Price] (Philadelphia, 1786), 2.

[45] Price, "Observations," in Peach, ed., *Richard Price and the American Revolution*, 208. The Abbé de Mably warned Americans against allowing "wealth" to "usurp an absolute empire" in the New World: avoid European manners, "vices," and "politics." The new republic must not become another Carthage, "at once *commercial and warlike*" (Gabriel Bonnot de Mably, *Observations on the Government and Laws of the United States* [Amsterdam, 1784], 120-121, my emphasis). For similar sentiments see "Letter from Turgot," in Peach, ed., *Richard Price and the American Revolution*, 222. On "agrarianism" see Lienesch, "Development," in his *New Order*, and, on the idealization of the middle stage of social development—and the "middle landscape"—see Leo Marx, *The Machine in the Garden: Technology and the Pastoral Ideal in America* (New York, 1964).

between agriculture, trade, and manufactures that American policymakers believed essential to western development.

Congressmen were impressed—and frightened—by the volatility of the frontier. They were convinced that the federal government's authority and property interests depended on effectively directing the course of western political and economic development. As a result, they were less interested in creating the material conditions for Price's "hardy yeomanry" than in sustaining links with—and control over—a rapidly dispersing frontier population. Under frontier conditions, the rustic simplicity and personal independence celebrated by foreign commentators posed a problem. In the new country, beyond the discipline both of established local institutions and of the marketplace, the lines between liberty and license, and between private enterprise and rampant privatism, inevitably blurred. Congressmen were skeptical about the possibility of republican self-government on the frontiers. They concluded that Congress would have to take an active role in regulating westward settlement and securing the union of East and West.

Students of early territorial history have generally held that this fear of anarchy prompted a reactionary insistence on social order by a new class of unelected, autocratic, territorial officials.[46] Certainly, the need for a more effective colonial authority in the West helped spur passage of the Northwest Ordinance in 1787. But even though policymakers came to believe that Congress had to impose strong government on the frontiers during the settlement period, they also recognized that union could not be indefinitely sustained by force alone. Jefferson's conclusion that if westerners "declare themselves a separate people, we are incapable of a single effort to retain them" was equally warranted by Congress's slender resources and by the potential power of western settlers united in opposition to its authority.[47] If force could not preserve the union, perhaps, Madison suggested, multiplying "ties of friendship, of marriage and consanguinity," would suffice.[48] Yet, as Jefferson argued (in the letter just cited), such ties would only serve to make recourse to force impossible: "our citizens can never be induced . . . to go there to cut the throats of their own brothers and sons."

Whatever their ideological affinities, most commentators concluded that the only effective bond between East and West was "interest." Exhortations to virtue and good citizenship were irrelevant in the absence of commercial connections. The genius of republican government decreed a separation unless both sections benefited equally. Colonial rule was seen

[46] Particularly Jack Ericson Eblen, *The First and Second United States Empires: Governors and Territorial Government, 1784-1912* (Pittsburgh, Pa., 1968), 17-51. But see Onuf, *Origins of the Federal Republic*, 166-171, and "From Constitution to Higher Law: The Reinterpretation of the Northwest Ordinance," *Ohio History*, XCIV (1985), 5-33.

[47] Jefferson to Madison, Jan. 30, 1787, in *Jefferson Papers*, XI, 93.

[48] Madison to Lafayette, Mar. 20, 1785, in *Madison Papers*, VIII, 251.

as a temporary necessity, both for maintaining order at the outset of settlement and for allowing common interests to develop, not as an enduring foundation for union. "No proud despot" would exercise authority in this "new-found world," wrote poet Philip Freneau; nor, added soldier-poet David Humphreys, would "feudal ties the rising genius mar."[49]

Freneau's poem "On the emigration to America" captured the prevailing sense of the importance of commercial development for westward expansion. The problem was not simply to establish trade links between settlements; far more than that, the West as a whole would have to be commercially transformed in order to become an integral part of the union. Freneau's description of western rivers epitomized his developmental, antipastoral vision:

> No longer shall they useless prove,
> Nor idly through the forest rove.

Instead, he continued, now addressing the rivers directly:

> Far other ends the fates decree,
> And commerce plans new freights for thee.[50]

The attraction of the West was not that it could provide a rural retreat for a virtuous yeomanry. Instead, Freneau imagined a western landscape redeemed from its natural state by the new uses decreed by advancing commerce.

An unimproved, undeveloped West was unimaginable. In the words of Manasseh Cutler, the land must be reduced to cultivation before it will "exhibit all its latent beauties, and justify those descriptions of travelers which have so often made it the garden of the world, the seat of wealth, and the center of a great empire."[51] Until touched by the white man's transforming hand, the western lands would remain "barren wilds" and "immense deserts." The promise of development was thus counterpointed to the dangers of underdevelopment, the reassertion of the wilderness's natural sway over savage man. Even while celebrating nature's bounty and asserting their natural rights to exploit it, Americans defined the "state of nature" as the lawless reign of anarchy and vice. The undeveloped, unconnected frontier provided the objective correlative to this conventional formula. In turn, conventional political ideas helped clarify and focus the alternative, radically distinct visions of the future, hopeful and

---

[49] Freneau, "On the emigration to America," *American Museum*, I (Feb. 1787), 159; Humphreys, "A poem on the happiness of America," *ibid*. (Mar. 1787), 249.
[50] *Ibid*. (Feb. 1787), 160.
[51] Cutler, *An Explanation of the Map which Delineates ... the Federal Lands ...* (Salem, Mass., 1787), in William Parker Cutler and Julia Perkins Cutler, *Life Journals and Correspondence of Rev. Manasseh Cutler, LL.D.*, 2 vols. (Cincinnati, Ohio, 1888), II, 400.

despairing, that the West evoked. By no means was it foreordained that the American "wilderness [would] be made to blossom like the rose."[52]

Political and economic concerns converged when polemicists and policymakers looked west. Union depended on commercial links that, in turn, depended on opportunities for profitable enterprise. In this light, the very fertility of the western lands constituted a problem for the new nation. Traditionally, republican theorists looked askance at luxury and therefore at commerce. How, they asked, could Americans be both virtuous and prosperous? American political economists who addressed this issue argued that an instrumental attitude toward natural abundance could resolve the dilemma. The challenge was to give settlers adequate incentives to exploit their property's commercial potential: useful labor should be suitably rewarded. This solution presupposed development, the creation of a context in which useful labor was possible.

The vision of economic development suggested a solution to the problem of natural abundance; it also promised to resolve chronic conflicts among interest groups. Tench Coxe, an enthusiastic supporter of manufactures, promoted internal improvements that would open the hinterland and so activate "the dormant powers of nature and the elements."[53] According to Coxe, farmers would provide primary materials for manufacturers, while both groups would depend on merchants to keep the wheels of trade turning. Promoters of development suggested that all market-oriented productive labor was essentially the same, whether in agriculture or manufacturing. By this logic, "land . . . must [be] consider[ed] as a raw material."[54] It is "our great staple," wrote William Barton, and agriculture is "our principal manufacture."[55]

Advocates like Barton argued that productive labor properly rewarded would help frontiersmen avoid the temptations of easy subsistence and make them into sober, industrious, and useful citizens. These publicists warned that the failure to guarantee development would be disastrous, for both the settlers themselves and the nation as a whole. Writing "on American Manufactures" in the first issue of the new *Columbian Magazine,* "Americanus" (probably Barton) appealed to the authority of British economist James Anderson, according to whom,

If the soil is naturally fertile, little labour will produce abundance; but, for want of exercise, even that little will be burthensome, and often neglected:—*want will be felt in the midst of abundance,* and the

[52] Jonathan Loring Austin, *An Oration, Delivered July 4, 1786* . . . (Boston, 1786), 15.

[53] Coxe, "An address to an assembly of the friends of American manufactures," Aug. 9, 1787, *American Museum,* II (Sept. 1787), 255.

[54] "Americanus" [William Barton?], "On American Manufactures," *Columbian Magazine,* I (Sept. 1786), 27. Both "Americanus" and Barton cited British economist James Anderson. See n. 56 below.

[55] "An American" [William Barton], *The True Interest of the United States, and Particularly of Pennsylvania* . . . (Philadelphia, 1786), 11.

human mind be abased nearly to the same degree with the beasts that graze the field. If the region is more barren, the inhabitants will be obliged to become somewhat more industrious, and therefore more happy—But miserable at best must be the happiness of such a people.[56]

"Want . . . in the midst of abundance": this, in a phrase, was the nightmare of underdevelopment. Only when industry was applied to abundance—not substituted for it—was true "happiness" attainable.

"Americanus" and like-minded promoters emphasized that the fate of the nation was inextricably linked to the future of the West. The same reasoning suggested that the failure to promote economic growth in settled areas would roll back the frontier. "A Plain, but Real, Friend to America," explained how the encouragement of manufactures would transform "sparse scattered settlements" into prosperous villages, "full of people, and as industrious as a bee-hive." But the collapse of infant industries and the decline of trade would make America over in the image of the frontier wasteland. The countryside would "wear a horrid deserted aspect"; without work, "our own poor" would be forced "to wander in the woods and wilds of the back countries, to live like Indians."[57]

Frontier whites, besotted with an effortless subsistence, might imagine themselves "happy." But in the developers' view this was a beggarly, savage happiness at best. After all, the native Americans were a melancholy race: they had failed to exploit nature's bounty, a failure reflected in their scattered and declining numbers. Properly developed, the West could support an infinitely larger, more prosperous people. In those pre-Malthusian days, the equations between population and power, and between population and prosperity, still made sense. To permit settlers to be satisfied with mere subsistence was to choose a small, semisavage population over the large, industrious, and civilized population that these fertile lands could so easily be made to support.[58]

Whatever America's role in the world, or as a world unto itself, the development of the West was essential. Even those who celebrated the redemptive influence of American agriculture conceded that frontier farms would have to be commercially viable. If federal lands were to have any value, purchasers had to be assured that they would find markets for their crops and a return on their investment. Congress was not about to give away its property, however attractive the idea of colonizing the West

[56] "Americanus" [Barton?], "On American Manufactures," *Columbian Magazine,* I (Sept. 1786), 27n, citing Anderson, *Observations on the Means of Exciting a Spirit of National Industry* (Edinburgh, 1777), Letter IV.

[57] "A Plain, but Real, Friend," Aug. 9, 1785, *Md. Jour.,* Aug. 16, 1785.

[58] Jefferson believed that it was America's destiny to spread its people across the new world, thus "doubling the numbers of mankind, and of course the quantum of existence and happiness" (Jefferson's Observations on Démeunier's Manuscript [1786], in *Jefferson Papers,* X, 57).

with virtuous farmers. Thus, while David Howell considered "cultivators of the soil" the true "guardians" of republicanism, he was also impressed by the "amazing prospect" of a "national fund" presented by the western lands. The "gods of the mountains" who settled on the frontiers would have to purchase their lands and thus pay for the privilege of defending American liberties.[59] Col. Humphreys hailed "agriculture! by whose parent aid, / The deep foundations of our states are laid." Through agriculture the western wilds would be conquered and so converted into an "Arcadian scene," poised between "too rude and too refin'd an age." Yet even Humphreys revealed developmental premises: agriculture was not only the "earliest friend of man"—the means of subsistence—but also, potentially, a "Great source of wealth" for enterprising Americans. The West would have to be developed to support agriculture, and agriculture would be the means of future development.[60]

Thomas Jefferson, the preeminent agrarian theorist, had no illusions about the future commercial character of the frontier or of his countrymen. Though from a global perspective Jefferson endorsed the idea that the new nation's "workshops" should remain in Europe and that a modern commercial-industrial economy constituted the leading threat to republican liberty, the opening of the West prompted him to assume a less doctrinaire posture.[61] Writing to Washington in March 1784, at a time when he was playing a key role in formulating congressional western policy, Jefferson dismissed the classic question of whether agriculture or commerce was the true source of man's happiness. "We might indulge" in such speculations, he wrote, "was it practicable to keep our new empire separated" from the rest of the world. But this could never be done. "All the world is becoming commercial," including the American people. "Our citizens have had too full a taste of the comforts furnished by the arts and manufactures to be debarred the use of them."[62]

The commercial character of the American people may have been regrettable, at least in theory, but in practice Jefferson sought to exploit the private pursuit of profit that he thought propelled the massive emigration to the West in order to advance the interests of his state and of the United States. Along with Washington and other like-minded Virginians, he was determined that Virginia command its fair share of the vast wealth to be created by western development. "Nature . . . has declared in favour of the Patowmac," he wrote, "and through that channel offers to pour into our lap the whole commerce of the Western world." Yet

---

[59] Howell to Jonathan Arnold, Feb. 21, 1784, in Staples, *Rhode Island in Congress*, ed. Guild, 479.

[60] Humphreys, "Poem on the happiness of America," *American Museum*, I (Mar. 1787), 251, 249.

[61] Jefferson, *Notes on the State of Virginia*, ed. William Peden (Chapel Hill, N.C., 1954), 164-165.

[62] Jefferson to Washington, Mar. 15, 1784, and to G. K. van Hogendorp, Oct. 13, 1785, in *Jefferson Papers*, VII, 26, VIII, 633.

nature's offer was contingent on Virginia's and Maryland's willingness to undertake extensive internal improvements. Other states were all too eager to divert the western trade into unnatural courses: Pennsylvanians, traditional rivals for economic control of the Ohio Valley, were busily promoting new routes west; even New Yorkers were beginning to consider ambitious proposals for connecting their state with the Great Lakes.[63] Responding to this incipient regional rivalry, Washington agreed (on Jefferson's urging) to head a company jointly sponsored by Virginia and Maryland to extend the navigability of the Potomac. Here, according to a Maryland legislator, David McMechen, was a potentially "immense source of wealth" for the Chesapeake region.[64] And now was the time, Washington insisted repeatedly throughout 1784 and 1785, for "fixing . . . a large portion of the trade of the Western Country in the bosom of this State irrevocably."[65]

Whether as a financial resource for governments straining under an "oppressive" burden of debt or as a source of commercial wealth for eastern entrepôts, the western lands had to be properly developed and integrated into the American and world economies. Commerce was an essential adjunct of western agricultural development: without access to markets settlers would have no incentive to improve the landscape. Similarly, political economists foresaw ample scope for the founding of new industries in the western world as well as vast new markets for eastern manufactures.

Promoters of manufactures were forced by their small numbers to embrace the vision of a harmony of interests and integrated economic development. Writers like Tench Coxe did not question the "preeminence of the agricultural interest." Indeed, the opening of the West, "the settlement of our waste lands, and subdividing our improved farms" would reinforce the dominance of agriculture. But it was a mistake to assume that the ascendancy of the agricultural interest would come at the expense of other interests. Instead, in Coxe's inflationary scheme, "agri-

---

[63] Jefferson to Washington, Mar. 15, 1784, ibid., VII, 26. For a plan to build a canal through New York see [Christopher Colles], Proposals for the Speedy Settlement of the Waste and Unappropriated Lands on the Western Frontiers of the State of New-York, and for the Improvement of the Inland Navigation between Albany and Oswego (New York, 1785).

[64] McMechen was parrying criticism of his vote in favor of the company in the Maryland Assembly (McMechen to Electors of Baltimore-Town, Sept. 20, 1785, Md. Jour., Sept. 23, 1785).

[65] Washington to Gov. Harrison, Oct. 10, 1784, in Fitzpatrick, ed., Washington Writings, XXVII, 480. See also Washington to Knox, Dec. 5, 1784, ibid., XXVIII, 3-5. Washington warned against allowing the "commerce of that country" to "embrace" the Mississippi route: "experience has taught us . . . how next to impracticable it is to divert it" (letter to Humphreys, July 25, 1785, ibid., 205).

culture appears to be the spring of our commerce, and the parent of our manufactures."[66]

Of course, for theorists like Coxe, the measure of agriculture's vitality was determined by market criteria—represented by the price of land—which depended in turn on the growth of other sectors of the economy. A "Farmer," writing in the *Maryland Journal* in early 1786, thus sought to "impress it on the minds of those who hold lands in this state, that they are as much interested in promoting its commerce, as the merchant can possibly be." "Farmer" surveyed land prices in neighboring states with a view to demonstrating that the value of land was not determined by fertility alone. The best lands were in Virginia, but they were worth considerably less than inferior lands in Pennsylvania. The explanation for this "great diversity in price" was "the great encouragement they [the Pennsylvanians] give to commerce."[67] Conspicuously missing from this account was any notion that agriculture should be privileged activity in the new nation, that its "value" consisted in the independence it afforded yeoman farmers at least relatively immune to market forces. On the contrary, it was a crucial premise for Barton, Coxe, and the many other writers who promoted economic development in the mid-1780s that "interests" were not only equal, and thus equally entitled to protection and assistance from government, but that they were, in essential respects, identical. Agriculture was really a form of manufacturing—the application of labor and capital to America's most abundant natural resource. In their varied but complementary pursuits, Americans were all driven by a "spirit of enterprize."[68] The result of all this busyness, according to Joel Barlow, would be "progress of arts, in agriculture, commerce, and manufactures"—if Americans acted prudently to secure the union and guarantee development.[69]

In one of the boldest formulations of the development idea, William Vans Murray pursued the new logic to the limits of republican theory. Murray rejected the old republican bias toward rustic, uncorrupted virtue, supported by equal distribution of landed property. He argued, instead, that only in an advanced state of civilization could a government be

[66] T[ench] C[oxe], "An Enquiry into the Principles on which a Commercial System for the United States should be founded," May 11, 1787, *American Museum*, I (June 1787), 499. For another invocation of the harmony of interests see New York [City] Chamber of Commerce, *Gentlemen. The Interest of the Landholder . . .* , broadside [New York, 1785]: "By the union of the farmer, the merchant and mechanic" the new nation had withstood "the open force of our enemies," New York Public Library.

[67] "Farmer," "To the Inhabitants of Maryland," Feb. 12, 1786, *Md. Jour.*, Feb. 17, 1786.

[68] Introductory Remarks to "The Happiness of America," *Columbian Magazine*, I (Oct. 1786), 67.

[69] Barlow, Oration to the Society of the Cincinnati, July 4, 1787, *American Museum*, II (Aug. 1787), 138.

"created under a just conception of human rights." Such rights would not, perhaps, be "relished by a rude society." The "perfect equality of rights" and "enlightened adoption of a free form of government" were possible in America because of its social maturity, not because it remained at some semideveloped, middle stage of civilization. Material abundance, or in Murray's forthright language, "luxury," was as "natural" to civilized Americans as poverty was to savages. It was simply a "romantic . . . fiction," Murray concluded, that "luxury and true liberty are incompatible in a democratic form."[70]

Murray showed how republican values could be transformed under the exigencies of nation making. Though many of his contemporaries would have stopped far short of his conclusions, he articulated some of the core values in American liberal theory. Proponents of commerce and economic development pressed the need to harmonize interests and create a true national community founded on free exchange and interaction. In this formulation, the public good—the creation of a more durable union— coincided with the pursuit of private interest. The crucial bridge between public and private realms, which classical theory sought to keep distinct, was a developing economy that rewarded private enterprise and directed it toward productive ends.

Independence Day orator John Gardiner described the American promise to a Boston crowd in 1785: "If we make a right use of our natural advantages we soon must be a truly great and happy people. When we consider the vastness of our country, the variety of her soil and climate, the immense extent of her sea-coast, and of the inland navigation by the lakes and rivers, we find a *world within ourselves*, sufficient to produce whatever can contribute to the necessities and even the superfluities of life."[71] Gardiner's world was a dynamic one, in which land was valued for what it could produce and self-sufficiency was the goal for a continent, not merely a household. Bodies of water affording easy communication and commerce were the most conspicuous natural features, the keys to future greatness. Made accessible by these natural highways, the western lands opened astonishing prospects for individual enterprise. But individual and collective success for the American people depended on making a "right use" of nature's gift.

The importance of development to Americans like Gardiner suggests, on the one hand, an enthusiastic endorsement of private initiatives from all sectors of society and, on the other, an awareness that the expansion of the union—perhaps even its perpetuation—was problematic. Development and union were counterpointed to underdevelopment, anarchy, and counterrevolution: both outcomes were plausible. This sense of contingency magnified the agency of the American people in determining their own, and the world's, future: according to Barlow, "every free citizen of

[70] Murray, "Political Sketches," Apr. 1787, *ibid.* (Sept. 1787), 237, 238, 233, 234.
[71] Gardiner, *An Oration, Delivered July 4, 1785* . . . (Boston 1785), 35.

the American empire ought now to consider himself as the legislator of half mankind."[72] In the developers' scheme the new world could expand or disintegrate depending on how or whether settlement was regulated and on what provisions voters would make for preserving and extending the union.

In development rhetoric, the ideas of enterprise, progress, and material abundance served as solvents for differences among sections as well as economic interests that, when conceived in static, mutually exclusive terms, appeared to pose a threat of destruction to the new nation. Economic growth would resolve the conflicts that grew out of scarcity: all interests would benefit from an expanding pie. Americans would come to see the interdependence of agriculture, manufacturing, and commerce that development proponents considered axiomatic; thus enlightened, they would no longer pursue shortsighted measures at each other's expense. Of course, the harmony-of-interest idea was often invoked as a rationale for promoting specific interests: manufacturers wanted protection, merchants wanted a coherent commercial policy, farmers wanted land. Differences among interests could not always be concealed by fulsome rhetoric, or by imaginary abundance. From this perspective, the dream of western development can be seen as a kind of oblique recognition of differences among Americans that often seemed intractable. Indeed, development schemes themselves often betrayed a distinct sectional bias. In the case of regional competition for control of the western trade, developers like Washington and Jefferson were expressing and promoting the very forces that a stronger, more developed union— their ostensible goal—was supposed to overcome.[73] Skeptics might reasonably conclude that national land policy, for instance, would simply enrich particular groups of well-situated traders and speculators. But the dream of development, even if traceable to self-interest, was broadly appealing. It represented an authentic impulse toward national integration, while giving a new legitimacy to the boundless ambitions of countless Americans. The developers taught that in a properly regulated new world economy the pursuit of private interest would rise above interest-group politics and guarantee the nation's wealth and power. Unlike the leaders of the Revolution, proponents of union through development sought to mobilize private interest and enterprise, not self-denial and sacrifice, to bring forth a new order.

[72] Barlow, Oration to the Cincinnati, *American Museum*, II (Aug. 1787), 138. For similar rhetoric see Amicus Reipublicae, *Address to the Public* . . . (Exeter, Mass. [1786]), 35.

[73] Washington emphasized the "political importance" of establishing "strong commercial bands" between East and West and thus strengthening the union, but conceded that the "commercial advantages"—to Virginia and Maryland—would be "immense" (letter to Knox, Dec. 5, 1784, in Fitzpatrick, ed., *Washington Writings*, XXVIII, 4).

III. UNION

The 1780s were a "critical period" for the union of American states. Congress's ordinances for distributing and governing the western lands in the national interest represented the first great effort to transcend sectional interests and provide for expansion of the union. To optimists like Washington, the westward movement of wealth and population would liberate Americans from insular loyalties and prejudices: "time" would "disarm localities of their power."[74] But a leap of faith was necessary before many of Washington's contemporaries could truly believe in the harmony of interests in an expanding republic. Such harmony defied the realities of American politics. Further, old-fashioned republicans questioned the wisdom of expansion: large polities were supposedly incompatible with individual and local liberties. The western problem thus raised urgent questions about the durability and desirability of union itself.

Congress's program for western development was designed to cement connections between East and West. The crucial first step was to create a national market in western lands. Only then would expansionists be able to answer arguments that expansion would depopulate and impoverish the old states. By positing the rapid integration of new settlements into the national economy, they could insist that all parts of the country would benefit. Controlled expansion would spur economic development, population growth, and internal improvements throughout the union. The growth of intersectional commerce would expand the scope of common interests and counter the effects of growing distances, making republicanism possible on a continental scale.

Some observers flatly denied that a continuing union between East and West was possible.[75] Many others entertained serious doubts. Madison outlined some of these for Jefferson in August 1784. Those who "remain in the Atlantic States" would be "sufferers by the encouragement of the Western settlem[en]ts," he explained. The old states would experience "depopulation," "depreciation" of land values, and the "delay of that maritime strength which must be their only safety in case of war." Finally, Madison concluded, the Confederacy itself would be endangered by "multiplying the parts of the Machine."[76]

All of the objections recounted by Madison were based on "zero-sum" premises; they assumed expansion without economic growth or development. Population was the central concern since population density was the key determinant of both land prices and political power. This focus on

[74] Washington to Grayson, June 22, 1785, *ibid.*, 172-173. Washington thought it would be a mistake for Congress to select a *"permanent* seat . . . at this time."

[75] These misgivings are discussed in Washington to Grayson, Apr. 25, 1785, *ibid.*, 136-139, and Archibald Stuart to Jefferson, Oct. 17, 1785, in *Jefferson Papers*, VIII, 646. See also Onuf, *Origins of the Federal Republic*, 159-160.

[76] Madison to Jefferson, Aug. 20, 1784, in *Madison Papers*, VIII, 108. See also Madison to Lafayette, Mar. 20, 1785, *ibid.*, 250-255.

population became clear in 1786 during debates over closure of the Mississippi. James Monroe was convinced that by acceding to Spain's conditions northerners meant to "make it the interest of the [western] people to separate" from the union, thus precluding the addition of new states and "throw[ing] the weight of population eastward and keep[ing] it there, to appreciate the vacant lands of New York and Massachusetts."[77] For their part, northerners such as Rufus King were persuaded that "an entire separation" between East and West was inevitable. If so, he asked, "in true policy ought the U.S. to be very assiduous to encourage their Citizens to become Settlers" in the trans-Appalachian region? If westerners were free to trade through the Mississippi, King added, "I should consider every emigrant to that country from the Atlantic States, as forever lost to the Confederacy."[78]

The challenge to western policymakers was to minimize the losses in population, wealth, and power that expansion apparently would entail. According to a typical complaint, "selling or settling" the West too "speedily" would open "a door for our citizens, to run off and leave us . . . depreciating all our landed property already settled, and disabling us from paying taxes, and funding the debt already contracted."[79] A program for the gradual extension of settlement, or what Washington called "progressive seating," would address these concerns. First, the "door" would not be flung wide open: the old states would retain populations sufficient to secure their welfare as well as customers for their land offices. But, at least in theory, regulated expansion would do more than this: by guaranteeing that westerners would become "useful" citizens, congressional land policy would increase the wealth of the entire union and provide an abundant subsistence for a growing population.

In practical terms, the population issue reduced to the question of where Congress would find suitably industrious settlers to develop the national domain. Many policymakers and commentators predicted that an influx of European immigrants would prevent the depopulation of the old states.[80] But those states were also producing population surpluses that could be directed west. Ezra Stiles of Connecticut, a diligent student of demographic trends, looked forward to a national population of fifty million by 1876 and concluded that even "if the present ratio of increase

[77] Monroe to Patrick Henry, Aug. 12, 1786, in William Wirt Henry, *Patrick Henry: Life, Correspondence, and Speeches*, 3 vols. (New York, 1891), II, 297; Monroe to Madison, Aug. 14, 1786, in *Madison Papers*, IX, 104-105.

[78] King to Gerry, June 4, 1786, in *Letters Cont. Cong.*, VIII, 380. For a discussion of Massachusetts's interest in preventing emigration to the Ohio region see Rufus Putnam to Washington, Apr. 5, 1784, in Cutler and Cutler, *Life of Cutler*, I, 174-176.

[79] "Extract of a letter from a gentleman in Maryland to his friend in Philadelphia," Aug. 15, 1785, *Independent Chronicle*, Sept. 8, 1785.

[80] Grayson told Washington that some congressmen thought it "true policy to get the money with[ou]t parting with inhabitants to populate the Country" (letter of Apr. 15, 1785, in *Letters Cont. Cong.*, VIII, 97).

should be rather diminished in some of the elder settlements, yet an *accelerated multiplication will attend our general propagation,* and overspread the whole territory westward for ages."[81] The result would not be an absolute loss of numbers for places like Connecticut: indeed, that state had continued to grow even as great numbers of its sons and daughters hived off to Vermont and Pennsylvania. Instead, Stiles and other population theorists forecast the ultimate equalization of rates of growth, not the redistribution of existing numbers or the simple extrapolation of the low densities that could be supported by subsistence agriculture.

Madison explained the connection between economic development and population growth in the same letter to Jefferson in which he reviewed conventional objections to western expansion. "Vacancies ... in an industrious country" caused by emigration "are not only Speedily filled but that population is ever increased by the demand of the emigrants & their descendants."[82] Simultaneous increase in the demand for products of the more densely settled, "industrious" parts of the country and expansion of commercial agriculture over fresh western lands would promote a continuing, reciprocal explosion of population.

The key factor in this conception of dynamic population growth, according to Benjamin Rush, was a distinctively American "passion for migration." "This passion," he wrote, may appear "strange and new," but it "is wisely calculated for the extension of population in America; and this it does, not only by promoting the increase of the human species in new settlements, but in the old settlements likewise." Local population surpluses, unless directed toward more promising regions, would retard growth, introducing a "languor in population."[83] The compelling conclusion was that the nation should encourage internal migration, even as it welcomed immigrants from abroad. Both were sources of increasing population, whether by redistributing excess population or by encouraging more rapid growth rates. In either case, the encouragement of population required freedom of movement. No one knew better than the people themselves when the material conditions for reproduction were most propitious. And no "political maxim [was] better established,"

---

[81] Stiles, *The United States Elevated to Glory and Honour* . . . , 2d ed. (Worcester, Mass., 1785), 60, my emphasis. For the best introduction to contemporary population theory see James Russell Gibson, "Americans versus Malthus: The Population Debate in the Early Republic" (Ph.D. diss., Clark University, 1982), esp. chap. 1. See also Drew R. McCoy, "Jefferson and Madison on Malthus: Population Growth in Jeffersonian Political Economy," *Virginia Magazine of History and Biography,* LXXXVIII (1980), 259-276.

[82] Madison to Jefferson, Aug. 20, 1784, in *Madison Papers,* VIII, 108. Madison argued at the Constitutional Convention that American populations would tend to equalize (speech of July 11, 1787, in Max Farrand, ed., *The Records of the Federal Convention of 1787,* 4 vols. [New Haven, Conn., 1911-1937], I, 585-586).

[83] "A Citizen of Pennsylvania" [Rush], "Account of the Progress of the Population, Agriculture, Manners, and Government in Pennsylvania," *Columbian Magazine,* I (Nov. 1786), 121.

William Barton wrote, than that "a high degree of population contributes greatly to the riches and strength of a state."[84]

Properly managed, the western lands would guarantee the future greatness of the new nation. But fulfillment of this promise depended on several related, problematic conditions. The free movement of population, particularly of the more industrious and useful sort, presupposed political stability, law and order, clear property titles, and peace with the Indians. The present disordered "state of things," Tench Coxe warned in 1787, "deters all who have the means of information" from coming to America.[85] Though Washington was confident that the western "Country ... will settle faster than any other ever did," its prospects clearly depended on preserving the peace.[86] He wrote Lafayette that he hoped to see the "sons and daughters of the world" flock to the "fertile plains of the Ohio," where they would find "agreeable amusement" in "fulfilling the first and great commandment, *Increase and Multiply*."[87] But this would be impossible in the event of the frontier warfare that unregulated settlement would necessarily provoke.

How could "freedom" be reconciled with regulation? Clearly, western policymakers did not sanction all private initiatives. Instead, they hoped to recruit from all over the world industrious immigrants eager to gain a better return on their capital and labor, as well as a more abundant subsistence. The population theorists assumed just this sort of rational, market-oriented behavior in their predictions of population growth. They expected not only that population would vary with the means of subsistence—a commonsense premise—but also that the spread of settlement would invigorate and accelerate interregional commercial transactions. Better-situated producers would be better equipped to satisfy each other's needs: through the workings of the marketplace they would become closer—more interdependent—even as they moved apart.

Population growth, linked with and fueling economic development, provided the American answer to traditional warnings against overlarge states. In "Lectures on Political Principles" Samuel Williams of Vermont argued against Montesquieu's "pernicious opinion" that "Civil Liberty can only exist in a Small Territory" and that only a despotic government could maintain order over extended territory. Williams identified political obligation with reciprocal interests and free exchange: "whatever be the

---

[84] Barton, *Observations on the Progress of Population* . . . ([Philadelphia], 1791), 1. Barton cited Richard Price: "The encouragement of population ought to be one of the first objects of policy, in every State."

[85] C[oxe], "Enquiry into Principles," *American Museum*, I (June 1787), 514. Joel Barlow asserted that "the blessings of a rational government will invite emigrations" (Oration to the Cincinnati, *ibid.*, II [Aug. 1787], 142). Lord Sheffield claimed that the Americans' "numbers . . . are certainly much decreased by the war and emigration" (*Observations on Commerce*, 105n).

[86] Washington to Knox, Dec. 5, 1784, in Fitzpatrick, ed., *Washington Writings*, XXVIII, 4.

[87] Washington to Lafayette, July 25, 1785, *ibid.*, 206.

size of the territory, the celerity of all motions would be greater in free constitutions." Under "judiciously constructed" republican institutions that permitted Americans to pursue their own ends freely, common interests would help overcome the growing distances entailed by expansion. But "tyranny" was unsuited to a large state because the imposition of the ruler's "caprices" guaranteed resistance by his subjects in defense of their interests. Tyrannical "motion" would be sluggish, not speedy, and the effective size of the state—defined by the difficulty of governing it—would increase.[88]

A liberal conception of civil society and civil liberty grounded on assumptions of rational economic behavior and the ultimate harmony of interests in the marketplace enabled theorists like Williams to imagine an expanding empire of liberty in the new world. Long-term trends, notably in population growth rates and in the demand for American agricultural products, seemed to justify optimism about expansion. From this perspective, the future of the American union was primarily a problem in political economy: no constitutional reforms could preserve the United States if the states were not bound together by common interests.[89] Therefore, congressional land policy, by determining the orientation of interests in the new settlements, was crucial to the prospects for continuing union between East and West. At the same time, the sale of federal lands spurred by western development promised virtually inexhaustible revenues to promote the common interests of all the states and strengthen the national government.

Throughout the 1780s, commentators who looked west for financial succor assumed that Congress's supply of lands soon would rapidly rise in value in response to a growing demand from a rapidly expanding population: the West would then become marketable at prices high enough to meet public revenue needs but not to discourage industrious settlers. In 1782, even before Congress had established its authority in the West, Pelatiah Webster confidently described "prospects of vast population and national wealth." These, he conceded, "may at first sight appear chimerical," but, supposing that the American population would continue to double every twenty-five years and given the renowned fertility of the western lands, "it will appear very probable that our own eyes may live to see the commencement of a great demand and rapid sale of our western territory."[90] But policymakers faced an immediate, practical problem in linking supply to demand. They had to create a market for a commodity, unimproved frontier land, that historically only had speculative value in anticipation of future development. Population pressure on a dwindling land supply might produce potential settlers, but Congress had to

[88] Williams, "On the Fallacy . . . that Civil Liberty can only exist in a Small Territory," *Columbian Magazine*, VI (Mar. 1791), 144.

[89] For further discussion see Cathy Matson and Peter Onuf, "Toward a Republican Empire: Interest and Ideology in Revolutionary America," *American Quarterly*, XXXVII (1985).

[90] Webster, "Essay on Western Lands," in his *Political Essays*, 498, 497.

persuade them that their capital would be safely and profitably invested in federal lands.

Congressmen were aware that the success of their land policy was by no means inevitable. They were convinced that the economic development of the West and the durability of its connections with the East hinged on drafting and enforcing effective regulations. Congress would have to introduce to the national frontier a new kind of settler-developer, capable of putting his property to immediate productive use and therefore justifying its price. The traditional growth of frontier settlements from semisavage subsistence to commercial farming would have to be collapsed into a single stage: the West would be commercial from the outset.[91] American antipathy to taxation reinforced the commitment to drawing revenue from the public land market instead of waiting for unregulated private initiatives to make land valuable, if this were possible, and hence capable of sustaining public burdens.

It thus becomes clear that the formulation of congressional land policy in 1784-1785 represented an effort to create a national market in western lands. The success of the effort depended on mobilizing national and even international demand for new, potentially productive lands. Congress would have to take an active role, at considerable expense, in guaranteeing that market conditions favorable to the nation's interests would prevail. Speculators and squatters were major obstacles to this program because, by claiming or occupying prime sites, they distorted supply and, by clogging the courts with conflicting claims, they scared off potential buyers.

Congress attempted to guarantee a vigorous national land market through a variety of related provisions in the May 1785 ordinance. First, it determined to remove its land offices from the frontier, thus neutralizing the advantage enjoyed by nearby settlers and speculators with firsthand knowledge of available lands. This crucial feature of the ordinance survived subsequent revision; a related provision, that federal lands be offered at auctions in each of the thirteen Atlantic states, was abandoned. Critics of this requirement thought that by fragmenting demand it would minimize competition and keep prices down; they also feared that multiple markets would deter foreign purchasers who would not know "when or where to apply for" lands.[92] But the underlying premise, that

[91] This point is also developed in Andrew R. L. Cayton, "Planning the Republic: The Federalists and Internal Improvements in the Old Northwest" (paper delivered at the meeting of the Organization of American Historians, Minneapolis, Minn., April 1985).

[92] Washington to the countess of Huntingdon, June 30, 1785, in Fitzpatrick, ed., *Washington Writings*, XXVIII, 181. Though Jefferson at first objected to this provision, he wrote David Hartley, Sept. 5, 1785, that it would guarantee a "proper mixture of the citizens from all the different states" (*Jefferson Papers*, VIII, 482-483). For the amendment to the land ordinance, stipulating that a single auction would be held at the seat of Congress, see resolution of Apr. 21, 1787, in *Jours. Cont. Cong.*, XXXII, 226.

Congress should not look to existing western settlements for settlers, was generally accepted. Washington, who knew these frontier people all too well, expected (and probably hoped) to see the West peopled from abroad.[93] Given the chaotic history of their own backcountry, at least some Virginians were predisposed to give New Englanders preference over their own people as prospective purchaser-settlers.[94] In any case, the guarantee that the eastern purchaser would have a fair chance to bid on western property promised to connect latent demand, where surplus population and wealth sought new opportunities, with an unlimited supply of potentially valuable property.

The most important feature of Congress's new land policy was the requirement of survey before settlement, with property lines following a grid system that made clear title possible, thus permitting easy sale and resale. Together with the triumph of the fee simple principle over feudal survivals such as primogeniture and entail, the grid helped transform landed property into a marketable commodity.[95] It was with this in mind that Washington advocated mapping the western lands on the basis of accurate surveys. In late 1784 he wrote fellow Virginian Richard Henry Lee, then president of Congress, recommending that the United States commission a map: "The expence attending this undertaking cou'd not be great, the advantages would be unbounded; for sure I am, nature has made such an ample display of her bounties in those regions, that the more the Country is explored, the more it will rise in estimation, consequently, the greater might the revenue be to the Union."[96]

As Washington suggested, the surveys that created the grid and guaranteed clear titles had the further advantage of providing purchasers with valuable information about Congress's lands. Potential settlers would know what they were getting.

To assure that citizens of all parts of the union would have equal access to information about the western lands, the ordinance stipulated that each

---

[93] "More than probably," the western population "will be composed in a great degree of Foreigners" (Washington to Lee, Aug. 22, 1785, in Fitzpatrick, ed., *Washington Writings*, XXVIII, 231).

[94] Edward Carrington to Monroe, Aug. 7, 1787, in *Letters Cont. Cong.*, VIII, 631. See the discussion in Onuf, "Settlers, Settlements, and New States," in Jack P. Greene, ed., *The American Revolution: The Unfinished Agenda* (forthcoming).

[95] John R. Stilgoe emphasizes the artificiality of imposing "urban" forms on the western lands (*Common Landscape of America, 1580 to 1845* [New Haven, Conn., 1982], 99-107). Of course, this artificiality was the key to the transformation of land into property. For a stimulating essay on perceptions of the landscape, see Hildegard Binder Johnson, "Perceptions and Illustrations of the American Landscape in the Ohio Valley and the Midwest," in *This Land of Ours: The Acquisition and Disposition of the Public Domain* (Indianapolis, Ind., 1978), 1-38.

[96] Washington to Lee, Dec. 14, 1784, in Fitzpatrick, ed., *Washington Writings*, XVIII, 11. Washington told John Filson that "it has long been my wish to see an extensive and accurate map of the Western Territory . . . founded upon actual surveys and careful observations" (letter of Jan. 15, 1785, *ibid.*, 30).

state nominate a surveyor to join geographer Thomas Hutchins in the field. The result, according to the Connecticut delegates, would be to diffuse "as generally as possible thro' the States a knowledge of the Nature and Quality of the Country so that the Citizens in general may be enabled to make their Purchases with Judgment and Discretion."[97] The goal, William Grayson told Washington, was that "the Country . . . be settled out of the bowels of the Atlantic States," each state "contributing it's [sic] proportion of emigrants."[98] The surveyors would not only act as the eyes and ears of potential purchasers but would help produce accurate surveys that would supply information about tree types and soil fertility as well as potential routes to markets.

The connection between knowledge and land values was axiomatic. New Hampshire's delegates wrote home shortly after the passage of the ordinance, urging that associations be formed to purchase western lands. "The general opinion of the goodness of the soil in this western country . . . has been increasing with every new investigation of it," they reported.[99] Of course, this "goodness" was a function of the knowledge that such investigations produced. In this sense, the survey of the West would represent an investment by Congress: it would create value by producing knowledge.

The crucial question, then, was access to knowledge. Speculators stood to benefit from general ignorance. A few insiders would monopolize information, either by conducting their own investigations and surveys or by abuse of public office.[100] The lack of specific information would deter purchasers prepared to put their property to productive use, and depressed land values would enable speculators to accumulate vast holdings. Government-run surveys thus were essential for guaranteeing both the public interest in land sales and the fullest possible participation of private purchasers in the western land market.

Congressmen recognized that this was a critical moment for the government to define its role in opening and developing the West.[101] Unregulated expansion would play into the hands of speculators who would exploit their local situation and superior knowledge to engross the best lands. Settlement would be retarded. The new nation would forfeit a golden opportunity to discharge its war debts without burdening productive citizens with oppressive taxes. Open, competitive bidding—a true market situation—would be impossible. This was the ultimate problem for western policymakers. Only through the creation of a market in western

---

[97] Delegates to Gov. Matthew Griswold, May 27, 1785, in *Letters Cont. Cong.*, VIII, 124.

[98] Grayson to Washington, Apr. 15, 1785, *ibid.*, 96.

[99] Delegates to Pres. Meshech Weare, May 29, 1785, *ibid.*, 130-131.

[100] For apposite comments on the poor prospects for farmers, as opposed to speculators, under Pennsylvania's land system see "A Little Land Jobber," "A few Short Hints," *Freeman's Jour.*, Mar. 23, 1785.

[101] Pickering to Gerry, Mar. 1, 1785, in Pickering, ed., *Life of Pickering*, I, 504.

lands could the United States guarantee economic development and preserve their union. A regime of unchecked privatism characterized by lawless violence, squatting, and land speculation jeopardized the long-term interests of enterprising settlers as well as public revenue. The challenge was to direct private initiatives toward the public good. As Pelatiah Webster wrote in his 1782 essay on the western lands, the "secret art, the true spirit of financiering" is "so to graft the revenue on the public stock, so to unite and combine public and private interests, that they may mutually support, feed, and quicken each other."[102]

The 1785 land ordinance was Congress's answer to the practical and pressing question of how it would secure, organize, and distribute the new national domain. The immediate results were disappointing. Delays in implementing congressional land policy exposed the fragile character of the market the ordinance was supposed to call into existence: surveys were expensive and time-consuming; when lands were finally offered for auction, few buyers appeared.[103] The defense of the Ohio frontier against squatters and speculators, as well as Indians, imposed a further drain on the Treasury. Nonetheless, Congress did succeed in holding the line against unauthorized encroachments on the public lands, thus assuring that the promise of national prosperity and power would not be foreclosed.

But more than the future of the West was at stake in the formulation of national land policy. In attempting to determine the pace and direction of western development, Congress grappled with the problem of union itself. This was a time when deepening sectional conflict, notably over the navigation of the Mississippi, prompted widespread doubts about the survival of the union. Could sectional interests merge harmoniously in western expansion? Would the union of East and West survive? The land ordinance represented affirmative answers to these questions. Congressmen hoped that the rapid development of frontier lands and the spread of commercial connections across the continent would preserve and extend republican government in America.

In elaborating the development theme, political economists stretched republican ideology to its limits. Intersectional economic development would reward and promote private enterprise and provide the foundation of a durable union. Therefore, they concluded, the pursuit of private interest did not jeopardize republican virtue: without common interests grounded in commercial exchange the survival of the extended republic was inconceivable.

Not all congressmen shared the economists' boundless enthusiasm for

[102] Webster, "Essay on Western Lands," in his *Political Essays*, 499.

[103] Only 72,934 acres were sold at the first auction, held in New York in autumn 1787 (*American State Papers: Documents, Legislative and Executive of the Congress of the United States*, 38 vols. [Washington, D.C., 1832-1861], *Public Lands*, III, 459).

commerce and development. But the western problem compelled careful thought about the need for economic as well as political connections between new settlements and old states. Congress's program for westward expansion represented a vote of confidence—an act of faith—in the face of pervasive doubts about the future of the union. The dangers of disunion, anarchy, and underdevelopment figured prominently in discussions of the western lands, anticipating themes that would be repeated during the "critical period." Juxtaposed to the grandiose visions of the development theorists, such warnings reinforced the sense that the fulfillment of America's destiny in world history depended on union and that union depended on development. The alternatives were unthinkable.

SLAVERY AND THE NORTHWEST ORDINANCE: A STUDY IN AMBIGUITY

Paul Finkelman

For many antebellum northerners the Northwest Ordinance's prohibition of slavery was almost a sacred text. A young Salmon P. Chase, writing well before he gained fame as an antislavery lawyer, described Article VI as a "remarkable instrument . . . the last gift of the congress of the old confederation to the country . . . a fit consummation of their glorious labors." To an aging Edward Coles, the antislavery former governor of Illinois, the legislation appeared "marvellous" and showed "the profound wisdom of those who framed such an efficacious measure for our country." Coles contrasted the sectional tensions of the 1850s following the Kansas-Nebraska Act to an earlier period, when "the Territories subject to it [the ordinance] were quiet, happy, and prosperous." Coles believed that if American politicians had followed the pattern set by the ordinance the turmoil of the 1850s might have been avoided. For men like Chase and Coles the ordinance was responsible for the creation of the free states along the Ohio River. Without it many antebellum northerners believed the Midwest would have become a bastion of slavery.[1]

Mr. Finkelman is a member of the Department of History at the State University of New York at Binghamton. He would like to thank Peter Onuf and Robert McColley for their helpful comments. An earlier version of this article was read in February 1984 at the Claremont Institute conference, "A New Order of the Ages?"

[1] Salmon P. Chase, ed., *The Statutes of Ohio and of the Northwestern Territory* (3 vols., Cincinnati 1833-1835), I, 18; Edward Coles, *History of the Ordinance of 1787* (Philadelphia 1856), 32-33. Peter S. Onuf, "From Constitution to Higher Law: The Reinterpretation of the Northwest Ordinance," *Ohio History*, 94 (Winter-Spring 1985), 5-7, 31-33, discusses nineteenth century views of the ordinance. For one politician's views of the ordinance, see Abraham Lincoln's various speeches between 1854 and 1860 in Roy P. Basler, ed., *The Collected Works of Abraham Lincoln* (9 vols., New Brunswick, N.J. 1953-1955), especially Lincoln's speech at Cincinnati, Ohio, in September 1859, at III, 454-457. Post-Civil War historians also interpreted the or-

JOURNAL OF THE EARLY REPUBLIC. 6 (Winter 1986). © 1986 Society for Historians and the Early American Republic.

In spite of the praise that Article VI received in the nineteenth century, recent scholars have, for the most part, ignored it. Although Ulrich B. Phillips described it as "the first and last antislavery achievement by the central government" in this period, a careful examination of the provisions and its implementation suggests that it is unclear exactly what the article was intended to accomplish. At the time of its passage the ordinance did not threaten slavery in the South. It may even have strengthened slavery there. Nor did the ordinance immediately or directly affect slavery in the territory north of the Ohio River. Slavery continued in the region for decades. Thus in the nineteenth century usage of the term, the ordinance was not abolitionist and was only barely "antislavery."[2]

---

dinance in this way. See B.A. Hinsdale, *The Old Northwest* (New York 1888), 263, 273; Wager Swayne, *The Ordinance of 1787 and the War of 1861* (New York [1892?]); and William Frederick Poole, *The Ordinance of 1787, and Dr. Manasseh Cutler as an Agent in Its Formation* (Cambridge, Mass. 1876). During the Missouri Compromise debates southerners denied that the ordinance could in fact prevent any state from adopting slavery once that state was admitted into the union. Glover Moore, *The Missouri Controversy, 1819-1821* (Lexington 1953), 121-122.

Whether the ordinance actually prevented slavery in the Northwest from ultimately surviving is open to question. Robert McColley, *Slavery and Jeffersonian Virginia* (Urbana 1964), 181, argues that "What prevented the slaveholding planters from dominating Illinois, and possibly even Indiana, was, of all things, cotton." McColley suggests that cotton pulled slavery south, because that was where slavery was most profitable. This variation on the "natural limits" theory of slavery is persuasive as a partial explanation of why slavery did not expand into Illinois. Had it not been for political factors, however, it is likely that Illinois would have become a slave state in the 1820s.

[2] U. B. Phillips, *American Negro Slavery* (New York 1918), 128. For nineteenth century analyses, see George Bancroft, *History of the United States of America, From the Discovery of the Continent* (6 vols., New York 1883-1885), VI, 290; J.P. Dunn, Jr., *Indiana: A Redemption From Slavery* (Boston 1888), 177-218; and Poole, *The Ordinance of 1787.* See also Hinsdale, *The Old Northwest,* 276-277, for his statement that "No act of American legislation has called out more eloquent applause than the Ordinance of 1787. . . . In one respect it has a proud pre-eminence over all other acts on the American statute-books. It alone is known by the date of its enactment, and not by its subject-matter."

Recent historiography is striking for the lack of interest in the ordinance in general, and the slavery provision in particular. Since World War II no article in either the *Journal of American History* (originally the *Mississippi Valley Historical Review*) or the *William and Mary Quarterly* has focused on the ordinance. The indexes of these two journals reveal that the ordinance is mentioned in only seven *MVHR/JAH* articles and only three *WMQ* articles during this period. The slavery provision is discussed in passing in only one article: William Cohen, "Thomas Jefferson and the Problem of Slavery," *Journal of American History,* 56 (Dec. 1969), 511. In his attempt to rehabilitate the image of the Founding Fathers, William W. Freehling mentioned Article VI of the

Certainly it is unlikely that all those who voted for the ordinance saw the provision as antislavery. The congressmen from the Deep South who voted for it were not consciously undermining slavery. On the contrary, some of the slaveholders who voted for the legislation may have believed that Article VI actually strengthened slavery. The fact that the ordinance was specifically limited to the territory north of the Ohio seemed to imply that the territories south of the river were open to slavery. This assumption was strengthened by the fact that an attempt in 1784 to prohibit slavery in *all* the western territories after the year 1800 had been defeated.[3] Furthermore, the ordinance's fugitive slave clause offered protection to the slaveowners whose property might escape into the territory. Since the Articles of Confederation contained no such protection, and the Constitutional Convention had not yet added a similar clause to the proposed new compact, this was an important victory for slavery.[4]

---

ordinance but did not analyze it in "The Founding Fathers and Slavery," *American Historical Review*, 77 (Feb. 1972), 87-89, and Robert F. Berkhofer, Jr., in "Jefferson, the Ordinance of 1784, and the Origins of the American Territorial System," *William and Mary Quarterly*, 29 (Apr. 1972), 231-262, briefly mentions Jefferson's attempt to prohibit slavery in the national territories in 1784 but does not discuss the Ordinance of 1787. Similarly, Jack Ericson Eblen, *The First and Second United States Empires: Governors and Territorial Government, 1784-1912* (Pittsburgh 1968), says little about the slavery provision, and the same is true of Peter S. Onuf's excellent book, *The Origins of the Federal Republic: Jurisdictional Controversies in the United States, 1775-1787* (Philadelphia 1983). Article VI of the ordinance is dealt with at some length in Donald L. Robinson, *Slavery in the Structure of American Politics, 1765-1820* (New York 1971). The only important article of the last two decades devoted to the slavery provision is Staughton Lynd's "The Compromise of 1787," reprinted in Lynd, ed., *Class Conflict, Slavery, and the United States Constitution* (Indianapolis 1967), 185-213.

State historical society journals have shown more interest in the ordinance. See Onuf, "From Constitution to Higher Law"; Ray A. Billington, "The Historians of the Northwest Ordinance," *Journal of the Illinois State Historical Society*, 40 (Dec. 1947), 397-413, and J. David Griffin, "Historians and the Sixth Article of the Ordinance of 1787," *Ohio History*, 78 (Autumn 1969), 252-260. See also Phillip R. Shriver, "America's Other Bicentennial," *The Old Northwest*, 9 (Fall 1983), 219-235.

[3] This analysis was first suggested by Staughton Lynd in "The Compromise of 1787," 189-200, to explain why southerners supported the slavery prohibition. The clause may also have strengthened slavery in the South by preventing competition between the Ohio Valley and Virginia or Kentucky. This point is discussed in more detail below.

[4] The fugitive slave clause of the ordinance was the first important protection given to slavery by the national government. The Constitutional Convention did not consider a fugitive slave provision until August 28, a month and a half after the ordinance provided such protection for slaveowners. It is likely that the South Carolinians at the convention who demanded this clause got the idea for such a clause from the ordinance. Max Farrand, ed., *The Records of the Federal Convention of 1787* (4 vols.,

While the ordinance gave support to slavery in the South, it did not destroy slavery north of the Ohio. Article VI was not an emancipation proclamation for the Northwest. No slaves were freed immediately because of the ordinance. Neither it nor the state constitutions of the free states in the Northwest led to an immediate end to slavery throughout the area.

In the long run, of course, Article VI helped set the stage for the emergence of five free states in the region. By discouraging slaveowners from moving into the region, the ordinance helped create a white majority in the Northwest that was hostile to slavery. This proved especially crucial in Illinois, where the attempt to amend the Illinois Constitution of 1818 to allow slavery was barely defeated. Yet, even after the defeat of the proslavery forces, slavery lingered in Illinois for nearly thirty years.[5] Slavery lingered so long in the Northwest at least in part because the ordinance itself was ambiguous, internally inconsistent, and written by men who were uncertain of their own objectives.

An examination of the transition from slavery to liberty in the Northwest illustrates the ambivalence of the founding generation over slavery, the naiveté of the early opponents of the peculiar institution, the tenacity of slaveowners in maintaining control over their "servants," even when they lived in theoretically "free" jurisdictions, and the support for slavery expansion that existed in the early national period.[6] Finally, this examination illustrates the difficulty of ending

---

New Haven 1911), II, 443, 453-454. The vigorous defense of slavery by the Deep South delegates at the constitutional convention stands in contrast to the adoption of Article VI of the ordinance, if that article is seen as "antislavery." It is likely, however, that the Deep South delegates in Congress thought Article VI would protect slavery where it was and allow it to spread to the Southwest. Thus, they may have seen the article as proslavery, or at least as protective of slavery.

[5] For a discussion of this see Onuf, "From Constitution to Higher Law," 23-29.

[6] Cases throughout the antebellum period raised the problem that persons might be held as slaves in an area where slavery itself was prohibited. See Paul Finkelman, *An Imperfect Union: Slavery, Federalism, and Comity* (Chapel Hill 1981). The problem of enslavement without the sanction of law persists to this day. In *United States* v. *Mussry*, 726 F 2d 1448 (1984), a federal court in California ruled that the coercion necessary to produce slavery need not be physical, but could be a result of threats, especially if those enslaved were aliens unfamiliar with the laws of the United States. In *Mussry* the court allowed the prosecution for enslavement of persons who had enticed Indonesian aliens to the United States, then seized their passports and return airline tickets, and told the Indonesians that they would suffer terrible penalties if they tried to escape. Such a case illustrates the power of a "master" over illiterate minorities, be they Indonesians in late twentieth century California or "indentured servants" in late eighteenth century Indiana and Illinois.

an entrenched institution merely by constitutional dictates and without the support of legislative enactments and executive enforcement.

The failure of the ordinance and state constitutions to end slavery immediately has a fourfold explanation. First, Article VI was drafted quickly and accepted without debate. Such debate might have clarified its intent and the meaning of its various clauses. After Article VI was added the rest of the ordinance was not changed to provide internal consistency in the document. Thus, specific dictates of the ordinance protected some slavery in the area. For example, throughout the ordinance there are references to "free" inhabitants of the territory, indicating that "unfree" inhabitants might also be allowed to live there.

Second, slavery had a certain staying power—a power of inertia—which made eradication of the institution difficult. Slavery existed in the Northwest before the ordinance was enacted, and the mere passage of a law by a distant and virtually powerless Congress could hardly effect immediate change. Nor would a state constitution necessarily end slavery immediately. Notions of private property fundamental to the ideology of the American Revolution further strengthened existing slavery in the territory. Was it fair, asked men raised on Lockean concepts of "life, liberty, and property," to deprive one man of his property to give another his liberty? For example, in 1815 Pennsylvania's Chief Justice William Tilghman concluded that property was as important as liberty. In denying the freedom claim of the slave Peggy he wrote: "I know that freedom is to be favoured, but we have no right to favour it at the expense of property." Tilghman articulated an attitude prevalent throughout the legal community. Thus, perhaps it is not surprising that the Illinois Constitution of 1818 protected slavery and involuntary servitude and that until 1845 the Illinois Supreme Court was unwilling to free all the slaves (or their descendants) in that state.[7]

Third, the abolition of slavery in the Northwest Territory created serious conflict-of-laws questions. The three most important antebellum states in the area—Ohio, Indiana, and Illinois—shared long borders

---

[7] *Marchand v. Negro Peggy*, 2 Sergeant & Rawle 18 (1815). Holding Peggy to be a slave, Tilghman declared: "The only just mode of extirpating the small remains of slavery in the state, would be by purchasing the slaves at a reasonable price, and paying their owners out of the public treasury." *Ibid.*, 19. In *Jarrot (colored man)* v. *Jarrot*, 2 Gilman (Ill.) 1 (1845), the Illinois Supreme Court held that the descendants of slaves owned by the original settlers, born after Illinois statehood, were free. It is significant that the Illinois court used the year of statehood, 1818, and not the year of the ordinance, to determine freedom.

with slave states. These borders were demarcated by the two great river highways of the American interior, the Ohio and the Mississippi. Numerous masters traveling with their slaves on these waterways found it necessary or convenient to land on the free side of these rivers. In later years the National Road would begin in the slave state of Maryland, but pass through two northwestern states and terminate in a third. If these states did not allow transit with slaves then comity among the states and harmony within the union would be disrupted. On the other hand, to allow such transit would require the states to violate their own constitutional prohibitions of slavery. This was so because even slaves temporarily in a free state were, nevertheless, slaves. As lawyers in England had successfully argued in *Somerset* v. *Stewart*, and as antislavery lawyers and politicians would argue in the antebellum period, freedom was essentially indivisible. It was impossible to bring slaves into a free jurisdiction without bringing some or all of the attributes of a system of slavery with them. If the slave followed the master into a free territory or state, so would the whip, the chain, and the coercion of the master.[8]

Finally, there was a lack of will on the part of many local officials, as well as officials of the national government, to actually enforce the spirit, and perhaps the precise letter, of the ordinance. Many of those theoretically opposed to slavery (such as Thomas Jefferson), or ambivalent about it, were willing to allow the institution to survive in the Northwest on the theory that the diffusion of slaves throughout the nation would benefit both the slaves and the white population. This theory was supported by many slaveholding settlers in the territory who were also not anxious to see the ordinance implemented.

The Northwest Ordinance directly addressed slavery in its last article:

There shall be neither slavery nor involuntary servitude in the said territory, otherwise than in the punishment of crimes, whereof the party shall have been duly convicted: provided always, that any person escaping into the same, from whom labour or service is lawfully claimed in any one of the original states, such fugitive may be lawfully reclaimed,

---

[8] *Somerset* v. *Stewart*, Loft 1 (1772); 20 Howell State Trials 1 (1772). See also William M. Wiecek, *The Sources of Antislavery Constitutionalism in America, 1760-1848* (Ithaca 1977), 20-39. On the problems of slavery and the conflict of laws, see Finkelman, *An Imperfect Union*. For discussions of slavery in the North see arguments of counsel in *Commonwealth* v. *Aves*, 18 Pickering (Mass.) 193 (1836), and *Lemmon* v. *The People*, 20 New York 562 (1860).

and conveyed to the person claiming his or her labour or service as aforesaid.[9]

Such language, on its face, appears to be straightforward and conclusive. The words "there shall be neither slavery nor involuntary servitude" seem to mean that all slavery is prohibited in the territory and that the status of "slave" cannot be recognized by the laws of the territory. Yet this apparently conclusive language was partially compromised by the fugitive slave provision of the same article. The article gives no hint as to how a fugitive slave was to be treated in the territory. Could a master beat his fugitive with impunity? Might a master rape his female fugitive slave? What would be the status of the child of a fugitive born in the territory? These questions, and similar ones, suggest that slavery presented problems that might not be easily overcome by a single article in the ordinance.

The apparent simplicity of Article VI is further undermined by other provisions of the ordinance and by the circumstances of the drafting of Article VI itself. The ordinance initially consisted of fourteen sections that outlined how the territory was to be governed, and five "articles" that would "forever remain unalterable, unless by common consent."[10] This proposed ordinance, with no mention of slavery, was discussed intermittently between May 1786 and May 1787. In April and May 1787 the proposal received two favorable readings in the Congress. A third reading, set for May 10, was postponed, and by May 12 Congress lacked a quorum. When Congress resumed its deliberations in July a new committee was formed to finish work on the ordinance. On July 11 that committee reported the ordinance, which did not contain the slavery clause. On the 12th the ordinance was given a second reading and scheduled for a final vote the next day. Again, no mention of slavery was made in the ordinance or on the floor of the Congress. On July 13 Nathan Dane, a delegate from Massachusetts, proposed the addition of Article VI. This amendment was apparently accepted without debate or protest. The ordinance, with the slavery prohibition now added to it, passed by a unanimous vote of all the states present.[11]

---

[9] Clarence Edwin Carter, ed., *The Territorial Papers of the United States* (18 vols., Washington 1934-1952), II, 49.

[10] Northwest Ordinance, Sec. 14, *ibid.*

[11] *Journals of the Continental Congress, 1774-1789* (34 vols., Washington 1904-1937), XXXII, 281-283, 292, 313-320, 333-334. The only dissenting vote in Congress came from Abraham Yates of New York.

Historians have long puzzled over this chain of events. Although Nathan Dane drafted Article VI in committee, some have doubted that he really deserved credit for the famous provision. While this point remains unresolved, it is not as compelling as the questions surrounding why the southern majority then in the Congress so readily accepted the clause.[12] Staughton Lynd offered two explanations: that southerners expected the Northwest to be sympathetic to southern issues even if it had no slaves; and that the Northwest Ordinance tacitly implied that the Southwest would remain open to slavery. More recently Peter Onuf has endorsed this position.[13]

The notion that the ordinance implied that the territory south of the Ohio would remain open to slavery is also supported by an economic explanation of southern support for the ordinance first offered by William Grayson. Grayson, a Virginian on the congressional committee that had drafted the ordinance, wrote to James Monroe that the slavery prohibition "was agreed to by the Southern members for the purpose of preventing Tobacco and Indigo from being made" in the Northwest. The ordinance would thus prevent the Northwest from competing with the emerging Southwest. The fugitive slave clause in Article VI doubtless helped gain the votes of southerners, and may have in fact been the necessary element in obtaining their support for the ban on slavery.[14]

---

[12] The nineteenth century historians cited above sought to determine who deserved the credit for the ordinance in general and Article VI in particular. In an attempt to duck the issue George Bancroft wrote: "Thomas Jefferson first summoned Congress to prohibit slavery in all the territory of the United States; Rufus King lifted up the measure when it lay almost lifeless on the ground . . . a congress . . . headed by William Grayson, supported by Richard Henry Lee, and using Nathan Dane as scribe, carried the measure to the goal . . . ." *History of the United States*, VI, 290. At the time the ordinance was passed only one state present, Massachusetts, had ended slavery. The five southern states present—Delaware, Virginia, South Carolina, North Carolina, and Georgia—would retain slavery until the Civil War. The two remaining states, New York and New Jersey, would be the last northern states to take steps to end slavery, not doing so until 1799 and 1804 respectively.

[13] Lynd, "Compromise of 1787," 199; Onuf, *Origins of the Federal Republic*, 169-171. Lynd also argues that the South was anxious to pass the ordinance so that the American side of the Mississippi River would be quickly settled. Such a settlement would strengthen America's hand in negotiations with the Spanish for access to New Orleans. This would explain why southerners were anxious to have some bill for organizing the territory, but does not explain why southerners should have been willing to give up slavery in the area.

[14] William Grayson to James Monroe, Aug. 8, 1787, in Edmund C. Burnett, ed., *Letters of Members of the Continental Congress* (8 vols., Washington 1921-1936), VIII, 631-633. Grayson's argument suggests that Deep South congressmen may have sup-

There is, finally, one other possible reason for southern support of the ordinance with an article prohibiting slavery: the need to pass an ordinance that would satisfy Manasseh Cutler, the lobbyist for the New England investors who formed the Ohio Land Company.

The final impetus for passage of the ordinance, for both southern and northern congressmen, was the possibility of selling some five million acres of land to Cutler and his associates. In two letters written immediately after passage of the ordinance Richard Henry Lee asserted that it was passed as "preparatory to the sale of that Country [Ohio]." Lee noted that as soon as the ordinance was passed Congress turned "to consider of [sic] a proposition made for the purchase of 5 or 6 millions of Acres, in order to lessen the domestic debt."[15] Evidence of this sort led the nineteenth century historian William F. Poole to conclude that the "chief motive of the Southern members in voting unanimously for the Ordinance was doubtless to relieve the financial embarrassment of the government, and to bring the public lands into the market at the highest price." Poole further argued that the slavery prohibition was placed in the ordinance at the insistence of Manasseh Cutler, because Congress felt it must frame "an instrument which would be satisfactory to the party proposing to purchase these lands." Perhaps informed by the realities of Gilded Age politics, Poole saw the lobbyist for the land company as the most important actor on the scene.[16]

Cutler came to New York on July 6 to lobby for the right to purchase land for the Ohio Company. On the 10th he presented the committee with some suggestions for amendments to the ordinance, and then immediately left New York for Philadelphia. On the 13th the ordinance, with the slavery prohibition, was adopted.[17] It is unknown

---

ported Article VI because prohibiting slavery in the Northwest would lower the price of slaves in the Southeast and Southwest while Upper South congressmen supported the ordinance to avoid economic competition from north of the Ohio River. See also Peter Force, "The Ordinance of 1787, and Its History," in William Henry Smith, ed., *The St. Clair Papers: The Life and Public Services of Arthur St. Clair* (2 vols., Cincinnati 1882), II, 611-612.

[15] Richard Henry Lee to Francis Lightfoot Lee, July 14, 1787, in Burnett, ed., *Letters of Members*, VIII, 619-620; Richard Henry Lee to George Washington, July 15, 1787, *ibid*, 620.

[16] Poole, *The Ordinance of 1787*, 27, 26.

[17] *Ibid.*, 29; *Journals of the Continental Congress*, XXXII, 343. Eblen, *First and Second United States Empires*, 43n, denies that Cutler could have had any effect on the ordinance because "it is clear that by the time Cutler arrived in New York in 1787, there was nothing really new to be offered." However, Article VI, containing the slavery prohibition and the quite new fugitive slave provision, was in fact added to

if Cutler would have agreed to purchase Ohio lands if the ordinance
had not contained the prohibition of slavery. His known antipathy
to slavery suggests that he was instrumental in persuading the committee, and the Congress, to accept the clause.[18] On the other hand,
he apparently was willing to accept the version of the ordinance he
read on July 10, which did not include the slavery prohibition, because
he left New York immediately after giving his suggested amendments
to the committee. Had he been overwhelmingly concerned with the
fate of his suggestions Cutler probably would have stayed in New York
for the vote on the thirteenth. It is impossible to know if Cutler's proposed amendments even included the prohibition of slavery, because
his diary entry on this subject gives absolutely no indication of what
the amendments were.[19] Poole's assertion that Cutler was responsible
for the slavery prohibition is, then, subject to the Scotch verdict—not
proved. Poole seems more correct in his conclusion that the "Ordinance
of 1787 and the Ohio purchase were parts of one and the same transaction. The purchase *would* not have been made without the Ordinance,
and the Ordinance *could* not have been enacted except as an essential

---

the ordinance *after* Cutler left New York. Eblen is also confused about when Cutler
appeared in New York. He states that Cutler arrived in New York on May 9 (page
37), and predicates his analysis accordingly. Cutler, however, did not come to New
York until July 6.

[18] *Cf.* Jay A. Barrett, *Evolution of the Ordinance of 1787* (1891, rep. New York
1971), 74-77, who argues against Cutler's antislavery credentials on the basis of subsequent votes in the United States Congress.

[19] Cutler's son Ephraim recalled in a statement written after Cutler's death, that
Cutler had personally claimed to be the author of the slavery prohibition. William
Parker Cutler and Julia Perkins Cutler, *Life, Journals and Correspondence of Rev. Manasseh
Cutler, LL.D.* (2 vols., Cincinnati 1888), I, 343-344. This claim, or the memory of
it by his descendants, may be a function of nineteenth century filiopietism common
among the descendants of the revolutionary era patriots. Cutler himself left no written documentation to support his claim of authorship. Cutler's presence at the Congress is ambiguous. He arrived on July 6, wrote down some suggestions for amendments to the pending bill, and left on the 10th. On the 11th, after Cutler had left
New York, the bill, as read to the Congress, did not include the antislavery amendments. Not until the 13th, when the bill had its third and final reading, did the slavery
prohibition appear. See also Edmund Cody Burnett, *The Continental Congress* (New
York 1941), 685. On July 19 when Cutler saw the final bill, as passed, he noted
in his diary that all but one of his suggestions had been accepted. At no time, however,
did Cutler indicate in his diary, or a letter, what those suggestions were. *Life, Journals
and Correspondence of Rev. Manasseh Cutler*, I, 230, 242, 293. The reliability of the printed
version of Cutler's journals has also been questioned, although not on this point.
Lee Nathaniel Newcomer, "Manasseh Cutler's Writings: A Note on Editorial Practice," *Mississippi Valley Historical Review*, 47 (June 1960), 88-101.

condition of the purchase.''[20] As noted above, the ordinance, in some form, had been under consideration since at least 1785.[21] It is likely that a version of the ordinance would have passed, sooner or later. But the evidence does suggest that Cutler's lobbying and the interest of the Massachusetts land speculators in purchasing land in Ohio did spur the Congress to act.

In the final analysis it may not matter who proposed Article VI, whether Cutler's lobbying made it possible, or why Congress enacted the ordinance when it did. What is important is that the history of the ordinance shows (1) that there was virtually no debate over the slavery provision; (2) that it was added at the last possible moment, without careful consideration; (3) that the rest of the ordinance was not redrafted to make it consistent with Article VI; and (4) that although the language of Article VI meant that slavery could not exist in the territory (except for fugitives), it is unlikely that the southern majority which passed the ordinance understood the article to mean this.

Whatever the reasons were, the prohibition of slavery was added to the ordinance at the eleventh hour. This was, of course, not the first time that a prohibition on slavery in the territories had been considered. In 1784 Jefferson had proposed the prohibition of slavery in *all* the national territories after 1800. It is difficult to imagine how Jefferson's proposal would have worked, had it been accepted; by 1800 some of the territories probably would have had large slave populations and politically powerful masters who would have worked to undermine the Ordinance of 1784, had it included Jefferson's prohibition. With no enforcement clause it is almost impossible to imagine a territorial or state legislature voluntarily ending slavery after the institution had been allowed to grow until 1800. There is no indication that anyone at the time considered or discussed how the proposal might have been implemented. Whatever enforcement problems Jefferson's clause might have caused were mooted when Congress defeated the proposal with strong and vocal opposition from the southern states.[22]

---

[20] Poole, *The Ordinance of 1787*, 31.

[21] Berkhofer, "Jefferson, the Ordinance of 1784, and the Origins of the American Territorial System"; Onuf, *Origins of the Federal Republic*, ch. 7.

[22] Berkhofer, "Jefferson, the Ordinance of 1784, and the Origins of the American Territorial System," discusses the defeat of Jefferson's prohibition on slavery. No one, as far as I know, discusses the potential enforcement problems of Jefferson's proposal. William Cohen, "Thomas Jefferson and the Problem of Slavery," 511, notes that under Jefferson's proposal "bondage would have been legal in the area for sixteen years; and it seems likely that, if the institution of slavery had been allowed to get a foothold in the territory, the prohibition would have been repealed."

In 1785 Rufus King proposed a similar provision, but it too was defeated without debate. Nor was the slavery prohibition debated in 1787. Nathan Dane, King's successor in Congress, also wanted slavery prohibited, but he initially excluded such a provision from the ordinance because he thought the attempt would be futile. Why it did pass is unclear. When the last minute amendment was accepted with apparently no discussion and little comment, Dane could offer no explanation. He wrote Rufus King that he "had no idea the States would agree to the sixth article, prohibiting slavery, as only Massachusetts of the Eastern States, was present," and thus he "omitted it" from the draft; "but finding the House favorably disposed on the subject, after we had completed the other parts, I moved the article, which was agreed to without opposition." No one in the Congress seemed to think this clause was extraordinary. Dane's comments on it in his letter to King were immediately followed by a discussion of what seemed to matter most to Dane, King, and Cutler: the purchase of land in Ohio. Besides Dane, only William Grayson, another member of the committee, commented on the slavery prohibition in any existing letter. The lack of debate on the article or comment on it by members of Congress, especially the many southerners present, suggests that the clause was not considered particularly important.[23]

The lack of debate on the clause, and the fact that it was tacked on to the document at the last moment, explains why the rest of the ordinance conflicts with the famed Article VI. Throughout the ordinance there are indirect references to slavery. Section 2 provides that "the French and Canadian inhabitants, and other settlers of the Kaska[s]kies, St. Vincent's, and the neighbouring villages, who have heretofore pro-

---

According to Merrill D. Peterson, the Ordinance of 1784 ultimately proved to be "ineffectual." *Thomas Jefferson and the New Nation* (New York 1970), 283. Thus, it is likely that even if Jefferson's slavery prohibition had been enacted it never would have been implemented.

[23] Nathan Dane to Rufus King, July 16, 1787, in Burnett, ed., *Letters of Members*, VIII, 621-622. The editors of the forthcoming edition of the letters of members of the Continental Congress at the Library of Congress have been kind enough to share their materials for this period. Except for the letters cited in notes 14, 15, and 23, there are no existing letters indicating that anyone in the Congress even mentioned the slavery prohibition in his correspondence. This in part may undermine Lynd's theory of concerted effort between the convention and the Congress. Manasseh Cutler could not have brought news of the slavery prohibition to the convention because he did not find out the exact wording of the ordinance until July 19. Of the sixteen letters written to or from southern congressmen in the month following the passage of the ordinance, only the Grayson letter cited in note 14 mentioned the slavery provision. *Ibid.*, VIII, 619-639.

fessed themselves citizens of Virginia [may retain] their laws and customs now in force among them, relative to the descent and conveyance of property." The main purpose of this clause was to allow the French settlers to follow French inheritance practices, rather than Anglo-American ones. Much of the property to be inherited, however, was slave property, and it is reasonable to believe that this "property" could still be conveyed through sales and passed on through wills. Much litigation in Missouri and Illinois would eventually focus on the status of the slaves owned by these early settlers of the Northwest.[24]

Article II of the ordinance provided protection for all private property, and required compensation for private property taken for the public good. Did Article VI provide an exception to Article II where slave property was concerned? Article II also provided that the territorial government could never pass legislation which would "interfere with, or affect private contracts or engagements, bona fide, and without fraud previously formed." It would not be farfetched to argue, as many slaveowners would, that slave property purchased or acquired before 1787 could not be taken—or freed—without compensation to the master, and that contracts for the purchase, sale, or rent of slaves, made before 1787, were still enforceable in the territory. Such an argument would ultimately be made by Chief Justice Taney in Dred Scott v. Sandford.[25] While Taney's notions of substantive due process may have been inapplicable for the introduction of slavery into a totally unsettled territory, the concept seems somewhat more reasonable for slaves already present in a territory when the federal government extended its jurisdiction over the area.

Another problem for the application of the slavery prohibition in Article VI is that in other places the ordinance refers to "free male

---

[24] For example, in Missouri see Merry v. Tiffin and Menard, 1 Mo. 725 (1827); Theoteste v. Chouteau, 2 Mo. 144 (1829); Nancy v. Trammel, 3 Mo. 306 (1836); Chouteau and Keizer v. Hope, 7 Mo. 428 (1842); Chouteau v. Pierre (of Color), 9 Mo. 3 (1845); and Charlotte (of Color) v. Chouteau, 11 Mo. 193 (1847), reargued at 21 Mo. 590 (1855), 25 Mo. 465 (1857), and 33 Mo. 194 (1862). In Illinois the leading case is Jarrot v. Jarrot, 2 Gilman 1 (1845). A number of other Illinois cases involved slaves brought into the Illinois territory after 1787 by the French settlers: Boon v. Juliet, 1 Scammon 258 (1836); Choisser v. Hargrave, 1 Scammon 317 (1836); and Borders v. Borders, 4 Scammon 341 (1843). Apparently a number of cases involving the "French" slaves went unreported. Roger D. Bridges, ed., "John Mason Peck on Illinois Slavery," Journal of the Illinois State Historical Society, 75 (Autumn 1982), 201. Slaves brought to Illinois before 1787 were referred to as "French" slaves even if they were owned by Anglo-Americans.

[25] 19 Howard (U.S.) 393 (1857). See also Don E. Fehrenbacher, The Dred Scott Case: Its Significance in American Law and Politics (New York 1978), passim.

inhabitants'' (Section 9) and "free inhabitants'' (Article II). Until Article VI was added at the very last moment, there was no doubt that slavery would be perfectly legal in the area. But, when Article VI was added and the rest of the ordinance was not rewritten, the document contained logical and linguistic contradictions. If there were "free inhabitants'' then there must also have been "unfree'' inhabitants. This language suggests that the congressmen who initially wrote the ordinance expected slaves to be there,[26] and that after Article VI was added they made no effort to insure that the rest of the language conformed with the new article. Had they done so, the sweeping language of Article VI might have been debated and clarified. Without such clarification and redrafting, the entire ordinance remained at odds with Article VI. These inconsistencies would enable slaveowners in the area to argue that their property rights had not been affected by Article VI.

Finally, Article IV of the ordinance provided for free navigation of the "waters leading into the Mississippi and St. Lawrence, and the carrying places between the same'' for all Americans.[27] It is doubtful if the congressmen from the southern states, as well as the representatives from such slave states as New York and New Jersey,[28] who

---

[26] It is unlikely that the congressmen were making a distinction between indentured servants and others when they used the term "free inhabitants.'' For one thing, indentured servants, like apprentices, were usually considered "free,'' even though they might be under some sort of long term contract. This is clearly the understanding of the Constitution's three-fifths clause (Article I, Section 2). The Articles of Confederation are less clear on this issue. Article IV talks about "the free inhabitants of each of these states'' and excludes "paupers, vagabonds, and fugitives from justice.'' It seems likely that this clause included indentured persons as "free inhabitants.'' Article IX of the Articles of Confederation allocates quotas for military enlistments based on ":the number of white inhabitants.'' This certainly included white indentured servants. In a strictly legal sense indentured servants were free persons who *voluntarily* contracted to serve someone for a term of years. As such they were not in "involuntary servitude.''

[27] In *State* v. *Hoppess*, 2 Western Law Journal 279 (1845), Judge Nathaniel Read of the Ohio Supreme Court refused to free a slave whose master voluntarily allowed him to leave a boat that was temporarily docked in Cincinnati. Read believed that the Ohio River and its wharves were open to unrestricted transit for all Americans, including masters traveling with their slaves. Finkelman, *An Imperfect Union*, 167-172.

[28] New York did not take steps to end slavery until 1799. "An Act for the gradual abolition of slavery,'' *New York Laws, 1799*, ch. LXII. New Jersey did not act until 1804. "An Act for the gradual abolition of slavery,'' *New Jersey Session Laws, 1804*, 251. In 1787 there was no indication that New York or New Jersey would end slavery in the near future. See Arthur Zilversmit, *The First Emancipation: The Abolition of Slavery in the North* (Chicago 1967). James Madison told the Virginia ratifying convention in 1788 that these two states "would, probably, oppose any attempts to annihilate

voted for the ordinance, understood it to mean that they could not take their slaves with them when traveling on the important inland water routes of the United States.

Despite the intentions of Dane and others to guarantee that the Northwest would be "free soil," Article VI of the ordinance was ill-suited to the task of ending slavery in the Northwest Territory. It contained no enforcement clause, as would the Civil War amendments to the United States Constitution. The article did not indicate what organ of government—the territorial governor, the territorial judiciary, the territorial legislature (which would not be formed until the territory's voting population reached five thousand), or the national Congress—would take action to end slavery.

Since an end to slavery would require an innovative change in public policy and social institutions, some governmental intervention was necessary. In its failure to provide a mechanism for enforcement Article VI must be compared and contrasted to other parts of the ordinance. Article III, for example, declared that "schools and the means of education shall forever be encouraged." But it neither required that schools be built nor did it provide an enforcement mechanism. In this way Article III and Article VI are similar. But the substance of the articles was so different that in one an enforcement mechanism was unnecessary while in the other it was vital.

A requirement that schools be built, or a declaration of what governmental body should do so, was unnecessary because for more than a century public schools had been built by local communities in America. Americans knew what schools were and knew how to build them. But few Americans had any experience with dismantling an entrenched social system that provided wealth for those who had political power at the expense of those who lacked all power. The education clause could be implemented by those who would benefit from the clause. But those people who would most directly benefit from Article VI were prohibited from participating in the political process, and thus could not insure the implementation of the article. Finally, both the creation of public schools and the abolition of slavery would have financial costs. While the Ordinance of 1787 provided no funds for either object, the Land Ordinance of 1785 had provided that one section in each township would be reserved "for the maintenance of public

---

this species of property" because they "had made no attempt, or taken any step, to take them from the people." Jonathan Elliot, ed., *Debates in the Several State Conventions on the Adoption of the Federal Constitution* (2nd ed., 5 vols., Philadelphia 1888), V, 459.

schools, within the said township."[29] Thus, the national government had committed financial resources to the education provisions of Article III but not to the prohibition of slavery required by Article VI.

Article III also dealt with Indians, admonishing the settlers to treat them fairly and not take their property without their consent. Unlike slaves, the Indians were in a position to defend their property rights, either in court or on the battlefield. Indeed, as Peter Onuf has recently noted, "emigration to the Northwest [was] . . . sluggish . . . because it took so long to pacify the Indian frontier." The settlers knew that peaceful relations with the Indians might be maintained if this provision of Article III were carried out. Thus, this part of the ordinance could be enforced. Just to make sure, however, Article III also explicitly reserved for Congress the right to declare war and explicitly directed that "laws founded in justice and humanity" would "be made" to protect Indian rights. The policy towards Indians was clear: either the settlers would observe "good faith" towards the Indians or the Congress would intervene.[30] No such threat of intervention existed for Article VI. Nor were the settlers in the territory even admonished to treat the slavery prohibition with "good faith."

The slavery prohibition compared unfavorably to both the education and the Indian provisions of Article III. Those who would benefit most from Article VI lacked the political power to implement it, the legal rights or support to enforce it in court, or the military might to fight for it on the battlefield. Neither the Congress nor the territorial government was directed to pass any enforcement legislation. Moreover, those in the territory who had the power to implement the slavery prohibition were the men least likely to do so.

---

[29] "An Ordinance for ascertaining the mode of disposing of Lands in the Western Territory," Act of May 20, 1785, *Journals of the Continental Congress*, XXVIII, 375-381, quotation, 378.

[30] Onuf, "From Constitution to Higher Law," 19. Article II of the ordinance protected such civil liberties as access to the writ of habeas corpus, jury trial, and bail while prohibiting "cruel or unusual punishments," excessive fines, and the taking of property without legal authority or just compensation. These protections could be enforced by the people of the territory through their elected representatives, through petitions to Congress, or by appeals to courts when they were created. With the exception of initiating legal action, slaves in the territory had no way to vindicate their rights. Initiating legal action was made more difficult by the low level of literacy among slaves, their lack of mobility, their lack of money to hire counsel, and laws that prohibited them from testifying against whites. A comparison between Articles II and VI suggests that granting constitutional rights to people is only effective if those people have the power, resources, and liberty to protect their rights.

The ordinance is worth reading and studying as an example of *how not to* draft a statute. It serves to remind legislators, lawyers, and jurists that hastily drafted and poorly planned amendments to legislation, added at the last minute, may not accomplish what their authors wish. Besides not giving any indication how the slavery prohibition was to be enforced, the framers of the ordinance did not resolve the internal contradictions created by Article VI. Thus, its meaning was left to whoever held power in the territory. Had there been a full-fledged debate over Article VI a clearer sense of its meaning might have emerged. In such a debate someone might have asked if the ordinance was meant to free the slaves then living in the territory. Similarly, a debate over Article VI might have clarified the status of the children of slaves in the region. Something modeled along Pennsylvania's gradual emancipation statute might have emerged, which would have specified the status of the existing slaves, their children, and any slaves brought into the territory, either as transients, sojourners, or residents. The ordinance was passed, however, when there were no delegates present from Pennsylvania, Rhode Island, or Connecticut, where gradual emancipation statutes already existed.[31] In fact, all of the delegates who voted for the ordinance came from states where emancipation had never been a political issue. Thus, the exact meaning of Article VI, and how it was to be implemented, was not debated and remained in doubt.[32]

In another context, the ordinance can be seen as an example of the tension between liberty and property inherent in revolutionary America. The "self-evident" truths of the Declaration of Independence—"that all men are created equal," and are endowed with the rights to "Life, Liberty and the pursuit of Happiness"— were, of course, written by a man who owned nearly two hundred

---

[31] "An Act for the Gradual Abolition of Slavery," *Pennsylvania Acts, 1780*; "An Act authorizing the manumission of negroes, mulattoes, and others, and for the gradual abolition of slavery," *Rhode Island Laws, 1784*; "An Act concerning Indian, mulatto, and negro servants and slaves," *Connecticut Laws, 1784*.

[32] Massachusetts had abolished slavery through its constitution and judicial decisions. Emancipation had been a political issue in Massachusetts only to the extent that the 1778 Massachusetts constitution did not have a free and equal clause and because it discriminated against blacks. Willi Paul Adams, *The First American Constitutions: Republican Ideology and the Making of State Constitutions in the Revolutionary Era* (Chapel Hill 1980), 184. However, to be charitable to Dane and others, when dealing with great social issues—with such monumental questions as human freedom—it may be better to pass what legislation you can, when you can, than to wait until something better can be accomplished at a later date.

slaves. There were numerous slaveowners in the Continental Congress and at the Constitutional Convention. Many of those who struggled against "enslavement" by King George III apparently had few scruples about enslaving others.[33]

Over the years "The Ordinance has become a symbol of the Revolution's liberalism" towards race, at least in part, because it was the only important act by the national government under the Articles of Confederation that indicated disapproval for the peculiar institution.[34] During the revolution Samuel Johnson chided the rebellious colonists by asking, "How is it that we hear the loudest *yelps* for liberty among the drivers of negroes?"[35] Unfortunately, there were no comfortable answers to the question. The American revolutionaries were trapped in an ideology of private property that made it almost impossible for them collectively to give up their own pursuit of happiness for the liberty of others.[36] In the ordinance the ideals of liberty came into conflict with the selfish happiness of the ruling race. Thus, the Congress could easily declare there would be no slavery in the Northwest Territory. It was quite another matter to eliminate the institution there.

Whatever it was supposed to accomplish, Article VI had little immediate impact on the legal status of slaves in the area that would become the states of Indiana and Illinois, where the bulk of the slaves in the territory lived.[37] This area had been French until 1763, when

---

[33] On the use of the term "slavery" in the rhetoric of the revolution, see Bernard Bailyn, *The Ideological Origins of the American Revolution* (Cambridge 1967), esp. ch. 6.

[34] Lynd, "The Compromise of 1787," 186. The only other obvious victories for "liberty" were the constitutional and statutory abolition of slavery in the North (see Zilversmit, *The First Emancipation*) and the Virginia manumission statute of 1782, "An act to authorize manumission of slaves," 11 Hening *Statutes of Virginia* 39, act of May 1782. For a different view see Freehling, "The Founding Fathers and Slavery."

[35] Quoted in Robinson, *Slavery in the Structure of American Politics*, 80.

[36] Linda Grant DePauw has demonstrated that very few Americans in the revolutionary period had the liberty to pursue happiness. Women, minors, propertyless white adult males, free blacks, and of course slaves faced numerous legal restrictions that limited their opportunities and rights. "Land of the Unfree: Legal Limitations on Liberty in Pre-Revolutionary America," *Maryland Historical Magazine*, 68 (Winter 1973), 355-368. Both the ordinances of 1784 and 1787 provided for universal adult male suffrage, although there is no record that free blacks were in fact allowed to vote in the Northwest.

[37] While population figures for this period are unreliable, all evidence indicates that nearly all the slaves in the Northwest lived in what would become Indiana and Illinois. All of the petitions to Congress in favor of allowing slavery in the Northwest came from that area. There were no doubt a few, but very few, slaves in what would

Britain took possession through the Peace of Paris. This treaty guaranteed the property rights of the original French settlers. In 1779 the Northwest was seized by George Rogers Clark, whose home state of Virginia claimed the area under its charter of 1609. Other states also claimed the territory under their charters. Although Virginia never intended to govern the area indefinitely, for a number of political reasons Virginia continued to assert authority over the area until it was ceded to the national government in 1784. Virginia's act of cession transferred possession of the area to the United States government but also protected the property rights of the residents of the territory. When the territory came into the hands of the United States, slaveowners were living there and the national government was obligated to protect their property.[38]

Although the ordinance contained no enforcement mechanism, and would in fact remain unenforced for many years, it nevertheless troubled the slaveowners living in the territory. The Franco-American slaveowners, coming out of a civil law tradition, may have believed that the ordinance was self-enforcing, or would be enforced by the national government.[39] Thus, shortly after the ordinance was adopted, various settlers in the area that later became Indiana and Illinois appointed Barthelemi Tardiveau as their agent to lobby Congress on matters involving land titles and other matters of concern to the Northwest. In July 1788 Tardiveau petitioned Congress "By order & in behalf of the french [sic] inhabitants of the Illinois [Country]." The petition asked Congress to secure certain land titles, reimburse the settlers for goods impressed by American soldiers, and to protect the rights of the French settlers in other ways. The last part of the petition noted:

There is in an Ordinance of Congress, an Ex post facto law . . . which declares that Slavery Shall not take place in the Western territory. Many

---

become the states of Ohio and Michigan. N. Dwight Harris, *The History of Negro Servitude in Illinois* (Chicago 1904); Emma Lou Thornbrough, *The Negro in Indiana: A Study of a Minority* (Indianapolis 1957).

[38] See Onuf, *Origins of the Federal Republic*, 75-77; William M. Malloy, ed., *Treaties, Conventions, International Acts, Protocols, and Agreements Between the United States of America and Other Powers, 1776-1937* (4 vols., Washington 1910-1938), I, 586; and "An act to authorize the delegates of this state in congress, to convey to the United States, in congress assembled, all the rights of this commonwealth to the territory north westward of the river Ohio," 11 Hening *Statutes of Virginia* 326.

[39] Little is written on the transition from civil law to common law in areas north of the present state of Louisiana. One excellent beginning is Morris S. Arnold, *Unequal Laws Unto a Savage Race: European Legal Traditions in Arkansas, 1686-1836* (Fayetteville 1985).

of the inhabitants of these districts have Slaves, and Some have no other property but Slaves. If they wish to preserve their property, they must transport themselves to the Spanish Side of the Mississipi [sic]; but if they do, they Shall lose the lands granted them by Congress. One law tells them: leave the country, or ye Shall forfeit your negroes: the other Saith; Stay in the country, or your lands shall be taken from ye.[40]

The French settlers hoped Congress would resolve their dilemma by allowing them to keep their slaves in the territory and thus hold on to their lands as well. When this request received no action Tardiveau presented a second petition that requested Congress either to modify the slavery prohibition of the ordinance or to "abrogate that part of their Resolve which binds them to a three years residence in the country in order to be entitled to the property of the lands granted them." Once again Tardiveau asserted that the slavery prohibition of the ordinance "operates as an Ex post facto law."[41]

The settlers of the Illinois Country believed the ordinance violated their property rights. The emancipation of slaves could not technically be considered an *ex post facto* law,[42] but the assertion that the ordinance was such a law underscored the popular hostility to it. *Ex post facto* laws symbolized tyranny and oppression; they were also simply bad policy. It was against such arbitrary lawmaking that the revolution was fought. The new national Constitution would prohibit such laws in the United States. The message from Tardiveau and the other French settlers was clear: by destroying property rights in slaves the Congress was violating its revolutionary commitment to fair government and the protection of private property. Justice and human liberty were not an issue for the slaveowners of the Northwest.

For many of those living in the Illinois Country the new United States was simply another "government." Since 1763 the area had been ruled by France, Great Britain, and Virginia. Certainly the settlers could not have felt great attachment for the United States. The

---

[40] "Memorial of Barthelemi Tardiveau, July 8, 1788," in Clarence W. Alvord, ed., *Kaskaskia Records, 1778-1790* (Springfield, Ill. 1909), 485-488. See also Arthur C. Boggess, *The Settlement of Illinois, 1778-1830* (1908, rep. Freeport, N.Y. 1970), 50-53.

[41] "Memorial of Barthelemi Tardiveau, September 17, 1788," in Alvord, ed., *Kaskaskia Records,* 491-493.

[42] An *ex post facto* law makes conduct criminal (or changes the punishment or penalty for such conduct, or the rules of evidence to prove such conduct) subsequent to the conduct. Since the holding of slaves was not made criminal under the ordinance, Article VI could not be considered an *ex post facto* law. The taking of property by the state, or altering the nature of property by the state, has never been considered *ex post facto* legislation.

revolution had not been *their* revolution. Thus, when the Congress failed to respond positively to their petitions many of the French settlers voted with their feet. In July 1789 Major John Hamtramck reported that "the King [of Spain] has permitted to the inhabitants living on the American side to settle themselves" in the Spanish territory west of the Mississippi. A few weeks later he noted that "A number of people had gone & were about going from the Illinois to the Spanish Side, in consequence of a resolve of Congress respecting negroes, who . . . were to be free."[43]

Tardiveau could not blame the slaveholding settlers for leaving. He explained to Governor Arthur St. Clair that "the wretched inhabitants of Illinois, who had seen themselves for ten years neglected by that [national] power from which alone they could expect protection, now found that the very first act of attention paid to them pronounced their utter ruin." With the passage of the ordinance "many aggravating circumstances rumored that the very moment" the territorial governor arrived "all their slaves would be set free." Thus, a "panic seized upon their minds" and the wealthiest settlers sought "from the Spanish Government that security which they conceived was refused to them" by the United States.[44]

Those slaveowners who remained in the Northwest Territory quickly discovered that the words of the ordinance were much like the words of the Declaration of Independence. They sounded idealistic but had little force. Although the Congress refused to modify the ordinance along the lines suggested by Tardiveau's petitions, neither did the Congress take any steps to see that the ordinance was implemented. Indeed, Tardiveau explained to St. Clair that he had failed to pressure Congress for a definitive answer to his memorial because "it was needless" and he had already "troubled that body with a number of petitions." Tardiveau assured St. Clair that certain unnamed "gentlemen" in Congress "remarked that the intention of the obnoxious resolution had been solely to prevent the future importation of slaves into the Federal country; that it was not meant to affect the rights of the ancient inhabitants." Tardiveau wanted St. Clair to convey this information to the settlers in the territory. In addition to informing St. Clair of this interpretation of the ordinance, in the summer of 1789 Tardiveau wrote friends in Illinois that "the resolve of

---

⁴³ Major John Hamtramck to General Josiah Harmar, July 29, Aug. 14, 1789, in Alvord, ed., *Kaskaskia Records*, 506-508, 508-509.

⁴⁴ Tardiveau to St. Clair, June 30, 1789, in Smith, ed., *St. Clair Papers*, II, 117-118.

Congress respecting the Slavery of this Country was not intended to extend to the negroes of the old French inhabitants.'' Major Hamtramck "immediately published" this information in an effort to stem the tide of emigration from the Northwest.[45]

Tardiveau was not entirely correct in his assessment of congressional intent. Congress had in fact made no dispositive interpretation of Article VI of the ordinance. Rather, Tardiveau's petitions had been referred to a committee made up of Abraham Clark of New Jersey, Hugh Williamson of North Carolina, and James Madison of Virginia. This committee of slave state congressmen offered a resolution which declared that the

> Ordinance for the government of the Western territory, shall not be construed to deprive the Inhabitants of Kaskaskies Illinois[,] Post St. Vincents and the other Villages formerly settled by the French and Canadians, of their Right and property in Negro or other Slaves which they were possessed of at the time of passing the said Ordinance, or in any manner to Manumit or Set free any such negroes or other persons under Servitude within any part of sd. Western territory; any thing in the said Ordinance to the contrary notwithstanding.[46]

This proposed resolution was never brought before the Congress for debate or a vote. Therefore, it could not really be said to explain congressional intent. At best it indicated what some men in Congress believed to be the best application of the ordinance. As the new Constitution of the United States went into effect, the meaning of the ordinance, passed under the old Articles of Confederation, remained unclear.

On another level, however, this committee report is a significant indication of sentiment on the issue. The report suggests how truly *uncommitted* the Founders were to ending slavery. James Madison's presence on this committee is particularly revealing. On the eve of the adoption of the Constitution the "father" of that document was unwilling to interpret the ordinance in an antislavery light, despite language in it which would have supported such an interpretation.

---

[45] *Ibid*; Hamtramck to Harmar, Aug. 14, 1789, in Alvord, ed., *Kaskaskia Records*, 508-509.

[46] *Journals of the Continental Congress*, XXXIV, 540-543, quotation, 541. Tardiveau wrote Governor St. Clair that privately a number of congressmen "remarked that the intention of the obnoxious resolution had been solely to prevent the future importation of slaves into the Federal country; that it was not meant to affect the rights of the ancient inhabitants." Tardiveau to St. Clair, June 30, 1789, in Smith, ed., *St. Clair Papers*, II, 117-118.

Although intellectually opposed to slavery, when given the opportunity Madison was unwilling to take any concrete steps to abolish it in one corner of the country where it was relatively weak. If Madison could not take a stronger position on liberating the slaves in the Northwest, then it is perhaps understandable that others of the founding generation failed to confront the problem of slavery where the institution was more entrenched and the number of slaves was greater.[47]

The committee report seemed to distort the plain meaning of the ordinance. The committee urged the Congress to "construe" it to mean that slaves living in the territory were not in fact emancipated, and that the French inhabitants (and by this time a good number of Anglo-American inhabitants as well) would not be deprived of their property. Slaveowners throughout the nation assumed that their property right in slaves included a right to the children of their female slaves. Thus, the committee report implied some sort of perpetual slavery for the descendants of those slaves living in the territory in 1787, in spite of the ordinance. The committee asked Congress to accept this construction, "any thing in the said Ordinance to the contrary notwithstanding." Such a statement implies that the committee felt the language of the ordinance was "to the contrary" and that the proffered construction violated the plain meaning of the clause.

Like the congressional committee, territorial Governor Arthur St. Clair had no interest in interfering in the master-slave relations of those he governed. Despite the language of the ordinance, the governor saw no reason to take action to end slavery. In 1790 he reported to President Washington that settlers were still moving west of the Mississippi to protect their slave property. To help stop this depopulation St. Clair told the president:

I have thought proper to explain the Article respecting Slaves as a prohibition to any future introduction of them, but not to extend to the liberation of those the People were already possessed of, and accquired

---

[47] At the Constitutional Convention Madison was also unwilling to confront the problem of slavery in the new republic. The most striking example of this was Madison's support of the electoral college. Madison told the Philadelphia Convention that he thought "the people at large" were "the fittest" to choose the president, but he supported the electoral college scheme because otherwise "the Southern States . . . could have no influence in the election on the score of the Negroes." Farrand, ed., *Records of the Convention*, II, 56-57. Madison's role in protecting slavery at the convention is discussed at length in Paul Finkelman, "Slavery and the Constitutional Convention: Making a Covenant with Death," in Richard Beeman *et al.*, eds., *Beyond the Confederation: Origins of the Constitution and American National Identity* (Chapel Hill 1986), 188-225.

[*sic*] under the Sanction of the Laws they were subject, at the same
time I have given them to understand that Steps would probably be
taken for the gradual Abolition of Slavery, with which they seem perfectly satisfied.[48]

This interpretation assumed that the ordinance was only a directive
to the territorial authorities, and that without further legislation slavery
might continue. St. Clair was concerned, however, about satisfying
the desires of his white, slaveholding constituency, and not with any
rights slaves might have under the ordinance. There is no extant record
that anyone in the new national government challenged St. Clair's
interpretation, perhaps because Washington and his cabinet agreed
with it.

A year later, however, St. Clair revealed to Secretary of State
Thomas Jefferson that neither he nor his constituents were happy with
his earlier interpretation of the ordinance. His initial understanding
would prevent the return of those slaveholders who had fled to the
Spanish territory because they thought the ordinance would free their
slaves. St. Clair felt that those slaveowners who had left the territory
should be allowed to return with their slaves. The governor was certain "that the [Spanish] Country itself is much less desirable than on
the american side—could they be allowed to bring them [their slaves]
back with them, all those who retired from that Cause would return
to a man."[49]

Two years later the territorial governor no longer wished to be
held to either of the interpretations he offered Washington and Jefferson. St. Clair wrote that the ordinance was "no more than the Declaration of a Principle which was to Govern the Legislature in all Acts
respecting that matter, and the Courts of Justice in their Decisions
upon Cases arising after the Date of the Ordinance." This idea had
been implied in his 1790 letter to Washington. Now he spelled it out.
But St. Clair went further still in reinterpreting the ordinance. He
asserted that "the Sense of Congress is very well to be known on this
Subject by what they have actually done—Viz: By making it unlawful
to import into any of the States any Negroes after a certain specified
Time, and which is yet to come—so that if any person after the Arrival of that period should import a Cargoe of Negroes there is no

---

[48] Governor Arthur St. Clair to President George Washington, May 1, 1790,
in Carter, ed., *Territorial Papers*, II, 244-248, quotation, 248.
[49] "Report of Governor St. Clair to the Secretary of State [Thomas Jefferson],"
Feb. 10, 1791, in Carter, ed., *Territorial Papers*, II, 332-337, quotation, 333.

Doubt that they would all be free while those that were in the Country before remain in Slavery according to the former Laws.'''⁵⁰

In his official duties St. Clair never had an opportunity to implement this interpretation of the ordinance. He did, however, use his office to discourage pro-freedom interpretations of it. In 1794 territorial Judge George Turner issued a writ of habeas corpus for slaves owned by another territorial official, Henry Vanderburgh. Turner asserted that all slaves were "free by the Constitution of the Territory" but before the case could come to trial a group of men, allegedly employed by Vanderburgh, kidnaped the blacks and reenslaved them. Turner sought indictments for kidnapping against Vanderburgh and his associates, but St. Clair interceded to protect the kidnappers. St. Clair also informed Turner that the ordinance was prospective only, and could not be used to emancipate slaves living in the territory before 1787.⁵¹

Turner later tried to liberate other slaves through the use of habeas corpus. Slaveowners complained to St. Clair about Turner, and residents of the Illinois Country petitioned Congress to remove him from office. The pressure was successful. In 1796 United States Attorney General Charles Lee reported to the House of Representatives that Turner should be prosecuted in a territorial court for abusing his office and, if convicted, he might then be impeached and removed from office. In 1797 a congressional committee concurred with Lee's advice, and under this threat Judge Turner resigned his office and left the territory.⁵²

At the end of Washington's administration the status of slaves in the Northwest remained substantially what it had been before the ordinance. The territorial governor had publicly and privately asserted that the ordinance applied only to those slaves brought into the Northwest *after* 1787. Slaveholders in the territory, who were often the most

---

⁵⁰ St. Clair to Luke Decker, Oct. 11, 1793, *ibid.*, III, 415-416. In *Groves* v. *Slaughter*, 15 Peters 449 (1841), the U.S. Supreme Court would make a similar analysis of a provision of the Mississippi Constitution of 1832, which prohibited the importation of slaves as merchandise. The court would assert that this provision could not become enforceable without legislative action.

⁵¹ Judge George Turner to Governor St. Clair, June 14, 1794, in Smith, ed., *St. Clair Papers*, II, 325-326; St. Clair to Turner, Dec. 14, 1794, *ibid.*, II, 330-332.

⁵² St. Clair to Winthrop Sargent, Apr. 28, 1795, *ibid.*, II, 340-343; "Inquiry into the Official Conduct of a Judge of the Supreme Court of the Northwestern Territory," *American State Papers*, Class X, *Miscellaneous* (2 vols., Washington 1834), I, 151-152, 157; Governor St. Clair to William St. Clair, June 3, 1795, in Smith, ed., *St. Clair Papers*, II, 372-373.

politically powerful men in the region, were not, however, content with this interpretation. Some had brought slaves into the territory since 1787. Others hoped to bring more slaves into the territory. As of 1797 no slaves appear to have been freed by the ordinance. But the language of the ordinance posed a potential threat to slavery north of the Ohio River, especially for those who owned slaves brought to the territory after July 1787. In the early years of the nineteenth century slaveowners would unsuccessfully petition Congress to modify the ordinance to protect their slaves.[53] In the meantime the territorial governments in Indiana and Illinois would adopt laws to protect slavery and involuntary servitude in those territories. Not until the second decade of the century would slavery begin to end in those jurisdictions. And not until the adoption of the second Illinois constitution in 1848, more than sixty years after the ordinance was passed, would all slavery end in the region.[54]

The sixty-year lag from the adoption of the ordinance to the final abolition of slavery in the Northwest reflects the ambiguous nature of the ordinance. As suggested at the beginning of this essay, many nineteenth century northerners venerated the Northwest Ordinance, in part because of Article VI. Much of this veneration was politically motivated. Those who opposed slavery sought to wrap themselves in the memory of the Founders. Article VI enabled them to do this. Thus, when an attempt was made to make Illinois a slave state, the words of the ordinance and the memory of those who were involved in its passage were important weapons for Edward Coles and his antislavery supporters. Similarly, in the Webster-Hayne debate, Daniel Webster

---

[53] These petitions are collected in Jacob Piatt Dunn, "Slavery Petitions and Papers," *Indiana Historical Society Publications* (Indianapolis 1894), II, 443-529. See esp. "Memorial of Randolph and St. Clair Counties, Jan. 17, 1806," 498; "Legislative Resolutions of 1807 [1806]," 507; "Petition of Randolph and St. Clair Counties, February 20, 1807," 510; "Legislative Petition of 1807," 515; and, against slavery, "Petition of Randolph County, February 20, 1807, Counter to the Preceding Petition," 512; "Counter Petition of Clark County," 518; and "Report on the Preceding," 521. "The Report of General W. Johnston, Chairman of the Committee to which the Petitions on the Slavery Question had been Referred," reprinted from the Vincennes *Sun*, Dec. 17, 1808, is at 522. See also "Slavery in the Indiana Territory," No. 222, 9th Cong., 2d sess., House of Representatives, *American State Papers, Miscellaneous*, I, 477-478; and "Slavery in the Indiana Territory," No. 222, 10th Cong., 1st sess., Senate, *American State Papers, Miscellaneous*, I, 484-486.

[54] "A Law concerning Servants. Adopted from the Virginia code, and published at Vincennes, the twenty-second day of September one thousand eight hundred and three . . . ," in Francis S. Philbrick, eds., *Laws of Indiana Territory, 1801-1809* (Springfield, Ill. 1930), 42; Illinois Constitution, 1848, Art. XIII, Sec. 16.

not only used the ordinance to his advantage but tried to claim that a Massachusetts man, Nathan Dane, deserved the credit for its passage. Thomas Hart Benton, who also opposed South Carolina's extremism, invoked the ordinance as well, but claimed the glory for a southerner, Thomas Jefferson.[55]

The use of the ordinance in the debates over slavery suggests its impact on the nation's political culture. But its impact on slavery in the Northwest, especially in what became Indiana and Illinois, is more ambiguous. Slavery continued in Indiana until after statehood. Not until 1820, in *State* v. *Lasselle*, did the Indiana Supreme Court declare that the institution violated the new state constitution. Even then, a few slaves were held until the 1830s.[56]

In Illinois the record is even bleaker. Here slavery remained vigorous throughout the territorial period. Illinois would most likely have adopted a full-fledged system of slavery in 1818 if the territorial leaders had not been certain that Congress would not have granted statehood under a constitution which allowed slavery.[57] Congressional opposition to slavery in Illinois was directly connected to the reverence that some northerners in Congress had for the ordinance. But it was the threat of rejection of a proslavery constitution by Congress, rather than the legal force of the ordinance itself, that preserved Illinois as a nominally free state. Nevertheless, slaveholders in Illinois were powerful enough to protect the institution in the state's Constitution of 1818 and in subsequent legislation.[58] No slaves living in the state were explicitly freed under the constitution and the Illinois Supreme Court did not follow Indiana's lead in interpreting the constitution to have ended slavery. On the contrary, the court continued to support slavery and servitude in the state until the 1840s. Not until the Constitution of 1848 did Illinois finally abolish slavery.[59]

---

[55] Poole, *Ordinance of 1787*, 8-9.

[56] *State* v. *Lasselle*, 1 Blackford 60 (1820). In 1820 the United States Census reported 190 slaves living in Indiana. As late as 1840 the census found 3 slaves in the state.

[57] Harris, *History of Negro Servitude in Illinois*, 18; Moore, *The Missouri Controversy*, 34, 54.

[58] Illinois Constitution, 1818, Art. VI, declared that slavery shall not "hereafter be introduced into this State," which implied that slaves already in the state could be retained. This article also upheld certain forms of indentured servitude, and allowed slaves to be brought from other states for limited amounts of time to work in the salt-making industry. See also Moore, *The Missouri Controversy*, 258-287. For a handy list of Illinois laws supporting slavery passed before 1840, see *Slave Code of the State of Illinois* (Julilet [sic] 1840), published by the Will County Anti-Slavery Society.

[59] For example, see *Hays* v. *Borders*, 1 Gilman (Ill.) 46 (1844), upholding inden-

Had the ordinance been drafted more clearly, it might have provided a better guide to the legislators of the Northwest. A requirement of gradual emancipation, such as Pennsylvania adopted in 1780, or one of absolute abolition, such as Vermont adopted in its first constitution, might have clarified the intent of the framers of the ordinance and given guidance to the settlers of the territory. Such clarification might have headed off the struggle to legalize slavery completely in Illinois in 1823-1824. It might also have led to freedom for the two to three thousand blacks who remained enslaved in the Northwest between 1787 and 1848.[60] In at least one small corner of revolutionary America the legacy of freedom written into Article VI would then have been a reality to those who were denied their natural rights under existing laws.

---

tures made before statehood that amounted to lifetime slavery. Illinois Constitution, 1848, Art. XIII, Sec. 16, finally abolished all slavery in the state.

[60] The exact number of slaves living in Indiana and Illinois is impossible to determine. The 1810 census listed 237 slaves and 393 free blacks in Indiana, "although many of the latter group were undoubtedly held under indentures." Thornbrough, *The Negro in Indiana*, 22. The 1820 census found 917 slaves in Illinois and 190 slaves in Indiana. Undoubtedly many of the 1,677 free blacks in those two states were also held in some form of servitude. As late as 1840 Illinois had 331 slaves. It is likely that more than 2,000 persons were held in slavery in Indiana and Illinois between 1787 and 1848.

Trial at Trenton

Robert J. Taylor*

O N January 10, 1783, Robert R. Livingston in a letter to Lafayette remarked that "the great cause between Connecticut
and Pennsylvania has been discided in favor of the latter. It is
a singular event. There are few instances of independent states submitting their Cause to a Court of Justice. The day will come tho' when
all disputes in the great republic of Europe will be tried in the same
way, and America be quoted to eximplify the wisdom of the measure."[1]
Livingston's optimism grew out of the trial held at Trenton from
November 12 to December 30, 1782, when the five commissioners,
acting under Article IX of the Confederation, declared that the territory
disputed between the two states was under the jurisdiction of Pennsylvania. This decision put an end to one phase of a struggle that had
then been going on for nearly thirty years, a struggle in which the
best legal talent had been employed and in which blood had been shed.
The trial, which was unique in being the only such action taken
under Article IX, raised interesting questions about the rights of Indians
and the validity of colonial charters.

The controversy between Connecticut and Pennsylvania had its
origin in land speculation. In 1754, a Connecticut group organized as
the Susquehannah Company had purchased from the Indians a tract of
land bounded on the south and the north by the southern and northern
boundaries of Connecticut extended westward across Pennsylvania and
on the east by a line ten miles east of the eastern branch of the Sus-
quehanna River and paralleling its meanderings. Westward the purchase ran 120 miles.[2] The company justified its action on the ground
that Connecticut's sea-to-sea charter gave that colony title to land west

---

* Mr. Taylor is a member of the Department of History, Tufts University. He
wishes to thank Miss Edith Henderson and the staff of the Harvard Law Library
and John Cushing, Librarian of the Massachusetts Historical Society, for help in
coping with the complexities of the legal citations.

[1] Livingston to Lafayette, Continental Congress Papers, item 118, foll. 380-381,
National Archives, Washington.

[2] The deed is printed in Julian P. Boyd, ed., *The Susquehannah Company Papers*
(Ithaca, 1962 [orig. publ., Wilkes-Barre, 1930]), I, 110-116.

of the Delaware River between the lines of latitude 41° and 42° 2'. While the Susquehannah Company tried often and hard to have Connecticut support its venture, the colony did not formally acknowledge ,its rights under the sea-to-sea clause until May 1771, and only after members of the company had organized heavy political pressure.[3] Once the step was taken, however, Connecticut vigorously pushed its claim both through attempted arbitration with the Penns and through legal efforts in England.[4] When the Revolution broke out, the case was awaiting hearings before the Privy Council. That body finally decided it would take no action until the struggle with America had terminated in favor of the mother country.[5]

The contest between Connecticut and the Pennsylvania proprietors before the Privy Council was far more than just a distant legal battle. Without the blessing of Connecticut, the Susquehannah Company had settled hundreds of families on both sides of the river in the Wyoming Valley, clustered in the vicinity of Wilkes-Barre. More than once they had been driven out, only to return. They came back permanently in 1771, and by the outbreak of the Revolution they numbered about three thousand.[6] Their persistence, their expansion, and their arrogant disregard for Pennsylvania law produced dangerous frictions on the frontier at a time when unity in the face of British enmity was essential. Thus Congress became the theater for further attempts to resolve the dispute between the two colonies; but committees appointed to find solutions wound up urging postponement of any solution, a freezing of the status quo.[7] Responsible leaders on both sides counseled caution and selfless devotion to the national cause, which dwarfed disputes over colonial boundaries. Nevertheless, Pennamites, that is, those who claimed land in the region through grants from Pennsylvania, found the Connecticut presence intolerable. Irritation among the speculators, as distinct from those Pennsylvanians who actually wanted to settle, was

[3] *Ibid.*, IV, xviii-xix, 215.

[4] See Robert J. Taylor, ed., *The Susquehannah Company Papers* (Ithaca, 1968-), V, Introduction, section III; and V-VI, *passim.*

[5] Richard Cumberland to Henry Wilmot, Nov. 19, 1776, Official Correspondence, Penn Papers, XII, 9, Historical Society of Pennsylvania, Philadelphia; see also Taylor, ed., *Susquehannah Co. Papers*, VII, no. 22.

[6] Oscar J. Harvey, *A History of Wilkes-Barre* . . . (Wilkes-Barre, 1909), II, 953. Harvey used a list of polls and ratable estates for his estimate.

[7] Taylor, ed., *Susquehannah Co. Papers*, VI, nos. 186, 195, 197, 199, 207, 217, 237, 240, and 241.

especially marked. The former pressed the provincial government hard. In December 1775, even while Congress was urging restraint, the Pennamites made a concerted effort to crush the Yankees. They were acting as a duly constituted posse authorized by Governor John Penn to arrest the Connecticut leaders, but their effort had all the marks of a military expedition. In the pitched battle that followed, the Pennamites suffered a severe defeat, leaving Connecticut claimants holding firm political control of the Wyoming Valley throughout the Revolution.[8] They came closest to losing their lands in 1778 after a British and Indian attack led by Colonel John Butler. The resulting terror nearly emptied their settlements.[9]

Despite harassment and even decimation of the population, the area of modern Wilkes-Barre and nearby places became truly an extension of Connecticut. First, in January 1774, the towns were lumped together into one township called Westmoreland, which was bigger than the rest of Connecticut proper and which regularly sent representatives to the Connecticut General Assembly. In October 1776 Westmoreland was made a county, coterminous with the town, and was given its own justices of the peace and county courts.[10] Westmoreland raised militia, contributed two companies to the Connecticut line, set up a committee of inspection, and in all ways played the role of a Connecticut county. By this time the quarrel that had begun with the Penns was taken over by the state of Pennsylvania.

That state, despairing of a resolution of the dispute through congressional committees, in 1779 sought action against Connecticut under Article IX of the Confederation, which the two states had ratified in 1778; Connecticut, however, regarded Pennsylvania's move as premature. It objected that the war was still in progress and that the Articles had not yet been ratified by all the states.[11] Thwarted, Pennsylvania

---

[8] *Ibid.*, nos. 200-203, 216, 219, 245, 246, and 248.

[9] William Maclay to Timothy Matlack, July 12, 1778, Gratz Collection, Case 1, Box 39, Historical Society of Pennsylvania; Taylor, ed., *Susquehannah Co. Papers*, VII, no. 35. Nathan Denison to Jonathan Trumbull, July 28, 1778, Massachusetts Historical Society, *Proceedings*, 2d Ser., III (Boston, 1888), 342-344.

[10] The acts creating the town and the county of Westmoreland are in J. H. Trumbull and C. J. Hoadly, eds., *Public Records of the Colony of Connecticut* (Hartford, 1850-1890), XIV, 217-218, and in C. J. Hoadly and L. W. Labaree, eds., *Public Records of the State of Connecticut* (Hartford, 1894-), I, 7.

[11] The copy of the resolution of the Pennsylvania General Assembly, Nov. 18, 1779, calling for implementation of Article IX, sent to Connecticut is in Susque-

began to cut off supplies to the troops garrisoned at Wyoming for protection of the frontier. In President Joseph Reed's view, these Connecticut soldiers, even though they were in Continental service, were surety for Connecticut's continued possession of the valley.[12] Pennsylvania's action stirred Congress to order General Washington to man the garrison with troops drawn from neither Connecticut nor Pennsylvania.[13] Feeling more comfortable with this choice, Pennsylvania bided her time. Then within a few weeks after the Confederation had been declared ratified by all the states, Pennsylvania was ready to press the implementation of Article IX. By January 1782 Connecticut reluctantly agreed to appoint agents for the purpose.[14]

Appointed were Jesse Root, Eliphalet Dyer, and William Samuel Johnson, who were also chosen as agents by the Susquehannah and Delaware companies.[15] Root was an established lawyer and political leader in his own state. Dyer, who had been a member and a leader of the Susquehannah Company from its start, was a familiar figure in Congress as well as in Connecticut. Johnson, while he had consistently deplored the Susquehannah scheme as unrealistic, had acted unofficially as the company's agent in England and officially as the agent of Connecticut there after the colony had adopted the western claim. He was one of the leading lawyers of his day.[16] Connecticut, incidentally,

---

hannah Settlers, I, 108, Connecticut State Library, Hartford. Connecticut's answering resolution is in *ibid.*, 110a-110b; printed in Taylor, ed., *Susquehannah Co. Papers*, VII, nos. 43 and 46.

[12] Reed to the Board of War, Nov. 20, 1780, Continental Congress Papers, Item 148, foll. 223-224; printed in Taylor, ed., *Susquehannah Co. Papers*, VII, no. 54.

[13] Dec. 12, 1780, Worthington C. Ford *et al.*, eds., *Journals of the Continental Congress* (Washington, 1904-1937), XVIII, 1147-1148.

[14] Resolution of the Pennsylvania General Assembly, Mar. 12, 1781, *Colonial Records of Pennsylvania* (Harrisburg, 1838-1853). XIII, 10; Connecticut's resolution, dated Jan. 1782, is given in Ford *et al.*, eds., *Journals of Continental Congress*, XXII, 346-347.

[15] The Susquehannah Company acted on Nov. 14, 1782. Minutes of meetings are in the Susquehannah Company Papers, Connecticut Historical Society, Hartford; printed in Taylor, ed., *Susquehannah Co. Papers*, VII, no. 125. The First and Second Delaware companies took action earlier, on Oct. 31, 1782; Jonathan Trumbull, Sr., Papers, XXI, 60a, 60c, Connecticut State Library; printed in Taylor, ed., *Susquehannnah Co. Papers*, VII, no. 119. The Delaware companies, organized soon after the Susquehannah Company, sought to settle lands between the Delaware River and the eastern boundary of the Susquehannah Company purchase: see Boyd, ed., *Susquehannah Co. Papers*, I, lxxxviii-lxxxix.

[16] All three Connecticut agents are included in the *Dictionary of American Biography*. For the activities of Dyer and Johnson in connection with the Susque-

expected the companies to pay better than half of the anticipated expenses of the forthcoming trial. This arrangement, which the companies accepted, perhaps suggests New England frugality, but even more, it reveals that the state had not yet defined the cause as a wholly public one. All the expenses of Pennsylvania, on the other hand, were borne by the state.[17]

Pennsylvania selected as its agents James Wilson, Joseph Reed, William Bradford, Jr., and Jonathan Dickinson Sergeant. Wilson and Reed, able lawyers both, were, of course, well known beyond the borders of their state. Wilson had a personal interest in the cause, for he was a heavy speculator in lands, some in the very area in dispute between the two states.[18] Bradford was the attorney general of Pennsylvania, and years later succeeded Edmund Randolph as attorney general of the United States. Sergeant had preceded Bradford in the office of state attorney general, in which he had made a reputation as a vigorous prosecutor of both criminals and Tories. A fifth man, Henry Osborne, played a solicitor's role in searching records and gathering evidence for the others to use. Of the five men representing Pennsylvania's interest, all but Wilson belonged to the Constitutionalist, or Radical, political faction. Some time after the trial this faction became more sympathetic than its rival, the Republicans, toward the Connecticut people settled in the disputed territory. In 1784 a Constitutionalist majority on the Council of Censors censured the General Assembly for its conduct toward the settlers. At no time, however, did either faction question Pennsylvania's right of jurisdiction in the disputed area.[19]

---

hannah Company, see the indexes of the various volumes of Taylor, ed., *Susquehannah Co. Papers*. See also George C. Groce, *William Samuel Johnson, A Maker of the Constitution* (New York, 1937), and George C. Groce, "Eliphalet Dyer: Connecticut Revolutionist," in Richard B. Morris, ed., *The Era of the American Revolution* (New York, 1939), 290-304.

[17] Hoadly and Labaree, eds., *Conn. State Rec.*, IV, 292; *Pennsylvania Col. Rec.*, XIII, 411. According to William Bradford's account with the state, Pennsylvania spent £1046 3s 2d on the trial. Records of the Supreme Executive Council, Executive Correspondence, 1783-1784, Record Group 27, Division of Archives and Manuscripts, Pennsylvania Historical and Museum Commission, Harrisburg.

[18] See James Wilson Papers, VIII, 72, 105, Historical Society of Pennsylvania; Charles Page Smith, *James Wilson, Founding Father* (Chapel Hill, 1956), Chap. XI; John F. Roche, *Joseph Reed, A Moderate in the American Revolution* (New York, 1957).

[19] Biographical details on Bradford and Sergeant are from the *DAB*. On factional politics see Robert L. Brunhouse, *The Counter-Revolution in Pennsylvania, 1776-*

Article IX provided that when disputes arose between states over boundaries, jurisdiction, and other matters, one state could petition Congress requesting a hearing, as Pennsylvania had done; and when Congress assigned a day for the agents of the disputing states to appear, they would then agree upon "commissioners or judges to constitute a court for hearing and determining the matter in question." The decision of such a court was to be "final and conclusive."[20] If the agents of the states could not agree upon commissioners, careful provision was made for Congress to select them. No state could indefinitely escape a determination by holding up the choice of a panel of judges or by refusing to appear before the court. While the agents of Connecticut and Pennsylvania had been instructed to come before Congress on the fourth Monday in June 1782, delays prevented a choice of commissioners until August.[21]

Dyer believed it was in Connecticut's interest to get as commissioners men from the landed states who would be apt to view more sympathetically her sea-to-sea claims. These were much on the minds of American political leaders at this time. As is well known, Maryland's delay in ratifying the Articles had come from her demand that the landed states cede their western claims to the United States. Less well known is that evidence for western claims was thought by some to be important in the forthcoming peace negotiations with Great Britain. The sea-to-sea clauses would reinforce the American demand for a western boundary at the Mississippi River. (Since the peace with France in 1763, it had been understood that the river was as far as the sea-to-sea claims could be pushed.)

In October 1780 Connecticut had offered to cede to the United States her western lands beyond the Susquehannah Company purchase provided settlement proceeded upon a township basis, but at the time her offer had been rejected by Congress, as had those of New York and Virginia.[22] All three were urged to cede their lands without condi-

1790 (Harrisburg, 1942), passim. Records of the Council of Censors, Journal, 1784, pp. 821-885, Division of Archives and Manuscripts, Pennsylvania Historical and Museum Commission.

[20] Ford et al., eds., Journals of Continental Congress, XIX, 217-218.

[21] Ibid., XXII, 351-352, 355-357, 389-392; Samuel Hazard, ed., Pennsylvania Archives (Harrisburg, 1852-1856), IX, 681-685.

[22] Hoadly and Labaree, eds., Conn. State Rec., III, 177-178; Ford et al., eds., Journal of Continental Congress, XIX, 99; XX, 704. Virginia had made a conditional offer of cession on Jan. 2, 1781; New York, on Mar. 1, 1781.

tions. Virginia's delegation became spokesman for the view of the landed states and leaders in manipulations to keep the importance of the claims in the forefront of the minds of the members of Congress. Virginia did not, of course, champion Connecticut's claim as such; in fact, Virginia later came to resent that state's pretensions.[23] But at least Virginia believed in sea-to-sea grants, and Dyer thought it was important to have that attitude well represented among the commissioners who would judge her dispute with Pennsylvania.

By a process of elimination, and after the men originally chosen had refused to serve,[24] the agents for the two sides mutually agreed upon seven men: William Whipple, Cyrus Griffin, David Brearley, William C. Houston, Welcome Arnold, Thomas Nelson, and Joseph Jones. Three of the seven were from Virginia—Griffin, Jones, and Nelson; two were from New Jersey—Brearley and Houston; and the other two, Whipple and Arnold, were from New Hampshire and Rhode Island respectively. This nice balance was upset when Jones and Nelson failed to serve. Jones insisted that he could not be at Trenton for the trial because he had to attend the Virginia House of Burgesses, and friends of Nelson gave a similar excuse for him.[25] The loss of two Virginians was a blow to Dyer, who saw his counterbalance to the men from the landless states denied him. He wrote to Governor Jonathan Trumbull, expressing his disappointment:

Tho the others have a good character for candor and impartiality, the local situation of four of them are not so agreable as we could wish; tho it is generally agreed that the extended charters of several of the United States will be considered very material in determining the extent and limits of the 13 United States when their sovereignty and independence are acknowledged in a peace establishment to be im-

[23] The Connecticut claim, of course, overlapped that of Virginia to the territory north and west of the Ohio River. When Connecticut in 1786 was making its final effort to have its land cession accepted by Congress, the Virginia delegation opposed Connecticut at every stage, for it was felt that the Virginia cession had already given Congress title to the land. See William Grayson to James Madison, May 28, 1786, in Edmund C. Burnett, ed., *Letters of Members of the Continental Congress* (Washington, 1921-1936), VIII, 372-373.

[24] Gen. Nathanael Greene and John Rutledge, Ford *et al.*, eds., *Journals of Continental Congress*, XXIII, 528.

[25] Eliphalet Dyer to Jonathan Trumbull, Sept. 25, 1782, Correspondence with Congressmen, 1780-1801, p. 6, Jonathan Trumbull, Jr., Papers, I, Connecticut Historical Society; printed in Taylor, ed., *Susquehannah Co. Papers*, VII, no. 111.

proved against the claims of Great Britain and to limit the territory of Canada. Yet those States who have not those extended charters affect to consider them in every other respect as vain and nugatory, and that every part which had not before the war been located and appropriated to individuals. . . .[26]

After the trial Dyer declared that the failure of Jones to attend was a reason for losing the cause.[27]

Of the five commissioners who went to Trenton, only Brearley and Griffin had had much judicial experience. Although men with little legal training and experience often served as judges in eighteenth-century America, this was no ordinary case. Much was at stake for hundreds of men and women, and the issue involved a number of fine legal points, as the lawyers were to demonstrate. Brearley had been chief justice of the New Jersey supreme court since 1779, and Griffin had been a judge of the Court of Appeals and Capture since 1780, a post in which he continued to serve for years afterwards. Whipple became an associate justice of the New Hampshire superior court in 1782, the year of the Trenton trial, but Houston was not even admitted to the bar until 1781, although in that year he became clerk of the supreme court of New Jersey. Arnold, innocent of any legal experience except as a mere justice of the peace, was a Providence businessman who had been a member of the legislature for several years.[28] Still, the Connecticut agents wrote to Governor Trumbull during the trial that the "judges all appear exceeding candid and to feel the importance of the cause they have to decide." Joseph Reed commented simply of the court that it was "pretty well as Courts go."[29]

[26] Dyer to Trumbull, Oct. 19, 1782, Massachusetts Historical Society, *Collections,* 7th Ser., III (Boston, 1902), 388.

[27] Dyer to William Williams, Jan. 1783, Correspondence with Congressmen, 1780-1801, p. 6, J. Trumbull, Jr., Papers, I; printed in Taylor, ed., *Susquehannah Co. Papers,* VII, no. 136.

[28] Except for Arnold, biographical details on the judges are from the *DAB.* For Arnold, see Tristam Burges, *A Memoir of Welcome Arnold* (n.p., 1850); *The Biographical Cyclopedia of Representative Men of Rhode Island* (Providence, 1881); and Joseph Jencks Smith, *Civil and Military List of Rhode Island* (Providence, 1900-1901), *passim.*

[29] Dyer, Johnson, and Root to Trumbull, Nov. 27, 1782, in Mass. Hist. Soc., *Collections,* 7th Ser., III, 401. Reed to George Bryan, Dec. 3, 1782, in William B. Reed, *Life and Correspondence of Joseph Reed* (Philadelphia, 1847), II, 389. But compare these with another judgment: "The Judges I doubt not are good men, tho' *Whipple* is a *Paltry* name and *Arnold* a bad one." See Edmund Pendelton to

The trial was scheduled to open November 12, 1782, at Trenton, the commissioners to receive expenses plus ten dollars per day each, with the costs shared equally by the two states.[30] Between August, when the commissioners were agreed upon, and November both sides laboriously copied old records, took depositions, hunted up Indian deeds, and pored over history books. Neither had to begin from scratch, for in the earlier clashes the two colonies had prepared elaborate defenses and counter-arguments. Moreover, newspaper polemicists and pamphleteers had rehearsed many of the main issues, their writings lacking only the subtle analysis of legal technicalities that the trial was to provide.[31]

After a few days' delay until the required quorum of five commissioners could be obtained, the court opened formally, only to have progress slowed by the "dilatory motions" of the Connecticut agents.[32] From the first the government of Connecticut had believed that going to trial before the peace had been established was a mistake, for such a contest could only be divisive at the time when national unity was paramount.[33] Besides, there was another reason. Many of the documents that Connecticut needed were presumably still in England, where they had been sent years before in preparation for a hearing. Among them, allegedly, was an Indian deed given in 1763 that Dyer, particularly, believed was essential to Connecticut's case.[34] To hold up proceedings, the Connecticut agents demanded that their opponents introduce the petition which Pennsylvania had filed with Congress to initiate action;

James Madison, Dec. 9, 1782, in William T. Hutchinson and William M. E. Rachal, eds., *The Papers of James Madison* (Chicago, 1962-), V, 383.

[30] Ford *et al.*, eds., *Journals of Continental Congress*, XXIII, 528-529.

[31] Taylor, ed., *Susquehannah Co. Papers*, V, nos. 97, 201, 213, 258, 271, 273, 274, 283, 289, 290; VI, nos. 1-5.

[32] The official record of the Trenton proceedings is given in Ford *et al.*, eds., *Journals of Continental Congress*, XXIV, 6-32. The phrase "dilatory motions" is Dyer's; see n. 29, above.

[33] Trumbull to Dyer and Root, Aug. 23, 1782, Correspondence with Congressmen, 1780-1801, p. 4, J. Trumbull, Jr., Papers, I; printed in Taylor, ed., *Susquehannah Co. Papers*, VII, 106.

[34] Dyer to Trumbull, Oct. 19, 1782, in Mass. Hist. Soc., *Collections*, 7th Ser., III, 388. While acting as the agent of the Susquehannah Company in England in 1764, Dyer had left various papers in the care of an English attorney, among them, according to Gov. Trumbull, "the Indian purchases by the Susquehannah and Delaware Companies, the Evidence of such Purchases and the Payment." See Trumbull to Thomas Life, Apr. 6, 1774, in Taylor, ed., *Susquehannah Co. Papers*, VI, no. 20. A list of papers left in England is in Jonathan Trumbull, Sr., Papers, XXI, 77, Connecticut State Library.

they questioned the validity of the commission under which the Pennsylvania agents acted; they asked the court to cite for appearance representatives of the Wyoming settlers whose interests were at stake in the trial; and they claimed the right to move for postponement at any point after the trial had begun.[35] Most of these motions failed—except in angering the opposing counsel, who saw only insincerity in these maneuverings. From the Pennsylvania viewpoint, these were but tactical delays designed to ward off a legal decision, since the longer Connecticut people actually held the land, the harder it would be for Pennsylvania to assert its rights both legally and physically.[36]

These preliminary skirmishes over, the trial proceeded in essentially three stages: (1) the offering of introductory statements, in which each side explained why the court should decide in its favor; (2) the presentation of "proofs and exhibits," in which enumerated arguments, called "positions," were supported by citation of records and works of history; and (3) the delivery of closing arguments, in which each lawyer except Bradford took a turn at presenting the case as he saw it and speaking to the arguments of his opponents. The order of speaking was Root, Sergeant, Dyer, Wilson, Johnson, and Reed. The official record of the proceedings gives in full only the introductory statements; research has disclosed what the positions of each side were and the exhibits produced for some of the positions; and notes taken by a clerk and by Reed give some idea of the closing arguments for every speaker except Dyer.[37] While the record is sparser than one would

[35] Ford et al., eds., Journals of Continental Congress, XXIV, 10, 11, 13, 26-27.
[36] Joseph Reed to William Moore, Nov. 23, 1782, in Hazard, ed., Pennsylvania Archives, IX, 691-692.
[37] The introductory statements of Pennsylvania and Connecticut are given in Ford et al., eds., Journals of Continental Congress, XXIV, 14-23. The positions of Pennsylvania and Connecticut are in Pennsylvania Archives, IX, 711-715, with some obvious inaccuracies in citations; reprinted in Taylor, ed., Susquehannah Co. Papers, VII, no. 128, viii, ix. The clerk's notes are printed very inaccurately in Pennsylvania Archives, XVIII, 621-629. The original document, once in Harrisburg, has been lost, but the Wyoming Historical and Geological Society, Wilkes-Barre, Pa., has a photostatic copy. These notes, hereafter cited as Clerk's notes, consist of 22 unnumbered pages, the notes on each speaker except Sergeant being identified as such. The notes on Sergeant are mistakenly placed after those on Johnson even though Sergeant was the second speaker and Johnson the fifth. No notes on Dyer's presentation remain. These are in Taylor, ed., Susquehannah Co. Papers, VII, no. 128, x, xii, xviii, xx, and xxii. Notes jotted down by Reed on Johnson's argument and for his own final statement are in the Joseph Reed Papers, X, New-York Historical Society, New York City. (Photostatic

like, one can discern the main lines of argument and the shift in thinking Connecticut had to make in the course of the trial.

From the start Pennsylvania based its case upon its charter boundaries, its purchases of land from the Indians, and its acquisition of territorial rights from the proprietors. For good measure, it declared that settlements had been made in the disputed territory before Connecticut made its claim. Pennsylvania, of course, had a long tradition of purchasing lands from the Indians to secure a clear title, in the interest of harmony occasionally even paying twice for the same land. In 1784 Pennsylvania was to make the last large purchase in acquiring title to the northwestern section of the state.[38]

Connecticut countered Pennsylvania's presentation of her case by pleading its own charter rights, its exercise of jurisdiction over the disputed lands since 1774, and the Indian deed obtained in 1754 by the Susquehannah Company.[39] Unhappily for the Connecticut cause, the deed had grave defects. It had erasures and neglected to mention a consideration given for the grant of land made. Although the Connecticut agents persuaded the court to allow introduction of depositions taken in 1763, nine years after the date of the deed, which testified to actual payment of a consideration, the Indian deed remained a weak prop because the purchase had been made without the authorization of

copies are in the Wyoming Historical and Geological Society.) These consist of 45 unnumbered pages. Hereafter cited as Reed's notes. These are in Taylor, ed., *Susquehannah Co. Papers,* VII, no. 128, xxi and xxiii. Both the clerk's and Reed's notes are sometimes so sketchy that the meaning can be ascertained only by checking every accompanying citation, but space limitations do not permit more than a suggestion of the material taken from legal treatises and works of history. In Taylor, ed., *Susquehannah Co. Papers,* VII, all citations are described fully. What I have sought to do here is to single out the main arguments and counterarguments without regard to the order in which they were developed and without indicating to what extent authorities cited had to be used to reconstruct arguments. One other set of notes deserves mention, those taken by Judge Griffin and printed in Julian P. Boyd, ed., *The Papers of Thomas Jefferson* (Princeton, 1950-), VI, 488-497. These are described as notes on "the arguments of the two outstanding figures, James Wilson and William Samuel Johnson." See *ibid.,* 479. Actually, Griffin blended together the positions of Pennsylvania and Connecticut, which he gave almost verbatim and in quotes, with notes taken not only on Wilson and Johnson but on Sergeant and Reed as well. At several points Griffin is helpful in being fuller, if not always accurate.

[38] Ford *et al.,* eds., *Journals of Continental Congress,* XXIV, 14-16; Brunhouse, *Counter-Revolution in Pennsylvania,* 149-150.

[39] Ford *et al.,* eds., *Journals of Continental Congress,* XXIV, 16-23.

the Connecticut government in violation of colonial law.[40] In the closing arguments both Root and Johnson built their cases without reliance upon the deed of 1754. Writing of Johnson's closing argument, Reed summed up the Connecticut difficulty with partisan vigor: "He gave up the Indian title wholly, which was prudent, as it was a scene of the vilest fraud and grossest forgery."[41]

Abandoning the Indian deed made it expedient for the Connecticut agents to call into question all Indian deeds as a basis for titles to land, for Pennsylvania had submitted many in her exhibits; they could not go unchallenged. Thus Root and Johnson raised the question of what right to the soil the Indians possessed. Citing Blackstone's *Commentaries,* Root held that only occupancy could give title to the soil. As simple hunters, the Indians when they sold land were merely selling the right to use land for hunting. No permanent landholding rights could be thus transferred. The very sparseness of Indian population argued that they had "no permanent property in lands. If otherwise it would Violate the Great Command (be fruitful etc.)."[42] Johnson took a somewhat different tack, basing soil rights on cultivation rather than on mere occupancy. Since the Indians were not cultivators in any more than a trifling sense, they acquired no true property rights. As savages, they had "no Records, no Papers, no Course of Descent. Necessity therefore compelled Europeans to depend on Crown Title."[43] When white men bought Indian lands, they were buying goodwill, not property. Johnson cited passages from both Thomas Hutchinson and Emmerich Vattel to give weight to the principle that cultivation alone gave right to the soil.[44]

Unfortunately, no record of Dyer's views on this point remain. Contemporary evidence suggests that he made a good deal of the introduction of the Indian deed at an earlier stage of the trial;[45] and that was to

[40] *Ibid.,* 24, 27-28. Sergeant cited a law passed in 1717 that prohibited securing land titles from the Indians without the consent of the Connecticut General Assembly. See *Acts and Laws of His Majesty's English Colony of Connecticut in New England in America* (New London, 1750 and 1769), 110-111.
[41] Reed to Bryan, Dec. 25, 1782, in Reed, *Joseph Reed,* II, 391.
[42] Clerk's notes, Taylor, ed., *Susquehannah Co. Papers,* VII, 185.
[43] Reed's notes, *ibid.,* 203-204.
[44] [Thomas Hutchinson], *A Collection of Original Papers Relative to the History of the Colony of Massachusetts-Bay* (Boston, 1769), 30. Emmerich Vattel, *The Law of Nations or Principles of the Law of Nature Applied to the Conduct and Affairs of Nations and Sovereigns* (London, 1760), I, Sections 81 and 91.
[45] Reed to Bryan, Dec. 3, 1782, Reed, *Joseph Reed,* II, 389.

be expected, for the whole claim of the Susquehannah Company, as distinguished from that of the state, rested upon the purchase made in 1754 from the Indians. If the deed were cast aside, the company would be wholly dependent upon the willingness of the Connecticut legislature to recognize the company's claim. Did Dyer resent the line that Root and Johnson took? If he did, he hid his feelings. After the trial, he wrote in high praise of the effort made by his colleagues, neither of whom was a member of the company although both were acting as its agents.[46] Perhaps Dyer was confident that the Connecticut government could be managed, for ever since 1774 supporters of the Susquehannah Company had been able to outvote their opponents, and the rights of the company had received recognition.

This dismissal of Indian deeds as not very significant brought rebuttals from both Sergeant and Reed, the one offering primarily an emotional or moralistic plea, the other examining closely Johnson's reasoning and his use of sources here, as on all other points. Judging from the outline he sketched in opening his argument, Wilson intended to discuss claims based on purchases from the Indians, but the notes that remain are too fragmentary to suggest his views. Sergeant defended the Indians' right to the soil by insisting that they were true proprietors and by reminding the court that in the early days white men had often found a good friend in the Indian, implying that Connecticut's denigration of the Indian rights smacked of ingratitude. Even the Dutch had shown the five Nations respect and kindness, he concluded.

Reed declared that Johnson in calling attention to the Indians' lack of records and papers was in effect introducing "A new Source of Property derived from superiour Understanding."[47] Heretofore only three origins of property rights had been commonly acknowledged: occupancy, purchase, and conquest of the soil. Johnson was defining a fourth. Reed then asked, "Can that be a civil Rule of acquiring Property which must ultimately end in Force because each must Judge and the Consequence destroy the Rule"?[48] Taking up Johnson's citation of Vattel, he noted that Vattel had approved purchases made from the Indians as "laudable." But if the purchases were praiseworthy, they were so because they were just. In saying that by purchase one acquired goodwill and thus security,

[46] Dyer to Williams, Jan. 1783, Correspondence with Congressmen, 1780-1801, p. 6, J. Trumbull, Jr., Papers, I.

[47] Reed's notes, Taylor, ed., *Susquehannah Co. Papers*, VII, 218.

[48] *Ibid.*

one was describing not a laudable act, but a prudent or even a selfish one. Furthermore, if one insisted upon cultivation as a means of acquiring title to lands, who was to say how much cultivation was necessary to establish a title? Compared with China, other parts of the globe were far behind; especially was this true of the New World. Reed declared that our ancestors regarded Indians as true proprietors and reminded his hearers that the Connecticut agents themselves had introduced a deed as part of their evidence earlier in the trial. Rather than the Crown being the only source of titles to land, as Johnson argued, the Crown merely granted a right of preemption for the purpose of governing relations among its subjects and of providing a mode of acquiring land from the Indians. Thus conflict among Englishmen was avoided, and those favored with grants could proceed to acquire titles from the Indians. Reed insisted, as did many men from the landless states, that ungranted western lands belonged to New York, which had obtained them from the Six Nations and was now ready to cede them to the United States. Connecticut did not come into the picture at all.

These exchanges over Indian rights, however, were not the heart of the closing arguments. The crux was the validity of the sea-to-sea clause in the Connecticut charter of 1662. In probing its meaning, opposing counsel delved deeply into legal treatises, documents, and historical works. Dispassionately viewed, the language of the charter and the circumstances of its issuance raised difficulties for both sides. The sea-to-sea clause of the Connecticut charter, which preceded by nineteen years that granted to William Penn, could be so defined that Penn's grant overlapped the older one to Connecticut. In fact, some eminent counsel in England had insisted that Connecticut's western claim was not an absurd one on its face, that the issue was worth a formal hearing.[49] But most of the difficulties were on the Connecticut side. As the Pennsylvania agents saw it, the Connecticut charter had been obtained through a misleading, if not downright fraudulent, plea at a time when men were ignorant of geography, and the document itself was defective for its omissions and its ambiguities of language.

A glaring weakness in the sea-to-sea claim was that the charter failed to include a "saving clause" exempting from Connecticut's jurisdiction any Christian people already settled within the bounds described. The

[49] See the legal opinion on Connecticut's State of the Case, *ibid.*, V, no. 201, pp. 243-245.

patent granted to the Council for New England in 1620 had included a saving clause, and specific reference to it was made in the Massachusetts-Bay charter of 1629. It was agreed on all sides that no English king could grant lands already possessed or inhabited by another Christian prince or people. Yet the sea-to-sea clause as Connecticut defined it would have included some of the settlements of the Dutch, for projection of Connecticut's north and south boundaries westward would have carried its territory right through New Netherlands. Clearly the Dutch were well established in 1662 at the time of the Connecticut charter; hence failure to include a saving clause constituted a "false recital," vitiating the charter.

The Connecticut agents met this argument in several ways. If we judge by the rather brief notes still extant, Root was the more simple and direct in his answer. Connecticut's first position as presented to the court had stressed prior discovery through the voyage of John Cabot; thus King James had made grants in a vacant country the right to which he had inherited. The English had priority over the Dutch. In the patent to the Council for New England, an exception had been made of lands actually settled; that exception by implication was carried into the Connecticut charter of 1662. Charles II granted the charter in answer to a plea which, among other things, declared that Connecticut had bought from George Fenwick, successor to John Winthrop, Jr., at Saybrook, jurisdictional rights to lands formerly granted to Lord Say and Sele and other lords and gentlemen. The grant to these men had in turn "derived from true royal Authority,"[50] that is, from the Council for New England patent. These antecedents freed the Connecticut charter of any vitiating omission.

Root's litany of grants prior to Connecticut's charter impressed neither Sergeant nor Reed. James I and Charles I had too often consulted their own interest and had violated their own acts by making later grants for the same areas. In Sergeant's opinion the early grants were a king's way of claiming title to as much land as possible. If the king could give away vast areas, it was presumed that the lands belonged to him. Reed

---

[50] The phrase comes from Connecticut's petition to the king for a charter. Root cited the petition, but the clerk's notes do not show that he used this quotation. The petition is in *Pennsylvania Archives*, XVIII, and formed part of the appendix to William Smith, *An Examination of the Connecticut Claim to Lands in Pennsylvania* . . . (Philadelphia, 1774), a source readily available at the time of the trial.

castigated the monopoly provisions of the old grants and their failure to provide for juries and representative government. Citing from both Thomas Hutchinson and William Douglass, Sergeant pointed out that the Council for New England as trustees had no right to convey soil or jurisdictional rights. Thus Lord Say and Sele and his associates could have obtained no true patent from such a source, and no rights by purchase could have been conveyed to Connecticut.

The patent to Lord Say and Sele did not exist except in being referred to in the records of the Connecticut colony; it had certainly never been signed by the king. Here, then, was a further vitiating factor. In asking for a charter Connecticut had falsely pleaded that she had bought former rights for a great consideration, rights that did not exist. When it came Johnson's turn to speak, he confessed himself willing to base Connecticut's claim on the charter of 1662. Its antecedents were only "historical facts" that conveyed no legal title, although they did convey an equitable one. He called the early settlers of Connecticut "associates" of Lord Say and Sele; indeed, all the Puritans were associates, and some kind of title had been obtained that way, a notion that brought a scoffing rebuttal from Reed.[51]

Although Johnson gave up the line of reasoning advanced by Root, he had still to deal with the problem of the Dutch, and he was fecund in his suggestions if not rigid in his logic. Not wanting to give up his "equitable" title, he insisted that the Dutch had made no true settlements prior to the patent of the Council for New England. The Dutch West India Company was not chartered until 1621, a year after the date of the Council's patent. The grant to the New Netherland Company, which gave a trading monopoly between the latitudes of 40° and 45°, and which lasted until 1618, was a "Settlement of Trade and not of Purchase."[52] Old maps that showed a vast extent of land west of the Dutch settlements which they called Nova Belgia only revealed the ignorance of their makers. Nova Belgia existed only as an idea, a convenient label for unknown territory. Citing Samuel Smith's history of New Jersey, Johnson pointed out that Governor Samuel Argall of Virginia had forced the Dutch to hold under the English because their country had been discovered by an Englishman, Henry Hudson.[53] When Reed held the floor,

[51] Reed's notes, Taylor, ed., *Susquehannah Co. Papers*, VII, 205-206.
[52] *Ibid.*, 206. The charter is given in E. B. O'Callaghan, ed., *Documents Relative to the Colonial History of the State of New York* (Albany, 1856), I, 11-12.
[53] Samuel Smith, *The History of the Colony of Novo Caesaria or New Jersey*

he reminded the court of the nationality of Cabot, whose discovery the Connecticut side had stressed. But no one could deny the Dutch presence in 1662. Johnson at one point declared that it was "the Spirit of the patent to except the Dutch possessions."[54] And he saw no difficulties in boundaries that overleaped the Dutch and then continued to run westward to the South Sea, an argument that Benjamin Trumbull had made much of some years earlier.[55]

Lawyer-like, Johnson strove to answer every contention of the opposition. If omission of a saving clause vitiated the charter of 1662, and if it was further vitiated by a false assertion that former rights had been purchased, the whole question of how charters were made void had to be gone into. What constituted false recital? Heavily emphasizing property rights, Johnson held that charters were not easily annulled. Using for his authority Matthew Bacon, he enumerated a set of principles defining circumstances in which mistakes occurring in grants would not invalidate them.[56] Reed did not quarrel with his law, but the Pennsylvania agent contended that the falsities of the charter and the Connecticut petition on which it was based were glaring. To demonstrate that the Dutch were indeed possessed of the land before 1620, he cited from the same historical work that Johnson had mentioned.[57]

But were not the sea-to-sea limits absurd in themselves? Had not the king out of ignorance of geography given away a princely domain and did not that ignorance itself invalidate the charter? On the question of whether men knew the distance to the South Sea the lawyers referred to a number of historical facts and works. James Wilson insisted that a mere twelve years before the date of the Connecticut charter men still

---

. . . *to the Year 1721* . . . (Burlington, 1765). Apparently this is one historical myth that has died out. Brodhead states that Argall's forcing the Dutch to submit in 1613 is "inconsistent with authentic state papers." See John R. Brodhead, *History of the State of New York* (New York, 1853), I, 54.

[54] Clerk's notes, Taylor, ed., *Susquehannah Co. Papers*, VII, 202. Although the clerk has Johnson making this statement, it is not found in Reed's notes on Johnson and is inconsistent with Johnson's view that the Dutch were intruders.

[55] Benjamin Trumbull, *A Plea, in Vindication of the Connecticut Title to the Contested Lands, Lying West of the Province of New York* . . . (New Haven, 1774); printed in Taylor, ed., *Susquehannah Co. Papers*, VI, no. 4.

[56] *A New Abridgement of the Law* (London, 1768), IV, 211. It is not certain that this was the edition used; many such legal works appeared in numerous editions, but the pagination remained the same.

[57] Smith, *History of the Colony of Novo Caesaria.*

believed the western ocean to be near at hand; but Johnson asserted that at the time of the surrender of the Plymouth patent, that is, in 1635, mention was made of "3000 Miles to the South Sea."[58] Wilson saw lurking behind the simple question of geography the larger one of intent in the interpretation of charters, and most of the notes on his argument that remain dwell upon this matter. He wheeled up a veritable battery of legal authorities—Blackstone, Vattel, Rutherforth, Bacon, Coke, Grotius, and Pufendorf—to demonstrate that in order to interpret a deed one had to go back into the past to ascertain the intention of those who drew it up.[59] Intention had to govern interpretation. Where the meaning of the words was not plain, one had to ascertain the common practice of the day, the motives of the parties, and the like, enlarging or contracting the meaning of the words as seemed suitable. It was remarkable, however, that "we have oftener reason to restrain then to enlarge" meaning in a legal instrument. "Would we judge of Charters we must not apply to the correct maps of the present Day but the Vague and uncertain knowledge the makers had of N. America."[60]

Johnson remained unpersuaded. He saw the size of the grant as no problem. A "grant of Lands generally will include all whether 5 or 500 Acres," and Connecticut's was a liberal grant, a royal grant, given to a people who had been "at great Expence and Hazard forming a Colony [that] extended Dominion 120 Miles." "You have been faithful in little you shall have much."[61] If the devil can quote scripture, a lawyer can cite treatises. Seizing upon some of Wilson's own authorities, Johnson insisted that interpretation "should be most against [the] Grantor" and that in grants, as distinct from laws, intention must be ascertained from the words alone.[62] Charles II was not deceived; John Winthrop, Jr., who secured the charter, said nothing about the South Sea. If there was

[58] Clerk's notes, Taylor, ed., *Susquehannah Co. Papers,* VII, 198, 201.
[59] William Blackstone, *Commentaries on the Laws of England* (Philadelphia, 1771); Vattel, *Law of Nations;* Thomas Rutherforth, *Institutes of Natural Law* . . . (Cambridge, Eng., 1754-1756, 1779); Matthew Bacon, *New Abridgement; The Sixth Part of the Reports of Sir Edward Coke* (London, 1738, 1776, 1777); Hugo Grotius, *The Rights of War and Peace in Three Books* (London, 1738); Samuel Pufendorf, *Of the Law of Nature and Nations* (London, 1729). The Blackstone edition given here was the first American one; Wilson, of course, may have used an English edition, but the pagination would not differ.
[60] Clerk's notes, Taylor, ed., *Susquehannah Co. Papers,* VII, 197-198.
[61] Reed's notes, *ibid.,* 205, 208.
[62] *Ibid.,* 205. Johnson cited Vattel, *Law of Nations,* II, Sections 264 and 300, and Bacon, *New Abridgement,* V, 525.

a mistake, it was the king's own. For Johnson, the sanctity of charter words was inviolate; property was beyond the reach even of Parliament.

The sanctity of property given by patent led both Johnson and Root to condemn the royal grant to the Duke of York in 1664. As will be recalled, the duke's bounds ran from the Delaware River to the Connecticut, from the Kennebec to the St. Croix and included Long Island as well as other islands. Johnson, about whose argument we have the most information, declared that this grant meant that Charles II had illegally and unwarrantably resumed lands previously granted to Connecticut in order to hand them over to his brother. Johnson noted that at the time, Connecticut had protested the loss of its towns on Long Island. When the Pennsylvania agents pointed out that a royal commission had established a boundary between New York and Connecticut, and that its work was "founded on and confirmatory of our Principle that the Settlement of a Christian Prince was an absolute Limit,"[63] Johnson asserted that the commission's business was with jurisdictional rights, not property; that the king was reaching for power, not settling property claims between Connecticut and his brother. Although Connecticut had claimed Dutch territory, it gave it up when it saw that the king had granted New Netherlands to the duke. Thus Connecticut had two western boundaries, one at New York and one at the South Sea. Root cited Bacon to prove that the king's grant should be so construed that it might take effect, meaning that the grant to the duke should have in no way interfered with Connecticut's claim to land west of the Delaware River.

Root and Johnson felt even more strongly about the royal grant to William Penn, which the latter called a junior patent, defective on its face because it was given for no true consideration, but only as a reward for Admiral Penn's merit.[64] Johnson went thoroughly into the question of royal regranting of land, describing the strict procedure that had to be followed to dissolve a corporation and divest it of its property. Analysis of dissolutions showed no reason to argue that Pennsylvania could be a regrant out of Connecticut's lands. Reed answered that Pennsylvania argued that land west of the Delaware River had never been granted at all, not that the king had resumed lands originally granted to Connecticut when he issued a charter to William Penn.

The Pennsylvania agents sought to buttress this interpretation and

[63] Reed's notes, Taylor, ed., *Susquehannah Co. Papers*, VII, 233.
[64] *Ibid.*, 214.

expose the pretensions of Connecticut by attacking the vagueness of the sea-to-sea bounds in the charter of 1662. Connecticut was described as bounded on the east by Narragansett Bay, on the north by the Massachusetts line, "on the South by the Sea, and in longitude as the lyne of the Massachusetts Colony, runinge from East to West," that is, from the bay on the east to the South Sea on the west.[65] How could the colony have the sea for its southern boundary and still run from the bay to the Pacific? The Pennsylvania agents announced that according to the charter, Connecticut had no southern boundary, and that the state did not know the boundaries of its own grant. This uncertainty was enough in itself to call the whole charter into question. There was even some quibbling over whether Long Island Sound could be called a sea or not.

Johnson, who undertook to answer these contentions, gave his mind free play. If the description of boundaries was vague, this defect did not threaten the charter; the court might be left to discover the real meaning of the words. If the sound was not a sea, why, one could skip over Long Island to the ocean. At any rate, the sea was a southern boundary as far as it extended; after that one could take as boundary the line of 40° of latitude, the old southern boundary of New England. Indeed, this would be the just construction, "but the Moderation of New England limits them. . . . Shall we lose by our Moderation?"[66] Johnson wanted to know. Reed remarked scornfully that the Connecticut agents were ready to overleap the sea and the continent as suited their purpose, that in their moderation they were willing to take something less than the whole state of Pennsylvania.

More than a quibble over definitions was at issue. The Pennsylvania agents maintained that the original Connecticut grant extended no farther west than the colony of New Haven, that clearly Charles II had not meant to include these settlements, for he wrote to that colony soon afterwards, addressing it as a separate government. If the Connecticut charter did not include the New Haven colony, then the purchases from the Indians made by New Haven people along the Delaware River and their attempted settlement there could not be used by Connecticut to strengthen its claims to lands west of the Delaware; and of course, a western line at New Haven made Connecticut's sea-to-sea claims ab-

[65] William MacDonald, ed., *Select Charters and Other Documents Illustrative of American History, 1606-1775* (New York, 1899), 119.
[66] Reed's notes, Taylor, ed., *Susquehannah Co. Papers*, VII, 209.

surd. In replying, Johnson made the distinction mentioned before, a distinction between jurisdictional and property rights. Although New Haven remained a separate jurisdiction for a few years after 1662, the lands were within the bounds described in the Connecticut charter. Jurisdiction concerned actual settlements, but right to the soil, right to property was a different matter. "Property and Privilidges are distinct in the Charter and ought to be kept so."[67] A patent gave title to land; governing rights were a wholly separate concern.

The Pennsylvania agents made some telling thrusts by recalling Connecticut's past convictions about her boundaries, by shifting from legal and verbal technicalities to the history of Connecticut's conduct. What stood out, of course, was that Connecticut people had not acted in accordance with the sea-to-sea clause until the Indian purchase of 1754, nearly one hundred years after the charter was issued. Further, the basis for that action received no recognition from the Connecticut government until 1771. Repeatedly, in answering official inquiries from England, Connecticut had described her bounds without mention of land west of the Delaware River. Sergeant pointedly observed that at one time the Susquehannah Company with Connecticut's blessing had sought a grant of lands directly from the king. If in 1662 Charles II had divested himself in favor of Connecticut of all the land that state was claiming in 1782 at Trenton, what need had there been for the Susquehannah Company to seek a royal grant? And how could Connecticut explain its failure to mention as a particular grievance the Quebec Act of 1774, often mentioned by Congress, which certainly infringed upon the boundaries claimed? Obviously Connecticut had not followed a consistent course, and its western claim was a recent innovation. James Wilson perhaps believed that time had destroyed any claim to land westward of New England, if indeed, that claim had ever had any basis, but extant notes give no clue to his development of the point. Reed not only mentioned Connecticut's long silence, but listed eleven instances in which Connecticut had positively indicated that her bounds were of narrow scope. His list included boundary agreements with the Dutch and with New York, laws passed by Connecticut, and letters from Connecticut governors disavowing claims to land west of the Delaware.[68]

Laboring under these blows, Johnson held steadfastly to his principle

[67] *Ibid.*, 208.
[68] *Ibid.*, 231-232. In 1754, Governors Roger Wolcott and Thomas Fitch, the latter

of the inviolability of property rights. No governor could give away the property of his people, and silence operated only against rights and privileges, not against property. Inconsistently, he dismissed the boundary agreements with the Dutch as irrelevant because Connecticut had not yet been vested with its property in 1650 and 1656, ignoring his earlier insistence upon an equitable title derived from older patents. As for the boundary agreement with New York in 1683, this was exacted through threat; Connecticut leaders feared that by not acquiescing they would jeopardize the charter. Other fears had kept them silent for many years thereafter, the dispute with the Mohegan Indians, for example, which had hung "like a Dagger over their Heads."[69] With the Mohegan dispute threatening the integrity of Connecticut territory, prudence and caution necessarily became the policy of the colony.

Finally, certain practical considerations injected into the closing arguments need to be mentioned. The distance of the western lands from the main part of Connecticut seemed to Sergeant to make the claim obviously ridiculous. The towns along the Connecticut River had created a separate jurisdiction because of their remoteness from Boston. "If the Government of Boston was too remote for Connecticut can a Country 1000 Miles distant be more convenient for the Government at Hartford?"[70] But Johnson held that there was no greater absurdity in Connecticut's claim than in Virginia's much larger one or in that of Massachusetts to Maine. Sergeant concluded by touching upon the "policy of the decision"[71] to be made at Trenton; the clerk, however, tells us nothing more. In summing up, Johnson stated that Sergeant believed that the interests of the United States in the west would be decided by "the strongest Arm."[72] The clerk's notes on Wilson show that he intended "to suggest the Advantages or inconveniences that are likely to flow from the Decision of this Court," but no hint remains of the line taken.[73]

Only in the notes on Johnson and Reed does the argument based on public policy become clear. If we can rely upon Griffin's notes, Johnson

more forthrightly than the former, had disavowed any wish to recognize encroachment upon Pennsylvania soil.

  [69] *Ibid.*, 213. Connecticut had had a protracted territorial dispute with the Mohegan Indians that was not settled until 1773.

  [70] Clerk's notes, *ibid.*, 191.

  [71] *Ibid.*, 192.

  [72] Reed's notes, *ibid.*, 216.

  [73] Clerk's notes, *ibid.*, 196.

deprecated the injection of policy issues, but only for an instant.[74] A decision in favor of Connecticut, he asserted, would stand the United States in good stead in coming negotiations over a western boundary, because upholding the sea-to-sea clause would give a legal basis for a boundary at the Mississippi. Neither conquest of the backlands nor presumed forfeiture of them to the United States afforded a secure basis for American territorial demands. For the one, British troops were still in possession of them; for the other, there was no body in the United States to which the lands could have been forfeited. The United States was a federal, not a corporate union; Congress had no imperial rights.[75] Reed countered these final assertions of Johnson by holding that conquest had given the United States a right to the back country, and that ungranted lands had belonged to New York, which had gained them from the Six Nations and had now ceded them to the American nation. His last word was that the right of declaring war and peace, which had been given to the Confederation, included "all the Objects that may be attained by War or Peace."[76]

Final arguments were heard on December 24. Apart from Pennsylvania's submission of a deposition from William Alexander, Lord Stirling, testifying to events surrounding the negotiations between the Indians and the Susquehannah Company, the trial was over. The decision given out on December 30 was notable for its brevity and its complete silence on the reasons why the judges awarded jurisdiction of the disputed territory to Pennsylvania.[77] They had agreed beforehand to announce their decision as a unanimous one and never to divulge the reasoning which led them to it.[78] Even though one must rely upon notes admittedly incomplete for the substance of the arguments, one feels justified in agreeing with the judges' award. Reed was genuinely surprised at the feebleness of Johnson's presentation.[79]

[74] Boyd, ed., *Papers of Jefferson*, VI, 497.

[75] Reed's notes, Taylor, ed., *Susquehannah Co. Papers*, VII, 216, 238.

[76] *Ibid.*, 238.

[77] Ford *et al.*, ed., *Journals of Continental Congress*, XXIV, 31-32.

[78] Cyrus Griffin to Barnabas Bidwell, Sept. 15, 1796, in Timothy Pickering Papers, LVIII, 350, Massachusetts Historical Society, Boston. Some time after the trial a conviction grew that two of the judges had really favored Connecticut. This notion first appeared in the *Connecticut Courant*, Jan. 25, 1785, in the course of a series of articles on the Trenton trial.

[79] Johnson was not well during the trial, according to Reed. See Reed to Bryan, Dec. 25, 1782, in Reed, *Joseph Reed*, II, 390.

Did the outcome of the trial justify Dyer's fear that the failure of two judges from landed states to participate would mean a decision unfavorable to Connecticut? In short, was the decision a political rather than a judicial one? Obviously no definitive answer is possible because the judges did not reveal the reasons for awarding jurisdiction to Pennsylvania, but a number of considerations may point to an answer.

The validity of western claims was most directly challenged by James Wilson, who believed that the English kings had never intended to grant such princely domains. As noted earlier, Wilson was speculating in lands in the disputed area, and his association with the Illinois-Wabash Company would naturally cause him to oppose the claims of landed states. In commenting upon his presentation, Joseph Reed remarked that Wilson's argument was "both labourious and judicious, he has taken much pains, having the success of Pennsylvania much at heart, both on public and private account."[80] But Wilson was a lawyer as well as a speculator; it behooved him to seize upon every argument that might influence the court. And he was part of a joint effort. His interest in overthrowing western claims can be overemphasized in the total range of Pennsylvania's argument. By far the greater part of that state's case was directed to the defects in Connecticut's charter and to the past conduct of Connecticut in agreeing to boundaries with New York and neglecting until 1771 to claim land west of the Delaware River.

Other than Wilson's questioning of sea-to-sea clauses, the importance of the western claims as such received only passing mention. In opposition to Johnson, the Pennsylvania agents took the line that such claims would be of no significance in the negotiations with Great Britain over a western boundary for the United States. Reed's position, it will be recalled, was that all the western territory had been ceded by New York.

Yet in Congress in 1786 when the acceptance of Connecticut's cession of western lands was at stake, Pennsylvania was one of the states to support Connecticut in her desire to have her cession accepted with its implied right to a western reserve. By voting with Connecticut, Pennsylvania was tacitly acknowledging that Connecticut had a claim to western territory; but Pennsylvania demanded a price for her support.[81]

[80] Reed to Bryan, Dec. 20, 1782, *ibid.*

[81] Ford *et al.*, eds., *Journals of Continental Congress*, XXX, 295-296, 299-304, 307-308, 310-311. Altogether eight votes were taken before acceptance of the Connecticut cession was achieved. Only once did Connecticut and Pennsylvania vote on opposite sides of this question; the split occurred on the third vote after Pennsylvania had of-

Involved in the congressional bargaining was James Wilson, despite the position he and other agents had taken at Trenton.[82] Connecticut met Pennsylvania's price by expressing her willingness formally to acquiesce in the Trenton decree of four years earlier and by suggesting that proprietors of the Susquehannah Company, who would be denied their claims within Pennsylvania, as distinguished from actual settlers in Wyoming, might get compensatory lands in the Reserve. It is useless to look for consistency among landless states on the issue of the western claims. They shifted their ground when it served their purposes to do so.

Local historians, aware of the prominent mention of the Trenton decree in the congressional debates over acceptance of Connecticut's cession, have concluded that Pennsylvania's support in 1786 had been secured at the trial in 1782, that some kind of bargain was struck sacrificing the interests of the Wyoming settlers to Connecticut's desire to obtain a reserved area west of Pennsylvania.[83] Such conclusions come from reading history backwards. No evidence supports the notion that the trial was a sellout or that an honest effort was not made on each side. The most disappointed man after Trenton, Eliphalet Dyer, was convinced that his colleagues had done their very best to convince the court.

In 1782 Pennsylvania did not see herself as a champion of a principle dear to landless states. Her concern was securing jurisdiction to lands within her charter boundaries. The larger question of Connecticut's right to territory west of Pennsylvania was not before the court. The judges viewed their commission narrowly: they were to settle a jurisdictional dispute between two states, no more and no less. That is why the judges cited their commission when the Connecticut agents asked that the Wyoming settlers be called to appear: the judges held that their

---

fered a motion providing that acceptance by the United States of any cession should not be interpreted as confirming the claim of the ceding state to any territory not ceded. In trying to protect the gains from the Trenton trial, Pennsylvania was jeopardizing Connecticut's right to a western reserve.

[82] Wilson offered one of the motions which recognized Connecticut's right to a reserved western area. Moreover, he had reputedly come to Congress in a mood to bargain. See Pelatiah Webster to William Samuel Johnson, Mar. 13, 1786, William Samuel Johnson Papers, IV, 37, Connecticut Historical Society.

[83] Henry T. Blake, before the Fairfield County Historical Society, 1893, and the editorial in the *Wyoming Republican and Farmer's Herald*, in 1837, both quoted in Oscar J. Harvey and Ernest G. Smith, *A History of Wilkes-Barre* (Wilkes-Barre, 1927), III, 1306.

appearance would have meant broadening the trial's scope to include private soil rights.[84] No one ever claimed that the Trenton decree officially affected Connecticut's larger claims. Quite the contrary. When Connecticut's cession was before Congress in 1786, one reason some of the states opposed any specific mention of the Trenton decree was their fear that formal acknowledgment of its validity might imply Connecticut's right to territory not covered by the Trenton decision.[85] Contemporaries did not see the trial as establishing a precedent with respect to interpretation of sea-to-sea clauses. Rather, for them the trial's importance lay in the fact that two sovereign states had chosen to settle a serious dispute through civilized means. This was the view of Robert Livingston quoted at the start of this essay. It was also the view of the only newspaper which gave any real coverage to the trial, the *Freeman's Journal*. The printer began his series of articles with this encomium:

This celebrated cause ... presents to the world a new and extraordinary spectacle: Two powerful and populous states, sovereign and independent (except as members of the federal union) contending for a tract of country equal in extent to many, and superior to some European kingdoms. Instead of recurring to arms, the *ultimo ratio* of kings and states, they submit to the arbitration of judges mutually chosen from indifferent states. ... Nothing is wanting to complete the honour and happiness of the United States on this event, but a chearful ready acquiescience in the definitive judgment: and it is not to be doubted but the usual wisdom and prudence of the state of Connecticut will be manifested on this occasion.[86]

His enthusiasm was premature, of course, as enthusiasm about man always is. But a number of others shared his view. Ironically, one of these was John Dickinson,[87] president of the Supreme Executive Council of Pennsylvania, whose term of office was to be marred by bickering

---

[84] Ford *et al.*, eds., *Journals of Continental Congress*, XXIV, 11.

[85] Charles Pettit to Jeremiah Wadsworth, May 27, 1786, Burnett, ed., *Letters of Members of the Continental Congress*, VIII, 368-369. In 1785, however, some members of Congress had apparently expressed the belief that the Trenton decision called into question Connecticut's right to any western lands; the Connecticut delegates to Gov. Matthew Griswold, Feb. 24, 1785, *ibid.*, 41.

[86] *Freeman's Journal*, Jan. 22, 1783. The newspaper printed the positions of Pennsylvania and Connecticut on Jan. 29 and Feb. 5.

[87] Dickinson to the General Assembly, Jan. 24, 1783, in *Pennsylvania Colonial Records*, XIII, 486-487.

and violence that erupted in 1783 and 1784 as Pennamites sought to give practical effect to the victory they thought they had won. During the trial the judges had informed participants that only jurisdictional rights could be ruled upon, and immediately after the trial was over the judges explained to Dickinson that private soil rights were a separate matter which could be determined only by a separate action under another clause of Article IX of the Articles of Confederation.[88] These distinctions were lost on Pennamite speculators. The issue of private soil rights remained for years to exacerbate Pennsylvania's relationships with the Wyoming settlers. On the other hand some of the Susquehannah Company leaders believed that they had evidence of fraud in the trial proceedings; repeatedly they sought to persuade Connecticut to reopen the case. In Congress in 1784 they were outmaneuvered in their effort to get the Trenton decision reconsidered, but long after that company leaders sought to pressure the Connecticut General Assembly into action on the company's behalf.[89]

It would have taken the wisdom of Solomon to satisfy both Pennamites and Yankees, but the establishment of political jurisdiction was never successfully challenged after 1782. There was that gain at least.

[88] William Whipple and others to Dickinson, Dec. 31, 1782, in *Pennsylvania Archives*, XVIII, 629-630.

[89] On the basis of hearsay evidence it was believed that documents sent from England had fallen into the hands of James Wilson and had been deliberately suppressed; Zebulon Butler to Elizur Talcott, May 16, 1783, Butler Papers, Wyoming Historical and Geological Society, Wilkes-Barre, Pa.; printed in Taylor, ed., *Susquehannah Co. Papers*, VII, no. 160. Julian P. Boyd has analyzed brilliantly the role of Jefferson in preventing Connecticut from reopening the trial issue in Congress. See Boyd, ed., *Papers of Jefferson*, VI, 501-505. In 1787, for example, leaders of the Susquehannah Company petitioned the Connecticut General Assembly to reopen the case. See Susquehannah Settlers, I, 172-175.

American Commercial Diplomacy in Russia, 1780 to 1783

David M. Griffiths*

OF the numerous failures experienced by American diplomacy in the course of the War for Independence none was more glaring than that of the Dana mission to St. Petersburg, 1781 to 1783. For two years Francis Dana, sent by Congress to conclude treaties of amity and commerce, resided at the Russian court, unrecognized and unwanted. For two years he suffered and endured, expecting recognition at any moment. And he departed the Russian capital lacking any realistic notion why his mission had proven so unfruitful.

In looking back at the event, historians have been prone to account for Dana's misadventures by a variety of facile but unconvincing explanations. Among the reasons most commonly offered are the Russian ruler's hatred for the American revolutionaries,[1] complex boudoir politics in which Dana was outclassed by the more versatile British ambassador,[2]

* Mr. Griffiths is a member of the Department of History, University of North Carolina at Chapel Hill. An earlier version of this article was read at a meeting of the American Association for the Advancement of Slavic Studies, Knoxville, Tenn., October 1969. Mr. Griffiths wishes to thank the Inter-University Committee on Travel Grants and the Office of Research Administration at the University of North Carolina for grants which helped further research for this article.

[1] See, for example, N. N. Bolkhovitinov, *Stanovlenie russko-amerikanskikh otnoshenii, 1775-1815* (Moscow, 1966), 59-60, 87; A. I. Startsev, "Amerikanskii vopros i russkaia diplomatiia v gody voiny S Sh A za nezavisimost," L. G. Beskrovnyi, ed., *Mezhdunarodnye sviazi Rossii v XVII-XVIII vv.* (Moscow, 1966), 468; G. P. Gooch, *Catherine the Great and Other Studies* (New York, 1954), 95; E. Dvoichenko-Markov, "The American Philosophical Society and Early Russian-American Relations," *Proceedings of the American Philosophical Society*, XLIV (1950), 554; Michael T. Florinsky, *Russia: A History and an Interpretation* (New York, 1953), I, 511.

[2] W. P. Cresson, *Francis Dana: A Puritan Diplomat at the Court of Catherine the Great* (New York, 1930), the only full-length biography of Dana, presents the history of the mission in terms of "boudoir politics." It should be added that the author used no Russian sources, choosing instead to rely upon an emigré Polish historian for his background. Startsev, "Amerikanskii vopros," in Beskrovnyi, ed., *Mezhdunarodnye sviazi*, offers the explanation of a cabal struck up between the British ambassador and Prince Potemkin, the empress's erstwhile favorite. (p. 465) See also Samuel F. Bemis, *The Diplomacy of the American Revolution* (New York, 1935), 166, n. 9.

and the failure of the French ambassador to lend Dana diplomatic support.[3] None of the explanations, singly or in combination, stands up to historical criticism; for, as we shall see, Catherine II was in no sense ideologically hostile to the Americans, boudoir politics were nothing more than an entertaining sidelight to court life, and the French ambassador in actuality did everything possible to forward the success of the mission. Where, then, lies the explanation for the failure? To a great extent the answer may be found in the conflicting assumptions reached by the two states. The Russian state, which since the seventeenth century had been borrowing so much from the West in order to compete with it, considered itself an integral part of the European balance of power system. As such, it pursued in alliance with Prussia traditional goals in Poland for the first half of Catherine's reign, and then in 1781 arranged an alliance with Austria directed against the Ottoman Empire.[4] In each case the alliance was based upon considerations of the direct military contribution to be expected from the other participant.

The United States, on the other hand, had little to offer prospective allies in the way of military support. But this ostensible disadvantage was thought to be insignificant in comparison with what the former British colonies did have to offer: their trade. The colonists proposed to the world a revolutionary system of free interchange of goods, the foundation of universal peace and prosperity. The system was predicated upon the

[3] The myth of French duplicity has its origins in the War for Independence itself, and has been taken at its face value by historians who have uncritically read the papers of Adams, Dana, and other anti-Gallicans. In her *History of the Rise, Progress and Termination of the American Revolution* (Boston, 1805), Mercy Otis Warren accounted for the failure of the Dana mission by "the intrigues of Britain, the arts of France, and the profound policy of the court of Petersburg." In an obvious allusion to Benjamin Franklin, the archenemy of the anti-Gallicans, she adds: "It was also suggested, that the double-dealings of some Americans of consideration, had their weight in frustrating the negotiation, and preventing a treaty between one of the most distinguished powers in Europe, and the United States of America." (II, 304-305) Although Franklin has since been exonerated, the French still stand accused. See J. C. Hildt, *Early Diplomatic Negotiations of the United States with Russia*, Johns Hopkins Studies in Historical and Political Science, 24 (Baltimore, 1906), 15-18; F. P. Renaut, *Les rélations diplomatiques entre le Russie et les États-Unis (1776-1825). Catherine II et les insurgés. La mission Dana (1776-1783)* (Paris, 1923), I, 179; Bolkhovitinov, *Stanovlenie*, 82, 87; Startsev, "Amerikanskii vopros," in Beskrovnyi, ed., *Mezhdunarodnye sviazi*, 461.

[4] A convenient English-language account is Isabel de Madariaga, "The Secret Austro-Russian Treaty of 1781," *Slavonic and East European Review*, XXXVIII (1959), 114-145.

assumption that each state was especially suited by nature to produce certain goods which it could exchange for those goods it was not suited to produce. Each state, regardless of military capacity, would have a guaranteed position—defined by nature—within the community of nations. Inherent in the concept was the belief that free trade was in accord with the natural law of the universe; once established, a new era of international friendship and cooperation would be ushered in. Free trade, in short, was to render power politics obsolete.

Accompanying this outlook was a condescending attitude toward the *ancien regime* and its traditional diplomatic patterns. National rivalries, power blocs, and mercantilism were declared unnatural—incrustations on the body politic, hindering progress toward universal happiness. The United States would have nothing to do with these corrupt practices. It would support the natural harmony of interests; substitute open for secret diplomacy; appeal to the commercial self-interest of nations—if necessary over the heads of the existing governments—in order to win converts to the cause. In the process this "new diplomacy" would contribute to the destruction of the British mercantile empire and the attainment of American independence.[5]

The American attempt to apply its presuppositions to the Russian case, and the complex factors governing Russia's response, have thus far remained outside the scope of historical research. In particular, it is important to ascertain just what the possibilities for commercial intercourse were and, even more importantly, how the two states viewed these possibilities.

Russia was one of the first nations to attract the attention of the colonists as a potential ally; even before the Declaration of Independence had been signed, there was talk of dispatching an agent to St. Petersburg.[6] Mingled with anticipation that Russia might provide valuable aid, however, was fear that this aid might be rendered the British. Concern on

[5] Various aspects of this commercial diplomacy may be found in: Felix Gilbert, *To the Farewell Address: Ideas of Early American Foreign Policy* (Princeton, 1961); Paul A. Varg, *Foreign Policies of the Founding Fathers* (Lansing, Mich., 1963); Gerald Stourzh, *Benjamin Franklin and American Foreign Policy* (Chicago, 1954); Merrill D. Peterson, "Thomas Jefferson and Commercial Policy, 1782-1793," *William and Mary Quarterly*, 3d Ser., XXII (1965), 584-610.

[6] Francis Wharton, ed., *The Revolutionary Diplomatic Correspondence of the United States* (Washington, 1889), II, 241, 288. Hereafter cited as *Diplomatic Correspondence.*

this account vanished in early 1780 with the Russian Declaration of Armed Neutrality. The proclamation, naively thought to have been directed solely against British naval practices, contained provisions for free ships—free goods, unhindered commerce by neutrals along the coasts of belligerents, narrow interpretation of contraband, and precise definition of a blockaded port. These, in sum, were the very principles enumerated in the model "Plan of Treaties" the colonists had drawn up in 1776, and in the commercial aspect of the Franco-American treaty of 1778. To the hard pressed rebels it appeared that Catherine II had presented herself as a champion of free trade and an enemy of British naval supremacy.

Reaction to the proclamation by American agents abroad was unanimous. By taking a stand for the defense of neutral shipping the empress had struck a blow for American independence. Exulted Benjamin Franklin: "The great public event in Europe of this year is the proposal by Russia of an armed neutrality for protecting the liberty of commerce."[7] These sentiments were echoed by John Adams: "They [the British] repeat the word neutrality, neutrality, but it is as decisive a determination against them as a declaration of war would have been; perhaps more so."[8] Adams assumed that a congress of the neutral powers would convene at St. Petersburg, and that one of its first actions would be the recognition of American independence. The United States, he concluded, must have an ambassador at the Russian court.[9]

News of the proclamation reached the shores of North America in the summer of 1780, and the recommendations to send an agent to the Russian capital arrived soon thereafter, and led to a series of events culminating in the appointment of an ambassador to the court of Catherine II. The first steps in this direction were formal adherence to the principles of the Declaration of Armed Neutrality, orders to naval captains to observe these principles, and instructions to envoys abroad to add their signatures to the league if permitted.[10] Following suggestions by Adams and Arthur

[7] *Ibid.*, IV, 24. For the complete history of the armed neutrality, see Isabel de Madariaga, *Britain, Russia and the Armed Neutrality of 1780* (New Haven, 1961).

[8] *Diplomatic Correspondence,* III, 632-633, and also 611, 631, 761, 861; Worthington C. Ford, ed., *Letters of William Lee . . .* (Brooklyn, 1891), III, 796-797.

[9] *Diplomatic Correspondence,* IV, 57-58, 193; Charles Francis Adams, ed., *Works of John Adams* (Boston, 1850-1856), III, 263-322.

[10] Worthington C. Ford *et al.,* ed., *Journals of the Continental Congress* (Washington, 1904-1937), XVIII, 905-906, 1008. Hereafter cited as *Journals of Continental Congress.*

Lee that a minister be sent to Russia, Dana was selected over Alexander Hamilton and Lee himself.[11]

The announced objective of the mission was "to engage Her Imperial Majesty to favor and support the sovereignty and independence of these United States, and to lay a foundation for a good understanding and friendly intercourse between the subjects of Her Imperial Majesty and the citizens of these United States, to the mutual advantage of both nations." Congress gave the new minister powers to accede to the League of Armed Neutrality, to conclude separate treaties with any neutral powers for the protection of trade, and to propose a treaty of amity and commerce based upon "principles of equality and reciprocity." Among Dana's instructions several are noteworthy: to communicate with and accept advice from Adams, Franklin, and the French minister at St. Petersburg; to have the latter sound out the empress's disposition towards the United States; and, if the investigations were to prove positive, to announce himself and his mission formally to the empress. Congress displayed a total misunderstanding of the aims of the armed neutrality by proclaiming a "leading and capital point" to be the admission of the United States "as a party to the convention of the neutral maritime powers for maintaining the freedom of commerce. This regulation, in which the Empress is deeply interested, and from which she has derived so much glory, will open the way for your favorable reception, which we have the greater reason to expect, as she has publicly invited the belligerent powers to accede thereto."[12] While the empress had invited the belligerents to accede to the principles of the armed neutrality, she had by no means invited them into the league itself. Indeed, what room could there be for a belligerent in a neutral league?

While it may at first seem odd that a relative unknown such as Dana would be chosen for the delicate task, there are several explanations. The anti-Gallicans, a melange of figures including the Adams cousins, the numerous Lees of Virginia, and James Lovell, had gained the upper hand in Congress in the late 1770s. It was their conviction that France—with the tacit support of American commissioner to Versailles, Benjamin Franklin—was attempting to maintain the American colonies in a state

---

[11] *Ibid.*, 1139, 1155-1156, 1164, 1166; Edmund C. Burnett, ed., *Letters of Members of the Continental Congress* (Washington, 1921-1936), V, 496. Hereafter cited as *Letters of Continental Congress.*

[12] *Journals of Continental Congress*, XVIII, 1166-1173.

of diplomatic subordination, so that it would not have to share the American market with later comers. If the former colonists could only make known to the European neutrals the trade benefits to be reaped through American independence, the argument ran, these nations would rush to America's succor, thus breaking France's monopoly by default. To this end American envoys trekked around Europe in fruitless search of alliances. An anti-Gallican, but not as outspoken as the Lees, Dana had a second consideration in his favor when it came time to select a minister to Russia: the quiet Massachusetts lawyer was already in Europe, acting as John Adams's secretary, and hence would not have to hazard the treacherous trans-Atlantic crossing.[13] But, unknown to Dana and the Continental Congress, an unofficial envoy had already preceded him to St. Petersburg.

Stephen Sayre, a College of New Jersey educated adventurer from Long Island, had been employed in London by the colonial merchant Dennys DeBerdt in the 1760s. Combining an interest in commerce with a passion for politics, Sayre managed to get elected sheriff of London in 1773 in the wake of the Wilkesite movement—a testimony to "what ignorance and impudence will do in London," a contemporary noted.[14] Sayre next stood for a seat in Parliament, lost, and claimed fraud. Worse was to follow. In the autumn of 1775, as political tension in the capital mounted higher and higher, the ex-sheriff was abruptly arrested and carried off to the Tower of London on a charge of high treason. With friend Arthur Lee serving as lawyer, Sayre was quickly released. He was not to enjoy his freedom for any length of time. Shortly thereafter the banking business he had formed went bankrupt, and Sayre went to debtor's prison.

Sayre emerged from confinement in February 1777, anxious to rebuild his fortune and at the same time contribute to the fortunes of his homeland. In pursuit of his twin goals he was to spend the next six years at various European capitals, often in the assumed guise of an agent of the Continental Congress. In Berlin, Sayre and Arthur Lee—the former serving as the latter's secretary—had their official papers stolen by the

[13] Massachusetts Historical Society, *Collections*, 7th Ser. (Boston, 1902), III, 176. *Letters of Continental Congress*, IV, 454.
[14] W. B. Reed, *Life of Esther DeBerdt* . . . (Philadelphia, 1853), 186. For the only published account of Sayre's activities see the brief sketch by Julian P. Boyd, "The Adventure of Stephen Sayre," *Princeton University Library Chronicle*, II (1940-1941), 51-64.

British ambassador while negotiating for a commercial agreement. Discouraged, Lee quarreled with his secretary and returned to Paris. Sayre stayed on in a futile attempt to convince Frederick the Great to acquire a neutral port in the West Indies through which trade could be carried on with the United States.[15] He presented a similar plan for a neutral port, either on St. Eustatius or St. Thomas, to Count Andreas Peter Bernstorff, the Danish foreign minister, in Copenhagen. It enjoyed no more success.[16] Nor did an interview with Gustav III of Sweden at a masked ball in Stockholm bring the desired results.[17] In Amsterdam the intrepid Sayre gained the trust of a group of merchants who provided credits for the construction of a ship to ply the route between that city and America via the West Indies. Just as he was preparing to make his maiden voyage news reached the Netherlands of the Declaration of Armed Neutrality. Sayre altered his plans to accommodate St. Petersburg.[18]

Long before the declaration the peripatetic merchant had disclosed to a sympathetic audience, and, incidentally, a British spy, some of his choicer projects. Among other items Sayre talked "*gravely* of going on to St. Petersburg to make a conquest of the Empress, who loves he says handsome men, and may have a curiosity for an American galant."[19] During his residencies in Copenhagen and Stockholm he had discovered for him-

---

[15] The relevant manuscript materials may be found in the following: Elliot to Suffolk, May 27 to Nov. 28, 1777, Foreign Office Papers, Class 353, Piece 4, 9-38, *passim*, Public Record Office. Hereafter cited as F. O. 353/4, 9-38. Pons to Vergennes, June 21 to Nov. 29, 1777, Correspondance Politique, Prussie, Vol. 195, Nos. 274-297, *passim*, Archives des Affaires Étrangères, Paris. For materials once in the Prussian archives see Marion D. Learned, *Guide to the Manuscript Materials Relating to American History in the German State Archives* (Washington, 1912), 20-24, and *Politische Correspondenz Friedrichs des Grossen* (Berlin, 1879-1939), XXXIX, 225, 227, 231, 239, 256.

[16] See State Papers, Class 75, Piece 133, 35, Public Record Office. Hereafter cited as S. P. 75/133, 35. Laval to Suffolk, Dec. 20, 1777, to May 2, 1778, S. P. 75/134, 1-3, 5, 14.

[17] Benjamin F. Stevens, *Facsimiles of Manuscripts in European Archives Relating to America, 1773-1783* (London, 1889-1895), V, 489-512; Sayre to Isaac Sears, Aug. 25, 1778, to Benjamin Franklin, Nov. 7, 1778, Jan. 23, Mar. 10, 21, Apr. 13, 1779, Franklin Papers, XXXIX, 162, XII, 115, XIII, 31, 181, 212, and XIV, 30, American Philosophical Society, Philadelphia. See several letters contained in a deposition by Sayre to George Washington, Jan. 3, 1795, State Papers, National Archives, Washington.

[18] Sayre to Franklin, Mar. 21, June 7, 9, Oct. 10, 1779, XIII, 212, XIV, 158, 165, and XVI, 23, Franklin Papers; Sayre to Washington, Oct. 15, 1790, State Papers, National Archives; W. H. de Beaufort, ed., *Brieven van en aan Joan Derck van der Capellen van de Poll* (Utrecht, 1879), 106, 154-163, 170, 240.

[19] Wentworth to Suffolk, May 15, 1777, Stevens, *Facsimiles*, VII, 694-704.

self that the northern neutrals looked to the Russian empress for initiative in maritime matters.[20] The Declaration of Armed Neutrality had settled the question.

We first find mention of the ex-sheriff in Russia in a dispatch of April 17, 1780, from James Harris, the British ambassador to St. Petersburg: "There arrived here about a week ago an Englishman by the name of Smith. From his language, way of living, and behavior, there are strong suspicions of his being either an American or a rebel agent."[21] Neither the alias nor a pose as a Leeward Islander sufficed to throw Harris off the track, and through his observations we may follow Sayre's activities in Russia.

Harris recorded several vain efforts by the American to obtain approval for a design to establish a Russian colony on an unidentified fertile, uninhabited island near Surinam, through which hemp and sailcloth were to be shipped in Russian vessels on their way past the British blockade of the North American mainland. In exchange for these naval stores the Americans were to provide rice and indigo, or else arrange a triangular trade and deliver sugar, cotton, and coffee from the West Indies. According to Harris, Sayre was supported in his solicitations by the Dutch resident Van Brienen, from whom he also received financial assistance. Van Brienen allegedly presented the proposal to A. R. Vorontsov, president of the Commerce College. The latter in turn passed it on to the empress, who "rejected it with disdain and comtempt." "Unless I saw here every day fresh and unheard of extravagances," continued Harris, "I should not think his ridiculous plan deserved a moment's attention."[22]

When the duchess of Kingston, whose celebrated bigamy trial had shared the London headlines with Sayre's treason trial a few years pre-

[20] Sayre to John Adams, Dec. 30, 1780, Adams Papers, Box 353, Massachusetts Historical Society, Boston. All papers emanating from Russia are dated in the Old Style or Julian calendar, which lagged eleven days behind the Western or Gregorian in the 18th century.

[21] Harris to Stormont, Apr. 17, 1780, S. P. 91/104, 37.

[22] Apr. 24, 1780, S. P. 91/105, 42; Sayre to Adams, Oct. 21, Dec. 30, 1780, Adams Papers, Box 353. Sayre's suggestion that the empress supply the money and the ships for the expedition was futile, for when Russian merchants desiring to set up trade with the East Indies made a similar request, her response was: "Suggest to the merchants to trade where they will. With regards to me, I will not give people, ships or money, and renounce all land and possessions in the East Indies and America for all times." See I. M. Kulisher, *Istoriia russkoi torgovli do deviatnadt-satogo veka vkliuchitelno* (St. Petersburg, 1923), 231-232. She enunciated her commercial philosophy to the philosophe Melchior Grimm in the following manner:

viously, rejected an application for a loan, the American announced his intention of leaving Russia.[23] But within a few days came more encouraging news. In an order to the Commerce College the empress made more explicit her determination to protect Russian merchants on the high seas. While contraband would not be tolerated, "all other goods, to whomever they may belong, and even if they belong to the subjects of one or another of the belligerent powers, may be freely transported on Russian vessels and shall enjoy, together with the goods of our subjects, the protection of the Russian flag." Presumably Sayre did not pause to read another provision: "We expressly forbid the merchants of our Empire to allow foreigners to sail ships or carry on commerce under their names,"[24] for he set right to work to take advantage of the new decree.

Having enlisted the cooperation of a Russian by name of Arsenev, a lieutenant-colonel in the hussars and former aide-de-camp to the director of the Admiralty, he received the Admiralty's sanction to construct a shipyard along the Neva River on land rented from a brewer. Under the company name of "Arsenev and Smith" the two began work on a large ship; but no sooner had the work gotten under way than a mysterious fire destroyed everything. Sayre immediately placed the blame upon the shoulders of the English.[25] Harris, in a formal written statement to the empress via the favorite, Potemkin, denied Sayre's accusations; the empress responded that she would not even deign to respond to the American's accusations.[26] Undaunted, "Arsenev and Smith" laid the keels for two new ships, this time with the assistance of a Russian carpenter

---

"Mon principe est que tout commerce aille comme il peut, et qu'il ne faut point donner de crocs-en-jambe au commerce comme à tout plein d'autres choses." *Sbornik imperatorskago russkago istoricheskago obshchestva,* XXIII (1878), 138.

[23] Harris to Stormont, May 1, 1780, S. P. 91/105, 47.

[24] The decree, together with the empress's order, may be found in fond 15 ("Gos. Arkhiv"), delo 457, Central State Archive for Ancient Acts, Moscow. The decree alone is published in F. Martens, *Recueil des traites et conventions conclus par la Russie avec les puissances étrangères* (St. Petersburg, 1874-1909), III, 271.

[25] Harris to Stormont, July 21, 1780, in S. P. 91/105, 86; L. H. Labande, ed., *Un diplomat français à la cour de Catherine II: Journal intime du Chevalier de Corberon, 1775-1780* (Paris, 1901), II, 326. The loss was later estimated by Sayre at £1,500: see Stephen Sayre, *The Case of Stephen Sayre* (Philadelphia, 1803), 8.

[26] Harris's statement is to be found in an enclosure to Stormont, July 21, 1780, S. P. 91/105, 86, and in Third Earl of Malmesbury, ed., *Diaries and Correspondence of Sir James Harris, First Earl of Malmesbury* (London, 1844), I, 327-328. The empress's reply was: "L'Américain ne peut vous faire nulle part, si peu de mal que chez moi; méprisez les bruits qu'on répand comme je les méprise: ils ne font aucune impression sur moi, et je croirois vous injurer si j'y faisois attention."

who, following in the footsteps of Peter the Great, had spent five years at Deptford Yard.[27]

Although Harris believed the ships too large ever to be launched, the empress put her faith in more concrete measures. She warned Arsenev that if an investigation showed him to be connected with Sayre, the ships would never enjoy the sanctuary of the Russian flag.[28] The empress also warned her governor-general in Archangel that an Englishman from that city had written to Franklin about the construction of a ship for the American cause. "You will realize that, aside from the illegal aid they would render the . . . colonies now rebelling against their king, such ships might be utilized against our commerce and that of friendly courts."[29] The unidentified "Englishman" to whom the empress referred was undoubtedly Sayre, who had earlier visited Archangel, and who carried on a voluminous—although one-sided—correspondence with Franklin. Work on the ships in St. Petersburg progressed, but they were launched in the autumn of 1782 under Arsenev's name alone, and confined their activities to transporting malt and hemp between the Russian capital and Brest.[30] That the empress would allow no commercial relations between Russia and America to jeopardize her already strained contacts with Great Britain is also the substance of a melodramatic account related to Adams on Sayre's return to Amsterdam in December 1781:

A certain native of America, who had been, as he thought, a great man in Europe, and who thought himself, and was thought by some others, to be the handsomest man in the world, both in face and figure, as well as a man of the most polished manners and irresistible address—this gentleman made a voyage or a journey, or both, to St. Petersburg, in the hopes of obtaining an audience of the autocratice *for the benefit of his country*. But the lady was as cold as marble. Neither the face nor the figure nor the address could procure a glance or an ogle from her.[31]

[27] Sayre to Adams, Oct. 21, 1780, Adams Papers, Box 353.

[28] Harris, Mar. 13, Apr. 27, 1781, F. O. 65/2, 40, 68. See also Malmesbury, ed., *Diaries*, I, 419-420.

[29] Letter of Apr. 1781, *Russkii Arkhiv*, 1893, I, 314.

[30] Harris to Stormont, Mar. 13, Apr. 27, Sept. 3, Oct. 21, 1781, F. O. 65/2, 40, 68, F. O. 65/4, 127, F. O. 65/5, 151. A note, dated Aug. 21, 1782, Correspondence Consulaire: St. Pétersbourg, 1778-1792, Affaires Étrangères, B1 989, no. 8, Archives Nationales, Paris, reveals that a "General Arsenev" had built and launched two ships. Sayre later confirmed that the ships carried malt and hemp between Russia and France. See Stephen Sayre, *A Short Narrative of the Life and Character of Stephen Sayre* (n. p., 1794).

[31] Adams to Mercy Warren, Aug. 8, 1801, Mass. Hist. Soc., *Collections*, 5th Ser. (Boston, 1885), IV, 445. In this letter Adams berates the 80-year-old Mrs. Warren

Thus Sayre's grandiose plans all fell through. To add insult to injury, his departure from Russia corresponded with the arrival of Dana, "who knew not two words of French, and very little of the world," bearing the coveted title of minister to St. Petersburg.[32]

To retrace the development of the Dana mission, the commissions and official instructions from Congress did not reach Europe until late March 1781. In accordance with his orders, Dana consulted Franklin, who attempted unsuccessfully to deflect him from his mission. Still following instructions, the eager American made an appointment with French Foreign Minister Vergennes, whom he knew to be opposed to militia diplomacy. Despite the obvious misgivings on both sides, the meeting proved relatively harmonious. Dana parried a suggestion, previously made by Franklin, that his credentials first be forwarded to Prince Dmitri Golitsyn, Russian ambassador at The Hague, for consideration, with the avowal that "a gentleman, not a native of the country, had written from thence [Russia] that some persons of rank, whether they were connected with the court at all I could not say, had expressed their wishes that some person should be sent there from America capable of giving information of the state of our affairs." The unidentified third party was apparently Sayre, who had intended that he himself be appointed minister. To Vergennes's all-too-well-founded fear that the empress in her role as mediatrix might be embarrassed by the presence of an American envoy, Dana responded that he would make the journey in a private capacity, and would make known his official assignment only after clear indications from the Russian court that formal relations were admissible. This last assurance appears to have mollified the foreign minister, who then reversed his previous opposition to the mission.[33]

Having received qualified approval from both Franklin and Vergennes, Dana now traveled to Holland, where Adams bestowed his blessing on the mission: "America, my dear sir, has been too long silent

---

for hinting in her history of the American Revolution that Francis Dana, Sayre's successor, should have resorted to more than conventional diplomacy to capture the attention of the Russian empress.

[32] Sayre to Washington, Oct. 15, 1790, State Papers, National Archives. It should be noted that Sayre himself knew no French.

[33] Vergennes to La Luzerne, Apr. 19, 1781, Correspondance Politique: États-Unis, Vol. 16, No. 16; Vergennes to Verac, Apr. 7, 1781, Correspondance Politique: Russie, Vol. 106, No. 14; *Diplomatic Correspondence*, IV, 349-351, 407-408, 722-723; *Journals of Continental Congress*, XX, 563.

in Europe. Her cause is that of all nations and all men; and it needs nothing but to be explained, to be approved," proclaimed Dana's former mentor.[34] The neophyte diplomat was thoroughly infected and, as he prepared to depart for St. Petersburg without disclosing his purpose to Golitsyn, he expressed an equally optimistic opinion: "The maritime powers want nothing but good information to convince them that it is for their substantial interest to form the most intimate connections with our country, and that speedily."[35]

From the very outset Dana's mission was doomed to failure. Language was a problem—the American spoke no French and the French ambassador to Russia, Verac, no English. More telling, Dana, as an anti-Gallican, deeply distrustful of French foreign policy and its representatives, determined to cut his own swath in the Russian capital. Notwithstanding Verac's warning that he move cautiously to avoid compromising himself and his nation, Dana—forgetting or ignoring the promise he had made to Vergennes to maintain the guise of a private citizen—at once began to envision himself as official ambassador to the court of St. Petersburg: "It appears to me," he wrote to Verac, "to be betraying the honor and dignity of the United States to seclude myself in a hotel, without making one effort to step forth into political life."[36] The cause of Dana's misplaced hopes at this point was a misinterpretation of the empress's intentions in her role as mediatrix. He had accepted the willingness of Catherine II to mediate between the belligerents as a willingness to recognize the existence, if not the independence, of the United States. Verac attempted to explain that while the imperial courts were mediating among Great Britain, France, and Spain, the British were to come to terms with their colonies *without the intervention of any other belligerent parties, not even that of the two imperial courts, unless their mediation shall be formally asked and granted for this object.*[37] This was far from tacit recognition. Yet the distinction drawn by Verac between the imperial mediation and the informal negotiations to be conducted paral-

---

[34] Adams to Dana, Apr. 18, 1781, in Adams, ed., *Works*, VII, 391-394.
[35] Dana to William Lee, May 17, 1781, Dana Family Papers, 1762-1793, Dana Papers, Massachusetts Historical Society.
[36] Dana to Verac, Aug. 23, 1781, Dana Papers, 1770-1782. The date is given in *Diplomatic Correspondence*, IV, 698, as Sept. 4 (n. s.). Where the Dana Papers have been published I shall cite the manuscript source only in case of omission, error, or divergence.
[37] *Diplomatic Correspondence*, IV, 705.

lel to it Dana viewed "as merely colorable terms, and a specimen of that finesse from which the politics of Europe can never be free."[38] Dana would have nothing to do with such obfuscations: "The United States trust to the justice of their cause and the rectitude of their intentions to open the way for them into the affections of the sovereigns of Europe. They have no sinister, no dishonorable propositions to make to any of them, but such only as they are persuaded will essentially promote the great interests and well-being of all," he self-righteously explained to the patient and tolerant French ambassador.[39] Dana, the New England lawyer, was arguing his moral case before a practiced diplomat well aware that legal briefs would have precious little effect upon the decisions of the Russian court.

For a variety of reasons—necessity of maintaining one's neutrality as mediatrix, commercial considerations, British diplomatic pressure, and desire to cater to the British whose help might be needed at a future date—the empress could not think of rendering Dana public recognition. This the French ambassador clearly understood. This the American envoy failed completely to fathom, despite explanations from Verac and from Sayre. Nothing could persuade him that diplomatic recognition was out of the question: "If I really thought with my correspondent [Verac] that her Imperial majesty had adopted the system mentioned to me in his letter . . . , viz., 'not to acknowledge the independence of the United States till Britain herself had done it,' I should soon bring the business to a conclusion, and take my leave of this court."[40] In the light of his subsequent experience, this would have been the wisest course of action.

The notion that it was beneath the dignity of the United States to resort to traditional diplomatic measures to obtain a hearing from the European courts was a fundamental principle of the anti-Gallicans. American diplomats were simply to appear at selected courts, outline the commercial advantages to be reaped from relations with the United States, and enter into negotiations for treaties of alliance and commerce. To a large extent Dana, a representative of mercantile Massachusetts, was a prisoner of this pattern of thinking, usually termed "militia diplomacy." Although not a merchant himself, he, like John Adams, numbered many influential

[38] *Ibid.,* 712.
[39] *Ibid.,* 698.
[40] *Ibid.,* V, 224.

New England merchants among his legal clients.[41] While serving as his secretary, Dana had more than ever come to share Adams's attitude concerning the overriding importance of commerce in the future system which was to be erected on the ruins of the old system of power politics. Combined with this firm faith in the morality and practicality of a system of international relationships governed by commercial arrangements was a desire to aid merchant friends with eyes on the Russian market. A close acquaintance, the Boston merchant Jeremiah Allen, hoped to establish direct trade between Russia and America, and used Dana to explore the prospects. Jonathan Thaxter, an American merchant operating out of Europe, expressed his interest in sharing in such a venture.[42] The extensive compilations of trade data—lists of exports to and from St. Petersburg and Riga (Allen was primarily interested in Riga) and their prices, import taxes, procedures for selling merchandise, legal rights of foreigners, and similar information—which are in the Dana Papers, bear witness to Dana's intention not only to establish direct relations between Russia and the United States, but also to his efforts to supply his merchant friends with the statistics necessary to initiate private trade. To Dana's way of thinking, the interests of Allen and Thaxter were those of the United States. And were not the interests of the United States also those of Russia?

It could be argued that there was a sufficient foundation of mutual interest for the establishment of direct commercial relations between the two nations. Prior to the outbreak of the War for Independence, American vessels did call at Russian ports, primarily for naval stores. Officially 1774 was the last year in which this trade was carried on.[43] There is, however, some evidence that at least in the earlier stages of the war some

[41] See Richard B. Morris, "Legalism versus Revolutionary Doctrine in New England," *New England Quarterly*, IV (1931), 211.

[42] Letters of Thaxter to Dana, Nov. 24, 1782, Mar. 31, 1783, Dana Papers, 1770-1782, 1783-1795.

[43] Specifically mentioned in the British and French archives are three American ships leaving St. Petersburg's port city of Kronstadt in 1774 for Boston, Lynn, and Philadelphia, laden with iron, hemp, cordage and deals. The English list is in S. P. 91/99, 137, and the French list in Correspondance Consulaire: St. Pétersbourg, 1773-1781, Affaires Étrangères, B1 988, no. 7. Norman E. Saul considers pre-Revolutionary trade with Russia to have made a significant contribution to the economy of Boston. He stresses the triangular trade, with Russian naval stores being highly prized in the colonies. See his "Beginnings of American-Russian Trade, 1763-1766," *Wm. and Mary Qtly.*, 3d Ser., XXVI (1969), 596-600.

smuggling took place. In 1775 the British Treasury Office reported a ship from Philadelphia attempting to acquire coarse linens at Hamburg and St. Petersburg.[44] After this we hear no more of American ships calling openly at Russian ports, but rather frequent are the complaints of British diplomatic agents in 1777 that ships flying Dutch colors would put in at St. Petersburg, pick up iron, hemp, and ships' masts, and only when they reached the comparative safety of the high seas replace their flag with the American flag.[45] Then there was the carrying trade in naval stores—legitimate in Russian eyes but illegitimate in British—carried on by the neutrals between Russia and the United States. Complained the British chargé d'affaires in late October 1775: "The number of French ships that have come to Petersbourg this year has been near five times as great as was ever known before; and their exportation of hemp very considerable. But this is what, I believe, is solely to be attributed to the unnatural rebellion of our Colonies, who have taken extraordinary supplies of that commodity from France."[46] Once the French entered the war the Dutch became the main suppliers of Russian naval stores to America.

Surviving records indicate that at least one Russian merchant was active in the Russian-American trade. Arvid Wittfooth, Swedish-born Russian consul at Bordeaux, had met with an unknown American "consul" who convinced him of the profitability of freighting Russian naval stores in Russian bottoms to America via Bordeaux.[47] Acting in a private capacity, Wittfooth chartered two ships, *La Marie Elisabeth* and *La Concorde,* and exported Russian products to America, a business which

---

[44] S. P. 91/99, 147.

[45] S. P. 91/101, 8, 42, 121. See also the report of Shairp, the British consul, Aug. 8, 1777, Great Britain: Embassy to Russia, 1774-1780, Bancroft Collection, New York Public Library, New York City.

[46] S. P. 91/100, 54. See also Shairp's report of Feb 7, 1777: "I suspect a great part of these commodities [hemp, iron, tallow, etc.] is intended for our American colonies; for I remember not many years ago, when 9 or 10,000 pieces of Russian sail cloth were not reckoned a large importation into London in one year, the greatest part of which was shipped afterwards to America; consequently that trade is now lost to our nation." S. P. 91/101, 27, and a letter in the same spirit, Sept. 19, 1777, S. P. 91/101, 188-189.

[47] Wittfooth to the Commerce College, May 12, 1778, fond 276, opis 1, ed. khr. 668, Central State Archive. Cited in Bolkhovitinov, *Stanovlenie,* 183-184, but with the incorrect fond number 246. Accurate mention of this document may be found in Frank A. Golder, *Guide to Materials for American History in Russian Archives* (Washington, 1917), I, 137. With regard to the unidentified consul, it may well have been Silas Deane, who is known to have visited Bordeaux.

proved quite lucrative. He encouraged other Russian merchants to follow his example, and appealed to them to send him iron, hemp, sailcloth, planks, tallow, and salted meat for reexport to America on commission.[48] Because of the political ramifications of the case the Commerce College chose not to come to any decision concerning the establishment of trade relations between Russia and the United States, preferring instead to pass the case on to the College of Foreign Affairs for judgment.[49] Although we do not know what action the College of Foreign Affairs, which was under the direction of Nikita Panin, took, we have indirect evidence that the arguments presented either convinced Panin or else coincided with his own opinions. For when in the summer of 1779 the empress, troubled by the possible repercussions of Spanish entry into the war, convened a special meeting of the Secret Committee of the College of Foreign Affairs to analyze and report on the situation, its recommendations reflected Wittfooth's attitude. The committee came to the conclusion that "the loss by England of her colonies on dry land would be not only unharmful, but might even be advantageous to Russian commercial interests, inasmuch as with time a new direct field of commerce between Russia and America might open up and be established for the satisfaction of mutual needs directly."[50] There were others who agreed with Wittfooth and Panin. In 1783, the year American independence was confirmed, there appeared books by two Russian subjects, each of which recommended that Russia open up commerce with America. One, by D. M. Ladygin, was entitled *Izvestie v Amerike o seleniiakh aglitskikh, v tom chisle nyne pod nazvaniem Soedinennikh Provintsii, vybrano perechenem iz noveishikh o tom prostrannykh sochinitelei* [Information in America concerning the English Settlements, including those now known as the United

---

[48] Wittfooth to the Commerce College, June (or possibly July) 30, 1782, fond 36, opis 1, delo 544, p. 84, Leningrad Branch of the Institute of History; Wittfooth to Montmorin, May 26, 1787, Correspondance Politique: Russie, Vol. 121, Docs. 35-36; V. Ulianitskii, *Russkie konsulstva za granitseiu v XVIII veke* (Moscow, 1889), I, 360-361; Bolkhovitinov, *Stanovlenie*, 183-186.

[49] Report of the Commerce College, Sept. 5, 1778, fond 276, opis 1, ed. khr. 668, p. 4, Central State Archive. Bolkhovitinov, *Stanovlenie*, 184, points out that one of the signers of the document is Aleksandr Radishchev.

[50] Order of the empress to Panin, July 26, 1779, of which copies may be found in fond 36, opis 1, delo 1161, p. 325, Leningrad Inst. of Hist., and fond 222, pachka V, ed. khr. 3, Manuscripts Division, Lenin State Library, Moscow. Copies of the report may be found here and published in P. I. Bartenev, ed., *Arkhiv Kniazia Vorontsova* (Moscow, 1870-1895), XXXIV, 388-405.

Provinces, selected from a list of the most recent composers on the subject] (St. Petersburg, 1783). A sixty-page work of a compilatory nature, the last several pages are devoted to a plea for the establishment of direct trade relations. Much more detailed is *Von den Handlungsvortheilen, welche aus der Unabhaengigkeit der Vereinigten Staaten von Nord-Amerika fuer das Russische Reich entspringen* [Concerning the trade advantages which arise out of the independence of the United States of America for the Russian empire] (Riga, 1783), by K. P. M. Snell, a German pastor serving as rector of a church school in Riga. The book, translated into Russian in 1786, made the following admission: "Wenn man nur betrachtet, was fuer einen Ueberfluss die Amerikaner an Masten, Bauholz, Hanf, Flachs, Theer, Pech, und Eisen haben, so ist es leicht, auf den Gedanken zu kommen, dass sie durch den Verkauf dieser Waaren dem russischen Handel grossen Abbruch thun werden, zumal wenn man dabey den grossen Umfang ihrer Provinzen und den Fleiss in Erwaegung ziehet, welchen sie nun, nach erhaltener Freiheit, anwenden werden, ihren Handel zu verbessern." [If one only considers what an abundance the Americans have in masts, building timber, hemp, flax, tar, pitch, and iron, it is easy to think that they would greatly diminish the Russian trade by selling these wares, particularly, if one considers the great spaciousness of their provinces and the diligence which they will use to improve their trade, now that they have received their freedom.] Snell concludes, however, that in the long run direct trade would be of mutual benefit.[51]

Not all Russians agreed with Wittfooth, Panin, Ladygin, and Snell— two of whom were non-Russian by birth in any case, while Panin had spent twelve years in Denmark and Sweden. Some feared that Russia and the United States, as extensive lands with roughly similar climates, would compete on the international market in naval stores, iron, and tobacco. As early as 1732 Thomas Coram, an agent for the colony of Georgia, had suggested the encouragement of the cultivation of hemp in the colonies to replace that normally imported from Russia, while five years later Prince Antiokh Kantemir, Russian envoy to London, was ordered by his superiors to study the problem of American iron and other prod-

[51] Unfortunately I have been unable to locate the Snell book anywhere. An excerpt from the book is given in V. A. Bilbasov, *Istoriia Ekateriny Vtoroi: Obzor inostrannykh sochinenii o Ekaterine II (1744-1796)* (Berlin, 1896), I, 284-285. Bolkhovitinov, *Stanovlenie,* 181, also unable to locate it, cites a review of the Russian translation of the book, evidently unaware that it first appeared in German.

ucts entering the British market in direct competition with Russian, and to come up with a method to keep them out.[52] With the outbreak of the War of Independence, the British government sought to implant doubt in Catherine's mind concerning the advantageousness of future Russian-American commercial exchange. In 1777 the Foreign Office issued a circular letter to the foreign diplomats resident in London to the effect that American and Russian commerce was competitive rather than complementary. If America were to gain its independence, the argument ran, its products would drive Russia's off the market.[53] Nor was the assertion easily put to rest, despite persistent claims by French diplomatic agents in St. Petersburg that American independence would benefit Russian commerce in view of the fact that Great Britain, once having lost its monopoly in the American colonies, would turn to Russia for naval supplies.[54] When the French chargé officially notified the Russian court of the signing of the Franco-American treaty, he perceived "une sensation très vive. Soit jalousie contre nous, soit prevention pour l'Angleterre, le premier mouvement a été de la plaindre, le second d'entrevoir de notre part une diminuation d'exportation des fournitures maritimes qui se trouvent en Amérique." The British, he noted, were doing their best to foster this fear.[55] Russian authorities could not be blamed for wondering if a newly independent United States might infringe upon their export market. They thought in terms of a finite market for exports, in which a new contestant could only prosper at the expense of the already established producers. And while Wittfooth stressed the advantages of direct Russian-American commerce, F. Brandenburg, the Russian consul at Cadiz, warned of American competition: "If North America confirms its independence," he predicted in September 1781, and "the number of inhabitants increases, they will then begin to raise there flax and hemp; and they already have timber, tar, pitch, wax, and other products which come from the North, and are in a position to satisfy with these all the southern areas at a better price and more conveniently than the North is

[52] Both instances are cited in A. V. Efimov, *Iz istorii velikikh russkikh geograficheskikh otkrytii v severnom ledovitom i tikhom okeanakh XVII i pervaia polovina XVIII v* (Moscow, 1950), 222.

[53] Cited from the *London Chronicle*, June 17-19, 1777, *Pennsylvania Magazine of History and Biography*, XVI (1892), 463-465.

[54] For variations on this theme see the correspondence between Vergennes and his representatives at St. Petersburg, Correspondance Politique: Russie, Vol. 99, No. 44, Vol. 100, No. 78, Vol. 101, Nos. 5, 11, 17, 20.

[55] Corberon, July 7, 1778, Correspondance Politique: Russie, Vol. 101, No. 27.

able to do." At least in part the problem for Russia was geographical: "Ships out of Boston arrive in Cadiz in from twenty to thirty days, while for northern ships and vessels from eighty to ninety days are needed for this voyage, and moreover they are sometimes forced to winter over in Norway."[56] Nor was it only the authorities and commercial agents abroad who feared American competition. A petition by a group of Russian merchants to the Commerce College in 1782, conjuring up the evil effects of American independence for Russian trade in hemp, flax, and iron, bears witness to a general wariness on the part of Russians concerning the economic ramifications of this independence.[57]

While the instances just examined might be labeled as mere apprehensions, the removal of American tobacco from the world market as a result of the War for Independence noticeably aided Russian exports. As early as 1714 Fedor Saltykov, Russian commercial agent in London, took note of the large profits derived by England from its tobacco plantations in America, and suggested that Russia grow its own rather than import American, as was the case at the time. Tobacco, he insisted, could be sold abroad as well as consumed at home.[58] But it was only under Catherine II that the cultivation of tobacco became a major enterprise. In 1763 the government began the free distribution of American tobacco seed with instructions for growing it.[59] Up to the beginning of the American Revolution, though, Russia still imported more than it exported, and most of the imported product came from the American colonies.

With the outbreak of hostilities in America, however, the shipment of tobacco to Europe almost ceased, leaving a considerable trade vacuum which Russia was the first to fill. The first partition of Poland and the successful conclusion to the first Turkish war had given her access to the Mediterranean through the Black Sea, a potentially economical way of transporting Ukrainian tobacco to France. Already in late 1776 Raimbert, a French merchant long interested in the exportation of Russian tobacco to France, began to negotiate with the foreign colonists established by

[56] Cited from Leningrad Inst. of Hist. by Bolkhovitinov, *Stanovlenie,* 179.

[57] Petition of the Riga merchants in fond 36, opis 1, delo 546, p. 63, Leningrad Inst. of Hist.

[58] Article 15 of Saltykov's reform project, cited in N. P. Pavlov-Silvanskii, *Proekty reform v zapiskakh sovremennikov Petra Velikogo* (St. Petersburg, 1897), II, 25.

[59] Heinrich Storch, *Statistische Uebersicht der Statthalterschaften des Russischen Reiches nach Ihren merkwuerdigsten Kulturverhaeltnissen* (Riga, 1795), 93; the same, *Tableau historique et statistique de l'Empire de Russie à la fin du dixhuitième siècle* (Basle, 1800), I, 260; Efimov, *Iz istorii,* 15.

the empress at Saratov.[60] He followed this up with a petition to Aleksandr Romanovich Vorontsov, president of the Commerce College, for permission to export tobacco. The interruption in the flow of American tobacco, he asserted, presented the ideal opportunity for Russian grown tobacco to capture the market.[61] The empress took up the suggestion by formulating new regulations for the export of tobacco. Soon what was to all appearances a flourishing business began.[62] It must be added, though, that hopes were not fully realized. The French Farmers-General complained about the quality of the tobacco and about the business practices of the Russians.[63] There was no real substitute for American tobacco, although this was not yet totally apparent when Dana made his appearance in St. Petersburg.

A major task confronting Dana, then, was to counter assertions that American trade would compete with Russian, an assertion he found to be widely accepted. The Russian authorities, he bemoaned, lacked an awareness of the benefits to be obtained from American trade.[64] He set about to correct this state of affairs with arguments that took three general directions. In the first place, there was an American market for iron, hemp, sailcloth, and cordage, while a legitimate Russian market existed for rice and tobacco. Secondly, there had once been a good deal of trade between the two via Great Britain, and with independence it would no longer have to be routed through the third party at the expense of the two producers. The final argument was less conclusive. Dana claimed that American naval stores had in the past enjoyed the benefit of British bounties. With independence these bounties would disappear, leaving Russia with a profitable market in Great Britain. Thus American independence would not prove harmful to Russian commercial interests. Tacked on was a warning that were Russia not

[60] Report of the British chargé, S. P. 91/100, 61, report of the French ambassador, Correspondance Politique: Russie, Vol. 99, No. 71; Jacob M. Price, *The Tobacco Adventure to Russia . . . (Transactions of the American Philosophical Society, LI* [Philadelphia, 1961]), Pt. 1, 95. For the French negotiations with Russia, see W. Kirchner, "Ukrainian Tobacco for France," *Jahrbuecher fuer Geschichte Osteuropas,* X (1962), 497-512.

[61] Mar. 11, 1777, fond 36, opis 1, delo 546, Leningrad Inst. of Hist.

[62] See the empress's additions to a Commerce College report of Feb. 10, 1778, Bartenev, *Arkhiv Kniazia Vorontsova,* XIII, 459-460; Shairp, May 14, 1778, S. P. 91/102.

[63] Raimbert, Nov. 14, 1780, Correspondance Politique: Russie, Vol. 105, No. 338.

[64] *Diplomatic Correspondence,* V, 322-323, 529-532, 781.

quick to recognize American independence and establish commercial relations, it would risk being shut out of the American market entirely.

His initial overtures met with little or no response. "I wish this country had a more commercial turn," he lamented. "We should then soon see a direct communication between the two countries opened and established, to the great benefit of both."[65] Since he had reason to think his mail was being opened at the post office, he took advantage of the situation to get across his point in a letter designed to be read by the authorities: "I have some reason to suppose," he hinted coyly, "this government not yet proporly informed . . . of the immense interest it has at stake relative to the commerce of our country." If Dana could only "do away all errors upon this subject of commerce, to establish the great mutual interests the two nations have in a close and intimate connexion with each other, . . . Her majesty would most certainly pursue the great interests of her empire, and not suffer herself to be diverted from that pursuit by any dazzling prospects of glory which the British, or any others, might hold out. She has too much wisdom not to change Her system when affairs have changed their face. . . . I agree with you [Adams] that glory and interest are both united in our case; that her majesty could not, by any line of conduct, more effectivally promote both than by stepping forth at this moment and acknowledging the independence of the United States and forming a commercial treaty with them."[66]

This measure having brought no results, Dana followed it up with his "Reflections to refute the assertion of the British that the Independence of the United States will be injurious to the commercial interests of the Northern Nations, and of Russia in particular," a lengthy polemic, the content of which is readily gleaned from the title. If one key passage may be extracted from the argument, it might be this: "Is not the great importance of the commerce of America to Russia beyond all question?"[67] This statement Dana considered axiomatic. Although

[65] *Ibid.*, 117.

[66] Dana to Adams, Apr. 12, 1782, *ibid.*, 322-323. In a footnote later provided by Dana himself we find the following remark: "This letter was written with a view of its being opened at the post office here, and accordingly was sent there under special conditions." Letters from St. Petersburg, 1782-1784, Dana Papers.

[67] Official Letters, 1782-1784, p. 105, Dana Papers. Bolkhovitinov, *Stanovlenie,* 178, came across this document in French in the Russian archives, and assumes it to be of Russian origin. A slightly different English version is found in *Diplomatic Correspondence,* V, 529-531.

an answer was not forthcoming, he continued his effort to "get through" to the empress by means of a detailed proposal for a commercial treaty between Russia and the United States.[68] Again, there was no response.

The Russian authorities were simply not convinced of the value of American trade. This was all the more true once Panin was forced out of office. Soon after his arrival in St. Petersburg Dana learned that "Count Panin will shortly return to court, and that he has the most favorable sentiments of the United States of any of her Imperial majesty's ministers."[69] As we have seen, he had issued a positive report on the potential of Russian-American commerce. But after leaving for his country estate in the spring of 1781 he was never allowed to resume his post as director of foreign affairs. He was replaced by I. A. Osterman, a pliant bureaucrat. In reality foreign affairs were now directed by the empress herself in conjunction with her closest advisors, Grigori Aleksandrovich Potemkin and Aleksandr Andreevich Bezborodko. Potemkin in particular was thought to be anti-American.[70] And Russian foreign policy underwent a drastic alteration. An Austrian alliance was consummated, and plans laid to partition the Ottoman Empire. If this goal were to be achieved, the British navy would have to remain passive. Would the relatively small amount of trade—if any at all—that Russia might strike up with America compensate for the estrangement from Great Britain that would almost certainly result? Would not British compliance in any projected offensive against the Turks (the second Russo-Turkish War actually broke out in 1787) prove more valuable to Russia, a nation without a flourishing mercantile tradition, but with a long history of conflict with the Turks and the Tatars, than a few more ships putting in at Riga and Kronstadt?

Failing to realize the obstacles in his path, Dana looked elsewhere for the cause of his difficulties. It was a cardinal point in the catechism of militia diplomacy that the French could not be relied upon for aid in seeking support from other European nations, for, it was believed, the French hoped to keep the Americans subordinated to their own

[68] Plan of a Commerical Treaty between Russia and the United States, in Box 588, Dana Papers. This document, as well as the "Reflections," is listed in Golder, *Guide*, 14, and photostatic copies are to be found in the Library of Congress.

[69] *Diplomatic Correspondence*, IV, 714.

[70] D. M. Griffiths, "Nikita Panin, Russian Diplomacy, and the American Revolution," *Slavic Review*, XXVIII (1969), esp. 18-20.

interests. If there were prominent Americans who seemed to fall in line with French reasoning on questions of foreign policy (Franklin was accused of being the chief perpetrator), they had sold out to the French for their own selfish gains. Adams came to this conclusion after Vergennes had informed him he would deal only with Franklin. Presumably it was from Adams that Dana acquired his mistrust of Franklin, Vergennes, and Verac.

Herein was to be found another cause for the abruptness with which Dana was treated by the Russian court: he had arrived in St. Petersburg without the least confidence in the French ambassador, to whose advice he had been bound by his instructions. On four occasions Dana approached the Frenchman to obtain his cooperation in communicating his mission to the Russian court (when news of Cornwallis's surrender was received, when Parliament proposed a new policy for America just prior to the collapse of the North government, when Charles James Fox announced that no preconditions would be attached to negotiations with the former colonies, and, finally, when Richard Oswald was empowered to treat of peace with the American commissioners). On all four occasions Verac recommended patience.[71] Dana, with his belief in the justice of the American cause and his conviction that he need only present the empress with the true story to be recognized, had a ready explanation for Verac's seeming hesitation: Vergennes had ordered him to prevent the success of the mission. "By all I have learned of Mr. Dana's negotiations in Russia, Mr. Jay's in Spain, and my own in Holland," announced Adams, "it is evident to me that the Comte de Montmorin, the Marquis de Verac, and the Duke de la Vauguyon have been governed by the same instructions; to wit, instead of favoring, to prevent, if possible, our success."[72] These suspicions coincided with Dana's, and provided him with an excuse for the apparent failure of his embassy. "I have the same idea of a certain policy which you have," he hinted darkly to Adams. When later editing his papers he added the clarifying notation that it was "the policy of the Court of Versailles to prevent the sovereigns of Europe acknowledging the independence of the United States during the war."[73] Dana seized upon Franco-

[71] Verac to Vergennes, Sept. 7, 1783, Correspondance Politique: Russie, Vol. III, No. 46.

[72] Adams, ed., Works, IX, 515.

[73] Dana to Adams, Oct. 7, 1782, Letters from St. Petersburg, 1782-1784, Dana Papers.

Russian negotiations for a commercial treaty to charge the French ambassador with hoping to squeeze the Americans out of the Russian trade. When he confided his apparent discovery to both Adams and Robert Livingston, the newly elected secretary for foreign affairs, the former concurred, while the latter was outraged at Dana's presumptuousness.[74]

The directness with which Dana had voiced his suspicions caused an extensive debate in Congress. And just prior to Dana's arrival in St. Petersburg, significant events had transpired back in Congress which made his mission even more untenable. Over the opposition of the Lees and the Massachusetts delegation a decision was taken to lend a more institutional structure to American diplomacy by the creation of a Department of Foreign Affairs to replace the committee of the Congress controlled by the Lee-Adams faction through James Lovell, its most active member. In the election for department secretary, Arthur Lee, nominated by Samuel Adams, took a first round lead over Livingston, the candidate of the more pro-Gallican forces. At this point the French minister stepped in and announced that the king would find it impossible to work with Lee. On the third round Livingston was named secretary.[75] The selection heralded the curbing of militia diplomacy. As the defeated candidate warned Dana in faraway St. Petersburg: "The present Secretary for Foreign Affairs, (R. R. Livingston) is a decided partizan of Dr. Franklin, and an enemy to Mr. Adams. Like a number of other parrots here, he praises the former by rote, and undertakes to tutor the other. Whatever you see or receive from him you may consider as dictated by the French Minister."[76] Franklin, Livingston, and the French, then, were all to be distrusted.

The first letters Livingston had received from his minister at St. Petersburg, full of vituperation against Verac, had convinced him of the necessity for restraining him. As the inimitable Lee phrased it: "The independent spirit which marked your proceedings when you arrived

[74] Dana to Livingston, Sept. 20, 1782, Official Letters, 1780-1782, Dana Papers, incorrectly dated 1781 in *Diplomatic Correspondence*, IV, 737. See also *ibid.*, V, 815-817. Vergennes had actually ordered his envoy to discontinue all negotiations for a commercial treaty. See his dispatch to Verac, Oct. 18, 1781, Correspondance Politique: Russie, Vol. 107, No. 27.

[75] La Luzerne to Vergennes, Aug. 11, 1781, Correspondence Politique: États-Unis, Vol. 20, No. 166.

[76] *Letters of Continental Congress*, VI, 379.

first at St. Petersburg did not please some. Upon this subject I have but one observation to make. That a foreign minister, if he attempt anything out of the hackneyed path, must do so at his own peril."[77] Livingston was not prepared to have Dana wander from the hackneyed path, and to prevent it devised a number of fences. Through the French minister to America he asked Verac to guide Dana in all his actions; he recommended that Dana be demoted from the rank of minister plenipotentiary to that of resident; and he ordered him to make no diplomatic overtures without "an absolute certainty" they would be acceptable.[78] For Dana himself the secretary had a stern letter of rebuke, a letter which was watered down by Congress, but which Livingston sent off in its original form.

While Livingston was hoping to rein Dana in, Adams at The Hague was urging him on. Once the preliminary peace treaty had been signed at Versailles, Adams advised Dana to disregard the advice tendered by Verac and Livingston:

You can no longer hesitate to make known your errand. Whether the advice if the Marquis de Verac is for or against it, I should think you would now go to the [Russian] minister. Your instructions are chains, strong chains. Whether you shall break them or not as we have been obliged to do, you are the only judge. There is Vulcan at Versailles [Vergennes] whose constant employment it has been to forge chains for American ministers. My advice to you is immediately to communicate your mission to the Minister of the Emperor and the Ministers of all the other courts which have acceded to the Armed Neutrality.[79]

It was to Adams that Dana listened, and not to Livingston.

In some manner Dana had managed to form an acquaintanceship with Maksim Alopeus, a Finn, and Panin's former secretary. Through Alopeus Dana established communication with a member of the College of Foreign Affairs, Petr Bakunin, another of Panin's former secretaries. After an exchange of letters and several personal meetings Dana was assured: "You may communicate your mission to the Vice-Chancellor [Count Osterman] at any time. It is possible you may not receive an

[77] July 6, 1782, Dana Papers, 1770-1782 (not included in the excerpt published in *Letters of Continental Congress*, VI, 379).
[78] La Luzerne to Verac, May 5, 1782, Correspondance Politique: Russie, Vol. 108, No. 256; La Luzerne to Vergennes, Mar. 17, 1782, Correspondance Politique: États-Unis, Vol. 20, No. 226; *Diplomatic Correspondence*, V, 209, 402.
[79] Adams, Feb. 22, 23, 1783, Dana Papers, 1783-1795.

answer immediately, but you need not be uneasy on that account, as the delay will not be occasioned by anything which concerns the United States or you personally; both your mission and your person are very agreeable to Her Imperial Majesty."[80] Informed of these conferences, Verac visited Dana, but the American had lost interest in the Frenchman's advice. On February 24, 1783, Verac received the following laconic note: "Je prens la liberté de vous informer que dans ce moment j'ai communiqué ma mission à son Excellence le Vice-Chancellor Comte d'Osterman."[81] A more detailed message was dispatched to Adams at The Hague: "I have this day communicated my mission to the Vice-Chancellor, Count Osterman, without having been advised to do so, by my correspondent; but I had *immediate* assurances that the way was clear. It is strange that anyone could have thought otherwise."[82]

The British ambassador, watching Dana's activities with increasing anxiety, reported to his superiors that the American

. . . had had several private meetings at a merchants by name of Stralborn and Wolff [Dana's banker] with Mr. Bacounin where he had proposed a commercial connection between Russia and America, and either from the apparent advantages he held forth to the Empire at large, or from having personally interested this gentleman in his behalf, Mr. Bacounin is become his strenuous advocate, and I understand has assured Mr. Dana that he would be openly acknowledged as minister out of hand, and his propositions for a treaty taken into immediate consideration.[83]

Bakunin may well have been the "B" the Dana Papers indicate was given "£50 for transmitting official papers."[84] As a member of the College of Foreign Affairs he also stood to gain from the conclusion of a commercial treaty, since by tradition the signers of any treaty received gifts of 6,000 rubles apiece. Harris had an explanation for Alopeus's complicity as well: "The whole has been a direct intrigue, in which Mr. Bacounin has had some share; but the chief promoter has been

<hr/>

[80] Conversation between Dana and "S," Feb. 22, 1783, *ibid.* A resumé of Dana's negotiations may be found in his Journal for 1783, *ibid.*

[81] Letters from St. Petersburg, 1782-1784, *ibid.*

[82] *Ibid.* A letter to Livingston, with the same information but more diplomatic in tone, is found in *Diplomatic Correspondence*, VI, 275-276. Dana's correspondence with Osterman is in Box 586, Dana Papers.

[83] Harris, Feb. 28, 1783, F. O. 65/9, 22.

[84] List of Expenses Submitted to Congress, Dana Papers, 1762-1793.

Alopeus, one of the principal secretaries to the Vice-Chancellor, who has been successively bought by Prussia and France, and who besides being paid by Dana, is now desirous of being sent from hence as minister to the new republic."[85] Although Dana lacked the necessary funds to bribe anyone, he had discussed with Adams his intention of administering the oath of allegiance to a non-Russian residing in St. Petersburg, who would then act as resident.[86] The person may well have been Alopeus.

A point-by-point recapitulation of Dana's extended negotiations with Count Osterman would add little to our present knowledge of official Russian-American diplomatic relations. Suffice it to say that Dana clung to his legalistic arguments for American recognition, while the vice-chancellor threw up every conceivable obstacle in his path. The American would be granted all the courtesies due a visitor from a friendly country, as would all other Americans. But recognition, Dana was informed, could not precede the conclusion of the definitive peace.[87] After months of fruitless bickering, Dana finally accepted the inevitable, and announced his intention to await the outcome of the definitive negotiations in Paris.

But after having suffered through two years of diplomatic frustration at St. Petersburg, Dana was administered the coup de grace by his own government. The ostensible cause was the necessity of presenting cash presents to all those who signed a commercial agreement, and Livingston seized upon this pretext to raise the question of Dana's recall before Congress. It would be preferable, he maintained, to break off negotiations rather than stoop to the level of bribery.[88] In general, the representatives seeking to protect Dana's position at St. Petersburg were from those states heavily involved in international trade and navigation, to whom Russia's iron and hemp seemed attractive. They were consistently supported by South Carolinians, who saw in Russia an un-

---

[85] F. O. 65/9, 24.

[86] Dana, Dec. 30, 1782, Letters from St. Petersburg, 1782-1784, *ibid.* It is also interesting to note that Alopeus had purchased a ship to transport goods from St. Petersburg to Bordeaux, but it is not clear if he was in any way connected with Wittfooth. See Labande, *Un diplomat français,* II, 353.

[87] For Dana's correspondence with Osterman, see Box 586, Dana Papers. For the Russian viewpoint, see "Précis sur les relations de la Cour Impériale de Russie avec les États-Unis de l'Amérique sur le règne de l'Impératrice Catherine II," photostat, Library of Congress, by Golder.

[88] *Diplomatic Correspondence,* VI, 388.

tapped market for rice.[89] Livingston, with assistance from James Madison and Alexander Hamilton, maneuvered through Congress resolutions which forbad Dana to pay for a treaty, or to sign one (although he could negotiate it), or even enter negotiations if he had not already done so. The resolutions reached the Russian capital in July 1783, finding the American awaiting the signature of the definitive peace.

Dana, bitter about his new orders, had had his heart set upon a reception at court, even going to the trouble of purchasing a carriage for his presentation. He had spent two years at a foreign court without a single accomplishment. As the British minister gloated maliciously: "Mr. Dana, after having made many unsuccessful attempts to be acknowledged here in a public capacity, is now going to return to Boston, and it will be probably many years before any other American will be desirous of being employed as minister at this court."[90] Dana's parting shot was a suggestion that the United States retaliate for the treatment rendered him by cultivating hemp and driving the Russian product off the market.[91]

The Dana mission, in conclusion, was an unmitigated disaster, the bitter aftertaste of which lingered on. It was to be more than twenty years before the United States saw fit to hazard another minister to Russia. As a member of the Russian College of Foreign Affairs noted in a candid moment: "Since the departure of Dana until the reign of His Majesty the Emperor our August Sovereign [Alexander] one sees hardly a trace of direct relations between Russia and the United States of America."[92] Wherein lay the fault? What role had French diplomacy played? Judging from Vergennes's despatches to Verac, France had taken the only position viable: Verac had been ordered to base his actions on the situation at court. If the Russian court were to manifest a desire to receive Dana formally—something Vergennes very much doubted—Verac was to lend the American assistance. If, however, the authorities manifested no inclination for recognition, Verac was to countenance no precipitous steps.[93] Despite the suspicions of Dana,

---

[89] *Journals of Continental Congress,* XXV, 966.
[90] Malmesbury, *Diaries,* II, 55.
[91] *Diplomatic Correspondence,* VI, 658.
[92] Golder, "Précis sur les relations de la Cour Impériale."
[93] After Vergennes's conference with Dana, Vergennes to Verac, Apr. 7, 1781, Correspondance Politique: Russie, Vol. 106, No. 14: "Mais si l'envie de se faire reconnoître dans sa capacité ministérielle le prenait, ou s'il cherchoit à introduire des

Adams, and their anti-Gallican friends, Vergennes in no manner sought to deter Russian recognition of America. Whatever may have been the case at other courts, all available evidence shows that Vergennes did everything in his power to encourage direct Russian-American relations, both diplomatic and commercial.[94]

What was the empress's attitude towards America? Ideologically she seems to have occupied no position at all. Nowhere in her writings does she indicate that she considered the War for Independence anything more than a colonial rebellion, closer in nature with the Corsican struggle with France, with which she sympathized, than with that form of social revolution with which she was only too familiar—the Pugachev rebellion. Her comments on the American Revolution are nothing more than witty epigrams, devoid of ideological content. It was not until the outbreak of the French Revolution, accompanied by reports from her ambassador in Paris linking the events with those in America of the preceding decade, that Catherine II discovered revolutionary content in the American contest. Until the storming of the Bastille the empress, together with the other monarchs of Northern Europe, tended to view the American situation within a traditional diplomatic framework.[95]

---

négociations, vous voudrez bien vous tenir à l'écart et n'y prendre aucune part, à moins que le gouvernement russe ne vous témoignât le désirer. C'est un égard que nous lui devons de ne faire aucune démarche qui pourroit announcer le dessein de le comprometter vis-à-vis de l'Angleterre." On Oct. 18, 1781, Vergennes repeated the same theme: "Sa manière d'être à Petersbourg dépendra nécessairement des événemens de la guerre, et en voulant se donner trop tôt une existence reconnue, il risqueroit de se mettre hors d'état de servir sa nation." (*Ibid.*, Vol. 107, No. 27.)

[94] The French foreign minister encouraged direct trade relations between Russia and the United States. See Labande, *Un diplomat français*, II, 270. According to Russian sources, Vergennes tried to convince both Russia and Denmark to negotiate directly with the United States. Startsev, "Amerikanskii vopros," in Beskrovnyi, ed., *Mezhdunarodnye sviazi*, 453-454.

[95] Frederick II of Prussia made the observation that the War for Independence in no way touched Russian interests. See *Politische Correspondenz*, XLV, 533. Neither Frederick II nor Gustav III of Sweden viewed the struggle in any other than traditional terms. See P. L. Haworth, "Frederick the Great and the American Revolution," *American Historical Review*, IX (1904), 460-478, and H. A. Barton, "Sweden and the War of American Independence," *Wm. and Mary Qtly.*, 3d Ser., XXIII (1966), 408-430. The sympathies of the Russian nobility, the most significant educated element in Russian society, seem to have been singularly muddled. M. M. Karamzin, an outstanding writer normally considered to be "liberal" in his younger Masonic days, notes that he hoped the British would reconquer the colonies. M. M. Karamzin, *Sochineniia* (St. Petersburg, 1848), II, 773. On the other hand for a neat example of the irrelevant way in which some

To Dana's dismay, Russia's commercial outlook was also traditional; the empress thought of trade more in terms of customs revenues than in strengthening the economy as a whole. The Russian merchant class was perhaps the most conservative in all Europe.[96] To this extent Russia's trade with a nation such as France, in which the former exported raw materials to the latter in exchange for luxury products which could be heavily taxed, would seem to have made more sense to Catherine, her advisors, and her merchants, than an unpredictable commerce with a new nation far across the ocean which in many respects seemed to be a competitor, especially in the realm of naval stores and tobacco.

Sweden, for instance, allowed American ships to trade freely in the port of Marstrand. When an English representative complained, he was informed by Count Scheffer that Gustav III "would still continue

members of the Russian nobility viewed the war, refer to the conversation Corberon related having had with Prince M. M. Shcherbatov, prominent historian and conservative ideologue: "Nous avons causé trois quarts d'heure sur les Américains et sur la forme des gouvernemens; il ne veut admettre que celle des républicains, même pour les grands états. Cela te paroitre bien systématique pour un Russe; mais il est de bonne foi, et c'est surement un des Russes les plus hônnetes." Labande, *Un diplomat français*, II, 49. It must be borne in mind that the four existing republics—the United Provinces, Switzerland, Venice, and Genoa—presented no challenge whatsoever to the existing social structure. The terms "republican" and "revolutionary" assumed ominous overtones for the Russian monarchy and aristocracy only with the advent of the French Revolution. For the report of the French ambassador to Paris in 1789 see *Literaturnoe nasledstvo*, XXIX and XXX (1937), 400.

[96] In a summation of the results of the Dana mission, Verac informed Vergennes that American "avait eut le tems d'étudier la nation, de connaître sa légèrité et son inconséquence, de voir par lui-même à quel excès on est ignorant sur les premières éléments du commerce, qu'on semble ne considérer que sous un point de vue entièrement fiscal et par le profit que les douanes, à force de vexations, peuvent donner au coffre de l'Impératrice." Sept. 7, 1783, Correspondance Politique: Russie, Vol. 111, No. 46. N. N. Firsov, in his detailed study of Russian society's attitude towards trade in Catherine's time, comes to conclusions concerning the empress and her ministers similar to those of the French ambassador. See his *Pravitelstvo i obshchestvo v ikh otnosheniiahk k vneshnei torgovle Rossii v tsarstvovanie Imperatritsy Ekateriny II* (Kazan, 1902), 29, 83-84. Prince Shcherbatov too had harsh things to say about the commercial principles of the Commerce College. See M. M. Shcherbatov, *Sochineniia* (St. Petersburg, 1896), I, 585. The Russian merchantry, by unanimous agreement, was abysmally ignorant of all modern concepts of trade. See Kulisher, *Istoriia*, 222-228, and Firsov, *Pravitelstvo i obshchestvo*, 8-20. N. L. Rubenshtein, a Soviet historian, has tried to prove that Russia in the second half of the 18th century had just entered the capitalist period, and its merchantry was channeling its attention into the domestic market. See N. L. Rubenshtein, "Vneshniaia torgovlia Rossii i russkoe kupechestvo vo vtoroi polovine XVIII veka," *Istoricheskie zapiski*, LV (1955), 360-361. Although Rubenshtein cites statistics, they tell us nothing about the attitudes of the merchant class.

to prevent their [American] agents from purchasing arms and ammunition in any port belonging to his dominions, in the same manner with which it has hitherto been done; but that it was His Swedish Majesty's wish on the other side, that the trade which last year had begun to be carried on with some American vessels at Marstrand, innocent as it was, would always be looked upon as such."[97] Long before the preliminary peace treaty between England and her former colonies had been concluded, Sweden began quiet negotiations with Franklin for a trade treaty. And before the conclusion of the definitive treaty, a Swedish-American trade agreement had been signed. One year later, in 1784, a treaty with Prussia, also patterned on the 1776 model "Plan of Treaties," was concluded. Denmark exhibited interest in trade with the United States.

But Russia held out. After hearing of the rejection of Dana's trade proposals, Adams approached Arkady Morkov, new Russian ambassador at The Hague. Morkov's response was that the matter could not even be considered until after the conclusion of the definitive peace treaty.[98] Again in 1784, when the American delegation expressed to Prince Bariatinsky, Russian ambassador to Paris, its desire to enter into commercial negotiations with Russia, it failed to receive an answer of any sort from the government.[99] As a result of Russian reluctance to establish formal relations, bilateral trade developed extremely slowly, even after the definitive peace treaty had been signed.[100] Nor did Russia quickly abandon the fear that the European market was insufficient for both Russian and American naval stores.[101] Thus Dana enjoyed no bargaining power whatsoever in his abortive negotiations.

[97] See letter of Doverfeld to William Eden, Apr. 7, 1778, S. P. 95/128, 71; and also S. P. 95/128, 4, 15.

[98] P. I. Bartenev, "Arkady Ivanovich Morkoy," *Russkaia Beseda*, IV (1857), addendum, 35; Startsev, "Amerikanskii vopros," in Beskrovnyi, ed., *Mezhdunarodnye sviazi*, 465.

[99] Bolkhovitinov, *Stanovlenie*, 188.

[100] Only two American ships called at Russian ports in 1783, on one of which was Dana's friend Allen, who took him back to Boston. Correspondance Politique: Russie, Vol. III, Nos. 461, 467, 471. Lists of goods exported from St. Petersburg and Riga, F. O. 97/340. Five ships arrived in 1784, still an inconsiderable number. Correspondance Politique: Russie, Vol. 112, Nos. 429, 431, 432. See also A. A. Rasch, "American Trade in the Baltic, 1783-1807," *Scandinavian Economic History Review*, XIII (1965), 44-49, and Alfred W. Crosby, Jr., *America, Russia, Hemp and Napoleon: American Trade with Russia and the Baltic, 1783-1812* (Columbus, 1965).

[101] See the concern expressed in the letters from the Russian ambassador to London, Bartenev, *Arkhiv Kniazia Vorontsova*, IX, 77-78, 81, 480.

Unlike Adams at The Hague, Dana was unable to appeal to public opinion over the heads of the authorities, for there was literally no public opinion to which to appeal. While Soviet scholars are prone to assert that leading or progressive circles (*peredovye krugi*) of Russian society looked with favor upon the American Revolution, the statement is almost meaningless for our purposes. In fact, one may count on one's fingers the number of Russians living within the country who in some way expressed themselves in this fashion. Among those in state service, only Panin and his secretaries (Dennis Fonvizin, Alopeus, and Bakunin) would seem to qualify, and all but Bakunin were pushed aside in 1781. Among the incipient intelligentsia, the names of Aleksandr Radishchev, Nikolai Novikov, and possibly Petr Bogdanovich apparently exhaust the list.[102] Either the intelligentsia was indifferent to the events in America, or else it was an insignificantly small group. The latter explanation is most probable.

Thus there was very little need for James Harris and British diplomacy to play the nefarious role often attributed to them. That the British ambassador had intrigued to his utmost cannot be denied. But we may dismiss the allegation that these intrigues influenced Russian policy to any great extent. The State Council, under the empress's supervision, had discussed Dana's application and rejected it even before Harris got wind of the proposals.[103] The empress was fully aware that consideration of Dana's trade proposals might jeopardize her uneasy relationship with Great Britain, and given Russia's traditional desire to deal decisively with the Turks, British friendship was a not insignificant factor. The Porte, in sum, was more important than the ports from the Russian viewpoint.[104]

[102] M. M. Shtrange in his *Demokraticheskaia intelligentsiia Rossii v XVIII veke* (Moscow, 1965) attempts to establish the existence of a non-noble intelligentsia in late 18th-century Russia. By his own admission, the list is hardly impressive. Bolkhovitinov, *Stanovlenie*, 91-129, deals extensively with those who apparently favored the American cause: A. N. Radishchev, N. I. Novikov, and P. I. Bogdanovich. To this list might be added N. I. Panin and D. I. Fonvizin among the nobility, and D. A. Golitsyn and F. V. Karzhavin among the expatriates. Although a few other individuals might have looked with favor upon the United States, there could never be a question of a "public opinion" to influence the decisions of the autocratic empress.

[103] I. Ia. Chistovich, ed., *Arkhiv Gosudarstvennogo Soveta* (St. Petersburg, 1869-1904), I, Pt. 1, 235. See also a letter of Bezborodko, Feb. 28, 1783, *Starina i Novizna*, XI (1900), 262-263.

[104] Verac to Vergennes, July 19, 1783, Correspondance Politique: Russie, Vol. III, No. 30.

The Longchamps Affair (1784–86), the Law of Nations, and the Shaping of Early American Foreign Policy

G. S. ROWE and ALEXANDER W. KNOTT

Among the pressing issues confronting Americans during and immediately after the Revolution was the need to determine whether or not there was "a legitimate sphere of national interest." If one did exist, it was equally crucial to judge whether or not Congress was worthy of sufficient powers and support to pursue and protect that interest.[1] Identifying the broad outlines of America's national goals—the achievement of political independence, national security, and commercial and territorial expansion—proved easier than reaching agreement on intelligent, effective, day-to-day policies and procedures to be employed in bringing these aspirations to fruition.[2] The latter decisions demanded a stand on the degree to which traditional European laws and customs would shape American reactions to foreign policy issues and the extent to which U.S. inchoate republican ideology necessitated both new institutions and novel courses of action.[3]

By 1784 the weakness of Congress in conducting foreign policy was apparent. Apart from its inability to prevail upon the individual states to accept a unified and coherent foreign policy, Congress had failed to execute extradition treaties with foreign powers and remained reluctant to face the responsibility for securing persons and property of foreign officials and residents in its territories. Closely related to these failures was congressional

---

[1] See, for instance, Jack N. Rakove, *The Beginnings of National Politics: An Interpretive History of the Continental Congress* (New York, 1979), pp. 342–52, esp. p. 350.

[2] Useful surveys include Samuel Flagg Bemis, *The Diplomacy of the American Revolution* (1935; reprint ed., Bloomington, IN, 1957); Reginald Horsman, *The Diplomacy of the New Republic, 1776–1815* (Arlington Heights, IL, 1985); and Lawrence S. Kaplan, *Colonies Into Nation: American Diplomacy, 1763–1801* (New York, 1972).

[3] For an examination of the literature focusing on republicanism and its impact on ideas, practices, and institutions in the early republic, see Robert E. Shalhope, "Towards a Republican Synthesis: The Emergence of an Understanding of Republicanism in American Historiography," *William and Mary Quarterly* 24 (April 1972): 49–80; and his "Republicanism and Early American Historiography," ibid. 39 (April 1982): 334–56.

unwillingness to accept the law of nations, as understood by Europe, or to force acceptance of that tradition, with modifications, upon America's thirteen states. At the heart of these failures were limitations imposed upon congressional authority in part by the Articles of Confederation and in part by historical tradition. Ultimately, answers to questions relating to the law of nations and to specific rights of diplomatic personnel under that tradition focused attention on the need for treaties with foreign nations that would clarify these issues. That, in turn, centered attention on the locus of sovereignty in the Confederation.

The unique relationship between the United States and France brought these critical issues to the forefront and forced private and public debate on them. The response of Pennsylvania and the Continental Congress to the activities of Charles Julien de Longchamps, a French inhabitant of Philadelphia who claimed noble status, was especially crucial. Longchamps's assault upon the French consul, Barbé de Marbois, in his legation at Philadelphia on 17 May 1784, and their confrontation in a public street two days later, forced state and national authorities to consider vital questions regarding both the source and shape of American foreign policy and the specific mechanisms to encourage and protect the foreign ambassadors and consuls who were largely responsible for the determination and implementation of those policies.[4]

Events triggered by Longchamps's actions helped both to define more clearly the direction of the American republic and to identify the role of foreign diplomatic personnel and protections to be accorded them in the United States. These decisions, born of the necessities of Confederation diplomacy and hammered out in the crucible of national politics, were written into the federal constitution in 1787 and into a rich harvest of treaties and consular agreements in the early republic. These developments helped to swell the demand for a stronger central government capable of determining and implementing a unified and coherent foreign policy.[5]

American relations with France were precarious by 1784. The end of hostilities lessened America's need for French military aid while increasing its desire for commerce with France. American republicans, uneasy with the presence of French troops in the United States during the war, feared that in the postwar period continental "indolence," "effeminacy," and "elitism" would

---

[4]For a discussion of the Longchamps-Marbois affair which focuses on its impact on Pennsylvania institutions and politics, see G. S. Rowe with A. W. Knott, "Power, Justice, and Foreign Relations in the Confederation Period: The Marbois-Longchamps Affair, 1784–1786," *Pennsylvania Magazine of History and Biography* 104 (July 1980): 275–307. An older study that contains numerous errors is Alfred Rosenthal, "The Marbois-Longchamps Affair," ibid. 63 (1939): 294–301. E. Wilson Lyon's *The Man Who Sold Louisiana: The Career of François Barbé-Marbois* (Norman, OK, 1942) describes Marbois's role in the incident but does not explore state or congressional materials.

[5]For a recent study that stresses problems in foreign affairs to explain the growing interest during the 1780s for a strong national government, see Frederick W. Marks III, *Independence on Trial: Foreign Affairs and the Making of the Constitution* (Baton Rouge, LA, 1973).

corrupt civic virtue.[6] Many Americans suspected that France harbored a subtle, but very real, antipathy toward U.S. interests and political forms. This attitude was not disspelled when France acquiesced in British retention of the northwest posts in violation of American sovereignty, or when it failed to press for prompt repayment of the Revolutionary War debt. France seemed to encourage a weak and divided America dependent upon it. Complaints often surfaced that French diplomatic personnel, especially consuls and vice-consuls, constituted a spy network within the country.[7]

French "adventurers" in the United States contributed additional tension to Franco-American relations by increasing the already growing crime rate in Philadelphia and routinely abusing and insulting French officials. Moreover, their various exploits helped to raise questions about the varied powers and jurisdictions between state courts and French consuls in residence.[8] They also exacerbated political divisions in Congress and in the country at large, thereby making resolution of differences all the more difficult. When several adventurers, taking fictitious names and pretending to be rich men of noble families, courted local women, Pennsylvania citizens protested vigorously.[9]

Against this background Longchamps, frustrated at the unwillingness of French diplomatic personnel at Philadelphia to confirm the titles he claimed, threatened Marbois in his legation on 17 May and then, two days later, forced him, as Thomas Jefferson later described it, "to box in the street like a porter."[10] Witnesses offered conflicting accounts of the second scuffle, but Marbois and his superior, the Chevalier de la Luzerne, French minister to the United States, wasted no time in alerting American officials of their desire to have Longchamps suffer severely for his impetuousness.[11]

Behind Luzerne's quick appeal for redress lay a variety of concerns. First and foremost he hoped to uphold the honor of his country and king and

---

[6]Gordon S. Wood, *The Creation of the American Republic, 1776–1787* (Chapel Hill, 1969), pp. 396–403, 413–25, esp. p. 423; William C. Stinchcombe, "Americans Celebrate the Birth of the Dauphin," in Ronald Hoffman and Peter J. Albert, eds., *Diplomacy and Revolution: The Franco-American Alliance of 1778* (Charlottesville, VA, 1981), p. 64.

[7]Marks, *Independence on Trial*, pp. 102, 107; William C. Stinchcombe, *The American Revolution and the French Alliance* (Syracuse, NY, 1969), p. 189; Richard Champion, *Considerations on the Present Situation of Great Britain and the United States of North America with a View to Their Future Commercial Connections* (London, 1784), p. 153.

[8]Lyon, *The Man Who Sold Louisiana*, p. 35; Luzerne to Comte de Vergennes, 17 May 1784, Archives diplomatique: Correspondence Politique, Ministère des Affairs Etrangères, 27:367–68 (hereafter cited as Ad:CP). French Reproductions, Manuscript Division, Library of Congress, Washington, DC. For a specific case described by Peter Stephen DuPonceau, see *Freeman's Journal* (Philadelphia), 21 July 1784.

[9]"Abishag," *Freeman's Journal*, 24 March 1784; "Leander," *Independent Gazetteer* (Philadelphia), 3 April 1784.

[10]Jefferson to Charles Thomson, 21 May 1784, in Julian P. Boyd, ed., *The Papers of Thomas Jefferson*, 21 vols. (Princeton, NJ, 1950–   ), 7:282.

[11]Luzerne to Vergennes, 17 May 1784, Ad:CP, 27:367–68; Luzerne to John Dickinson, 19 May 1784, *Pennsylvania Archives*, 9 ser., 138 vols. (Philadelphia, 1852–1949), 1st ser., 11:462–64.

to avenge his colleague. Beyond that, he recognized the opportunity to pressure American authorities into accepting the law of nations and the protections accorded diplomatic personnel explicit in that tradition. Luzerne, a long-time advocate of a stronger national voice in the United States, preferred that the impetus for resolving these difficulties, particularly the adoption of the law of nations, would emanate from the national government. If Congress would take the initiative in this matter, it could accrue power at the expense of individual states. Finally, Luzerne hoped for a consular agreement that would strengthen the hand of the national Congress while binding the states to its provisions.[12]

On 19 May, the same day Longchamps assaulted Marbois in the streets of Philadelphia, Luzerne demanded satisfaction from Pennsylvania and notified Congress the next day. He insisted that American officials recognize the offense as a clear violation of the law of nations and, consistent with its provisions, return Longchamps to France so that he might be "punished, according to the Laws of the Kingdom." Should Longchamps not face French justice for his abuse of Marbois, Luzerne warned, all foreign diplomatic personnel at Philadelphia would join the French staff in believing that "the security of all those who . . . reside here in a public character" were unsafe and might follow Congress's example in removing their legations. Pressed by Luzerne, Marbois added his complaints to those of his superior.[13]

If Congress were alarmed by the Longchamps case and its implications for the law of nations, so too were American diplomatic personnel. Jefferson, on the eve of his departure to Paris, was sensitive to issues touching the law of nations, particularly those related to the protection of private American citizens in France. Americans, he complained to James Monroe, were "unprotected by the laws of nations," and therefore they were "liable to the jurisdiction of the country." It was important to Jefferson for the two countries to sort out and agree to rules that would protect both officials and citizens in each country.[14]

Not surprisingly, Jefferson quickly recognized the seriousness of Longchamps's assault upon Marbois and the French legation's unbounded fury over the incident. He expressed his opinion to Charles Thomson, secretary to Congress, that Longchamps's "very daring insult" to Marbois would complicate his job in France. Jefferson therefore promised Thomson that he would "make [himself] acquainted with the facts because it will possibly be the cause of something disagreeable here, & perhaps on the other side of the water."

---

[12]Luzerne to Dickinson, 19 May 1784, ibid., pp. 462–64. For background on Luzerne, consult William E. O'Donnell, *The Chevalier de La Luzerne: French Minister to the United States, 1779–1784* (Bruges, 1938).

[13]Entry of 20 May 1784, Despatch Books, 1779–1789, vol. 3 (1781–86), p. 102, in *Papers of the Continental Congress*, National Archives Microfilm Project, Item 95 (hereafter cited as *PCC*); Luzerne to Dickinson, 19 May 1784, *Pennsylvania Archives*, 1st ser., 11:462–64.

[14]Jefferson to James Monroe, 21 May 1784, and Jefferson to James Madison, 25 May 1784, in Boyd, *Papers of Thomas Jefferson*, 7:279, 289.

He voiced even graver concern to James Madison four days later, after learning more about the details surrounding Longchamps's attack and the French response. Jefferson feared that the case would "go next to France and bring on serious consequences." He groused that Congress had "the will but not the power to interpose."[15]

The French were aided in their attempts to pressure Congress into embracing the law of nations by Peter John Van Berckel, Luzerne's colleague and friend, and minister to the United States from the Netherlands. If the United States would not recognize the law of nations, and if Longchamps was not surrendered to French authorities for punishment in accordance with international law, the French and Dutch delegations were prepared to remove their legations from Philadelphia. On 22 May, at a meeting with Thomas Mifflin, president of Congress, Luzerne and Van Berckel warned that members of the Swedish and Spanish diplomatic corps were prepared to follow suit.[16] Their complaints admitted no ambiguity in the law of nations as it related to American responsibility in the Longchamps case.

Torn by disagreements on how to deal with the Longchamps case and divided over its long-range implications for Franco-American relations, congressional committees assigned to respond to French demands reacted cautiously. The committees' tasks were made no easier by Pennsylvania's inept handling of the matter.[17] Congress managed to pass a resolution on 28 May, declaring it essential to the safety and harmony of the American union to make the law of nations an integral part of American law, but it was unprepared to take more direct action until Pennsylvania's course of action became clearer.[18]

Developments at the state level became more apparent when Pennsylvania authorities took Longchamps into custody on 27 May. While he remained incarcerated and under heavy guard, President John Dickinson and the judges of the state's Supreme Court debated his fate. Dickinson privately admitted his own preference for turning Longchamps over to the French, although he conceded the serious political and constitutional obstacles to such a move. For one, the law of nations spoke of sovereign rulers and their responsibilities, but, as Dickinson recognized, in the republican governments of the United

---

[15]Jefferson to Thomson, 21 May 1784, and Jefferson to Madison, 25 May 1784, ibid., pp. 281–82, 289.
[16]Luzerne to Vergennes, 19 June 1784, Ad:CP, 27:424–31; Luzerne to Vergennes, 1 November 1784, quoted in O'Donnell, *The Chevalier de La Luzerne*, p. 246n; report of P. J. Van Berckel, Algemeen Rijksarchief, Legatie Archieen, no. 1161, The Hague, the Netherlands. The same pressure was applied to Pennsylvania. See Dickinson to McKean, 25 May 1784, Thomas McKean Papers, Historical Society of Pennsylvania, Philadelphia (hereafter cited as McKean Papers).
[17]For Pennsylvania's efforts to capture Longchamps and for later permitting him first to escape and then to be released on bail, see Rowe with Knott, "Power, Justice, and Foreign Relations in the Confederation Period," pp. 280–83.
[18]Worthington C. Ford et al., eds., *Journals of the Continental Congress, 1774–1789*, 34 vols. (Washington, DC, 1904–37), 27:502, 504, 564 (hereafter cited as *JCC*); "Law of Nations," Committee Report, 28 May 1784, Item 107, nos. 40 and 41, *PCC*.

States the people were sovereign. Dickinson and members of his Supreme Executive Council were merely representatives of the sovereign people of Pennsylvania.[19] The Supreme Court justices maintained that Pennsylvania had no power arbitrarily to release the prisoner to the French. They pointed out that normally cases of this nature were covered by consular treaties, but, since no such treaty defined rights and legalities or recognized the law of nations as part of American law, jurisdiction fell to local courts. Chief Justice Thomas McKean of Pennsylvania believed that the state would have to determine Longchamps's fate, and he rescheduled the Philadelphia oyer and terminer proceedings to facilitate a solution.[20]

Before Luzerne embarked for France, he commanded Marbois, now chargé d'affaires, to continue to urge Congress and state officials to terminate the Longchamps case in accordance with the law of nations. Marbois was ordered to "insist constantly" that Longchamps be extradited under heavy guard to France for trial there, or, "at the very least,". to demand that he be incarcerated in the United States until the king could make known his wishes. Should Marbois suspect that Pennsylvania authorities intended to ignore precedents established by the law of nations, try Longchamps under the laws, and simply assign to him a perfunctory fine and brief confinement, Marbois was told to protest vigorously that this was "contrary to [the] written assurances given on several occasions by Congress, and by . . . Pennsylvania." Moreover, if Pennsylvania's judges should put Longchamps "at liberty," Marbois was to "withdraw immediately to the Congressional residence to await orders."[21]

As a central figure in the case, Marbois was unable to remain as detached from Pennsylvania's efforts to try Longchamps as both he and Luzerne wished. The French believed that Pennsylvania had no authority to try Longchamps; the state was obliged only to confine him until he could be turned over to French authorities. Marbois's personal discomfiture increased when the state pushed ahead to indict Longchamps and prepared for his trial. Despite constant pleadings from William Bradford, Pennsylvania's attorney general, who argued that the state's case against Longchamps would suffer without Marbois's testimony, the latter refused to agree to a public deposition. He believed that such participation on his part would facilitate proceedings he opposed. In addition, Marbois thought that his appearance in an American courtroom would demean him if he were "compared with the criminal."[22]

Pennsylvania's trial of Longchamps, which began on 24 June 1784, provided a partial victory for French authorities and American congressmen sympathetic to France. Conscious that this was "a case of the first impression in the United States," McKean and Judges George Bryan and Jacob Rush

---

[19]Dickinson to McKean, 25 May 1784, and also 2 and 26 June 1784, McKean Papers. These also appear in *Pennsylvania Archives*, 1st ser., 11:478, 484.
        [20]McKean and the judges to Dickinson, 7 June 1784, *Pennsylvania Archives*, 1st ser., 11:484–85.
        [21]Luzerne to Marbois, 20 June 1784, Ad:CP, 27:432.
        [22]Bradford to Marbois, 11 June 1784, ibid., pp. 443–46; Marbois to Bradford, 11 June 1784, ibid.; Marbois to Vergennes, 1 July 1784, ibid., 28:3.

accepted the prosecution's claims that Longchamps's assault upon Marbois was a crime under the law of nations and punishable under its provisions. They also accepted the prosecution's contention that only a verdict leaving no doubt that the law of nations was an integral part of Pennsylvania law would assure respect of the world at large. The court agreed with Bradford's assertion that "the law of nations, which makes part of the common law of all nations, requires no particular forms of legal proceedings, but always adopts those of the municipal laws of the different countries where it is in force." The jury, after some hesitation, concurred. It convicted Longchamps on all counts.[23]

The trial did not determine, however, whether or not the law of nations was also a part of national law and, therefore, if Congress had jurisdiction in similar cases. If the law of nations was not a part of national law, Congress must continue to defer to state power and face the possibility that similar occurrences, or more potentially dangerous ones capable of provoking war with a foreign power, lay within state prerogative.[24] The judges also ignored Longchamps's fate. Because they postponed his sentencing to a later date, the court adjourned before determining whether or not the French could still reclaim Longchamps. In this important respect, the Longchamps affair continued to be a serious problem for Congress and the nation.

If Congress hoped to grapple with the Longchamps conundrum in relative peace and secrecy, it was disappointed. As Pennsylvania's judges contemplated the options still open to them, public debate over the case accelerated. "An Independent Patriot," writing on 27 June, argued that the Longchamps matter and the question of the law of nations were crucial to the American republic. At stake here, according to "An Independent Patriot," was the very independence of the United States and its laws. Should either Pennsylvania or Congress uncritically embrace the law of nations and, as a result, return Longchamps to France, not only would his rights be violated, but such action also would endanger the rights of all American citizens; it would expose American-law as impotent to deal with state and national concerns. The writer argued that Longchamps was a citizen of the United States because he had taken an oath of allegiance the day following his attack upon Marbois.[25] Longchamps's rights, therefore, were American rights. Failure to rely upon American law to punish the transgressions of its citizens, according to "An Independent Patriot," would identify the United States as a slavish puppet to

---

[23]Alexander J. Dallas, ed., *Reports of Cases in the Supreme Court of Pennsylvania* (Philadelphia, 1790–1807), 1:111–18; *Freeman's Journal*, 11 August 1784.

[24]James Madison in particular complained that it should not be up to "part of the community" to implicate or endanger "the whole." Quoted in Marks, *Independence on Trial*, p. 14.

[25]Longchamps took an oath one day after threatening Marbois at the French legation. See Thomson to Franklin, 13 August 1784, Benjamin Franklin Bache Papers, American Philosophical Society, Philadelphia. Bradford, during the trial, suggested that the oath taken by Longchamps on 18 May implied at best "a partial allegiance" to the United States. He emphasized that Longchamps continued to view himself as a French citizen because he persisted in wearing his French uniform.

French wishes and would seriously undermine independence and cherished rights.[26]

A second writer, calling himself "A Spectator," denounced the notion that the law of nations was, or should be, part of American law; it should not be operable in the Longchamps case. Such conclusions would not only wreak an injustice upon Longchamps but also undermine American independence and commit the United States to pernicious ideas. The law of nations, "A Spectator" protested, permitted any number of "unjust practices," such as piracy and poisoned weapons. Acceptance of these and other barbarous practices would frustrate attempts by the United States to become a truly enlightened republic. "Customs or precedents militating against the welfare and safety of a body of people (for instance, pretended rules for surrendering the inhabitants of a FREE country and transporting them abroad for trial) are incompatible with the grand original principles on which they ought to be founded." He concluded by pointing out that "precedents or customs ténding to make people unhappy can, with no propriety of character, be quoted only by those to whom the misery of man is a delight."[27]

Alarmed by the public interest in the case and the impact it would have upon French diplomats, Thomson sent "a minute detail" of the matter to American ministers at Paris to prevent "any disagreeable consequences." At the same time, he warned Bradford to preserve scrupulously all records of the trial in case they were needed to explain American actions. Thomson also struggled to placate the French consul by insisting that language in a 4 June congressional resolution regarding Longchamps's assault be changed to assuage "M[arbois] whose dignity has been insulted and whose feelings are all alive."[28]

The French remained intransigent while vacillating between a desire to get their way from Pennsylvania and a hope that they could achieve their aims through Congress. On 1 July Marbois sent to Paris a detailed account of developments in the state, along with the copy of a letter signed by "An Independent Patriot." Maréchal de Castries, minister of the marine, reviewed Marbois's correspondence and earlier letters from Luzerne and informed Comte de Vergennes, the French foreign minister, that the king demanded that Longchamps be returned and tried in a French court. Castries himself believed it was essential that Longchamps "be judged by one of the Tribunals of the Kingdom."[29]

---

[26]*Freeman's Journal*, 30 June 1784. A series of articles on the Longchamps case appeared in *Courier d'Amérique* and was reprinted in the *Freeman's Journal*, 21 July, and 4, 11, and 18 August 1784. Other articles appeared in the *Pennsylvania Packet* and *Independent Gazetteer*. The *Gazetteer* (3 July) quoted a Pennsylvania leader to the effect that, "if they send [Longchamps] off, I think I shall not long be safe myself."

[27]*Freeman's Journal*, 14 July 1784; see also "A. B." in ibid., 21 July 1784.

[28]Thomson to the chairman of the Committee of the States, 2 and 5 July 1784, in Edmund Cody Burnett, ed., *Letters of Members of the Continental Congress*, 8 vols. (Washington, DC, 1921–36), 8:846, 847 (hereafter cited as *LMCC*).

[29]Marbois to Vergennes, 1 July 1784, Ad:CP, 28:3; Castries to Vergennes, 8 August 1784, ibid., p. 90.

Vergennes did not relay this information to Marbois until 12 October 1784 when he told the consul that the king had "reacted with indignation . . . to the threats and actual acts that Longchamps [had] made against [Marbois]." The king desired that Marbois "formally demand the extradition of Long-champs," offering some type of reciprocity, if necessary. Only when Marbois had "lost all hope of obtaining the first," was he to "insist that at least the guilty one be punished in the U.S. in a manner which can satisfy the King."[30]

Pennsylvania's sentencing of Longchamps to two years in prison and a fine of $200 on 7 October forced Marbois to shift his attention more purposefully to Congress.[31] Although French influence in that body had dwindled by summer 1784, several developments made Congress vulnerable to increased French pressure. In the spring of 1783, Stephen Higginson of Massachusetts had observed "for a long time a party in Congress so thoroughly in the interests of France as to have preferred her interest to ours, whenever they came into competition." The membership of Congress had changed since then, however, and Marbois proved less effective than Luzerne before him in dealing with the congressmen.[32] But Benjamin Franklin, U.S. minister to France, now favored giving "satisfaction" to Marbois and so informed Thomson on 11 November 1784. Thomson, who wielded impressive powers in Congress—indeed, in the absence of John Jay he was for all purposes the foreign minister—remained sympathetic to French interests.[33] Pennsylvania added its own pressure for congressional action when its Supreme Executive Council, despite Dickinson's apparent lingering hopes of a legislative settlement,[34] announced that the state had done all it could do and was now prepared to "rely upon the Wisdom of Congress." By December, Marbois also was convinced that Congress was eager to chastise Pennsylvania for its failure to defer to the king in the Longchamps affair by refusing to return to that state.[35]

---

[30]Vergennes to Marbois, 12 October 1784, ibid., pp. 319–20.

[31]Dallas, *Reports*, 1:118. Marbois, who viewed the sentence as light, charged it to the judges' "timidity," the influence of popular opinion on the state government, fears of riots, and the need of the state to encourage foreign immigration, especially among Germans. Marbois to M. de Cabres, 7 November 1784, Archives Nationales, Affaires Etrangères, B1, 946, pp. 169–72 (hereafter cited as ANAE), French reproductions, Manuscript Division, Library of Congress, Washington, DC.

[32]Edmund C. Burnett, *The Continental Congress* (1941; reprint ed., New York, 1964), pp. 590ff.; Ralph L. Ketchum, "France and American Politics, 1763–1793," *Political Science Quarterly* 78 (June 1963): 207–08.

[33]Franklin to Thomson, 11 November 1784, Item 127, 2:222, *PCC*; Fred S. Rolater, "Charles Thomson, 'Prime Minister' of the United States," *Pennsylvania Magazine of History and Biography* 101 (July 1977): 332–38.

[34]On 21 July Dickinson called the Pennsylvania Assembly into special session to deal with the Longchamps case and to consider legislation recognizing the law of nations and identifying penalties for crimes against diplomatic personnel. See *Minutes of the Provincial Council of Pennsylvania*, 16 vols. (Harrisburg, PA, 1851–53), 14:163–64, 172–73. See also *Minutes of the Third Session of the Eighth General Assembly* (Philadelphia, 1784), pp. 256, 267, 268–69, 273, 277–78, 283, 359–60; and *Minutes of the First Session of the Ninth General Assembly* (Philadelphia, 1784), pp. 7, 20, 22, 35, 38, 65.

[35]Dickinson to the president of Congress, 22 November 1784 and "Committee Book, 1781–1785," Item 197, p. 174, *PCC*.

The presence of the Marquis de Lafayette at Philadelphia after 9 August gave an additional boost to those looking to the national government for a more vigorous, perhaps even a final, equitable solution to the Longchamps case. From the moment he arrived at Philadelphia, Lafayette pleaded for a stronger national government for the United States, and he made no secret that he believed America's current constitutional balance hurt its interests abroad. Even before his arrival in the United States, he had indefatigably promoted Franco-American trade and "a stronger federal head" in the new republic. Lafayette told Madison that in politics "his three hobby-horses are the alliance between France and the United States, the Union of the latter, and the manumission of the slaves."[36]

Longchamps was an embarrassment to Lafayette and his scheme for closer Franco-American relations. Initially, Lafayette simply remained silent on the issue; eventually, he conceded privately that he "wish[ed] the devil had carried [Longchamps] off six months ago." In a sense, however, Longchamps's presence worked to Lafayette's purpose. The "Longchamps fiasco," as historian Louis Gottschalk has observed, advertised for all to see "the confederation's inadequacy." Lafayette advised Jay and members of Congress that the affair might increase dissatisfaction with American policies in the French court. He made no effort, so far as the records show, to persuade state officials to surrender Longchamps or to convince Congress to try to force Pennsylvania to do so. He was content to remind them, if they needed such a reminder, that the dangers of an impotent Confederation were very real, and that the unwillingness of the states to surrender sovereignty to Congress had become "notorious." Upon his departure in December, he called once more for a stronger central government.[37]

As Lafayette departed American shores, Jay formally assumed his powers as secretary of foreign affairs and confronted the issue of Longchamps's fate. Because of the unsettled conditions in Congress, Marbois had held off the formal presentation of the king's demand for Longchamps's extradition. Congress had met at Trenton in November to reclaim its affairs from the committee of the states which had handled congressional matters since 3 June, but it had adjourned shortly thereafter. By January 1785 the peripatetic Congress had moved to New York. Marbois seemed satisfied to permit Congress to "settle in" before making his formal appeal for Longchamps. Thus, although Edward Bancroft, the British agent who kept the ministry informed, and others

---

[36]Louis R. Gottschalk, *Lafayette Between the American and the French Revolutions, 1783–1789* (Chicago, 1950), pp. 25, 29, 37, 39, 57, 73, 85–86; Franklin to Robert Morris, 25 December 1783, in Albert H. Smyth, ed., *The Writings of Benjamin Franklin*, 10 vols. (New York, 1905–07), 9:139; Madison to Jefferson, 17 October 1784, in Boyd, *Papers of Thomas Jefferson*, 7:446.

[37]Quoted in Gottschalk, *Lafayette Between the American and the French Revolutions*, p. 94. See also ibid., pp. 132, 134, 135–36.

were aware of the king's decision to demand Longchamps's extradition, Congress had not been officially notified.[38]

Marbois's own shifting attitudes toward Longchamps also contributed to his hesitancy to approach Congress. By late 1784, Marbois and his wife Elizabeth, the American-born daughter of Pennsylvania politician William Moore, had concluded that the prisoner should be freed. Marbois confided to M. de Cabres, an undersecretary in the Ministry of Navy and Colonies, that he "desire[d] personally, and believe[d] [himself] presently obligated to work to end this man's captivity." Perhaps he and his wife succumbed to threats against them should Longchamps be returned to France, or perhaps, as he told Cabres, he hoped by his actions to prevent "further attempts against privileged persons." In any case, he wrote Cabres that Longchamps's punishment had been "really extraordinary" from the viewpoint of American practice. He argued, too, that Congress already had offered some satisfaction to France, "though indirectly," by rebuffing Pennsylvania's desires that Congress return to Philadelphia.[39]

Marbois believed he had a plan that would satisfy all concerned. He proposed to Cabres that he be permitted to demand from Congress Longchamps's return and then ask for a pardon for Longchamps upon his release. In that way, French principles could be protected and a degree of justice secured for Longchamps as well. If Congress should refuse his request, Marbois believed the king should conditionally pardon Longchamps. In that way, France could maintain that Longchamps was not returned because the king did not want him to be. Such a strategy, "compromising no one," would be an indirect way to withdraw French demands. Otherwise, should Congress refuse the king's demands—and that possibility seemed very likely to Marbois—it would "hurt the King's dignity to send further ministers here." He reminded Cabres that Longchamps would still be under heavy bond to keep the peace for another seven years, whatever the case. Marbois urged Cabres to approach Castries with his proposal.[40]

On 10 February, without waiting for a reply from Versailles, Marbois formally requested from Congress Longchamps's extradition, proclaiming him

---

[38]Burnett, *Continental Congress*, p. 618ff.; Marbois to Vergennes, 26 December 1784, Ad:CP, 28:461; Edward Bancroft to the Marquis de Carmarthen, 8 December 1784, British Foreign Office, ser. 4, 221/110, British reproductions, Manuscript Division, Library of Congress, Washington, DC.

[39]Marbois to Cabres, 6 January 1785, B1, 946, pp. 190–91, ANAE. For Marbois's growing concern with "adventurers" in Philadelphia, see his letter to Vergennes, 16 February 1785, Ad:CP, 29:48–50. On 26 December (ibid., pp. 79–80), Marbois informed Vergennes that Congress was in New York, and "there is hope that the King would not hold all the States responsible for the refusals and misconduct of one state, especially when he recalls that Congress had been the first victim of the vices of the Pennsylvania Constitution." For one threat against Marbois, see unknown to Marbois, 4 February 1785, "Domestic Letters of the Department of State, 1784–1906," 1:35–36, National Archives, Washington, DC.

[40]Marbois to Cabres, 6 January 1785, B1, 946, pp. 190–91, ANAE. Elizabeth Moore Marbois also wrote to the queen seeking her help to interest the king in a pardon for Longchamps. Elizabeth Marbois to the queen, 1 January 1785, ibid., pp. 192–93.

a subject of the king and a man convicted of a crime against the law of nations. Implicit in Marbois's demand was the French insistence that Congress either pressure Pennsylvania into giving up the prisoner, or override the state's jurisdiction. In a separate and private note to Jay, Marbois expressed his desire that a pardon for the prisoner be worked out at some point in the extradition process.[41] The reply of the French court, made two days before Marbois's formal appeal to Congress but without his knowledge, stated that the king was content to drop the matter, believing that further requests "would not succeed."[42]

In the meantime, unaware of the king's change of heart but cognizant of the French consul's private hopes for a pardon, Jay submitted the Marbois materials to Congress. Jay was not happy with the persistence of the French in demanding Longchamps's release because, as he told Mifflin, the issue "excited much uneasiness." For the record, Jay informed Marbois that he "foresaw great problems in this affair," and he reminded the consul that Longchamps already had been found guilty by a state court and had served part of his sentence. Longchamps's punishment had been "more severe than it would have been if a similar offense had been made against the first magistrate of the state." He drew Marbois's attention to the fact that "it was difficult in a country where the government [was] made up of the people to give complete satisfaction in a novel case like this one." He expressed his hope that the king "would take into consideration the differences between the governments of Europe and the one of the United States."[43]

These moves were taken against a backdrop of continuing public discussion of the law of nations. A "memoir addressed to free and independent citizens of the United States, concerning the affair of the Chevalier Charles Julien de Longchamps," appeared in Boston's *Independent Chronicle*, reviewing the case's history and demanding that Longchamps not be surrendered to French jurisdiction. The anonymous author argued that Longchamps's fate was not simply the concern of the people of Pennsylvania or members of Congress. Every American, every republican, he insisted, had a stake in

---

[41] Marbois to Congress, 10 February 1785, Ad:CP, 29:45. Lafayette played an important role in convincing the French government to relinquish its claims, according to Gottschalk in *Lafayette Between the American and the French Revolutions*, p. 155.

[42] Vergennes to Marbois, 8 February 1785, Ad:CP, 29:43.

[43] Jay to Thomas Mifflin, 15 February 1785, "Domestic Letters of the Department of State, 1784–1906," 1:18, National Archives; Marbois to Vergennes, 16 February 1785, Ad:CP, 29:48–50. Jay told John Adams on 11 February that he "wish[ed] that Matter had not been pressed." See "Foreign Letters of the Continental Congress and the Department of State, 1785–1790," pp. 3–4, National Archives. Edward Livingston in New York wrote to DuPonceau at Philadelphia on 15 February that "the affair of Mr. Longchamps engrosses the conversation of this place. It is said the [*sic*] De Marbois has made a positive demand of him from the Congress. I can give reports only, as our Fathers in Congress affect great mystery when spoken to on the subject and studiously avoid its discussion. . . . Be so kind as to send me the publications relative to this business." Quoted in Thomas R. Meehan, "The Pennsylvania Supreme Court in the Laws and Commonwealth of Pennsylvania, 1776–1790" (Ph.D. diss., University of Wisconsin, 1960), p. 393.

Longchamps's fortunes. The law of nations, according to Emerich de Vattel, held that "the ambassador's secretary is one of his domesticks, but the secretary of the embassy has his commission from the sovereign himself, which makes him a kind of public minister, and he . . . enjoys immunities independent of the ambassador." But the author of the memoir denied that Marbois was a "direct representative" of the king, or that he was a public minister. He was, instead, merely a "representative of the commercial sector," a man charged with managing commerce among his countrymen. Therefore, contrary to Marbois's claim, he was not protected by the law of nations.[44]

One week after receiving Marbois's formal demand for the extradition of Longchamps, Jay informed Congress of his position. He conceded the French everything—and nothing. He pointed out that even if Longchamps were clearly a French citizen who had offended the king, even if the United States were clearly bound by treaty to deliver him up, and even if the American government conceded that the king had every right to demand Longchamps's extradition, the United States could not acquiesce in French demands under its current constitutional arrangements. Marbois's demand was premature. Since Longchamps had violated Pennsylvania law, that state's authorities had the legal right to try, convict, and punish him for his crime. Jay recommended refusing French demands for the moment. He promised to reopen the issue after 4 July 1786 when Longchamps's incarceration was to end, but only if the French persisted.[45]

Congress was not altogether persuaded by Jay's arguments. Several congressmen complained that refusal to relinquish Longchamps to the French would result in the recall of the French and Dutch ministers, and perhaps other ministers as well. Such a move would reflect badly on the national government and seriously weaken its capacity to function among the nations of the world. On the other hand, the weakening of diplomatic relations clearly appealed to others.[46] Marbois wrote Vergennes that a number of congressmen "want no ministers here from creditor nations. . . . Some would like to see foreign ties broken so foreign debts wouldn't have to be paid."[47]

Marbois's observation was only partly accurate. The desire of men such as Francis Dana and Elbridge Gerry to rid the United States of foreign ministers and to restrict American representatives abroad stemmed more from a wish to pursue a truly independent course and to jettison many of the hoary ideals

---

[44]Emerich de Vattel, *The Law of Nations: Applied to the Conduct and Affairs of Nations and Sovereigns* (1760; reprint ed., New York, 1787), book 4, chap. 9, p. 724; copy of *Independent Chronicle*, n.d., found in Ad:CP, 29:51–55. Justice George Bryan had anticipated and rejected this last argument in his address to the jury in June 1784. See Dallas, *Reports*, 1:115.

[45]Jay's report, "An Affair of Longchamps," 17 February 1785, Item 124, 1:16, *PCC*.

[46]Ibid. Among the congressmen serving between 1784 and 1786 who favored reducing the number of foreign ministers and their staffs in the United States were David Howell (RI), Francis Dana (MA), Elbridge Gerry (MA), Hugh Williamson (NC), Richard Henry Lee (VA), John Francis Mercer (VA), and Samuel Osgood (MA). See, for instance, Dana to Gerry, 18 June 1784, *LMCC*, 7:558.

[47]Marbois to Vergennes, 7 May 1785, Ad:CP, 29:233.

and practices of the European past than from a bid to avoid repaying bills. They also desired to strengthen the states at the expense of the national government, to guarantee a decentralized republic. Dana observed that

> there is nothing clearer in my opinion than that our Interests will be more injured by the residence of foreign ministers among us, than they be promoted by our ministers abroad. The best way to get rid of the former is not to send the latter. And therefore let those already appointed die off, or resign as fast as they may. . . . We have the World to ourselves, and if we not know how at present, we shall learn to govern it as well at least as any other part of the Globe is governed, and sooner and better without foreign interference than with it.[48]

The committee assigned to evaluate Jay's recommendation, and its chairman, New Yorker Robert R. Livingston, preferred to stall for as long as possible any formal congressional response. Livingston's committee did not report until 27 April, and then it offered only a series of half measures to replace Jay's forthright move to refuse extradition. It called upon the secretary of foreign affairs to express to France the sincerest apologies of the United States for the delay in responding to its claims and to seek the king's understanding of the complexity of the case. The report concluded that "difficulties . . . may arise on this head from the nature of a federal union in which each State retains a distinct and absolute sovereignty in all matters not expressly delegated to Congress leaving to them only that of advising in many of those cases in which other governments decree."[49]

Jay sought to circumvent the committee report by offering a ploy through which Congress could leak his report to Lafayette. The Frenchman then could "diffus[e] certain sides at Versailles on that subject, which would promote our views without making Congress responsible for them, and tend to check any desire they may have to press us farther about the matter." Jay suggested that there be no formal vote on the report and that no copy of it appear in the journal. It was probably Jay's stratagem that Rufus King had in mind when he wrote Gerry that "we now have it in our power to conduct the business in a mode consistent with our honor, and satisfaction to the other party—I cannot be particular—the delay of a discussion has been very convenient."[50]

---

[48]Quoted in Rakove, *The Beginnings of National Politics*, p. 347.

[49]*JCC*, 28:314–15.

[50]Jay to Mifflin, 28 April 1785, Item 80, no. 149, *PCC*; Rufus King to Gerry, 1 May 1785, *LMCC*, 8:108. John Adams at Auteuil outside Paris was shocked to learn from Jay that the French were continuing their demands for Longchamps. He suggested that "it may not . . . be amiss for the French Government to keep up a claim which may be a standing restraint to their own subjects in all foreign countries." If he had seen Franklin's consular agreement with Vergennes, he put the best face on it; he had no doubt that the French now appreciated American rights to refuse their earlier demands concerning Longchamps and realized that both nations recognized that "no positive stipulation between the two powers [existed whereby] criminals shall be mutually given up." Adams was correct only in the sense that the treaty had yet to be ratified, and no clear mechanism existed by which the state could be forced to submit to its provisions. Adams to Jay, 24 April 1785, Item 84, p. 381, *PCC*.

Despite continuing dissension within Congress and lingering fears by some that refusal to release Longchamps would provoke diplomatic retaliation, most congressmen had concluded by the spring of 1785 that Longchamps should not be given up. To turn him over to the French would not only defeat many U.S. foreign policy aims but also compromise several of America's most cherished domestic goals. It was not exclusively the constitutional difficulties that explain congressional reluctance to surrender Longchamps but rather Congress's belief that such a move was incompatible with the interests of an enlightened, independent, and republican government. The position of Congress was clear; what remained to be determined was its strategy in maintaining that position. As the Connecticut delegation reported to Governor Mathew Griswold, "[Longchamps] will not, we Imagine, be Deliver'd up, but the Question is what Answer shall be given and upon what grounds the denial may be most prudently placed."[51]

The important problem of whether or not the law of nations would be embraced formally by the national government—and, if so, in what form it would be embraced—remained unresolved. Left unsettled as well was whether or not Congress, if it accepted the law of nations or a modified Americanized version of it, could compel the states to recognize that law. That question struck at the heart of a powerful congressional dilemma: the inability to coerce the states. Jefferson came to understand, as did others, that provisions in the law of nations relating to consuls and ministers—and protections accorded them—were also those normally incorporated into consular agreements among nations. Such conventions, so essential to the welfare of the American union, could not be guaranteed until Congress held power to conduct foreign policy.[52]

On 27 April, the same day that Livingston's committee responded to Jay's proposal, Congress urged the states to pass specific laws to afford protection to foreign diplomats. While none did so, the Pennsylvania Assembly drafted such a bill and came within a few votes of passing it.[53] Virginia in 1786 gave Congress the power to regulate its commerce, and in that role to govern commercial agents, including consuls. Virginia also authorized the extradition of citizens guilty of crimes within another jurisdiction if proof of

---

[51]Connecticut delegates to Mathew Griswold, 24 February 1785, *LMCC*, 8:41–42.

[52]This issue was debated for the next several years. In his 1787 pamphlet "The Weakness of Brutus Exposed, or Some Remarks in Vindication of the Constitution Proposed by the Late Federal Convention Against the Objections and Gloomy Fears of the Writer Humbly Offered to the Public," Pelatiah Webster wrote that, until the federal government was empowered "to punish any individual or state, who shall violate our treaties with foreign nations, insult their dignity or abuse their citizens, and compel due reparation in such cases," the threat of being drawn into a European war was very real. Others also perceived that federal power to enforce the law of nations was essential to save the American republic. See Webster's pamphlet in Paul L. Ford, ed., *Pamphlets on the Constitution of the U.S. Published During Its Discussion by the People, 1787–1788* (Brooklyn, NY, 1888), p. 121; and Marks, *Independence on Trial*, p. 178. An examination of America's interest in the law of nations taken from a different perspective is provided by Gregg L. Lint, "The American Revolution and the Law of Nations, 1776–1789," *Diplomatic History* 1 (Winter 1977): 20–34.

[53]See note 34 above.

their guilt were first submitted to Congress. As early as 25 May 1784, Jefferson had argued for such a step. "[F]or God's sake," he had written Madison, "while this instance of the necessity of providing for the enforcement of the law of nations is fresh on men's minds, introduce a bill which shall be effectual and satisf[act]ory on the subject." Upon hearing of Virginia's 1786 legislation, Jefferson agreed that "the politics of Europe render it indispensably necessary that with respect to everything external we be one nation only, firmly hooped together."[54]

Partly as a result of the Longchamps developments, Congress began in 1786 to consider reforms to ensure its greater effectiveness and efficiency. Among the proposed reforms was the creation of a federal court empowered to interpret the law of nations and, equally important, to coerce the states into compliance with its provisions.[55] The Longchamps case had illustrated the futility of permitting thirteen governments to interpret the law of nations for the country as a whole, or to reject it on a whim. Subsequent discussion of the law of nations revealed the general bankruptcy of congressional power. Many congressmen and American government representatives abroad realized that much of Congress's impotence could and should be overcome through calculated, judicious treaties, including consular agreements, with foreign powers.

Luzerne had understood from the start that French desires to avenge Marbois at the expense of Longchamps were intimately connected to the need for a consular agreement between the two countries. He recognized better than most the difficulties for Franco-American relations inherent in the Longchamps developments. For two years he had worked assiduously to conclude a consular agreement designed to confront and resolve many of these problems. To that end, as early as July 1781 he had submitted to Congress a draft for a consular convention which subsequently had been debated and amended in January 1782. Much of the debate over Luzerne's draft had centered on Article 13, which provided that Americans living in France who committed offenses against other Americans, and Frenchmen living in the United States who committed crimes against other French citizens, were to be subject to the law and authorities of their own government. This provision, which granted potentially immense powers to French consuls in America at the expense of both state and national governments, generated the greatest heat in Congress.[56]

The complaints by Luzerne and Marbois to Congress regarding Longchamps's actions on 19 May 1784 touched a raw nerve. Congressmen were extremely sensitive to their impotence in foreign affairs and their inability to persuade the thirteen states to follow their lead. A part of its failure stemmed

---

[54]Marbois to Vergennes, 22 February 1785, Ad:CP, 29:71; Madison to Jefferson, 9 January 1785, and Jefferson to Madison, 25 May 1784, and 8 February 1786, in Boyd, *Papers of Thomas Jefferson*, 7:593–94, 289; 9:264.
[55]*JCC*, 31:494, 497.
[56]Ibid., 21:792–93, 804–10; 22:17, 18–27, 46, 52, 54.

from vacant leadership chairs, but the absence of a ratified consular agreement between the two countries was even more important.[57] Preliminary negotiations between Franklin and Vergennes for the consular agreement were under way, although Congress was ignorant about the progress of those deliberations. Congress realized only that as a body it was deeply divided over the issue. Congressmen James Lowell, Dana, and Gerry opposed the consummation of such an agreement, and Jay, the incoming secretary of foreign affairs, was also known to be cool toward it. He believed that a consular agreement would bind the fledgling republic too closely to France, while Lowell, Dana, and Gerry thought that it would compromise American sovereignty in general.

The Longchamps incident could not be easily divorced from the issue of a consular agreement. Any such understanding would necessarily identify the powers, privileges, and protections accorded foreign consuls. It also would raise the question of French influence in the United States. But even congressmen promoting a consular understanding with the French knew that such a treaty would not, under current conditions, sufficiently bind the states. The question of the consular convention, like that of the law of nations, then, forced Americans to reassess congressional power.

Immediately before taking office as secretary of foreign affairs, Congressman Jay moved to clarify developments closely related to Longchamps's fate. On 14 December he argued successfully that, if Franklin had not yet signed the consular agreement with Vergennes, Congress should take decisive steps to see that it was not signed. Richard Henry Lee, who supported Jay's move, wrote Franklin that same day to inform him that Congress now harbored severe reservations concerning the draft treaty of 25 January 1782. A committee headed by Jay and composed of Samuel Hardy, Hugh Williamson, William S. Johnson, Monroe, and Gerry was appointed to revise the earlier draft. Still at issue was the ambiguous language concerning the powers of consuls. Unfortunately for Jay and his supporters, Franklin had affixed his signature to the treaty on 29 July 1784 and had forwarded a copy to Congress for ratification.[58]

When Marbois had made his demands to Congress in December 1784 for Longchamps's release, Jay had mixed feelings. Unhappy with the French demands and interested in dismissing them, he still appreciated how the particulars of the case could work to his advantage in opposing any consular understanding with the French. No better example existed in the memories

---

[57]No minister of foreign affairs had been active for some time, although Jay had been elected to that post on 7 May. He was not scheduled to assume office for another seven months, however, and rumors circulated that he would not, in fact, shoulder the burdens of that office. Ibid., 26:355.

[58]Ibid., 27:685–86; 28:7n, 158n, 480; Richard H. Lee to Franklin, 14 December 1784, *Diplomatic Correspondence of the United States from the Signing of the Definitive Treaty of Peace, 10th September 1783, to the Adoption of the Constitution, 4 March, 1789*, 3 vols. (Washington, DC, 1837), 1:95, 204. James Monroe became head of this committee.

of congressmen to underscore the dangers inherent in the wording of Article 13 of the congressional draft of the consular agreement.[59]

France's desire to avenge Marbois at the expense of Longchamps and the issue of a Franco-American consular convention became even more apparent, at least in the minds of many congressmen, following the arrival of Franklin's proposed treaty on 6 June 1785. One year earlier Chief Justice McKean had observed that "there is no doubt but [that] the consular power . . . extends to cases of this kind, between subjects of the same Sovereign by a particular convention or Treaty." Because McKean and his associates on the Pennsylvania bench had "not heard of any such between His Most Christian Majesty and the United States," the justices had ordered Dickinson to proceed with the state's trial against Longchamps.[60]

Franklin and Vergennes had signed the consular treaty after Longchamps's trial but before his sentencing. Thomson saw Congress's dilemma and sought to use it to the advantage of those like himself who favored a stronger central government. He prepared a private memorandum to persuade Congress to institute essential reforms, particularly those entrusting Congress with powers to coerce the states. Thomson proposed that state judges be compelled to recognize national interests when foreign treaties or conventions like the consular agreement were concerned. Livingston, too, was anxious for such reforms. As his last act as secretary of foreign affairs in April 1783, he issued a circular letter to the states urging them to recognize and adhere to national treaties.[61] The particulars of the Longchamps case and the consular agreement could not be divorced from the growing movement to strengthen the central government and, in fact, heightened the debate. Without some means of binding states to national policy and interests, the United States might be rendered vulnerable to foreign intrigue and machinations.[62]

Efforts to diffuse such a possibility with France continued throughout the spring of 1785, along with efforts to Americanize the law of nations by introducing U.S. ideals and practices into treaties. The Longchamps particulars were not the deciding factors in Jay's opposition to Franklin's recently signed consular treaty, but the shadow of the case hung over the entire ratification proceedings in July. Jay, like Gerry, Lee, and others, distrusted France's aims and believed that its consuls would compromise American sovereignty. They viewed any agreement that legitimized consular exchanges as potentially destructive.[63]

While desiring to afford safeguards for foreign diplomatic personnel, Jay denounced many of the provisions of Franklin's treaty, labeling them repugnant "to the spirit and genious [sic] of America." His thorough, almost clinical, examination of the treaty on 6 July established that, among other

[59]*JCC*, 22:52.
[60]McKean to Dickinson, 25 May 1784, McKean Papers.
[61]Rakove, *The Beginnings of National Politics*, p. 344; Kaplan, *Colonies Into Nation*, p. 152.
[62]Hugh Williamson to Samuel Johnston, 30 May 1788, *LMCC*, 8:744.
[63]*JCC*, 29:500–15.

weaknesses in the agreement, Article 9, which permitted acts and declarations made before foreign consuls and vice-consuls to be admitted to state courts, appeared to render foreigners residing in the United States subject to consular jurisdiction. Article 12 gave French consuls the power to send captains, masters, passengers, or entire ships back to France. Jay and others feared that the word "passengers" might be construed to permit France to reclaim Longchamps or individuals like him. Jay also pointed out that the treaty did not clearly determine who should have jurisdiction in cases similar to that of Longchamps. Articles 11 and 13 seemed to be contradictory in this respect.[64]

Jay's devastating critique doomed Franklin's treaty.[65] In addition to Jay's criticisms, when the treaty called for foreign consuls to present their commissions to assume their duties to the respective states, it created the wrong impression in the minds of congressmen seeking to strengthen the national voice.[66] Accordingly, Congress instructed Jefferson, now minister plenipotentiary, to seek revisions. In particular, Congress sought to reduce the immunities, privileges, and powers of consuls, and to minimize areas of extraterritoriality.[67]

In the meantime, Lafayette's letters to Jay of 8 February and 11 May 1785, which privately confirmed French aims to withdraw all claims on Longchamps, provided the stimulus for Congress to encourage termination of the matter. On 20 July the committee appointed to grapple with Longchamps's fate was discharged, and all its papers were returned to Jay. Late in July, Marbois formally approached Jay about ending the affair. Marbois merely requested that all materials relating to Longchamps, including his own official request for Longchamps's extradition, be returned to him "as if no such Demand had been made." Such a move would eliminate any need for Congress to reply officially to France. Marbois asked only that Congress continue to encourage states to make the law of nations common to their courts. On 22 August Jay urged Congress to comply with Marbois's request and his attendant stipulations. Congress concurred, and on 31 August the matter was closed.[68]

For more than two years the Longchamps case held the attention of Congress. Its preoccupation with the particulars flowed logically from its

---

[64]Ibid., esp. p. 506.

[65]Ibid; Dumas Malone, *Jefferson and the Rights of Man* (Boston, 1951), pp. 199–200.

[66]*JCC*, 29:502. The convention omitted the requirement that consuls "present their Commissions in the First Instance to the United States in Congress assembled." That requirement appears in Article 1 of the original "scheme."

[67]*Diplomatic Correspondence of the United States*, 1:233; Malone, *Jefferson and the Rights of Man*, pp. 198–202; Boyd, *Papers of Thomas Jefferson*, 14:67–92; Samuel Flagg Bemis, ed., *The American Secretaries of State and Their Diplomacy*, 10 vols. (New York, 1927–29), 1:252–59.

[68]*JCC*, 29:564n, 598–99; Jay to Mifflin, 2 August 1785, "Domestic Letters of the Department of State," 1:391–92, National Archives; Jay's report, 22 August 1785, Item 124, p. 139, *PCC*; Jay to Marbois, 31 August 1785, "Domestic Letters of the Department of State," 1:423–24, National Archives; Jay to Adams, 6 September 1785, "Foreign Letters of the Continental Congress and the Department of State, 1785–1790," pp. 124–28.

recognition that the Marbois-Longchamps affair sparked fundamental questions regarding the nature and spirit of the young republic. Congressmen correctly sensed that the diplomatic embroglio set in motion processes by which America's foreign policy would be shaped. The affair coerced citizens of the early republic into confronting their obligations toward foreign diplomatic personnel and into weighing the wisdom of embracing the law of nations. If the republic embraced the established law of nations, a choice would be made to accept traditional norms of behavior and the nation-state system within which these laws and customs had evolved. To grapple intelligently with those two issues, they needed to struggle as well with the question of which level of government—state or national—should determine the outcome of these questions. As such, Longchamps's assault upon Marbois helped to raise crucial questions about the legitimacy and efficacy of the Confederation and, in the process, contributed heavily to the reform movement which bore fruit one year later at the Philadelphia convention.

Jefferson's attitudes helped to establish the connection between the Longchamps affair and the questions it raised about the powers of the central government. Like others, he associated the Longchamps particulars with the proposed consular agreement with France and with the need to strengthen "the federal head." He came to believe that foreign commerce and its associated enterprises offered Congress the opportunity to increase its powers at the expense of the states. "The moment these [commercial] treaties are concluded the jurisdiction of Congress over commerce of the states springs into existence," he wrote in June 1785, "and that of the particular states is superseded." He also came to appreciate that consuls were the "creatures of a treaty." Because the Articles of Confederation permitted Congress to conclude treaties with foreign powers and, as Jefferson noted, to define the powers of consuls through treaties, such agreements would be "paramount to the laws of the states." By September 1786 he rejoiced that commercial developments and the Longchamps case had created "a [di]sposition to center in the hands of Congress all powers re[spec]ting our connection with foreign nations [which] is becoming universal."

Thus, even when Jefferson did not approve of all the changes proposed by Jay in Franklin's draft of the consular convention, he agreed to push for their acceptance. Without a treaty, he reasoned, states would not be obliged to conform to provisions of either draft. In brief, a single line of logic led Jefferson from Longchamps's assault on Marbois, to the need for consular agreements, and finally to the need for a strong central government with sufficient power to conclude the types of treaties enabling the federal government to solve problems similar to that of Longchamps.[69]

---

[69]Jefferson to Monroe, 16 June 1785, Jefferson to David Hartley, 5 September 1785, Jefferson to William Carmichael, 22 August 1786, Jefferson to C. W. F. Dumas, 22 September 1786, and Jefferson to Jay, 9 January 1787, in Boyd, *Papers of Thomas Jefferson*, 8:230–31, 484–85; 10:285–86, 397; 11:31.

The new constitution in 1787 enhanced "the federal head." A variety of forces and events contributed to its creation, but its Article 3, section 2, in part reflected developments from the Longchamps case and the French claims for his extradition and punishment. French demands for jurisdiction over Longchamps initially had led to a consideration of the law of nations which, in turn, had led to congressional efforts in August 1786 to form a federal court with jurisdiction over matters relating to international law and empowered to bind states to its decisions. The national court subsequently established in the federal constitution accomplished both. Edmund Randolph spoke for many when, in his appeal for the new federal constitution in 1787, he complained that in most state constitutions "the law of nations [was] unprovided with sanctions in many cases, which deeply effect the . . . public dignity and public justice." Without the new constitution, he argued, the Confederation will "be doomed to be plunged into war, from its wretched impotency to check offenses against this law."[70]

For all the furor raised against the new constitution in general, and Article 3 in particular, no complaints surfaced in the various ratification conventions or in the public at large against the new court's proposed power to grapple with international law or its jurisdiction over "cases effecting ambassadors, other public Ministers, and Consuls." Nor did critics see fit to question the provision in Article 3, section 2, that in all cases involving ambassadors, foreign ministers, and consuls "in which a state shall be a Party, the supreme Courts shall have original Jurisdiction." By 1787 Americans familiar with the Longchamps affair accepted the necessity of their federal government to have an instrument through which to embrace and interpret the law of nations.[71]

Although the new federal government did not formally adopt the law of nations, it did write portions of that tradition into its laws, with American modifications. The tumult surrounding the Longchamps case made clear American support for the law of nations and widespread acknowledgment that a necessary part of being accepted fully by the other nations of the world must be a willingness to admit the legitimacy of that tradition. From the beginning of the Longchamps case, the lawyer Peter DuPonceau maintained that "this affair is one of those which interests every sovereign and every community, and will make a remarkable era in the history of the Law of Nations."[72]

Equally evident from the debate and developments in the Longchamps matter, however, were American hopes to modify the law of nations to reflect more clearly republican priorities and assumptions. "A Bill to Promote the Progress of the Useful Arts," passed by the first federal Congress on 30 April 1790, proclaimed that "to assault, strike, wound, imprison, or in any other

---

[70]Edmund Randolph, *Letter on the Federal Convention*, in Ford, *Pamphlets on the Constitution of the United States*, pp. 262–63.

[71]Henry S. Commager, ed., *Documents of American History*, 6th ed. (New York, 1958), p. 144. See also Merrill Jensen, ed., *The Documentary History of the Ratification of the Constitution*, vol. 2, *Pennsylvania* (Madison, WI, 1976), esp. pp. 625, 630.

[72]*Freeman's Journal*, 4 August 1784.

manner infract the law of nations, by offering violence to the person of an ambassador, or other public minister, such persons so offending on conviction shall be imprisoned not exceeding three years, and fines at the discretion of the court." The penalties that the bill called for were virtually the same as those leveled against Longchamps in October 1784, a move that surprised no one aware of the case.[73]

Additional elements of the law of nations were incorporated into the consular agreement with France, which finally was ratified in 1788. Signed by Jefferson and French Foreign Minister L. C. de Montmorin, the agreement both clarified several provisions of Franklin's 1782 draft relating to consular powers and jurisdictions and met Jay's objections regarding infringements on American sovereignty. Article 2 established that "consuls and vice consuls, and persons attached to their functions . . . shall enjoy a full and entire immunity for their chancery and the papers which shall be therein contained." Consuls, no longer required to present their commissions to the states, now received authority to exercise their functions from Congress. They still had the power to arrest captains, masters, and seamen of their own vessels, as stated in Article 9, but no mention was made of passengers or others who might be forced to return to France. Jay's concern about who should have jurisdiction in cases like that of Longchamps was resolved by Article 10, which gave jurisdiction to the courts of the respective countries. Finally, a new article limiting the duration of the convention to twelve years was included to see "if after the Experience of a few Years, it should be found to answer the Purposes intended by it."[74]

Longchamps had disappeared from public view by the time the new federal government was created in 1787, but in the constitution that created that government, as well as in the laws and treaties written under its auspices regarding its early foreign policy assumptions, aspirations, and institutions, his spirit lingered on. Dickinson had warned his colleagues at the Philadelphia convention that "experience must be our only Guide." He intended experience to mean both political wisdom gained by studying past events but, equally important, that obtained through participation in events.[75] It is little wonder that those who had struggled with Longchamps and the implication of his activities wove into the fabric of the early republic's foreign policy the agreements and institutional safeguards against a repetition and, in the process, gave shape and definition to America's foreign policy.

---

[73]Annals of the Congress of the United States: First Congress, 2 vols. (Washington, DC, 1834), 1:990–91, 996–97; 2:2279; Herbert W. Briggs, ed., The Law of Nations: Cases, Documents, and Notes, 2d ed. (New York, 1952), p. 766. The law was modeled after 7 Anne c. 12 but altered to include protection to the person of the diplomat.

[74]JCC, 22:46–54; Jay to Jefferson, 3 October 1786, in Boyd, Papers of Thomas Jefferson, 10:430; Hunter Miller, ed., Treaties and Other International Acts of the United States of America, 8 vols. (Washington, DC, 1931–48), 2:228–44, esp. pp. 229, 230, 237–38.

[75]Max Farrand, ed., Records of the Federal Constitution of 1787, 4 vols. (New Haven, CT, 1911–37), 2:entry for 13 August; Douglas Adair, "Experience Must Be Our Guide: History, Democratic Theory, and the United States Constitution," in Jack P. Greene, ed., Reinterpretations of the American Revolution (New York, 1968), pp. 399–400.